TAFSIR AL-QURTUBI

Classical Commentary of the Holy Qur'an

VOLUME

I

TAFSIR AL-QURTUBI

Classical Commentary of the Holy Qur'an

TRANSLATED BY

AISHA BEWLEY

VOLUME

I

DAR AL-TAQWA

ISBN 1-870582-22-5

Translation: Aisha Bewley

Editor: Abdalhaqq Bewley and
Printed and Bound by The Bath Press

Production: Bookwork, Norwich

Cover design by Sohail Nakhooda
Floral ornament by Ibrahim Batchelder

Published by:
Dar Al Taqwa Ltd.
7A Melcombe Street
Baker Street
London NW1 6AE

بسم الله الرحمن الرحيم

In the name of God, most Gracious, most Merciful

The publisher of Imam Al-Qurtubi inspiring book, Tafseer Al-Qurtubi are deeply grateful to His *Excellency*, *Mr. Easa Saleh Al-Gurg*, *CBE*, for his generosity in making the publication of the book possible. In these days of high production costs of even the most valuable texts, such help as given by *His Excellency* is greatly valued as it enables the book to reach a wider readership.

FOREWORD

I am delighted to have this opportunity to contribute in some way to the publication of al-Qurtubi's Tafsir, which represents a landmark in the history of commentaries on the Holy Qur'an in the English language. The appearance of this translation will give English-speaking readers access to one of the great classical commentaries and the wealth of knowledge that it contains.

Authoritative exposition of the meanings of the Qur'anic text requires consideration of many different aspects including the spiritual, linguistic, legal and historical ones. Imam al-Qurtubi's Tafsir is remarkable in many ways, but he was especially interested in the legal interpretation of the Scripture. This is clear from the original title of his work, which is al-Jami 'li-ankam al-Qur'an ("The Compendium of Qur' anic Decrees"). I congratulate the publishers of this work, Dar al-Taqwa, and the translators on their initiative in making available a major classic of Islamic literature. May Allah Most High accept their efforts, and may this work inspire the ambitions and aid the efforts of many students and scholars in their research on the meaning of the Glorious Qur' an.

Easa Saleh Al-Gurg, CBE.

Table of Contents

Preface

There is a marked dearth in the English language of translations of classical *tafsīr* literature and the overriding intention of the translators in undertaking this abridged translation of *al-Jāmi' li-Aḥkām al-Qur'ān* (The Comprehensive Legal Rulings of the Qur'ān) by Abū 'Abdullāh Muḥammad ibn Aḥmad al-Anṣārī al-Qurṭubī (d. 671/1273) has been to give access to English speaking readers of the Qur'ān to one of the great classical commentaries of the Qur'ān and to the enormous wealth of traditional understanding of the Qur'ānic *āyat*s which it contains.

The explanation of the meaning of Allah's words to mankind in His final Revelation requires many different facets to be taken into consideration – linguistic, spiritual, historical, legal, etc. – and the great commentators, while, of course, covering all of these aspects in general, tended to concentrate on one in particular. As his title makes clear, the special interest of al-Qurṭubī was legal, and his commentary looks in depth at all the legal implications contained in the *āyats* of the Qur'ān. Elucidation of this aspect of the Revelation is, of course, essential to understanding those passages with direct legal significance, as well as providing an extremely illuminating insight to other *āyat*s whose legal import is not immediately obvious, and the approach also shows vividly how the Qur'ān impinges on and should be applied to our daily lives.

However, in his desire to clarify the details of every legal judgement which can be extrapolated from the Qur'ānic *āyat*s, the author tends to digress into the examination of every possible branch of the matter concerned in a way that goes considerably beyond what is necessary for the complete understanding of the *āyat* under discussion. After than simply concentrating on the particular legal ruling derived from the *āyat*, he will provide a detailed explanation of the entire fiqh of the area concerned, including all the differing opinions of different fuqahā', and the weight of their respective arguments. Since the primary object of presenting this work was to provide a tool to enable English speakers to gain a greater understanding of the meaning of the Qur'ān rather than to produce a manual of Islamic law of which there are many available, in their abridgement the translators have cut out the passages which go into extraneous legal detail, aiming to leave only that legal material which serves to really contribute to the understanding of the *āyat* in question. This is one of the ways in which the original work has been abridged.

Further abridgement has taken place through the omission of numerous grammatical and philological points which only relate to the original Arabic and have no bearing when the meaning has been transposed into English.

There are several occasions when a *ḥadīth*, which the author has quoted to assist in the explanation a particular *āyat,* has been followed by other versions of the same *ḥadīth*, often only differing one from the other in the smallest of details. In these instances usually only the first version has been included. The *isnād*s of the *aḥādīth* have also been curtailed to avoid excessive lists of names, as have discussions about the comparative strengths of the different *isnāds* when that has no bearing on the eventual use of the *ḥadīth* involved. Certain other *aḥādīth* have been omitted when they are quoted to demonstrate the linguistic use of a certain word, rather than the subject of the *āyat* itself.

Another thing which has been cut out is several poems which were included in the original, together with the complex discussion on the linguistic usages involved in them, whose translation does not add to the general understanding of the *āyat*s when translated into English.

One other point worth mentioning is that both the Arabic text of the Qur'ān used and also the English rendering of the *āyat*s, which throughout is from the Noble Qur'ān published by Bookwork and is also the work of the present translators, employ the Warsh reading, which is doubly appropriate in this instance since it was undoubtedly the reading which al-Qurṭubī originally studied and the one which was most widespread in the area in which this famous work was originally published. This means that readers may notice a few slight differences between this and other versions with which they may be familiar. It also means that the *āyat* numbering will not be exactly the same as that used in texts and translations based on the Ḥafṣ reading. It should be noted in this regard that there is, in fact, no particular numbering of the *āyat*s which absolutely definitive, and even varies in different printings of the Warsh version, as readers will discover when they read al-Qurṭubī's introduction.

Anyone not familiar with Warsh may wonder about the heavy black dots inserted under or over some letters in the Arabic text. These are used to indicate various points of pronunciation depending on where they are situated. Some mark an *imāla* which means that the pronunciation of the vowel concerned is narrowed and not so open as it would otherwise be. At other times it marks where the hamza would be if the reciter were beginning with word concerned rather than eliding it with the word before. The point is that the unfamiliar reader should realise that this is the normal way in which the Warsh text is written and not an aberration of some kind.

In conclusion, it is important to reiterate that this translation never set out to be a work of dry scholarship, intended to give an exact and literal translation of the original text, but rather is intended to give modern readers access to the immense learning of Imām al-Qurṭubī in such a way that it will illuminate for them the meaning of Allah's words in the Qur'ān and open to them through his wisdom depths of understanding which have not previously been open to them.

We ask Allah to accept this from us and to forgive its many shortcomings and to make it a means to the greater understanding of His Noble Book.

Abdalhaqq and Aisha Bewley
Norwich

Introduction

In the Name of Allah, the All-Merciful, Most Merciful

We seek His help and may Allah bless our master Muḥammad and his family and Companions and grant them abundant peace.

Praise belongs to Allah who began by praising Himself before any praiser praised Him! I testify that there is no god but Allah alone with no partner, the Lord who is One and Self-Sustaining, the Living, Self-Subsistent who does not die, the Master of Majesty and Nobility and immense gifts, He who has spoken the Qur'ān, He who created the human being and blessed him with faith and sent His Messenger Muḥammad, may Allah bless him and grant him peace, with the clarification. He sent him with the Clear Book which distinguishes between doubt and certainty which eloquent men cannot oppose and intelligent men cannot contradict. They cannot bring its like, even if they help one another. He made its examples lessons for those who reflect on them and His commands guidance for those who study them. In it He explains the obligatory judgements and differentiates the lawful and unlawful. In it He repeats admonitions and stories for understanding and different types of metaphors and reports about matters of the Unseen.

The Almighty says, *"We have not omitted anything from the Book."* (6:38) He addresses it to His friends and they understand, and He explains to them what He means in it and they know it. So those who recite the Qur'ān bear a concealed secret of Allah and guard His preserved knowledge. They are the khalifs of His Prophets and His trustees, who are His people, elite and chosen ones. The Messenger of Allah, may Allah bless him and grant him peace, said, "Allah has placed two kinds of people among us."

They asked, "Who are they, Messenger of Allah?" He replied, "They are the people of the Qur'ān, the people of Allah and His elite." (Ibn Mājah and Abū Bakr al-Bazzār)

Anyone who knows the Book of Allah and remembers what has been explained to him in it should be restrained by its prohibitions and fear Allah, be mindful of Him and be ashamed before Him. He has taken on the burdens of the Messengers and has become a witness in the Rising against the opponents among the people of other religions. Allah Almighty said, *"In this way We have made you a middlemost community, so that you may act as witnesses against mankind."* (2:143) The argument is against the one who knows it and neglects it, more than against the one who is lacking in it and ignorant of it. If someone is given knowledge of the Qur'ān and does not benefit from it, is not constrained by its prohibitions and is not deterred by it and commits ugly sins and vile crimes, the Qur'ān is an argument against him. The Messenger of Allah, may Allah bless him and grant him peace, said, "The Qur'ān is an argument for you or against you." (Muslim)

Therefore it is obligatory for anyone chosen by Allah to memorise His Book to have proper respect for it, reflect on the truth of its words, understand its marvels and clarify what is unusual in it. The Almighty says, *"It is a Book We have sent down to you, full of blessings, so let people of intelligence ponder its Signs"* (38:29) and *"Will they not then ponder the Qur'ān or are there locks upon their hearts?"* (47:24) May Allah make us among those who respect it properly, reflect on it deeply, implement its justice, fulfil its conditions and do not seek guidance elsewhere. May He guide us to its outward signs and radiant definitive judgements and by it combine for us the best of this world and the Next! He is worthy to be feared and entitled to forgive.

Then He gave to His Messenger clarification of what was unspecified, explanation of what was difficult, and determination of what was probable, so that, as well as conveying the Message, he showed his special competence in the Revelation which was entrusted to him. Allah says, *"And We have sent down the Reminder to you so that you can make clear to mankind what has been sent down to them."* (16:44) Then, after the Messenger of Allah, may Allah bless him and grant him peace, the scholars were appointed to extract the meanings which it indicates and to point out its principles in order that through *ijtihād* they may reach the knowledge of what is meant. By that they were distinguished from others and they are singled out for reward on account of their efforts. Allah Almighty says, *"Allah will raise in rank those of you who believe and those who have been given knowledge."* (58:11) So the Book became the basis and the *Sunna* its clarification and the deduction of the scholars its exposition and elucidation. Praise be to Allah who has made our breasts the vessels of His Book, our ears the springs of the *Sunna* of His Prophet, and our aspirations directed to learning the Qur'ān and investigating its meanings and unusual words, and by that seeking to please the Lord of the worlds and, by it, to rise to knowledge of the *dīn*.

The Book of Allah is the source of all the sciences of the *Sharī'a* which convey the *Sunna* and the obligatory. It was brought down by the Trustworthy One of heaven to the Trustworthy One of the earth. I thought that I should devote myself to it for my entire life and devote my strength to that cause by writing a brief commentary on it containing some points of *tafsīr*, linguistics, grammar, and recitations, refutation of the people of deviation and misguidance as well as several *aḥādīth* which attest to what we mention regarding judgements and the revelation of *āyat*s, thereby combining the meanings of both and explaining what is abstruse in them using the statements of the *Salaf* and those who followed them. I have done this to remind myself and as a security for the day when I am buried and as a righteous action after my death. Allah says, *"On that Day man will be told what he did and failed to do"* (75:13) and *"Each self will know what it has sent ahead and left behind."* (82:5) The Prophet, peace be upon him, said, "When a man dies, his actions are cut off except for three – an ongoing *ṣadaqa* and knowledge which brought benefit and a virtuous child who makes supplication for him."

I intend in this book to attribute statements to their speakers and *aḥādīth* to their compilers. It is said that part of the blessing of knowledge is to ascribe a statement to its speaker. Many *aḥādīth* are reported in books of *tafsīr* and *fiqh* unattributed and so the one who reads them does not know who transmitted them. Therefore someone without information about that remains confused and does not know the sound from the weak. It is a vast science. Therefore he does not accept it as evidence until he knows to whom it is ascribed among the famous imāms and reliable scholars of Islam. We have indicated some of that in this book. Allah is the one who grants success. I have only used those stories of commentators and reports of historians which are necessary for clarification.

Its title is: *The General Judgements of the Qur'ān and Clarification of what it contains of the Sunna and Āyats of Discrimination.* May Allah make it sincerely for His sake and grant me and my parents the benefit of it. He hears the supplication and is quick to respond. Amen.

The General Virtues of the Qur'ān and encouragement to study it. The excellence of the one who seeks it, recites it, listens to it and acts by it.

This topic is vast and scholars have written many books on it. We will mention some points which point out the excellence of the Qur'ān and what Allah has prepared for its people when they are sincere for His sake and act by it. The first aspect of the excellence of the Qur'ān that the believer should be aware of is that it is from the Lord of the worlds and is uncreated. It consists of unparalleled words and has a quality which has no equivalent or like. It comes from the light of Allah's Essence. Recitation is the voices of the reciters and their tunes. It is their acquisition, and they are commanded to do it as an obligation in certain acts of worship and it is recommended at many times. They are forbidden to recite it when they are in a state of major impurity, and are rewarded for doing it and punished for abandoning it. This is part of what the Muslims, the people of the Truth, agree on. Traditions state that and well-known reports prove it.

Reward and punishment are only connected to what is part of what people earn, as will be explained. Were it not that Allah had placed in the hearts of His slaves the strength to bear it so that they can reflect on it, study it and remember what it contains of His obedience, worship and performing His duties and obligations, they would be too weak and would collapse under its weight or perish. How could they bear it when Allah says, *"Had We sent down this Qur'ān onto a mountain, you would have seen it humbled, crushed to pieces out of fear of Allah"* (59:21)? What is the strength of hearts compared to that of the mountains? But Allah provided His slaves with the strength to bear what He wishes as a favour and mercy from Him.

As for traditions about this topic, the first is what at-Tirmidhī transmitted from Abū Sa'īd that the Messenger of Allah, may Allah bless him and grant him peace, said, "The blessed and exalted Lord said, 'If anyone is distracted from asking Me by the Qur'ān and remembering Me, I will give him better than what I give the askers.'" He also said, "The excellence of the words of Allah over all other words is like the excellence of Allah over His creation." (*ḥasan gharīb ḥadīth*) As-Samarqandī reported in his *Musnad* that 'Abdullāh said, "The seven long *sūra*s are like the Torah. The [*sūra*s with] a hundred *āyat*s are like the Gospel. and the *Mathānī* is like the *Zabūr.* The rest of the Qur'ān is excellent."

In at-Tirmidhī, 'Alī reported, "I heard the Messenger of Allah, may Allah bless him and grant him peace, say, 'There will be trials like patches of dark night.' I asked, 'Messenger of Allah, how can one escape them?' He replied, 'The Book of Allah, Blessed and Exalted, contains your history, information about what came before you, news about what will come after you and correct judgement between you. It is decisive, not a jest. Allah will crush any tyrant who abandons it and Allah will misguide whoever seeks guidance from other than it. It is the Firm Rope of Allah, His Clear Light and the Wise Reminder. It is the Straight Path. Passions are not misguided by it, the tongues do not become sated with it, and the godfearing do not become bored by it. It does not wear out when it is recited a lot and its wonders do not cease. It is that which the *jinn* did not leave once they had heard it. They said, *"We heard a wonderful Qur'ān which guides to right guidance."* (72:1-2) Whoever knows it has knowledge which takes precedence. Whoever utters it speaks the truth. Whoever judges by it is just. Whoever acts by it is rewarded. Whoever calls to it is guided to a straight path. Take it, one-eyed.'"[1]

Al-Anbārī says in his book, *The Refutation of the One who Opposes the Recension of 'Uthmān*, transmitting from 'Abdullāh ibn Mas'ūd, that the Messenger of Allah, may Allah bless him and grant him peace, said, "This Qur'ān is the Banquet of Allah. Learn as much as you can from His banquet. This Qur'ān is the Rope of Allah, and it is the Clear Light and Useful Healing. It is a protection for the one who clings to it and a rescue for the one who follows it. It is not crooked and so puts things straight. It does not deviate so as to be blamed. Its wonders do not cease. It does not wear out with much repetition. So recite it. Allah will reward you with ten good deeds for every letter of its recitation. I do not say that *Alif-Lām-Mīm* is a letter nor two *alifs*, one placing its foot on the other. You should not stop reciting *Sūrat al-Baqara*. Shayṭān flees from a house in which *Sūrat al-Baqara* is recited. The house most devoid of good is a house empty of the Book of Allah." In *Gharīb* Abū 'Ubayd quotes 'Abdullāh (ibn Mas'ūd): "This Qur'ān is the Banquet of Allah. Whoever enters it is safe." He said, "The interpretation of the *ḥadīth* is that it is a metaphor. The Qur'ān is likened to something Allah has prepared for people. They have good and benefits in it. Then He invited them to it."

Al-Bukhārī transmits from 'Uthmān ibn 'Affān that the Prophet, may Allah bless him and grant him peace, said, "The best of you is the one who learns the Qur'ān and teaches it." Muslim transmitted from Abū Mūsā that the Messenger of Allah, may Allah bless him and grant him peace, said, "The metaphor of a believer who recites the Qur'ān is that of a citron – its scent is fragrant and its taste is good. The metaphor of a believer who does

1. This is Ibrāhīm an-Nakhā'ī, who had one eye (*a'war*).

not recite the Qur'ān is that of a date – it has no scent but its taste is sweet. The metaphor of a hypocrite who recites the Qur'ān is that of basil – its scent is fragrant but its taste is bitter. The metaphor of a hypocrite who does not recite the Qur'ān is that of colocynth – it has no scent and its taste is bitter."

Abū Bakr al-Anbārī mentioned that when someone finished the Qur'ān, Abū 'Abdu'r-Raḥmān as-Sulamī would sit him before him and put his hand on his head and say to him, "You! Fear Allah! I do not know of anyone better than you if you act by what you know." Ad-Dārimī reported that Wahb ad-Dhimārī said, "If Allah gives someone the Qur'ān and he stands reciting it at the ends of the night and the ends of the day and acts by what is in it and dies in obedience, on the Day of Rising Allah will raise him up with the angels and Prophets."

Muslim related that 'Ā'isha reported that the Messenger of Allah, may Allah bless him and grant him peace, said, "Someone who recites the Qur'ān and is fluent in it is with the noble pious angels. Someone who recites the Qur'ān and stammers in it has two rewards as it is difficult for him." He will have one reward for the recitation and one reward for the difficulty. The levels of the fluent reciter are all above that because the Qur'ān was difficult for him and then he rose beyond that to be like the angels. Allah knows best.

At-Tirmidhī reports from 'Abdullāh ibn Mas'ūd that the Messenger of Allah, may Allah bless him and grant him peace, said, "Whoever recites a letter of the Book of Allah earns a good deed, and each good deed is worth ten like it. I do not say that *'Alif-lām-mīm'* is one letter, but that *alif* is a letter, *lām* is a letter, and *mīm* is a letter." (*ḥasan ṣaḥīḥ gharīb*)

Muslim reported that 'Uqba ibn 'Āmir said, "The Messenger of Allah, may Allah bless him and grant him peace, came out to us while we were in the *Ṣuffa* and asked, 'Which of you would like to go every day to Buṭḥān or to al-'Aqīq and bring two large-humped she-camels from it without wrongdoing?' We said, 'Messenger of Allah, all of us would like that!' He said, 'Does not one of you go to the mosque and teach or recite two *āyat*s from the Book of

Allah? That is better for him than two camels, and three verses are better for him than three camels, four verses are better than four camels, and so on regarding the number of camels.'"

Abū Hurayra reported that the Messenger of Allah, may Allah bless him and grant him peace, said, "Allah will relieve anyone who relieves a believer of one of the afflictions of this world of one of the afflictions of the Day of Rising. Allah will give ease in this world and the Next to anyone who eases the hardship of another. Allah will veil anyone who veils another Muslim in this world and the Next. Allah will help His slave as long as His slave is helping his brother. Whoever travels a path on which he seeks knowledge, Allah will make the path to the Garden easy for him. People do not meet in one of the houses of Allah to recite the Book of Allah and study it together without tranquillity descending on them, mercy covering them, angels encircling them and Allah mentioning them to those who are with Him."

Abū Dāwūd, an-Nasā'ī, ad-Dārimī, and at-Tirmidhī reported that 'Uqba ibn 'Āmir heard the Prophet, may Allah bless him and grant him peace, say, "The one who recites the Qur'ān publicly is like the person who gives his *ṣadaqa* publicly. The one who recites the Qur'ān secretly is like the person who conceals his *ṣadaqa*." (*ḥasan gharīb*) At-Tirmidhī reported from Abū Hurayra that the Prophet, may Allah bless him and grant him peace, said, "The Qur'ān will come on the Day of Rising and say, 'O Lord, robe him!' and He will put on him the crown of nobility.' It will say, 'O Lord, more!' and He will put on him the robe of honour. Then it will say, 'O Lord, be pleased with him!' and He will be pleased with him. It will be said, 'Recite and ascend,' and he will be increased with a good deed for every *āyat*." (*ṣaḥīḥ*)

Abū Dāwūd reported from 'Abdullāh ibn 'Amr that the Messenger of Allah, may Allah bless him and grant him peace, said, "Those who know the Qur'ān will be told, 'Recite and ascend. Recite slowly as you did in the world below. Your station will be at the last verse you recite.'" Ibn Mājah transmitted that Abū Sa'īd al-Khudrī reported that the Messenger of Allah, may Allah bless him and grant him peace, said, "The one who knows the Qur'ān will be told, 'Recite and ascend.' He will recite and rise a degree by every *āyat* until he reaches the last thing he has."

Al-Anbārī transmitted from Umm Umāma al-Ḥimṣī that the Messenger of Allah, may Allah bless him and grant him peace, said, "Whoever is given a third of the Qur'ān has been given a third of Prophethood. Whoever is given two-thirds of the Qur'ān has been given two-thirds of Prophethood. Whoever recites all of the Qur'ān has been given all of Prophethood although he has not received any revelation. On the Day of Rising he will be told, 'Recite and ascend.' He will recite an *āyat* and rise a degree until he finishes what he knows of the Qur'ān. Then he will be told, 'Take,' and he will take. Then he will be asked, 'Do you know what is in your hands? Eternity is in your right hand and bliss in your left.'"

Al-Marwazī reported from 'Alī that the Messenger of Allah, may Allah bless him and grant him peace, said, "If someone reads the Qur'ān, recites it and memorises it, Allah will admit him to the Garden and let him intercede for all the people of his family for whom the Fire is mandatory." Umm ad-Dardā' said, "I visited 'Ā'isha and asked her, 'What is the excellence of the one who recites the Qur'ān over the one who does not recite it among those who enter the Garden?' 'Ā'isha replied, 'The number of the *āyat*s of the Qur'ān is according to the number of degrees of the Garden. No one will enter the Garden better than the one who recites the Qur'ān.'" Abū Muḥammad Makkī mentioned it. Ibn 'Abbās said, "If anyone recites the Qur'ān and follows what is in it, Allah has guided him from misguidance and will protect him on the Day of Rising from an evil reckoning. That is because Allah says, *'All those who follow My guidance will not go astray and will not be miserable.'* (20:123)" Ibn 'Abbās said, "Allah has guaranteed that the one who follows the Qur'ān will not go astray in this world nor be wretched in the Next." Makkī also mentioned that. Al-Layth said, "It was said that mercy does not come quicker to anyone than to the one who listens to the Qur'ān according to the words of the Almighty, *'When the Qur'ān is recited, listen to it and be silent so* *that hopefully you will gain mercy.'* (7:204)" The word "hopefully" makes it mandatory for Allah.

In the *Musnad* of Abū Dāwūd aṭ-Ṭayālisī, it is reported from 'Abdullāh ibn 'Amr that the Messenger of Allah, may Allah bless him and grant him peace, said, "Anyone who stands [in prayer] for ten *āyat*s will not be written among the heedless. Anyone who stands for a hundred *āyat*s will be written among the obedient. Anyone who stands for a thousand *āyat*s will be written among those with heaps [*qinṭar*s] of reward." There are many traditions about this, and what we have mentioned is adequate. Allah is the One who grants success.

How to recite the Book of Allah and what is disliked and forbidden in it, and people's disagreement about that.

Al-Bukhārī transmitted that Qatāda said, "I asked Anas about the recitation of the Messenger of Allah, may Allah bless him and grant him peace, and he said, 'He would lengthen syllables when he recited, "In the Name of Allah, the All-Merciful, Most Merciful." He would extend the name *"Allāh"*, extend *"ar-Raḥmān"* (the All-Merciful) and extend *"ar-Raḥīm"* (the Most Merciful).""'

At-Tirmidhī reported that Umm Salama said, "The Messenger of Allah, may Allah bless him and grant him peace, used to put stops in his recitation. He would say, *'Praise be to Allah, the Lord of the worlds,'* and stop, *'the All-Merciful, Most Merciful,'* and stop. Then he would recite, *'Master of the Day of Repayment.'*" (*gharīb*, Abū Dāwūd transmitted a similar *ḥadīth*.)

It is related that the Prophet, may Allah bless him and grant him peace, said, "The person with the best voice is the one that I see fears Allah Almighty when he recites." It is related that Ziyād an-Numayrī came with the reciters to Anas ibn Mālik and was told to recite. He raised his voice and intoned. He had a loud voice and Anas uncovered his face, as he had a black cloth over it, and said,

"You! what is this you are doing?" When he saw something he objected to, he would remove the cloth from his face.

It is related that Qays ibn 'Ubbād said, "The Companions of the Messenger of Allah used to dislike raising the voice in *dhikr*." Those who disliked raising the voice in recitation of the Qur'ān included Sa'īd ibn al-Musayyab, Sa'īd ibn Jubayr, al-Qāsim ibn Muḥammad, al-Ḥasan, Ibn Sīrīn, an-Nakhā'ī and others. Mālik ibn Anas and Aḥmad ibn Ḥanbal also disliked it. All of them disliked raising the voice with the Qur'ān and intoning it. It is related that Sa'īd ibn al-Musayyab heard 'Umar ibn 'Abdu'l-'Azīz leading the people and he intoned in his recitation. Sa'īd sent a message to him saying, "May Allah put you right! Imāms should not recite like that." So 'Umar stopped singing. Al-Qāsim ibn Muḥammad said, "A man recited in the mosque of the Prophet and intoned and al-Qāsim objected to that. He said, Allah Almighty says, *'Truly it is a Mighty Book. Falsehood cannot reach it from before it or behind it.'* (41:41-42)" Mālik related that he was asked about *nabr* (raising the voice) when reciting the Qur'ān in the prayer and he disliked that strongly and objected to the raising of the voice in recitation. Ibn al-Qāsim related from him that he was asked about melody in the prayer and he said, "I do not like it." He said, "It is a kind of singing which they do and for which they are paid money."

One group permit raising the voice in the Qur'ān and intoning it. That is because, when someone beautifies his voice in it, it settles more deeply in the selves and the hearts listen more to it. They find evidence in the words of the Prophet, may Allah bless him and grant him peace, "Adorn the Qur'ān with your voices." Al-Barā' ibn 'Āzib transmitted it as did Abū Dāwūd and an-Nasā'ī. The Prophet, may Allah bless him and grant him peace, said, "He who does not sing the Qur'ān is not one of us." (Muslim). There is also what Abū Mūsā told the Prophet: "If I had known that you listened to my recitation, I would have beautified it for you." 'Abdullāh ibn Mughaffal said, "In a journey in the year of the Conquest, the Messenger of Allah, may Allah bless him and grant him peace, recited *Sūrat al-Fatḥ* on his mount and he used a quavering tone in his recitation." Some of those who believed this were Abū Ḥanīfa and his people, ash-Shāfi'ī, Ibn al-Mubārak and an-Naḍr ibn Shumayl. It is the choice of aṭ-Ṭabarī, Abū'l-Ḥasan ibn Baṭṭāl, Qāḍī Abū Bakr ibn al-'Arabī and others.

The first position is sounder because of what we already mentioned and will mention. As for using the first *ḥadīth* as evidence, it is not apparent. It is an example of the reversal of the normal order and in fact means, "Adorn your voices with the Qur'ān." Al-Khaṭṭābī said, "That is how more than one of the Imāms of *Ḥadīth* have explained it, saying it is reversal."

Al-Khaṭṭābī related from al-Barā' that the Messenger of Allah, may Allah bless him and grant him peace, said, "Adorn the Qur'ān with your voices." He said, "It means be melodious in the recitation and employ your voices to do it and take it as a sign and adornment." It is said that it means to encourage people to recite the Qur'ān and persist in it. It is related from Abū Hurayra that he heard the Messenger of Allah say, "Adorn your voices with the Qur'ān." It is related that 'Umar said, "Make your voices good with the Qur'ān."

It is to this sense that the words of the Prophet, may Allah bless him and grant him peace, refer when he said, "The one who does not sing the Qur'ān is not one of us," meaning "the one who does not make his voice good with the Qur'ān is not one of us." That is how 'Abdullāh ibn Abī Mulayka interpreted it. 'Abdu'l-Jabbār ibn al-Wird said that he heard Ibn Abī Mulayka say that 'Abdullāh ibn Abī Yazīd said, "Abū Lubāba passed us and we followed him until he went into his house. He was a man of shabby appearance. I heard him say, 'I heard the Messenger of Allah, may Allah bless him and grant him peace, say, "He who does not sing the Qur'ān is not one of us."'" 'Abdu'l-Jabbār said, "I asked Ibn Abī Mulayka, 'Abū Muḥammad, what do you think of the one who does not have a good voice?' He replied, 'He makes it as good as he can.'" (Abū Dāwūd)

This is also the meaning of Abū Mūsā's words to the Prophet, may Allah bless him and grant him peace: "If I had known that you were listening to my recitation, I would have made my voice good in the Qur'ān, adorned it and used *tartīl* (slow recitation)."

This indicates that he was quick in his recitation with a good natural voice. If he had known that the Prophet, may Allah bless him and grant him peace, was listening, he would have extended his recitation and used *tartīl* as he usually did when he recited to the Messenger of Allah. He used to do that in order to increase the beauty of his voice when reciting.

We seek refuge with Allah from interpreting what the Messenger of Allah, may Allah bless him and grant him peace, said as meaning that the Qur'ān is adorned by voices or anything else! Whoever interprets it in this way has committed something terrible in saying that the Qur'ān is in need of someone to adorn it. It is Light, Illumination, and the Highest Adornment for the one who wears its splendour and is illuminated by its light. It is said that the command to adorn means to learn the readings and to adorn them with our voices. That implies: "adorn the recitation with your voices," since "*qur'ān*" means recitation as Allah says, *"The recitation (*qur'ān*) of dawn."* (17:78) According to this interpretation, it is valid that it simply means "to recite" as we made clear.

It is said that the word understood as "singing" (*yataghanna*) comes from *istighnā*, "not having any need", not from *ghinā'* (singing). This was the interpretation adopted by Sufyān ibn 'Uyayna and Wakī' ibn al-Jarrāḥ. Sufyān related that from Sa'd ibn Abī Waqqāṣ. Another point is also related from Sufyān which Isḥāq ibn Rāhawayh mentioned, which is that it means "to be enriched and without need of other words". This is the interpretation preferred by al-Bukhārī when he dealt with the verse, *"Is it not enough for them that We have sent down to you the Book which is recited to them?"* (29:51) What is meant by being enriched by the Qur'ān is not being in need of the history of nations. Interpreters have said that.

It is said that *"yataghanna"* means to display sorrow. In other words sorrow should appear in the reciter when he reads and recites, and it does not come from "*ghunya*" (being able to dispense with) because a different form of the verb would have been used for that. A group of scholars believed that, including Imām Ibn Ḥibbān al-Bustī. Their evidence was what Muṭarrif ibn

'Abdullāh ibn ash-Shikhkhīr related from his father: "I came to the Messenger of Allah, may Allah bless him and grant him peace, while he was praying and his chest was heaving like a cauldron from weeping." They said, "This report makes it clear that what is meant is displaying sorrow. This is also supported by what the Imāms related from 'Abdullāh: "The Prophet, may Allah bless him and grant him peace, said, 'Recite to me.' So I recited *Sūrat an-Nisā'* to him until I reached the *āyat, 'How will it be when We bring a witness from every nation and bring you as a witness against them?'* (4:41) I saw his eyes overflowing with tears."

These are four interpretations and none of them indicate that recitation is done with tunes or quavering voices. Abū Sa'īd al-A'rabī said about "He who does not sing the Qur'ān is not one of us": "The Arabs were keen on singing and using verse in most of what they said. When the Qur'ān was revealed, they wanted to use the Qur'ān as their chant instead of singing, and the Prophet said this."

The fifth interpretation is what some claim as evidence for quavering and singing. 'Umar ibn Shayba said, "I told Abū 'Āṣim about Ibn 'Uyayna's interpretation regarding 'singing' meaning 'beyond need' and he said, 'Ibn 'Uyayna did not do well.'" Ash-Shāfi'ī was asked about the interpretation of Ibn 'Uyayna and said, "I know better than this. If the Prophet, may Allah bless him and grant him peace, had meant not having need, he would have said it. He said, 'singing' and so we know that he meant singing." Aṭ-Ṭabarī said, "What is known in our view is that *taghannin* is singing in the language of the Arabs, which is using a good voice with quavering." As for those who claim that it means 'being without need', that is not part of the language and poems of the Arabs. We do not know any of the people of knowledge who said that.

In respect of what aṭ-Ṭabarī claimed about *taghanna* not meaning *istighnā* in Arabic, al-Jawharī stated what we mentioned as did al-Harawī. There is nothing to prevent it meaning *istighnā*, as it is indeed more appropriate to accept that which is related from a great Companion as Sufyān reported. Ibn Wahb said about Sufyān,

"I have not seen anyone with better knowledge of the interpretation of *aḥādīth* than Sufyān ibn 'Uyayna."

A sixth interpretation is what has come in the form of an addition in *Ṣaḥīḥ* Muslim which is that Abū Hurayra heard the Messenger of Allah, may Allah bless him and grant him peace, say, "Allah does not listen to anything so gladly as He listens to a Prophet with a good voice chanting the Qur'ān aloud." Aṭ-Ṭabarī said, "If it had been as Ibn 'Uyayna said, there would be no point in mentioning a good voice and aloud." The word "aloud", can be part of the words of the Prophet, Abū Hurayra or someone else. If it is the first, which is unlikely, it is evidence of lack of warbling (*tatrīb*) and quavering because he did not say that. He said, "aloud", meaning so that he and those around him can hear him as the Prophet said to someone he heard raising his voice in the *shahāda*, "O mankind! Be kind to yourselves. You are not calling out to someone dead or absent." So there is no evidence for what they claim. Some of our scholars preferred this interpretation, saying that it is the most likely because the Arabs use the term translated as "singing out" for the one who raises his voice and directs it to someone absent even if it had no tune. He said, "This is the explanation of the Companion, and he knows their manner of speaking far better."

Abū'l-Ḥasan ibn Baṭṭāl argues for the school of ash-Shāfi'ī and says, "The removal of the difficulty in this question is found in what Ibn Abī Shayba reported … from 'Uqba ibn 'Āmir who said that the Messenger of Allah, may Allah bless him and grant him peace, said, "Learn the Qur'ān, sing it and write it. By the One who has my soul in His hand, it is more likely to escape than a camel from the hobble." Our scholars said, "Even if this *ḥadīth* has a sound *isnād*, what is known absolutely and definitively refutes it: the recitation of the Qur'ān has reached us *mutawātir* from many shaykhs, generation after generation back to the noble era and to the Messenger of Allah, may Allah bless him and grant him peace, and there was no making of tunes or intoning (*tatrīb*) related by them while they go into depth regarding the pronunciation of the letters, *madda, idghām, iẓhār* and other types of recitation."

Furthermore, in quavering and intoning, there is putting a *hamza* on what does not have a *hamza* and a lengthening of what should not be lengthened. So the single *alif* will be made into two *alif*s and one *wāw* into two. That leads to an increase in the Qur'ān which is forbidden. If that occurs in a place where there is *hamza*, they make several *hamza*s. It may be said that 'Abdullāh ibn Mughaffal said that the Messenger of Allah, may Allah bless him and grant him peace, recited on his camel in the Year of the Conquest of Makka (8/630) and quavered, which al-Bukhārī mentioned. He said, describing it, *"a' a' a'"* three times. That may mean *ishbā'* which is lengthening the vowel of the *madda* in its proper place.

It is also possible that the story of his voice has to do with the rocking of his camel, as it happens to someone in a loud voice when he is riding and his voice tightens and is cut because of the rocking of the camel. Since this is possible, then there is no evidence in it. 'Abdu'l-Ghanī ibn Sa'īd transmitted from the *ḥadīth* of Qatāda from 'Abdu'r-Raḥmān ibn Abī Bakr who reported that his father said, "The recitation of the Messenger of Allah, may Allah bless him and grant him peace, was extended (*madd*) but there was no quavering (*tarjī'*)." Ibn Jurayj reported that Ibn 'Abbās said, "The Messenger of Allah had a *mu'adhdhin* who intoned. The Messenger of Allah, may Allah bless him and grant him peace, said, "The *adhān* should be easy and smooth (i.e. without trilling). If your *adhān* is not easy and smooth, then do not give the *adhān*." (ad-Dāraquṭnī) If the Prophet, may Allah bless him and grant him peace, forbade it in the *adhān*, it is more likely that he would not permit it in the Qur'ān which the All-Merciful preserves as Allah says, *"It is We who have sent down the Reminder and We will preserve it."* (15:9)

This disagreement regarding recitation is a result of the meaning of the Qur'ān not being understood due to the repetition of voices and the great amount of quavering. If the matter goes further so that the meaning cannot be understood, then that is agreed to be forbidden. This is done by reciters in the towns of Egypt who recite before kings and at funerals and receive wages and stipends for doing so. Their effort is misguided and their work is ruined. By so doing they allow the alteration of the Book of Allah and it makes it easy for them to be bold against Allah by adding to His revelation what was not in it out of ignorance in their *dīn*, deviation from the *Sunna* of their Prophet, rejecting the course of the righteous *Salaf* in respect of that matter, and longing for what Shayṭān has made seem attractive in what they do. They "suppose that they are doing good" while they repeat their error and play with the Book of Allah. We are returning to Allah, but the Truthful One, may Allah bless him and grant him peace, reported that that would happen and so it is as he, may Allah bless him and grant him peace, reported it would be.

Imām Razīn and at-Tirmidhī al-Ḥakīm in *Nawādir al-Uṣūl* reported the *ḥadīth* transmitted by Ḥudhayfa in which the Messenger of Allah, may Allah bless him and grant him peace, said, "Recite the Qur'ān with the tunes and voices of the Arabs and beware of the tunes of the people of passionate love and the tunes of the People of the two Books [meaning the Torah and Gospel]. After you will come a people who quaver their voices while reciting the Qur'ān, as is done in singing and wailing. That will not go beyond their throats. Their hearts are tempted and attracting the hearts of those who admire them is what really concerns them." "Tunes" refers to intoning, quavering the voice and being good in recitation, poetry and singing.

Our scholars state that this is like those of the reciters of our time who do that before prayers and in gatherings, using foreign tunes which the Prophet, may Allah bless him and grant him peace, forbade. Quavering (*tarjī'*) in recitation is to repeat the letters like the Christians do. *Tartīl* in reciting the Qur'ān is to recite slowly and deliberately, and to make the letters and vowels clear. It is like the petals of the daisy. It is desirable when reciting the Qur'ān. Allah says, *"Recite the Qur'ān distinctly."* (73:4) Umm Salama was asked about the recitation and prayer of the Prophet, peace be upon him, and she said, "What do you have to do with his prayer! He prayed and then slept the amount he prayed. Then he prayed the amount he slept and then he slept the amount he prayed until morning." Then she described his recitation, which was an explanatory recitation, letter by letter. An-Nasā'ī, Abu Dāwūd and at-Tirmidhī transmitted it as being *ḥasan ṣaḥīḥ gharīb*.

Cautioning the people of the Qur'ān and scholars against showing off

Allah Almighty says, *"Worship Allah and do not associate anything with Him"* (4:36) and the Almighty also says, *"So let him who hopes to meet his Lord act rightly and not associate anyone in the worship of his Lord."* (18:110). Muslim reported from Abū Hurayra that he heard the Messenger of Allah, may Allah bless him and grant him peace, say, "The first of people to be judged on the Day of Rising will be a man who was martyred. He will be brought forward and will be informed of the blessings he had and will acknowledge them. Allah will ask, 'What did you do with them?' He will say, 'I fought for You until I was martyred.' Allah will say, 'You lie. Rather you fought so it would be said, "A bold man!" And so it was said.' Then the command will be given and he will be dragged on his face until he is thrown into the Fire.

"There will also be a man who studied knowledge and taught it and recited the Qur'ān. He will be brought and informed of his blessings which he will acknowledge. Allah will say, 'What did you do with them?' He will reply, 'I studied knowledge and taught it and I recited the Qur'ān for You.' Allah will say, 'You lie. Rather you studied so that it would be said, "A scholar!" and you recited so that it would be said, "He is a reciter!" And so it was said.' Then the command will be given and he will be dragged on his face until he is thrown into the Fire.

"There will also be a man to whom Allah gave a lot of wealth and all sorts of property. He will be brought and informed of his blessings which he will acknowledge. Allah will ask, 'What did you do with them?' He will answer, 'There was no path in which You like spending to be done but that I spent in it for You.' Allah will say, 'You lie. Rather you did it so that it would be said, "He is generous." and so it was said.' Then the command will be given and he will be dragged on his face until he is thrown into the Fire."

In the *Raqā'iq*, Ibn al-Mubārak transmitted from al-'Abbās ibn 'Abdu'l-Muṭṭalib that the Messenger of Allah, may Allah bless him and grant him peace, said, "This *dīn* will be victorious until it passes the sea and until you plunge into the sea with horses in the Way of Allah Almighty. Then there will come a people who recite the Qur'ān. When they recite it, they will say, 'Who reads more than us? Who knows more than us?'" Then he turned to his Companions and said, "Do you think that there will be any good in those?" "No," they replied. He said, "Those are from you and those are from this Community and those are the fuel of the Fire." Abū Dāwūd and at-Tirmidhī transmitted that the Messenger of Allah said, "Anyone who learns knowledge which should be learned for the sake of Allah, the Mighty and Majestic, only to obtain by it goods of this world, will not experience the scent of the Garden on the Day of Rising." At-Tirmidhī said it is a *ḥasan ḥadīth.*

It is reported that Abū Hurayra reported that the Messenger of Allah, may Allah bless him and grant him peace, said, "Seek refuge with Allah from the Pit of Sorrow." They asked, "Messenger of Allah, what is the Pit of Sorrow?" He replied, "It is a valley in Hell from which Hell seeks refuge a hundred times a day." He was asked, "Messenger of Allah, who will enter it?" He replied, "Those who recite to show off their actions." (*gharīb*) In the book of Asad ibn Mūsā it is reported that the Prophet, may Allah bless him and grant him peace, said, "There is a valley in Hell, and Hell seeks refuge from the evil of that valley seven times a day. In that valley is a pit, and Hell and that valley seek refuge from the evil of that pit. In that pit is a serpent and Hell, the valley and the pit seek refuge with Allah from the evil of that serpent seven times. Allah has prepared it for the wretched among those who know the Qur'ān and disobey Allah."

So the one who knows the Qur'an and seeks knowledge should fear Allah regarding himself and act sincerely for Allah. If he does anything which is disliked, he should hasten to repent and begin to show sincerity in his goal and his actions. The one who knows the Qur'ān must guard himself more carefully than others, as he has a wage which others do not have. At-Tirmidhī transmitted that Abū'd-Dardā' reported that the Messenger of Allah, may Allah bless him and grant him peace, said, "Allah revealed in one of the Books to one of the Prophets, 'Warn those who seek understanding for other than the *dīn* and learn for other than action and seek this world by the deeds of the Next world. They will wear sheep-skins in front of people to give the impression of meekness while their hearts are like the hearts of wolves. Their tongues are sweeter than honey while their hearts are more bitter than aloes. They will try to deceive Me and will make light of Me. I will send them trials which will leave even the forbearing bewildered.'"

At-Ṭabarī transmitted in *Adab an-Nufūs* that one of the Companions of the Prophet said that the Messenger of Allah, may Allah bless him and grant him peace, said, "Do not try to deceive Allah. If anyone tries to deceive Allah, Allah will deceive him. It is his own self which is deceived if he were only aware." They asked, "Messenger of Allah, how can someone try to deceive Allah?" He replied, "By doing what Allah has commanded you while you seek other than Him by it. Fear showing-off. It is *shirk*. The one who shows off will be summoned before witnesses on the Day of Rising by four names which he is called: 'O unbeliever! O loser! O perfidious! O deviant! Your actions are lost and your reward is nullified. You have no share today. Seek your reward from those you acted for, O impostor!"

It is reported from 'Alqama that 'Abdullāh ibn Mas'ūd said, "How will you feel when you are enveloped by a trial in which children grow old and the old become senile and people will act according to an innovated *sunna*? When any of it is changed, it will be said, 'The *sunna* has been changed.'" He was asked, "When will that be, Abū 'Abdu'r-Raḥmān?" He replied, "When your reciters are many and your *fuqahā'* are few, and your leaders are many and your trusted ones are few, and this world is sought by the actions of the Next World and people learn *fiqh* for other than the *dīn*." Sufyān ibn 'Uyayna said, "I heard that Ibn 'Abbās said, 'If those who know the Qur'ān had taken it as it should be taken and in the way that is proper, Allah would love them. But they seek this world by it and so Allah hates them and they are indulgent with people.'" It is related from Muḥammad ibn 'Alī about the words of the Almighty, *"They will be bundled headfirst into it, they and the misled"* (26:94), "This refers to people who describe the truth and justice with their tongues and then oppose it by espousing something other than that."

What the one who knows the Qur'ān must do and not neglect to do

The first thing is to be sincere in seeking it for Allah as we mentioned. You should make yourself recite the Qur'ān night and day, in the prayer or outside the prayer, so that you do not forget it. Muslim transmitted from Ibn 'Umar that the Messenger of Allah, may Allah bless him and grant him peace, said, "The example of the one who knows the Qur'ān is like the one who has hobbled camels. If he takes care of them, he will keep them. If he releases them, they will go off. When the one who knows the Qur'ān stands and recites it night and day, he remembers it. If he does not do that, he forgets it." So someone who knows the Qur'ān must praise Allah, be thankful for His blessing, remember Him, rely on Him, seek His help, desire Him and cling to Him. He must remember death and prepare for it. He should fear his wrong actions and hope for his Lord's pardon. His fear when his health is good should be stronger since he does not know what his seal will be. When he is close to dying, his hope should be stronger in himself because of his good opinion of Allah. The Messenger of Allah, may Allah bless him and grant him peace, said, "None of you should die except with a good opinion of Allah." This means you should think that He will have mercy on you and forgive you.

He should know the people of his time, preserve himself from the ruler, and strive to save himself and save his life, having to hand what he can of the goods of this world, striving for himself in that as much as he can. His greatest concern should be scrupulousness in his *dīn*, fearfulness of Allah and watchful awareness of Him in what He commands and forbids. Ibn Mas'ūd said, "The one who recites the Qur'ān should be known by his nights when people are asleep and his days when people are awake, his weeping when people laugh, his silence when people delve into improper matters, his humility when they are arrogant and his sorrow when they are happy." 'Abdullāh ibn 'Umar said, "The one who knows the Qur'ān should not delve with those who delve, nor be ignorant with the ignorant, but he should pardon and overlook by the right of the Qur'ān because inside of him are the words of Allah Almighty. He must protect himself from doubtful paths and laugh little and speak little in the gatherings of the Qur'ān and elsewhere concerning anything in which there is no benefit. He must be forbearing and grave.

He should be humble to the poor and avoid arrogance and vanity. He should withdraw from this world and its people if he fears temptation for himself, and should abandon argumentation and dispute. He should make an effort to be kind and show proper *adab*. He should be with those from whose evil he is safe, whose good he hopes for and from whose injury he is safe. He should not listen to those who slander in his presence and should keep the company of those who lead him to what is good and direct him to truthfulness and noble character, those who adorn him and do not sully him.

He must learn the rulings of the Qur'ān and understand what Allah means and what He obliges. Then he will benefit from what he reads and act by what he recites. How vile is the one who knows the Qur'ān and recites its obligations and rulings by heart but does not understand what he recites. How can the one who does not understand what it means act? How ugly it is that he is asked about the *fiqh* of what he recites but does not know it. The example of someone with a state like this is only like *"a donkey who carries volumes"* (62:5).

He should know the Makkan from the Madinan *sūra*s so that by that he can distinguish between what Allah told His slaves at the beginning of Islam and what was recommended for them at the end, what He obliged on them at the beginning of Islam and those obligations He added to it at the end. The Madinan abrogates the Makkan in most of the Qur'ān. It is not possible for the Makkan to abrogate the Madinan because the abrogated was revealed before the abrogating. Part of his perfection is to know the *i'rāb* (inflection/grammar) and the unusual. That is part of what will make it easy for him to know what he reads and will remove doubt from him in what he recites.

Aṭ-Ṭabarī said, "I heard al-Jarmī say, 'For thirty years, I have been giving people *fatwās* in *fiqh* taken from the book of Sibuwayh [i.e. based on grammar].'" Muḥammad ibn Yazīd said, "That was because Abū 'Umar al-Jarmī knew *aḥādīth*. When he learned the book of Sibuwayh, he learned *fiqh* in *ḥadīth* since it is from the book of Sibuwayh that he learned investigation and *tafsīr*. Then he looked into the *sunna*s which are firmly transmitted from the Messenger of Allah, may Allah bless him and grant him peace. It is by means of them that the seeker reaches what Allah means in His Book and that opens up for him the judgements of the Qur'ān. Aḍ-Ḍaḥḥāk said about the words of the Almighty, *'Be people of the Lord because of your knowledge of the Book.'* (3:79), 'It is a duty for whoever learns the Qur'ān to be a *faqīh*.'"

Ibn Abī'l-Ḥawārī mentioned, "A group of us went to Fuḍayl ibn 'Iyāḍ in 185 AH and stopped at his door, but he did not give us permission to enter. One of the people said, 'If he comes out for anything, he will come out to recitation of the Qur'ān.' So we ordered a reciter to recite and he appeared to us from a window. We said, 'Peace be upon you and the mercy of Allah.' He said, 'And peace upon you.' We asked, 'How are you, Abū 'Alī?' He replied, 'I am in well-being from Allah and harm from you. What you are doing is something new in Islam. We belong to Allah and are returning to Him! This is not how we seek knowledge! We used to go to the shaykhs and would not see ourselves worthy of sitting with them. We sat below them and eavesdropped. When a *ḥadīth* was given, we would ask them to repeat it and we would retain it. You seek knowledge with ignorance. You waste the Book of Allah. If you had sought the Book of Allah, you would have found in it healing for what you want.' We said, 'We have studied the Qur'ān.' He said, 'Your study of the Qur'ān is work enough for your lives and the lives of your children!' We asked, 'How, Abū 'Alī?' He replied, 'You will not learn the Qur'ān until you know its *i'rāb,* its *muḥkam* from its *mutashābih*, and its abrogating from its abrogated. When you know that, then you will have no need of the words of Fuḍayl and Ibn 'Uyayna.' Then he said, 'I seek refuge with Allah, the All-Hearing, All-Knowing from the Accursed Shayṭān. In the Name of Allah, the All-Merciful, the Most Merciful. *"O mankind! An admonition has come to you from your Lord and also healing for what is in the breasts and guidance and mercy for the believers. Say: 'It is the favour of Allah and His mercy that should be the cause of their rejoicing. That is better than anything they accumulate.'"'* (10:57-58)"

When the reader of the Qur'ān obtains these ranks, he will be fluent in the Qur'ān and know the Discrimination. He will be close to the one who brings him close to it. He will not benefit from any of what we have mentioned until he has a sincere intention for Allah when he seeks it, or continues to have a sincere intention after learning it, as was already stated. A seeker of knowledge may begin by desiring reputation and honour in the *dīn*. Then his understanding of knowledge continues until it is clear to him that he has erred in his belief, and so he repents of that and makes his intention sincere for Allah. He benefits from that and improves his state. Al-Ḥasan said, "We used to seek knowledge for this world and it dragged us to the Next World." Sufyān ath-Thawrī said that. Ḥabīb ibn Abī Thābit said, "We sought this matter and we had no intention in it. The intention came afterwards."

The syntax of the Qur'ān, learning it and studying it and the reward for the one who recites the Qur'ān with proper inflections

Al-Anbārī said, "The Prophet, his Companions and their Followers all mention the excellence of proper understanding of the syntax of the Qur'ān and the encouragement to learn it and censure and dislike poor grammatical understanding. This obliges the reciters of the Qur'ān to strive to learn it."

One aspect of that is in what is related from Abū Hurayra who reported that the Prophet, peace be upon him, said, "Use the proper syntax in the Arabic of the Qur'ān and search out its unusual words." It is reported from Ibn 'Umar that the Messenger of Allah, may Allah bless him and grant him peace, said, "If someone recites the Qur'ān without its correct grammar, an angel is entrusted to him to write for him, as is revealed, ten good deeds for every letter. When he uses correct grammar for some of it and fails to do so for some of it, two angels are entrusted who write down every letter with twenty good deeds. If he inflects it correctly, four angels are entrusted to him to write down seventy good deeds for every letter." Aḍ-Ḍaḥḥāk reported that 'Abdullāh ibn Mas'ūd said, "Recite the Qur'ān well and adorn it with your voices and employ its correct syntax. It is Arabic and Allah loves the correct syntax to be employed." Mujāhid reported that Ibn 'Umar said, "Use correct syntax in the Qur'ān."

Abū Bakr and 'Umar said, "We prefer some syntax of the Qur'ān to simply memorising its letters." Ash-Sha'bī reported that 'Umar said, "Anyone who recites the Qur'ān with its syntax has the reward of a martyr with Allah." Makḥūl said, "We were told that anyone who recites with correct syntax has double the reward of someone who recites without it." Ibn 'Abbās reported that the Messenger of Allah, may Allah bless him and grant him peace, said, "Love the Arabs for three reasons: because I am an Arab, the Qur'ān is in Arabic and the language of the people of the Garden will be Arabic." Abū Ḥamza said, "Al-Ḥasan was asked about people studying Arabic and he said, 'They do well. They learn the language of their Prophet.'" Al-Ḥasan was told, "We have an imām who uses ungrammatical Arabic." He said, "Dismiss him."

Ibn Abī Mulayka said, "A bedouin arrived in Madina in the time of 'Umar ibn al-Khaṭṭāb and asked, 'Who will recite some of what was revealed to Muḥammad, may Allah bless him and grant him peace?' A man recited *Sūrat at-Tawba* to him. He said, 'Allah is free of the idolaters and His Messenger' (9:3) using the genitive for Messenger (*rasūlihi*).' The bedouin said, 'Allah is free of His Messenger? If Allah is free of His Messenger, we are more free of him.' 'Umar heard what the bedouin had said so he summoned him and said, 'Bedouin, are you free of the Messenger of Allah?' He replied, '*Amīr al-Mu'minīn*, I came to Madina with no knowledge of the Qur'ān. I asked someone to recite it to me and he recited this *Sūra at-Tawba* and said, "Allah is free of the idolaters and His Messenger." So I said, "Allah is free of His Messenger? If Allah is free of His Messenger, we are more free of him."' 'Umar said, 'That is not how it is, bedouin.' He said, 'How is it then, Amīr al-Mu'minīn?' He said, 'Allah is free of the idolaters, as is His Messenger (*rasūluhu*).' The bedouin said, 'We, by Allah, are more free of what Allah and His Messenger are free of!' So 'Umar ibn al-Khaṭṭāb commanded that only those who knew proper grammar should recite to people and he commanded Abū'l-Aswad to set out the grammar."

'Alī ibn al-Ja'd reported that he heard Shu'ba say, "The metaphor of someone who knows the *ḥadīth* but does not know Arabic is that of a donkey which has a nosebag with no fodder in it." Ḥammād ibn Salama said, "The one who seeks *ḥadīth* and does not learn grammar – or Arabic – is like a donkey who has a nosebag in which there is no barley." Ibn 'Aṭiyya said, "The syntax of the Qur'ān is a basic principle in the *Sharī'a* because it is that by which its meanings, which are the *Sharī'a*, are established."

Ibn al-Anbārī said, "The Companions of the Prophet and their Followers provide evidence for using language and poetry to explain unusual and problematic words in the Qur'ān and that demonstrates the soundness of the school of the grammarians respecting that and the falsity of those who deny that. It is reported from 'Ikrima that Ibn 'Abbās said, "When you ask me about the unusual words of Allah, look for them in poetry. Poetry is the lexicon of the Arabs." Sa'īd ibn Jubayr and Yūsuf ibn Mihrān were heard to mention that they heard Ibn 'Abbās being asked about something in the Qur'ān and he replied. "It means such and such. Have you not heard the poet say such-and-such?"

What is reported about the excellence of *tafsīr* of the Qur'ān and those who do it

Our scholars say that part of what is transmitted from the Companions and Followers about the excellence of *tafsīr* is that 'Alī ibn Abi Ṭālib mentioned Jābir ibn 'Abdullāh and described him as having knowledge. A man said to him, "May I be your ransom! You describe Jābir as having knowledge when you are who you are!" He said, "He knew the *tafsīr* of the words of Allah, *'He who has imposed the Qur'ān upon you will most certainly bring you back home again.'* (28:85)" Mujāhid said, "The dearest of creatures to Allah Almighty is the one who has the most knowledge of what is revealed." Al-Ḥasan said, "Allah has not revealed an *āyat* but that He wants people to know about what it was revealed for and what it means." Ash-Sha'bī said, "Masrūq travelled to Basra for the *tafsīr* of an *āyat* and was told that the one who could explain it had travelled to Syria. So he made preparations and travelled to Syria to learn its *tafsīr*."

'Ikrima said about the words of the Almighty, *"If anyone leaves his home, making* hijra *to Allah and His Messenger"* (4:100), "I sought for the name of this man 'who left his home, emigrating for Allah and His Messenger' for fourteen years until I found him." Ibn 'Abdu'l-Barr said that it was Ḍamra ibn Ḥabīb. Ibn 'Abbās said, "I remained for two years wanting to ask 'Umar about the two women who helped each other against the Messenger of Allah, may Allah bless him and grant him peace, and only awe of him prevented me from asking. Finally I asked him and he replied that it was Ḥafṣa and 'Ā'isha." Iyās ibn Mu'āwiya said, "The metaphor of those who recite the Qur'ān without knowing its *tafsīr* is that of some people to whom a letter comes from their king at night when they have no lamp. They are alarmed, not knowing what the letter contains. The metaphor of the one who knows the *tafsīr* is that of a man who brings them a lamp so that they can read what the letter says."

What is reported about the one who is a bearer of the Qur'ān, who he is and those who are hostile to him

Abu 'Umar said, "It is related by various paths that the Prophet, may Allah bless him and grant him peace, said, 'Part of esteem for Allah is honouring three: a just ruler, a Muslim with white hair and a bearer of the Qur'ān who is neither excessive in it nor turns away from it.'" Abū 'Umar said that the bearers of the Qur'ān are those who know its rulings, its lawful and unlawful and act by what it contains. Anas reported that the Messenger of Allah, may Allah bless him and grant him peace, said, "The Qur'ān is better than everything. Whoever respects the Qur'ān has respected Allah. Whoever makes light of the Qur'ān has made light of the right of Allah Almighty. The bearers of the Qur'ān are those who are encircled by the mercy of Allah, exalting the Word of Allah, touched by the light of Allah. Allah befriends whoever befriends them and Allah is hostile to whoever is hostile to them. Such people have made light of the right of Allah."

The respect and esteem for the Qur'ān which is mandatory for someone who recites and bears the Qur'ān

In *Nawādir al-Uṣūl*, at-Tirmidhī al-Ḥakīm said, "Part of respect for the Qur'ān is to only touch it when pure. Part of respect for it is to recite it in a state of purity. Part of respect for it is to use the tooth-stick (*siwāk*), clean between the teeth and make the mouth clean as the mouth is its pathway. Yazīd ibn Abī Mālik said, 'Your mouths are the pathways of the Qur'ān, so purify and clean them as much as you can.'

"Part of respect for it is to dress as you would dress to visit the amir because you are speaking privately. Part of respect for it is to face *qibla* to recite it. When Abū'l-'Āliyya recited he would put on a turban, dress, wear a mantle and face *qibla*. Part of respect for it is to rinse your mouth when you spit. Shu'ba reported from Abū Ḥamza from Ibn 'Abbās that he had a spittoon in front of him and when he spat, he would rinse his mouth and then begin recitation. Whenever he spat, he rinsed. Part of respect for it is that when you yawn, you should stop reciting, because when one recites, one is addressing and conversing with the Lord. Yawning is from Shayṭān. Mujāhid said, 'When you yawn while reciting the Qur'ān, stop reciting out of respect until you stop yawning.' 'Ikrima said, 'By that he meant to respect the Qur'ān.'

"Part of respect for it is to seek refuge with Allah from the accursed Shayṭān when starting to recite it. You should say 'In the Name of Allah, the All-Merciful, the Most Merciful' when beginning to recite it from the first *sūra* or from wherever you start. Part of respect for it is that, when you begin to recite it, you should not stop for a time to speak to people without need. Part of respect for it is that you should not stop reciting it when someone interrupts you by speaking to you and mix recitation with your reply. That is because when you do that, you remove the effectiveness of the formula of seeking refuge which you uttered at the beginning. Part of respect for it is to recite it deliberately, slowly and carefully.

"Part of respect for it is to deploy your mind and intelligence in understanding what is addressed to you. Part of respect for it is to stop at an *āyat* of promise and have hope in Allah and ask Him for His bounty, and to stop at an *āyat* of warning and seek refuge with Allah from the threat. Part of respect for it is to stop at its metaphors and visualise them. Part of respect for it is to investigate its unusual words. Part of respect for it is to give every letter its due so that the words are fully articulated and then you will receive ten good deeds for every letter.

"Part of respect for it is to end its recitation by proclaiming the truthfulness of its Lord and testifying to its delivery by His Messenger and testifying that that is true. You say, 'Our Lord has spoken the Truth and His Messengers conveyed it and we testify to that. O Allah, make us among the witnesses to the Truth, establishing justice.' Then you make supplication.

"Part of respect for it is that when you recite, you do not take *āyat*s piecemeal from each *sūra* and recite them. It is related to us that the Messenger of Allah, may Allah bless him and grant him peace, passed by Bilal who was reciting a little from each *sūra* and he commanded him to recite the entire *sūra*.

"Part of respect for it is that when you put down a copy of the Qur'ān, you do not leave it open and you do not put any other book on top of it. It should always be on top of any other books, be they books of knowledge or other books. Part of respect for it is that when you recite, you put it in your lap or on top of something in front of you and do not put it on the ground. Part of respect for it is not to erase the board it is written on with spit, but rather use water. Part of respect for it is that when it is washed with water you avoid impurities from various places and in the places where it is put. That washing is respect. Some of the *Salaf* before us used to use that water to heal themselves. Part of respect for it is to not take a page when it is worn out and brittle out of fear for the writing. That is great coarseness. It should be erased with water.

"Part of respect for it is to not let a day pass without looking at least once at the Qur'ān. Abū Mūsā used to say, 'I am ashamed not to look once a day at the contract of my Lord.' Part of respect for it is to give the eyes their share of it. The eye leads to the self. Between the self and the breast is a veil and the Qur'ān is in the breast. When you recite it by heart the ear listens and conveys it to the self. When you look at its writing, the eye and the ear both convey it. That is more likely to achieve the conveyance. Then the eye has its share just as the ear does. Zayd ibn Aslam reported from 'Aṭā' ibn Yasār from Abū Sa'īd al-Khudrī that the Messenger of Allah, may Allah bless him and grant him peace, said, 'Give the eyes their portion of worship.' They asked. 'Messenger of Allah, what is their portion of worship?' He replied, 'To look at the Qur'ān and reflect on it and study its wonders.' Makḥūl reported from 'Ubāda ibn aṣ-Ṣāmit that the Messenger of Allah, may Allah bless him and grant him peace, said, 'The best worship of my community is to read the Qur'ān with the eyes.'

"Part of respect for it is not to resort to it when offered worldly goods. It is reported … that Ibrāhīm [an-Nakhā'ī] used to dislike to resort to any of the Qur'ān when he was offered worldly goods. That is like saying to a man who comes to you, '*You have arrived at the pre-ordained time, Mūsā,*' (20:40) and like saying, *'Eat and drink with relish for what you did before in days gone by'* (69:24) when food is served, and other such things. Part of respect for it is not to say *Sūrat an-Naḥl*, *Sūrat al-Baqara* and *Sūrat an-Nisā',* but to say, 'The *sūra* in which such-and-such is mentioned.' (This, however, is contrary to the words of the Prophet, may Allah bless him and grant him peace, 'If anyone recites the two *āyat*s from the end of *Sūrat al-Baqara* at night, they will be enough for him.') (al-Bukhārī and Muslim from 'Abdullāh ibn Mas'ūd)

"Part of respect for it is to not invert its order as some teachers of children do in order to show off cleverness and fluency. That is opposition to Allah. Part of respect for it is to not deepen its recitation as is done by those obstinate innovaters who intensify the pronunciation of the *hamza* and pronounce words with affectation. That is an innovation which *Shayṭān* suggested to them which they accepted. Part of respect for it is not to recite it using musical tunes like the tunes of the people of depravity nor with the quavering of the Christians nor chanting of the monks. All of that is deviation.

"Part of respect for it is to make its letters bold. Abū Ḥukayma reported that he used to copy out the Qur'ān in Kufa. 'Alī passed by him, inspected his writing and ordered, 'Make your pen thicker.' 'So I took the pen and cut off part of it and then wrote while 'Alī was standing and looking at my writing. He said, 'Like that. Give light to it as Allah gave it light.'"

"Part of respect for it is not to compete in loudness in recitation so that it becomes spoiled for him and he hates what he hears and it becomes like a contest. Part of respect for it is not to argue or quarrel about its recitations or say to a person, 'It is not like that.' Perhaps that recitation is a sound and permitted one and then you would be denying the Book of Allah.

"Part of respect for it is not to recite it in the market or in places of clamour, worthless talk, and the places where fools congregrate. Do you not see that Allah Almighty mentioned the slaves of the All-Merciful and praised them because, when they pass by worthless talk, they pass by it with dignity? (cf. 25:72) This is about simply passing by those engaged in worthless talk. So how could they recite the Qur'ān in the midst of worthless talk and a gathering of fools?

"Part of respect for it is not to use it as a pillow or lean on it or throw it to someone when he wants it to be passed to him.

"Part of respect for it is not to make it small. ... It is reported that 'Alī said, 'Do not make the Qur'ān small.' It is related that 'Umar ibn al-Khaṭṭāb saw a small Qur'ān in the hand of a man and asked, 'Who wrote it?' 'I did,' he replied, and then 'Umar struck him with his whip and said, 'Esteem the Qur'ān.' It is related that the Prophet, may Allah bless him and grant him peace, forbade people to say, 'a little mosque or a little Qur'an' (using the diminutive).

"Part of respect for it is not to adorn it with gold or write it in gold so that it is mixed with the adornment of this world. Mughīra related that Ibrāhīm disliked adorning the Qur'ān or writing it with gold or putting marks at the beginning of *āyat*s or making it small. It is related from Abū'd-Dardā' that the Messenger of Allah, may Allah bless him and grant him peace, said, 'When you adorn your mosque and decorate your Qur'ān, then ruin is upon you.' When Ibn 'Abbās saw a Qur'ān adorned with silver he observed, 'You tempt the thief with it. Its adornment is inside it.'

"Part of respect for it is that it should not be written on the ground or on a wall as is done in modern mosques.... It is reported that 'Umar ibn 'Abdu'l-'Azīz said, 'The Messenger of Allah, may Allah bless him and grant him peace, passed by some writing on the ground and said to a lad of the tribe of Hudhayl, 'What is this?' He replied, 'It is from the Book of Allah. A Jew wrote it.' He said, 'May Allah curse the one who did this. Only put the Book of Allah in its proper place.' Muḥammad ibn az-Zubayr said that 'Umar ibn

'Abdu'l-'Azīz saw a son of his writing the Qur'ān on a wall and beat him.

"Part of respect for it is that when its writing is washed for treating an illness, it should not be poured on a rubbish heap or in a place of impurity or in a place where people walk, but in a place where people do not walk, or a hole should be dug in a pure place so that it can be poured into it, or it can be poured into a large river.

"Part of respect for it is that, whenever someone completes the recitation of the entire Qur'ān, he recites some of the beginning so that it does not have the form of something abandoned. That is why when the Messenger of Allah, may Allah bless him and grant him peace, finished reciting, he would recite about five *āyat*s from the beginning so that it would not be in an abandoned form. Ibn 'Abbās said that a man came and asked, 'Messenger of Allah, which action is best?' He replied, 'You must have the embarking state.' 'What is the embarking state?' he asked. He replied, 'The one with the Qur'ān who starts from its beginning until he reaches its end and then starts at the beginning. Whenever he alights, he immediately travels on.'

It is recommended to gather your family when you finish the Qur'ān. Al-Anbārī reported … from Qatāda that when Anas ibn Mālik finished reciting the Qur'ān, he would gather his family and make supplication. It is reported that when Mujāhid, 'Abda ibn Abi Lubāba and various people were about to complete the recitation, they would summon people since mercy descends at the conclusion of the Qur'ān. It is reported that Ibrāhīm at-Taymī said, "When someone finishes the Qur'ān at the beginning of the day, the angels bless him until evening. When someone finishes the Qur'ān at the beginning of the night, the angels bless him until morning." He said, "They recommended that it should be finished at the beginning of the night or at the beginning of the day."

"Part of respect for it is that you should not write the refuge *sūra*s from it and then enter the lavatory unless they are inside a covering of leather or silver or something else. Then it is as if it were inside his breast.

"Part of respect for it is that when you write it out [for medicinal purposes] and then drink it, you should say the Name of Allah for every breath and have a very strong intention. Allah will give to you according to your intention. Mujāhid said, 'There is no harm in writing out the Qur'ān and then having a sick person drink it.' Abu Ja'far said, 'If someone has hardness in his heart, he should write *'Yasin'* on a goblet with saffron and drink it.'

"Part of respect for it is not to say, 'What a short *sūra*!' Abū'l-'Āliyya disliked saying 'what a short or large *sūra*'. When he heard someone say that, he would retort, 'You are smaller than it. All of the Qur'ān is immense.'" Abū Dāwūd related the contrary of this from the *ḥadīth* of 'Amr ibn Shu'ayb from his grandfather which states that one can use those terms. 'Amr said, "No small or large *sūra* is part of the *Mufaṣṣal*."

What is reported regarding threats against engaging in *tafsīr* of the Qur'ān by means of opinion (*ra'y*) or being bold in that, and the ranks of the commentators

It is related that 'Ā'isha said, "The Messenger of Allah, may Allah bless him and grant him peace, did not explain the Book of Allah except for some *āyat*s which Jibrīl taught him." Ibn 'Aṭiyya said, "The meaning of this *ḥadīth* is that it is about the unseen things of the Qur'ān, explaining what is ambivalent (*mujmal*) and the like to which there is no way to uncover except with Allah's help. Part of that are those unseen matters which Allah has not made known, like the time of the Rising and the number of blasts on the Trumpet and the order of the creation of the heavens and the earth."

At-Tirmidhi reported from Ibn 'Abbās that the Prophet, may Allah bless him and grant him peace, said, "Fear attributing words to me which you do not know. Anyone who deliberately tells a lie regarding me will take his seat in the Fire. Anyone who speaks about the Qur'ān by own opinion, should take his seat in the Fire." It is also reported from Jundub that the Messenger of Allah, may

Allah bless him and grant him peace, said, "Anyone who speaks on the Qur'ān by his own opinion and is right is still wrong." This is a *gharīb ḥadīth* in Abū Dāwūd and one of its transmitters is questionable. Razīn added, "Whoever speaks by his opinion and errs has disbelieved."

Al-Anbārī said in the *Kitāb ar-Radd*, "There are two interpretations of the *ḥadīth* of Ibn 'Abbās. One is that someone who speaks on problematic things (*mushkil*) in the Qur'ān by what he does not know, differing from the position of the first Companions and Followers, exposes himself to the anger of Allah. The second, which is the firmer and sounder of the two, is that when someone says something about the Qur'ān knowing the truth to be different, he should take his seat in the Fire."

Regarding the *ḥadīth* of Jundub, some of the people of knowledge say that "opinion" here means "whim". Whoever speaks about the Qur'ān according to his own whims and does not take from the Imāms of the *Salaf* and happens to be right is still wrong since he has judged the Qur'ān by something whose basis is not recognised and is not based on the position of those with expertise in traditions and transmission. Ibn 'Aṭiyya says, "The meaning of this is that a man is asked about a meaning of the Book of Allah and hurries to explain it by his own opinion without looking at what the scholars have said and what the rules of knowledge like syntax and *uṣūl* demand." Not included is the explanation of grammarians and linguists of its grammar and the *fuqahā'* of its meaning where each speaks by his *ijtihād* based on the rules of his own branch of knowledge and investigation.

This is sound and more than one scholar prefers it. The one who speaks according to what pops into his imagination and occurs to his mind without seeking evidence for it in the fundamental principles errs. Anyone who derives its meanings by basing himself on the fundamental principles which are agreed upon is praised.

Some scholars said that *tafsīr* is dependent on oral transmission since Allah says, *"If you have a dispute about something, refer it back to Allah and His Messenger."* (4:59) This is false because the prohibition against explaining the Qur'ān is either that what is desired is to confine oneself to transmission and not investigate, or it is something else. It is false that what is meant is that no one should say anything about the Qur'ān other than what he has heard. The Companions recited the Qur'ān and differed about its interpretation in some cases. Not all of what they said was what they heard from the Prophet. The Prophet, may Allah bless him and grant him peace, made supplication for Ibn 'Abbās and said, "O Allah, give him understanding in the *dīn* and teach him interpretation." If interpretation is confined to Revelation and Prophetic reports, what is the point of singling him out for that? This is clear and undoubted.

The prohibition against *tafsīr* applies to two instances. The first is when the interpreter has opinion about something on the basis of his nature and passion and, therefore, interprets the Qur'ān according to his opinion and passion in an effort to justify his position. If it had not been for that opinion and passion, that meaning about the Qur'ān would not have occurred to him. This can sometimes be conscious, as in the case of someone who uses some *āyat*s of the Qur'ān to prove the validity of an innovation, when he knows that that is not what is meant by the *āyat*, but his aim is to confuse his opponent. Sometimes it is done in ignorance which may happen when an *āyat* can be applied in various ways and his understanding inclines to the meaning which coincides with his position. He prefers that interpretation because of his opinion and passion and so he interprets it according to his own opinion. If it had not been for his opinion, he would not have preferred that meaning.

Sometimes someone has a sound purpose and seeks evidence for it in the Qur'ān and uses what he knows of it as evidence for what he wants, like the one who calls people to strive against a hard heart. Allah says, *"Go to Pharaoh. He has overstepped the bounds."* (20:24) He points to his heart and suggests that that is what is meant by 'Pharaoh' in this *āyat*. This kind of interpretation is used by some preachers with good motives to make their words effective and encourage their listeners. This is forbidden because it is unacceptable linguistic analogy and is not permissible. The esotericists use the same method to false purposes with the goal of deluding people and calling them to their false beliefs. They use the Qur'ān according to their opinion and position in matters that they absolutely know are not meant. This is one of the aspects of *tafsīr* that is forbidden.

The second instance is when an interpreter hastens to explain the Qur'ān according to the literal meaning of the Arabic without the help of transmission about what the unusual words of the Qur'ān mean and what has been passed down about the ambiguous and interchangeable words, conciseness, elision, concealment and reversal of order it contains. Someone who does not have a firm grasp of the literal *tafsīr* and then sets out to derive meanings by simple understanding of Arabic often errs and joins the company of those who interpret the Qur'ān according to their own opinions.

Transmission is necessary first of all in the primary *tafsīr* so that one avoids error, and then after that one employs understanding and deduction to expand on it. The unusual words which are only understood via transmission are numerous, and one cannot hope to reach the inward before having a firm grasp of the outward. Do you not see that the Almighty says, *"We gave Thamūd the camel as a visible sign (*mubṣira*) and then they mistreated her"* (17:59)? It means a visible sign and they wronged themselves by killing it. Someone who looks at the literal Arabic might think that it means that the camel could see (*mubṣira*) and therefore not know what they did wrong and how they wronged others and themselves. This is part of elision and concealment. There are many such examples in the Qur'ān. In cases other than these two, there is no prohibition against interpretation, and Allah knows best.

Ibn 'Aṭiyya said, "Most of the righteous *Salaf* like Sa'īd ibn al-Musayyab, 'Āmir ash-Sha'bī and others used to be overawed at the prospect of making interpretation of the Qur'ān and would refrain from it out of scrupulousness and cautiousness for themselves in spite of their perfection and precedence." Al-Anbārī said, "The imāms of the *Salaf* were too scrupulous to explain the problematic parts of the Qur'ān. One supposed that his *tafsīr* might not coincide with what Allah meant and so refrained from speaking. Another feared that he would become an imām in *tafsīr* and people might follow his method, when he might hesitate to explain a single letter according to his own opinion or to err about it and then his follower might say, 'My imām in the *tafsīr* of the Qur'an by opinion is so-and-so, the imām of the *Salaf*.'" Ibn Abī Mulayka said, 'Abū Bakr aṣ-Ṣiddīq was asked about the *tafsīr* of a letter of the Qur'ān and said, "Which heaven will cover me and which earth will bear me? Where will I go? What will I do if I say about a letter of the Book of Allah other than what Allah Almighty meant?"

Ibn 'Aṭiyya said, "Several of the *Salaf* used to explain the Qur'ān and made the Muslims continue in that. As for the beginning of the commentators on whom they relied, there was 'Alī ibn Abī Ṭālib, and he was followed by 'Abdullāh ibn 'Abbās, who devoted himself to the subject and perfected it. He was followed by scholars like Mujāhid, Sa'īd ibn Jubayr and others. More is transmitted from him in that than is retained from 'Alī. Ibn 'Abbās said, 'What I took of *tafsīr* of the Qur'ān was from 'Alī ibn Abī Ṭālib.' 'Alī used to praise the *tafsīr* of Ibn 'Abbās and encouraged people to take it from him. Ibn 'Abbās used to say about himself, 'An excellent translator of the Qur'ān is 'Abdullāh ibn 'Abbās.' 'Alī said about him, 'It is as if Ibn 'Abbās looks at the unseen through a fine curtain.'"

He was followed by 'Abdullāh ibn Mas'ūd, Ubayy ibn Ka'b, Zayd ibn Thābit, and 'Abdullāh ibn 'Amr ibn al-'Āṣ. All that is taken from the Companions has excellent preference because they witnessed the revelation and its descent in their language. 'Āmir ibn Wāthila said, "I saw 'Alī ibn Abī Ṭālib speaking. I heard him say in his *khuṭba*, 'Ask me. By Allah, you will not ask me about anything that will happen until the Day of Rising but that I will tell you about it. Ask me about the Book of Allah. By Allah, there is no *āyat* but that I know whether it was revealed at night or in the day, revealed on flat ground or on a mountain.'" Ibn al-Kawwā' rose and asked about *Sūrat adh-Dhāriyāt* (51).

'Abdullāh ibn Mas'ūd said, "If I knew of anyone with more knowledge of the Book of Allah than me, who could be reached by mounts, I would go to him." A man asked him, "Have you not met 'Alī ibn Abī Ṭālib?" 'Yes," he replied, "I have met him." Masrūq said, "I found some of the Companions of Muḥammad, may Allah bless him and grant him peace, like pools which water one person, some like pools which water two, and some such that if all people had come to it, it would satisfy them. 'Abdullāh ibn Mas'ūd was one those pools."

Abū Sa'īd al-Khudrī reported that the Messenger of Allah, may Allah bless him and grant him peace, said, "The most merciful to my community is Abū Bakr, the strongest in the *dīn* of Allah is 'Umar, the most truly modest is 'Uthmān, the one with the most knowledge of judgement is 'Alī, and the one with most knowledge of the shares of inheritance is Zayd. The one with the most recitation of the Book of Allah is Ubayy ibn Ka'b. The one with the most knowledge of the lawful and unlawful is Mu'ādh ibn Jabal. The trustworthy representative of this community is Abū 'Ubayda ibn al-Jarrāḥ. Abū Hurayra is a vessel of knowledge and Salmān is a sea of knowledge which is not perceived. Vegetation has not shaded nor has the earth supported anyone with a more truthful tongue than Abū Dharr."

Ibn 'Aṭiyya said, "The prominent Followers (*Tābi'ūn*) included al-Ḥasan al-Baṣrī, Mujāhid, Sa'īd ibn Jubayr and 'Alqama. Mujāhid studied recitation with Ibn 'Abbās coupled with understanding the meaning, stopping at every *āyat*. 'Ikrima and aḍ-Ḍaḥḥāk followed them. Even if aḍ-Ḍaḥḥāk did not meet Ibn 'Abbās, he studied with Ibn Jubayr. As for as-Suddī, 'Āmir ash-Sha'bī attacked him and Abū Ṣāliḥ because he thought that they fell short in investigation."

Then the *tafsīr* was transmitted by just men of every generation, as the Prophet, may Allah bless him and grant him peace, said, "This knowledge will be carried by just men of every generation, discarding from it the deviation of the excessive, the ascriptions of the falsifiers and the interpretation of the ignorant." (Abū 'Umar and others related it). Al-Khaṭīb al-Baghdādī said, "This testimony from the Messenger of Allah, may Allah bless him and grant him peace, shows that Qur'ānic interpreters are scholars of the *dīn* and imāms of the Muslims because they guard the *Sharī'a* against deviation and the ascription of falsehood and refute the interpretation of ignorant fools. One must consult them and rely on them in the business of the *dīn*."

The Book being explained by the *Sunna*, and what has been transmitted about that

Allah says, *"And We have sent down the Reminder to you so that you can make clear to mankind what has been sent down to them"* (16:44), and *"Those who oppose his command should beware of a testing trial coming to them or a painful punishment striking them"* (24:63) and *"Truly you are guiding to a Straight Path."* (42:52) It is made obligatory to obey the Prophet, may Allah bless him and grant him peace, in more than one *āyat* of the Book and that is connected to obeying Allah, Allah says, *"Whatever the Messenger gives you you should accept and whatever He forbids you you should forgo."* (59:7) Ibn 'Abdu'l-Barr mentioned that 'Abdu'r-Raḥmān ibn Yazīd saw a *muḥrim* wearing his ordinary clothes and he forbade him to do that. The man said to him, "Bring me an *āyat* from the Book of Allah which removes my clothes." He recited to him, *"Whatever the Messenger gives you you should accept and whatever He forbids you you should forgo."* (59:7) Hishām ibn Ḥujayr said, "Ṭāwūs prayed two *rak'āt*s after *'Aṣr* and Ibn 'Abbās said, 'Stop performing them.'' He said, 'It is only forbidden to take them as a *sunna*.' Ibn 'Abbās said, 'The Messenger of Allah, may Allah bless him and grant him peace, forbade praying after *'Aṣr*. I do not how whether you will be punished or rewarded for them because Allah says, *"When Allah and His Messenger have decided a thing it is not for any believing man or believing woman to have a choice about it."* (33:36)'"

Abū Dāwūd related from al-Miqdām ibn Ma'dīkarib that the Messenger of Allah, may Allah bless him and grant him peace, said, "I was given the Book and its like with it. It will not be long before a satiated man on his throne declares, 'This Qur'ān is all you need. Make lawful whatever you find lawful in it and make unlawful whatever you find unlawful in it.' But domestic donkeys are not lawful for you nor is eating any beast of prey with fangs nor is something dropped by someone who has a treaty with you until its owner declares himself free of it. If someone stops off with some people, they must give him hospitality. If they do not, he can legally pursue them for the equivalent cost of his due hospitality."

Al-Khaṭṭābī said that the words, "I was given the Book and its like with it," can be interpreted in two ways. One is that it means he was given hidden revelation which is not recited in the same way that he was given the outward recited part. The second is that he was given the Book as recited revelation and was given clarification like it, meaning permission to explain what was in the Book, making it general and specific, adding to it and legislating what is in it. Therefore it is mandatory to act by that and to accept it like the outward recited Qur'ān. The *ḥadīth* is a warning against opposing those established *sunan* which are not in the Qur'ān, as was done by the Khārijites and Rāfiḍites. They attached themselves to the literal text of the Qur'ān and abandoned the *sunna*s which contain the clarification of the Book. This *ḥadīth* contains evidence that there is no need to compare the *ḥadīth* with the Book. Whatever is confirmed as being from the Prophet is evidence in itself. As for what some relate, "When a *ḥadīth* comes to you, compare it with the Book. If it agrees with it, take it. Otherwise, discard it," it is a baseless false *ḥadīth*.

The clarification is of two types: a general clarification of the Book, like clarifying the five prayers, their times, prostration, *rukū'* and all their rulings, the amount and time of *zakāt* and the types of property from which it is taken, and the details of the practices of *ḥajj*. When the Prophet, may Allah bless him and grant him peace, performed the *ḥajj* with the people, he said, "Take your practices from me," and he said, "Pray as you saw me praying." (al-Bukhārī) 'Imrān ibn Ḥusayn said to a man, "You stupid man! Do you find *Ẓuhr* in the Book of Allah as four *rak'at*s in which recitation is not aloud?" Then he enumerated for him the prayer, *zakāt* and the like and then said, "Do you find this explained in the Book of Allah? The Book of Allah Almighty did not define this while the *Sunna* explains it!"

Al-Awzā'ī reported that Ḥassān ibn 'Aṭiyya said, "Revelation descended on the Messenger of Allah, may Allah bless him and grant him peace, and Jibrīl brought him the *Sunna* which explains that." ... Al-Awzā'ī also reported that Makḥūl said, "The Qur'ān is more in need of the *Sunna* than the *Sunna* is of the Qur'ān." Yaḥyā ibn Abī Kathīr said, "The *Sunna* judges the Book and the Book does not judge the *Sunna*." Al-Fuḍayl ibn Ziyād said that he heard Aḥmad ibn Ḥanbal being asked about this *ḥadīth* and he said, 'I am not so bold as to say it, but I say that the *Sunna* explains and clarifies the Book."

How to learn and understand the Book of Allah and the *Sunna* of His Prophet. It is reported that it used to be easier to act by it than to memorise it

In the *Kitāb al-Bayān*, ad-Dānī reports from 'Uthmān, Ibn Mas'ūd and Ubayy that the Messenger of Allah, may Allah bless him and grant him peace, used to recite ten *āyat*s to them, and they did not go on to another ten until they knew what action was connected to those *āyat*s. So we should learn the Qur'ān and how to act by it at the same time. It is reported that as-Sulamī said, "When we learned ten *āyat*s of the Qur'ān, we did not learn the ten after them until we knew what they contained of the *ḥalāl* and *ḥarām*, of prohibitions and commands." In the *Muwaṭṭā'*, Mālik reported that he heard that 'Abdullāh ibn 'Umar spent eight years learning *Sūrat al-Baqara*. In his book, *The Names of Those who Transmitted from Mālik*, Aḥmad ibn 'Alī ibn Thābit mentions that Nāfi' transmitted that Ibn 'Umar said, "'Umar learned *al-Baqara* over twelve years. When he finished, he slaughtered a camel." Al-Anbārī reports that 'Abdullāh ibn Mas'ūd said, "It was difficult for us to memorise the words of the Qur'ān, but easy for us to act by them. After us will be people for whom it is easy to memorise the Qur'ān, but hard to act by it."

It is reported that Ibn 'Umar said, "The best of the Companions of the Messenger of Allah, may Allah bless him and grant him peace, at the beginning of this Community only memorised a *sūra* or two of the Qur'ān. They were given the gift of acting by the Qur'ān. The last of this community will recite the Qur'ān – children and blind – and will not be given the gift of acting by it." Khalaf ibn Hishām al-Bazzār was heard to say, "I only think that the Qur'ān in our hands has been denuded [of action]. That is because we were told that 'Umar ibn al-Khaṭṭāb memorised *Sūrat al-Baqara* over the course of about ten years. When he had memorised it, he slaughtered a camel to thank Allah. In our time, a boy sits before me and recites a third of the Qur'ān without missing out a single letter. I only reckon that the Qur'ān is denuded in our hands."

The meaning of the words of the Prophet, "The Qur'ān was revealed in seven *aḥruf* (dialects/modes)."

In the *Ṣaḥīḥ* of Muslim, Ubayy ibn Ka'b reported that the Prophet, peace be upon him, was with the Banū Ghifār when Jibrīl came to him and said, "Allah commands you to recite the Qur'ān to your Community in one mode." He said, "I ask Allah for His pardon and forgiveness. My Community will not be able to do that." Then he came a second time and said, "Allah commands you to recite the Qur'ān to your Community in two modes." He said, "I ask Allah for His pardon and forgiveness. My Community will not be able to do that." He came a third time and said, "Allah commands you to recite the Qur'ān to your Community in three modes." He replied, "I ask Allah for His pardon and forgiveness. My Community will not be able to do that." He came a fourth time and said, "Allah commands you to recite the Qur'ān to your Community in seven modes. Whichever mode they recite, it is correct." At-Tirmidhī reported that Ubayy said, "The Messenger of

Allah, may Allah bless him and grant him peace, met Jibrīl and said, 'Jibrīl, I was sent to an illiterate community. Some of them are old women and old men, boys and girls, and men who do not read at all.' He said to him, 'Muḥammad, the Qur'ān was revealed in seven modes.'" (*ṣaḥīḥ*) This story is confirmed in the main authorities: al-Bukhārī, Muslim, the *Muwaṭṭā'*, Abū Dāwūd, an-Nasā'ī and other books in the form of the story about Hishām ibn Ḥakīm with 'Umar which we will mention later.

Scholars disagree about what is meant by the seven modes, and there are thirty-five things mentioned by al-Bustī. We will mention five of them here:

- This is the position of most of the people of knowledge, such as Sufyān ibn 'Uyayna, 'Abdullāh ibn Wahb, aṭ-Ṭabarī, aṭ-Ṭaḥāwī and others. What is meant are the seven manners of synonyms with different expressions, like *aqbala, ta'āla* and *halluma* (all of which mean "come here"). Aṭ-Ṭaḥāwī said, "The clearest elucidation of that is what is mentioned in the *ḥadīth* of Abū Bakra, 'Jibrīl came to the Prophet, may Allah bless him and grant him peace, and said, "Recite in one mode." Mikā'īl said, "Increase it." He said, "Recite it in two modes." Mikā'īl said, "Increase it," until it was seven modes. He said, "Recite it. Each is adequate unless you confuse an *āyat* of mercy for an *āyat* of punishment or an *āyat* of punishment with an *āyat* of mercy."' That is like *halluma, ta'āla, aqbala, adhhaba, asra'a* and *'ajjala*." It is related from Ibn 'Abbās that Ubayy ibn Ka'b used to recite "wait for us" (57:13) *"undhurūnā"* as *"umhulūnā"*, *"akhkhirūnā"*, and *"arqubūnā"*. With the same *isnād*, it is reported that Ubayy recited in 2:20 *"marrū"* instead of *"mashaw"* and *"sa'aw"* (they walk). In al-Bukhārī, az-Zuhrī said, "These modes are about the same matter. They do not differ in respect of the *ḥalāl* and *ḥarām*."

  Aṭ-Ṭaḥāwī said, "There was scope for people in the letters since they were unable to take the Qur'ān in other than their dialects because they were illiterate and only a few of them could write. It was hard for someone with a dialect to change to another. If he wanted to do that, it would have entailed great hardship and so they were given scope regarding different expressions as long as the meaning was the same. They remained like that until many of them could write and the dialects reverted to that of the Messenger of Allah, may Allah bless him and grant him peace. Then they were able to memorise those words and they no longer had the allowance to recite differently." Ibn 'Abdu'l-Barr said, "It is clear that scope for the seven modes was at a particular time out of necessity. When that necessity was removed, the ruling of the seven was removed, and the Qur'ān was recited in one mode."

• Some people say that the seven dialects in the Qur'ān are the seven dialects of all the Arabs, both Yamanī and Nizār, because the Messenger of Allah, may Allah bless him and grant him peace, was not ignorant of any of them. He was "given all the words". It does not mean that the one mode has seven aspects, but these seven dialects are in different parts of the Qur'ān. Some of it is in the dialect of Quraysh, some in that of Hudhayl, some in Hawāzin, and some in Yamanī. Al-Khaṭṭābī said, "That is how the Qur'ān is recited in seven ways." This is the meaning of the Qur'ān being revealed in seven modes. Al-Qāsim ibn Sallām believed that and Ibn 'Atiyya preferred it. Some tribes used writing more than others. Anas mentioned that when 'Uthmān told them to copy out the Qur'ān, he said, "When you and Zayd differ, then write in the dialect of Quraysh. It was revealed in their dialect." (al-Bukhārī)

Qāḍī Ibn aṭ-Ṭayyib [al-Bāqillānī] said, "The meaning of 'Uthmān's words that it was revealed in the dialect of Quraysh, means most of it. It is not a definitive proof that it is all in the dialect of Quraysh since there are words and letters which differ from the dialect of Quraysh. This indicates that it was revealed in all the language of the Arabs, and no one can say that it was just Quraysh or one part of the Arabs rather than others." Ibn 'Abdu'l-Barr said that this meant that most of it was revealed in the dialect of Quraysh because other than the dialect of Quraysh exists in sound readings with the use of the *hamza*s and the like. Quraysh did not use the *hamza*. Ibn 'Aṭiyya said that the meaning of the "seven modes" is that the expressions of the seven tribes are in it.

• These seven dialects are all from the tribes of Muḍar. Some people said that. They used as evidence what 'Uthmān said, "The Qur'ān was revealed in the language of Muḍar." They said, "It is possible that part of it is that of Quraysh, part Kināna, part Asad, part Hudhayl, part Taym, part Ḍaba, and part Qays. They said these tribes of Muḍar contain the seven dialects in these ranks. Ibn Mas'ūd used to like those who copied out the Qur'āns to be from Muḍar. Others objected to the idea that it was all from Muḍar and said that there are rare usages in Muḍar with which it is not permitted to write the Qur'ān.

• What is related from some scholars is exemplified by Qāḍī Ibn aṭ-Ṭayyib who said, "I have reflected on the aspects of the differences in recitation and have found them to be seven. Some involve changes of voweling while the meaning and form remain, like *aṭharu* and *aṭhara* in 11:78; some do not change their form but change their meaning through inflection, as in 34:19, reading *bā'id* or *bā'ida*; some retain their form and change their meaning with different letters; some change the form while the meaning remains as in 101:5 where both *'ahn* and *ṣūf* mean wool; some change their form and meaning; some entail a change of order; and some consist of addition or reduction."

• What is meant by the seven modes are meanings in the Book of Allah: command and prohibition, promise and threat, stories, arguments and parables. Ibn 'Aṭiyya says that this is weak because that is not called *aḥruf*. Furthermore there is consensus that it does not occur in making the lawful lawful or changing any of the meanings. Qāḍī Ibn aṭ-Ṭayyib mentioned a *ḥadīth* along these lines from the Prophet, may Allah bless him and grant him peace, and then said, "This is not part of what it is allowed for them to recite." *Ḥarf* in this means 'manner' as Allah says, *'one who worships Allah on an edge.'* (22:11). That is the meaning of the *ḥadīth* about the seven means of allowing and forbidding and the like.

It is also said that what is meant by the seven *aḥruf* are the seven readings that we have because all of that is sound as the Prophet, may Allah bless him and grant him peace, stated. This, however, is not correct, as we will now explain.

Section on the seven readings

Most scholars, like ad-Dāwūdī, Ibn Abi Ṣufra and others said that these seven readings which are ascribed to the seven readers are not the seven *aḥruf* for which the Companions had allowance to recite. They refer merely to one *ḥarf* of those seven, which is what 'Uthmān collected in the copy of the Qur'ān which he authorised. Ibn an-Naḥḥās and others mentioned that. These seven famous readings (*qirā'āt*) are the selections of those Imāms of recitation. That is because each of them chose what he related and the aspect he knew of the recitations which he considered to be the best and most appropriate. Each held to a path, related and recited it, and became famous for it. He is known for it and it is ascribed to him, like the mode of Nāfi' and the mode of Ibn Kathīr. One of them did not forbid choosing another nor object to it. He allowed it. Each of those seven has two or more choices related from him. All are sound.

Muslims at this time have agreed to rely on what is soundly transmitted from these imāms regarding those readings which they related and recorded in books. The consensus remains that they are correct, and the preservation of the Book which Allah promised has been secured. This is the position of the earlier imāms and excellent reliable men like Qāḍī Abū Bakr ibn aṭ-Ṭayyib, aṭ-Ṭabarī and others. Ibn 'Aṭiyya said, "These seven readings have lasted through different times and places and the prayer is performed using them as their soundness is established by consensus. As for the rare (*shādhdh*) readings, the prayer is not performed using them because there is no consensus on that. As for what is related from the Companions and the Followers about that, it can only be believed that they transmitted that. As for what is related from Abū's-Sammāl and those connected to him, one does not rely on it."

Someone else said, "As for the rare (*shādhdh*) readings of the copies of the transmitted Qur'ān, they are not considered to be the Qur'ān, and are not acted on as if they were part of it. It is most probable that they are clarification of the interpretation of the position of the one to whom they are ascribed, like the reading of Ibn Mas'ūd. If the transmitter is explicit about having heard it from the Messenger of Allah, may Allah bless him and grant him peace, then scholars have two positions about acting on it: negative or positive . The negative position is based on the fact that the transmitter did not relate it as a *ḥadīth*, but as Qur'ān, and it is not affirmed as such and so is not confirmed. The positive position is that even if it is not affirmed as Qur'ān, it is affirmed as *sunna*, and that obliges action, just as the case with all single *aḥādīth*.

Section: The *ḥadīth* of 'Umar and Hishām

Ibn 'Aṭiyya said, "Allah allowed these seven modes to His Prophet, may Allah bless him and grant him peace, and Jibrīl brought them to him in a way which ensured inimitability and precise cohesion. His words, *'Recite what is easy of it,'* did not permit any of the Companions to change any expression in one of these dialects as he wished. If that had been the case, then the Qur'ān would not have been inimitable, as people would have changed this and that and then it would have become other than what was revealed from Allah. The permission was for the seven modes of the Prophet, may Allah bless him and grant him peace, in order to give ample scope to his Community. Once he recited to Ubayy what Jibrīl brought him, and once to Ibn Mas'ūd what had been presented to him.

This was the crux of the difference between 'Umar ibn al-Khaṭṭāb's reading of *Sūrat al-Furqān* and that of Hishām ibn Ḥakīm. Otherwise how was it proper for the Prophet, may Allah bless him and grant him peace, to say about the recitation of each of them which differed, 'That was how Jibrīl recited it to me.' Was it only that he recited it once like that and once like this? This is the meaning of what Anas said when he recited *'aṣwab'* instead of *'aqwam'* in *Sūrat al-Muzzammil* (73:6) meaning "more conducive". He was told, 'We recite it "*aqwam*".' He replied, '"*Aṣwab*", "*aqwam*" and "*ahya*"' are all the same." This is the sense of what is reported from the Prophet, may Allah bless him and grant him peace. If anyone had been permitted to do that, that would have invalidated the words of Allah, '*It is We who have sent down the Reminder and We will preserve it.*' (15:9)."

Al-Bukhārī, Muslim and others related that 'Umar ibn al-Khaṭṭāb said, "I heard Hishām ibn Ḥakīm reciting *Sūrat al-Furqān* in a different way from how I read it, and the Messenger of Allah, may Allah bless him and grant him peace, himself had recited it to me. I almost grabbed him, but I waited until he had finished. Then I got him by his cloak and took him to the Messenger of Allah, may Allah bless him and grant him peace. I said, 'Messenger of Allah, I heard this one reciting *Sūrat al-Furqān* differently to how you recited it to me!' The Messenger of Allah, may Allah bless him and grant him peace, said, 'Let him recite.' He recited it as I had heard him recite it. The Messenger of Allah, may Allah bless him and grant him peace, said, 'That is how it was revealed.' Then he told me, 'Recite.' I recited it and he said, 'That is how it was revealed. This Qur'ān was revealed in seven modes, so recite whatever you find easy of it.'"

Similar to this *ḥadīth* is what Muslim transmitted from Ubayy ibn Ka'b. He said, "I was in the mosque when a man came in to pray. He recited a reading to which I objected. Then another man entered and recited a different recitation to that of his companion. When they finished the prayer, we all went to the Messenger of Allah, may Allah bless him and grant him peace, and I said, 'This one recited a reading to which I objected and the other entered and used a different recitation to that of his companion.' The Prophet, may Allah bless him and grant him peace, commanded them to recite, and the Prophet commended what they had done. Then doubt entered my heart such as had not even affected me in the *Jāhiliyya.* When the Prophet, may Allah bless him and grant him peace, saw what had overpowered me, he struck my chest and I started to sweat, feeling alarm as if I had been looking at Allah. He said to me, 'Ubayy, I was sent a message to recite the Qur'ān in one mode and I replied that I wanted it to be made easy for my community. A second message commanded me to recite it in two modes, and I replied that I wanted it to be made easy for my community. Then I was told the third time, "Recite it in seven modes. You can ask for something for each time you returned to ask." I said, "O Allah, forgive my Community! O Allah, forgive my Community!" I delayed the third until a Day when all creation even Ibrāhīm, peace be upon him, will ask of me.'"

Ubayy meant that he felt confusion and astonishment, in other words he had an impulse from Shayṭān which sullied his state and muddied his mind at that moment. The difference of the readings seemed terrible to him while it was not in itself terrible. Otherwise what would entail denial of the difference in the recitations, when that is not necessary? Praise be to Allah who abrogated what is greater than a reading! When the Prophet, may Allah bless him and grant him peace, saw the thought that occurred to him, he woke him up by striking his chest. The result of that was the expansion of his breast and inward illumination so that the unveiling and expansion took him to a state of vision. When the ugliness of that thought was clear to him, he feared Allah and sweated profusely out of shame before Allah. This thought is the type of thing about which the Prophet, may Allah bless him and grant him peace, spoke when they said to him, "We find things in ourselves which one of us finds too terrible to speak about." He asked, "Do you experience that?" "Yes," they replied. He said, "That is clear faith." (Muslim from Abū Hurayra)

The collection of the Qur'ān and the reason 'Uthmān had copies of the Qur'ān copied out and burned the rest. The memorisation of the Qur'ān by the Companions in the time of the Prophet

In the time of the Prophet, the Qur'ān was scattered in the breasts of men. People wrote some of it on pages, on skins and on white stones and flat stones, scraps and other things. Then a great number of the reciters were killed in the Battle of Yamāma in the time of Abū Bakr. Something like 700 of them were killed in a single day and 'Umar ibn al-Khaṭṭāb suggested to Abū Bakr to collect the Qur'ān out of fear that the shaykhs of the reciters such as Ubayy, Ibn Mas'ūd and Zayd would all die. Zayd ibn Thābit recommended that, and so after great effort. he collected it together without putting the *sūra*s in order.

Al-Bukhārī reports that Zayd ibn Thābit said, "After the slaughter in the war of Yamāma, Abū Bakr sent for me, and 'Umar was with him. Abū Bakr said, ''Umar has come to me and said, "Many people were killed in the Battle of Yamāma, and I fear that many Qur'ān reciters will be killed in other places and so much of the Qur'ān will be lost unless you collect it. I think that you should collect the Qur'ān together."' Abū Bakr said, 'I said to 'Umar, "How can I do something which the Messenger of Allah did not do?" 'Umar said, "By Allah, it is better." 'Umar kept on at me about it until Allah opened my breast to it. I think what 'Umar thinks.'" Zayd ibn Thābit continued, "'Umar was sitting with him, not speaking. Abū Bakr said, 'You are an intelligent young man and we have no doubts about you. You used to write down the revelation for the Messenger of Allah, may Allah bless him and grant him peace. Therefore you are to search out the Qur'ān and collect it.' By Allah, if he had obliged me to move one of the mountains, that would not have been weightier for me than his command to me to collect together the Qur'ān. I replied, 'How can the two of you do something which the Messenger of Allah, may Allah bless him and grant him peace, did not do?' Abū Bakr said, 'By Allah, it is better.' He continued to keep on at me until Allah opened my breast to that which Allah had opened the breasts of Abū Bakr and 'Umar. So I began to search out the Qur'ān and collect it from the parchments, shoulder-blades, palm fronds and the breasts of men until I found two *āyat*s of *Sūrat at-Tawba* with Khuzayma al-Anṣārī that I did not find with anyone else: *'A Messenger has come to you from among yourselves...'* (9:128) The copy of the Qur'ān in which the Qur'ān was collected remained in the possession of Abū Bakr until Allah took him, and then it was with 'Umar until Allah took him, and then it was with Ḥafṣa bint 'Umar."

If it is asked what was the point of 'Uthmān unifying people under a single copy of the Qur'ān when Abū Bakr had already achieved that, then the response is that the aim of 'Uthmān was not to gather people in order to compile the Qur'ān. Do you not see that he sent to Ḥafṣa to ask her to give him the copy of the Qur'ān so that it could be copied out and then returned to her? 'Uthmān did that because people were disagreeing about the various recitations owing to the fact that the Companions had spread to different areas and had begun to strongly disagree, such as the conflict which took place between the people of Iraq and the people of Syria according to Ḥudhayfa.

They joined an expedition to Armenia and each group recited what had been transmitted to them. They disagreed and quarrelled and some of them called the others unbelievers, renouncing them completely, cursing one another. Ḥudhayfa was alarmed at what he saw. As soon as he arrived back to Madina, according to al-Bukhārī and at-Tirmidhī, before returning to his house he went to 'Uthmān and said, "This Community has reached the stage where it will be destroyed!" "Why?" asked 'Uthmān. He said, "It is about the Book of Allah. I was on this expedition and some of the people of Iraq, Syria and the Ḥijāz came together." Then he described what had happened and said, "I fear that they will differ about their Book as the Jews and Christians differed."

This is evidence of the falseness of those who say that the seven *aḥruf* are the seven present readings because there is no disagreement about them. Suwayd ibn Ghafala reported from 'Alī ibn Abī Ṭālib that 'Uthmān said, "What do you think about the copies of the Qur'ān? The people have disagreed about the reciters until a man says, 'My reading is better than your reading. My reading is more excellent than your reading.' This is equivalent to disbelief." He replied, "What is your view, *Amīr al-Mu'minīn*?" He said, "I think that we people should agree on one reading. If you differ today, those after you will disagree more strongly." 'Alī said, "The correct opinion is yours, *Amīr al-Mu'minīn*." So 'Uthmān sent a message to Ḥafṣa saying, "Send us the pages in your possession and we will copy them and then return them to you." She sent them to him and he ordered Zayd ibn Thābit, 'Abdullāh ibn az-Zubayr, Sa'īd ibn al-'Āṣ, and 'Abdu'r-Raḥmān ibn al-Ḥārith ibn Hishām to make copies of them. 'Uthmān told the group of Qurayshis, "When you and Zayd ibn Thabit disagree about any of the Qur'ān, write it in the dialect of Quraysh. It was revealed in their language." They did that. When they had copied it out, 'Uthmān returned the pages to Ḥafṣa and he sent a copy of what they had copied out to every region and commanded that every sheet or copy which had any other form of the Qur'ān should be burned. 'Uthmān did this after gathering the *Muhājirūn* and *Anṣār* and a group of Muslims and consulting them about it. They agreed to collect what was sound and firm of the well-known readings from the Prophet, may Allah bless him and grant him peace, and discard anything else. They thought that what he decided was right and correct. May Allah have mercy on him and all of them.

Ibn Shihāb said that he was told by 'Ubaydullāh ibn 'Abdullāh that 'Abdullāh ibn Mas'ūd disliked Zayd ibn Thābit copying out the Qur'ān and said, "Company of Muslims, withdraw from making copies and entrusting it to one man. By Allah, I became Muslim while he was in the loins of an unbelieving father!" meaning Zayd ibn Thābit. That is why 'Abdullāh ibn Mas'ūd said, "People of Iraq, conceal the copies of the Qur'ān you have and conceal them. Allah says, *'Those who misappropriate will arrive on the Day of Rising with what they have misappropriated.'* (3:161). Meet Allah with the copies of the Qur'ān." (at-Tirmidhī)

Abū Bakr al-Anbārī said, "The fact that Abū Bakr, 'Umar and 'Uthmān chose Zayd in the matter of collecting the Qur'ān does not mean that they were putting him over 'Abdullāh ibn Mas'ūd. 'Abdullāh was better than Zayd, older in Islam, had attended more battles and possessed more virtues. Zayd, however, knew more of the Qur'ān than 'Abdullah since he had memorised it all during the lifetime of the Messenger of Allah, may Allah bless him and grant him peace, whereas 'Abdullāh had only memorised about seventy *sūras* while the Messenger of Allah, may Allah bless him and grant him peace, was alive and learned the rest after his death. The one who knew the entire Qur'ān and memorised it while the Messenger of Allah, may Allah bless him and grant him peace, was alive was more entitled to compile the Qur'ān and to be preferred and chosen to do so. No ignorant person should suppose that this is an attack on 'Abdullāh ibn Mas'ūd since the fact that Zayd had the better memory of the Qur'an of the two does not mean that he should be preferred to him in general terms because Zayd also knew more Qur'ān than Abū Bakr and 'Umar, and he was certainly not better than them or equal to them in virtue."

Abū Bakr al-Anbārī said, "The objection which 'Abdullāh ibn Mas'ūd made was done in anger and is not acted upon or accepted. There is no doubt that once he was no longer angry he was satisfied with the excellence of the decision of 'Uthmān and the Companions of the Messenger of Allah, may Allah bless him and grant him peace, and concurred with their agreement and abandoned his opposition to them."

One scholar said that 'Abdullāh ibn Mas'ūd died before learning all the Qur'ān. Yazīd ibn Hārūn said, "The two *sūra*s of refuge have the same status as *al-Baqara* and *Āli 'Imrān*. Anyone who claims that they are not part of the Qur'ān has rejected Allah Almighty." He was asked, 'What about what 'Abdullāh ibn Mas'ūd says about them?" He replied, "There is no disagreement among the Muslims that 'Abdullāh ibn Mas'ūd died before memorising all of the Qur'ān." This requires some investigation, as will come.

Ḥammad said – I think quoting Anas ibn Mālik – "They disagreed about an *āyat* and would say, 'The Messenger of Allah, may Allah bless him and grant him peace, recited it to so-and-so.'

He might be three days from Madina and he would be sent for and would be asked, 'How did the Messenger of Allah, may Allah bless him and grant him peace, recite such-and-such an *āyat* to you?' and they would write it as he said." Ibn Shihāb said, "One day they disagreed about *tābūt*. Zayd said *tābūh*. Ibn az-Zubayr and Sa'īd ibn al-'Āṣ said, *tābūt*. The disagreement was taken to 'Uthmān who said, 'Write it with *tā'*. It was revealed in the language of Quraysh." (al-Bukhārī and at-Tirmidhī)

'Uthmān had several copies of the Qur'ān made. Some say there were seven while the majority say that there were four. They were sent to various areas. Matrix copies were sent to Iraq, Syria and Egypt, and the reciters of the cities relied on them and none of them differed from the original copy in the manner in which it was conveyed. There is not found among the seven reciters any real difference in the words, neither more nor less. That is because they all relied on what was conveyed in 'Uthmān's copy.

Al-Anbārī quoted Suwayd ibn Ghafala in *Kitāb ar-Radd*, "I heard 'Alī ibn Abī Ṭālib say, 'Company of people! Fear Allah and beware of excess about 'Uthmān and calling him "The burner of Qur'āns". By Allah, he only burned them on the basis of the advice of a council of us, the Companions of Muḥammad, may Allah bless him and grant him peace.'" It is also reported that 'Alī said, "If I had been ruler at the time of 'Uthmān, I would have done to the copies of the Qur'ān the same thing that 'Uthmān did."

Section

Our scholars say that what 'Uthmān did refutes the Ḥulūlīs and Ḥashwites who say that the letters and sounds are eternal and that recitation and reading are eternal and that faith is eternal and the *rūḥ* is eternal. The Community and all groups of the Christians, Jews and Brahmans believe – and indeed, every theist and unitarian – that that which is eternal is unaffected by any event, and no one's power can affect it by any aspect or means. Non-existence is not possible for the eternal and the eternal does not become temporal and the temporal does not become eternal. As for the eternal, there is no beginning to its existence whereas the temporal is that which exists after it was not.

Section

The Rāfiḍites attack the Qur'ān and say, "One person is sufficient to confirm the transmission of an *āyat* and mode just as you have done. You confirmed the statement of a single man, Khuzayma ibn Thābit, in reporting about the end of *Sūrat at-Tawba* and the *āyat* in *Sūrat al-Aḥzāb 'Among the believers are men... '* (33:23)." The reply to them is that when Khuzayma mentioned these words, many of the Companions remembered them and Zayd himself recognised them. That is why he said, "The last two *āyat*s of *Sūrat at-Tawba* were missing." If he had not already known them, he would not have known that anything was missing. So the *āyat* was in fact established by consensus, not by Khuzayma alone. The second answer is that it was established by the testimony of Khuzayma alone and the evidence of its soundness is found in the description of the Prophet, may Allah bless him and grant him peace, and so has no need for another witness, which is not the case of the *āyat* in *al-Aḥzāb*. That is established by the testimony of Zayd and Abu Khuzayma who heard it from the Prophet. It is mentioned that Abu Khuzayma is not the same Khuzayma with whom the *āyat* of *at-Tawba was* found and he was known among the Anṣār. Anas knew him. The one with whom the *āyat* of *al-Aḥzāb* was found was Khuzayma ibn Thābit. There is no confusion in the story.

In Muslim and al-Bukhārī, Anas ibn Mālik said, "The Qur'ān was gathered together in the time of the Prophet, may Allah bless him and grant him peace, by four, all of whom were from the Anṣār: Ubayy, Mu'ādh ibn Jabal, Zayd ibn Thābit, and Abū Zayd." Anas was asked, "Who is Abū Zayd?" and he replied, "One of my paternal uncles." Also in al-Bukhārī, Anas said, "When the Prophet died, may Allah bless him and grant him peace, only four knew all the Qur'ān: Abū'd-Dardā', Mu'ādh ibn Jabal, Zayd and Abū Zayd."

Ibn aṭ-Ṭayyib said, "These traditions do not indicate that the Qur'ān was not memorised in the time of the Prophet and that only four of the Anṣār knew it by heart as Anas stated. It is confirmed by multiple paths of transmission that the entire Qur'ān was also known by 'Uthmān, 'Alī, Tamīm ad-Dārī, 'Ubāda ibn aṣ-Ṣāmit, and 'Abdullāh ibn 'Amr ibn al-'Āṣ." Anas' words mean that only these four took it directly from the mouth of the Messenger of Allah, may Allah bless him and grant him peace. Most of them learned it from one another.

The Qāḍī did not mention 'Abdullāh ibn Mas'ūd and Sālim, the client of Abū Ḥudhayfa, although they were among those who knew the entire Qur'ān. It is reported that 'Umar ibn al-Khaṭṭāb said, "I was with the Messenger of Allah, may Allah bless him and grant him peace, and with him were Abū Bakr and whomever Allah wished. We passed 'Abdullāh ibn Mas'ūd who was praying. The Messenger of Allah, may Allah bless him and grant him peace, asked, 'Who is reciting the Qur'ān?' He was told, ''Abdullāh ibn Umm 'Abd.' He said, ''Abdullāh recites the Qur'ān fresh as it was revealed.'"

One scholar said that this meant that he recited the first *ḥarf* in which the Qur'ān was revealed rather than the other seven which the Messenger of Allah, may Allah bless him and grant him peace, was allowed after the Messenger of Allah, Jibrīl, recited the Qur'ān to him in Ramaḍān. It is related that Abū Ẓubyān said, "'Abdullāh ibn 'Abbās asked me, 'Which of the recitations do you recite?' I replied, 'The first recitation, that of Ibn Umm 'Abd.' He told me, 'Rather it was the last. The Messenger of Allah, may Allah bless him and grant him peace, used to present the Qur'ān to Jibrīl once a year. In the year that he died, the Messenger of Allah read it to him twice. 'Abdullāh was present and knew what was abrogated and changed in that.'" In Muslim, 'Abdullāh ibn 'Amr stated that he heard the Messenger of Allah, may Allah bless him and grant him peace, say, "Take the Qur'ān from four: Ibn Umm 'Abd – and he began with him – Mu'ādh ibn Jabal, Ubayy ibn Ka'b and Sālim, the client of Abū Ḥudhayfa."

These reports indicate that 'Abdullāh knew all the Qur'ān in the lifetime of the Messenger of Allah, contrary to what was said, and Allah knows best. In *Kitāb ar-Radd*, al-Anbārī transmitted that 'Abdullāh ibn Mas'ūd said, "I learned 72 (or 73) *sūra*s from the Messenger of Allah, may Allah bless him and grant him peace, and I read to him from *al-Baqara* as far as *'Allah loves those who repent'* (2:222)." Abū Isḥāq says that he learned the rest of the Qur'ān from Mujammi' ibn Jāriya al-Anṣārī. If this is true, the consensus which Yazīd ibn Hārūn mentioned is true and that is why Qāḍī Ibn aṭ-Ṭayyib did not mention him among those who knew the Qur'ān by heart in the time of the Messenger of Allah, may Allah bless him and grant him peace. Allah knows best.

Part of what will indicate the soundness of Ibn Mas'ūd's knowledge of the Qur'ān is that the people with the readings among the people of the Ḥijāz, Syria and Iraq all traced their readings which they chose back to one of the Companions who read it to the Messenger of Allah, may Allah bless him and grant him peace. 'Āṣim traced his reading to 'Alī and Ibn Mas'ūd, Ibn Kathīr to Ubayy as did Abū 'Amr ibn al-'Alā', and 'Abdullāh ibn 'Āmir traced his to 'Uthmān. All of them said that they had read it to the Messenger of Allah. The *isnād*s of these readings are continuous and the transmitters are reliable, as al-Khaṭṭābī stated.

What has come about the order of the *sūra*s and *āyat*s of the Qur'ān, its vowelling and dots, its *ḥizb*s and tens, the number of its letters, *juz'*s, words and *āyat*s

Ibn aṭ-Ṭayyib said, "Some say that the *Salaf* differed about the order of the *sūra*s of the Qur'ān and some of them wrote the *sūra*s in the order that they were revealed and put the Makkan before the Madinan, and some put *al-Ḥamd* (*Fātiḥa*) at the beginning, and others put *al-'Alaq* at the beginning. This was the case in the first copy of 'Alī. As for the copy of Ibn Mas'ūd, it begins with '*Master of the Day of the Dīn*' (1:4) and then *al-Baqara*, and then *an-Nisā'* with a different order. The copy of Ubayy began with *al-*

Ḥamd, then *an-Nisā'*, then *Āl 'Imrān*, then *al-An'ām*, then *al-A'rāf*, then *al-Mā'ida*. There were significant differences."

Ibn aṭ-Ṭayyib's answer is that it is possible that the order of the *sūras* as we have today in the Qur'ān is by *ijtihād* on the part of the Companions. Makkī mentioned this in the *tafsīr* of *Sūrat at-Tawba*. He mentioned the order of the *āyat*s in the *sūra* and that the placing the *basmala* at the beginnings of them was from the Prophet, peace be upon him. Since he did not command that for *Sūrat at-Tawba*, it was left without a *basmala*. This is the soundest of what is said about it.

In the *Jāmi'*, Ibn Wahb stated that Sulaymān ibn Bilāl heard Rabī'a being asked why *al-Baqara* and *Āl 'Imrān* were put first when there were about eighty *sūra*s revealed before them and they were revealed in Madina. Rabī'a said, "They were put first and the Qur'ān was arranged according to the knowledge of those who arranged it and had knowledge of that. This is what we ended up with and we do not ask about it." It is reported from Qatāda that Ibn Mas'ūd said, "Whoever of you seeks a model, should model himself on the Companions of the Messenger of Allah. They have the best hearts of this community, the deepest knowledge, least artifice, straightest guidance and the best state. Allah chose them to be the Companions of His Prophet and to establish His *dīn*. So acknowledge their excellence and follow in their footsteps. They followed straight guidance."

Some scholars say that the arrangement of the *sūra*s of the Qur'ān which we find in our copies of the Qur'ān was at the instruction of the Prophet, may Allah bless him and grant him peace. What is related about the differences between the copies of Ubayy, 'Alī and 'Abdullāh was before the final presentation. The Messenger of Allah, may Allah bless him and grant him peace, arranged those *sūra*s for them after they had done that. It is reported from Ibn Wahb that he heard Mālik say, "The Qur'ān was arranged according to what they heard from the Messenger of Allah, may Allah bless him and grant him peace."

Al-Anbārī mentioned in *Kitāb ar-Radd*, "Allah Almighty revealed the Qur'ān all at once to the lowest heaven, and then it came down in parts to the Prophet over twenty years. A *sūra* would be revealed about a matter which happened and an *āyat* would answer an inquiry. Jibrīl would give the Messenger of Allah, may Allah bless him and grant him peace, the place of the *sūra* and the *āyat*. So the *sūra*s are in order as the *āyat*s and letters are in order. All of it is from Muḥammad, the Seal of the Messengers, peace be upon him, from the Lord of the Worlds. Whoever changes the order of the *sūra*s is like someone who invalidates the order of the *āyat*s and changes the letters and the words. There is no argument against the people who possess the truth in putting *al-Baqara* before *al-An'ām* when *al-An'ām* was revealed before *al-Baqara* because the order is taken from the Messenger of Allah. He said, "Put this *sūra* in such-and-such a place.'"

Al-Barā' said, "The last of the Qur'ān to be revealed was, '*They will ask you for a fatwā. Say: "Allah gives you a fatwā about people who die without direct heirs."*'" (4:176). Abū Bakr ibn 'Ayyāsh said, "Abū Isḥāq erred because it is reported from Ibn 'Abbās that the last part of the Qur'ān to be revealed was, *'Show fear of a Day when you will be returned to Allah. Then every self will be paid in full for what it earned. They will not be wronged'* (2:281). Jibrīl told the Prophet, peace be upon both of them, 'Muḥammad, put it as the beginning of 281 of *al-Baqara*.'"

Ibn Baṭṭāl said, "Whoever says this, does not say that the recitation of the Qur'ān in the prayer and lessons must be in the order that it is in copies of the Qur'ān. Rather it is only mandatory to put the *sūra*s in order when writing them down, and it is not known that any of them said that the same order is mandatory in the prayer, in recitation of the Qur'ān and study or that it is not lawful for someone to learn *al-Kahf* before *al-Baqara* or *al-Ḥajj* before *al-Kahf*. Do you not see that 'Ā'isha told the person who asked about this, 'There is nothing wrong in whichever you recite first. The Prophet used to recite one *sūra* in a *rak'at* and then would recite in the next *rak'at* a different *sūra* than the one that follows it.'

As for what is reported from Ibn Mas'ūd and Ibn 'Umar about it being disliked to recite the Qur'ān out of order, claiming that it upsets the heart, what they meant by that was reciting the *sūra* out of order and beginning from its end and then working backwards, because that is forbidden. Some people do this with the Qur'ān and poetry to subject the tongue to that and facilitate memorisation. Allah forbade doing this in the Qur'ān because it disorders His *sūra*s and is counter to what He meant by it."

Part of what indicates that it is not obliged to use the chronological order of revelation in copies of the Qur'ān is that it is confirmed that certain *āyat*s were revealed in Madina and then placed in Makkan *sūra*s. 'Ā'isha said, "*Sūrat al-Baqara* and *Sūrat an-Nisā'* were revealed when I was with him (i.e. in Madina), but they come in the copies of the Qur'ān before earlier *sūra*s of the Qur'ān revealed in Makka."

Section

As for the vowelling of the Qur'ān and its dots, it is reported that 'Abdu'l-Mālik ibn Marwān commanded them to be added, and that was undertaken by al-Ḥajjāj in Wāsiṭ. He worked on the task and added its *ḥizb*s. He commanded the governor of Iraq, al-Ḥasan, and Yaḥyā ibn Ya'mur to do that. After that he wrote a book in Wāsiṭ on the readings in which he compiled what was related about the disagreement of people in relation to the script. People used that book for a long time until Ibn Mujāhid wrote his book on the readings. In *Kitāb aṭ-Ṭabaqāt* az-Zubaydī quotes al-Mubarrad as saying that the first person to use dots in the Qur'ān was Abū'l-Aswad ad-Du'alī. Ibn Sīrīn also mentioned that he had a copy of the Qur'ān in which Yaḥyā ibn Ya'mur had put the dots.

Section

As for the position regarding the division of the Qur'ān into groups of ten *āyat*s, Ibn 'Aṭiyya said, "In one of the histories I read that the 'Abbāsid al-Ma'mūn commanded that to be done. It is also said that al-Ḥajjāj did it." In the *Kitāb al-Bayān*, ad-Dānī said that 'Abdullāh ibn Mas'ūd disliked the marking of tens in the copies of the Qur'ān and that he erased them. Mujāhid is reported to have disliked the tenths in copies of the Qur'ān.

Ashhab said, "I heard Mālik being asked about the tens which are in the Qur'ān in red and other colours and he disliked that, saying, 'There is nothing wrong in marking the tens with [normal] ink.' He was asked about copies of the Qur'ān in which the ends of *sūras* were written along with the number of *āyat*s in every *sūra*. He said, 'I dislike for anything [additional] to be written or vowelled in the master copies. As for those copies by which children learn, I see no harm in doing that.'" Ashhab said, "Then he produced for us a copy of the Qur'ān which had belonged to his grandfather. He had written it when 'Uthmān had the Qur'ān copied out. We saw the ends were written in ink in something resembling a chain which extended for an entire line and I saw that the *āyat*s had diacritical marks in ink."

Qatāda said, "They began with the dots, then with marking the division of the fives and then the tens." Yaḥyā ibn Abī Kathīr said, "The Qur'ān was bare in the original copies and the first thing that they did was to put dots on the *bā'*, *tā'* and *thā'*. They said, 'There is nothing wrong in it. It makes it clearer.' Then they put dots at the ends of *āyat*s and then they put openings and ends of *sūra*s."

Abū Ḥamza said, "Ibrāhīm an-Nakhā'ī noticed in my copy of the Qur'ān the opening of such-and-such a *sūra*. He said to me, 'Erase it. 'Abdullāh ibn Mas'ūd said, "Do not mix with the Book of Allah something which is not part of it."'" Abū Bakr as-Sarrāj said, "I asked Abū Rāzin, 'Do I write '*Sūra* such-and-such' in my copy of the Qur'ān?' He replied, 'I fear that people will come who do not know it and think that those words are part of the Qur'ān.'"

Ad-Dānī said, "All these reports which allow the marking of tens and fives and beginnings of *sūra*s and the beginnings of *āyat*s say that it was done by the Companions whose *ijtihād* led them to that. I think that those of them who objected to that objected to the use of colours like red, yellow and so forth, although the Muslims in other areas agreed on their use in the master copies and other copies, and prohibition and error were removed from them in what they agreed upon, Allah willing.

Section

As for the number of its letters and *juz*'s, Sallām al-Ḥimānī said, "Al-Ḥajjāj ibn Yūsuf gathered the reciters, *ḥuffāẓ* and scribes and said, 'Tell me how many letters are in the entire Qur'ān.' I was one of that group. We calculated and agreed that the Qur'ān had three hundred and forty thousand, seven hundred and forty (340,740) letters. Then he said, 'Tell me which letter ends half of the Qur'ān.' It was in *al-Kahf*, on the *fā'* of *wa layatalaṭṭaf* [18:19, *"he should go about with caution."*] He said, 'Tell me the thirds.' The first third was found to be at the beginning of 9:100 and the second at the beginning of 26:100 or 101. The last third was the rest of the Qur'ān. He said, 'Tell me the sevenths of the letters.' We did so."

Sallām, Abū Muḥammad, stated, "We did that over four months. Every night al-Ḥajjāj would read a fourth. The end of the first fourth was at the end of *al-An'ām,* the second in *al-Kahf*, the third at the end of *az-Zumar* and the fourth consisted of the rest. This is contrary to what is mentioned by ad-Dānī in *Kitāb al-Bayān*.

Section

As for the number of the *āyat*s of the Qur'ān in the first Madinan copy, Muḥammad ibn 'Īsā said, "The number of the *āyat*s of the Qur'ān in the first Madinan copy was six thousand." Abū 'Amr said, "It is the number related by the people of Kufa from the people of Madina, and they did not name anyone specifically on whom they relied in that."

As for the final Madinan copy, according to Ismā'īl ibn Ja'far, it has six thousand two hundred and fourteen (6214) *āyat*s. Al-Faḍl said, "The number of the *āyat*s of the Qur'ān according to the Makkans was six thousand two hundred and nineteen (6219). That is the number related by Sālim and al-Kisā'i from Ḥamza. Al-Kisā'i attributed it to 'Alī." Muḥammad said, "The number of the *āyats* of the Qur'ān according to the Basrans was six thousand two hundred and four (6204), which is the number which their *Salaf* passed down. As for the number of the people of Syria, Yaḥyā ibn al-Ḥārith adh-Dhamārī said it was six thousand two hundred and twenty-six (6226). One transmission has six thousand two hundred and twenty-five (6225)." Ibn Dhakwān said, "I think that Yaḥyā did not count the *basmala*."

As for the number of its words, al-Faḍl ibn Shādhān said, "The total number of the words of the Qur'ān according to 'Aṭā' ibn Yasār is seventy-seven thousand four hundred and thirty-nine (77,439) and its letters are three hundred and twenty-three thousand and fifteen (323,015)." This differs from what al-Ḥimānī said. Ibn Kathīr reported that Mujāhid said, "This is what we counted of the Qur'ān: it has three hundred and twenty-one thousand, one hundred and eighty (321,180) letters. This also differs from what al-Ḥimānī mentioned.

The meaning of the words *sūra*, *āyat*, *kalima* (word) and *ḥarf* (letter)

The word "*sūra*" which means chapter, wall or fence in Arabic is used in the Qur'ān to make each chapter clear and distinct from every other *sūra*. The chapters are called that because in them one ascends from one degree to the next. It is said that they are called that because of their honour and elevation, as is said of walls which are raised up in the land. It is said that they are called that because the one who reads them looks forward at what lies ahead, like the walls of a building. All these are without *hamza*. It is said that they are called that because they are cut out from the Qur'ān on their own, as the Arabs call a leftover *su'r*. In that case the word would have a *hamza* which was replaced with a *wāw*. It is said that they are called that because of their completion and perfection as this word is used for a fine camel.

An *āya*[*t*] is a sign. It is a sign since it is separate and distinct from the words before it and the words after it; it is clear from other signs and is on its own. It can mean a proof or token. It is said that it is called that because it is a collection of letters of the Qur'ān, as one says, "The people went forth with their full company (*āya*)." It is said that it is called *āya* because it is a wonder which people are unable to imitate.

Grammarians disagree about the root of *āya*. Sibuwayh said that it is *ayaya* and because the *yā'* is vowelled and has a *fatḥa* before it, it becomes *alif* and so it is *āya*. Al-Kisā'ī said that its root is *āyaya* and the *yā'* accepts the *alif* with a *fatḥa* before it and is elided because they are similar. Al-Farrā' says that its root is *ayyaya* and it accepts the *alif* out of dislike of the doubling and becomes *āya*.

As for the word *kalima*, it is a composite structure which is made up of a mixture of letters. The longest words in the Book of Allah are eleven letters long, like *"la-yastakhlifannahum"* (24:55) and *"a-nulzimukumūhā"* (11:28) and the like. As for *"fa-asqaynākumūhu"* (15:22), it is ten in writing and eleven in articulation. The shortest have two letters, like *mā*, *lā, laka*, *lahu*, and the like. Some words are just one letter, such as the interrogative *hamza* and the conjunctive *wāw*, but are not spoken alone.

Sometimes a complete *āyat* is comprised of a single word, as in *"wa'l-fajr"*, *"wa'd-duḥā"*, and *"wa'l-'aṣr"*. That is also the case in *"alif-lām-mīm"*, *"alif-lām-mīm-ṣād"*, *"ṭā-hā"*, *"yā-sīn"*, and *"ḥā-mīm"* according to the Kufans. That occurs at the beginnings of *sūra*s, but not inside them. Abū 'Amr ad-Dānī said, "I do not know of any word which on its own is an *āyat* except for *'mudhāmmatān'* in *Sūrat ar-Raḥmān* (55:64)." Two words may become connected and be two *āyat*s, as in *"ḥā-mīm. 'ayn-sīn-qāf"* according to the Kufans.

It is possible that elsewhere a single word may stand for a complete and self-sustaining *āyat*. Allah says, *"The most excellent Word of your Lord was fulfilled for the Tribe of Israel for their steadfastness."* (7:137) It is said that "word" here refers to Allah's words: *"We desired to show kindness to those who were oppressed in the land..."* (28:5-6) The Almighty says, *"He bound them to godfearing self-restraint (lit. word of* taqwā*)"* (48:26). Mujāhid said that the "word" is: *"There is no god but Allah."* The Prophet, may Allah bless him and grant him peace, said, "Two words are light on the tongue, heavy in the balance, beloved to the All-Merciful: 'Glory be to Allah and by His praise. Glory be to Allah, the Immense.'" The Arabs sometimes call an entire ode and story a "word".

The word *ḥarf* (letter) is the shape which stands alone in a word of which it is made up. A letter can be called a word and a word a letter as we made clear. Abū 'Amr ad-Dānī said, "Are the letters of the alphabet at the beginnings of *sūra*s, such as *ṣād*, *qāf*, and *nūn* letters or words? I say that they are words, not letters. That is because a letter is not unvowelled nor is it alone in a *sūra* nor separate from what is mixed with it. But these are unvowelled, alone, separate, like words which are distinct."

Does the Qur'ān contain words which are not Arabic?

There is no disagreement among the Arabs that the Qur'ān contains words composed in a non-Arabic mode and names of people which are not Arabic, like Isrā'īl, Jibrīl, 'Imrān, Nūḥ and Lūṭ. They disagree about whether there are words other than proper names which are non-Arabic. Qāḍī Ibn aṭ-Ṭayyib, aṭ-Ṭabarī and others believe that there are no non-Arabic words in it and the Qur'ān is pure Arabic, and whatever words which are found in it ascribed to other languages happen to be common to both, and so the Arabs, Persians, Abyssinians and others used them. Some claim that non-Arabic words exist in the Qur'ān but that since they are so few that does not preclude the Qur'ān being pure Arabic and the Prophet from speaking the language of his people. *Mishkāt* (24:35) is a niche, *nasha'a* means "to rise in the night" as in *"nāshi'ata'l-layl"* (73:6), *qaswara* (74:51) is a lion and *kiflatayn* (57:28) means "double". These are found in Abyssinian. *Ghassāq*

(38:57) means "foul" in Turkish. *Qisṭās* (17:35; 26:182) means "balance" in Greek. *Sijjīl* (21:104; 15:74; 105:4) means "stones" in Persian. *Ṭūr* (2:63; 2:93, etc.) is a mountain and *yamm* (7:136. etc.) means sea in Syriac. *Tannūr* (11:40; 23:27) is the surface of the earth in Persian.

Ibn 'Aṭiyya said, "The truth about the expression of these words is that their origin is foreign, but the Arabs used them and Arabicised them and so they are Arabic. When the Qur'ān was revealed in their language, the Arabs had mixed with other languages via trade and travel." And Allah knows best.

Points about the inimitability of the Qur'ān, preconditions of the miracle and its reality

A miracle *(mu'jiza)* is the evidence of the Prophets which indicates their truthfulness. It is called that [the verb means "to be unable to do"] because no human being is able to do the like of it. It has five preconditions. If one of them is missing, it is not a miracle.

- It must be something which only Allah can do. This precondition is necessary because if someone comes at a time in which it is possible for there to be Messengers and claims to be a Messenger and makes his miracle consist of moving and being still, standing and sitting, that is not a miracle nor evidence of his truthfulness since another creature can do that. Miracles consist of things like splitting the sea, splitting the moon and other such things.

- It must break normal patterns. If someone comes at night and his sign is that the night will come after the day or the sun rise in the east in the morning, that is not a miracle because it is something which only Allah can do and it was not done for his sake. Things which break normal patterns are like turning a staff into a snake, the rock splitting and the she-camel emerging, or water springing from fingers like a spring.

- It must be claimed to testify to the Message.
- It must occur in order to support this claim against those who challenge him as when he says, "I am a Prophet and my sign is that this she-camel will speak."
- It must be that no one successfully comes up with the like of what he is challenged to do.

It is not said that the miracle with the five preconditions is limited to the truthful, because the Dajjāl, as our Prophet, may Allah bless him and grant him peace, said, will have immense matters appear at his hands. The difference is that one claims to be a Messenger and the other to be a Lord, and there is a great difference between the blind and the seeing.

Section

If you affirm this, know that there are two types of miracle. The first is that which is famous and whose time ended at the death of the Prophet, and the second are those transmitted by multiple traditions as being sound and confirmed and hence must be known. The precondition is that many people transmitted it and have knowledge of what they transmit and the whole chain is reliable so that it is impossible that there be any falsehood in it. This is the case with the Qur'ān which has been transmitted from large numbers of people continuously and has gone to many lands. The Qur'ān will remain a miracle until the Day of Rising whereas the miracles of other Prophets ended with their death. The Qur'ān will not be changed or altered as happened with the Torah and Gospel.

There are ten aspects to the inimitability of the Qur'ān.

- Its wondrous composition differs from every usual order in Arabic and other languages because its arrangement is not poetry at all, as Allah says, *"We did not teach him poetry nor would it be right for him."* (36:69) In the *Ṣaḥīḥ* Collection of Muslim, it is reported that Unays, the brother of Abū Dharr, told Abū Dharr, "In Makka I met a man who claims that Allah sent him." He asked, "What do people say about him?" He replied, 'They say: he is a poet, a soothsayer and a sorcerer." Unays was a poet and said, "I have heard the words of the soothsayers and this is not like their words. I compared him with the reciters of poetry and it was not like them. No one after me should err and say he was a poet. He is truthful and they are liars." When 'Utba ibn Rabī'a heard the Qur'ān, he affirmed that it was not sorcery or poetry and that he had never heard anything like it.

- Its style differs from all the styles of the Arabs.

- It has a lucid, eloquent style which could never come from a creature at all. Reflect on that in *Sūrat Qāf* (50) and *Sūrat az-Zumar* (39) and you will clearly see its eloquencc which a creature could not possibly originate.

Ibn al-Ḥaṣṣār said, "These three – arrangement, style and lucid eloquence are found in every *sūra*, indeed, in every *āyat*, and the combination of these three distinguishes what is heard of every *āyat* and every *sūra* from the words of ordinary humans. By this there is a challenge [to opponents] and inimitability. Every *sūra* has these three, although other aspects of the ten may be ascribed to it as well. *Sūrat al-Kawthar* (108) consists of only three short *āyat*s, being the shortest *sūra* in the Qur'ān, and it contains reports about the unseen matters: about Kawthar and its immensity and abundance which indicates that the Prophet will have the greatest number of Followers. The second is about al-Walīd ibn al-Mughīra, who was a wealthy man with many children when this was revealed, and then later he was destroyed.

- The Arabic usage used in it is beyond what any Arab could master and they all agree that it is correct.

- It talks of matters which occurred from the beginning of the world until the time of its revelation, all this issuing from the mouth of someone illiterate who could neither read nor write. It reports about the stories of Prophets with their communities and past generations as well as those matters the People of the Book asked about when they challenged him about the People of the Cave, al-Khiḍr and Mūsā, and Dhū'l-Qarnayn. Qāḍī Ibn aṭ-Ṭayyib points out that we know that there was no way for him to learn this because he did not have contact with people with knowledge of history or frequent a teacher so that he could take from them, and so it is known that it could only have come by way of revelation.

- There is the fulfilment of Allah's promises which were visually perceived in all that He promised in the Qur'ān. That is divided into general reports, like promising His Messenger, peace be upon him, victory and expelling those who expelled him, and promises which have preconditions like, *"If someone trusts in Allah, He is enough for him."* (65:3)

- There are reports about unseen matters in the future which could only be known by revelation. Part of that is Allah's promise to His Prophet that his *dīn* would overcome all other *dīns*, as happened. When Abū Bakr sent his armies on expeditions, he would inform them of Allah's promise to make His *dīn* victorious so that they would be confident of victory and certain of success. 'Umar also did that, and the conquests continued in the east and west. Allah says, *"Allah has promised those of you who believe and do right actions that He will make them the successors in the land as He made those before them the successors."* (24:55)

- There is the knowledge that the Qur'ān contains, which is the basis for all people regarding the lawful and unlawful and other rulings.

- There are eloquent expressions of wisdom which do not normally issue from a human being.

- The perfect symmetry of the entire Qur'ān, outward and inward without disparity or inconsistency, is a final factor. Allah says, *"If it had been from other than Allah, they would have found many inconsistencies in it."* (4:82)

These are ten points and an eleventh, mentioned by an-Naẓẓām[1] and some Qadarīs, is that the meaning of inimitability is the impossibility of opposition and being prevented from undertaking to meet the challenge. They said that the prohibition and diverting people from attempting to do that are the miracle rather than the Qur'ān itself. That is because Allah directed their aspirations away from undertaking the challenge to bring a *sūra* like it. This is false because the consensus of the community without any disagreement is that the Qur'ān itself is the miracle, not the diversion and prohibition because its eloquence and lucidity are beyond normal patterns. If there had been any words like it, it would not be the case.

Information about *aḥādīth* forged about the excellence of the *sūra*s of the Qur'ān and other matters

One does not pay any attention to what forgers devise and opponents create of false *aḥādīth* and baseless reports about the excellence of the *sūra*s of the Qur'ān and other virtuous actions. Many people do this, and their goals and aims vary. Some of them are *zindīq*s, like al-Mughīra ibn Sa'īd al-Kūfī and Muḥammad ibn Sa'īd ash-Shāmī. They forged *aḥādīth* and used to create doubt in the hearts of people. Part of that is what Muḥammad ibn Sa'īd related from Anas ibn Mālik about the words of the Prophet, may Allah bless him and grant him peace, "I am the seal of the Prophets and there will be no Prophet after me except as Allah wishes." He added the exception and that is heresy on his part. This is mentioned by Ibn 'Abdu'l-Barr in the *Kitāb at-Tamhīd*.

1. A famous Mu'tazilite in Baghdād, d.c. 221/836.

Some forged *aḥādith* to support a sect to which they called people. One of the Khārijites said after he repented, "These *aḥādīth* are the *dīn*. So look to whom you take your *dīn*. When we desire something, we make up a *ḥadīth* about it."

A group forged *aḥādīth* about rewards, calling people to virtuous actions, as related from Nūḥ ibn Maryam al-Marwazī, Muḥammad ibn 'Ukkāsha al-Kirmānī, Aḥmad ibn 'Abdullāh al-Juwaybārī and others. He was asked, "Where did you get what you have from 'Ikrima from Ibn 'Abbās about the virtue of certain *sūra*s?" He replied, "I saw that people turned from the Qur'ān and busied themselves with the *fiqh* of Abū Ḥanīfa and the expeditions of Muḥammad ibn Isḥāq and so I made up this *ḥadīth* about rewards." There are other examples like this, like the long *ḥadīth* reported from Ubayy about the virtues of each *sūra* of the Qur'ān.

Some beggars who stand in markets and mosques forge *aḥādīth* with *isnād*s from the Prophet, may Allah bless him and grant him peace, which they have memorised. They mention these forged *aḥādīth* along with their *isnāds*. Aṭ-Ṭayālasī said, "Aḥmad ibn Ḥanbal and Yaḥyā ibn Ma'īn prayed in the Ruṣāfa mosque and a storyteller stood before them and said, 'Aḥmad ibn Ḥanbal and Yaḥyā ibn Ma'īn related to me from 'Abdu'r-Razzāq from Ma'mar from Qatāda from Anas that the Messenger of Allah, may Allah bless him and grant him peace, said, 'If anyone says, "There is no god but Allah," a bird is created from every word whose beak is of gold and feathers of coral.' He began a story which would cover about twenty pages. Aḥmad looked at Yaḥyā and Yaḥyā looked at Aḥmad. He asked, 'Did you say this?' He said, 'By Allah, I only just heard it at this moment.'

"They remained silent until he finished his story. Then Yaḥyā asked him, 'Who told you this *ḥadīth*?' 'Aḥmad ibn Ḥanbal and Yaḥyā ibn Ma'īn,' he replied. He said, 'I am Ibn Ma'īn and this is Aḥmad ibn Ḥanbal and we have not heard this at all in the *aḥādīth* of the Messenger of Allah. This must be a lie.' 'You are Yaḥyā ibn Ma'īn?' he asked. 'Yes,' he replied. He said, 'I had not heard that Yaḥyā ibn Ma'īn was a fool and I did not know it until this moment!' Yaḥyā asked, 'And why do you say that I am a fool?' He replied, 'It is not as if there was no Yaḥyā ibn Ma'īn and Aḥmad ibn Ḥanbal in the world but you two! I have written from seventeen Aḥmad ibn Ḥanbals other than this.' Aḥmad hid his face in his sleeve and said, 'Let him go.' He went as if he was mocking them." These groups lie about the Messenger of Allah, may Allah bless him and grant him peace.

If they had confined themselves to what is established in the *Ṣaḥīḥ* collections and *Musnad*s and other books made by scholars related by the imams, they would have had enough. They abandoned his warning, "Fear Allah when reporting from other than those you know. Whoever deliberately lies about me should take his seat in the Fire." So he, may Allah bless him and grant him peace, warned his Community about lying, indicating that he knew that it would happen. His warning was about what is forged by the enemies of Islam and the *zindīq*s in encouragement and warning and other things. Those who do the greatest harm are those who ascribed asceticism to themselves and forged *aḥādīth* about rewards that they claim. People accepted their forgeries and relied on them, and so they were misguided and misguided others.

What has come on the refutation of those who attack the Qur'ān and oppose the text of 'Uthmān by adding to it or removing some of it

There is no disagreement in the Community between the Imāms of the *Sunna* that the Qur'ān is the name used to designate the Words of Allah which Muḥammad, may Allah bless him and grant him peace, brought as a miracle, as we have said. It is preserved in the hearts, recited on the tongues, written in the copies of the Qur'ān, and known by necessity in *sūra*s and *āyat*s. It is free of any addition or increase in words and letters. There is no need for a definition to define it nor number to contain it. Anyone who claims increase or decrease in it has declared the consensus false and such an action astonishes people. We read what Allah said about what the Messenger, may Allah bless him and grant him peace, brought of the Qur'ān revealed to him, "*Say: 'If both men and jinn banded together to produce the like of this Qur'ān, they could never produce anything like it, even if they backed each other up.'*" (17:88). That is an attempt to invalidate the Sign of the Messenger because if it had been something someone was capable of doing, it would not be a proof or a sign and therefore not a miracle.

Those who say that there is addition and decrease in the Qur'ān reject the Book of Allah and what the Messenger has brought. It is like someone who states that the obligatory prayers are fifty, one can marry nine women and that Allah obliged extra days to be fasted together with the days of Ramaḍān, and so forth. As all of that is refuted by consensus, so consensus about the Qur'ān is more binding and necessary.

Seeking Refuge with Allah from Shayṭān

Allah orders people to seek refuge at the beginning of every recitation, when He says, *"Whenever you recite the Qur'ān, seek refuge with Allah from the cursed Shayṭān."* (16:98) This command is a recommendation according to the position of the majority for every time of recitation other than the prayer. There is disagreement where the prayer is concerned. An-Naqqāsh reported from 'Aṭā' that seeking refuge is mandatory in it. Ibn Sīrīn, Ibrāhīm an-Nakhā'ī and some other people sought refuge in the prayer in every *rak'at* and treated the command of Allah to seek refuge as applying in every case. Abū Ḥanīfa and ash-Shāfi'ī sought refuge in the first *rak'at* of the prayer and considered all the recitation during the prayer to constitute a single act of recitation. Mālik did not think that there was any need to seek refuge in the obligatory prayers but thought it should be done in night prayers in Ramaḍān.

Scholars agree that the formula of seeking refuge is not part of the Qur'ān nor an *āyat* of it. It is the words of the reciter, *"A'ūdhu bi'llāhi min ash-shayṭāni'r-rajīm* ('I seek refuge with Allah from the Accursed Shayṭān')." This formula is that on which the majority of scholars agree because it concurs with the expression in the Book of Allah. It is related that Ibn Mas'ūd said, "I say, 'I seek refuge with Allah, the All-Hearing, All-Knowing from the accursed Shayṭān.'" The Prophet, may Allah bless him and grant him peace, said to him, "Ibn Umm 'Abd, I seek refuge with Allah from the accursed Shayṭān as Jibrīl read it to me from the Preserved Tablet from the Pen."

Abū Dāwūd and Ibn Mājah related in their *Sunan* collections that Jubayr ibn Muṭ'im saw the Messenger of Allah, may Allah bless him and grant him peace, praying. ('Amr said, "I do not know which prayer it was.") He said, "Allah is very much greater. Allah is very much greater (three times). Praise be to Allah abundantly. Praise be to Allah abundantly (three times) Glory be to Allah morning and evening (three times). I seek refuge with Allah from Shayṭān and his blowing, spitting and spurring." Spurring is madness, spitting is poetry and blowing is pride.

Abū Dāwūd also related that Abu Sa'īd al-Khudrī said that when the Messenger of Allah, may Allah bless him and grant him peace, rose at night, he would say the *takbīr* and then say, "Glory be to You, O Allah, and by your praise. Blessed is Your Name and exalted are You. There is no god but You." Then he said, "There is no god but Allah" three times, "Allah is very great" three times, and "I seek refuge with Allah, the All-Hearing, all-Knowing from the Accursed Shayṭān from his spurring, blowing and spitting." Then he would recite.

Sulaymān ibn Sālim related from Ibn al-Qāsim that the refuge formula is: "I seek refuge with Allah, the Immense from the Accursed Shayṭān. Allah is the All-Hearing, All-Knowing. In the Name of Allah, the All-Merciful, Most Merciful." Ibn 'Aṭiyya stated, "Those who recite often change the attribute of the Name of Allah and that of the other, as when one says 'I seek refuge with Allah the <u>Glorious</u> from the <u>rebellious</u> Shayṭān,' and the like. I do not say that this is a good innovation nor that it is not permitted."

Al-Mahdawī said, "The reciters agree about reciting the refuge formula at the beginning of the *Fātiḥa* except for Ḥamza who does it silently. As-Suddī related that the people of Madina used to begin recitation with the *basmala*. As-Samarqandī related from some of the commentators that seeking refuge is an obligation. When the reciter forgets it and then remembers at some point in his recitation, he stops and seeks refuge and then begins from the beginning again. One of them said that he seeks refuge and then returns to where he stopped. The first is the position of the authorities of the Ḥijāz and Iraq and the second is that of the authorities of Syria and Egypt.

Az-Zahrāwī said, "The *āyat* was revealed about the prayer, and it was recommended to seek refuge outside the prayer, but it is not an obligation." Another said, "It was an obligation only for the Prophet, may Allah bless him and grant him peace, and we emulate him."

It is related from Abū Hurayra that the refuge formula should be recited after recitation. Dā'ūd said that. Abū Bakr ibn al-'Arabī said, "Not knowing the correct way led people to say that when the reciter finishes reciting the Qur'ān, he should seek refuge with Allah from the Accursed Shayṭān." Abū Sa'īd al-Khudrī reported that the Prophet, may Allah bless him and grant him peace, used to seek refuge in the prayer before the recitation. This is a confirmed text.

If it is asked, "What is the benefit of seeking refuge from the Accursed Shayṭān at the time of recitation?" the reply is that the benefit lies in obeying the command. The only benefit of prescribed matters lies in obeying them if they are commands or avoiding them if they are prohibitions. It is said that its benefit is to obey the command to seek refuge from the whispering of Shayṭān in recitation as Allah says, *"We did not send any Messenger or any Prophet before you without Shayṭān insinuating something into his recitation while he was reciting."* (22:52).

Ibn al-'Arabī said, "Very strange is what we find of the words of Mālik in the Collection regarding the *tafsīr* of this *āyat*, '*Whenever you recite the Qur'ān, seek refuge with Allah from the cursed Shayṭān*' (16:98) when he says, 'That is after the recitation of the Umm al-Qur'ān for the one who recites in the prayer.' This position has no effect and investigation does not support it. If it is as some people say about the seeking refuge being after the recitation, it specifies that that is after the *Fātiḥa* in the prayer. That is a vast claim and does not resemble the basic principle or understanding of Mālik. Allah best knows the secret of this transmission."

Regarding the excellence of seeking refuge, Muslim related that Sulaymān ibn Ṣurad said, "Two men were quarrelling in the presence of the Prophet, may Allah bless him and grant him peace. One of them became angry and his face turned red and his veins stood out. The Prophet looked at him and said, 'I know a statement which, if you say it, will remove what you feel: "I seek refuge with Allah from the accursed Shayṭān."' A man who had heard the Prophet, may Allah bless him and grant him peace, went to the man and said, 'Do you know what the Messenger of Allah said? He said, "I know a statement which, if you say it, will remove what you feel: I seek refuge with Allah from the accursed Shayṭān."' The man said to him, 'Do you think I am mad?'" (al-Bukhārī)

Muslim reported that 'Uthmān ibn Abī'l-'Āṣ said, "I went to the Prophet, may Allah bless him and grant him peace, and said, 'Messenger of Allah, Shayṭān comes between me and my prayer and recitation and confuses me.' He said, "That is a shayṭān called Khinzab. When you feel that, seek refuge in Allah from him and spit to your left three times.' I did that and Allah removed it from me."

Abū Dāwūd reported that Ibn 'Umar said, "When the Messenger of Allah, may Allah bless him and grant him peace, travelled, and night was coming he said, 'O earth, my Lord and your Lord is Allah. I seek refuge with Allah from your evil and the evil of what He creates in you, from the evil of what crawls on you, from the lion and the black scorpion, from snakes and scorpions and the dwellers of the land, and the parent and what he begets.'"

Khawla bint Ḥakīm reported that she heard the Messenger of Allah, may Allah bless him and grant him peace, say, "If anyone makes camp and then says, 'I seek refuge with the complete words of Allah from the evil of what He created,' he will not be harmed by anything until he sets out again." (*Muwaṭṭā'*, Muslim and at-Tirmidhī)

The refuge formula (*isti'ādha*) in Arabic is seeking protection in something so that it will guard a person against what he dislikes.

The name "Shayṭān" comes from a root which means to be far from good. *Shaṭūn* is a deep well. *Shaṭan* is a rope. It is called that because its ends are from far from one other. The Arabs describe a refractory horse as a shayṭān. Shayṭān himself is called that because he is far from the truth and is rebellious; and the word is used for every rebellious one among the jinn and animals. It is said that "*shayṭān*" is derived from *shāṭa* which is a word used for someone who is destroyed or burned. *Ar-rajīm* (accursed) means to be far from good and humiliated. Its root means "stoning". "Stoning" is a metaphor for killing, cursing, exile and abuse.

It is reported from 'Alī ibn Abī Ṭālib, "I saw the Messenger of Allah, may Allah bless him and grant him peace, at Ṣafā, facing an individual in the form of an elephant whom he was cursing. I asked, 'Who are you cursing, Messenger of Allah?' He replied, 'This is the accursed Shayṭān.' I said, 'Enemy of Allah, by Allah, I will kill you and relieve the Community of you!' He said, 'This is not my repayment from you.' I asked, 'And what is your repayment from me, enemy of Allah?' He said, 'By Allah, no one will hate you at all unless I had a share of him with his father in his mother's womb.'"

The *Basmala*

بِسْمِ ٱللَّهِ ٱلرَّحْمَٰنِ ٱلرَّحِيمِ ١

In the Name of Allah, the All-Merciful, the Most Merciful

Scholars say that "In the Name of Allah, the All-Merciful, Most Merciful" is an oath from our Lord which He revealed at the beginning of every *sūra*. By it, He swears to His slaves, "What I have laid down for you, My slaves, in this *sūra* is true. I will fulfil for you all that I guarantee in this *sūra* of My promise, kindness and gentleness." "In the Name of Allah, the All-Merciful, Most Merciful" is part of what Allah revealed in His Book, and this is special for this Community after Sulaymān. Some scholars say that "In the Name of Allah, the All-Merciful, Most Merciful" contains all the *Sharī'a* because it indicates the Essence and the Attributes.

Sa'īd ibn Abī Sakīna said that he heard that 'Alī ibn Abī Ṭālib looked at a man who had written, "In the Name of Allah, the All-Merciful, Most Merciful," and told him, "Do it well. If a man does it well, he will be forgiven." Sa'īd said, "I heard that a man looked at a parchment on which was written 'In the Name of Allah, the All-Merciful, Most Merciful,' and kissed it and placed it on his eyes and was forgiven on account of that." There is a similar story from Bishr al-Ḥāfī. When he picked up a rag on which was "the Name of Allah" and perfumed it, his own name became honoured. Al-Qushayrī mentioned that.

An-Nasā'ī reports from Abū'l-Malīḥ about a man who rode behind the Messenger of Allah that he mentioned that the Messenger of Allah, may Allah bless him and grant him peace, said, "When your animal stumbles with you, do not say, 'Shayṭān has made it stumble!' because that puffs him up until he becomes like a house and says with strength, 'I have done it.' Rather say, 'In the Name of Allah, the All-Merciful, Most Merciful' and Shayṭān will become small until he is like a fly.'"

'Alī ibn al-Ḥasan said about the words of the Almighty, *"When you mention your Lord alone in the Qur'ān, they turn their backs in flight"* (17:46), "That refers to when you say, 'In the Name of Allah, the All-Merciful, Most Merciful.'" It is reported that 'Abdullāh ibn Mas'ūd said, "Whoever wants Allah to rescue him from the nineteen *Zabāniyya* should recite, 'In the Name of Allah, the All-Merciful, Most Merciful' so that Allah will make each letter a shield for him against one of them. The *basmala* contains nineteen letters according to the number of the angels of the Fire who Allah says are also nineteen. (74:30) They say in all that they do, 'In the Name of Allah, the All-Merciful, Most Merciful.' That is their strength and they take their strength from the name of Allah."

Ibn 'Aṭiyya said, "The like of this is what they say about the Night of Power being the 27th night, taking note of the position of the word "*hiya*" in the words of the *sūra*, *Al-Qadr* (97:1-5). [It is the twenty-seventh word in the *sūra*.] That is like what they say about the number of angels who hastened to report the words of the one who said, 'My Lord, praise is Yours, abundant, excellent and blessed,' [after rising from *rukū'* when the Prophet said, "Allah hears the one who praises Him."] It is about thirty letters. That is why the Prophet, may Allah bless him and grant him peace, said, 'I saw about thirty angels racing to see which would be the first to write it down.'" Ibn 'Aṭiyya said, "This is an elegant *tafsīr*, but not a firm *tafsīr*."

Ash-Sha'bī and al-A'mash report that the Messenger of Allah, may Allah bless him and grant him peace, wrote, "In Your Name, O Allah" until he was commanded to write "In the Name of Allah," and then he wrote that. When it was revealed, *"Say: 'Call on Allah or call on the All-Merciful"* (17:110), he wrote, "In the Name of Allah, the All-Merciful." When there was revealed, *"It is from Sulaymān and says, 'In the Name of Allah, the All-Merciful, Most Merciful'"* (27:30), he wrote that. In Abū Dāwūd, ash-Sha'bī, Abū Mālik, Qatāda and Thābit ibn 'Umāra said that the Prophet did not write "In the Name of Allah, the All-Merciful, Most Merciful" until *Sūrat an-Naml* (27) was revealed.

It is reported that Ja'far aṣ-Ṣādiq said that the *basmala* is the crown of the *sūra*s. This indicates that it is not an *āyat* of the *Fātiḥa* or other *sūra*s. People disagree about this and have three positions regarding it.

- It is not an *āyat* of the *Fātiḥa* or any other *sūra*. This is the position of Mālik.

- It is an *āyat* of every *sūra*, and this is the position of 'Abdullāh ibn al-Mubārak.

- Ash-Shāfi'ī said that it is an *āyat* of the *Fātiḥa* and what he says about the other *sūra*s varies. Sometimes he says that it is an *āyat* of every *sūra* and sometimes that it is only one of the *Fātiḥa*. There is no disagreement that it is an *āyat* of the Qur'ān inside *Sūrat an-Naml*.

Ash-Shāfi'ī's evidence is what ad-Dāraquṭnī related from Abū Hurayra that the Prophet, may Allah bless him and grant him peace, said, "When you read *'Praise belongs to Allah, the Lord of all the worlds,'* then recite *'In the Name of Allah, the All-Merciful, Most Merciful'*. It is the Mother of the Qur'ān, the Mother of the Book, and the Seven *Mathānī*. *'In the Name of Allah, the All-Merciful, Most Merciful'* is one of its *āyat*s."

The evidence of Ibn al-Mubārak and one of the positions of ash-Shāfi'ī is what Muslim reports from Anas: "One day while the Messenger of Allah, may Allah bless him and grant him peace, was among us he nodded off and then he raised his head smiling. We asked, 'What has made you smile, Messenger of Allah?' He replied, 'A *sūra* was just revealed to me. It is: "*In the Name of Allah, the All-Merciful, Most Merciful. Truly We have given you the Great Abundance. So pray to your Lord and sacrifice. It is the one who hates you who is cut off without an heir.*"' (108)"

The sound position is that of Mālik because the Qur'ān is not established by single reports, but by way of definitive multiple transmission about which there is no disagreement. Ibn al-'Arabī said, "It is enough for you that there is no disagreement between people about the Qur'ān. There is no disagreement about the Qur'ān." Sound reports which cannot be attacked indicated that the *basmala* is not an *āyat* of *al-Fātiḥa* or any other *sūra* except for *Sūrat an-Naml*. Muslim reported that Abū Hurayra said, "I heard the Messenger of Allah, may Allah bless him and grant him peace, say, 'Allah says, "I have divided the prayer into two halves between Me and My slave, and My slave will have what he asks for. When My slave says, *"Praise be to Allah, the Lord of all the worlds,"* Allah says, 'My slave has praised Me." He says, *"the All-Merciful, the Most Merciful,"* and the Lord says, "My slave has lauded Me." My slave says, *"the King of the Day of Judgement,"* and Allah says, "My slave has magnified Me (or entrusted to Me)." The slave says, *"You alone we worship. You alone we ask for help,"* and Allah says, "This is between Me and My slave and My slave will have what He asks for." The slave says, *"Guide us on the Straight Path, the Path of those whom You have blessed, not of those with anger on them, nor of the misguided,"* and Allah says, "Those are for My slave and My slave will have what He asks for.""'"

Allah said, "I have divided the prayer", meaning the *Fātiḥa*, and he called it "prayer" because the prayer is not valid except with it. So He designated the first three *āyat*s for Himself, singling them out for Himself, and the Muslims do not disagree about that. Then he made the fourth between Him and His slave because it contains the abasement of the slave and seeking help from Him. That contains esteem for Allah. Then three *āyat*s conclude the seven. They are three, because He uses the plural, not the dual in "Those are for My slave," So *"those You have blessed"* is an *āyat*. Ibn Bukayr reported that Mālik said that *"those You have blessed"* is an *āyat*.

This is confirmed by the division and by what the Prophet said to Ubayy when he asked the Prophet, "How do you recite when you begin the prayer?" He replied, "I recited, *'Praise be to Allah, the Lord of all the worlds'* to the end." The *basmala* was not part of it. That was the position of the people of Madina, the people of Syria and the people of Basra. Most reciters counted *"those You have blessed"* as an *āyat*. This is also related from Abū Naḍra from Abū Hurayra who said that the sixth *āyat* is *"those You have blessed"*. The people of Kufa count the *basmala* as part of it and do not count *"those You have blessed"*.

If it is said that it is confirmed in the copies of the Qur'ān that the *basmala* is written and transmitted as it is transmitted in *an-Naml* and that this is multiple transmission, we reply that that is sound, but is it because it is Qur'ān, or is it a divider between *sūra*s as is related from the Companions, "We did not know the end of the *sūra* until *'In the Name of Allah, the All-Merciful, Most Merciful'* was revealed." (Abū Dāwūd) Or it may be for the blessing, in the same way that the Community agrees to write it at the beginning of books and letters. All of that is possible. Al-Jurayrī said, "Al-Ḥasan was asked about 'In the Name of Allah, the All-Merciful, Most Merciful' and said 'At the beginning of letters.'" He also said, "'In the Name of Allah, the All-Merciful, Most Merciful' was not revealed in any of the Qur'ān except *an-Naml*." The criterion is that the Qur'ān is not established by logic and deduction. It is established by definitive multiple transmission. So the statement of ash-Shāfi'ī about the *basmala* being at the beginning of each *sūra* is unsound because the *basmala* is not an *āyat* of each *sūra*. Praise belongs to Allah.

It is reported that a group related that the *basmala*s are part of the Qur'ān. Ad-Dāraquṭnī dealt with all of that. We do not deny the transmission of that and we have indicated it, but we have firm reports which counter it which are related by reliable imāms and *fuqahā'*. In *Ṣaḥīḥ Muslim*, 'Ā'isha is reported as saying, "The Messenger of Allah, may Allah bless him and grant him peace, used to begin the prayer with the *takbīr* and the recitation of 'Praise be to Allah, the Lord of all the worlds.'" Muslim also reported that Anas ibn Mālik said, "I prayed behind the Prophet, Abū Bakr and 'Umar, and they began with 'Praise be to Allah.' They did not mention 'In the Name of Allah, the All-Merciful, Most Merciful', either at the beginning or the end of recitation."

So our school prefers that, and it is logical. That is because the Mosque of the Prophet in Madina passed through many years from the time of the Messenger of Allah, until the time of Mālik and during all that time no one recited, "In the Name of Allah, the All-Merciful, Most Merciful," following the *Sunna*. This refutes the *aḥādīth* you cite. Our people, however, prefer to recite it in the voluntary prayers, and there are traditions (*āthār*) about reciting it or an allowance for doing that. Mālik said, "There is no harm in reciting it in the *nāfila* or simply reading the Qur'ān."

A group of the school of Mālik and his people said that it is not part of the *Fātiha* or any other *sūra*, and it is not read by the one who prays the obligatory or any other prayer, either silently or aloud. It is permitted to recite it in *nāfila* prayers. This is well-known in his school and with his people. There is another transmission that it is recited at the beginning of the *sūra* in *nāfila* prayers but not at the beginning of the *Fātiḥa*. It is related that Ibn Nāfi' began his recitation with it in the obligatory and *nāfila* prayers and did not ever omit it. Some of the people of Madina say that there must be "In the Name of Allah, the All-Merciful, Most Merciful," among them Ibn 'Umar and Ibn Shihāb. Ash-Shāfi'ī, Aḥmad, Isḥāq, Abū Thawr and Abū 'Ubayd said that. That indicates that it is a matter of *ijtihād* and not definitive, as some ignorant individuals claim.

A group of scholars believe that it is recited silently with the *Fātiḥa*. They include Abū Ḥanīfa and ath-Thawrī. That is related from 'Umar, 'Alī, Ibn Mas'ūd, 'Ammār and Ibn az-Zubayr. It is also the view of al-Ḥakam and Ḥammād, and it is stated by Aḥmad ibn Ḥanbal and Abū 'Ubayd. Something similar to that is related from al-Awzā'ī. The evidence is the report from Anas ibn Mālik: "The Messenger of Allah, may Allah bless him and grant him peace, led us in the prayer and we did not hear him recite, 'In the Name of Allah, the All-Merciful, Most Merciful.'"

This is a good position, and the traditions (*āthār*) reported from Anas agree on it and remove the disagreement about the recitation of the *basmala*. It is related that Sa'īd ibn Jubayr said, "The idolaters used to come to the mosque. When the Messenger of Allah, may Allah bless him and grant him peace, recited, *'In the Name of Allah, the All-Merciful, Most Merciful,'* they said, 'This Muḥammad mentioned the Raḥmān of Yamāma,' meaning Musaylima. So he was commanded to recite it silently and it was revealed, *'Do not be too loud in your prayer or too quiet in it.'* (17:110)" At-Tirmidhī al-Ḥakīm said, "That has lasted until now, even if the cause no longer exists, as running remains in *ṭawāf* even if the cause no longer exists and silence in the day prayers even if the cause no longer exists."

The Community agree that it is permitted to write it at the beginning of every book of knowledge and letter. There is disagreement about books of poetry and whether or not it should be written in them.

The Sharī'a recommends mentioning the *basmala* at the beginning of every action, like eating, drinking, slaughtering, sex, purification, embarking on a ship and the like. Allah says, *"Eat that over which the name of Allah has been mentioned"* (6:118) and *"He said, 'Embark in it. In the name of Allah be its voyage and its landing!'"* (11:41) The Prophet, may Allah bless him and grant him peace, said, "Lock your door and mention the Name of Allah. Put out your lamp and mention the Name of Allah. Cover your vessel and mention the Name of Allah. Tie up your waterskin and mention the Name of Allah." He said, "If anyone of you wants to go to his wife, he should say, 'In the Name of Allah. O Allah, keep Shayṭān away from us and keep Shayṭān away from what You provide us with.' If a child is decreed for them, Shayṭān will not harm him at all." He told 'Umar ibn Abī Salama, "Boy, say the name of Allah Almighty and eat with your right hand and eat what is in front of you."

When 'Uthmān ibn Abī'l-'Āṣ complained to him of a pain he had in his body since he had become Muslim, the Messenger of Allah said to him, "Place your hand on that part of your body which pains you and say 'In the Name of Allah' three times and then say seven times, 'I seek refuge in the might and power of Allah from the evil of what I feel and am on my guard against.'" Ibn Mājah and at-Tirmidhī report that the Prophet said, "The veil between the jinn and the private parts of the sons of Ādam when he enters the privy is to say, 'In the Name of Allah.'" Ad-Dāraquṭnī reported that 'Ā'isha said, "When the Prophet touched his *wuḍū'* vessel, he said the Name of Allah and then poured the water on his hands."

Our scholars say that this refutes the Qadarites and others who say that our actions are decreed for us. The argument against them in that is that Allah commanded us to begin every action with the *basmala*.

The meaning of "In the Name of Allah" is "by Allah", and the meaning of "by Allah" is by His creation and determination to reach what is reached. Some say that "In the Name of Allah" means "I begin with the help, success and blessing of Allah." This is Allah teaching His slaves to mention His Name at the beginning of actions.

There is disagreement about the derivation of *ism* (Name), with two basic positions. The Basrans say that it is derived from *sumū*, which means height and elevation. It is said that *ism* means that the person is in an elevated place. It is said that the name lifts the named from others. It is said that the name is called that because it is higher than the other parts of speech by its strength. The noun (*ism*) is stronger by agreement because it is the root. These are three statements.

The Kufans say that it is derived from *sima*, which means a sign, because the Name is a sign of the One to whom it is given. So the root of *ism* is *wasam*. The first is sounder because of the form of the diminutive and the form of plural which is *asmā'*. Another disagreement indicates the soundness of that, and it is the next point.

If it is true that *ism* is derived from height, Allah was described by it before creation existed, after it existed and will be when it is annihilated, and creatures have no effect on the Names or Attributes. This is the position of the people of the *Sunna*. Those who say that it is derived from *sima*, say that before time Allah was without name or attribute. When He created creatures, they gave Him Names and Attributes. When He annihilates them, He will again have no name or attribute. This is the position of the Mu'tazilites, and it is contrary to that on which the Community agree. It is worse than their error when they say, "His Word is created." Exalted above that is Allah! It is according to this that there is a disagreement about the Name and Named.

The people of truth believe, as Qāḍī Abū Bakr ibn aṭ-Ṭayyib al-Bāqillānī mentioned, that the name is the thing named and Ibn Fūrak is content with that. It is the position of Abū 'Abīda and Sibuwayh. If someone says, "Allah is Knowing" his words indicate the Essence which is described as being knowing. So the Name is Knowing and it is what is Named. It is the same when someone says, "Allah is the Creator." The Creator is the Lord and it is the Name itself. So their view is that the Name is the Named itself with no distinction.

Ibn Ḥaṣṣār said, "Those among the innovators who deny the attributes claim that namings have no meaning except the Essence. That is why they say that the Name is not the Named. Whoever affirms the Attributes, affirms that the Names have meanings which are the qualities of the Essence. They are not expressions, but they are Names in their view. More of this will come in *al-Baqara* and *al-A'rāf.*

Allah is the greatest and most comprehensive of all the Names, so that one scholar said that it is the Greatest Name of Allah and no one else has it. That is why it has no dual nor plural. That is one of two interpretations of the words of the Almighty, *"Do you know of any other with His Name?" (*19:65), in other words anyone named with His Name which is Allah. Allah is the Name of the True Existent who has all the Divine Attributes and is described as Lord and alone possesses real existence. There is no god but Him. Glory be to Him! It is said that it means the One who should be worshipped. It is said that it means the One whose existence is necessary who always was and always will be. The meaning is the same.

There is disagreement about whether this Name is derived or is a unique designation for the Divine Essence. Many of the people of knowledge believe the first but then disagree on its actual derivation and root. Sibuwayh reported from al-Khalīl that its root is *ilāh*, on the measure of *fi'āl*. The *alif* and *lām* replace the *hamza*. Sibuwayh said that it is like *an-nās* (people) whose root is *anās*. It is said that its root is *lāh* and the *alif* and *lām* are added to exalt it. This is what Sibuwayh preferred. Al-Kisā'ī and al-Farrā' said that *"bismillāh"* is made up of *bismi - al-ilāh* and elision has occurred and the first *lām* assimilated into the second and so becomes a double *lām*.

It is said that the name Allah is derived from *walaha*, to be bewildered. *Walah* means loss of intellect, and someone who is *wālih* is bewildered. Allah bewilders minds when they think on the realities of His attributes and reflect on gnosis of Him. So the basis of *ilāh* is *walāh* and the *hamza* is changed from the *wāw*. That is also reported from al-Khalīl. It is related that aḍ-Ḍaḥḥāk said, "He is called Allah because creatures devote (*ta'allaha*) themselves to Him in their needs and make supplication to Him in times of hardship. It is related that al-Khalīl ibn Aḥmad said something similar. It is also said that it is derived from elevation and that the Arabs used to use "*lāha*" for something elevated and they used the verb for sunrise.

It is said that the name Allah is derived from the word *ilāh* (god), which means an object of worship so that the meaning of "Allah" is the Object of Worship. So what the unifiers say, "There is no god but Allah" means "there is no object of worship other than Allah." Here "*illā*" means "other", not "except." Some claim that the root is *al-hā'* which alludes to the third person. That is since they affirm Him as existing in their natural intellects and indicate Him with the letter of allusion. Then the *lām* of possession is added to it since they know that He is the Creator and Master of things, and *laha* then is added for magnification.

The second position is taken by a group of scholars, including ash-Shāfi'ī, Abu'l-Ma'ālī, al-Khaṭṭābī, al-Ghazālī, al-Mufaḍḍal and others, and is related from al-Khalīl and Sibuwayh. It is that the *alif* and *lām* are a necessary part of it and cannot be elided from it. Al-Khaṭṭābī said that the evidence that the *alif* and *lām* are an intrinsic part of the structure of this name and not added for definition is that it is included in the vocative, as "*Yā Allāh!*" The vocative is not combined with the definite article *alif-lām*. One does not say, *"Yā ar-Raḥmān."* Allah knows best.

There is also disagreement about the derivation of *ar-Raḥmān*. Some of them said that it has no derivation because it is one of the names particular to Him and if it had been derived from mercy (*raḥma*), it would be connected to the one shown mercy and it would be possible to say, "Allah is *Raḥmān* to His slaves" as one does with *raḥīm*. If it had been derived from *raḥma*, the Arabs would not have denied it when they heard it because they did not deny the mercy of their Lord. Allah says, *"When they are told to prostrate to the All-Merciful, they say, 'And what is the All-Merciful?'"* (25:60)

At al-Ḥudaybiyya, when 'Alī wrote at the command of the Prophet "In the Name of Allah, the All-Merciful, Most Merciful," Suhayl ibn 'Amr said, "As for 'In the Name of Allah, the All-Merciful, Most Merciful,' we do not know 'In the Name of Allah, the All-Merciful, Most Merciful'! Rather write 'In Your Name, O Allah.'" Ibn al-'Arabī says that this indicates that they did not know the attribute rather than the One Described. Evidence is found in the fact that they said, "What is the Raḥmān?" not "Who is the Raḥmān?" Ibn al-Ḥaṣṣār said, "It is as if he [the one who said this] had not recited the other *āyat*, *'Yet they still reject the All-Merciful.'* (13:30)" One group believe that it is derived from *raḥma*, and is intensive, meaning the One who possesses mercy such as no one else has. It has no plural or dual whereas *raḥīm* can be dual or plural.

Ibn al-Ḥaṣṣār said that part of what indicates the derivation is what at-Tirmidhī transmitted as sound from 'Abdu'r-Raḥmān ibn 'Awf. He heard the Messenger of Allah say, "Allah Almighty says, 'I am the All-Merciful. I created kinship (*raḥīm*) and split it as a name from My Name. Whoever maintains ties, I maintain ties with him. Whoever severs it, I sever him.'" This is a text for its derivation and so there is no point in contention about it. The denial of the Arabs was simply due to their ignorance of Allah and what is mandatory for Him.

Al-Anbārī mentions that al-Mubarrad stated that *ar-Raḥmān* is a Hebrew name. Aḥmād ibn Yaḥyā also said that. This view is unwarranted. Abū'l-'Abbās says that the attribute is for praise. Quṭrub says that it is possible to combine the two for stress.

There is disagreement about whether the two names *Raḥmān* and *Raḥīm* have one meaning or two meanings. It is said, that they mean the same, as do *nadmān* and *nadīm*. It is said that *Raḥmān* is a special name with general action and *Raḥīm* is a general name with a particular action. This is the position of the majority.

Abū 'Alī al-Fārisī said that *Raḥmān* is a general name for all types of mercy for which Allah is singled out. *Raḥīm* can be used for how He is towards the believers, as He says, *"He is merciful to the believers."* (33:43). Al-'Arazamī says that *Raḥmān* is merciful to all His creatures with rain, physical and general blessings, and *Raḥīm* is merciful to the believers in guiding them and being kind to them. Ibn al-Mubārak said that when the *Raḥmān* is asked He gives and when the *Raḥīm* is not asked, He is angry. Ibn 'Abbās said that they are two fine (*raqīq*) names, and one is finer than the other, meaning that it has more mercy.

Al-Khaṭṭābī said, "This is problematic because fineness has no place in any of the attributes of Allah." Al-Ḥusayn ibn al-Faḍl al-Bajalī said, "This is an error on the part of the transmitter because fineness (*riqqa*) is not part of the attributes of Allah at all. Rather, they are two compassionate (*rafīq*) names, one more compassionate than the other. Compassion is one of the Attributes of Allah Almighty. The Prophet, may Allah bless him and grant him peace, said, 'Allah is Compassionate. He loves compassion and gives for compassion what he does not for harshness.'"

Most scholars agree that the name *ar-Raḥmān* is used only for Allah Almighty and it is not permitted to call anyone else by it. Do you not see that He says, *"Say: 'Call on Allah or call on the All-Merciful'"* (17:110)? So it is equal to the Name in which none but Him share. He says, *"Ask those We sent before you as Our Messengers: Have We ever designated any gods to be worshipped besides the All-Merciful?"* (43:445) So they reported that the *Raḥmān* deserved worship. Musaylima the Liar[1] – may Allah curse him – was outrageous and called himself "the *Raḥmān* of Yamāma" and so was called "the Liar".

Ar-Raḥīm is general and can be used in respect of creatures. As *ar-Raḥmān* is universal as we said, *ar-Raḥīm* provides harmony and balance in the revelation. Al-Mahdawī stated that. It is said that the meaning of *ar-Raḥīm* is: "It is by the *Raḥīm* that you reach to the *Raḥmān*." So *ar-Raḥīm* is the attribute of Muḥammad, may Allah bless him and grant him peace, and Allah described him with that. He says, "compassionate, merciful" when describing

1. Musaylima the Liar: a false Prophet of the Banū Ḥanīfa in Yamāna who was one of the leaders of the Ridda.

him. So it is as if the meaning of saying, "In the Name of Allah, the All-Merciful, the Most Merciful" is "It is by Muḥammad, may Allah bless him and grant him peace, that you will reach Me," in other words by following him and what he has brought, you will reach My reward, honour and the vision of My face." Allah knows best.

It is related that 'Alī ibn Abī Ṭālib said, "*Bismillāh* is healing from every illness and protection against every disease. *Ar-Raḥmān* is a help for everyone who believes in Him. It is a name not used for anyone else. *Ar-Raḥīm* is for those who repent, believe and perform righteous actions."

Some of them explained the meaning according to the letters. It is related that 'Uthmān ibn 'Affān asked the Messenger of Allah, may Allah bless him and grant him peace, about the interpretation of "In the Name of Allah, the All-Merciful, Most Merciful." He said, "The *bā'* is the trial (*balā'*) of Allah, His relief, brilliance and radiance (*bahā'*). The *sīn* is the splendour (*sanā'*) of Allah. The *mīm* is the kingdom (*mulk*) of Allah. As for Allah, there is no god but Him. The *Raḥmān* is kind to both the pious and impious of His creatures. The *Raḥīm* is kind only to the believers." It is reported that Ka'b al-Aḥbar said, "The *bā'* is His radiance (*bahā'*), the *sīn* is His splendour (*sanā'*), and there is nothing higher than it. The *mīm* is His kingdom, and He has power over all things and nothing is hard for Him."

It is said that every letter is the opening of one of His Names. The *bā'* is the key to His Name *Baṣīr* (All-Seeing). The *sīn* is the key to His Name, *Samī'* (All-Hearing). The *mīm* is the key to His Name, *Malīk* (Master). The *alif* is the key to His Name, Allah. The *lām* is the key to His Name, *Laṭīf* (Kind). The *hā'* is the key to His Name, *Hādī* (Guide). The *rā'* is the key to His Name, *Rāziq* (Provider). The *ḥā'* is the key to His Name, *Ḥalīm* (Forbearing). The *nūn* is the key to His Name, *Nūr* (Light). The meaning of all this is supplication of Allah at the beginning of everything.

There is disagreement how *'ar-Raḥīm'* is connected in recitation to *'al-ḥamdu lillāh'*. Umm Salama related that the Prophet recited *'ar-Raḥīm'* with a *sukūn* on the *mīm*, stopping there and then beginning with a fresh *alif*. Some of the Kufans recited it in that way. Most people recite, *'ar-Raḥīmi'l-ḥamdu'*, with a *kasra* on the *mīm* and connecting it to the *alif* in *al-ḥamd*. Al-Kisā'ī reported that some Arabs read it *'ar-Raḥīma'l-ḥamdu'*, with *fatḥa* on the *mīm* and connected to the *alif*, as if the *mīm* was in fact silent, but with an elision into the *alif*. Ibn 'Aṭiyya said, "This recitation is not reported from anyone I know."

1
Sūrat al-Fātiḥa

بِسۡمِ ٱللَّهِ ٱلرَّحۡمَٰنِ ٱلرَّحِيمِ ١
ٱلۡحَمۡدُ لِلَّهِ رَبِّ ٱلۡعَٰلَمِينَ ٢ ٱلرَّحۡمَٰنِ
ٱلرَّحِيمِ ٣ مَٰلِكِ يَوۡمِ ٱلدِّينِ ٤
إِيَّاكَ نَعۡبُدُ وَإِيَّاكَ نَسۡتَعِينُ ٥
ٱهۡدِنَا ٱلصِّرَٰطَ ٱلۡمُسۡتَقِيمَ ٦
صِرَٰطَ ٱلَّذِينَ أَنۡعَمۡتَ عَلَيۡهِمۡ غَيۡرِ
ٱلۡمَغۡضُوبِ عَلَيۡهِمۡ وَلَا ٱلضَّآلِّينَ ٧

In the Name of Allah, the All-Merciful, Most Merciful

Praise be to Allah, the Lord of all the worlds,
the All-Merciful, the Most Merciful,
the King of the Day of Repayment.

You alone we worship.
You alone we ask for help.

Guide us on the Straight Path,
the Path of those whom You have blessed,
not of those with anger on them,
nor of the misguided.

Its Virtues

At-Tirmidhī related from Ubayy ibn Ka'b that the Messenger of Allah, may Allah bless him and grant him peace, said, "Allah has not revealed anything like the Mother of the Qur'ān (the *Fātiḥa*) in either the Torah or the Gospel. It is the Seven *Mathānī*, and it is divided between Me and My slave. My slave will have what He asks for." Mālik also transmitted this as a *mursal ḥadīth* from Abū Hurayra.

Al-Bukhārī transmitted from Abū Sa'īd ibn al-Mu'allā, "I was praying in the mosque when the Messenger of Allah, may Allah bless him and grant him peace, called me and I did not answer. I said, 'Messenger of Allah, I was praying.' He said, 'Did not Allah say, *"Respond to Allah and to the Messenger when He calls you"* (8:24)?' Then he said, 'Shall I teach you the greatest *sūra* of the Qur'ān before you leave the mosque?' He took my hand. When we were about to leave, I said, 'Messenger of Allah, you said, "I will teach you the greatest *sūra* of the Qur'ān?"' He said, '"Praise be to Allah, Lord of the worlds" (the beginning of the *Fātiḥa*) are the seven *Mathānī* and the "Immense Qur'ān" which I was given.'"

Ibn al-Anbārī said in *Kitāb ar-Radd*, "My father related to me from Abū 'Ubaydullāh al-Warrāq from Abū Dāwūd from Shaybān from Manṣūr that Mujāhid said, 'Iblīs, may Allah curse him, lamented four times: when he was cursed, when he fell from the Garden, when Muḥammad, may Allah bless him and grant him peace, was sent, and when the *Fātiḥa* of the Book was revealed, and it was revealed in Madina.'"

Scholars disagree about the relative excellence of some *sūra*s and *āyat*s over others, and some of the Beautiful Names of Allah over others. Some people say that none of them are better than any other because all are the Word of Allah, and the same lack of preference applies to His Names. Shaykh Abū'l-Ḥasan al-Ash'arī, Qāḍī Abū Bakr ibn aṭ-Ṭayyib, Abū Ḥātim Muḥammad ibn Ḥibbān as-Sibtī and a group of *fuqahā'* believed this, and something to that effect is related from Mālik. Yaḥyā ibn Yaḥyā said that it is an error to consider one part of the Qur'ān better than other parts.

Similarly Mālik disliked the repetition of one particular *sūra* rather than others. In reference to the words of Allah Almighty, *"We bring one better than it or equal to it,"* (2:106) Mālik says that this means "one containing judgement rather than one subject to abrogation." Ibn Kināna related the same as that from Mālik.

Some of them use the following argument: "The best is only recognised by comparison with what might be considered slightly less excellent but the essential nature of all *āyat*s is one and the same. They are all part of the Word of Allah and there can be no deficiency in the Word of Allah." As-Sibtī stated: "The meaning of the words 'Allah has not revealed anything like the *Umm al-Qur'ān* in either the Torah or the Gospel' is that Allah Almighty does not give those who recite the Torah or Gospel a reward like that which He gives to the one who recites the *Umm al-Qur'ān* since Allah favoured this community over other communities and He gave a greater excellence to the recitation of His Words in His final Revelation than He gave to others for reciting His Words in previous Revelations. It is a favour from Him to this community. The *Fātiḥa* is the greatest *sūra* in respect of its reward. The Prophet's words do not mean that some parts of the Qur'ān are better than other parts."

Some people have said that there is a certain kind of superiority which may be seen in such *āyat*s as the words of the Almighty: *"Your God is One God. There is no god but Him, the All-Merciful, the Most Merciful,"* (2:163), the Throne Verse, the end of *Sūrat al-Ḥashr*, and *Sūrat al-Ikhlāṣ,* which are among the proofs of His Oneness and His attributes, and that does not exist, for instance, in such *āyat*s as *"Perish the hands of Abū Laḥab"* (111:1) and those like it. Superiority occurs through the wondrous meanings and how numerous they are, not in respect of the quality of the language. This is the truth. Those who said that there was preference included Isḥāq ibn Rāḥawayh as well as other scholars and *mutakallimūn*. It is the position preferred by Qāḍī Abū Bakr ibn al-'Arabī and Ibn al-Ḥaṣṣār who go by the *ḥadīth* of Abū Sa'īd ibn al-Mu'allā and the *ḥadīth* of Ubayy ibn Ka'b in which he said, "The Messenger of Allah, may Allah bless him and grant him peace, said to me, 'Ubayy, which of the *āyat*s in the Book of Allah is the greatest?' I said, *'Allah, there is no god but He, the Living, the Self-Sustaining.'* (2:255, i.e. the *Āyat al-Kursī*) He struck my chest and said, 'May knowledge give you joy, Abū'l-Mundhir!'" (al-Bukhārī and Muslim) Ibn al-Ḥaṣṣār said, "I am surprised at those who differ when such texts exist."

The *Fātiḥa* possesses attributes which other *sūra*s do not possess to the extent that it is said that the entire Qur'ān is contained in it. It consists of twenty-five words which embrace all the sciences of the Qur'ān. Part of its honour is that Allah has divided it between Himself and His slaves, and the prayer is only valid with it and no action is necessary to gain a reward for it. It is in this sense that it is the Mother of the Qur'ān. *Sūrat al-Ikhlāṣ* is considered to be equivalent to one third of the Qur'ān because the Qur'ān contains *tawḥīd*, judgements and admonition, and *Sūrat al-Ikhlāṣ* contains all of *tawḥīd*. It also explains the words of the Prophet to Ubayy, "Ubayy, which of the *āyat*s in the Book of Allah is the greatest?" to which he replied, *"Allah, there is no god but He, the Living, the Self-Sustaining."* (*Āyat al-Kursī,* 2:255) It is the greatest *āyat* because it contains every aspect of *tawḥīd*. In the same way the Prophet's words, "The best of what I and the Prophets before have said is: 'There is no god but Allah alone with no partner'" indicate that that is the best form of *dhikr* because they are words which contain all the knowledges of *tawḥīd*. The *Fātiḥa,* on the other hand, contains *tawḥīd*, worship and admonition so that all the aspects of the Qur'ān are summed up in it.

'Alī ibn Abī Ṭālib, may Allah be pleased with him, related that the Messenger of Allah, may Allah bless him and grant him peace, said, "The *Fātiḥa* of the Book, the *Āyat al-Kursī*, *'Allah bears witness that there is no god but Him'* (3:18) and *'Say: "O Allah, Master of the Kingdom"'* (3:26): these *āyat*s are suspended from the Throne. There is no veil between them and Allah." (Abū 'Umar ad-Dānī)

Its Names

The *Fātiḥa* has many names. Some of them are:

- ***aṣ-Ṣalāt* (The Prayer)**, since Allah Almighty said in a *ḥadīth qudsī*, "I have divided the prayer between Myself and My slaves."
- ***Sūrat al-Ḥamd* (*Sūra* of Praise)**, because praise is mentioned in it. This is similar to the way other *sūra*s are named, such as "The *Sūra* of the Battlements", or "Booty", "Repentance" and the like.
- **The *Fātiḥa* (Opener) of the Book**. This name is undisputed among the scholars. It is called that because it opens the recitation of the Qur'ān and the writing of every copy of the Qur'ān opens with it, and the prayer also opens with it.
- ***Umm al-Kitāb*** (The Mother of the Book). There is some disagreement concerning this name. Some allow it while Anas, al-Ḥasan and Ibn Sīrīn disliked it. Al-Ḥasan said, "The *Umm al-Kitāb* is the *ḥalāl* and the *ḥarām*. Allah Almighty says, *'Āyats containing clear judgements – they are the* Umm al-Kitāb *– and others which are open to interpretation.'* (3:7)" Anas and Ibn Sīrīn said that the *Umm al-Kitāb* is the name of the Preserved Tablet. Allah Almighty says, *"It is in the* Umm al-Kitāb *with Us."* (43:4)
- ***Umm al-Qur'ān*** (The Mother of the Qur'ān). There is also disagreement about this. The majority allow it while Anas and Ibn Sīrīn dislike it. Firm *aḥādīth* refute these two opinions. At-Tirmidhī transmitted from Abū Hurayra that the Messenger of Allah, may Allah bless him and grant him peace, said, "*'Praise belongs to Allah'* is the Mother of the Qur'ān, the Mother of the Book and the Seven *Mathānī*." He said that this *ḥadīth* is *ḥasan ṣaḥīḥ*. In Al-Bukhārī we find: "It is called Mother of the Book (because it begins the writing of copies of the Qur'ān and begins its recitation in the prayer." Yaḥyā ibn

Ya'mar said, "The Mother of Towns is Makka, the Mother of Khorasan is Merv, and the Mother of the Qur'ān is the *Fātiḥa*." It is said that it was called The Mother of the Qur'ān because it is the beginning of it and contains all its sciences. It is for that reason that Makka is called the Mother of the Towns because it was the first town on earth, and civilisation spread out from it.

• **Al-Mathānī** (The Repeated, the Exceptional). It is called that because it is repeated in every *rak'at* of the prayer. It is said that it is called that because it is exclusively for this Community and it was not revealed to anyone before because it was a treasure stored up for this Community.

• **The Immense Qur'ān**. It is called that because it contains all the sciences of the Qur'ān. That is because it contains praise of Allah Almighty with the qualities of His Perfection and Majesty, the command to perform acts of worship and to be sincere in them, acknowledgement of the inability to do any of it except with His help, entreaty to Him for guidance to the Straight Path, and being spared the states of those who violate the contract, and clarification of the final fate of the deniers.

• **Healing**. Ad-Dārimī related from Abū Sa'īd al-Khudrī that the Messenger of Allah, may Allah bless him and grant him peace, said, "The *Fātiḥa* of the Book is healing from every poison."

• ***Ar-Ruqya*** (the Charm). This name is taken from a *ḥadīth* of Abū Sa'īd al-Khudrī in which the Messenger of Allah, may Allah bless him and grant him peace, said to a man who recited it as a charm for someone with a snake-bite, "What taught you that it was a charm?" He replied, "Messenger of Allah, something that came into my heart."

• ***Al-Asas*** (The Core). A man complained to ash-Sha'bī of abdominal pain and he said, "You must have the Core of the Qur'ān, the *Fātiḥa* of the Book. I heard Ibn 'Abbās say, 'Everything has a core. The core of this world is Makka because civilisation spread out from it. The core of the heavens is 'Arīb, which is the seventh heaven. The core of the earth is 'Ajīb, and it is the lowest earth. The core of the Gardens is the Garden of 'Adn, and it is the navel of the gardens and on it the Garden is founded. The core of the Fire is Jahannam, which is the lowest level on which the other levels are based. The core of creatures is Ādam, and the core of the Prophets is Nūḥ. The core of the tribe of Israel is Ya'qūb. The core of the Qur'ān is the *Fātiḥa* and the core of the *Fātiḥa* is "In the Name of Allah, the All-Merciful, Most Merciful."' When you are ill, you should recite the *Fātiḥa* and you will be healed."

- ***Al-Wāfiya*** (the Complete). Sufyān ibn 'Uyayna said that it is because it may not be halved or broken up. In the case of other *sūra*s, if one reads half in a *rak'at* and half in the other *rak'at*, that is allowed. If the *Fātiḥa* is divided between two *rak'at*s, that does not satisfy the legal requirements.

- ***Al-Kāfiya*** (the Sufficient). Yaḥyā ibn Abī Kathīr said that it is because it suffices for others while others do not suffice for it. This is indicated by what Muḥammad ibn Khallād al-Iskandāranī mentioned that the Prophet, may Allah bless him and grant him peace, said: "The *Umm al-Qur'ān* is a substitute for other than it, and other than it is not a substitute for it."

Al-Muhallab said, "The charm is in the words *'You alone we worship and You alone we ask for help'*." It is also said that the entire *sūra* is a charm, based on the words of the Prophet, peace be upon him, to the man: "What taught you that it was a charm?" and he did not say, "that there is a charm in it." This indicates the entire *sūra* is a charm because it is the *Fātiḥa* of the Book and its beginning and contains all of its sciences, as has been already stated. Allah knows best.

The fact that it bears the names *al-Mathānī* and *Umm al-Kitāb* does not prevent other things from having those names as well. Allah Almighty says, *"A Book consistent in its frequent repetitions* (mathānī)*"* (39:23) and so He called His whole Book *'Mathānī'* because things are repeated in it. The seven long *sūra*s are also called *Mathānī* because of the obligations and stories repeated in them. Ibn 'Abbās said, "The Messenger of Allah, may Allah bless him and grant him peace, was given the Seven *Mathānī*." He said they are the seven long suras. An-Nasā'ī mentioned that and said they extend from *al-Baqara* to *al-A'rāf*, but they disagree about the seventh. Some people say it is *Yūnus*, and some *al-Anfāl* and some *at-Tawba*. The last is the position of Mujāhid and Sa'īd ibn Jubayr.

Its Revelation

The Community agree that the *Fātiḥa* of the Book has seven *āyat*s except for a report from Ḥusayn al-Ju'fī that it only has six, which is unusual. There is also a report from 'Amr ibn 'Ubayd that "*You alone We worship*" is an *āyat*, and so it is eight *āyat*s, but this is an exception (*shādhdh*). Allah's words, *"We have given you the Seven Oft-repeated"* (15:87), and the *ḥadīth qudsī*, "I have divided the prayer..." refute these two statements.

The Community also agree that it is part of the Qur'ān. There are those who counter this by saying that if it were part of the Qur'ān, then 'Abdullāh ibn Mas'ūd would have written it in his copy of the Qur'ān, and the fact that he did not write it indicates that it is not part of the Qur'ān, nor indeed are the two *sūra*s of refuge in his view. The answer to that was given by Abū Bakr al-Anbārī. He reported that al-A'mash said, "'Abdullāh ibn Mas'ūd was asked, 'Why have you not written the *Fātiḥa* of the Book in your copy of the Qur'ān?' He said, 'If I had written it, I would have written it with every *sūra*.'" Abū Bakr said, "He was referring to the way that every *rak'at* is begun with the *Umm al-Qur'ān* before the *sūra* recited after it." He said, "I made things shorter by omitting it. It is safely preserved because all the Muslims memorise it and so I did not write it anywhere to avoid having to write it with every *sūra* since it precedes all of them in the prayer."

There is disagreement about whether it is Makkan or Madinan. Ibn 'Abbās, Qatāda, Abū'l-'Āliyya ar-Riyāḥī Rufay' and others said that it is Makkan. Abū Hurayra, Mujāhid, 'Aṭā' ibn Yasār, az-Zuhrī and others said that it is Madinan. It is said that half of it was revealed in Makka and half in Madina, as is related by Abū'l-Layth Naṣr ibn Muḥammad ibn Ibrāhīm as-Samarqandī in his *tafsīr*. The first position is considered sounder because of the words of the Almighty, *"We have given you the Seven Oft-repeated and the Magnificent Qur'ān,"* from the end of *Sūrat al-Ḥijr* and it is agreed that *al-Ḥijr* is a Makkan *sūra* and there is no disagreement that the prayer was made obligatory in Makka. It has not been recorded anywhere that the prayer in Islam was ever performed without reciting *"Praise be to Allah, the Lord of the worlds."* This is backed up by the words of the Prophet, "There is no prayer without the *Fātiḥa* of the Book."

Qāḍī ibn aṭ-Ṭayyib mentioned people's disagreement about the first part of the Qur'ān to be revealed. It is said that it was *al-Muddaththir* (74) or *al-'Alaq (96)* or the *Fātiḥa*. Al-Bayhaqī mentioned in the *Proofs of Prophethood* from Abū Maysara 'Amr ibn Sharaḥbīl that the Messenger of Allah, may Allah bless him and grant him peace, said to his wife Khadīja, "When I was alone, I heard a voice calling and, by Allah, I fear that this is an affliction." She said, "We seek refuge with Allah! Allah would not do that to you. By Allah, you return people's trusts, maintain ties of kinship and give *ṣadaqa*..." When Abū Bakr entered when the Messenger of Allah, may Allah bless him and grant him peace, was not there, Khadīja mentioned the matter to him and said, "'Atīq, go with Muḥammad to Waraqa ibn Nawfal." When the Messenger of Allah, may Allah bless him and grant him peace, came in, Abū Bakr took his hand and said, "Let us go to Waraqa." He asked, "Who told you?" "Khadīja," he replied.

So they went to him and told him the story. He said, "When I was alone, I heard a voice calling behind me, 'O Muḥammad, O Muḥammad!' and I began to run away from that place." He said, "Do not do that. When it comes to you, be firm so that you can hear what it says. Then come and tell me." When he was alone, he was called and told: "O Muḥammad! Say: 'In the Name of Allah, the All-Merciful, Most Merciful. *Praise be to Allah, the Lord of the worlds …to… misguided.'* 'Say: There is no god but Allah.'" So he went and told Waraqa and Waraqa said to him, "Good news and good news again! I testify to you that you are the one of whom 'Īsā son of Maryam gave the good news and you have received the like of the *Nāmūs* of Mūsā and you are a sent Prophet. You will be commanded to do *jihād* at some future date. If I am still alive, I will strive with you."

When Waraqa died, the Messenger of Allah, may Allah bless him and grant him peace, said, "I have seen the priest in the Garden wearing a silk garment because he believed in me and affirmed me." He meant Waraqa. Al-Bayhaqī said, "This [*ḥadīth*] is *munqaṭa'*." It is preserved and so it may be a report about the revelation of the *Fātiḥa* after the revelation of "Read in the name of your Lord." (96:1) and *Sūrat al-Muddaththir* (74).

Ibn 'Aṭiyya said that some scholars think that Jibrīl did not bring down the *Sūra* of Praise because of the *ḥadīth* in which Muslim reported that Ibn 'Abbās said, "While Jibrīl was sitting with the Prophet, may Allah bless him and grant him peace, he heard a crack above him. He lifted his head and said, 'This is a door of heaven being opened today which has not been opened until now.' An angel descended from it and he said, 'This is an angel who has descended to earth who has not descended before today.' He greeted them and said, 'Good news of two lights which you have been given which no Prophet before you was given: the *Fātiḥa* of the Book and the Seals of *Sūrat al-Baqara* (2:285-286). You will not read a single letter of them without being rewarded for it.'" Ibn 'Aṭiyya said, "It is not as they think. This *ḥadīth* indicates that Jibrīl came before the other angel to the Prophet, may Allah bless him and grant him peace, to inform him of it and of what he brought down. Accordingly Jibrīl participated in its revelation, but Allah knows best."

It is clear that this *ḥadīth* indicates that Jibrīl did not teach the Prophet, may Allah bless him and grant him peace, any of the *Fātiḥa*. We explained that it was revealed in Makka and that Jibrīl brought it down since Allah says, *"The Faithful* Rūḥ *brought it down."* (26:193) This means all of the Qur'ān. So Jibrīl brought down its recitation in Makka and the angel brought down its reward in Madina, but Allah knows best. It is said that it is Makkan/Madinan and that Jibrīl brought it down twice, as ath-Tha'labī related. What we mentioned is more likely since it combines the Qur'ān and the *Sunna*. Praise and favour belong to Allah.

Its Judgements

It has already been made clear that the *basmala* is not an *āyat* of the *Fātiḥa* according to the sound position. Given that, then the ruling for those doing the prayer is that, after the *takbīr*, they begin straightaway with "*al-ḥamdu lillāhi rabbi'l'ālamīn*" and are not silent and do not recite any *tawjīh* or *tasbīh.*[1] This is verified by the *ḥadīth* of 'Ā'isha, Anas and others. There are other *āḥadīth* which contain the *tawjīh*, *tasbīḥ* and silence, and a group of scholars follow that position. It is related that, when they began the prayer, 'Umar ibn al-Khaṭṭāb and 'Abdullāh ibn Mas'ūd used to say: "Glory be to You, O Allah, and by Your praise. Blessed is Your Name and exalted is Your Majesty. There is no god but You." Sufyān, Aḥmad, Isḥāq and the people of opinion follow that. Ash-Shāfi'ī used to say what is related from 'Alī from the Prophet, may Allah bless him and grant him peace, which is that when he began the prayer, he said the *takbīr* and then *"I have turned my face..."* (6:79) Muslim mentioned it and it will come in full at the end of *Sūrat al-An'ām.* At this point what we have said here is enough concerning this matter, Allah willing.

Ibn al-Mundhir said, "It is verified that when the Messenger of Allah, may Allah bless him and grant him peace, said the *takbīr* for the prayer, he was silent for a time before starting the recitation, during which time he said, 'O Allah, put as much distance between me and my errors as You have put between the east and the west. O Allah, cleanse me of my errors as the white garment is cleansed of dirt. O Allah, wash me of my errors with snow, ice and hail.' Abū Hurayra acted according to that. Abū Salama ibn

1. *Tawjīh* (a formula of directing oneself) and *tasbīḥ* (glorification) precede recitation of the *Fātiḥa* in some legal schools.

'Abdu'r-Raḥmān said, 'The imām has two silences, so take advantage of them with recitation.' Al-Awzā'ī, Sa'īd ibn 'Abdu'l-'Azīz and Aḥmad ibn Ḥanbal inclined to the *ḥadīth* of the Prophet, may Allah bless him and grant him peace, regarding this matter."

Scholars disagree about the exact nature of the obligation of reciting the *Fātiḥa* in the prayer. Mālik and his people say that it is incumbent on the imām and anyone praying alone in every *rak'at*. Ibn Khuwayzimandād al-Baṣrī al-Mālikī said, "There is no disagreement about the position of Mālik in respect of someone forgetting it in one *rak'at* of a two-*rak'āt* prayer, when it is clear that the prayer is then invalid and does not satisfy the obligation. There is disagreement about his position regarding someone who forgets it in one *rak'at* of a three or four-*rak'āt* prayer. Once he said that he must repeat the prayer and another time that he should do the prostration of forgetfulness. That is transmitted by Ibn 'Abdu'l-Ḥakam and others from Mālik." Ibn Khuwayzimandād said, "It is said that he repeats that *rak'at* and then does the prostration of forgetfulness after the *salām*." Ibn 'Abdu'l-Barr said, "The sound position is that he discounts that *rak'at* and does another to replace it, like someone who omits a prostration out of forgetfulness. That is the preference of Ibn al-Qāsim."

Al-Ḥasan al-Baṣrī, many of the people of Baṣra, and al-Mughīra ibn 'Abdu'r-Raḥmān al-Makhzūmī al-Madanī said, "If someone recites the *Umm al-Qur'ān* once during the prayer, it satisfies the obligation and he does not have to repeat it because it is a prayer in which the *Umm al-Qur'ān* was recited. It is complete according to the words of the Prophet, peace be upon him, 'The prayer of anyone who does not recite the *Umm al-Qur'ān* is invalid,' and the Prophet recited the *Fātiḥa."*

It is possible that the prayer of anyone who does not recite it in every *rak'at* is invalid and it is possible that the prayer of someone who does not recite it in most of the *rak'at*s is invalid. This is the reason for the disagreement, and Allah knows best.

Abū Ḥanīfa, ath-Thawrī and al-Awzā'ī said, "If it is omitted intentionally throughout the entire prayer and something else is recited instead, that satisfies the requirements," although al-Awzā'ī had some disagreement about that. Abū Yūsuf and Muḥammad ibn al-Ḥasan said, "Its minimum is three *āyat*s or a long *āyat*, like the *Āyat* of Debt (2:282)."

Aṭ-Ṭabarī said, "Someone who prays should recite the *Umm al-Qur'ān* in every *rak'at*. If he does not recite it, the requirement is only satisfied by reciting its equivalent in the Qur'ān in respect of the number of *āyat*s and the letters it contains." Ibn 'Abdu'l-Barr said, "This makes no sense because the specification of it and the text on it specify it and nothing else. It is not permissible for the one for whom it is obliged to do something else in its place and to leave it when he is able to recite it. He must do it and repeat it, like he must fulfil all other specific obligations in acts of worship."

If someone following the imām catches the *rukū'* with the imam, the recitation of the imām is considered sufficient for him since there is consensus that when someone catches the *rukū'* he just says his *takbīr al-iḥrām* and bows without reciting anything else. If he finds the imām standing, he should recite. No one should fail to recite behind the imām in one of the silent prayers. If he does so, he has acted badly but, according to Mālik and his people, he owes nothing. When the imām recites aloud, those following the imām do not recite the *Fātiḥa* or anything else according to the well-known position from the school of Mālik since Allah Almighty said, *"When the Qur'ān is recited listen to it and be quiet."* (7:204) The Messenger of Allah, may Allah bless him and grant him peace, said, "I would not contend with the Qur'ān." He said about the imām, "When he recites, be silent" and "If someone has an imām, the recitation of the imām is his recitation."

Ash-Shāfi'ī said in what al-Buwaytī and Aḥmad ibn Ḥanbal reported, "No one's prayer is satisfied unless he recites the *Fātiḥa* of the Book in every *rak'at*, imām or follower, whether the imām recites aloud or silently." In Iraq ash-Shāfi'ī used to say about the follower, "He recites when it is silent but not when it is aloud," like the well-known position of the school of Mālik. He said in Egypt that there are two positions about when the imām recites aloud. One is that the follower should recite, and the other is that the requirements of the prayer are satisfied if he does not recite, the recitation of the imām being sufficient. Ibn al-Mundhir related this view while Ibn Wahb, Ashhab, Ibn 'Abdu'l-Ḥakam, Ibn Ḥabīb and the Kufans said that the follower should not recite anything, whether the imām recites aloud or silently since the Prophet, peace be upon him, said, "The recitation of the imām is his recitation." This is general. It is also because Jābir said, "Whoever prays a *rak'at* in which he does not recite the *Umm al-Qur'ān* has not prayed – except behind an imām."

The position of ash-Shāfi'ī and Aḥmad is that the *Fātiḥa* is incumbent in every *rak'at* on everyone in general by the words of the Prophet, may Allah bless him and grant him peace, "There is no prayer for the one who does not recite the *Fātiḥa* of the Book in it," and his words, "If anyone prays a prayer in which he does not recite the *Umm al-Qur'ān*, it is incomplete," three times. Abū Hurayra said, "The Messenger of Allah, may Allah bless him and grant him peace, commanded me to call out: 'There is no prayer except with the recitation of the *Fātiḥa* of the Book.'" (Abū Dāwūd)

As the prostration or *rukū'* of a *rak'at* does not replace that of another *rak'at*, so the recitation of one *rak'at* does not replace that of another. That is stated by 'Abdullāh ibn 'Awn, Ayyūb as-Sakhtiyānī, Abū Thawr and others among the people of ash-Shāfi'ī and Dā'ūd ibn 'Alī. The same thing is reported from al-Awzā'ī and Makḥūl also said it. It is related that 'Umar ibn al-Khaṭṭāb, 'Abdullāh ibn 'Abbās, Abū Hurayra, Ubayy ibn Ka'b, Abū Ayyūb al-Anṣārī, 'Abdullāh ibn 'Amr ibn al-'Āṣ, 'Ubāda ibn aṣ-Ṣāmit, Abū Sa'īd al-Khudrī, 'Uthmān ibn Abi'l-'Āṣ and Khawwāt ibn Jubayr said, "There is no prayer except with the *Fātiḥa* of the Book." It is the position of Ibn 'Amr, famous in the school of al-Awzā'ī. Those Companions are models and examples and all of them obliged the *Fātiḥa* in every *rak'at*.

Imām Abū 'Abdullāh Muḥammad ibn Yazīd ibn Mājah al-Qazwīnī transmitted something in his *Sunan* which removes any disagreement. He said that it is reported from Abū Sa'īd al-Khudrī that the Messenger of Allah, may Allah bless him and grant him peace, said, "There is no prayer for someone who does not recite in every *rak'at* the *Fātiḥa* and another *sūra*, be it a *farḍ* prayer or any other." In the *Ṣaḥīḥ* of Muslim, Abū Hurayra reported that the Prophet, peace be upon him, told someone to whom he taught the prayer, "Do that throughout all your prayer."

Ibn al-'Arabī said, "He said, 'There is no prayer for the one who does not recite the *Fātiḥa* of the Book.' People disagree about this principle and whether the negation applies to doing it in full or to a part. The *fatwā* varies according to the different states of those who investigate. The best known and strongest in this principle is that the negation is general. The strongest comes from the transmission of Mālik that the prayer of someone who does not recite the *Fātiḥa* is invalid. Then we look at its repetition in every *rak'at*. Whoever reflects on the words of the Prophet, may Allah bless him and grant him peace, 'Do that in all your prayer' obliges him to repeat the recitation as he repeats the *rukū'* and prostration, but Allah knows best."

Scholars agree that there is no prayer without recitation and they agree that there is no particular amount specified beyond the *Fātiḥa* of the Book, although they recommend that only one *sūra* should be recited with the *Fātiḥa* because that is the maximum which has come from the Prophet, may Allah bless him and grant him peace. Mālik said, "The *sunna* of recitation is to recite the *Umm al-Qur'ān* and a *sūra* in the first two *rak'at*s and only the *Fātiḥa* in the last two." Al-Awzā'ī said, "You should recite the *Umm al-Qur'ān*. If you do not recite the *Umm al-Qur'ān* and recite something else instead, that satisfies the requirements." Ath-Thawrī said, "In the first two *rak'at*s, you recite the *Fātiḥa* and a *sūra*, and you can glorify in the last two if you wish, or if you wish, you may recite. If you neither recite nor glorify, your prayer is still allowed." That is the position of Abū Ḥanīfa and the rest of the Kufans. Ibn al-Mundhir said, "We related that 'Alī ibn Abī Ṭālib said, 'Recite in the first two and glorify in the last two.'"

An-Nakhā'ī reported that Sufyān said, "If someone does not recite in three *rak'at*s, he must repeat the prayer because the recitation in one *rak'at* is not sufficient." He said, "The same applies if someone forgets to recite in one *rak'at* in the *Fajr* prayer." Abū Thawr said, "A prayer is only satisfied with the recitation of the *Fātiḥa* in every *rak'at*, which was the Egyptian position of ash-Shāfi'ī, and a group of the people of ash-Shāfi'ī also say that." It is like that in that which Ibn Khuwayzimandād al-Mālikī said. He said, "We consider recitation of the *Fātiḥa* to be mandatory in every *rak'at*. This is the sound position regarding this question." Muslim related that Abū Qatāda said, "The Messenger of Allah, may Allah bless him and grant him peace, used to lead us in the prayer and he would recite the *Fātiḥa* of the Book and two *sūra*s in the first two *rak'at*s of *Ẓuhr* and *'Aṣr*. Sometimes we could hear the *āyat*. He was long in the first *rak'at* of *Ẓuhr* and short in the second, and did the same in *Ṣubḥ*." In one variant, "He used to recite the *Fātiḥa* in the last two *rak'ats*." This is a clear text and sound *ḥadīth* supporting what Mālik believed.

The majority believe that what is additional to the *Fātiḥa* in the recitation is not mandatory according to what Muslim related from Abū Hurayra. He said, "There is recitation in every prayer. What the Prophet, may Allah bless him and grant him peace, made us hear, we make you hear, and what he hid from us we hide from you. If anyone recites the *Umm al-Qur'ān*, it is enough for him. If anyone recites more, that is good." Al-Bukhārī said, "If there is more, it is good." Many of the people of knowledge reject abandoning the *sūra*, with or without necessity, including 'Imrān ibn Ḥusayn, Abū Sa'īd al-Khudrī, Khawwāt ibn Jubayr, Mujāhid, Abū Wā'il, Ibn 'Umar, Ibn 'Abbās and others. They said, "There is no prayer for the one who does not recite the *Fātiḥa* in it and some of the Qur'ān with it." Some of them stipulate two *āyat*s, or one *āyat*, and some do not give a limit. He said, "Something of the Qur'ān with it."

If someone finds it impossible after his best efforts to learn the *Fātiḥa* or anything of the Qur'ān, he should mention Allah in place of the recitation using whatever formula he can: *takbīr*, *lā ilāha illā'llāh*, praise, glorification, magnification or *"lā ḥawla walā quwwata illā bi'llāh*" when he prays alone or with an imām in the silent prayer. Abū Dāwūd and others reported that 'Abdullāh ibn

Abī Awfā said, "A man came to the Messenger of Allah, may Allah bless him and grant him peace, and said, 'I cannot learn any of the Qur'ān. So teach me what will compensate that for me.' He said, 'Say: "Glory be to Allah and praise be to Allah. There is no god but Allah and there is no strength or power except by Allah."' He said, 'Messenger of Allah, this is for Allah. What is for me?' He said, 'Say: "O Allah, show mercy to me, protect me, guide me and provide for me."'"

If someone is unable even to learn any of these expressions, he should not fail to try to pray with the imām. The imām will bear that responsibility for him if Allah wishes. He must, however, always persevere in trying to memorise the *Fātiḥa* of the Book and more of the Qur'ān until death intervenes. He is engaged in striving so that Allah will excuse him. If someone cannot speak Arabic, the Arabic supplication is translated for him into a language which he understands so he can perform his prayer. That will be good enough, Allah willing. If someone recites the prayer in Persian when he has good Arabic, it is not allowed according to the position of the majority. Abū Ḥanīfa said, "Recitation in Persian satisfies it, even if he is good in Arabic because the goal is to grasp the meaning." Ibn al-Mundhir said, "That does not satisfy it because it is contrary to what Allah commanded and contrary to what the Prophet, may Allah bless him and grant him peace, taught and contrary to what the Community of Muslims do. We do not know of anyone agreeing with this statement of his."

Saying Āmīn

It is *sunna* for the reciter of the Qur'ān to say *"āmīn"* when he finishes the *Fātiḥa,* after a moment of silence following the *nūn* of *"ḍāllīn"* to distinguish what is part of the Qur'ān from what is not.

It is established from the *ḥadīth* of Abū Hurayra that the Messenger of Allah, may Allah bless him and grant him peace, said, "When the imām says *āmīn*, say *āmīn*. If someone's *āmīn* coincides with that of the angels, he will be forgiven his past wrong actions." Our scholars say that the forgiveness of wrong actions is dependent on four conditions which are contained in this *ḥadīth*. The first is the imām saying *āmīn*, the second is those behind him saying *āmīn*, the third is the *āmīn* of the angels, and the fourth is the coinciding of the *āmīn*s. Some say that the coinciding refers to the answer, some that it is about the time, and some say that it is about sincerity in supplication as is made clear by the words of the Prophet, "Call on Allah and be certain of the answer. Know that Allah does not answer the supplication of a heedless negligent heart."

Abū Dāwūd related that Abū Muṣabbaḥ al-Maqrānī said, "We used to sit with Abū Zuhayr an-Namīrī, one of the Companions, and he related the best statement about this. When one of us made a supplication, he said, 'End it with *āmīn*. *Āmīn* is like the seal on the page.'" Abū Zuhayr said, "Shall I tell you how I know that? One night we went out with the Messenger of Allah, may Allah bless him and grant him peace, and came to a man who was intense in his asking [of Allah]. The Prophet, may Allah bless him and grant him peace, stood listening to him and he said, 'It is guaranteed if he seals it.' A man of the people said to him, 'With what is it sealed?' He said, 'With *āmīn*. If he seals it with *āmīn*, it is guaranteed.' The man who asked the Prophet, may Allah bless him and grant him peace, went to the man and said, 'Did you seal it, so-and-so?' and he gave him the good news." In a *ḥadīth* we also find, "Jibrīl taught me *āmīn* when I finished the *Fātiḥa* and it is like the seal on the Book." And in another *ḥadīth*, "*Āmīn* is the seal of the Lord of all the worlds."

The meaning of *āmīn* according to most of the people of knowledge is, "O Allah, give us an answer", which acts as a kind of supplication. Some people say that it is one of the Names of Allah. That is related from Ja'far ibn Muḥammad, Mujāhid, and Hilāl ibn Yasāf. Ibn 'Abbās is also said to have related it from the Prophet, may Allah bless him and grant him peace, but the transmission is not sound. Ibn al-'Arabī said that as well. It is also said that the meaning of *āmīn* is "Let it be like that". Al-Jawharī said that. Al-Kalbī related from Abū Ṣāliḥ that Ibn 'Abbās said, "I asked the Messenger of Allah, may Allah bless him and grant him peace, the meaning of *āmīn*. He said, 'Lord, do it.'" Muqātil said, "It strengthens the supplication and asks for the descent of blessing." At-Tirmidhī said, "It means: 'Do not disappoint our hopes'."

There are two ways of pronouncing *āmīn*: with both vowels long like *Yāsīn*; and with the first vowel short like *yamīn*. Doubling the *mīm* is an error, according to al-Jawharī. The doubling is related from al-Ḥasan and Ja'far aṣ-Ṣādiq. It is the position of al-Ḥusayn ibn al-Faḍl, who derived it from *amma* meaning to aim for something, which gives it the meaning: "we aim for You." This occurs in Allah's words, *"or those heading* (āmmīn) *for the Sacred House..."* (5:2)

Scholars disagree about whether the imām says it at all and, if he does, whether he says it out loud. Ash-Shāfi'ī and Mālik believe in the transmission of the Madinans regarding that whereas the Kufans and some Madinans say that it should not be said out loud. Ibn al-Qāsim related from Mālik that the imām does not say *āmîn* but those behind him do. That is the position of Ibn al-Qāsim and the Egyptian scholars of Mālik. Their evidence is the *ḥadīth* of Abū Mūsā al-Ash'arī: "The Messenger of Allah, may Allah bless him and grant him peace, addressed us, made our *sunna* clear to us and taught us our prayer. He said, 'When you pray, then make your rows straight. Then let one of you lead the prayer. When he says the *takbīr*, say the *takbīr*. When he says, *'not of those with anger on them nor of the misguided,'* say *āmīn* and Allah will answer you." (Muslim) Al-Bukhārī has a chapter on "the imām saying *āmīn* out loud".

The people of Abū Ḥanīfa said that it is more appropriate to say *āmīn* silently rather than out loud because it is supplication and Allah Almighty says, *"Call on your Lord humbly and secretly."* (7:55) They said, "The evidence for it is what is related about the interpretation of the words of the Almighty, *'Your request is answered.'"* (10:89) They said, "Mūsā and Hārūn used to make supplication using *āmīn* and so Allah called them both supplicators. The answer is that making supplication silently is better in order to avoid any showing-off. As for the group prayer, attending it is in order to publicise an outward obligation and to promote a duty which people are recommended to observe. The imām has to articulate the recitation of the *Fātiḥa* which contains supplication and *āmīn* at the end of it. When supplication is of that sort which is *sunna* to say aloud, then *āmīn* follows at the end of the supplication and is also *sunna*. This is clear.

The meaning of the *Fātiḥa* and its various readings

بِسْمِ ٱللَّهِ ٱلرَّحْمَٰنِ ٱلرَّحِيمِ ١
ٱلْحَمْدُ لِلَّهِ رَبِّ ٱلْعَٰلَمِينَ ٢ ٱلرَّحْمَٰنِ
ٱلرَّحِيمِ ٣ مَلِكِ يَوْمِ ٱلدِّينِ ٤
إِيَّاكَ نَعْبُدُ وَإِيَّاكَ نَسْتَعِينُ ٥
ٱهْدِنَا ٱلصِّرَٰطَ ٱلْمُسْتَقِيمَ ٦
صِرَٰطَ ٱلَّذِينَ أَنْعَمْتَ عَلَيْهِمْ غَيْرِ
ٱلْمَغْضُوبِ عَلَيْهِمْ وَلَا ٱلضَّآلِّينَ ٧

1 *In the Name of Allah, the All-Merciful, Most Merciful*

2 *Praise be to Allah, the Lord of all the worlds,*
3 *the All-Merciful, the Most Merciful,*
4 *the King of the Day of Repayment.*

5 *You alone we worship.*
You alone we ask for help.

6 *Guide us on the Straight Path,*
7 ***the Path of those whom You have blessed,***
not of those with anger on them,
nor of the misguided.

Praise be to Allah

Abū Muḥammad 'Abdu'l-Ghanī ibn Sa'īd related from Abū Hurayra and Abū Sa'īd al-Khudrī that the Prophet, may Allah bless him and grant him peace, said, "When the slave says, *'Praise be to Allah,'* Allah says, 'My slave has truly praised Me.'" Muslim related from Anas ibn Mālik that the Messenger of Allah, may Allah bless him and grant him peace, said, "Allah is pleased with the slave who eats and praises Him for it or takes a drink and praises Him for it." Al-Ḥasan said, "There is no blessing but that the words 'praise be to Allah' are better than it." Ibn Mājah related from Anas ibn Mālik that the Messenger of Allah, may Allah bless him and grant him peace, said, "When Allah gives someone a blessing and he says, 'praise be to Allah', what he says is better than what he receives."

In *Nawādir al-Uṣūl*, Anas ibn Mālik reported that the Messenger of Allah, may Allah bless him and grant him peace, said, "If the entire world, lock, stock and barrel, were to be in the hand of a man of my Community and then he said, *'Praise be to Allah,'* his praise of Allah would be greater than everything he possessed." Abū 'Abdullāh said, "We find that its meaning is that he has been given this world and is then given these words to say after it. The words are better than all of this world because this world will end while the words will remain, being one of the enduring good actions. Allah says, *'In your Lord's sight, right actions which are lasting are better both in reward and end result.'* (19:76)"

This world is from Allah and the words of praise are also from Him. He gave him this world and made him rich. He gave him the words and honoured him by them in the Next World. Ibn Mājah related from Ibn 'Umar that the Messenger of Allah, may Allah bless him and grant him peace, said to them, "One of the slaves of Allah said, 'O Lord, praise is Yours as befits the majesty of Your face and the immensity of Your power.' His two recording angels were puzzled by it. They did not know how to record it, so they rose to heaven and said, 'Our Lord, Your slave said something which we do not know how to record.' Allah Almighty, Who knows better what His slave said, asked, 'What did My slave say?' They replied, 'O Lord, he said, "O Lord, praise is Yours as befits the majesty of Your face and the immensity of Your power."' Allah said to them, 'Continue to write it as My slave said it until he meets Me and I will repay him for it.'"

Scholars disagree about which is better: the words, "Praise be to Allah, the Lord of all the worlds," or the words, "There is no god but Allah." One group say that "Praise be to Allah, the Lord of all the worlds" is better because it incorporates the *tawḥīd* contained in "There is no god but Allah". It thus contains both *tawḥīd* and praise whereas "There is no god but Allah" contains *tawḥīd* alone. Another group say that "There is no god but Allah" is better because it repels disbelief and idolatry and because people are fought for refusing to say it. The Messenger of Allah, may Allah bless him and grant him peace, said, "I was commanded to fight people until they say, 'There is no god but Allah.'" Ibn 'Aṭiyya preferred this and said that this view is entailed by the words of the Prophet, may Allah bless him and grant him peace, "The best of what I and the Prophets before me said is, 'There is no god but Allah alone with no partner.'"

The word "praise" (*ḥamd*) in the language of the Arabs means comprehensive praise. The definite article is used since the category includes all forms of praise. Allah deserves all praise since He has the Most Beautiful Names and sublime attributes. It is an all-inclusive expression. The name "Muḥammad" which is derived from it means the one who has many praiseworthy qualities. Praise is the opposite of blame.

Praise is more universal than thankfulness. Abū Ja'far aṭ-Ṭabarī and Abū'l-'Abbās al-Mubarrad believed that praise and thankfulness have the same meaning. Abū 'Abdu'r-Raḥmān as-Sulamī stated that in *al-Ḥaqā'iq*, quoting Ja'far aṣ-Ṣādiq and Ibn 'Aṭā'allāh. Ibn 'Aṭā'allāh said, "It means 'Thanks be to Allah' since there is blessing from Him in teaching it to us so that we praise Him." Some scholars say that "thanks" is more general than praise because it is shown with the tongue, the limbs, and the heart whereas praise is made only with the tongue. It is said that praise is more general because it contains the meaning of thanks and the meaning of praise and is therefore more universal than thanks because praise can include thanks but thanks does not include praise.

It is related that Ibn 'Abbās said, "'Praise be to Allah' is the statement of every thankful person." When he sneezed, Ādam said, "Praise be to Allah." Allah said to Nūḥ, *"Then say: 'Praise be to Allah who has rescued us from the people of the wrongdoers!'"* (23:28). Ibrāhīm said, *"Praise be to Allah Who, despite my old age, has given me Ismā'īl and Isḥāq."* (14:39) Dā'ūd and Sulaymān said, *"Praise be to Allah who has favoured us over many of His slaves who are believers."* (27:15) He said to His Prophet, may Allah bless him and grant him peace, *"Praise be to Allah Who has had no son."* (17:111). The people of the Garden say, *"Praise be to Allah who has removed all sadness from us."* (35:34) *"The end of their call is: 'Praise be to Allah, the Lord of all the worlds!'"* (10:10)

The sound position is that the word "praise" is used for the qualities of a person praised without the need of any prior act of charity on that person's part. Thankfulness is praise for the one thanked because of some good that he has done. Based on this definition, our scholars say that praise is more universal than thanks because it comprises both praising and thanking. Thanks is particular, being directed towards someone who did good to you. So the word "praise" is more general and is used in the *āyat* because it is more than thanks.

It is mentioned that Ja'far aṣ-Ṣādiq said, "'Praise be to Allah' is a way of praising Him with the attributes with which He has described Himself, and the word *ḥamd* is used because it is made up of the letters *ḥā'*, *mīm* and *dāl*. *Ḥā'* is from oneness (*wa**ḥ**dāniyya*), *mīm* is from dominion (***m**ulk*), and *dāl* is from everlastingness (***d**aymūmiya*). This is the real meaning of '*al-ḥamdu* *lillāh'*." Shaqīq ibn Ibrāhīm said in the explanation of "Praise be to Allah" that it has three aspects. The first is that when Allah gives you something you acknowledge the One who gave it to you. The second is that you show you are pleased with what He has given you. The third is that, as long as there is still strength in your body you do not disobey Him. These are the preconditions of praise.

The meaning of the words *"Praise be to Allah, the Lord of all the worlds"* is "My prior praise of Myself before any created being praises Me. My praise of Myself before time does not have a cause and praise of Me by My creatures is sullied by causes." Our scholars said, "It is repugnant for a creature who has not been given perfection to praise himself for bringing benefits and repelling harms." It is said that since He knew His slaves' inability to praise Him, He praised Himself by Himself for Himself before time. No matter how much His slaves try, they are unable to praise Him sufficiently. Do you not see how the Master of the Messengers displayed inability when he said, "I cannot number Your praises." It is said that Allah praised Himself before time because He knew the great number of His blessings to His slaves and their inability to fulfil the obligation of praising Him. So He praised Himself for them in order that His blessings would be more enjoyed by them since He removed the burden of praising Him for them.

All seven readings and the majority of people agree that there is a *ḍamma* on the *dāl* of *ḥamd*, making it *ḥamd**u***. *Ḥamd**a*** is related from Sufyān ibn 'Uyayna and Ru'ba ibn al-'Ajjāj. Sībuwayh says that, grammatically, if someone uses the nominative *ḥamd**u***, it has the meaning of "I praise Allah greatly." Praise is from him and from all of creation for Allah. If someone uses the accusative *ḥamd**a***, he is saying praise is from him alone for Allah. It is said that His praise of Himself is to inform His slaves of it. What is implied, according to this, is, "Say: praise be to Allah." Aṭ-Ṭabarī said, "*Praise be to Allah* is praise by which He praises Himself. It contains a command for His slaves to praise Him and so it is as if He were saying, 'Say: praise be to Allah.'"

the Lord of all the worlds

"The Lord of all the worlds" is their Master. Every kingdom has its Lord and the Lord is the Master (*mālik*). In the *Ṣaḥīḥ* collections we find that "Lord" (*ar-Rabb*) is one of the Names of Allah Almighty. It is only used of someone else in a relative sense. They sometimes used it to designate a king in the time of *Jāhiliyya*.

So the word "Lord" means Master. That is demonstrated by the words of the Almighty in *Sūra Yūsuf*, "*Mention me when you are with your lord.*" (12:42) In a *ḥadīth* we find, "When the slavegirl gives birth to her mistress (*rabba*)." The Lord is the one who puts things right, manages, compels and preserves. Al-Hurawī and others said that it is used of the one who tries to put a thing right. *Rabbāniyyūn* (divines) are so called because of their guarding of the Revealed Books. The Lord is the One worshipped. Some scholars say that it is the greatest name of Allah because of the great number of those who make supplication using it. Consider its use in the Qur'ān, as at the end of *al-Baqara and Āl 'Imrān*, and in *Sūrat Ibrāhīm* and other *sūra*s. By this quality of Lordship we are made aware of the quality of the relationship between the Lord and the slave which involves kindness, mercy and need in every state.

There is disagreement about the derivation of the word *rabb*. Some say that it is derived from *tarbīya* (upbringing). So Allah Almighty manages His creation and nurtures them. We find that borne out in the words of the Almighty, *"Your foster daughters in your care."* (4:23) He called a foster daughter *rabība* because the husband cares for her. On the basis that Allah manages His creation and nurtures it, *Rabb* reflects an attribute connected to Divine Action, and, in as far as *Rabb* means king and master, it is an attribute of the Divine Essence.

When the definite article is affixed to "Lord" on its own it can only mean Allah Almighty because it is defined, but if it is made possessive, it can be shared between Allah and His slaves. It is said, "Allah is the Lord of the slaves, Zayd is the lord of the house and Allah is the Lord of the lords." Allah owns both the owner and what is owned. He created him and provides for him. No lord except for Allah can be either a creator or a provider. A slave can become an owner after he was not an owner and ownership can also be removed from him. He can own one thing and not own another. The attribute of lordship when it is applied to Allah is different from this. He everlastingly owns everything in existence. This is the difference between the attribute of the Creator and the created.

The meaning of the word "worlds" (*'ālamīn*) is the subject of much discussion among interpreters. Qatāda said that it is the plural of *'ālam*, and means every existent thing except Allah. It is said that the people of every age are 'a world'. Al-Ḥusayn ibn al-Faḍl said that, by the words of Allah, *"Of all beings* ('ālamīn)*, do you lie with males?"* (26:165), he means people. Ibn 'Abbas said that *'ālamīn* means the jinn and human beings. The evidence for his position is the words of the Almighty, *"So that he can be a warner to all beings* ('ālamīn)." (25:1) He was not a warner to the animals but he was to the jinn. Al-Farrā' and Abū 'Ubayda said, "The word 'world' (*'ālam*) designates all who have understanding and they constitute four communities: people, jinn, angels and shayṭāns. 'World' is not used for beasts, because it is a word only used for those with intelligence."

Abū 'Amr ibn al-'Alā' said, "They are those with a *rūḥ*." Ibn 'Abbās also said, "It means everything with a *rūḥ* crawling on the face of the earth." Wahb ibn Munabbih said, "Allah has eighteen thousand worlds. This world is just one of them." Abū Sa'īd al-Khudrī said, "Allah has forty thousand worlds, and this world from east to west is just one of them." Muqātil said, "There are eighty thousand worlds. Forty thousand are on the land and forty thousand in the sea."

The first position is the soundest of these, because it includes every creature and existent thing. Evidence for it is found in the words of the Almighty, *"Pharaoh said, 'What is the Lord of all the worlds?' He said, 'The Lord of the heavens and the earth and everything between them.'"* (26:23-24) The word is derived from *'alam* (sign) and *'alāma* (token) because it indicates the One who brought it into existence. That is like what az-Zajjāj said: "The word "worlds" refers to all that Allah created in this world and the Next." Al-Khalīl said, "*'Alam*, *'alāma* and *ma'lam* are what indicates a thing, so *'ālam* indicates that it has a Creator and Director. This is clear." It is mentioned that a man said in the presence of al-Junayd, "Praise be to Allah." He said to him, "Complete it as Allah did. Say: 'Lord of all the worlds'." The man said, "What are these worlds that they should be mentioned with the Real?" He said, "Say it, my brother. When the temporal is connected to the timeless, no trace of it remains."

Although the word "Lord" is usually considered to be genitive (*Rabb**i***), it can also be read as nominative (*Rabb**u***) or accusative (*Rabb**a***). If it is read as accusative it becomes the object of the praise, and if it is read as nominative it is the beginning of a new sentence, implying: "He is the Lord of all the worlds."

The All-Merciful, Most Merciful

After calling Himself "the Lord of all the worlds" Allah then describes Himself as "the All-Merciful, Most Merciful". Because His description as "the Lord of all the worlds" causes fear, He followed it by "the All-Merciful, Most Merciful" since that contains reassurance, so that His qualities will induce both awe of Him and also desire for Him. This helps people in their obedience to Him. He does the same in several places in His Book. He says elsewhere: *"Tell My slaves that I am the Ever-Forgiving, the Most Merciful, but also that My punishment is the painful punishment."* (15:49-50) And in another place: *"The Forgiver of wrong action, the Accepter of repentance, the Severe in retribution, the Possessor of abundance."* (40:3) In the *Ṣaḥīḥ* of Muslim we find a *ḥadīth* in which Abū Hurayra reported that the Messenger of Allah, may Allah bless him and grant him peace, said, "If the believers knew the punishment of Allah, no one would hope for His Garden. If the unbelievers knew the mercy of Allah, no one would despair of His Garden." The meanings of these two Names have already been given.

the King of the Day of Repayment

Muḥammad ibn as-Samayqa' has "King" in the accusative, and there are four readings of it: *mālik*, *malik*, *malk*, and *malīk.*

Scholars disagree about which is the more comprehensive: *malik* (king) or *mālik* (master). The two variants are transmitted from the Prophet, may Allah bless him and grant him peace, Abū Bakr and 'Umar, may Allah be pleased with them both. At-Tirmidhīi mentioned both readings. It is said that "King" (*malik*) is more general and intensive than "Master" (*mālik*) since every king is a master but not every master is a king. and because a king has authority over the property of a master. Abū 'Ubayda and al-Mubarrad also held that opinion. It is said that "Master" is more comprehensive because He is the Master of people and other creatures and so is more far reaching and greater in His power of disposal since He sees to the imposing of the laws of the *Shari'a.*

Abū 'Alī said that Abū Bakr ibn as-Sirāj transmitted from some of those who preferred to recite *mālik* that Allah describes Himself as being the Master of everything in His words "Lord of all the Worlds", and so there is no point in the recitation of *mālik* because that would be a repetition. Abū 'Alī said, "This is not a valid argument because the Revelation contains many similar instances, where the general comes first and then the particular. One example is Allah's words: *"He is Allah, the Creator, the Maker, the Giver of Form."* (59:24) Creator is general, and the Giver of Form is mentioned because it calls attention to what is created and the existence of wisdom. Another instance is when the Almighty says, *"They are certain about the Next World"* after saying *"those who believe in the Unseen."* (2:3) The Unseen contains the Next World and other things, but He mentioned it because of its immensity and to call attention to the obligation to believe in it and to refute the unbelievers who deny it. Yet another example of particular relevance to the *Fātiḥa* is the formula, *"the All-Merciful, Most Merciful"* when *Raḥmān* is general for all existence and *Raḥīm* is mentioned after it to make it specific to the believers in the Next World, something made explicit by His words, *"merciful to the believers"* (33:43)".

Abū Ḥātim said that *mālik* is more intensive when praising the Creator than *malik*, and *malik* is more intensive when praising creatures than *mālik*. The difference between them is that a master in the case of creatures can be other than a king. When Allah is a master, He is also a king. This position was chosen by Qāḍī Abū Bakr ibn al-'Arabī. He mentioned three reasons. One is that it can be applied to both the particular and general and so you can say "master of a house, land and garment", in the same way that you say "master of a kingdom". The second is that it is applied to the master of little or a lot. When you reflect on these two statements, you find that they are the same. The third is that you say, "Master of the Kingdom" (*mālik al-mulk*) not "King of the Kingdom" (*malik al-mulk*). Ibn al-Haṣṣār said that that is the case because the word "master" indicates property (*milk*) and does not necessarily entail a kingdom (*mulk*). Property comprises both matters and so it is more intensive.

Some of them argue that *mālik* is more intensive because it has an extra letter and so its reciter receives ten more good actions than the one who reads *malik*. This is looking at form rather than meaning. The recitation of *malik* is established and it has meanings which *mālik* does not have, and Allah knows best.

It is said that it is not permitted to give anyone this name nor to call other than Allah Almighty by it. Al-Bukhārī and Muslim related from Abū Hurayra that the Messenger of Allah, may Allah bless him and grant him peace, said, "Allah will seize the earth on the Day of Rising and roll up heaven in His right hand and then say, 'I am the King. Where are the kings of the earth?'" Abū Hurayra also reported that the Messenger of Allah, may Allah bless him and grant him peace, said, "The most abased man in the sight of Allah is a man who calls himself, 'the King of Kings.'" Muslim added, "There is no king except Allah Almighty." Sufyān said, "Like the Persian term *Shahanshah*." The Messenger of Allah, may Allah bless him and grant him peace, said, "The man with whom Allah will be angriest is a man who calls himself, 'the king of kings.' There is no king except Allah." Ibn al-Ḥaṣṣār said, "It is like that with 'King of the Day of Judgement' and 'Master of the Kingdom.'" There is no disagreement that this title is forbidden to all creatures in the same way that 'the King of kings' is.

It is, however, permitted to be described as king or master if what is intended is what is customarily understood by those terms. Allah says, *"Allah sent you Ṭālūt as a king."* (2:247) The Prophet, may Allah bless him and grant him peace, said, "Some people from my community were shown to me raiding in the way of Allah, riding the middle of this sea like kings on thrones."

It may be asked why does Allah say *"King of the Day of Repayment,"* when the Day of Judgement has not yet arrived? How can He describe Himself as being the King of something He has not yet brought into existence? The response to this is that the word used is an active participle from the verb *malaka*, and the active participle in Arabic can be used to indicate something which is still to come. The form can be used for the future, and that is the case in the words, *"King of the Day of Repayment,"* meaning that He will be the King of it.

A second point is that the interpretation of the phrase refers to power, meaning that Allah has power on the Day of Judgement or over the Day of Judgement and is bringing it about because the king of a thing can dispose of a thing as He wills and has power over it. Allah is the King of all things and disposes of them as He wills. Nothing is impossible for him. The first aspect is closer to Arabic and more effective. Abū'l-Qāsim az-Zajjāji said that.

A third point is to ask why Allah singled out the Day of Repayment, when He is King of that Day and all other days? The answer is because, in this world, there is contention about who has sovereignty, as is displayed in what Pharaoh, Nimrod and other tyrants did. On that Day no one will contend with Him for sovereignty and all of them will be humbled to Him, as He says, *"To whom does the kingdom belong today?"* (40:16) The answer of all creatures is: *"to Allah, the One, the Conqueror."* (40:16) Glory be to Him! There is no god but Him.

If the reading *malik* (King) is employed, it is one of the attributes of the Divine Essence. If *mālik* (Master) is used, it is one of the attributes of Divine Action.

The word "day" normally designates the time from the rising of dawn until the moment when the sun sets. It is used metaphorically here for the time from when the Resurrection takes place until the time when the people of Paradise and Hell take up their respective abodes.

"Repayment" (*dīn*) here means requital for actions and reckoning for them. That is what Ibn 'Abbās, Ibn Mas'ūd, Ibn Jurayj, Qatāda and others said. This understanding is related from the Prophet, may Allah bless him and grant him peace. It is indicated by the words of the Almighty, *"On that Day Allah will repay them what is due to them."* (24:25) He says, *"Every self will be repaid today for what it earned."* (40:17) *"Today you will be repaid for what you did."* (45:28) *"Will we face a reckoning?"* (37:53).

Linguists report that *dayn* is debt and *dīn* is repayment. Another aspect of it is *ad-Dayyān* as an attribute of the Lord, meaning "the Repayer". A *ḥadīth* states, "The clever one is he who reckons himself," using the same verbal root. It is said that it means judgement and this is also related from Ibn 'Abbās. *Dīn* can also mean obedience. Tha'lab said, "*Dāna* is used for a man when he obeys, when he disobeys, when he is exalted, when he is abased and when he is overcome, and so it is one of the words with opposite meanings. *Dīn* is also used for custom and affair.

You alone we worship

With this phrase the third person changes to the second person. From the beginning to this point the *sūra* has been description of Allah and praise for Him. There are several other examples of this happening in Allah's Book. We find in *Sūrat al-Insān*: *"Their Lord will give them a pure drink."* which then changes to: *"This is your reward."* (76:21-22) Then we find the reverse in *Sūrat Yūnus*: *"When some of you are on a boat, running before a fair wind"* which changes to *"and then a violent squall comes upon them"* (10:22).

The word "worship" here means obedience. Worship is obedience and humility. A smooth (*mu'abbad*) road is one which is easy for travellers to travel on. Al-Harawī said, "When those subject to the *Sharī'a* say this they are acknowledging Allah's Lordship and affirming the worship of Allah alone since other people worship other than Him in the form of idols and other things."

You alone we ask for help

The meaning of "ask for help" (*ista'āna*) is to seek aid, support, and success. This is a sentence added to the previous one. Yaḥyā ibn Waththāb and al-A'mash recite *"nista'īn"*. That is the dialect of the tribes of Tamīm, Asad, Qays and Rabī'a.

As-Sulamī says in *al-Ḥaqā'iq*, "I heard Muḥammad ibn 'Abdullāh ibn Shādhān say that he heard Abū Ḥafṣ al-Farghānī say, 'Whoever recites *"You alone we worship and You alone we ask for help"* cannot be considered guilty of espousing either the doctrine of fatalism or that of absolute free will.'"

If it is asked why the object is put before the verb, the answer is that it is put ahead because of its importance. The Arabs tend to put the most important thing first. It is mentioned that a bedouin cursed another and so the cursed turned from him and the curser said, "You from me!" And the other replied, "From you I turn." They put the object of emphasis first. It also ensures that the created slave is not put before the object of worship.

Most reciters and scholars double the *yā'* in *iyyāka* in both places, although 'Amr ibn Fā'id recited it as *iyāk*. That is because he disliked the doubling of the *yā'* since it is heavy and because there is a *kasra* before it.

Guide us on the Straight Path

The words "guide us" are a supplication, implying that this is something desired by the speaker from their Lord. It means: "Direct us to the Straight Path and guide us on it. Show us Your guidance which will lead us to intimacy with You and nearness to You." Some scholars say that Allah made this *sūra* a model for all supplication. Half of it comprises His praise and half comprises our needs. The supplication which is in the *sūra* is the best which one can use for supplication because these are words spoken by the Lord of the Worlds. When you use it you make supplication using His words which He spoke. In a *ḥadīth* we find, "There is nothing Allah considers more noble than supplication," and so by this token the *Fātiḥa* is the most noble of the noble and among the best things it is possible for a human being to say.

It is said that it means: "Guide us to follow the *Sunna* in performing all the obligations we owe to You." It is said that the root of the word "guide" is inclination towards something. That can be seen in the words of the Almighty: *"We have truly turned* (hudnā) *to You."* (7:156), meaning we have inclined towards You. Another facet of its meaning can be gleaned from the word *hadiya* (gift) which is so called because it moves from one owner to another. Another aspect of its meaning can be inferred from the word *hady* which is the term used for an animal driven to the *Masjid al-Ḥarām*. From all this we can see that the meaning is: Incline our hearts to the Truth.

Al-Fuḍayl ibn 'Iyāḍ said that the Straight Path is the path of *ḥajj*. This is a very specific meaning and a general meaning is far more likely. Muḥammad ibn al-Ḥanafiyya said about the words, *"Guide us to the Straight Path"* that they mean to the *dīn* of Allah and that no other kind of worship is accepted. 'Āṣim al-Aḥwal said that Abū'l-'Āliyya said, "The Straight Path is the Messenger of Allah, may Allah bless him and grant him peace, and his two Companions after him," 'Āṣim said, "I said to al-Ḥusayn that 'Abū'l-'Āliyya said that the Straight Path was the Messenger of Allah, may Allah bless him and grant him peace, and his two companions after him." He said, "He spoke the truth and was faithful."

The root meaning of *ṣirāṭ* in Arabic is "a way". It is also related with a *sīn* rather than a *ṣād*, from *istirāṭ*, meaning "swallowing", implying the swallowing up of the Path by the one who travels on it. It is related that it should be pronounced between a *zāyy* and a *ṣād*. It is related with a pure *zāyy*, but *sīn* is the root. Salama related that al-Farrā' said that *zirāṭ* with a pure *zāyy* is the dialect of 'Udhra, Kalb and the Banū'l-Qayn.

"Straight" is an adjective describing "Path" and it means one which has no crookedness or deviation in it. We find it used in the words of the Almighty, *"This is My Path and it is straight, so follow it."* (6:153)

the Path of those whom You have blessed

This "Path" is the same as the first and the meaning is: "continue to guide us". Someone may be guided to the path and then prevented from going along it. It is said that it is another path and means knowledge of Allah Almighty and recognition of Him. Ja'far ibn Muḥammad said that.

There are ten readings of the word normally recited as *'alayhim* used in this phrase. It can be recited as *'alayhum, 'alayhim, 'alayhimī, 'alayhimū, 'alayhumū, 'alayhumu*. These are the six forms related from the imāms among the reciters. There are four other possibilities transmitted from the Arabs, but not related from the reciters. 'Umar ibn al-Khaṭṭāb and Ibn az-Zubayr recited *ṣirāṭa man* (the path of him who) instead of *ṣirāṭa alladhīna* (the path of those who).

People disagree about the identity of those who are blessed. The majority of commentators say that it means the Prophets, the people of truth, the martyrs and the righteous. They deduce that from the *āyat* in *Sūrat an-Nisā'*: *"Whoever obeys Allah and the Messenger will be with those whom Allah has blessed: the Prophets and the true, the martyrs and the righteous. What excellent company such people are!"* (4:69) It is clear from this *āyat* that these are the people who have been blessed by Allah and therefore those who are referred to in the *Fātiḥa* as following the Straight Path. So what we are asking for in the *Fātiḥa* is to be taken on the path which they have followed. Everything which has been said on this subject boils down to this and so there is no sense in mentioning all the different positions, and Allah is the One whom we ask for success.

This *āyat* contains a refutation of the Qadariyya, Mu'tazilites and Shi'a because they believe that the will of a human being alone is enough to initiate his actions, obedience or disobedience. They believe that man is the creator of his own actions and so he does not need his Lord to originate them. Allah refutes them in this *āyat* since in it we ask Him for guidance to the Straight Path. If the matter had really been in their hands and the choice really been theirs and not their Lord's, they would not need to ask Him for guidance or to repeat that request in every prayer. They also pray to Him to avert from them what is disliked which are those things contrary to guidance. They say, *"The path of those whom You have blessed, not of those with anger on them nor of the misguided."* As they ask Him to guide them, they also ask Him not to misguide them. That is how they pray, saying, *"Our Lord, do not make our hearts swerve aside after You have guided us."* (3:8)

Not of those with anger on them, nor of the misguided

There is also disagreement about the identity of "those with anger on them" and the "misguided". The majority say that those with anger on them are the Jews and the misguided are the Christians. That was explained by the Prophet, may Allah bless him and grant him peace, in the *ḥadīth* of 'Adī ibn Ḥātim and the story of how he became Muslim, transmitted by Abū Dāwūd in his *Musnad* and at-Tirmidhī in his *Collection*. That explanation is also attested to by the Almighty who says about the Jews, *"They brought down anger from Allah upon themselves"* (2:61, 3:112) and He says, *"Allah is angry with them."* (48:6) He says about the Christians that they, *"were misguided previously and have misguided many others, and are far from the right way."* (5:77)

It is said that those with anger on them are the idolaters and that the misguided are the hypocrites. It is said that those with anger on them are those who omit the obligation of reciting this *sūra* in the prayer, and the misguided are those who lose the blessing of its recitation. In *al-Ḥaqā'iq*, as-Sulamī said, as did al-Māwardī in his *tafsīr,* that this is nonsense. Al-Māwardī said that this view is rejected. It is said that "those with anger on them" refers to people who follow innovations and that the misguided are those who lose the *sunna* of guidance. This is good. The explanation of the Messenger of Allah, may Allah bless him and grant him peace, is more appropriate, higher and better.

Linguistically "*ghaḍab*" (anger) means intensity of feeling. A man who is *ghaḍūb* is prone to anger. *Ghaḍūb* is a serpent which is malignant because of its severity. *Ghaḍba* is a shield made from camel hide, one part of which is folded over the other. It is called that because of its strength. The meaning of anger when it is attributed to Allah is the desire to punish and it is an attribute of the Essence since the will of Allah is one of the attributes of the Essence. Some people say it is the punishment itself. A corroboration of that view is the *ḥadīth*, "*Ṣadaqa* extinguishes the anger of the Lord."

The word "misguidance" (*ḍalāl*) in Arabic means "missing the target and straying from the path of Truth". One way the word is used is when milk disappears (*ḍalla*) in water. It is also used in the *āyat*, *"When we have been absorbed* (ḍalalnā) *into the earth"* (32:10), i.e. we disappear by death and become dust.

'Umar ibn al-Khaṭṭāb and Ubayy ibn Ka'b inserted a second *ghayri* before *ḍāllīn.* The word *ghayri* makes something definite because it can only be one of two things, as you say, "The living is not (*ghayri*) the dead; the one who is still is not (*ghayri*) the one moving, and the one standing is not (*ghayri*) the one sitting."

2
Sūrat al-Baqara

We will first mention its revelation, excellence and summarise its contents. We will do that with each *sūra*.

Sūrat al-Baqara is Madinan and parts of it were revealed at various times. It is said that it was the first *sūra* to be revealed in Madina, except for Allah's words *"Have fear of a Day when you will be returned to Allah."* (2:281) which was the last *āyat* to be revealed. It was revealed on the Day of Sacrifice during the Farewell Ḥajj, at Mina. The *āyat*s about usury were also numbered the last *āyat*s to be revealed of the Qur'ān.

The excellence of this *sūra* is unsurpassed and the reward for reciting it is enormous. It is called the Pavilion (*fusṭāṭ*) of the Qur'ān. Khālid ibn Ma'dān said that. That is due to its greatness and splendour and the great number of rulings and warnings it contains. 'Umar, may Allah be pleased with him, spent twelve years learning it, its *fiqh* and contents and his son spent eight years. Ibn al-'Arabī said, "I heard one of our shaykhs say, 'It contains a thousand commands, a thousand prohibitions, a thousand rulings and a thousand reports.'" The Messenger of Allah, may Allah bless him and grant him peace, sent an expedition consisting of a number of men and he put the youngest of them in charge of them because he knew *Sūrat al-Baqara*. He told him, "Go! You are its commander." (At-Tirmidhī from Abū Hurayra, *ṣaḥīḥ*). Muslim related from Abū Umāma al-Bāhilī, "I heard the Messenger of Allah, may Allah bless him and grant him peace, say, 'Read *Sūrat al-Baqara*. Learning it is a blessing, abandoning it is a cause of regret, and sorcerers are impotent before it.'"

It is also related from Abū Hurayra that the Messenger of Allah, may Allah bless him and grant him peace, said, "Do not turn your houses into graveyards. Shayṭān flees from a house in which *Sūrat al-Baqara* is recited." Ad-Dārimī related that Ibn Mas'ūd said, "There is no house in which *Sūrat al-Baqara* is recited but that Shayṭān leaves it breaking wind." The Prophet, may Allah bless him and grant him peace, also said, "Everything has a hump and the hump of the Qur'ān is *Sūrat al-Baqara*. Everything has a core and the core of the Qur'ān is the *Mufaṣṣal.*[1]" In the *Ṣaḥīḥ* of al-Bustī, Sahl ibn Sa'd reported that the Messenger of Allah, may Allah bless him and grant him peace, said, "Every thing has a hump and the hump of the Qur'ān is *Sūrat al-Baqara*. If someone recites it in his house at night, Shayṭān will not enter his house for three nights. If someone recites it during the day, Shayṭān will not enter his house for three days." Al-Bustī says that what is meant are the rebellious shayṭāns.

Ad-Dārimī reported in his *Musnad* from ash-Sha'bī that 'Abdullāh ibn Mas'ūd said, "If anyone recites ten *āyat*s of *Sūrat al-Baqara* in the night, Shayṭān will not enter that house that night until morning. They are: the four at the beginning of it, the *Āyat al-Kursī* and the two following it, and the three at the end, which begin *'Everything in the heavens and everything in the earth belongs to Allah'* (2:284)." Ash-Sha'bī said that neither Shayṭān nor anything he dislikes will come near him or his family that day. They are not recited over a mad person without him recovering. Al-Mughīra ibn Subay', one of the companions of Ibn Mas'ūd, said, "And he will not forget the Qur'ān." Isḥāq ibn 'Īsā said, "He will not forget what he has memorised."

We read in the *Kitāb al-Isti'āb* of Ibn 'Abdu'l-Barr: "Labīd ibn Rabī'a was one of the poets of the *Jāhiliyya*. He lived until the time of Islam and became a good Muslim and abandoned his poetry after entering the *dīn.* While he was khalif, 'Umar asked him about his poetry and asked him to recite some. He recited *Sūrat al-Baqara* and 'Umar said, "I asked about your poetry." He said, "I have not uttered a line of poetry since Allah taught me *al-Baqara* and *Āl 'Imrān.*" 'Umar liked what he said, and gave him a large sum of money and then added more. Many historians say that Labīd did not utter any poetry from the time he became Muslim.

1. *Mufaṣṣal*: the *sūras* of the Qur'ān starting from *Sūrat Qaf* (50) to the end of the Qur'ān.

الٓمٓ ﴿١﴾

1 Alif. Lam. Mim.

Interpreters disagree about the letters at the beginnings of the *sūra*s. ‘Āmir ash-Sha‘bī, Sufyān ath-Thawrī and a group of *ḥadīth* scholars say that Allah has a secret in each of His Books and these letters are Allah’s secret in the Qur’ān. They form part of the *mutashābih* (open to interpretation) *āyat*s in the Qur’ān about which only Allah knows. It is not necessary to discuss them but one should simply believe in them and recite them as they have come. This position was related from Abū Bakr aṣ-Ṣiddīq and ‘Alī ibn Abī Ṭālib. Abū’l-Layth as-Samarqandī related that ‘Umar, ‘Uthmān and Ibn Mas‘ūd said, “The ‘separated’ letters are part of a hidden knowledge which cannot be explained.” Abū Ḥātim said, “We only find the ‘separated’ letters in the Qur’ān at the beginning of the *sūra*s. We do not know what Allah means by them.”

This was also stated by Abū Bakr al-Anbārī, who reported via an *isnād*, that ar-Rabī‘ ibn Khuthaym said, “Allah Almighty revealed this Qur’ān and He has kept the knowledge of whatever He wishes for Himself and He has acquainted you with what He wishes. As for what He has kept to Himself, you will not acquire it, so do not ask about it. As for what He has acquainted you with, it is that which you can ask and report about. You do not know the entire Qur’ān and you will not teach all that you know.” Abū Bakr said, “This tells us that the meanings of the letters of the Qur’ān are concealed from everyone as a test from Allah Almighty. Anyone who believes in them is rewarded and is fortunate. Anyone who rejects and doubts them sins and is far from Allah’s mercy.” ‘Abdullāh ibn Mas‘ūd said, “A believer does not have any belief in anything better than belief in the unseen.” Then he recited, *“those who believe in the Unseen.”* (2:3)

This is the basic position and ruling about the *mutashābih*. It is sound according to the evidence which will be presented when the matter is again addressed at the beginning of *Āl ‘Imrān*, Allah willing. The position of a large group of scholars, however, is that we should speak about this matter and search out the benefits it contains and the ideas which can be deduced from it. People disagree about the letters and say many different things. It is related from Ibn 'Abbās and 'Alī that the "separated" letters in the Qur'ān are the greatest Name of Allah, though we do not know how it is composed from them.

Quṭrub, al-Farrā' and others say that it is simply about the letters of the alphabet – and Allah knows best – so that when the Arabs were challenged by the Qur'ān to produce something like it, it would be clear that it is composed of the same letters which are the basis of their normal language. That would make their inability to duplicate it all the more apparent in the proof against them since there is nothing in it outside of the letters they use in their everyday speech. Quṭrub said, "They used to run away when they heard the Qur'ān. When they heard, *'Alif Lām Mīm'* and *'Alif Lām Mīm Ṣād'*, they did not know this expression and so they stopped to listen to him, may Allah bless him and grant him peace, and he then presented the familiar Qur'ān to them so that it would be firm in their hearing and ears and would be evidence against them." Some people say as corroboration for this, "It is related that, when the idolaters refused to listen to the Qur'ān in Makka and said, '*Do not listen to this Qur'ān. Drown it out*' (41:26), these letters were revealed so that they would find it odd and start to listen. So they began listening to the Qur'ān and the evidence against them was clearly established."

Another group said that they are letters which indicate the names of things from which they are taken. Ibn 'Abbās and others said that *Alif* is from Allah, *Lām* from Jibrīl and *Mīm* from Muḥammad, may Allah bless him and grant him peace. It is said that *alif* is the beginning of the Divine Name Allah, *lām* is the beginning of the Divine Name *Laṭīf*, and *Mīm* is the beginning of the Divine Name *Majīd*. Abū'ḍ-Ḍuḥā related from Ibn 'Abbās that *"Alif Lām Mīm"* means: "I, Allah, know best." *"Alif Lām Rā"* means: "I, Allah, see." And *"Alif Lām Mīm Ṣād"* means: "I, Allah, bestow." So the *alif* indicates the idea "I", *lām* indicates the name Allah, and *mīm* indicates the meaning "I know." Az-Zajjāj preferred this position and said, "I believe that each letter has a meaning. "

Zayd ibn Aslam said, "They are the names of the *sūra*s." Al-Kalbī said, "They are oaths which Allah Almighty swore by due to their excellence and honour. They are an aspect of His Names." Ibn 'Abbās also said that. Some scholars refute this position saying that it is not valid for them to be oaths because an oath is always connected to a particle, such as *inna*, *qad*, *laqad* or *mā*. None of these is used here and so it is not correct to say that they are oaths. The reply to that is that the object of the oath is His words, "*without any doubt*". If a man were to swear, saying, "By Allah, there is no doubt in this Book," then the words would be correct. "*Lā*" [no] is the complement of the oath. So the position of al-Kalbī and what is reported from Ibn 'Abbās is confirmed as being both correct and valid.

If it is asked what the wisdom is in an oath from Allah Almighty, when people in that time were in two groups: those who accepted and those who denied since those who accept do so without an oath and those who deny will not believe even with an oath, the answer is that the Qur'ān was revealed in the language of the Arabs and when one of the Arabs wanted to stress his words, he would swear to what he said. Allah Almighty wanted to stress the proof to them and so He swore that the Qur'ān was from Him.

Some say that *"alif lām mīm"* means: "This Book was revealed to you from the Preserved Tablet." Qatāda said, "*Alif Lām Mīm* is one of the Names of the Qur'ān." It is related that Muḥammad ibn 'Alī at-Tirmidhī said, "Allah Almighty summed up all the rulings and stories which are in that *sūra* in the letters which are mentioned at the beginning of it. That can only be understood by a Prophet or a *walī*. Then He made that clear throughout the entire *sūra* so that all people would understand it." Other things are said as well, and Allah knows best.

ذَٰلِكَ ٱلْكِتَٰبُ لَا رَيْبَ فِيهِ هُدًى لِّلْمُتَّقِينَ ۝٢

2. ***That is the Book, without any doubt.***
In it is guidance for the godfearing:

That is the Book

It is said that *"That is the Book"* really means "This is the Book". The word "that" is used here to indicate what is present, even if its normal usage is to indicate something absent, just as Allah says about Himself, *"That is the Knower of the Unseen and the Visible, the Almighty, the Most Merciful."* (32:6) So the word "that" indicates the Qur'ān. In short the meaning is: "*Alif Lām Mīm*. This Book is without any doubt." That is the position of Abū 'Ubayda, 'Ikrima and others. We find support for it in the words of the Almighty, *"That* (tilka) *is the argument We gave to Ibrāhīm."* (6:83) and *"Those* (tilka) *are Allah's Signs which we recite to you with truth."* (2:252). But when they become as if they were distant, the word "that" is used. In al-Bukhārī we find, "Ma'mar said, 'That Book is the Qur'ān.'"

There are many other things said about the meaning of these words. It is said that *"That is the Book"* refers to the Book which accompanies all human beings, containing the information about whether they will be happy or wretched in the Next World, their lifespan and their provision, and the whole phrase means that there is no way of altering it. It is said that *"That is the Book"* means: "That which I wrote for Myself before time: 'My mercy precedes My anger.'" In the *Ṣaḥīḥ* of Muslim, Abū Hurayra reported that the Messenger of Allah, may Allah bless him and grant him peace, said, "When Allah finished creation, He wrote in His Book which is with Him, 'My mercy predominates over (or precedes) My anger.'"

It is said that Allah Almighty promised His Prophet, peace be upon him, that He would send down on him a Book which water would not erase. It indicates the promise which is referred to in the

Ṣaḥīḥ of Muslim in the *ḥadīth* of 'Iyāḍ ibn Ḥimār al-Majāsha'ī when the Messenger of Allah, may Allah bless him and grant him peace, said, "Allah looked at the people of the earth and hated them, Arabs and non-Arabs, except for the remainder of the People of the Book. He said, 'I sent you to test you and to test others by you. I sent down to you a Book which cannot be washed away by water. You recite it asleep and awake.'"

It is said that this phrase indicates the part of the Qur'ān which was promised in Makka. It is said that when Allah Almighty revealed to His Prophet, may Allah bless him and grant him peace, in Makka, *"We will impose a weighty Word upon you"* (73:5), the Messenger of Allah, may Allah bless him and grant him peace, continued to wait for this promise to be fulfilled by his Lord. When *"Alif Lām. Mīm. That is the Book, without any doubt"* (2:2) was revealed to him in Madina, it had the meaning: this Qur'ān which was revealed to you in Madina is that Book which you were promised and which I revealed to you in Makka.

It is said that the word "That" indicates what was revealed in the Torah and Gospel concerning the Qur'ān. The implication is that it is that Book which was foretold by the Torah and Gospel. The Gospel and Torah testify to its soundness and it deals with what is in them as well as containing things which are not in them. It is said that *"That is the Book"* is a reference to the Torah and Gospel themselves, so that the meaning is "*Alif Lām Mīm.* Those two Books" or the like of those two Books, meaning that this Qur'ān contains what is in those two Books. So the word "that" indicates two, the possibility of which is attested to in the Qur'ān when Allah Almighty says, *"A cow, not old or virgin, but somewhere between the two* (dhālika)" (2:68), making it clear that the word "that" can refer to two things.

It is said that *"That is the Book"* refers to the Preserved Tablet, that Book on which the destinies of all existent things are recorded. Al-Kisā'ī said that it refers to the Qur'ān in heaven which had not yet been revealed. It is said that Allah Almighty promised the people of the Book that He would send down a Book to Muḥammad, may Allah bless him and grant him peace, and so it indicates that promise. Al-Mubarrad said that the meaning is that this Qur'ān is that Book by which you seek victory against the unbelievers.

It is also said that it means all the letters of the alphabet, out of which all books are composed. This is somewhat borne out by the derivation of the word *kitāb* (book) which is a verbal noun from *kataba, yaktubu*. From it comes *katība* (squadron), so called because it is composed of horsemen gathered together and *takattaba* is used when horses are deployed in squadrons. *Kutba* is a seam, and the plural is *kutab*. So *kitāb* is the writing by the scribe of the letters of the alphabet joined together in words. It is called a Book, even if it is just writing. The word *kitāb* also denotes obligation, judgement, prescription and the decree.

without any doubt.

The word "doubt" (*rayb*) has three meanings. One is doubt, the second is suspicion, and the third is need. So there is no doubt and no suspicion about the Book of Allah Almighty. It means that it is true in itself and it is revealed from Allah and is one of His qualities, uncreated and not within time, even if the unbelievers doubt that. It is said that the phrase is a prohibition, meaning "Do not doubt." The words end as if He were saying, "That Book is true." The word *rāba* is used when you have doubt and fear about something.

In it is guidance

The word *hudā* (guidance) in Arabic means right guidance and clarification, in other words it involves unveiling, guidance and increased clarification for the people who recognise it.

There are two types of guidance. Guidance can mean pointing out the way and this is what the Messengers and their followers are able to do. Allah says, *"Every people has a guide."* (13:7) He said, *"You are guiding to a straight path."* (42:52) So he has given you that aspect of guidance which entails direction, calling to the truth and admonition. That aspect of guidance, however, which involves people actually following the path and reaching the goal is the business of Allah alone. He says to his Prophet, may Allah bless him and grant him peace, *"You cannot guide those you would like to."* (28:56) Guidance here means filling the heart with faith. Further examples of this are when Allah says, *"They are the people guided by their Lord,"* (2:5) and *"He guides whoever He wills"* (35:8) where guidance means being actually moved to the path of guidance.

Abū'l-Mu'ālī said, "Guidance means 'bringing to' and it entails guiding the believers to the paths of the Garden and roads which lead to it, as in the words of Allah describing those who do *jihād*, *'He will not let their actions go astray. He will guide them...'* (47:4-5) or in the case of the unbelievers to the Fire, as in His words, *'Guide them to the Path of the Blazing Fire'* (37:23)."

for the godfearing:

Allah Almighty singled out the godfearing for His guidance, even though the Qur'ān, in fact, is guidance for all creatures, in order to honour them because they believe and affirm what it contains. It is related that Abū Rawq said, "*'Guidance for the godfearing'* means honour for them. It is ascribed to them out of esteem and honour for them and to show their excellence."

The word "godfearing" is derived from *taqwā* whose linguistic root is said to mean to be sparing of words. Ibn Fāris related that. That is indicated by the *ḥadīth*, "The godly (*taqī*) is sparing in his words and the godfearing (*muttaqī*) is above both the believers and the obedient." He is someone who protects himself, by his righteous actions and sincere supplication, from Allah's punishment. It is derived from guarding oneself against the disliked by putting a barrier between you and it.

It is reported that Ibn Mas'ūd said one day to his nephew, "Nephew, do you see how many people there are?" "Yes," he replied. He said, "There is no good in any of them except those who turn to Allah or are godfearing." Then he added, "Nephew, do you see how many people there are?" "Yes," he replied. He said, "There is no good in them except for a man of knowledge or a student." Abū Yazīd al-Bisṭāmī said, "A godfearing person is someone whose words are for Allah when he speaks and whose actions are for Allah when he acts." Abū Sulaymān ad-Dārānī said, "The godfearing are those from whose hearts love of appetites has been stripped away." It is said that a godfearing person is one who is protected from *shirk* and free of hypocrisy. Ibn 'Aṭiyya said, "This is false because someone could be like that and still be a deviator." In relation to *taqwā* 'Umar ibn al-Khaṭṭāb asked Ubayy, "Have you ever taken a path between thorny bushes?" "Yes," he replied. He said, "What did you do?" He said. "I gathered in my clothes and was careful." He said, "That is *taqwā*."

Taqwā comprises all good. It is Allah's directive to all human beings and it is the best acquisition a person can get. Abū'd-Dardā' was asked, "Your companions utter poetry but you do not memorise any of it." He refuted them, declaiming:

A man wants to be given his desire
but Allah only gives him what He wills.
A man says, 'My profit and my property,'
but *taqwā* of Allah is the best thing that can be acquired.

ٱلَّذِينَ يُؤْمِنُونَ بِٱلْغَيْبِ وَيُقِيمُونَ ٱلصَّلَوٰةَ وَمِمَّا
رَزَقْنَٰهُمْ يُنفِقُونَ ٣

3 ***those who believe in the Unseen***
and establish the prayer
and spend from what We have provided for them;

those who believe

The word "believe" here means hold to be true. Linguistically *īmān* (faith, belief) is affirmation. In the Revelation the words of the brothers of Yūsuf *"You will not believe us,"* (12:17) mean "believe that we are telling the truth". Qatāda is reported as saying, "Son of Ādam, if the only time you want to do good is when you are feeling enthusiastic, you should know that it is the nature of the self to incline to ennui, indifference and boredom; the believer, however, is the one who spurs himself on; the believer is the one who takes heart; the believer is the one who remains strong. The believers are those who cry out to Allah night and day. By Allah, a true believer continues to say, 'O Lord' secretly and openly until he is answered secretly and openly."

in the Unseen

In the language of the Arabs, the *ghayb* (Unseen) denotes everything which is hidden from you. It is used for the setting of the sun. *Mughība* is used for a woman when her husband is absent. We fall into a *ghayba*, meaning a hole in the ground. *Ghayāba* is a forest, which is a group of trees into which one disappears. It is also used for low-lying ground, because it is out of sight.

Scholars disagree about the meaning of the word here. Some say that what is meant by "Unseen" in this *āyat* is Allah Himself. Ibn al-'Arabī said that this is weak. Others have said that it is the Decree; others that it is the Qur'ān and the unseen things it contains; others that the Unseen are those matters about which the Messengers report which are beyond the scope of human intellect: the signs of the Last Hour, the punishment of the grave, the Gathering, the Resurrection, the *Sirāṭ*, the Scales, the Garden and the Fire. Ibn 'Aṭiyya said that these statements are not mutually exclusive. The Unseen refers to all of them.

It is, in fact, the prescribed faith indicated in the *ḥadīth* of Jibrīl when he said to the Prophet, may Allah bless him and grant him peace, "Tell me about faith (*īmān*)." He replied, "It is to believe in Allah, His angels, His Books, His Messengers, and the Last Day, and to believe in the decree, both its good and its evil." He said, "You have spoken the truth." 'Abdullāh ibn Mas'ūd said, "There is no faith better for the believer than faith in the Unseen." Then he recited, *"Those who believe in the Unseen."* (2:3)

In the Qur'ān we find, *"We are never absent* (ghā'ibīn)" (7:7), and also, *"Those who fear their Lord in the Unseen."* (21:49). Allah cannot be seen by the eyes and cannot be seen in this dimension of existence but He is not absent to investigation and deduction. The believers believe that they have a powerful Lord who will repay all their actions. They fear Him in their hearts and fear Him when they are alone where others cannot see them, through their knowledge that He is aware of them. These *āyat*s agree and there is no contradiction in them. Praise be to Allah!

"Unseen" is also said to mean their consciences and hearts. According to this understanding, the words *"they believe in the Unseen"* mean "they believe in their hearts". In other words, their hearts are filled with faith in contradistinction to the hearts of the hypocrites which are empty of faith. That is what al-Ḥasan said.

and establish

Establishing the prayer means performing it together with its pillars, *sunna*s and positions at the correct time as will be explained. *Qāma* here does not have the normal meaning of "stand" but rather means to continue with and firmly establish.

The call known as the *iqāma* of the prayer is well-known. It is *sunna* with the majority so that, if someone fails to recite it, he does not have to repeat the prayer. Al-Awzā'ī, 'Aṭā', Mujāhid, and Ibn Abī Laylā, however, made it obligatory and anyone who forgets it has to repeat the prayer. Some scholars say that, if someone abandons it intentionally, he should repeat the prayer. That is not because it is obligatory since, if it that were the case, those who forget and those who abandon it deliberately would be subject to the same judgement. It is for making light of the *sunna*. Allah knows best.

the prayer

Linguistically the root of the word "*ṣalāt*" (prayer) means supplication. Evidence for that is the words of the Prophet, "When one of you is invited for food, he should accept. If he is not fasting, he should eat, and if he is fasting, he should make supplication (*ṣallā*)." When Asmā' gave birth to 'Abdullāh ibn az-Zubayr, she sent him to the Prophet, may Allah bless him and grant him peace. Asmā' said, "He wiped his head and prayed (*ṣallā*) for him," meaning made supplication.

Some people say that it is derived from the word *ṣalā*, which is the cord in the middle of the back which separates at the base of the spine and goes round it. From it is also derived the word *muṣallā* for the second horse in a horse race, because at the end of the race, his head is at the rump (*ṣalwān*) of the horse in front. So the derivation of the *ṣalāt* from this is either because it is the second pillar after the declaration of faith and so it resembles someone coming second immediately behind another horse, or because the back of the one who bows in the prayer is bent, in which case *ṣalā* refers to the bending of the horse's back. 'Alī said, using the word with this meaning, "The Messenger of Allah, may Allah bless him and grant him peace, came first, Abū Bakr second (*ṣallā*) and 'Umar third."

It is also said to be taken from the idea of warming a branch with fire to straighten it and make it supple by heat since *ṣilā'* means roasting by fire, thus referring to how the one who prays straightens himself by his efforts and makes himself supple and humble. *Ṣalāt* can also mean supplication and mercy, as in "O Allah, bless (*ṣalli*) Muhammad." *Ṣalāt* is also an undefined act of worship. Allah says, *"Their prayer* (ṣalāt) *at the House"* (8:35), meaning their worship.

There is disagreement about what is meant by "the prayer" in this instance. It is said that it is both the obligatory and voluntary prayers, and that is the sound position because the expression is undefined.

The prayer is only valid if all its preconditions and obligatory elements are fulfilled. Among its preconditions is purity. Its rulings will be explained in *Sūrat an-Nisā'* and *Sūrat al-Mā'ida.* The private parts must be covered, which will be dealt with in *Sūrat al-A'rāf*, Allah willing. Its obligatory elements are facing the *qibla*, the intention, the *takbīr al-iḥrām* and standing for it, reciting the *Fātiḥa* and standing for it, *rukū'* and being still in it, rising from *rukū'* and standing up straight, prostration and being still in it, rising from prostration, sitting between the two prostrations and being still in it, the second prostration and being still in it, and the final sitting and being still in it.

The source for all this is the *ḥadīth* of Abū Hurayra about the man who had prayed incorrectly whom the Prophet, may Allah bless him and grant him peace, taught. He told him, "When you stand for the prayer, do *wuḍū'* thoroughly and then face the *qibla*. Say the *takbīr* and then recite what is easy of the Qur'ān. Then bow and remain still in it and then come up until you are standing straight. Then prostrate until you are still in prostration. Then come up until you are still in sitting. Then do the like of that in all your prayer." (Muslim)

Our scholars said, "The Prophet, may Allah bless him and grant him peace, explained to us the pillars of the prayer. He said nothing about the *iqāma*, raising the hands, the amount of recitation, the *takbīr*s for the movements, the glorification in *rukū'* and prostration, the middle sitting, the *tashahhud* for the final sitting and the *salām*. As for the *iqāma* and the specific requirement of the *Fātiḥa*, they have already been discussed.

The prayer is one of the causes of provision, as will be explained in *Sūra TāHā*, Allah willing, in the explanation of the *āyat*, *"Instruct your people to do the prayer..."* (20:132). The prayer also contains healing for stomach pains and other things. Ibn Mājah related that Abū Hurayra said, "I prayed and then sat down. The Prophet, may Allah bless him and grant him peace, turned to me and said in Persian, 'You have a stomach ache?' I said, 'Yes, Messenger of Allah.' He said, 'Then pray. There is healing in prayer.'" After that, when something serious happened to him, he devoted himself to the prayer.

and spend from what We have provided for them;

The word "provided" means "given to". Provision, according to the people who follow the *Sunna,* refers to everything which can be used, *ḥarām* or *ḥalāl*, as opposed to the Mu'tazilites who say that the *ḥarām* is not provision because it is not valid for a person to own it. According to them Allah does not "provide" the *ḥarām*, He only "provides" the *ḥalāl*; only something which is validly owned can properly be called provision. So, according to them, if a child grows up with thieves and only eats what the thieves eat until he is adult and strong and then himself becomes a thief and remains a thief and eats what he steals until he dies, Allah has not provided him with anything, since everything he ever consumed was *ḥarām* and he did not validly own it. He dies, therefore, without having consumed any of Allah's provision. This is false and the evidence for it is that, if provision had meant legally valid ownership, it would mean that no child could receive provision, nor could any animal which grazes in the wilderness, nor could a lamb because its mother's milk belongs to its owner and not to the lamb.

The Community agree that children, lambs and beasts are provided for and that Allah Almighty provides for them, even though they are not the owners of anything, because it is known that nourishment is an aspect of provision. The Community also agree that slaves are provided for and that Allah Almighty provides for them although they are not owners. So it is clear that provision is what we have said, not what the Mu'tazilites say.

All nourishment is provision and there is no provider except Allah: *"Is there any creator other than Allah providing for you from what is in heaven and the earth."* (35:3) He says, *"Allah is the Provider, the Possessor of Strength, the Sure."* (51:58) He says, *"There is no creature on the earth which is not dependent upon Allah for its provision."* (11:6) This is definite. Allah Almighty is the true Provider in every instance. The son of Ādam is a mere recipient because his ownership of property is, in fact, only metaphorical as we have made clear in our commentary on the *Fātiḥa*. He is provided for, like the animals which truly own nothing. If the thing is something he is permitted to obtain, it is *ḥalāl* for him and if it is not permitted, it is *ḥarām* for him, but nevertheless all of it is provision. One great man of knowledge explained the words of Allah, *"Eat of your Lord's provision and give thanks to Him, a bountiful land and a forgiving Lord."* (34:15) by saying the adjective "forgiving" (*ghafūr*) used in it indicates that provision may contain what is unlawful.

The word for "those who spend" (*yunfiqūn*) means "to bring something out". "Spending" is to give out money with the hand. *Nafaqa*, in regard to a sale, means to transfer money from the hand of the seller to the hand of the buyer. *Nafaqa* is used for an animal when its life leaves it. From the same root comes *nāfiqā'*, the other entrance of the hole of the jerboa from which it emerges when it is attacked from the other entrance. We also have the word *munāfiq* (hypocrite), so called because he leaves belief or belief leaves his heart. *Nayfaq* is used for trousers because the legs emerge from them. *Nafaqa* is also used for something which is spent, used up or comes to an end. An example of that usage is in the words of Allah, *"You would still hold back out of the fear it would run out."* (17:100)

Scholars disagree about what is meant by the giving of provision in this instance. It is said that it refers to obligatory *zakāt*. That is related from Ibn 'Abbās and is because the prayer accompanies it. It is said that it refers to what a man spends on his family. That is related from Ibn Mas'ūd because that is the best type of expenditure. Muslim related from Abū Hurayra that the Messenger of Allah, may Allah bless him and grant him peace, said, "Out of a dinar which you spend in the way of Allah and a dinar which you spend on freeing a slave and a dinar which you give to a poor person and a dinar which you spend on your family, the one with the greatest reward is the one which you spend on your family." It is related from Thawbān that the Messenger of Allah, may Allah bless him and grant him peace, said, "Is not the best dinar a man spends the dinar which he spends on his family and the dinar which he spends on his mount in the way of Allah and the dinar which he spends on his companions in the way of Allah?" Abū Qilāba said, "He began with the family," and then he continued, "What man could have a greater reward than someone who spends on a young family to keep them virtuous, or Allah gives them the benefit of him and he enriches them."

It is also said that what is meant here is voluntary *ṣadaqa*. That is related from aḍ-Ḍaḥḥāk in reference to the fact that obligatory *zakāt* is only referred to with the expression particular to it, which is the word *zakāt*. When a word other than *zakāt* is used, it may be obligatory or voluntary. When the word "spend" is used, it is only voluntary. Aḍ-Ḍahhāk said, "Spending was, at first, a kind of sacrifice by which a person drew near to Allah Almighty according to his effort in it until Allah revealed the obligations of *zakāt* in *Sūrat at-Tawba* (9) which abrogated that." It is said that it refers to obligatory rights on wealth other than *zakāt* because by connecting it to the prayer, Allah Almighty, is indicating that they are obligatory, and the fact that He uses another expression shows that this is an obligation other than *zakāt*.

It is said that its meaning is general and that is a sound position because Allah praises all kinds of spending out from what we are provided with. In that case the meaning is that they pay the *zakāt* obliged by the *Sharī'a* and also spend in other ways in which it is recommended for them to spend. It is said that *"belief in the Unseen"* is the portion of the heart, *"establishing the prayer"* is the portion of the body and *"spending from what they are provided with"* is the portion of wealth. This is evident. Some early scholars said in their interpretation of the words of Allah Almighty, *"they spend from what We have provided them,"* that they refer to people teaching others some of what Allah has taught them.

وَالَّذِينَ يُؤْمِنُونَ بِمَآ أُنْزِلَ إِلَيْكَ وَمَآ
أُنْزِلَ مِن قَبْلِكَ وَبِالْآخِرَةِ هُمْ يُوقِنُونَ ﴿٤﴾

4 ***those who believe in what has been sent down to you***
and what was sent down before you,
and are certain about the Next World.

those who believe in what has been sent down to you and what was sent down before you,

It is said that what is meant here are the believers of the people of the Book, like 'Abdullāh ibn Salām, and that it was revealed about him. The previous *āyat* was revealed about the believers of the Arabs. It is said that both this *āyat* and the previous one are about believers in general.

Allah's words *"what has been sent down to you,"* refer to the Qur'ān, and His words *"and what was sent down before you"* refer to previous books, so this differs from what the Jews and Christians did, since they only believed in their own Books as

Allah tells us later in this *sūra*: *"When they are told, 'Believe in what Allah has sent down,' they say, 'We believe in what was sent down to us.'"* (2:91)

It is said that when this *āyat* was revealed and the words *"those who believe in the Unseen"* came, the Jews and Christians said, "We believe in the Unseen." When Allah said, *"establish the prayer"* (2:3), they said, "We establish the prayer." When He said, *"they spend from what We have provided for them,"* they said, "We spend and give alms." When He said, *"those who believe in what has been sent down to you and what was sent down before you,"* they were averse to that.

There is a question which arises here. How can one believe in all the various Revelations when it is clear that their rulings conflict? Two answers are given. One is that one believes that all of them came from Allah. This is the position of those who abolish all the acts of worship prescribed by prior *sharī'a*s. The second is that one believes in those things in them which have not been abrogated. This is the position of those who say it is obligatory to abide by prior *sharī'a*s, a judgement which will be explained in the proper place.

and are certain about the Next World

The words *"and are certain about the Next World"* refer to the Resurrection after death. Certainty is knowledge free of all doubt. Various forms of this verb (*yaqina*) can be used to express this idea. Sometimes it is possible for this word to indicate the opposite meaning of "conjecture", and we find it in this sense elsewhere in the Qur'ān and in many poems.

أُوْلَٰٓئِكَ عَلَىٰ هُدًى مِّن رَّبِّهِمْۖ وَأُوْلَٰٓئِكَ
هُمُ ٱلْمُفْلِحُونَ ۝٥

5 ***They are the people guided by their Lord.***
They are the ones who have success.

They are the people guided by their Lord.

Our scholars say that the words *"by their Lord"* refute the Qadariyya who say that they themselves are the creators of their own faith and their own guidance. Allah is too exalted for their position to be true. If that had been the case, Allah would have said, "by their own selves". The meaning of the word "guidance" *(hudā)* has already been discussed in the commentary on the second *āyat* of this *sūra*.

They are the ones who have success.

The linguistic root of *"falāḥ"* (success) is *falḥ*, which has the meaning of splitting or cleaving. From it comes *filāḥa*, tillage of the earth when it is ploughed for cultivation. Abū 'Ubayd said that. That is why a ploughman is called a *fallāḥ*. Someone with a split lower lip is called *aflaḥ*. It is as if the one with success cuts through adversity until he reaches his goal. It is used for success and continuation, which is also another aspect of its linguistic root.

The meaning of *"the ones who have success"* in this context is those who win the Garden and remain in it. Ibn Abī Isḥāq said, "The successful are those who attain what they seek and are saved from the evil from which they flee. The meaning is the same." The word *falāḥ* is also used for *saḥūr* (the pre-dawn meal in Ramaḍān), as in the *ḥadīth* recorded by Abū Dāwūd: "Until we almost missed *falāḥ* with the Messenger of Allah, may Allah bless him and grant him peace." It was asked, "What is *falāḥ*?" The answer was, "*Saḥūr.*"

إِنَّ ٱلَّذِينَ كَفَرُوا۟ سَوَآءٌ عَلَيْهِمْ ءَأَنذَرْتَهُمْ
أَمْ لَمْ تُنذِرْهُمْ لَا يُؤْمِنُونَ ٦

6 ***As for those who disbelieve,***
it makes no difference to them
whether you warn them or do not warn them,
they will not believe.

As for those who disbelieve,

After mentioning the believers and their states, Allah then mentions the unbelievers and their end. *Kufr* (disbelief) is the opposite of *īmān* (belief) and that is what is meant in this *āyat*. *Kufr* can also mean ingratitude for blessings and gifts received. The Prophet, peace be upon him, used it in that way when he spoke about women in the eclipse *ḥadīth*: "Then I saw the Fire – and I have never seen anything more hideous than what I saw today – and I saw that most of its inhabitants were women." They asked, "Why, Messenger of Allah?" He replied, "For their *kufr*." It was asked, "Do they reject Allah [or Are they ungrateful to Allah]?" He said, "They are ungrateful to their husbands, and they are ungrateful for good behaviour (towards them). Even if you were to behave well to one of them for a whole lifetime and she were to see you do something (that she did not like) she would say that she had never seen anything good from you." (al-Bukhārī and others)

The root of the verb *kafara* in Arabic indicates covering and hiding. Night is called *kāfir* because it covers everything in darkness. *Kāfir* can also mean a sea or huge river and is also used with the meaning of cultivator – someone who covers seeds with earth. Its plural in that case is *kuffār* rather than *kāfirūn*. Allah Almighty says, *"Like the plant-growth after rain which delights the cultivators (kuffār)"* (57:20). Ashes are called *makfūr* when the wind has swept the dust so that it has covered them. Land which is *kāfir* is that which is so far off the beaten track that people almost never stop in it or pass by it. Those who do stop in such places are people of *kufūr*. It is also said that *kufūr* means isolated villages.

it makes no difference to them

The words *"it makes no difference to them"* mean that it is the same to them whether you warn them or do not.

whether you warn them

His words, *"whether you warn them"* mean to announce and convey warning. The word used here for "warn" (*andhara*) is almost only ever used to alarm people when there is time for them to take measures to avoid the thing they are being warned about. If the situation does not allow for such a time of preparation, it is called announcement (*ish'ār*) and not warning.

Scholars disagree about the interpretation of this *āyat*. It is said to refer to people in general, indicating those against whom the decree of punishment will be carried out. It is an established fact that Allah already knows that these people will die in *kufr*. Allah wanted to tell people about those whose state is like that without being specific.

Ibn 'Abbās and al-Kalbī said that the *āyat* was revealed about the leaders of the Jews in Madina, including Ḥuyayy ibn al-Akhṭab, Ka'b ibn al-Ashraf and those like them. Ar-Rabī' ibn Anas said, "It was revealed about the leaders of the idolaters who were killed at Badr." The first position is sounder. Anyone who says it was revealed about a particular person, can only be referring to someone whose *kufr* was revealed from the Unseen after his death. That is one aspect of the *āyat*.

خَتَمَ ٱللَّهُ عَلَىٰ قُلُوبِهِمْ وَعَلَىٰ سَمْعِهِمْ وَعَلَىٰٓ
أَبْصَٰرِهِمْ غِشَٰوَةٌ وَلَهُمْ عَذَابٌ عَظِيمٌ ٧

7 *Allah has sealed up their hearts and their hearing*
and over their eyes is a blindfold.
They will have a terrible punishment.

Allah has sealed up

The words, *"Allah has sealed up"* make it clear that in this *āyat* Allah debars such people from having faith. The word "*khatama*" (sealed up) means covering a thing and fastening it up so that nothing can enter it. It is used for letters and other such things so that what is inside them cannot be reached or replaced.

Interpreters say that, in His Book, Allah describes the hearts of the unbelievers as having ten qualities: as being sealed up, stamped, constricted, sick, rusted up, dead, hard, turning away, fanatically enraged and in denial. On being in denial, He says: *"Their hearts are in denial and they are puffed up with pride."* (16:22) On fanatical rage: *"When those who disbelieve filled their hearts with fanatical rage."* (48:26) On turning away: *"Then they turn away. Allah has turned their hearts away because they are a people who do not understand."* (9:127) On being hard: *"Woe to those whose hearts are hardened against remembrance of Allah."* (39:22) and: *"Then your hearts became hardened after that."* (2:74) On being dead: *"Someone who was dead and whom We brought to life."* (6:122) and: *"Only those who can hear respond. As for the dead, Allah will raise them up,"* (6:36) On being rusted up: *"No indeed! Rather what they have earned has rusted up their hearts."* (83:14) On being sick: *"Those with sickness in their hearts."* (47:29) On being constricted: *"When He desires to misguide someone, He makes his breast narrow and constricted."* (6:125) On being stamped: *"Their hearts have been stamped so that they do not understand."* (9:87) and: *"Allah has stamped them with* kufr.*"* (4:155) On being sealed up, He says, *"Allah has sealed up their hearts."* (2:7) All will be explained in its proper place, Allah willing.

Sealing up can be physical, as we have made clear, and also spiritual as in this *āyat*. In respect of the heart, being sealed up entails the inability to absorb Allah's words, understand what He says and reflect on His *āyat*s. In respect of hearing, it entails the inability to understand the Qur'ān when it is recited or to respond to the call to believe in the Oneness of Allah. The blindfold over the eyes entails the inability to be guided by means of reflecting on His creatures and the wondrous things He has made. This is what Ibn 'Abbās, Ibn Mas'ūd, Qatāda and others have said about this.

We find in this *āyat* definitive proof of the fact that it is Allah Who is the author of guidance and misguidance, *kufr* and *īmān*. So we can only be amazed at the obtuseness of the minds of the Qadariyya who say that they are the authors of their own faith and guidance. The "sealing up" referred to in the *āyat* is the stamp of *kufr* so how could someone subject to that come to have *īmān*, no matter how hard his striving was? Allah has sealed up their hearts and their hearing and a blindfold has been placed over their eyes. How are they going to be guided and who is going to guide them after Allah when He has misguided them, made them deaf, and blinded their eyes. *"And no one can guide those whom Allah misguides."* (39:23) That action of Allah is nevertheless just, since He does not place any real impediment in the way of those He misguides and disappoints, preventing them from fulfilling those things which are obligatory for them. So the attribute of justice is not negated. He denies them His grace, He does not prevent them doing what was obliged for them.

Some say that the words *"khatm"* (sealing), "*ṭab'*" (stamping) and "*ghishāwa*" (covering) are used metaphorically and are really a way of designating them as unbelievers, judging them to be unbelievers, and reporting that they are unbelievers and are not to be taken as retaining their literal meaning. We say that this is not the case because the reality of this sealing and stamping is an action by which the heart actually becomes sealed and stamped, so it is not correct to take it metaphorically. Do you not see that when it is said, "So-and-so stamped the book and sealed it," it means that the book in question is actually stamped and sealed, not designated or judged. There is no disagreement concerning this among people with knowledge of the language, and the whole community agree that Allah Almighty has described Himself as sealing and stamping the hearts of the unbelievers to repay them for their disbelief, as He says, "*Allah has stamped them with disbelief.*" (4:155). So the sealing and stamping are something which Allah does to a heart which prevents faith entering it. There is evidence for this in His words, *"In that way We insert it into the evildoers' hearts. They do not believe in it,"* (15:12) and He says, *"We have placed covers on their hearts, preventing them from understanding it."* (6:25)

their hearts

Putting the heart first indicates the excellence of the heart over all other limbs and faculties. The core and the noblest part of anything is its heart. The heart is the locus of reflection. The Arabic word for heart, *qalb*, is a verbal noun which means to turn something over completely so that it is returned to how it was at the beginning. "*Qalaba*" (to turn) a vessel is to turn it upside down. Then this image is transferred and used for this organ, the noblest part of the creature, owing to the speed with which thoughts revolve in it. Ibn Mājah reported from Abū Mūsā al-Ash'arī that the Prophet, may Allah bless him and grant him peace, said, "The metaphor of the heart is that of a feather moved by the winds in the desert." This is the meaning which the Prophet expressed when he said, "O Allah, Who makes hearts firm, make our hearts firm in your obedience."

Even though the limbs follow the heart and it is their leader and master, they nevertheless affect it, because the actions they perform make a connection between the outward and the inward. The Prophet, may Allah bless him and grant him peace, said, "A man gives *ṣadaqa* and a white spot is engraved in his heart. A man lies and his heart goes black." At-Tirmidhī reports as a *ṣaḥīḥ ḥadīth* from Abū Hurayra, "A man may commit a sin and his heart becomes black. If he repents, his heart is polished." He said, "That is the rust which Allah mentions in the Qur'ān when He says, *"No indeed! Rather what they have earned has rusted up their hearts."* (83:14) Mujāhid said, "The heart is like a hand which holds a sin with every finger and then is sealed." The Prophet, may Allah bless him and grant him peace, said, "There is a lump of flesh in the body. When it is sound, the entire body is sound, and when it is corrupt, the entire body is corrupt – it is the heart."

Muslim relates a *ḥadīth* from Ḥudhayfa: "The Messenger of Allah, may Allah bless him and grant him peace, related two *ḥadīth*s to us. I have seen one of them come true and am still waiting for the other. He related to us that the quality of trustworthiness had descended into the hearts of men. Then the Qur'ān came down and they knew it from the Qur'ān and they knew it from the *Sunna*. Then he related that trustworthiness would be removed, and he said, 'A man will go to sleep and trustworthiness will be taken from his heart and its trace will remain like a small scar. Then he will go to sleep and trustworthiness will be taken from his heart and its trace will remain like a superficial blister, such as you see when an ember rolls onto someone's foot and it blisters up.' Then he took some pebbles and rolled them onto his foot. 'And people will continue to trade but practically no one will fulfil his trust, to such a point that it will be said, "There is a trustworthy man among the Banū so-and-so!" and until it will be said of a man, "How tough he is! How elegant! How intelligent!" when he does not have even a speck of belief in his heart.' There was a time when I did not care whom I did business with. If he was a Muslim, his *dīn* was sufficient assurance for me, and if he was a Christian or a Jew, his Muslim patron was sufficient assurance for me. Today I only do business with so-and-so and so-and-so among you."

Hudhayfa said that he heard the Messenger of Allah, may Allah bless him and grant him peace, say, "Trials will come upon the hearts, following one after another like the reeds in a woven mat. Any heart which opens the door to them will have a black mark put in it. Any heart which rejects them will have a white mark put in it. Thus hearts will be of two kinds: those which are white like marble which will not be harmed by trial as long as the heavens and the earth endure, and those which are black and dust-coloured like an upset earthen jug, not recognising what is right or rejecting what is wrong, totally permeated by base desires."

The heart is sometimes referred to by the word *fu'ād* and also by the term *ṣadr* (breast). Allah Almighty says, *"It is so that We can fortify your heart* (fu'ād*) by it."* (25:32) He said, *"Did We not expand your breast for you?"* (94:1). In both places it is the heart which is meant. The heart is also often equated with the intellect. Allah Almighty says, *"There is a reminder in that for anyone who has a heart."* (50:37), meaning intelligence, because the heart is the locus of the intellect according to most authorities. *Fu'ād* is the locus of the *qalb* and the breast is the locus of the *fu'ād*. Allah knows best.

and their hearing

The fact that hearing comes before sight in this *āyat* is used as evidence by those who say the hearing is better than vision. Allah also says, *"Say: 'What do you think? If Allah took away your hearing and your sight…'"* (6:46) He said, *"He gave you hearing, sight and hearts."* (32:9) This is said to be because hearing is always receptive from every direction, both in light and darkness, while sight is only effective in one direction at a time and needs light to function. However, most people put sight above hearing because hearing only perceives sounds and words, while sight perceives bodies, colours and all forms. They said, "Something which embraces more things is better."

and over their eyes is a blindfold.

The pronoun "their" applies to those whom Allah knows will not believe among the unbelievers of Quraysh, or to the hypocrites or the Jews, or to all unbelievers, which is more correct because it is universal. The seal is what covers hearts and hearing and the blindfold covers the eyes. The word used for blindfold is *ghishā'* which simply means a covering. From it comes *ghāshiya*, a saddle cover, so-called because it goes right over it.

Some commentators say that the covering applies to the hearing and the eyes and that it is only the hearts which are sealed. Others say that the seal covers all of them and that blindfold is another way of saying seal.

They will have a terrible punishment.

"They" here refers to the unbelievers who deny the "terrible punishment" they are going to receive. The word "punishment" (*'adhāb*) includes things like whipping, burning with fire, cutting with steel and other things which inflict pain and suffering on a person. In the Qur'ān we find: *"A number of believers should attend their punishment."* (24:2) The word is derived from a root meaning imprisonment and prevention. Linguistically one can say, "I will punish him," meaning restrain him. The same root is used for the sweetness (*'adhūba*) of water because it becomes sweet by being confined in a vessel so that it is pure and separated from what it is mixed with. We also find it used in the words of 'Alī, "Keep (*a'dhibū*) your women from going out." Punishment is called that because the person being punished is held and kept from everything which is conducive to his comfort and afflicted with the opposite.

وَمِنَ ٱلنَّاسِ مَن يَقُولُ ءَامَنَّا بِٱللَّهِ وَبِٱلْيَوْمِ
ٱلْءَاخِرِ وَمَا هُم بِمُؤْمِنِينَ ۝٨

8 *Among the people there are some who say,*
"We believe in Allah and the Last Day,"
when they do not believe.

Ibn Jurayj related that Mujāhid said, "Four *āyat*s were revealed in *Sūrat al-Baqara* about the believers, two about the unbelievers, and thirteen about the hypocrites. As-Suddī said that "people" here refers to the hypocrites. Sufi scholars say that the word "people" is a generic noun and one does not use the generic to address friends.

Grammarians disagree about the derivation of the word "people" (*an-nās*). It is said that it is the plural of *insān* (human being). In this case the word *nās* comes from *naws*, which means movement. The word is used to mean moving about and it is found with that significance in *ḥadīth*. It is also said that the word comes from the word "forget" (*nasī*), in which case its root would be *nasiya*. Ibn 'Abbās said, "Ādam forgot (*nasā*) the covenant with his Lord and was named *insān*." He said, "Ādam forgot and so his descendants forgot." This is borne out in the Qur'ān when Allah says, *"We made a contract with Ādam before, but he forgot."* (20:115)

Allah Almighty mentions the believers first because of their nobility and excellence. Then He mentions the unbelievers next because disbelief and belief are two opposites. Then after that He mentions the hypocrites and connects them to the unbelievers to deny that they have faith with the words, *"They do not believe."* This refutes the Karrāmite thesis that faith is confirmed by affirmation of it on the tongue even if the heart does not believe. Their evidence is the words of Allah, *"Allah will reward them for what they say."* (5:85) He does not say "for what they say and their belief in it." They also used as evidence the words of the Prophet, "I was commanded to fight people until they say, 'There is no God but Allah.' When they have said it, their blood and property are protected from me."

This is wrong and fails to look into what the Qur'ān and *Sunna* actually say about acting by both statement and belief. The Messenger of Allah, may Allah bless him and grant him peace, said, "Faith is recognition in the heart, articulation by the tongue and acting according to the pillars." (Ibn Mājah in the *Sunan*) That which Muḥammad ibn Karrām as-Sijistānī and his people say is hypocrisy and schism. We seek refuge with Allah from disappointment and corrupted belief.

Our scholars say that there are two types of believer: a believer whom Allah loves and protects, and a believer whom Allah loves and does not protect, but with whom He is angry and towards whom He is hostile. Allah loves and protects all those whom He knows will end up as believers. Allah hates and is angry with and hostile towards all those whom He knows will end up as unbelievers – not, of course, on account of their belief but because of the disbelief and misguidance which will overpower them. Likewise there are two types of unbeliever: an unbeliever who will be punished and an unbeliever who will not be punished. The one who will be punished is the one who ends up with disbelief and so Allah is angry with him and hostile towards him. The one who will not be punished is the one who ends up with belief: Allah is not angry with this one nor does he hate him. He loves him and protects him, not for his disbelief, but for the belief which will overtake him.

This means that it is not permitted to make the following general statement: A believer deserves the reward and an unbeliever deserves the punishment. Rather such a statement must be made conditional to the end result. Because of this we say that Allah was pleased with 'Umar even while he was worshipping idols and always meant to reward him and admit him to the Garden, not, of course, for his worship of idols, but for his ultimate belief. On the other hand, Allah was angry with Iblīs even while he was worshipping Him because of his ultimate disbelief.

The Qadariyya differed regarding this matter. They said that Allah was not angry with Iblīs when he worshipped Him nor pleased with 'Umar when he was worshipping idols. This is false since it is confirmed that Allah knew how Iblīs would end up and how 'Umar would end up even though this had not yet happened. So it is confirmed that He was angry with Iblīs and loved 'Umar. The consensus of the *Umma* indicates that Allah would never show love for anyone He knew was going to be one of the people of the Fire; He would be angry with him. He does, however, love the one He knows will be one of the people of the Garden.

The Messenger of Allah, may Allah bless him and grant him peace, said, "Actions are revealed by their results." That is why Sufi scholars say that faith is not what the slave is adorned with in word and deed, but faith is the preordainment of happiness before time. As for its outward appearance on individuals, that may be either empty of reality or actually true.

This is confirmed in the *Ṣaḥīḥ* of Muslim and elsewhere from 'Abdullāh ibn Mas'ūd that the Messenger of Allah, may Allah bless him and grant him peace, said, "The way that each of you is created is that you are gathered in your mother's womb for forty days as a sperm-drop and then for a similar length of time as a blood-clot and then for a similar length of time as a lump of flesh. Then an angel is sent and he breathes the spirit into you and is encharged with four commandments: to write down your provision, your life-span, your actions, and whether you will be wretched or happy. By Him, apart from Whom there is no god, one of you can do the actions of someone destined for the Garden until there is only an armspan between him and it, and then what is written will overtake him and he will do the actions of someone destined for the Fire and enter it. And one of you can do the actions of someone destined for the Fire until there is only an armspan between him and it, and then what is written will overtake him and he will do the actions of someone destined for the Garden and enter it."

Abū Muḥammad 'Abdu'l-Ghanī ibn Sa'īd al-Miṣrī transmitted a *ḥadīth* about the *zindīq*s from Muḥammad ibn Sa'īd ash-Shāmī going back to Abū Razīn al-'Uqaylī who said, "The Messenger of Allah, may Allah bless him and grant him peace, told me, 'Abū Razīn, you and I will drink from a milk whose taste is unaltered.' Then I asked, 'How will Allah bring the dead to life?' He said, 'Have you passed by a land which is barren and then you pass by it and it is lush, and then you pass by it again and it is barren and you pass by it again and it is lush?' I replied, 'Yes.' He said, 'That is how the Resurrection is.' I asked, 'How will I know that I am a believer?' He said, 'None of this Community (or My Community) does an action and knows that it is good and that Allah will reward it, or does an evil action and knows that it is bad and that Allah will either punish it or forgive it, without that showing that he is a believer.'"

Even if the *isnād* of this *ḥadīth* is not strong, its meaning is sound. It does not contradict the *ḥadīth* of Ibn Mas'ūd. That depends on the seal as the Prophet, may Allah bless him and grant him peace, said, "Actions are by their seals." This indicates that he is actually a believer, and Allah knows best.

Linguists say, "A hypocrite (*munāfiq*) is called a hypocrite when he displays outwardly something different from what he is concealing inside himself, like the jerboa whose hole is called a *nāfiqā'*. That is because it burrows into the earth leaving some fine soil near the surface. When it is alarmed, it covers the mouth of its hole with dirt and leaves, so the outside of its hole seems to be solid earth whereas the inside is really hollow. Thus the outside of the hypocrite has the appearance of faith while inwardly it is really disbelief.

يُخَٰدِعُونَ ٱللَّهَ وَٱلَّذِينَ ءَامَنُواْ وَمَا يُخَٰدِعُونَ
إِلَّآ أَنفُسَهُمْ وَمَا يَشْعُرُونَ ٩

9 *They think they deceive Allah and those who believe.*
They deceive no one but themselves
but they are not aware of it.

They think they deceive Allah and those who believe.

Our scholars have said that their imagined deceit of Allah is in themselves and in their thinking. It is said that it is by their actions which are those of a deceiver. It is said that there is something elided here, and that what is really meant is deceit of the Messenger of Allah, may Allah bless him and grant him peace. Al-Ḥasan and others said that. Allah has made their deceit of His Messenger equivalent to deceit of Himself because the Prophet called them using Allah's Words. The same applies to their deceit of the believers as a whole: in reality they are deceiving Allah. Their deceit lies in their display of faith which differs from the disbelief they conceal. This results in their lives and property being spared and makes them think that they are safe and have been successful in deceiving the believers. Some interpreters said that.

Linguists say that the root of the word "*khadā'a*" (deceit) means corruption. So the meaning is that they corrupt their faith and actions, in respect of what is between them and Allah, by showing off. This is explained by the Prophet. Its root is also said to signify concealment, from which comes *mikhda'*, the cabinet in which something is kept in the house. One form of the word is used of a hyena concealing itself in its den.

They deceive no one but themselves

The words, *"They deceive no one but themselves,"* mean that the end result of what they do is that only they are deceived. There is a saying: "Whoever tries to deceive someone who is not deceived has deceived himself." This is true because deceit can only occur in respect of someone who does not know the inward reality. Any attempt to deceive someone who knows what is really going on is inevitably self-deceit. This is proof that the hypocrites do not recognise Allah since they do not know that He is not deceived. The Prophet, peace and blessing be upon him, said, "Do not deceive Allah. If anyone deceives Allah, Allah deceives him and his self deceives him while he is not aware." They said, "Messenger of Allah, how can Allah be deceived?" He replied, "By your doing what Allah has commanded while seeking the pleasure of another by it." The full extent of this deception will be seen in the interpretation of Allah's words: *"Allah is mocking them."* (2:15)

Nāfi', Ibn Kathīr and Abū 'Amr read, *yukhādi'ūna* for "deceive" both times it occurs, whereas 'Āṣim, Ḥamza, al-Kisā'ī and Ibn 'Āmir read *yakhda'ūna,* without the middle *alif* the second time.

but they are not aware of it.

This means that they do not understand that the evil of their deception will come back on them; they think that they will be saved and win by their deceit. That may seem to be the case in this world but in the Next World they will be told, *"Go back and look for light."* (57:13)

فِي قُلُوبِهِم مَّرَضٌ فَزَادَهُمُ اللَّهُ مَرَضًا وَلَهُم
عَذَابٌ أَلِيمٌ بِمَا كَانُوا يُكَذِّبُونَ ﴿١٠﴾

10 ***There is a sickness in their hearts***
and Allah has increased their sickness.
They will have a painful punishment
on account of their denial.

There is a sickness in their hearts

In the words "a sickness in their hearts", sickness is a metaphor for the corruption caused by their lack of faith. That is either doubt and hypocrisy or denial and repudiation. The meaning is that their hearts are sick since they lack the protection, success and support which come from true faith. Ibn Fāris, the linguist, says that sickness is that which brings man out from health through illness, hypocrisy, or shortcoming in something.

and Allah has increased their sickness.

The meaning of these words is that Allah has increased them in doubt and hypocrisy on top of their disbelief and lack of support and lack of power. So this *āyat* indicates the permission to pray against the hypocrites and expel them because they are the worst of Allah's creatures. Indeed one possibility is that the words actually are a supplication against them with the meaning, "May Allah increase their sickness". It is said that the phrase is simply information from Allah about their increased sickness, meaning sickness on top of their sickness. He says in another *āyat*, *"It adds defilement to their defilement."* (9:125)

Those with knowledge of the precise use of language say that the first "sickness in their hearts" is because of their reliance on this world and their love for it and their neglect of the Next World and their turning away from it. Then Allah's words "Allah has increased their sickness" mean that He has thrown them back on themselves and loaded them with the cares of this world, so that they are unable to break through them and turn to concern for the Next World. Al-Junayd said, "Sickness of the heart comes from following the lower desires, and sickness of the limbs comes from the sickness of the body itself."

on account of their denial

This refers to their denial of the Messengers and rejection of Allah. It is their denial of His *āyat*s.

Scholars disagree about why the Prophet, may Allah bless him and grant him peace, left the hypocrites alone even though he knew that they were hypocrites. There are basically four positions.

- Some scholars say that he did not kill them because he was the only one who knew their state. Without exception, scholars agree that a *qāḍī* may not issue a sentence of execution on the basis of personal knowledge. They disagree about lesser sentences.

- The people of ash-Shāfi'ī say that he did not kill them because a *zindīq*, who is someone who conceals disbelief and shows faith, is asked to repent and is not killed. Ibn al-'Arabī said, "This is weak. The Prophet did not ask them to repent and no one transmits that and no one says that it is obligatory to ask *zindīq*s to repent. The Prophet, may Allah bless him and grant him peace, left them alone in spite of his knowledge of them."

- He did not kill them in order to bring hearts closer to him and so that people would not be alienated. The Prophet, may Allah bless him and grant him peace, indicated this when he said to 'Umar, "I seek refuge with Allah from people saying that I kill my Companions." (al-Bukhārī and Muslim) He used to give people things to bring their hearts closer although he knew about their weak belief. This is the position of our scholars and others. Ibn 'Aṭiyya said that this is the approach of the people of Mālik when talking about the Messenger of Allah, may Allah bless him and grant him peace, refraining from the hypocrites as stated by Muḥammad ibn al-Jahm, Qāḍī Ismā'īl, al-Abhari and Ibn al-Mājishūn.

As for those who use the words of Allah Almighty, *"If the hypocrites and those with sickness in their hearts do not desist"* to the words *"mercilessly put to death"* (33:60-61) as justification for killing hypocrites, Qatāda said that this only applies when they make their hypocrisy public. Mālik said, "Hypocrisy in the time of the Messenger of Allah, may Allah bless him and grant him peace, is like *zandaqa* among us today. If there is firm evidence against him a *zindīq* is killed without being asked to repent." This is one of the positions of ash-Shāfi'ī.

Mālik said that the Messenger of Allah, may Allah bless him and grant him peace, refrained from killing hypocrites to make it clear to his Community that a ruler is not permitted to judge by personal knowledge when there is no other clear evidence against someone. Qāḍī Ismā'īl said, "There was no witness against 'Abdullāh ibn Ubayy except for Zayd ibn Arqam alone, nor against al-Julās ibn Suwayd except 'Umayr ibn Ṣa'd, his foster son. If two men had testified to the disbelief and hypocrisy of either of the two men, they would have been killed."

Ash-Shāfi'ī gave the evidence for the other position when he said: "The *sunna* about someone against whom there is evidence of *zandaqa* and who then denies it and proclaims his faith and that he is free of every *dīn* except Islam is that it is forbidden to shed his blood." That is what was stated by the people of opinion *(ra'y)*, Aḥmad, aṭ-Ṭabarī and others. Ash-Shāfi'ī and his people said, "The Messenger of Allah, may Allah bless him and grant him peace, forbade killing hypocrites as long as they display Islam, even when it is known that they are hypocrites, because what they display must be accepted."

Aṭ-Ṭabarī said, "Allah Almighty made the rulings between his slaves dependent on the outward and entrusted judgement about their secret beliefs to none of His creation. No one can judge against what is apparent because that would be judgement by supposition. If anyone had been entitled to do that, the most entitled would have been the Messenger of Allah. He judged the hypocrites as Muslims because of what they displayed and left their secrets to Allah."

There is debate about this distinction. The Prophet, may Allah bless him and grant him peace, used to know them – or many of them – by their names and persons by Allah's informing him of who they were. Ḥudhayfa also knew who they were since the Prophet told him so that 'Umar used to ask him, "Ḥudhayfa, who are they?" He refused to answer.

- Allah preserved the Companions of his Prophet since he made them firm against the efforts of the hypocrites to corrupt them or corrupt their *dīn*, and for this reason there was no harm in their remaining. That is not the case today because we are not safe from the *zindīq*s corrupting our common people and the ignorant among us.

وَإِذَا قِيلَ لَهُمْ لَا تُفْسِدُوا۟ فِى ٱلْأَرْضِ قَالُوٓا۟
إِنَّمَا نَحْنُ مُصْلِحُونَ ﴿١١﴾

11. ***When they are told,***
"Do not cause corruption on the earth,"
they say, "We are only putting things right."

When they are told, "Do not cause corruption on the earth,"

Corruption is the opposite of rightness. Its reality is turning from rectitude to its opposite. The meaning in the *āyat* is: Do not cause corruption on the earth through disbelief and friendliness with unbelievers and making people abandon their faith in Muḥammad, may Allah bless him and grant him peace, and the Qur'ān. It is said that the earth, before the Prophet, may Allah bless him and grant him peace, was sent, was full of corruption and acts of disobedience were done in it. When the Messenger of Allah, may Allah bless him and grant him peace, was sent, the corruption was eliminated and the earth put right. Then when people again perpetrated acts of disobedience, they corrupted the earth after it had been put right, as Allah says in another *āyat*, *"Do not corrupt the earth after it has been put right."* (7:56)

The word for earth (*arḍ*) is feminine and is a generic term so that it means the earth in general. Everything under the sky is earth. The word *arīḍ* means wide. A common curse is, "May you have no land (*arḍ*)." *Arḍ* also means the shakes and shaking. It also means catarrh. One derived word means a young palm-tree which is an off-shoot. *Irāḍ* is a large carpet of wool or hair. A man who is *arīḍ* is lowly and disposed to do good.

they say, "We are only putting things right."

"Putting things right" (*ṣalāḥ*) is the opposite of corruption. They say this because they are under the illusion that their corruption is putting things right. One aspect of it is what they do for the unbelievers under the false impression that they are setting things right between them and the believers.

أَلَآ إِنَّهُمْ هُمُ ٱلْمُفْسِدُونَ وَلَٰكِن لَّا يَشْعُرُونَ ﴿١٢﴾

12 ***No indeed! They are the corrupters,***
but they are not aware of it.

No indeed! They are the corrupters,

These words are to refute their claims and to deny what they have said. Those with knowledge of the precise use of language say that it shows that their claim is a lie. Do you not see that Allah says, "They are corrupters." This is the truth.

but they are not aware of it.

There are two opinions about this. One is that they do corruption secretly and display righteousness and are not aware that their business was known by the Prophet. The other aspect is that they consider their corruption to be righteousness and are not aware that it is corruption and that they have disobeyed Allah and His Messenger by not making the truth clear and then following it.

وَإِذَا قِيلَ لَهُمْ ءَامِنُوا۟ كَمَآ ءَامَنَ ٱلنَّاسُ قَالُوٓا۟ أَنُؤْمِنُ كَمَآ
ءَامَنَ ٱلسُّفَهَآءُ ۗ أَلَآ إِنَّهُمْ هُمُ ٱلسُّفَهَآءُ وَلَٰكِن لَّا يَعْلَمُونَ ﴿١٣﴾

13 ***When they are told, "Believe***
in the way that the people believe,"
they say, "What! Are we to believe
in the way that fools believe?"
No indeed! They are the fools, but they do not know it.

When they are told,

"They" refers to the hypocrites, according to Muqātil and others.

"Believe in the way that the people believe,"

This means to affirm Muḥammad, may Allah bless him and grant him peace, and his *Sharī'a* in the same way that the Muhājirūn and the people of Yathrīb who had become Muslim affirmed them.

They say, "What! Are we to believe in the way that fools believe?"

This was said by the hypocrites who used to say it when they mocked and made fun of Islam, referring to the Companions of Muḥammad, may Allah bless him and grant him peace. Ibn 'Abbās said that, and he also said that it was the believers of the People of the Book who were intended by their words. Allah acquainted His Prophet and the believers with what they said.

No indeed! They are the fools,

Allah confirmed that they possess foolishness, lack of understanding and lack of insight, and they are the ones properly described by that. He reported that they are the fools but they do not realise that they are because of the rust covering their hearts.

Al-Kalbī related from Abū Ṣāliḥ from Ibn 'Abbās that this *āyat* was revealed about the Jews so that, when it was said to them, *"Believe in the way that the people believe,"* 'Abdullāh ibn Sallām and his companions said, *"What! Are we to believe in the way that fools believe?"* meaning the ignorant and superstitious Arabs.

The root of *safah* (foolishness) is lightness and shallowness. It is used of woven cloth when it is flimsy and badly woven and suggests shabbiness. It is used for the wind which makes the branches of a tree move. It is used to disparage a person. *Safah* is the opposite of *ḥilm* (forbearance).

but they do not know it.

These words are like "They are not aware of it." Knowledge is recognising and knowing something for what it is.

وَإِذَا لَقُواْ الَّذِينَ ءَامَنُواْ قَالُوٓاْ ءَامَنَّا وَإِذَا خَلَوْاْ إِلَىٰ
شَيَٰطِينِهِمْ قَالُوٓاْ إِنَّا مَعَكُمْ إِنَّمَا نَحْنُ مُسْتَهْزِءُونَ ﴿١٤﴾

14 ***When they meet those who believe,***
they say, "We believe."
But then when they go apart with their shaytans,
they say, "We are really with you.
We were only mocking."

This *āyat* was revealed about the hypocrites.

But then when they go apart with their shayṭāns,

Commentators disagree about the meaning of "shayṭāns" here. Ibn 'Abbās and as-Suddī said that they are the leaders of the hypocrites. Al-Kalbī said that they are the shayṭāns of the jinn. A group of commentators said that they are the soothsayers. 'Shayṭāns' means people distant from faith. The best course is to combine all of these meanings. Allah knows best.

they say, "We are really with you. We were only mocking."

This is the proof against them because, with these words, they negate their claim to be believers. It is said that it means making fun of the believers. *Haz'* is mockery and playing about.

اللَّهُ يَسْتَهْزِئُ بِهِمْ وَيَمُدُّهُمْ فِي طُغْيَٰنِهِمْ يَعْمَهُونَ ﴿١٥﴾

15 ***But Allah is mocking them, and drawing them on,***
as they wander blindly in their excessive insolence.

But Allah is mocking them,

This means taking revenge on them and punishing them. He mocks them and repays them for their mocking. The punishment they receive has the same name as the wrong action they commit. This is the statement of the majority of scholars and is a common Arabic usage.

Al-Kalbī related from Ibn 'Abbās that this *āyat* refers to the hypocrites of the People of the Book. He mentioned them and their mocking and that when they withdraw to their shayṭāns, meaning their leaders in disbelief, they said, "We are with you in your *dīn*. We were only mocking the Companions of Muḥammad." Allah will mock them in the Next World and open for them a door between *Jahannam* and the Garden and they will be told, "Come," and they will come swimming in the Fire while the believers are on beds in alcoves looking at them. When they reach the door, it will be shut against them and the believers will laugh at them. According to this understanding the words *"Allah is mocking them"* refer to something which happens in the Next World. The believers will laugh at them when the doors are locked against them. That is confirmed by the words of the Almighty, *"those who believe are laughing at the unbelievers, on couches, gazing in wonder"* (83:34-35) at the people of the Fire. *"Have the unbelievers been rewarded for what they did?"* (83:36)

Some people say that Allah's mocking takes the form of drawing them on by degrees in allowing them to experience the blessings of this world. Allah Almighty shows them kindness in this world, contrary to the reality of their situation which is hidden from them, and veils them from the punishment of the Next World so that they think that He is pleased with them when, in fact, the Almighty has foreordained their punishment. The human being considers this to be mocking, deceit, and tricking.

The Prophet, may Allah bless him and grant him peace, indicated this interpretation in his words: "When you see Allah Almighty giving a slave what he wants when he continues to perform acts of disobedience, that is part of drawing on." Then he finished with this *āyat*: *"When they forgot what they had been reminded of, We opened up for them the doors of everything, until, when they were exulting in what they had been given, We suddenly seized them and at once they were in despair. So the last remnant of the people who did wrong was cut off. Praise belongs to Allah, the Lord of the worlds."* (6:44-45). Some scholars say that the meaning of the *āyat*, *"We will lead them on from where they do not know."* (7:182) is that when they commit a sin, they receive a blessing.

and drawing them on,

This phrase means allowing them a long period of respite, as we find in Allah's words, "*We only allow them more time so that they will increase in evildoing."* (3:178) The verbal root means increase. Yūnus ibn Ḥabīb said, "It is said that Allah supplies them when they commit evil in just the same way that He supplies them when they do good. Allah Almighty says, *"We supplied you with property and sons."* (17:6) He says, *"We will supply them with fruit and meat that they desire."* (52:22) Al-Akhfash said, "It means to give." Al-Farrā' and al-Laḥyānī said, "It is to give more of the same. It is used for giving support, as when you reinforce an army."

they wander blindly

Mujāhid said, "They go back and forth, confused in disbelief. The scholars of language use it for when someone is confused and vacillates. It is used for camels who do not know which way to go. *'Amā* signifies blindness of the eyes and *'amah*, as is used here, signifies blindness of the heart.

in their excessive insolence.

Their disbelief and misguidance. The basic meaning of the words "excessive insolence" comes from the idea of overflowing or going over the limits of something. We find the same root used in the words of the Almighty, *"When the waters rose,"* (69:11), meaning rose high and overflowed the banks of the reservoir. It is also used of Pharaoh when Allah says, *"He overstepped,"* (20:24), meaning that he was excessive in his claim, when he said, *"I am your Lord Most High."* (79:24) The meaning in the *āyat* is to extend the length of their lives so that they increase in insolence and so that their punishment will in turn be increased.

أُولَٰئِكَ ٱلَّذِينَ ٱشْتَرَوُا۟ ٱلضَّلَٰلَةَ بِٱلْهُدَىٰ فَمَا رَبِحَت
تِّجَٰرَتُهُمْ وَمَا كَانُوا۟ مُهْتَدِينَ ﴿١٦﴾

16 ***Those are the people***
who have sold guidance for misguidance.
Their trade has brought no profit; they are not guided.

Those are the people who have sold guidance for misguidance.

Selling here is a metaphor. It means that these people have preferred disbelief to belief, because the act of buying and selling only occurs when someone desires one thing rather than another. No real exchange is involved here, however, because the hypocrites are not really believers in the first place so in fact they have no faith to sell. Ibn 'Abbas said, "They take misguidance and abandon guidance." It means that they choose disbelief over belief. The business metaphor is appropriate because buying and selling refer to replacing one thing with another and the Arabs used it in this way.

Misguidance (*ḍalāl*) is bewilderment. Forgetfulness is called misguidance because of the confusion it entails. It can mean being forgotten. Death is also sometimes called misguidance as in Allah's words: *"They said, 'When we have been absorbed (*ḍalalnā*) into the earth.'"* (32:10)

Their trade has brought no profit.

Allah ascribed profit to trade since it is the custom of the Arabs to use terms related to commerce metaphorically in this context. It means that they have made no profit in the transaction they have made.

They are not guided.

There is misguidance in the transaction they have made. It is said that it is in the prior knowledge of Allah. Guidance is the opposite of misguidance.

مَثَلُهُمْ كَمَثَلِ الَّذِي اسْتَوْقَدَ نَارًا فَلَمَّا أَضَاءَتْ مَا حَوْلَهُ
ذَهَبَ اللَّهُ بِنُورِهِمْ وَتَرَكَهُمْ فِي ظُلُمَاتٍ لَا يُبْصِرُونَ ﴿١٧﴾

17 ***Their likeness is that of people who light a fire,***
and then when it has lit up all around them,
Allah removes their light
and leaves them in darkness, unable to see.

Some of this *āyat* is in the singular and some in the plural. Some people say that the word *alladhī,* which is usually singular, has a plural meaning here and means people who light, and this is borne out by the fact that the *āyat* begins and ends with the plural usage of "their" and "them". Others say that the singular is used because it only takes one person to actually light the fire among the group who undertake to do it. When the light is gone, the effect is the same for all of them and so Allah says, "their light." The pronoun "their" refers to the hypocrites, and this depicts their state in the Next World, as Allah does in another place when He says: *"A wall will be erected between them with a gate in it."* (57:13) Someone who lights a fire in darkness can only see a short distance, just as the hypocrite remains lost in his confusion and vacillation.

The *āyat* is a metaphor which illustrates the reality of the hypocrites. They make a show of faith, taking advantage of the judgements of Islam in respect of marriage, inheritance, booty, and other such things and giving security to themselves, their children and their property. This is like someone who lights a fire on a dark night and it gives him just enough light to see what he needs to protect himself. But when it goes out he is no longer safe from harm and he becomes confused. That is how the hypocrites are when they imagine that they are deceiving the believers by uttering the words of Islam. Then, after they die, they will go to the painful punishment since, *"The hypocrites are in the lowest level of the Fire"* (4:145) and their light vanishes. They say, *"Let us borrow some of your light."* (57:13). Others things are said. The word for fire (*nār*) is derived from the word for light (*nūr*), as fire gives light.

صُمٌّ بُكْمٌ عُمْيٌ فَهُمْ لَا يَرْجِعُونَ ﴿١٨﴾

18 ***Deaf, dumb, blind.***
They will not return.

Deaf, dumb, blind.

The word for deafness in Arabic (*ṣumm*) comes from a word which means to be blocked, like a canal which is silted up or like a vial with a stopper in it. So a deaf person is someone whose hearing is blocked up. The word for dumb (*bukm*) used here refers to those who cannot speak or understand. If he can understand, the word used is *akhras*. It is also said that they mean the same thing. The word *'umy* (blind) is used of those who have lost their sight. It is also said that someone is "blind" when he is confused. What is meant here is not the actual senses themselves, rather what is intended is the negation of the ability to perceive the truth. Qatāda said of this that they are deaf to hearing the truth, dumb to speaking it and blind to seeing it. This meaning was used by the Prophet, may Allah bless him and grant him peace, in describing the rulers when the Final Hour is near in the *ḥadīth* of Jibrīl. Allah knows best.

They will not return.

They will not return to the truth. Allah says this from the position of His prior knowledge of them.

أَوۡ كَصَيِّبٖ مِّنَ ٱلسَّمَآءِ فِيهِ ظُلُمَٰتٞ وَرَعۡدٞ وَبَرۡقٞ يَجۡعَلُونَ
أَصَٰبِعَهُمۡ فِيٓ ءَاذَانِهِم مِّنَ ٱلصَّوَٰعِقِ حَذَرَ ٱلۡمَوۡتِۚ وَٱللَّهُ
مُحِيطُۢ بِٱلۡكَٰفِرِينَ ﴿١٩﴾

19 ***Or that of a storm-cloud in the sky,***
full of darkness, thunder and lightning.
They put their fingers in their ears
against the thunderclaps, fearful of death.
Allah encompasses the rejectors.

Or that of a storm-cloud in the sky,

At-Ṭabarī says that the "or" here, in fact, means "and", and it is also said that the "or" is in order to give a choice between the two metaphors so as not to confine the description of the hypocrites to just one of them.

The word for sky, *samā'*, which means sky or heaven, is everything that is above you and covers you. So the roof of a house is sometimes called *samā'*. The word can also designate the rain because rain descends from the sky. Herbage is also sometimes called *samā'* in Arabic because it covers the ground. Heaven is what is above and the earth is what is underneath.

full of darkness, thunder and lightning.

The word *ẓumulāt* (darkness) is in the plural, indicating both the darkness of night and the darkness of the clouds which are piled up.

Scholars disagree about what thunder is. At-Tirmidhī reports that Ibn 'Abbās said, "The Jews asked the Prophet, may Allah bless him and grant him peace, what thunder was. He said, 'One of the angels is entrusted with the clouds and wields a fiery sword with which he drives the clouds wherever he wishes.' They said, 'What is this sound we hear?' He said, 'He hits the clouds when he pushes them until they go wherever Allah has commanded.' They said,

'You have spoken the truth.'" It is a long *ḥadīth*. Many scholars accept this explanation. Thunder is the name of the sound heard. 'Ali said that. It is reported from Ibn 'Abbās that thunder is a wind caught between the clouds which causes that sound.

They also disagree about lightning. It is reported from 'Alī, Ibn Mas'ūd and Ibn 'Abbās that lightning comes from the iron bar in the hand of an angel with which he drives the clouds. This is the literal meaning of the *ḥadīth* of at-Tirmidhī. Ibn 'Abbās also said that it is a whip of fire in the hand of an angel with which he drives the clouds.

Scientists say that thunder is the sound of the collision of the clouds, and lightning is what is sparked by their collision. This is rejected and not transmitted and Allah knows best. It is said that the root of thunder (*ra'd*) means movement. Hence *ri'dīd* for a coward. One form of the word means to tremble. The root of the word for lightning, *barq,* means "glittering" and "a bright light".

Ibn 'Abbās reported, "We were with 'Umar ibn al-Khaṭṭāb on a journey between Madina and Syria with Ka'b al-Aḥbār. There was a wind and then rain, strong wind and hail. The people separated. Ka'b told me, 'If someone hears the thunder and then says, "Glory be to the One *'whom the thunder glorifies His praise and the angels from fear of Him,'"* (13:13) he is safe from what is in those clouds, hail and thunderclaps.' I said it as did Ka'b. In the morning, the people gathered and I said to 'Umar, '*'Amīr al-Mu'minīn*, we were in a different situation to everyone else.' 'And why is that?' he asked. I told him the *ḥadīth* of Ka'b. He said, 'Glory be to Allah! Why didn't you tell us so that we could say the same as you said!'" Ibn 'Umar reported about the Prophet, "When he heard thunder and lightning, he said, 'Oh Allah, do not kill us with Your anger or destroy us with Your punishment, and protect us from them.'"

They put their fingers in their ears

So that they will not hear the Qur'ān and thereby believe in it and in Muḥammad, peace be upon him. That was disbelief for them and disbelief is death.

against the thunderclaps,

To protect them from the thunderclaps. Ibn 'Abbās, Mujāhid and others said that, when the force of the thunder is very strong, there is an angel who wields the fire from within, which is the lightning. Al-Khalīl said, "It is the strong event arising from the sound of the thunder which is accompanied by flashes of fire which burn what they strike." Abū Zayd said, "The fire falls from the sky in strong thunder." The word "thunderclaps" is also used for the blast and "the Shout" which is a punishment with which Allah strikes the unbelievers.

In this *āyat* Allah likens the states of the hypocrites to the darkness, thunder, lightning and thunderclaps which are found in a cloudburst. Darkness resembles their disbelief, and thunder and lightning is like what they fear. Blindness is also darkness. It contains a threat and rebuke which is the thunder, and radiant proofs which can be dazzling like the lightning. The thunderclaps represent what the Qur'ān contains of being summoned to fight and the threat of the punishment in the Hereafter. It is said that the "thunderclaps" are the burdens of the *Sharī'a* which they hate, such as *jihād*, *zakāt* and other things.

Allah encompasses the rejectors.

They cannot evade Him. This linguistic term is used when someone is hemmed in on all sides. Allah encompasses all creatures, meaning they are in His grasp and under His power. This means that He knows everything about them. It is said that it means He will destroy them and bring them all together.

يَكَادُ الْبَرْقُ يَخْطَفُ أَبْصَارَهُمْ ۖ كُلَّمَا أَضَاءَ لَهُم
مَّشَوْا فِيهِ وَإِذَا أَظْلَمَ عَلَيْهِمْ قَامُوا ۚ وَلَوْ شَاءَ اللَّهُ لَذَهَبَ
بِسَمْعِهِمْ وَأَبْصَارِهِمْ ۚ إِنَّ اللَّهَ عَلَىٰ كُلِّ شَيْءٍ قَدِيرٌ ٢٠

20 ***The lightning all but takes away their sight.***
Whenever they have light, they walk in it
but whenever darkness covers them, they halt.
If Allah wished, He could take away
their hearing and their sight.
Allah has power over all things.

The lightning all but takes away their sight.

The word for "take" (*khaṭafa*) used here means taking extremely quickly or snatching. It is used of birds of prey because of their speed. If one takes the Qur'ānic metaphor of lightning as indicating alarm, the expression means that their fear of what will happen to them almost takes away their sight. If one takes it as indicating the Qur'ānic commands to the believers, it means that it is those which nearly blind them.

Whenever they have light, they walk in it but whenever darkness covers them, they halt.

Al-Mubarrad says that what is implied is: "Whenever the lightning lights up the road for them." The meaning is that when they hear *āyats* of the Qur'ān which they understand and agree with, they accept them and act by them. But when some *āyat*s are revealed about which they are confused and which they do not understand or find burdensome, they "halt", in other words they remain fixed in their hypocrisy, as Ibn 'Abbās said. It is said that the meaning is that, when their crops and cattle were flourishing and they had continuous blessings, they said, "The *dīn* of Muḥammad is a blessed *dīn*." But when hardship befell them and difficulties afflicted them, they became angry and remained fixed in their hypocrisy, as Ibn Mas'ūd and Qatāda said. The soundness of this is indicated by the words of the Almighty: *"Among the people there is one who worships Allah right on the edge. If good befalls him, he is content with it, but if trial befalls him, he reverts to his former ways."* (22:11)

Sufi scholars say that this is a metaphor which Allah made for someone whose initial state is made unsound by a self-seeking intention and who, because of that lays claim to the states of the great. His initial state would have continued to give him illumination if it had remained sound by being accompanied by correct *adab*. But when he adulterates it with false claims, Allah removes the light from him and he remains in the darkness of his false claims, not seeing any way to emerge from them.

It is also related from Ibn 'Abbās that the people meant here are the Jews since, when the Prophet, may Allah bless him and grant him peace, was victorious at Badr, they were greedy and said, "This, by Allah, is the Prophet of whom Mūsā gave good news. There is no banner which will resist him." When he suffered a reverse at Uḥud, they went back on that and were full of doubt. This is weak. The *āyat* is about the hypocrites, and this is sounder from Ibn 'Abbās. The meaning can apply to all.

If Allah wished, He could take away their hearing and their sight.

This means that, if Allah had wished, he could have informed the believers about them and removed the protection and power of Islam from them by overwhelming them, killing them and expelling them from their houses. Hearing and sight are specifically mentioned since they were already mentioned in the *āyat* or because they are the noblest senses of the human body.

Allah has power over all things.

This is general. According to the *mutakallimūn*, it means that it is permitted to describe Allah with the attribute of power. The Community agree that Allah has the name *al-Qadīr*, the Powerful. Allah has power over every possibility whether it is brought into existence or remains non-existent. All responsible people are obliged to know that Allah possesses power to act as He wills and He does whatever He wishes according to His knowledge and choice. They must also know that human beings possess a certain limited power through which they obtain what Allah has decreed for them according to normal means, but this power is not self-generated. Allah singled out the attribute of power in this instance because He already mentioned the action which results from the threat and intimidation contained in the *āyat*s, and so power is fitting here. Allah knows best.

The *āyat*s up to this point form an introductory section to the Book of Allah. The first four describe the believers, the next two describe the unbelievers and the rest are about the hypocrites.

يَٰٓأَيُّهَا ٱلنَّاسُ ٱعْبُدُوا۟ رَبَّكُمُ ٱلَّذِى خَلَقَكُمْ وَٱلَّذِينَ
مِن قَبْلِكُمْ لَعَلَّكُمْ تَتَّقُونَ ﴿٢١﴾

21 ***Mankind! worship your Lord,***
Who created you and those before you,
so that hopefully you will be godfearing.

Mankind!

'Alqama and Mujāhid said that every *āyat* which begins with "Mankind!" was revealed in Makka and every one which begins with "You who believe!" was revealed in Madina. That is refuted by the fact that this *sūra* and *Sūrat an-Nisā'* are definitely Madinan and both contain *āyat*s beginning "Mankind!". But what they said about "You who believe" is true. 'Urwa ibn az-Zubayr said, "All *ḥudūd* and legal obligations were revealed in Madina, and what is mentioned about Divine punishment was revealed in Makka." This is clear.

There is disagreement about who is meant by "mankind". There are two positions. One is that it refers to the unbelievers who do not worship Allah, which is indicated by His words, "*If you have doubts...* " (2:23) The second is that it is all people, in which case the believers are being told to remain constant in their worship and the unbelievers to begin it.

worship your Lord,

The word "worship" here designates affirming Allah's unity and holding to the laws of His *dīn*. The root of *'ibāda* (worship) means humbleness and abasement. The word *mu'abbada* is used for a path made by people's feet. *'Ibāda* also means obedience, devotion and religious practices.

Who created you

Allah mentions His quality as Creator since the Arabs acknowledged that Allah created them. He mentioned that as an argument against them and to rebuke them. It is said that by that He reminded them of His blessings to them. There are two aspects to the basic meaning of creation. The first is determination and the second is origination, innovation and genesis.

and those before you,

It is said that if they admit that He created them, they must admit that He created others. The answer is that the words are notification and reminding so that it will be more extensive in warning. He reminds them about those before them so that they will know that the One who made those before them die, having created them, will also make them die. They should reflect on the circumstances of those before them and how they died. They know that they will be tested as those others were tested. Allah knows best.

so that hopefully you will be godfearing.

This is clearly connected to "worship your Lord," not to "created you" because if Allah created someone for Hell, He obviously did not create him to be godfearing.

There are three interpretations of the term *la'alla* (hopefully). The first is its usual meaning of hope and anticipation. Such qualities are within the scope of human beings. It is as if He were saying: "Do that with the hope and desire that you will be godfearing." This is the position of Sibuwayh and leading grammarians. The second is that Arabs often use the term to mean "in order to" and so it would mean "in order for you to be godfearing". Aṭ-Ṭabarī says this. The third is that it means to bring a thing within reach. It is as if He were saying, "Do that because by accepting Allah's command you will have protection from the Fire."

الَّذِي جَعَلَ لَكُمُ الْأَرْضَ فِرَاشًا وَالسَّمَاءَ بِنَاءً وَأَنزَلَ مِنَ
السَّمَاءِ مَاءً فَأَخْرَجَ بِهِ مِنَ الثَّمَرَاتِ رِزْقًا لَّكُمْ ۖ فَلَا
تَجْعَلُوا لِلَّهِ أَندَادًا وَأَنتُمْ تَعْلَمُونَ ﴿٢٢﴾

22 ***It is He who made the earth a couch for you***
and the sky a dome.
He sends down water from the sky
and by it brings forth fruits for your provision.
Do not, then, knowingly make others equal to Allah.

It is He who made the earth a couch for you

The word "made" (*ja'ala*) can mean "create" as is used in the *āyat "He who created/appointed (*ja'ala*) the darkness and the light."* (6:1) and can also mean "designate" as in *"We have made (*ja'alnā*) it an Arabic Qur'ān"* (43:3) and *"They have assigned (*ja'alū*) to Him a portion"* (43:15).

A "couch" is something on which people lie and rest. So this description cannot apply to mountains, wild areas and seas because one of the characteristics of a couch is that it is something on which one reclines. The mountains, however, are described as pegs, as we find in *"Have We not made the earth a flat carpet and the mountains its pegs?"* (78:6-7) and other places, and the seas are something on which one travels to gain benefit as in *"the ships which sail the seas to people's benefit"* (2:164) and elsewhere.

and the sky a dome.

The sky is to the earth like a roof is to a house. Allah says elsewhere, *"We made the sky* (samā') *a preserved and protected roof."*

(21:32). *Samā'* is used for everything which is high and gives shade, as was mentioned earlier.

He sends down water from the sky and by it brings forth fruits for your provision.

The words *"and by it brings forth fruits for your provision"* mean that Allah produces various kinds of fruits and plants for us. "Provision" means food for us and fodder for our animals. This is clear from His words, *"We pour down plentiful water. Then split the earth into furrows. Then We make grain grow in it. And grapes and herbs. And olives and dates. And luxuriant gardens. And orchards and meadows. For you and your livestock to enjoy."* (80:25-32) We have already discussed the meaning of provision. If it is asked how provision can be used for fruits before they are owned by any owner, the reply is that they are ready to be owned and sound for use and so they constitute provision.

This *āyat* indicates that Allah spares the human being from being dependent on any other creature. The Prophet, may Allah bless him and grant him peace, indicated this when he said, "It is better for one of you to take a rope and carry firewood on his back than for him to go to a man and beg from him who then may give to him or refuse to do so." (Muslim). All forms of work are meant by this. Anyone who makes himself dependent on another human being like himself out of laziness, hope and desire for the things of this world has taken the path of someone who makes another equal to Allah.

A Sufi scholar said, "In this *āyat* Allah speaks about the path of poverty, which is that you make the earth your bed, the sky your cover, water your perfume and grass your food, and do not worship anyone in this world of creatures for the sake of this world. Allah Almighty has given you what you need without owing anything to anyone." Nawf al-Bikālī said, "I once saw 'Alī ibn Abī Ṭālib go out and look at the stars. He said, 'Nawf, are you asleep or awake?' I replied, 'Awake, *Amīr al-Mu'minīn*.' He said, 'Blessed are those who make do with little of this world and desire the Next World. Those are the people who take the ground as a bed, its soil as a mattress, its water as a perfume, and the Qur'ān and supplication as a blanket. They reject this world, taking the path of the Messiah.'"

Do not then, knowingly, make others equal to Allah.

Meaning His likes and peers. Ibn 'Abbas said that "knowingly" is addressed to the unbelievers and hypocrites. It might be asked, "How can they be described as knowing when Allah has already described them with the attributes of sealing, deafness and blindness?" The answer has two aspects. One is that "knowingly" means the specific knowledge that Allah Almighty created creatures, sent down the rain and made provision grow. So they know that He is their Blesser without any equal. The second is that the meaning is that you, in fact, have the strength and ability to know His oneness if you were only to reflect and consider. Allah knows best.

This *āyat* contains evidence for the command to use the evidence of the intellect and invalidates blind imitation. Ibn Fūrak said, "It is possible to apply this *āyat* to the believers in which case it means, "O believer, do not apostatise and make others equal to Allah when you know that Allah is One."

وَإِن كُنتُمْ فِي رَيْبٍ مِّمَّا نَزَّلْنَا عَلَىٰ عَبْدِنَا فَأْتُوا بِسُورَةٍ مِّن
مِّثْلِهِۦ وَادْعُوا شُهَدَآءَكُم مِّن دُونِ اللَّهِ إِن كُنتُمْ صَٰدِقِينَ ﴿٢٣﴾

23 ***If you have doubts about what***
We have sent down to Our slave,
produce another sūra equal to it,
and call your witnesses, besides Allah,
if you are telling the truth.

If you have doubts about what We have sent down

This refers to the Qur'ān and is addressed to the idolaters who are being challenged by Allah. When they heard the Qur'ān, they said, "This does not seem to us like the words of Allah. We have doubts about it." So the *āyat* was revealed. It is connected to the previous *āyat* since in that Allah has mentioned evidence of His oneness and power and now gives evidence for the Prophethood of His Prophet, showing that what he brings is not a forgery.

to Our slave,

"Our slave" (*'abd*) is Muhammad, may Allah bless him and grant him peace. *'Abd* is derived from *ta'abbud*, meaning abasement. A slave is so-called because he is submissive. Some people said that *'ibāda* is the noblest of qualities and that being called "*'abd*" is the noblest of designations, and so Allah calls His Prophet a slave.

produce another *sūra* equal to it,

Ibn Kaysān said that this is a command which, in fact, means that they lack the power to do so because Allah knew that they would be unable to do it. In the words "equal to it" the "it" refers to the Qur'ān according to the majority, while some say that it refers to the Torah and Gospel. Some say that "it" should be read "him" and refers to the Prophet, meaning "produce a mortal who does not read or write like him who is able to produce such words."

and call your witnesses, besides Allah,

This means your helpers and supporters. Al-Farrā' says it means your gods. Ibn Kaysān said, "If someone asks why witnesses are mentioned here when witnesses testify to a matter, or inform about the matter to which they have witnessed, yet here they are told 'to produce a *sūra*', the answer is that they are ordered to seek the help of their scholars and summon them to witness what they bring. So the *āyat* will refute all of them and be a stronger proof. Mujāhid said that it means, "summon people to be your witnesses," in other words to testify that you are against it.

if you are telling the truth.

This is regarding what you say about being able to match it, since they said elsewhere, *"If we wanted, we could say the same thing."* (8:31) Truthfulness is the opposite of lying. The root meaning of *ṣidq* (truthfulness) is the firmness of a spear. *Ṣiddīq* is someone who is devoted to truthfulness. *Ṣadāqa* (friendship) is derived from the same root and indicates truthfulness in counsel and love.

فَإِن لَّمْ تَفْعَلُواْ وَلَن تَفْعَلُواْ فَاتَّقُواْ النَّارَ الَّتِي
وَقُودُهَا النَّاسُ وَالْحِجَارَةُ أُعِدَّتْ لِلْكَٰفِرِينَ ﴿٢٤﴾

24 ***If you do not do that – and you will not do it – then fear the Fire whose fuel is people and stones, made ready for the unbelievers.***

If you do not do that – and you will not do it –

You will not be able to produce another *sūra* equal to it. Some commentators say that the *āyat* is about not being able to call witnesses. This is one of the unseen things about which the Qur'ān reported before it could happen. Ibn Kaysān said that they were not telling the truth when they said that it was lies, forged, magic, poetry or myths of earlier peoples, as we find elsewhere in the Qur'ān. They claimed to have knowledge but could not produce anything like it.

then fear the Fire whose fuel is people and stones,

Fear and safeguard yourself against the Fire by believing the Prophet and obeying Allah. The word "*waqūd*" (fuel) refers to firewood and *wuqūd* is burning. The word "people" is usually general, but its meaning here is particular to those who have been decreed to be the fuel of the Fire. May Allah protect us from it! The "stones" in this *āyat* are said to be black sulphur by Ibn Mas'ūd and al-Farrā'. It is singled out because it has five qualities of punishment which other minerals do not: speed of burning, foul smell, much smoke, clinging strongly to bodies, and great intensity of heat when it is burned. It is said that "stones" means idols since Allah says elsewhere, *"You and what you worship besides Allah are fuel for Hell."* (21:98)

This *āyat* does not mean that only people and stones are in the Fire. There are indications elsewhere that the jinn and shayṭāns will be in it as well. It is a warning that the Fire is so hot that it burns stones as well as burning people. According to one interpretation, the stones are part of the punishment and the people of the Fire are punished with fire and stones.

A *ḥadīth* of the Prophet, peace be upon him, says, "Every harmful thing will be in the Fire." This has two interpretations. One is that everyone who harms others in this world will be punished by Allah in the Next World with the Fire. The second is that everything which harms people in this world – wild animals, vermin and other things – will be in the Fire to punish the people of the Fire. Some interpreters believe that this fire with stones is particular to the Fire of the unbelievers. Allah knows best.

Muslim related from 'Abbās, "I said, 'Messenger of Allah, Abū Ṭālib used to protect you and support you. Will that benefit him?' He replied, 'Yes. I found him in the midst of the Fire and I brought him to a shallow part. If it were not for me, he would have been in the lowest level of the Fire.'"

made ready for the unbelievers.

The literal meaning of this phrase would seem to imply that only the unbelievers enter the Fire, but that is not the case, as is mentioned in the threat to wrongdoers and in the firm *aḥādīth* about intercession.

It also contains an indication of what the people who hold the true position say about the Fire being already created and in existence, which differs from innovators who state that it still has not yet been created. Muslim reported that 'Abdullāh ibn Mas'ūd said, "We were with the Messenger of Allah when he heard something fall. He said, 'Do you know what that was?' We said, 'Allah and His Messenger know best.' He said, 'It was a stone which was thrown into the Fire seventy years ago, and it has been falling through the Fire right up until now when it hit the bottom.'"

Al-Bukhārī related from Abū Hurayra that the Messenger of Allah, may Allah bless him and grant him peace, said, "The

Garden and the Fire argued and the Fire said, 'I have the tyrants and the arrogant.' The Garden said, 'I have the weak and poor people.' Allah Almighty said to the Fire, 'You are My punishment by which I punish whomever I will,' and He said to the Garden, 'You are My mercy by which I show mercy to whomever I will. Each of you will have its fill.'" The Prophet, peace be upon him, saw them both during the Eclipse prayer and in his Night Journey and entered the Garden, and this is irrefutable. Success is by Allah.

وَبَشِّرِ ٱلَّذِينَ ءَامَنُوا۟ وَعَمِلُوا۟ ٱلصَّـٰلِحَـٰتِ أَنَّ لَهُمْ جَنَّـٰتٍ
تَجْرِى مِن تَحْتِهَا ٱلْأَنْهَـٰرُ ۖ كُلَّمَا رُزِقُوا۟ مِنْهَا مِن ثَمَرَةٍ رِّزْقًا
قَالُوا۟ هَـٰذَا ٱلَّذِى رُزِقْنَا مِن قَبْلُ ۖ وَأُتُوا۟ بِهِۦ مُتَشَـٰبِهًا ۖ
وَلَهُمْ فِيهَآ أَزْوَٰجٌ مُّطَهَّرَةٌ ۖ وَهُمْ فِيهَا خَـٰلِدُونَ ﴿٢٥﴾

25 ***Give the good news***
to those who believe and do right actions
that they will have Gardens
with rivers flowing under them.
When they are given fruit there as provision,
they will say, 'This is what we were given before.'
But they were only given a simulation of it.
They will have there spouses of perfect purity
and will remain there timelessly, for ever.

Give the good news to those who believe

Whenever Allah mentions the repayment of the unbelievers, He also mentions the repayment of the believers. Good news (*bushrā*) means a report about something which produces an effect which is seen on the outer skin (*bashara*). It is usually used for joy connected to the news of some good occurrence, but can also be used for news of a sorrowful or evil type. Allah says, using the same word, *"Give him the news of a painful punishment."* (45:8)

and do right actions

This refutes those who say that *īmān* alone is sufficient to gain Divine reward, because if that had been the case, Allah would not have added right actions. The Garden is obtained by faith and right actions. It is also said that the Garden is obtained by faith and the different degrees in it by right actions. Allah knows best.

that they will have Gardens.

The "Gardens" are given that name because they shade those in them with their trees.

with rivers flowing under them.

It is related that the rivers of the Garden are not in channels, but flow on the surface, held in place by Divine power, flowing wherever its inhabitants wish.

When they are given fruit there as provision, they will say, 'This is what we were given before.'

"Before" means in this world. There are two aspects to this. One is that their words mean, "This is what we were promised in the world below," and the second is that they actually mean, "This is what we were given in the world below" because the colour of the fruits they receive resembles the colour of the fruits of this world. But when they eat it, they find the taste different. It is said that "before" refers to earlier during their time in the Garden because they were given provision there and then later are given more provision. They are given food and fruit at the beginning of the day and eat it and then, when they are given it at the end of the day, they say this, but then they find that the taste is different.

But they were only given a simulation of it.

This means that it is similar in appearance but differs in taste. Ibn 'Abbās, Mujāhid, al-Ḥasan and others said that. 'Ikrima said that it resembles the fruit of this world but differs from it in almost every way. Ibn 'Abbās said, "This is an expression of wonderment. There is nothing of this world which is in the Garden except the names of things. So it is as if they wonder when they see the excellence of the fruit and its great size."

They will have there spouses of perfect purity

"Spouse" in Arabic can refer to husband or wife. "Purity" means that they are free of menstruation, phlegm and all human impurities. Mujāhid said that they do not urinate, defecate, give birth, menstruate, ejaculate or expectorate.

and will remain there timelessly, for ever.

Remaining timelessly, for ever (*khulūd*) means staying for time without end, from which comes "the Garden of Eternity". It is used metaphorically for something which is of extremely long duration.

إِنَّ ٱللَّهَ لَا يَسْتَحْيِۦٓ أَن يَضْرِبَ مَثَلًا مَّا بَعُوضَةً فَمَا
فَوْقَهَا ۚ فَأَمَّا ٱلَّذِينَ ءَامَنُوا۟ فَيَعْلَمُونَ أَنَّهُ ٱلْحَقُّ مِن
رَّبِّهِمْ ۖ وَأَمَّا ٱلَّذِينَ كَفَرُوا۟ فَيَقُولُونَ مَاذَآ أَرَادَ ٱللَّهُ
بِهَٰذَا مَثَلًا ۘ يُضِلُّ بِهِۦ كَثِيرًا وَيَهْدِى بِهِۦ كَثِيرًا ۚ وَمَا
يُضِلُّ بِهِۦٓ إِلَّا ٱلْفَٰسِقِينَ ﴿٢٦﴾

26 ***Allah is not ashamed to make an example of a gnat***
or of an even smaller thing.
As for those who believe,
they know it is the truth from their Lord.
But as for those who disbelieve,
they say, 'What does Allah mean by this example?'
He misguides many by it and guides many by it.
But He only misguides the deviators.

Allah is not ashamed to make an example of a gnat

Ibn 'Abbās said, "When Allah Almighty made the two earlier metaphors for the hypocrites (2:17 and 2:19), people said 'Allah is too high and exalted to make metaphors.' Therefore Allah revealed this *āyat*."

In the transmission of 'Aṭā' from Ibn 'Abbās we find: "When Allah mentioned the gods of the idolaters, and said, *'If a fly steals something from them, they cannot get it back,'* (22:73), and He mentioned the stratagems of their gods and compared them to a spider's web (cf. 29:41), they said, 'Do you see that Allah mentions flies and spiders in the Qur'ān He revealed to Muḥammad? How can He possibly do that?' So Allah revealed this." Al-Ḥasan and Qatāda said that when Allah mentioned flies and the spider in the Book, the Jews laughed and said, "This has got nothing to do with Divine Revelation," and so Allah revealed this *āyat*.

Commentators disagree on the meaning of the word "*yastaḥyī*" (ashamed) in this *āyat*. It is said that it means, "does not fear," which aṭ-Ṭabarī prefers. Others say that it means, "does not fail to" or "does not refuse to". The root means to withdraw from doing a thing and refuse to do it out of fear of the occurrence of something ugly. This is impossible for Allah. In the *Ṣaḥīḥ* Collection of Muslim, Umm Salama mentioned that Umm Sulaym came to the Prophet, may Allah bless him and grant him peace, and said, "Messenger of Allah, Allah is not ashamed of the truth," meaning that He commanded people not to be to embarrassed to ask about it.

or of an even smaller thing.

"Wa mā fawqahā" (lit. "what is above it") means linguistically – and Allah knows best – what is smaller than it. Qatāda and Ibn Jurayj, however, said that it means what is larger.

they know it is the truth from their Lord.

The pronoun "it" refers to the example, meaning that the example is the truth and the truth is the opposite of the false.

they say, 'What does Allah mean by this example?'

This is not really a question; they are just denying it.

He misguides many by it and guides many by it.

It is said that these are the words of the unbelievers, who say, "What does Allah means by this example by which people are divided between guidance and misguidance?" It is also said that it is a reply from Allah Almighty and this interpretation is more likely because they affirm that guidance is from Him. In this case it is: "Say: He misguides many by it and guides many by it," meaning He gives success to some and disappoints others. This is a refutation of the position of the Mu'tazilites and others who say that Allah did not create misguidance or guidance. They said that the meaning of "misguides many" is only descriptive, in other words He describes such a person as being misguided because in reality Allah Himself does not misguide anyone. This understanding is in fact an example of their misguidance, and differs from the statements of the commentators and is linguistically improbable.

But He only misguides the deviators.

He does not misguide anyone except the deviators who He already knew He would not guide. Nawf al-Bikālī says, "'Uzayr said, when speaking to his Lord, 'My God, You create creatures and misguide whomever You wish and guide whomever You wish.' A voice said, ''Uzayr, turn from this! You should turn from this or I will remove your Prophethood from you. I will not be asked about what I do but they will be asked.'" The basic meaning of "*ḍalāl*" (misguidance) is disintegration. It is used when milk is dispersed in water, and Allah says, using that meaning of the word, *"When we have been absorbed into the earth."* (32:10). The root of "*fisq*" (deviation) is to come out from something, and it is used, for instance, to describe a date-stone coming out of its skin and a mouse leaving its hole. In a *ḥadīth* we find, "Five animals are all deviant (*fawāsiq*) and can be killed in the Ḥaram and out of it: snakes, crows, mice, rabid dogs and kites." ('Ā'isha in Muslim). One variant has scorpions instead of snakes. The Prophet, may

Allah bless him and grant him peace, used the word *fisq* for them because of the harm they do. When a man is *fāsiq* he is impious.

ٱلَّذِينَ يَنقُضُونَ عَهْدَ ٱللَّهِ مِنۢ بَعْدِ مِيثَٰقِهِۦ وَيَقْطَعُونَ مَآ أَمَرَ ٱللَّهُ بِهِۦٓ أَن يُوصَلَ وَيُفْسِدُونَ فِى ٱلْأَرْضِ ۚ أُو۟لَٰٓئِكَ هُمُ ٱلْخَٰسِرُونَ ﴿٢٧﴾

27 ***Those who break Allah's contract***
after it has been agreed,
and sever what Allah has commanded to be joined,
and cause corruption on the earth,
it is they who are the lost.

Those who break Allah's contract

"Those" refers back to the "deviators" in the previous *āyat*. The word used here for "break" (*naqaḍa*) means to nullify what has been concluded of a marriage contract, treaty or other agreement. *Nuqaḍa* means unravelled when applied to a rope and *munāqaḍa,* when used in respect of words, means that they contradict one another.

People disagree about the nature of the "contract" alluded to here. It is said that it is the one which Allah made with all the descendants of Ādam when He brought them forth from his loins. (cf. 7:172) It is said that it is Allah's directive to His creatures, commanding them to obey His commands and forbidding them to disobey Him. This is found in His Books, revealed on the tongues of all His Messengers. "Breaking it" is to abandon acting by it. It is said that the clear evidence of His Oneness in the heavens and the earth constitutes the contract and breaking it is not grasping it. It is also said that it is Allah's contract with those given the previous Books to make the Prophethood of Muḥammad, may Allah bless him and grant him peace, clear and not to conceal it. In this case, the *āyat* is about the People of the Book. Abū Isḥāq az-Zajjāj said,

"The contract is the one He made with the Prophets and those who follow them not to reject the Prophet, may Allah bless him and grant him peace. The evidence for that is found in *'When Allah made a covenant with the Prophets ... "undertake my commission on that condition?"'"* (3:81) The most likely position is that the *āyat* refers to the unbelievers.

after it has been agreed,

The word for "agreed" (*mithāq*) used here is employed when a contract has been confirmed by oath. It implies firmness in the strength of the contract.

and sever what Allah has commanded to be joined,

Scholars disagree about what Allah has commanded to be joined. It is said that it means to maintain the ties of kinship. It is said that He commanded that words must be joined to action and their severing is by speaking without acting. It is said that the "joining" refers to Allah's command to affirm all His Prophets but they severed this by affirming some of them and denying others. It is said that it refers to the *dīn* of Allah and His worship on earth, establishing His laws and observing the limits He has imposed. It is general, in that case, to everything that Allah Almighty commanded be joined. This is the statement of the majority. Kinship is, of course, a part of that.

and cause corruption on the earth

This refers to the fact that they worship other than Allah Almighty and commit injustice in what they do in order to fulfil their lower appetites. This is extreme corruption.

it is they who are the lost.

They have lost their fortunes and their honour. This is misguidance and destruction. One who is lost will find he has lost himself and his family on the Day of Rising and will be denied a place in the Garden.

This *āyat* directs people to be trustworthy in their contracts and to hold to that. It is not permitted to break any permissible contract to which you commit yourself, whether it is with a Muslim or anyone else, since Allah Almighty censured those who break their contracts. He says, *"Fulfil your contracts"* (5:1), and He said to His Prophet, peace be upon him, *"If you fear treachery on the part of a people, then revoke your treaty with them mutually."* (8:58). He forbade treachery and that is nothing other than the breaking of a contract, as will be made clear in its proper place.

كَيْفَ تَكْفُرُونَ بِاللَّهِ وَكُنتُمْ أَمْوَاتًا فَأَحْيَاكُمْ
ثُمَّ يُمِيتُكُمْ ثُمَّ يُحْيِيكُمْ ثُمَّ إِلَيْهِ تُرْجَعُونَ ﴿٢٨﴾

28 ***How can you reject Allah,***
when you were dead and then He gave you life,
then He will make you die and then give you life again,
then you will be returned to Him?

This question conveys amazement. It is extraordinary how anyone can disbelieve when the proof has been established. If it is asked how this can be addressed to the People of the Book when they have not rejected Allah, the answer is that, when they did not affirm the Prophethood of Muḥammad, may Allah bless him and grant him peace, and accept what he brought, then they associated something else with Allah because they did not acknowledge that the Qur'ān was from Him. Anyone who asserts that the Qur'ān is the words of a mortal has associated something else with Allah and therefore broken his contract. It is said that the rebuke means: "How can you be ungrateful for His blessings to you and reject His power to do this?" Al-Wāsiṭī said that this is used to rebuke them because dead things and inanimate things cannot contend with their Maker in any way at all. Dispute only issues from bodies which possess a *rūḥ*.

and then give you life again,

There is disagreement among the people of interpretation on the order of these two deaths and lives, and how many deaths and lives a human being has. Ibn 'Abbās and Ibn Mas'ūd said that it means that you were dead and non-existent before you were created and then He gave you life by creating you. Then He will make you die when your term has come to an end. Then He will bring you to life on the Day of Rising. Ibn 'Aṭiyya said, "This is what is meant by the *āyat*. It is a position which the unbelievers must hold since they acknowledge their life and previous non-existence. When the selves of the unbelievers concede that they were dead and non-existent and are now alive in this world, the fact that they will be made to die should make them more open to the possibility of another revivification. Yet they still deny that it has any valid relevance to them."

Someone else said, "According to this interpretation, the life in the grave has the same judgement as the life of this world." It is also said that it means that you were dead in the loins of Ādam and then Allah brought you out from him like atoms and then He made you die the death of this world and then He will resurrect you.

Another interpretation is that it means that you were dead as sperm in the loins of a man and the womb of a woman and then He took you out of the womb and gave you life. Then He will make you die after that in this life and give you life in the grave for the questioning. Then He will make you die in the grave and then give you the life of the resurrection for the Gathering, which is the life after which there is no more death. According to this interpretation, there are three deaths and three lives. If they were dead in Ādam's loins, brought out from his back and made to testify before they were sperm in the loins of men and wombs of women, then there are four deaths and four lives.

It is even said that Allah Almighty brought them into existence before He created Ādam, like dust, and then made them die. According to this, there are five deaths and five lives. There is a sixth death for the rebels of the Community of Muḥammad, may Allah bless him and grant him peace, when they enter the Fire, based on the *ḥadīth* of Abū Sa'īd al-Khudrī in which the Messenger of Allah, may Allah bless him and grant him peace, stated, "As for the true people of the Fire, who are its eternal inhabitants, they do not die in it nor live. The Fire, however, will smite some people for their wrong actions and Allah will make them die until they are coals. Then He will grant intercession on their behalf and they will be brought out group by group. They will be scattered by the rivers of the Garden and it will be said to the people of the Garden, 'Pour water on them.' And they will grow like seeds which are carried by a flood." A man of the people remarked, "It seems as if the Messenger of Allah, may Allah bless him and grant him peace, must have grazed sheep in the desert!" (Muslim)

then He will make you die

These words indicate a real death because they are stressed by the use of the verbal noun. That is to honour them. It is said that it is permitted for *"make you die"* to be a metaphor about their being absent from its pains by sleep and not a real death. The first is sounder. Grammarians agree that, when a verb is intensified by a verbal noun, it is not a metaphor, but indicates a reality, as when Allah says, *"Allah spoke directly to Musa."* (4:164) It is said that the meaning of "you were dead" means you were obscure and then He brought you to life by making you mentioned and honoured by this *dīn* and the Prophet who came to you. Then He will make you die and your fame will die and then He will bring you to life for the resurrection.

then you will be returned to Him.

You will be returned to His punishment on account of your disbelief returns. It is said it is to return to life and to the questioning as the Almighty says, *"As We originated the first creation, so We will regenerate it."* (21:104). So their return is like their beginning.

هُوَ ٱلَّذِى خَلَقَ لَكُم مَّا فِى ٱلْأَرْضِ جَمِيعًا ثُمَّ
ٱسْتَوَىٰٓ إِلَى ٱلسَّمَآءِ فَسَوَّىٰهُنَّ سَبْعَ سَمَٰوَٰتٍ وَهُوَ
بِكُلِّ شَىْءٍ عَلِيمٌ ﴿٢٩﴾

29 ***It is He who created***
everything on the earth for you
and then directed His attention up to heaven
and arranged it into seven regular heavens.
He has knowledge of all things.

It is He who created everything on the earth for you

"Created" means originated and brought into existence after non-existence. All of this was created for our sake. "Everything" means that all of the earth's blessings are for us. It is said that this fact indicates the Divine Unity and demands reflection on our part.

Those who say that the basic position, in respect of things which are useful, is that they are all permissible use this *āyat* and those like it as evidence. Another example is: *"He has made everything in the heavens and everything on the earth subservient to you."* (45:13) This applies until there is specific evidence that something is forbidden. The holders of this view support this by saying that tasty foods were created while it was possible that they would not be created. They were not created to no purpose and so they must have a use. That cannot be for Allah because He has no need of anything and so they must be for our benefit. That benefit consists either in our enjoying them, or in our avoiding them because they are a test for us, or in our reflecting on them. Those things can only come about through our tasting them and therefore they must be permissible.

This is unsound reasoning because we cannot accept as true the proposition that something which is not created to give benefit is to no purpose. Allah created things as they are and the principle of bringing benefit is not compulsory for Him. He is the only One who can makes things compulsory. So we cannot require the imposition of some benefit as such people claim, nor can we state that some of those benefits can only be obtained by means of taste. Other matters can also be deduced from foods, as is done by biologists. Another objection to their position is found in the case of substances which are feared to be lethal poisons. So those who espouse this position are countered by those people who forbid certain things. Others do not come down on either side, saying that there is no action about which we know either good or bad but that it is possible for it to be good in itself without that being specified before the *Sharī'a* came and therefore its ruling had to wait for the arrival of the *Sharī'a*. These are three statements made by the Mu'tazilites.

Shaykh Abū'l-Ḥasan [al-Ash'arī] and his adherents, most Mālikīs and aṣ-Ṣayarifī say that one suspends judgement about this question. That means that there is no judgement about the thing in that case, and that the *Sharī'a* will judge whatever it wishes when it comes. The intellect cannot judge something to be obligatory or not. Its portion in the matter is simply to recognise matters for what they are.

The sound meaning of *"created everything on the earth for you"* is that it means that it is food for reflection. That is indicated by the lessons which precede and follow it: giving life, making die, creation, direction to the heaven and arranging it. The One who does such things does not lack the power to bring you back to life again.

It is said that the meaning of "for you" is "all for your use". What is meant by it is "for you to reflect upon" because of what we mentioned. If one were to ask what the benefit of reflecting on scorpions and snakes is, we reply that by means of harmful things a person is reminded of the punishments which Allah has prepared for the unbelievers in the Fire, and that induces him to believe and abandon disobedience. This is the greatest consideration. Ibn 'Arabī said, "There is nothing in this phrase which involves prohibition, permission or suspension of judgement. This *āyat* is evidence and clarification of Allah's Oneness."

Those with a firm grasp of meanings say about *"It is He who created everything on the earth for you"* that it implies that people should use these things to strengthen their obedience to Allah and not use them in ways that involve disobedience. Abū 'Uthmān said, "He gave it all to you and subjected it to you as proof of the vastness of His generosity and so that you would have confidence in the generous gifts He has guaranteed to you in the Hereafter. But do not allow His great kindness to lead you to be content with few actions since He showed you immense blessings before action. That is *tawḥīd*."

'Umar said that a man came to the Messenger of Allah, may Allah bless him and grant him peace, and asked him to give to him. The Messenger of Allah said, "I do not have anything, but buy in my name and when something comes to me, we will pay it." 'Umar said to him, "Give something when you have something to give! Allah has not obliged you to do what you are unable to do." The Prophet disliked what 'Umar said. Then a man of the Anṣār said, "Messenger of Allah! Spend and do not fear diminution from the Master of the Throne!" The Messenger of Allah, may Allah bless him and grant him peace, smiled and joy could be seen in his face at the words of the Anṣārī. Then the Messenger of Allah said, "That is what I am commanded to do."

Our scholars say that fear of diminution is having a bad opinion of Allah because Allah Almighty created the earth and what is in it for the sons of Ādam, quoting the phrase, *"He created everything on the earth for you."* All these things are subjected to the human being absolutely as evidence against him so that he will be Allah's slave as he was created to be. When the slave has a good opinion of Allah, he does not fear diminution because he knows that Allah will replace it. *"Anything you expend will be replaced by Him. He is the Best of Providers,"* (34:39) and *"My Lord is Rich Beyond Need, Generous."* (27:40) The Messenger of Allah said, "Allah Almighty said, 'My mercy precedes My anger. Son of Ādam, spend and I will spend on you.' The right hand of Allah is full and pouring forth, not decreased by any of the night or day." The Messenger of Allah, may Allah bless him and grant him peace, also said, "There is no day which dawns on the slaves of Allah without two angels descending and one of them saying, 'O Allah, refund those who give money' and the other saying, 'O Allah, ruin those who withhold it.' The same happens in the evening." This is all sound and related by the Imāms, praise be to Allah.

If someone has an illuminated breast and knows that his Lord is wealthy and generous, he spends and does not fear diminution. That is how it is with someone whose appetites are dead to this world and is content with a little nourishment to keep him alive and whose desires for himself are cut off. This person gives in both wealth and constriction and does not fear diminution. The person who relies on himself fears diminution. When he gives today and tomorrow has desire for something, he fears that he will not get it tomorrow and the business of the expenses of the day worry him because of fear of diminution.

Muslim reported that Asmā' bint Abī Bakr said, "The Messenger of Allah, may Allah bless him and grant him peace, told me, 'Spend, (or give out or expend) and do not hold back, or Allah will hold back from you. Do not refuse to spend your surplus or Allah will deny you His.'" An-Nasā'ī reported that 'Ā'isha said, "Once a beggar came to me while the Messenger of Allah was with me and I gave instructions for something to be given to him and then summoned him and looked at him. The Messenger of Allah said, 'Do you want nothing to enter or leave your house except with your knowledge.' 'Yes,' I replied. He said, 'Don't worry, 'Ā'isha. Do not hold back, or Allah will hold back from you.'"

and then directed His attention up to heaven

In His words "then directed", the word "then" is simply a narrative aid and does not imply any time sequence in the matters referred to. Linguistically the word "directed" (*istawā*) means to ascend to and be on top of something as in *"When you and those with you settled in the ship."* (23:28). It is used for the sky over your head and the birds over your head.

This *āyat* is one of those which are considered problematic. Regarding it and others of a similar nature people take three views.

One of them is that we should read it and believe in it and not seek to explain it, which is the position of most of the Imāms. An example of this attitude is what is related from Mālik when a man asked him about the words of Allah, *"The All-Merciful was established firmly on the throne."* (20:5) Mālik said, "The meaning of *istawā* (established firmly) is not unknown but the how of it is not intelligible; belief in it is mandatory; and asking about it is an innovation. I think you are an evil man!" Others say that we should read it and understand it literally. This is the position of the anthropormorphists. Yet others say that we should read it and interpret it metaphorically and cannot take it literally.

Al-Farrā' said about this *āyat*, "*Istawā* in Arabic has two usual meanings. One refers to people reaching full maturity. The second is being free from crookedness. A third possibility is someone directing himself to something. This is its meaning in this *āyat*, and Allah knows best." Ibn 'Abbās said that *istawā* here means to ascend. All these things are possible in Arabic. Sufyān ibn 'Uyayna said that it means "to aim for it", in other words its creation. It is said that the meaning of the word is without limitation or definition, as aṭ-Ṭabarī preferred. Abū'l-'Āliyya ar-Riyāḥī said, "It means to rise."

It would appear from this *āyat*, if you take the word "then" as having a temporally sequential meaning, that Allah created the earth before the heavens whereas in *Sūrat an-Nāzi'āt* (79) He describes the heavens being created before the earth. This was the position of Qatāda: heaven was created first. Aṭ-Ṭabarī related it from him. Mujāhid and other commentators say that Allah dried the water on which His Throne rested and turned it into the earth and made smoke rise from it and made heaven. Thus earth was created before heaven. I believe that what Qatāda said is sound, Allah willing: that Allah first created the smoke of heaven and then created the earth and directed Himself to heaven, which was smoke and arranged it and then He smoothed out the earth.

Part of what indicates that smoke was created before the earth is what is related from Ibn Mas'ūd and some Companions about this *āyat*: the Throne of Allah Almighty was on the water and He did not create anything before water. When He desired to bring about creation, He produced smoke from the water and it rose above it and was high above it (*samā*) and so He called it heaven (*samā'*). Then He dried the water and made it earth and then split it up and made it into seven earths.

The basic element of the creation of all things is water as is reported by Ibn Mājah and Abū Ḥātim al-Bustī from Abū Hurayra. He asked the Messenger of Allah, "When I see you my self is happy and my eye delighted. Tell me about the origin of all things." He said, "All things were created from water." He asked, "Tell me about something by virtue of which, I will enter the Garden." He said, "Feed people, extend the greeting, maintain ties with your kin, and stand in prayer at night when people are asleep, and you will enter the Garden in peace."

Ibn 'Abbās said that the Messenger of Allah, may Allah bless him and grant him peace, said, "The first thing that Allah created was the Pen and He commanded it to write down all that would be." Al-Bayhaqī said, "Allah knows best, but he meant that the first thing that Allah created after water, wind and the Throne was the Pen." Ṭāwūs said that a man came to 'Abdullāh ibn 'Amr ibn al-'Āṣ and asked, "What was creation created from?" He said, "From water, fire, darkness, wind and earth." The man asked, "And from what were these created?" He replied, "I do not know." Then the man went to 'Abdullāh ibn az-Zubayr and asked him and he gave the same answer as 'Abdullāh ibn 'Amr. Then he went to 'Abdullāh ibn 'Abbās and he answered the same. When he asked the second question, Ibn 'Abbās recited, *"He has made everything in the heavens and everything on the earth subservient to you."* (45:13) The man said, "This could only come from a man of the people of the House of the Prophet!"

and arranged it into seven regular heavens.

Allah mentions seven heavens but does not give a clear number of earths in the Revelation. The only possible reference to seven earths is found in His words, *"and of the earth the same number (*mithlahunna*)."* (65:12) There is disagreement about the meaning of that but it is said that it is referring to their number (lit. "their like"), and the number is also used in several *aḥādīth* with reference to the number of earths.

He has knowledge of all things.

He has knowledge of all He created. Since He created things, He must know them. He says, *"Does He who created not then know?"* (67:14). He knows all known things with timeless pre-eternal knowledge which He alone possesses.

وَإِذْ قَالَ رَبُّكَ لِلْمَلَٰٓئِكَةِ إِنِّي جَاعِلٌ فِي ٱلْأَرْضِ خَلِيفَةً ۖ قَالُوٓا۟
أَتَجْعَلُ فِيهَا مَن يُفْسِدُ فِيهَا وَيَسْفِكُ ٱلدِّمَآءَ وَنَحْنُ نُسَبِّحُ
بِحَمْدِكَ وَنُقَدِّسُ لَكَ ۖ قَالَ إِنِّيٓ أَعْلَمُ مَا لَا تَعْلَمُونَ ۝٣٠

30 ***When your Lord said to the angels,***
'I am putting a khalif on the earth,'
they said, 'Why put on it
one who will cause corruption on it and shed blood
when we glorify You with praise
and proclaim Your purity?'
He said, 'I know what you do not know.'

When your Lord said to the angels,

It is possible that there is an elided word here in which case the meaning would be, "Remember when ..." It is also said that it goes back to His words, *"Worship your Lord who created you,"* (2:21) in which case the meaning would be, "When the One who created you said to the angels."

The fact that Allah addressed the angels indicates that they existed and understood. He addressed them not to consult them or to ask for their opinion but simply to inform them.

'I am putting a khalif on the earth,'

"Putting" in this context means creating, as aṭ-Ṭabarī said. The earth means Makka. The Prophet, may Allah bless him and grant him peace, said, "The earth was smoothed out from Makka," which is why it is called the Mother of Cities. *Khalīfa* (khalif) has the form of an active participle, meaning "the one who replaced the angels before him on the earth", or other than the angels, according to what has been reported. It is also possible that it is in the passive mode, in which case it means one who is sent as a representative.

This *āyat* is sound evidence for having a leader and a khalif who is obeyed so that he will be a focus for the cohesion of society, and the rulings of the khalifate will carried out. None of the Imāms of the Community disagree about the obligatory nature of having such a leader, except for what is related from al-Aṣamm (lit. the Deaf), who lived up to the meaning of his name and was indeed deaf to the *Sharī'a*, and those who take his position who say that the khalifate is permitted rather than mandatory if the Community undertakes all their obligations on their own without the need for a ruler to enforce them.

The Companions agreed to make Abū Bakr khalif after the disagreement which took place between the Muhājirūn and the Anṣār. If it had been a definite obligation that the ruler had to be from Quraysh, there would have been no point in the argument and debate which took place. When Abū Bakr died, he delegated the task of being khalif to 'Umar and no one said that it was not mandatory. Its obligatory nature indicates that it is one of the pillars of the *dīn* which support the Muslims. Praise be to Allah, the Lord of the worlds.

They said, 'Why put on it one who will cause corruption on it and shed blood,

We know definitely that the angels only know what they are informed about and have no foreknowledge. That applies to all angels because Allah says, *"They do not precede Him in speech,"* (21:27) in praise of them.

As to why they asked this question, it is said that it means that when they heard the word "khalif", they understood that the sons of Ādam would cause corruption since the task of the khalif is to put things right. They, however, made the label of disobedience apply to all human beings. So to cheer their hearts, Allah made it clear to them that some humans would cause corruption and some would not. That was confirmed when Allah taught Ādam the names and unveiled knowledge to him which had been hidden. It is said that they asked the question because they had seen the corruption and bloodshed of the jinn who had inhabited the earth before the creation of Ādam. So Allah sent Iblīs against them with an army of angels and they killed them and drove them into the seas and to the tops of the mountains. That was when pride entered Iblīs's heart. Their words, "Why put?" is thus a simple question. "Is this khalif going to be like the jinn or not?"

Ibn Zayd and others said that Allah informed them that the khalif's descendants would cause corruption and shed blood and so they asked this, either from astonishment that Allah was appointing a species who would disobey him or because they considered both the appointment and the disobedience terrible.

when we glorify You with praise

Its meaning is "We disassociate You from any attribute which is not appropriate for You." By their glorification they disassociate Him from all defects through His exaltation. Ṭalḥa ibn 'Ubaydullāh said, "I asked the Messenger of Allah, may Allah bless him and grant him peace, about the meaning of 'Glory be to Allah', and he said, 'It is disassociating Allah from every defect.'" It is derived from the verbal root *sabḥ*, which means swimming and travelling a long distance.

Interpreters disagree about the interpretation of the glorification of the angels. Ibn Mas'ūd and Ibn 'Abbās said that it is their prayer, as in the words of Allah: *"If it had not been that he was a man who glorified Allah,"* (37:143) meaning "one of those who pray". It is said that their glorification is raising their voices with *dhikr*, as al-Mufaḍḍal says. Qatāda said that it is saying

"Subhānallāh" as is usual linguistically. That is confirmed according to what is related by Abū Dharr from the Messenger of Allah, may Allah bless him and grant him peace, who, when he was asked, "Which words are best?" replied, "Those which Allah chose for His angels and slaves: 'Glory be to Allah with His praise.'" (Muslim) 'Abdu'r-Raḥmān ibn Qurṭ reported that the Messenger of Allah, may Allah bless him and grant him peace, said during the Night Journey, "Glory be to the High, the Most High. Glory be to Him and exalted is He!" (al-Bayhaqī)

and proclaim Your purity?'

"We exalt You, praise You and purify Your Name from those things which are not appropriate for You which heretics have ascribed to You," as Mujāhid, Abū Ṣāliḥ and others said. Aḍ-Ḍaḥḥāk and others said that it means: "We purify ourselves for you, seeking Your pleasure." Some people said that Qatāda said it means: "pray" and that *taqdīs* is prayer, but this is weak according to Ibn 'Atiyya. I say that it is a sound meaning. Prayer contains exaltation, proclamation of purity and glorification. The Messenger of Allah, may Allah bless him and grant him peace, used to say in his *rukū'* and prostration, "Glorious, Pure, Lord of the angels and the *Rūḥ*." ('Ā'isha in Muslim) It means purification as is seen elsewhere in the Qur'an. The prayer is purification from wrong actions. Allah knows best.

He said, 'I know what you do not know.'

Scholars disagree about the meaning of the words "what you do not know". Ibn 'Abbās said, "Iblīs was proud when He was honoured and made the treasurer of heaven. He believed that it was his prerogative and he despised the potential for disbelief and disobedience inherent in Ādam. The angels said this, not knowing what Iblīs had inside him which was different to what they had. Then Allah told them, "I know what you do not know," meaning that He knew what Iblīs really felt about Ādam. Qatāda said that it refers to the Prophets, men of virtue and people of obedience who Allah would place on earth. It is also possible that the meaning is general and includes all of that

وَعَلَّمَ ءَادَمَ ٱلْأَسْمَآءَ كُلَّهَا ثُمَّ عَرَضَهُمْ عَلَى ٱلْمَلَٰٓئِكَةِ
فَقَالَ أَنۢبِـُٔونِى بِأَسْمَآءِ هَٰٓؤُلَآءِ إِن كُنتُمْ صَٰدِقِينَ ﴿٣١﴾

31 ***He taught Adam the names of all things.***
Then He arrayed them before the angels and said,
'Tell me the names of these if you are telling the truth.'

He taught Adam the names of all things.

"Teaching" here means "inspiring with the necessary knowledge". It is possible that it took place by means of the angel Jibrīl. Sufi scholars say, "He knew them when Allah taught him and remembered them when He made him do so but forgot the contract he had made because, in it, he relied on himself. Allah says, *'We made a contract with Ādam before, but he forgot. We did not find that he had a firm resolve.'*" (20:115) Ibn 'Aṭā' said, "If those names had not been unveiled to Ādam, he would not have been able to tell them to the angels."

Ādam's *kunya* is Abū'l-Bashar, which means "the father of humanity". Abū Muḥammad is also used since Muḥammad is the Seal of the Prophets, as as-Suhaylī said. It is said that his *kunya* was Abū Muḥammad in the Garden and Abū'l-Bashar on the earth.

There is disagreement about the derivation of the name Ādam. It is said that it is derived from the crust (*adam*) and surface (*adīm*) of the earth and he was called that because he was created from it. Ibn 'Abbās stated that. It is said that it is derived from *adma*, which is brownness. Aḍ-Ḍaḥḥāk claimed that it is duskiness. An-Naḍr claimed that it is whiteness and that Ādam was white, since they use this word for a white camel. I believe that the sound view is that it is derived from the surface of the earth. Sa'īd ibn Jubayr said, "Ādam received his name because he was created from the surface of the earth and he was called *insān* (human being) because he forgot (*nasī*)."

The people of interpretation disagree about the meaning of the "names" mentioned in this *āyat*. Many say that it is all things, large and small.

Then He arrayed them before the angels

Interpreters disagree about whether the presentation of the names involved the presentation of the things themselves or simply the names themselves to the angels. Ibn Mas'ūd says that it means to display the actual things. Others say that it just means the names.

and said, 'Tell Me the names of these if you are telling the truth.'

"If the sons of Ādam are simply going to cause corruption on the earth, then show me that you have the same knowledge that I have taught this new creature." In other words there is far more to a human being than the angels were able to perceive. Al-Mubarrad says that "*ṣādiqīn*" (telling the truth) means "knowing".

قَالُواْ سُبْحَٰنَكَ لَا عِلْمَ لَنَآ إِلَّا مَا عَلَّمْتَنَآ إِنَّكَ أَنتَ
ٱلْعَلِيمُ ٱلْحَكِيمُ ٣٢

32 ***They said, 'Glory be to You!***
We have no knowledge
except what You have taught us.
You are the All-Knowing, the All-Wise.'

"Glory be to You" above anyone but You knowing the Unseen. This is their answer to "Tell me." They answered that they only know what Allah has taught them. From this comes the obligation for someone who is asked for knowledge he does not possess to say, "Allah knows best, I do not know," in imitation of the angels,

Prophets, and virtuous scholars. The Prophet, may Allah bless him and grant him peace, told us, however, that, when the scholars died, true knowledge would disappear and we would be left with ignorant people who would be asked for *fatwā*s and give *fatwā*s according to their own opinion. So they will be misguided and also misguide others.

قَالَ يَٰٓـَٔادَمُ أَنۢبِئْهُم بِأَسْمَآئِهِمْ ۖ فَلَمَّآ أَنۢبَأَهُم بِأَسْمَآئِهِمْ
قَالَ أَلَمْ أَقُل لَّكُمْ إِنِّىٓ أَعْلَمُ غَيْبَ ٱلسَّمَٰوَٰتِ وَٱلْأَرْضِ
وَأَعْلَمُ مَا تُبْدُونَ وَمَا كُنتُمْ تَكْتُمُونَ ﴿٣٣﴾

33 ***He said, 'Adam, tell them their names.'***
When he had told them their names,
He said, 'Did I not tell you that I know
the Unseen of the heavens and the earth,
and I know what you make known
and what you hide?'

He said, 'Adam, tell them their names.'

Allah commanded him to tell them their names after they were arrayed before the angels so that they would know that He knows best what He asked them about. This was in order to demonstrate Ādam's excellence and high position. He was better than them since he had greater knowledge than them and they were made to prostrate before him and become his students and ordered to learn from him, and so he had the rank of majesty and greatness.

Some scholars use this as evidence for the Prophethood of Ādam before he was in the Garden since Allah says, *"Tell them their names,"* and so Allah commanded him to inform the angels of that which they had no knowledge.

This *āyat* contains evidence for the excellence of knowledge and its people. In a *ḥadīth* we find, "The angels lower their wings to anyone who seeks knowledge for the pure pleasure of seeking it." They only do that for the scholars alone because that is what Allah obliged them to do in the case of Ādam and so they continue to behave in the same way. When knowledge appears in a person, they are humble to him out of respect for knowledge and its people and pleasure at him seeking it and being involved with it. This is merely for the seekers of knowledge, so how much more must that be in the case of its masters!

Scholars disagree about who is better: the angels or the sons of Ādam. Some people say that the Messengers among human beings are better than the Messengers from the angels and that human *awliyā'* are better than the *awliyā'* of the angels. Some people say that the Highest Assembly is better. Their argument is that they are *"honoured slaves, who do not precede Him in speech,"* (21:26-27) and other similar *āyat*s. There is also the *ḥadīth qudsī* in which Allah says, "If he mentions Me in an assembly, I mention him in an assembly better than them."

Those who seek evidence for the superiority of the sons of Ādam, quote the *āyat*: *"Those who believe and do right actions, they are the best of creatures."* (98:7) and the words of the Prophet, "The angels lower their wings to anyone who seeks knowledge for the pure pleasure of seeking it." There are other *aḥādīth* in which Allah boasts of mankind to the angels and He only boasts of the best. Allah knows best.

Some scholars have said that there is no way of concluding that the Prophets are better than the angels or that the angels are better than them, because the only way of doing so would be if there was a definitive report from Allah or from His Messenger or the consensus of the Community, and nothing of that sort exists.

He said, 'Did I not tell you that I know the Unseen of the heavens and the earth,

This is proof that no one knows anything of the Unseen except what Allah informs Him of, like the Prophets or those whom Allah teaches. Astrologers, soothsayers and such people are all liars. This will be discussed in *Sūrat al-An'ām.*

and I know what you make known

This refers to their words about Allah putting someone on the earth who would cause corruption there.

and what you hide?'

Ibn 'Abbās, Ibn Mas'ūd and Sa'īd ibn Jubayr said that what is being referred to is the pride and rebellion which Iblīs concealed in himself. Mahdī ibn Maymūn said, "We were with al-Ḥasan when al-Ḥasan ibn Dīnar asked him, 'What did the angels hide?' He replied, 'When Allah created Ādam, the angels saw an extraordinary creature. It was as if something about that worried them. Then they turned confidentially to one another and said, "Why are we concerned about this creature! Allah has not created anything but that we are more honoured than it in His sight."'"

وَإِذْ قُلْنَا لِلْمَلَٰٓئِكَةِ ٱسْجُدُوا۟ لِءَادَمَ فَسَجَدُوٓا۟ إِلَّآ إِبْلِيسَ أَبَىٰ
وَٱسْتَكْبَرَ وَكَانَ مِنَ ٱلْكَٰفِرِينَ ﴿٣٤﴾

34 ***We said to the angels, 'Prostrate to Adam!'***
and they prostrated, with the exception of Iblis.
He refused and was arrogant
and was one of the unbelievers.

We said to the angels, 'Prostrate to Ādam!' and they prostrated,

"Prostrate" here means to be humble and submit. Those who say that Ādam and his sons are better than the angels find evidence in Allah's words to the angels here: *"Prostrate to Ādam!"* They say that this indicates that he was better than them. The answer to that is that the meaning of this "prostrate" simply means to be humble in front of Ādam. If someone were to ask, "If he was not better than them, what was the point of telling them to prostrate to him?", the answer is that, when the angels exulted in their glorification and praise, Allah commanded them to prostrate to something other than Him in order to show them that He had no need of them and their worship. Some say that they criticised and belittled Ādam and did not recognise the special nature of what Allah had created and so they were commanded to prostrate. It could be that it was a punishment for them because of what they said.

It is said that Ibn 'Abbās found evidence for the supreme excellence of human beings in the fact that Allah swore by the life of His Messenger, may Allah bless him and grant him peace, and said, *"By your life! They were wandering blindly in their drunkenness,"* (15:72) and granted him security from punishment in His words, *"So that Allah may forgive you your earlier errors and any later ones."* (48:2)

People disagree about how the angels prostrated to Ādam although they agree that the prostration was not worship. Most say that this command to the angels was for them to place their foreheads on the ground as is done in the prayer because the form of prostration is clear in both custom and the *Sharī'a.* Thus the prostration was to honour him because of his excellence and to obey Allah's command to them. Ādam acted as their *qibla.* Some people say that it was not the *"sajda"* (act of prostration) which is known today but rather refers to the basic linguistic meaning of the word, which is abasement and obedience. So the meaning is that they humbled themselves before Ādam and acknowledged his virtue. So "prostrated" simply means "did what they were commanded".

There is also disagreement about whether the prostration was exclusively to Ādam, so that it is not permitted to prostrate to anyone else in existence except Allah, or whether such prostration was permitted until the time of Ya'qūb, based on the words of Allah, *"He raised his parents up onto the throne. The others fell prostrate in front of him."* (12:100). Most, however, say that this kind of prostration was permitted right up until the time of the Messenger of Allah, may Allah bless him and grant him peace. When the trees and camels prostrated before him, the Companions said to him, "We are more entitled to prostrate to you than trees and stray camels." He told them, "It is not permitted to prostrate to anyone except the Lord of the worlds." (Ibn Mājah and al-Bustī) When Mu'ādh came from Syria, he prostrated to the Messenger of Allah who said, "What is this?" He said, "Messenger of Allah, I went to Syria and saw them prostrate before their patriarchs and bishops. So I wanted to do that with you." He stated, "No one should do that."

with the exception of Iblīs.

The exception is connected to what was just mentioned before (i.e. the angels), as is generally stated. Ibn 'Abbās, Ibn Mas'ūd, Ibn Jurayj and others said that Iblīs was one of the angels. Ibn 'Abbās said, "His name was 'Azāzīl and he was one of the noblest of the angels. He had four wings and then was deprived of his angelic status. When he disobeyed Allah, He cursed him and he became Shayṭān. Sa'īd ibn Jubayr said, "The jinn were a tribe of the angels, created from fire and Iblīs was one of them. The rest of the angels were created from light." Ibn Zayd, al-Ḥasan and Qatāda said, "Iblīs was the father of the jinn in the same way that Ādam was the father of human beings. He was not an angel." A similar statement is also related from Ibn 'Abbās. He said that his name was al-Ḥārith in Arabic. Sahr ibn Ḥawshab and others say, "He was one of the jinn who were on earth. The angels fought them and captured him as a child and he worshipped with the angels."

Others find their evidence in Allah's description of the angels: *"They do not disobey Allah in respect of any order He gives them and carry out what they are ordered to do,"* (66:6) and in the *āyat*, *"Iblīs was one of the jinn."* (18:50) The jinn are not angels. The proponents of the first position answer that nothing prevents Iblīs from issuing from the angels as a whole, since Allah knew that he would be wretched and He is not asked about what He does. Others say that he was one of the guardians of the Garden but not one of the angels of heaven. Sometimes the angels are referred to as "jinn" because of their being hidden from sight in the same way.

He refused and was arrogant

He refused to prostrate because he thought he was better than Ādam. This means that he considered the command and wisdom of Allah to be foolish. This is the arrogance about which the Prophet said. "Anyone who has an atom's weight of pride in his heart will not enter the Garden!" When a man said to the Prophet that a man likes his clothing and appearance to be good, he said, "Allah is beautiful and loves beauty. Pride is to disregard the truth and to despise people." (Muslim)

Ibn al-Qāsim said, "I heard that the first disobedience was envy and pride when Iblīs envied Ādam and Ādam desired to eat from the tree." Qatāda said, "Iblīs envied Adam for the honour he had been given. He complained, 'I am made of fire and this one is only made of clay.'" So the first wrong action was pride, then greed which caused Ādam to eat from the tree, and then envy when the son of Ādam envied his brother.

and was one of the unbelievers.

This "was" means "became". Most interpreters say that the meaning is: Allah knew that he would become an unbeliever because an unbeliever has one reality and a believer another and Allah knows them both. This is sound because of what the Prophet said in al-Bukhārī, "Actions are by their seals." It is said that Iblīs worshipped Allah for eighty thousand years and had leadership and was a guardian of the Garden during all of which time he was gradually being drawn on, in the same way that hypocrites say the *shahāda* with their tongues and that Bal'am had the greatest Name on his tongue. He had leadership but pride was firmly rooted in him. Ibn 'Abbās said, "He thought that he had greater excellence than the angels which is why he said, "I am better than him." This is why Allah said, *"What prevented you from prostrating to what I created with My own Hands? Were you overcome by arrogance or are you one of the exalted?"* (38:75) The basis of his creation was the fire of Might, which is shown by the fact that He swore by it when he said, *"By Your might, I will mislead all of them."* (38:82). Might brings about pride so that he thought that he was better than

Ādam. Abū Ṣāliḥ said, "The angels were created from the light of might and Iblīs from the fire of might."

Our scholars say that, if someone is not a Prophet and Allah displays miracles and the breaking of normal patterns at his hand, it does not necessarily indicate that he is saint. This is opposed to what the Sufis and Shi'ites say about this matter, indicating that if he had not been a *walī*, Allah would not have made appear on his hands what He did. Our proof is that the knowledge that one of us is a *walī* of Allah can only be validated after it is clear that he has died a believer. If it is not known that someone died a believer, we cannot unequivocally state that he is the *walī* of Allah. That is only proven by faith.

There is disagreement about whether there was any unbeliever before Iblīs or not. Some say that Iblīs was the first to disbelieve and it is also said that there were unbelievers of the jinn before him, who were on the earth. There is also disagreement about whether his *kufr* was ignorance or obstinacy, both things being said by the people of the *Sunna*.

وَقُلْنَا يَٰٓـَٔادَمُ ٱسْكُنْ أَنتَ وَزَوْجُكَ ٱلْجَنَّةَ وَكُلَا مِنْهَا رَغَدًا
حَيْثُ شِئْتُمَا وَلَا تَقْرَبَا هَٰذِهِ ٱلشَّجَرَةَ فَتَكُونَا
مِنَ ٱلظَّٰلِمِينَ ﴿٣٥﴾

35 ***We said, 'Adam, live in the Garden,***
you and your wife,
and eat freely from it wherever you will.
But do not approach this tree
and so become wrongdoers.'

We said, 'Adam, live in the Garden, you and your wife

There is no disagreement that Allah expelled Iblīs when he became an unbeliever and put him far from the Garden and that, afterwards, He commanded Ādam "to live" (*uskun*) in the Garden, in other words, to abide there and take up residence there. *Sakan,* from the same root, means any place that one feels at home in; *sikkīn* is a knife, which is so called because it stills the movement of the slaughtered animal; *miskīn* (indigent) is derived from the same root since a poor person cannot move about through lack of means; *sukkan* is the rudder of the ship because it keeps it steady.

The *āyat* shows that living in a place does not necessarily constitute ownership of it. One of the gnostics said that the use of the word *"uskun"* (live) shows that it was for a time which would come to an end. So the original entry of Ādam and Ḥawwā' into the Garden was one of a temporary and not a permanent nature. If this understanding is correct, there is evidence in it for what most scholars say: that if someone gives a man a place to live, the man does not own it by living there and the owner can evict him when he decides to terminate the tenant's residency.

Ādam's wife was Ḥawwā' who was created from his rib without Ādam being aware of it. If pain had been involved in that process, men would not have affection for their wives.

We ignore what the Mu'tazilites claimed about it not being the Garden of Eternity, but a garden on the earth. That is because Allah uses the definite article for it and the fact that when someone asks Allah for the Garden, using the definite article, He only means the Garden of Eternity.

It is not logically impossible that Iblīs entered the Garden to tempt Ādam. It is agreed that the angels enter and leave the Garden and that during the Night Journey, the Prophet, peace be upon him, entered it and left it. If someone claims that what is meant is the Holy Land, which Allah purified of sins, that is ignorance on their part, because Allah commanded the tribe of Israel to enter the Holy Land, which was greater Syria. The people who follow the *Sharī'a* agree that Allah purified the Holy Land, but nevertheless acts of rebellion, disbelief and lying occurred in it. These things were not prevented by its being sanctified.

But do not approach this tree

Do not go near it to eat from it. It is said that it means "do not touch it" or "do not go close to it". Ibn 'Aṭiyya said that this is a clear example of *sadd adh-dharā'i'* (the legal principle of barring the means to wrong action). Some of those who have a fine grasp of the use of language say that the instruction not to approach, in itself, indicates that they were, in fact, going to fall into error and leave the Garden and not dwell in it forever because someone who is eternal is not commanded or forbidden anything. The evidence of this is in the words of Allah, *"I am putting a khalif on the earth,"* (2:30) showing that Adam was definitely going to leave it.

A tree is a plant with a trunk. Interpreters disagree about what type of tree this was. Ibn Mas'ūd, Ibn 'Abbās, Sa'īd ibn Jubayr and others say that it was a grapevine and that is why wine was forbidden us. Ibn 'Abbās, Abū Mālik and Qatāda say that it was wheat. Wahb ibn Munabbih said that when Allah relented towards Ādam, he made it the food of his descendants. Ibn Jurayj said that some of the Companions said that it was a fig tree as is reported from Qatāda. Ibn 'Aṭiyya said that there is no specification of what it was which can be reliably relied upon. What is correct is to believe that Allah forbade Ādam a particular tree and then he went to it and disobeyed Him by eating from it. The tree was a test.

They also disagree about how he could eat from it in the light of the threat which follows it, *"and so become wrongdoers."* Some people said that they ate from other than the tree which was indicated and did not interpret the prohibition as applying to the entire species, which suggests that Iblīs deluded them into taking an over-literal understanding of Allah's instruction to them. Ibn al-'Arabī said, "It was the first act of disobedience according to this view." It is also said that Ādam ate out of forgetfulness, forgetting the threat. That is sound by the report from Allah about that in His Book, *"We made a contract with Adam before, but he forgot. We did not find that he had a firm resolve."* (20:117)

It is said that the first of the two to eat from it was Ḥawwā' because Iblīs misled her and that the first of his words were to her because she could whisper to her husband, and it was the first trial for men from women. When she mentioned it to Ādam, he rejected it and mentioned the contract. Iblīs persisted with Ḥawwā' who, in turn, persisted with Ādam until she said, "I will eat before you. If anything happens to me, you will be safe." She ate and was not harmed and went to Ādam and said, "I ate and it did not harm me." So he ate and then their private parts became clear to them and they fell into wrong action. This is because the command to them was in the dual. So there was no punishment until they both did it. It is sound that there was no full disobedience until they had both done it. Ādam did not see this fact and so he forgot the ruling.

Scholars disagree about whether the Prophets can commit minor wrong actions for which they are punished, or not, although there is a consensus that they are protected from great wrong actions and every vice in which there is disgrace or imperfection. Aṭ-Ṭabarī and other *fuqahā'*, *mutakallimūn* and *ḥadīth* scholars say that minor wrong actions are possible for them, while the Shi'ites say that they are protected from all of that. Some of the *fuqahā'* of Mālik, Abū Ḥanīfa and ash-Shāfi'ī say that they are protected from all minor wrong actions as they are protected from all major wrong actions because we are commanded to follow them in their actions and conduct completely without attention to context. If they were allowed minor wrong actions, it would not be possible to follow them since it would not be possible to judge which of their actions were right and which were wrong. Some later scholars took the former position, saying that Allah would report about any wrong actions which occurred and rebuke them for them so we would know which they were. This does not detract from their position. As al-Junayd said, "The good actions of the pious are the evil actions of those brought near."

and so become wrongdoers.'

The root of the word for wrongdoers, *ẓulm*, means to put something in other than its proper place. Land which is 'wronged' (*maẓlūma*) is land which had no well and then a well was dug. *Ẓalīm* is also used for milk which is drunk before becoming thick. A man who is *ẓalīm* inflicts great injustice. *Ẓulm* is *shirk* as Allah says, *"Associating others with Him is a terrible wrong (ẓulm)."* (31:13)

فَأَزَلَّهُمَا ٱلشَّيْطَٰنُ عَنْهَا فَأَخْرَجَهُمَا مِمَّا كَانَا فِيهِ ۖ
وَقُلْنَا ٱهْبِطُوا۟ بَعْضُكُمْ لِبَعْضٍ عَدُوٌّ ۖ وَلَكُمْ فِى ٱلْأَرْضِ
مُسْتَقَرٌّ وَمَتَٰعٌ إِلَىٰ حِينٍ ٣٦

36 ***But Shayṭān made them slip up by means of it,***
expelling them from where they were.
We said, 'Go down from here
as enemies to each other!
You will have residence on the earth
and enjoyment for a time.'

But Shayṭān made them slip up by means of it,

The word for "slip up" comes from the root *zilla* which means error, so he made them fall into error. Allah says elsewhere, *"Shayṭān made them slip for what they had done."* (3:155) This took place by means of whispering, which caused them to enter into error through their own disobedience. Shayṭān has no power to physically make a person do anything. His only power is to persuade people to commit an error on their own account, and so the reason for Ādam's moving from one place to another was his own wrong action. It is said that the meaning is their actual slipping down from the Garden when Allah expelled them from it.

expelling them from where they were.

Their expulsion from the Garden to the earth was because they were created from it and so that Ādam could be a khalif in the earth. Iblīs did not intend to expel him from the Garden but simply wanted to make him fall from his rank and to put him far from

Allah in the position he enjoyed. So Iblīs did not obtain his goal and, for this reason, his rancour, resentment and foul opinion increased even more. In fact the opposite took place. Allah says, *"Then his Lord chose him and turned to him and guided him."* (20:122) So Ādam became the khalif of Allah on the earth after he had been near Him in His abode. Adam's high rank can be said to be Iblīs's doing because he was the reason for it and for the error which brought it about.

The commentators do not disagree that Iblīs undertook to make Ādam err but they disagree about how he did it. Ibn Mas'ūd, Ibn 'Abbās and the majority say that he did it as himself, while some say that he entered the Garden in the form of a snake. It is said that the snake was a servant of Ādam in the Garden and it betrayed him by giving the enemy of Allah power over itself. It was cursed because of this and so it is one of the creatures that can be killed while in *iḥrām.*

We said, 'Go down from here

This is addressed to Ādam, Ḥawwā', the snake and Shayṭān according to Ibn 'Abbās. Al-Ḥasan said that only Ādam, Ḥawwā' and the whisperer are intended. Mujāhid and al-Ḥasan said it was all the descendants of Ādam and Iblīs. The word from which "go down" is derived is *hubūṭ,* meaning "to descend from a higher to a lower place". Ādam landed in a place called Sarndib in India on a mountain called Budh borne by a wind from the Garden which lingered among its trees and valleys and filled them with fragrance. Hawwā' landed in Jadda, Iblīs in Ubulla, and the snake in Baysan or Sijistan. Sijistan is full of snakes.

as enemies to each other!'

Some scholars say that this applies to the human body itself. They find evidence in the words of the Prophet: "When a person's limbs say to his tongue, 'Fear Allah regarding us. If you are straight, we are straight. If you are crooked, we are crooked.'"

It is important to realise that Allah Almighty did not expel Ādam from the Garden and make him go down from it as a punishment, because He only sent him down after he had repented and He had accepted his repentance. He sent him down either to discipline him or to make the test hard. The truth, however, is that his being sent down to live on the earth stemmed from a pre-eternal wisdom governing the whole matter. It was so that his descendants would spread throughout the earth and so that they could be given responsibility and tested there, and then be given their rewards and penalties in the Next World, since the Garden and the Fire are not dimensions where accountability applies. The eating of the tree was the necessary condition for Ādam's descent from the Garden, and Allah does whatever He wills.

You will have residence on the earth

This means a place of residence. As-Suddī, however, says that it refers to their graves, meaning a more permanent resting place. Allah's words, *"He made the earth a stable dwelling place"* (27:61) can bear either meaning. Allah knows best.

and enjoyment

The word used here for enjoyment (*matā'*) applies to what is enjoyed of food, clothes, life, conversation, intimacy and other such things. From it is taken the *mut'a* (temporary) marriage since it gives a man temporary enjoyment of a woman.

for a time

Interpreters disagree about the word "*ḥīn*" (time). One group say that it means until death. This is the position of those who say that "residence" refers to our lifetime on the earth. Some say that it means until the Last Hour, and this is the position of those who say that "residence" refers to the grave. *Ḥīn* sometimes means a distant time and can also refer to a period of time. It can also mean a moment or a segment of time.

Linguists disagree about the meaning of this word as do our scholars and others. Al-Farrā' stated that *"ḥīn"* can designate two types of time: a time which is undefined and a time which Allah mentions: *"It bears fruit regularly by its Lord's permission"*

(14:25), which is six months. Ibn al-'Arabī says that the meaning of "time" is unknown and no judgement is connected to it. A "known time" is that which is connected to judgements and legal responsibility. The maximum of a known time is a year, although Mālik says it is a month. There is no point in this line of thought because there is no valid analogy for its amounts nor any text from the Prophet, peace be upon him, saying what its length is.

فَتَلَقَّىٰٓ ءَادَمُ مِن رَّبِّهِۦ كَلِمَٰتٍ فَتَابَ عَلَيْهِ إِنَّهُۥ
هُوَ ٱلتَّوَّابُ ٱلرَّحِيمُ ٣٧

37 Then Adam received some words from his Lord
and He turned towards him.
He is the Ever-Returning, the Most Merciful.

Then Ādam received some words from his Lord

"Received" here means understood, grasped or learned. Interpreters disagree about the "words" mentioned in this *āyat*. Al-Ḥasan, Sa'īd ibn Jubayr, aḍ-Ḍaḥḥāk and Mujāhid said that it refers to Ādam's words in *Sūrat al-A'rāf*, *"Our Lord, we have wronged ourselves. If You do not forgive us and have mercy on us, we will be among the lost."* (7:23) Mujāhid also said that the words were, "Glory be to You, O Allah. There is no god but You. My Lord, I have wronged myself, so forgive me. You are the Ever-Forgiving, Most Merciful." One group say that he saw written on the pedestal of the Throne, "Muḥammad is the Messenger of Allah" and sought intercession through that. Another group say that what is meant is weeping, modesty and supplication, or regret, asking forgiveness and sorrow.

and He turned towards him.

This means that Allah accepted his repentance. That occurred on the Day of 'Āshūrā' which was a Friday as has been reported.

When a person repents, he returns to obedience to his Lord. The root of the word for repentance (*tawba*) means to return.

If it is asked why the pronoun "him" is used and not "them" when both Ādam and Ḥawwā' participated in the wrong action, the answer is that, when Adam was addressed at the beginning with "live" in the masculine singular, he was singled out for receiving. It is also because the woman is respected and concealed and so Allah wished to conceal her fault. That is why He does not mention her in connection with the act of disobedience when He says, *"Ādam disobeyed his Lord and became misled."* (20:121) It is also because the woman usually follows the man. Similarly Mūsā's servant is not mentioned with Mūsā when he is addressed in the second person singular, *"Did I not tell you?"* (18:75)

He is the Ever-Returning, the Most Merciful.

The word "Ever-returning" (*tawwāb*) can be used for both people and Allah. Scholars have three positions about the meaning when it is used for Allah. One is that it is permitted for the Lord and is used for Him in the Qur'ān and *Sunna* and it should not be interpreted. Others say that it is a real description of Allah and it is used when Allah turns towards His slave when he turns from disobedience to obedience. The third view is that when Allah turns to a person, it means that He accepts His repentance.

The form of the word *tā'ib*, even if it may be permissible linguistically, cannot be used for Allah because we cannot apply any names or attributes to Him except what He or His Prophet or the community of the Muslims have used for Him.

No one has the power to generate repentance unilaterally because Allah Almighty alone creates all actions. This differs from the position of the Mu'tazilites and those who follow them. In the same way no one else can forgive wrong actions, and this is why our scholars say that the Jews and Christians disbelieved when they took their religious leaders as Lords by ascribing this power to them.

قُلْنَا ٱهْبِطُوا۟ مِنْهَا جَمِيعًا ۖ فَإِمَّا يَأْتِيَنَّكُم مِّنِّى هُدًى فَمَن تَبِعَ هُدَاىَ
فَلَا خَوْفٌ عَلَيْهِمْ وَلَا هُمْ يَحْزَنُونَ ﴿٣٨﴾

38 ***We said, 'Go down from it, every one of you!***
Then when guidance comes to you from Me,
those who follow My guidance
will feel no fear and will know no sorrow.'

We said, 'Go down from it,

Allah repeats the command by way of stress and harshness. It is said that, the first time, it is connected to transgression and the second to bringing guidance. It is also said that the first is the descent from the Garden to heaven and the second the descent from heaven to earth. This would indicate that the Garden was in the seventh heaven.

every one of you!

Wahb ibn Munabbih said, "When Ādam descended to earth, Iblīs said to the wild animals, 'This is your enemy, so destroy him.' They gathered and elected the dog as their leader, saying, 'You are the boldest of us.' When Ādam saw that, he was confused. Jibrīl came to him and said, 'Stroke the dog's head.' He did so. When the animals saw that the dog was friendly to Ādam, they scattered. The dog sought security and Ādam gave it to him and he remained with him and his sons from then on."

Then when guidance comes to you from Me,

There is disagreement about the meaning of *"hudā"* (guidance). As-Suddī said that it is the Book of Allah. It is said to be success in following Allah's guidance. A group say that it refers to the Messengers who came to Ādam from the angels and those who came to his descendants from among mankind. "From Me" is another indication that the actions of people are created by Allah, which differs from the position of the Qadariyya and others.

will feel no fear and will know no sorrow.'

"Khawf" (fear) is anxiety and it applies only to the future. *"Ḥuzn"* (sorrow) is the opposite of happiness and applies only to the past. So the meaning is that they have no fear about what lies ahead of them in the Next World nor are they sorrowful about anything that passed them by in this world. This does not deny the terrors of the Day of Rising and the fear which the people of obedience will experience, because Allah and His Messenger have stated that the hardships of the Rising will not be lessened for those who obeyed Allah. It is when they go to the Garden that they will feel no fear, and Allah knows best.

وَالَّذِينَ كَفَرُوا وَكَذَّبُوا بِآيَاتِنَا أُولَٰئِكَ أَصْحَابُ النَّارِ
هُمْ فِيهَا خَالِدُونَ ﴿٣٩﴾

39 ***But those who disbelieve and deny Our Signs***
are the Companions of the Fire,
remaining in it timelessly, for ever.

Those who disbelieve commit *shirk*. The word *"Aṣḥāb"* (Companions) comes from the root *ṣuḥba*, which means to be connected to a thing in any state and at any time. It entails clinging to the thing and mixing with it.

يَا بَنِي إِسْرَائِيلَ اذْكُرُوا نِعْمَتِيَ الَّتِي أَنْعَمْتُ عَلَيْكُمْ
وَأَوْفُوا بِعَهْدِي أُوفِ بِعَهْدِكُمْ وَإِيَّايَ فَارْهَبُونِ ﴿٤٠﴾

40 ***Tribe of Israel! remember the blessing***
I conferred on you.

Honour My contract and I will honour your contract. Have dread of Me alone.

Tribe of Israel!

Isrā'īl was Ya'qūb. Abū'l-Faraj said that he is the only Prophet to have two names except for Muḥammad, may Allah bless him and grant him peace, who has many names. I say, however, that it is said that the Messiah is a name of 'Īsā, and Allah also named him *Rūḥ* (Spirit) and Word. Al-Khālid ibn Aḥmad said that there were five Prophets with two names: Muḥammad was also called Aḥmad, may Allah bless him and grant him peace, 'Īsā was called the Messiah, Ya'qūb was called Isrā'īl, Yūnus was called Dhū'n-Nūn, and Ilyās was called Dhū'l-Kifl.

remember the blessing I conferred on you.

"Dhikr" (remembrance) is a word with several possibilities of meaning according to the context. When applied to the heart, it implies remembrance rather than forgetfulness. When applied to the tongue, it implies speech rather than silence. Ibn al-Anbārī said, "The meaning is to remember to be grateful for Allah's blessing." It is said that it means to remember with the heart which is certainly much to be desired, in other words: "do not forget or overlook the blessing which I bestowed on you." *"Ni'ma"* (blessing), although singular, has a comprehensive meaning.

Among Allah's blessings to them were that He saved them from the people of Pharaoh, appointed Prophets from among them, sent down the Books and manna and quail to them, made fountains gush out from the rock for them, and included the mention of Muḥammad, may Allah bless him and grant him peace, in the Torah. Blessings to fathers are blessings to sons because they are ennobled by the nobility of their fathers.

Those with a precise grasp of the use of language say that Allah connected blessings to the tribe of Israel but did not mention that regarding the Community of Muḥammad, may Allah bless him and grant him peace; rather He says, *"Remember Me and I will remember you,"* (2:152) so the other communities look from the blessing to the Blesser while the Community of Muḥammad looks from the Blesser to the blessing.

Honour My contract and I will honour your contract.

There is disagreement about the contract referred to here. Al-Ḥasan said it is what is found in Allah's words, *"Take hold vigorously of what We have given you"* (2:63 and elsewhere). Az-Zajjāj said that what is meant are the words in the Torah about following Muḥammad, may Allah bless him and grant him peace.

Allah's honouring of the contract is generally taken to mean that they will receive the reward of the Garden. It is also said that it means that, if they perform their obligations with sincerity, then Allah will accept them from them. It is said that, if they perform acts of worship, Allah will look after their affairs. It is said that it means that, if they preserve their behaviour outwardly Allah will adorn their hearts inwardly. It is also said that it is general to all His commands and prohibitions and what is mentioned about Muḥammad, may Allah bless him and grant him peace, in the Torah and elsewhere. This is the position of most scholars, and it is sound. His side of the contract is that He will admit them to the Garden.

Have dread of Me alone.

The command is a threat.

وَءَامِنُوا۟ بِمَآ أَنزَلْتُ مُصَدِّقًا لِّمَا مَعَكُمْ وَلَا تَكُونُوٓا۟
أَوَّلَ كَافِرٍۭ بِهِۦ ۖ وَلَا تَشْتَرُوا۟ بِـَٔايَٰتِى ثَمَنًا قَلِيلًا وَإِيَّٰىَ فَٱتَّقُونِ ﴿٤١﴾

41 ***Believe in what I have sent down,***
confirming what is with you.
Do not be the first to reject it
and do not sell My Signs for a paltry price.
Have fear of Me alone.

Believe in what I have sent down,

This means the Qur'ān.

confirming what is with you.

"What is with you" is the Torah.

Do not be the first to reject it

Ibn Jurayj said that the third person pronoun translated as "it" refers to the Qur'ān, but according to Abū'l-'Āliyya it refers to Muḥammad, may Allah bless him and grant him peace, in which case it would be "him".

If it is asked why *"kāfir"* (reject) is in the singular and not the plural, it is said that there is an elision which implies: "Do not be the first group to reject it." Al-Akhfash and al-Farrā' say that it goes back to "the first", in other words: "do not be the first of those who reject it."

Do not sell My Signs for a paltry price.

Do not take a bribe to change the description of Muḥammad, may Allah bless him and grant him peace, as found in the Torah. The rabbis used to do that when they were forbidden to do it. Some interpreters, al-Ḥasan and others said that. It is said that they received food in return for knowledge like a stipend when they were forbidden that. It is said that the rabbis used to teach their *dīn* for a wage and were forbidden to do that. Abū'l-'Āliyya said that it means: "do not sell My commands, prohibitions and Signs for a paltry price," meaning do not abandon them for this world and its substance and for the sake of a livelihood which is insignificant.

This *āyat* is here addressed to the tribe of Israel and is about getting something for what they did. It can thus refer to anyone who takes a bribe for altering or falsifying the truth, refusing to teach what is obliged for him, or refusing to convey what he knows and which is incumbent on him to convey unless he is paid for it. All that is included in the *āyat*, and Allah knows best. Abū Hurayra reported that the Messenger of Allah, may Allah bless him and grant him peace, said, "Anyone who learns knowledge which should be learned for the sake of Allah, the Mighty and Majestic alone, simply to obtain by it goods of this world, will not experience the scent of the Garden on the Day of Rising." (Abū Dāwūd)

Scholars disagree about taking a wage for teaching the Qur'ān and knowledge of the *dīn* because of this *āyat* and others like it. Az-Zuhrī and the exponents of opinion *(ra'y)* forbade that, saying that it is not permitted for anyone to take a wage for teaching the Qur'ān because teaching it is one of the obligations which require sincerity and the intention of drawing near to Allah. Therefore there can be no wage for someone who does that just as there can be none for fasting or the prayer.

Ibn 'Abbās related that the Prophet, may Allah bless him and grant him peace, said, "Your children's teachers are the worst of you, the least merciful to orphans and the harshest to the poor." Abū Hurayra said that he asked, "Messenger of Allah, what do you say about other teachers?" He said, "Their dirhams are unlawful, their clothes are unlawful, and their words are hypocrisy." 'Ubāda ibn aṣ-Ṣāmit said, "I taught the Qur'ān and writing to some of the people of the Ṣuffa and one of them gave me a bow. I said, 'It is not money and I can shoot it in the Way of Allah.' I asked the Messenger of Allah about it and he said, 'If you are happy to wear a collar of fire, accept it.'" Mālik, ash-Shāfi'ī, Aḥmad, Abū Thawr and most scholars permit accepting a wage for teaching, based on the words of the Prophet in the *ḥadīth* of Ibn 'Abbās, "You are most entitled to take wages for the Book of Allah." (al-Bukhārī) This *ḥadīth* is an evidentiary criterion which removes any dispute and can be relied on.

To make an analogy between such teaching and the prayer and fasting is incorrect. There is a clear difference between the two things. The prayer and fasting are individual actions of worship for a person while teaching the Qur'ān is an act of worship which can be done by other than the teacher himself. Therefore he is permitted to receive a wage for his attempt to convey the meaning of the Qur'ān, just as he would for teaching someone how to write the Qur'ān.

Some say that this *āyat* only applies to the tribe of Israel and there is disagreement about whether what was legislated for them applies to us.

It is also said that the *āyat* is about those who should teach and refuse to do so unless they are paid. If it is not incumbent on someone, he is permitted to take a wage based on the evidence of the *Sunna*. It might be specifically incumbent on him except in the case of a teacher who does not have enough to support himself and his family. If that is the case, then the ruler should support him for sake of the establishment of the *dīn*. If he does not, it is up to the Muslims to do so. When Abū Bakr became khalif, he did not have enough to support his family and so he took some cloth and went to the market. He was asked about that and said, "How else will I support my family!" They sent him back and allotted a sufficient amount to cover his needs.

As for the *aḥādith* about teachers mentioned above, none of them are reliable. The *ḥadīth* of Ibn Abbās has someone abandoned in the *isnād*. The *ḥadīth* of Abū Hurayra has someone who is unknown in the *isnād*. The *ḥadīth* of 'Ubāda has someone in its *isnād* who is known for "denounced" (*munkar*) *aḥādīth*. It is also related that the Messenger of Allah, may Allah bless him and grant him peace, said, "The best of people and the best of those who walk on the surface of earth are teachers. Whenever they renew the *dīn*, give to them and do not employ them and constrict them. When a teacher tells the child to say, 'In the Name of Allah, the All-Merciful, Most Merciful,' and the child says, 'In the Name of Allah, the All-Merciful, Most Merciful,' Allah writes the freeing of the child, the freeing of his teachers and the freeing of his parents from the Fire."

Scholars disagree over the ruling about someone who takes a wage for leading the prayer. Ashhab related that Mālik was asked about praying behind someone who was hired to lead the people in Ramaḍān. He said, "I hope that there will be no harm in it." It is more strongly disliked in the obligatory prayer. Ash-Shāfi'ī and his people and Abū Thawr said, "There is no harm in that or in praying behind him."

Another point concerning this matter is found in what is related by ad-Dārimī from aḍ-Ḍahhāk ibn Mūsā: "Sulaymān ibn 'Abdu'l-Mālik passed through Madina on the way to Makka and stayed there for a few days. He inquired, 'Is there anyone in Madina who met any of the Companions of the Prophet, may Allah bless him and grant him peace?' They replied, 'Abū Ḥāzim.' He sent for him and when he came, he asked, 'Abū Ḥāzim, what is this concealment?' Abū Ḥāzim said, 'Amir al-Mu'minīn, what concealment are you referring to?' He said, 'The notable people of Madina came to me but you did not!' He said, 'Amīr al-Mu'minīn, I ask you to seek refuge with Allah from saying what is not the case. You did not know me before today and I did not see you!'

"He turned to Muḥammad ibn Shihāb az-Zuhrī who said, 'The shaykh is right and you are wrong.' Sulaymān said, 'Abū Ḥāzim! Why do we hate death?' He replied, 'Because the Next World tests you and this world makes you prosper and so you dislike to move from prosperity to ruin.' He said, 'You are right, Abū Ḥāzim. How will our presentation before Allah tomorrow be?' He said, 'For the one who did good it will be like someone returning to his family after an absence. But as for the one who did evil, he will be like a runaway slave being brought back to his owner.' Sulaymān wept and said, 'Would that I knew what I have with Allah!' He said, 'Examine your actions in the light of the Book of Allah.' He asked, 'Where should I look?' He said, *'The truly good will be in perfect Bliss and the dissolute will be in a Blazing Fire.'* (82:13-14)'

"Sulaymān asked, 'Where is the mercy of Allah, Abū Ḥāzim?' Abū Ḥāzim said, 'The mercy of Allah is near those who do good.' Sulayman said, 'Abū Ḥāzim, which of Allah's slaves are the noblest?' He replied. 'Those with integrity and intelligence.' He asked 'Which works are best?' Abū Ḥāzim said, 'Performing obligations while avoiding prohibitions.' Sulaymān asked, 'Whose supplication is heard?' He replied, 'The supplication of a good-doer for a good-doer.' He asked, 'Which *ṣadaqa* is best?' He said, 'That given to a despairing beggar and to someone who is destitute in which there is no question of indebtedness or insult.' He asked,

'Which words are fairest?' He replied, 'Speaking the truth in the presence of someone you fear or have hopes of.' He said, 'Which of the believers is the cleverest?' He replied, 'A man who obeys Allah and directs other people to it.' He said, 'Which of the believers is the most stupid?' He replied, 'A man who sinks to his brother's passion when he is a wrongdoer and sells the Next World for this one.'

"Sulaymān told him, 'You are right. So what do you say about us?' He said, 'Amīr al-Mu'minīn, will you let me go?' Sulaymān said, 'No, rather give me advice.' He said, 'Amīr al-Mu'minīn, your fathers overpowered the people with swords and took this kingdom by force without consulting the Muslims or without their pleasure until they killed many of them. They have left us. If only you had been aware of what they said and what was said to them!' A man in the gathering said to him, 'Abū Ḥāzim! What you have said is bad!' Abū Ḥāzim said, 'You lie. Allah has taken a covenant from scholars to make things clear to people and to not conceal them.' Sulaymān said to him, 'So how can we put things right?' He replied, 'Leave aside conceit, hold to integrity and divide equally.' Sulaymān said to him, 'What is our approach?' He replied, 'Take from the lawful and give it to its people.'

"Then Sulaymān asked him, 'Abū Ḥāzim, will you keep our company so that you can take from us and we from you?' He replied, 'I seek refuge with Allah!' Sulaymān asked, 'Why is that?' He replied, 'I fear that I would lean towards them a little and then Allah would let me taste a double punishment in life and a double punishment in death.' (cf. 17:75) Sulaymān said, 'Tell us your needs.' He answered, 'That you save me from the Fire and make me enter the Garden.' Sulaymān told him, 'That is not up to me!' Abū Ḥāzim stated, 'I have no need of anything else from you.' He said, 'Make supplication for me.' Abū Ḥāzim said, 'O Allah, if Sulaymān is your friend, ease him to the good of this world and the Next World. If he is Your enemy, take him by the forelock where You want and please.' Sulaymān said to him, 'Enough!' Abū Ḥāzim said, 'I was short but it is a lot if you are one of its people. If you are not one of its people, I should not shoot from a bow with no string.'

"Sulaymān said, 'Give me some advice.' He said, 'I will advise you and be brief. Exalt your Lord and free Him from seeing you where He forbade you to be and from not seeing you where He commanded You to be.'

"When he left him, he sent him a hundred dinars and wrote to him, 'Spend it and you will have the like of it many times more.' He returned it to him and wrote to him, 'Amīr al-Mu'minīn, I seek refuge with Allah from your asking me being a joke or my reply to you being a surrender. I am not pleased with it for you, so how could I be pleased with it for myself? When Mūsā ibn 'Imrān, peace be upon him, arrived at the water of Madyan, he found shepherds drawing water there. Standing apart from them, he found two women, holding back their sheep. He questioned them and they said, "We cannot draw water until the shepherds have driven off their sheep. You see our father is a very old man." So he drew water for them and then withdrew into the shade and said, "My Lord, I am truly in need of any good You have in store for me." That was when he was hungry and fearful and without security. In spite of that he asked his Lord alone and did not ask people.

"'The shepherds did not notice, but the women noticed. So when they returned to their father, they told the story to him and recounted what he had said. Their father, who was Shu'ayb, said, "This is a hungry man." He told one of them, "Go and invite him." When she came to him, she respected him and covered her face and said, "My father invites you so that he can pay you your wage for drawing water for us." It grieved Mūsā when she said, "your wage for drawing water for us." He, however, found that he had no alternative but to follow her because he was hungry and alone in a strange place. When he followed her the wind blew and began to blow her garment against her back so that the shape of her buttocks showed. Mūsā looked to the side at times and lowered his eyes at others.

"'When his patience was exhausted, he called her and said, "Slave of Allah! Go behind me and direct me to the way by words." When he reached Shu'ayb, supper was being prepared. He told him, "Sit, young man and eat." Mūsā said to him, "I seek refuge with Allah." Shu'ayb asked, "Why? Aren't you hungry?" "Yes," he replied, "but I fear that this may be a recompense for drawing water for them and I am from the people of a house who do not sell anything of their *dīn* even for the entire earth filled with gold." Shu'ayb said to him, "No, young man, but it is my custom and the custom of my fathers to give hospitality to a guest and feed him." So Mūsā sat and ate.

"'If these hundred dinars are recompense for what I said, then carrion, blood and pig meat in a state of need are more lawful than it. If it is connected to the treasury, then there are others who deserve it as much as I do. If it is between us, then I have no need of it.'"

This is how one follows the Book and the Prophets. Look at this virtuous imām and scholar and how he would not take any payment for his knowledge, his advice or his counsel. He openly made the truth clear and did not show any fear in doing so. The Messenger of Allah, may Allah bless him and grant him peace, said, "Awe of someone should not prevent any of you from speaking the truth wherever he is." In the Revelation we find: *"They strive in the Way of Allah and do not fear the blame of any censurer."* (5:54)

وَلَا تَلْبِسُوا۟ ٱلْحَقَّ بِٱلْبَٰطِلِ وَتَكْتُمُوا۟ ٱلْحَقَّ وَأَنتُمْ تَعْلَمُونَ ﴿٤٢﴾

42 ***Do not mix up truth with falsehood***
and knowingly hide the truth.

Do not mix up truth with falsehood

A thing is mixed up when it is mixed with something similar to it. Then it is not clear. Qatāda said that the meaning of the phrase is "do not mix up Judaism and Christianity with Islam."

The word used for "falsehood" is *bāṭil* which means when something becomes unsound and worthless. It can also mean "in vain". The False (*al-Bāṭil*) is one of the names of Shayṭān. A hero is also called *baṭl*, using the same root, because he makes the courage of his opponent "in vain". *Baṭāla* is unemployment.

Interpreters disagree about what is meant by "truth with falsehood". Ibn 'Abbās and others said that it means do not mix what you have of the truth in the Book with falsehood by alteration or substitution. The Jews said, "Muḥammad, may Allah bless him and grant him peace, was sent, but not to us." So their affirmation of his mission was the truth but their denial that he was sent to them was falsehood. Ibn Zayd said that what was meant by the truth was the Torah, and the falsehood was the changes they made to it. Ibn 'Abbās's statement is the most correct because it is general and so includes all the other statements.

and knowingly hide the truth.

This can be joined as "Do not mix and do not hide," or there can be an elision, meaning, "Let there not exist among you mixing the truth and concealing it." Ibn 'Abbās said, "It means their concealing the genuineness of the Prophet, may Allah bless him and grant him peace, in spite of the fact that they recognised him." So their rejection was one of obstinacy not ignorance. Allah is not attesting that they have knowledge, but is rather forbidding them to conceal what they know to be true. The wrong action is made all the more serious because it is done in spite of knowledge.

وَأَقِيمُوا۟ ٱلصَّلَوٰةَ وَءَاتُوا۟ ٱلزَّكَوٰةَ وَٱرْكَعُوا۟ مَعَ
ٱلرَّٰكِعِينَ ﴿٤٣﴾

43 ***Establish the prayer and pay zakāt***
and bow with those who bow.

Establish the prayer and pay *zakāt*

This is a command which entails a definite obligation.

The root meaning of *"zakāt"* is grow and increase. It is used for crops and wealth when they increase. A man who is *zakī* is someone with increased wealth. Paying this tax out from wealth is called *zakāt*, even though doing it seems to produce the opposite of increase since it involves reducing that wealth. The reason is because it increases the wealth in *baraka* or with the reward for paying it. It is also said that its root meaning is approbation, from which is taken the attestation of a witness's character by the *qāḍī*. So whoever pays *zakāt* obtains approbation for himself. It is further said that the root meaning of *zakāṭ* is purification. It is as if the one who pays it has purified himself of the liability of the right to which the poor are entitled and which Allah has imposed on him. Do you not see that the Prophet, may Allah bless him and grant him peace, called what was paid as *zakāt* the "filth of people". Allah says, *"Take* zakāt *from their property to purify and cleanse them."* (9:103)

There is disagreement about what is meant by *zakāt* here. It is said that it is referring to the obligatory *zakāt* since it is connected to the prayer. It is also said to be the *zakāt al-fiṭr*. Mālik stated that according to Ibn al-Qāṣim. The first is the position of the majority of scholars. According to them, the *zakāt* mentioned in the Book is general and was then clarified by the Prophet, may Allah bless him and grant him peace.

and bow

Linguistically the root of the word "bow", *raka'a*, means to bend the body. It is used metaphorically for descending in station. People disagree about why this act is specifically mentioned here. Some people say that, as bowing (*rukū'*) is one of the pillars of the prayer, it is used here to designate the prayer as a whole. This is not particular to the word "bowing" alone since the word "recitation" and the word "prostration" are also used to designate the whole prayer as well. Allah says, *"The recitation of fajr* (dawn)*,"* (17:78) meaning the *Fajr* prayer, and the Messenger of Allah, may Allah bless him and grant him peace, said, "Whoever catches a prostration of the prayer has caught the whole prayer."

It is said that bowing was singled out because the tribe of Israel did not have that in their prayer. It is said that it was more onerous for the people in the *Jāhiliyya* so that one of those who became Muslim, I think it was 'Imrān ibn Ḥusayn, told the Prophet, "Provided that I do not have to prostrate except standing," meaning "not bow". When Islam was firm in him and he was at peace with it, he performed *rukū'* in the way he was commanded to.

The legal *rukū'* is that a person bends his spine and makes his back and neck level while his fingers clasp his knees and he remains bowing, saying, "Glory be to My Lord, the Immense" three times. That is the minimum. It is a *farḍ* by the Qur'ān and *Sunna*, as is prostration. The *Sunna* added the stillness to it and the standing between *rukū'* and prostration.

with those who bow.

The word "with" implies both togetherness and simultaneity. That is why some of those who interpret the Qur'ān say that the command to pray did not at first entail attending the group prayer, but when Allah said "with" in this *āyat*, He commanded people to pray as a group. Scholars have two different positions about attending the group prayer. The majority say that it is one of the confirmed *sunna*s and a penalty is mandatory for anyone who regularly fails to attend it without an excuse. Some of the people of knowledge make it mandatory when there is ability. Ibn 'Abdu'l-Barr says, "It is confirmed, by consensus, that it is not permitted to agree to make all the mosques empty of group prayers. If there is a group prayer in the mosque and an individual prays in his home, that is permitted because the Prophet, may Allah bless him and grant him peace, said, 'The group prayer is seventy-seven degrees better than the prayer of the person praying alone.'" (Muslim)

Scholars disagree about the excellence connected to the group and whether it is for the group alone wherever it is or whether it is for a group in the mosque. The first is more evident because the group is what the judgement is connected to, and Allah knows best.

أَتَأْمُرُونَ ٱلنَّاسَ بِٱلْبِرِّ وَتَنسَوْنَ أَنفُسَكُمْ وَأَنتُمْ
تَتْلُونَ ٱلْكِتَٰبَ أَفَلَا تَعْقِلُونَ ﴿٤٤﴾

44 ***Do you order people to devoutness***
and forget yourselves,
when you recite the Book?
Will you not use your intellect?

Do you order people to devoutness

This is a question implying a rebuke. What is meant according to the people of interpretation are Jewish scholars. Ibn 'Abbās said, "The Jews used to command their followers to follow the Torah but they contradicted it in their denial of the description of Muḥammad, may Allah bless him and grant him peace, in it." Ibn Jurayj said, "The rabbis encouraged people to obey Allah while they committed acts of disobedience themselves." One group said, "They encouraged others to give *ṣadaqa* but were themselves miserly." All these ideas are similar. The people who deal in indications (*ishārāt*) say that the meaning is: "Do you ask people for the realities of meanings when you disobey their outward meaning?"

There will be a severe punishment for someone who is like this. Anas reported that the Messenger of Allah, may Allah bless him and grant him peace, said, "On my Night Journey I passed by some people who were cutting off their lips with scissors of fire. I asked, 'Jibrīl, who are they?' He said, 'Those are the speakers of the people of this world who commanded people to devoutness and forgot themselves.'" This indicates that the punishment of the one who knows what is right and wrong and that it is obligatory to perform the requirements of both is worse than that of someone who does not know. That is because it is as if he were making light of the prohibitions and rulings of Allah. He does not benefit from his knowledge. The Messenger of Allah, may Allah bless him and grant him peace, said, "The worst of people on the Day of Rising will be a scholar whom Allah does not make benefit from his knowledge."

Know that the rebuke in the *āyat* is for abandoning acts of devoutness, not for ordering them. This is why in His Book Allah censures those who command acts of devoutness but do not perform them themselves. He says it in the present tense because it is a rebuke which will last until the Day of Rising. Ibrāhīm an-Nakhā'ī said, "I dislike attributing a specific cause to three *āyat*s: *'Do you order people to devoutness...'* (2:44), *'Why do you say what you do not do?'* (61:2) and *'I would clearly not want to go behind your backs and do something I have forbidden you to do.'* (11:88)"

The word for "devoutness" (*birr*) means obedience and righteous action. It also means truthfulness. It also means a fox cub and the bleating of sheep when they are herded. So it is a shared word. *Burr* is wheat and *barr* is respectfulness and esteem, such as that which should be shown to one's parents.

and forget yourselves

This means "fail to do them yourselves" which is a common usage of the word *"nasā"* (forget) as it is used in the Qur'ān. The root can also designate the opposite of remembrance and memory.

when you recite the Book?

The Book is the Torah and it also applied to anyone who does the same as they did. The root of "*tilāwa*" (recitation) means "to follow", which is why it is used for recitation because words follow one another so that they form a sequence.

Will you not use your intellect?

Will you not prevent yourselves from being in this state? The word "*'aql*" (intellect) implies restraint, from which comes the hobble (*'iqāl*) of the camel because it prevents it from moving. The word is also sometimes used for blood money because it prevents the relative of the victim from killing the perpetrator. *I'tiqāl* is a spasm of the stomach or restraining of the tongue. Az-Zajjāj says, "The *'āqil* is the one who does what Allah has obliged him to do. If someone does not do it, he is ignorant."

The people who follow the truth agree that the intellect is an existent thing which is neither timeless nor non-existent because, if it had been non-existent, it would describe some essences and not others. Since it exists, it is impossible to say it is timeless since there is nothing timeless except Allah.

وَاسْتَعِينُوا بِالصَّبْرِ وَالصَّلَوٰةِ وَإِنَّهَا لَكَبِيرَةٌ إِلَّا عَلَى الْخَاشِعِينَ ﴿٤٥﴾

45 ***Seek help in steadfastness and the prayer.***
But that is a very hard thing,
except for the humble:

Seek help in steadfastness and the prayer.

The root meaning of the word used for "*ṣabr*" (steadfastness) means restraint and is used for binding a person, and it also means endurance. Allah has commanded us to persist in obedience to Him and to restrain ourselves from committing acts of disobedience in His Book by telling us to be steadfast. It is said that a person first refrains (*ṣabara*) from acts of disobedience, and once he has done so he becomes steadfast (*ṣābara*) in obedience. This is the soundest of what is said.

Ṣalāt (the prayer) is mentioned rather than other acts of worship. When something happened to the Prophet, he sought refuge in the prayer. Ibn 'Abbās was once told about the death of his brother – or, it is said, a daughter of his – when he was on a journey and he said, "A weak spot Allah has protected, a burden Allah has spared us, and a reward which Allah will bring." Then he went off the road and prayed and went back to his camel, saying, *"Seek help in steadfastness and the prayer."*

Some people say that what is meant is supplication according to linguistic usage. This is like the *āyat* of Allah, *"When you meet a troop, then stand firm and remember Allah"* (8:45) because firmness is *ṣabr* and *dhikr* is supplication. A third position was espoused by Mujāhid who said that, in this *āyat*, *ṣabr* referred to fasting. The month of Ramaḍān is called "The month of *Ṣabr*". The reason for this is that fasting curbs appetites and makes one ascetic in this world and the prayer keeps one from lewd action and what is disliked. Allah knows best.

Steadfastness in the face of injury and in performing acts of obedience is part of striving against the self and curbing it from its appetites and preventing it from becoming proud. It is one of the qualities of the Prophets and Righteous. Yaḥyā ibn al-Yamān said, "Steadfastness is not to desire any state except that which Allah has placed you in and to find pleasure in whatever He has decreed for you in this world and the Next." 'Alī said, "Steadfastness in relation to faith is like the head in relation to the body." Aṭ-Ṭabarī agreed with 'Alī and said, "That is because faith is recognition by the heart, affirmation with the tongue and action with the limbs. If someone is not steadfast in acting with his limbs, he does not truly have faith."

Allah describes the reward for various actions and puts a limit on it. He says, *"Those who produce a good action will receive ten like it."* (6:160) But He makes the reward of the steadfast limitless and praises the people who have it: *"The steadfast will be paid their wages in full without any reckoning."* (39:10) and *"But if someone is steadfast and forgives, that is the most resolute course to follow."* (42:43)

One of the virtues of *ṣabr* is that Allah describes Himself as having it, as in the *ḥadīth* of Abū Mūsā when the Prophet said, "There is no one or nothing with more patience in the face of an insult which he hears than Allah Almighty. They claim that He has a son and yet He gives them health and provides for them." (al-Bukhārī) Our scholars say that, in the case of Allah, *ṣabr* has the meaning of forbearance, in that He defers the punishment from those who deserve it. The description of Him as having *ṣabr* does not come in the Revelation, but in this *ḥadīth* where it is interpreted by scholars to mean forbearance, and so one of His Names is *aṣ-Ṣabūr*, because of His great forbearance towards those who disobey Him.

But that is a very hard thing,

Interpreters disagree about what the word "that" refers to here. It is said to refer to the prayer alone because it is harder for people than fasting, given that steadfastness here refers to fasting. The prayer is the prison of the lower self while fasting is just denial of its appetites. Someone who denies one or two appetites is not the same as someone who denies all his appetites. Fasting denies the appetite for women, food and drink but one is able to enjoy other appetites like talking, walking and looking and other such things. So there is consolation for the denied appetites. The one who prays, however, is denied all those things and all his limbs are restrained in the prayer from all appetites. That is why prayer is harder for the self and a greater burden on it. It is said to refer to both of them but usually it is taken to mean the prayer. It is also said to refer to worship as a whole which entails both fasting and the prayer. It is said to be a use of the verbal noun here, in which case it would mean that "seeking help" is what is difficult. It is said to refer to responding to Muḥammad, may Allah bless him and grant him peace, because *ṣabr* and prayer are part of that to which he called.

except for the humble:

Qatāda said, "*Khushū'*(humility) is in the heart where it takes the form of fear and appears outwardly as the lowering of the eye in the prayer." Az-Zajjāj said, "A humble person is one in whom the effect of abasement can be seen." The word is used of a house which has fallen down. This is the root meaning. A "humble" place is one which has nothing to indicate where it is. The verb is used for lowering the voice and lowering the eyes. *Khush'a*, which comes from the same root, means a low hill. A land which is *khāshi'* is a place covered in dust with no place where one can alight.

Al-A'mash said that he asked Ibrāhīm an-Nakhā'ī about humility and he said, "A'mash! You want to be an imam for the people and do not know what humility is! Humility does not consist of eating coarse food and wearing coarse clothes and bowing the head. Humility is to see the noble and lowly as having the same right and to be humble towards Allah in every obligation He has imposed on you." 'Umar ibn al-Khaṭṭāb looked at a young man with a bowed head and said, "You! Lift your head up! Humility is not more than what is in the heart!" 'Alī said, "Humility is in the heart and that your hands are gentle with the Muslims and that you do not look about during the prayer." So someone who makes a display of humility, beyond what is in his heart, displays hypocrisy on top of hypocrisy. Sahl ibn 'Abdullāh said, "A person is not humble until every hair in his body manifests humility by the words of Allah, *'The skins of those who fear their Lord tremble.'*" (39:23)

This is praiseworthy humility because when the heart is still, the outward must also be humble and the person who has it will inevitably display it; so you will see him with his head bowed, courteous and submissive. The *Salaf* used to strive to be like that. The blameworthy form is artificial, pretending to weep with a bowed head as the ignorant do in order to be viewed with respect. That is deceit from Shayṭān.

ٱلَّذِينَ يَظُنُّونَ أَنَّهُم مُّلَٰقُواْ رَبِّهِمْ وَأَنَّهُمْ إِلَيْهِ رَٰجِعُونَ ﴿٤٦﴾

46 ***those who are aware that they will meet their Lord and that they will return to Him.***

This describes the humble. The word for being aware, *ẓann*, means certainty in this context according to the majority of scholars. The normal meaning of *ẓann* entails some doubt but it can be used to mean certainty as in this *āyat* and elsewhere.

يَٰبَنِيٓ إِسۡرَٰٓءِيلَ ٱذۡكُرُواْ نِعۡمَتِيَ ٱلَّتِيٓ أَنۡعَمۡتُ عَلَيۡكُمۡ
وَأَنِّي فَضَّلۡتُكُمۡ عَلَى ٱلۡعَٰلَمِينَ ٤٧

47 ***Tribe of Israel! remember the blessing***
I conferred on you
and that I preferred you over all other beings.

He means the beings of their time. It is said that the preference was because they had a lot of Prophets and other advantages.

وَٱتَّقُواْ يَوۡمٗا لَّا تَجۡزِي نَفۡسٌ عَن نَّفۡسٖ شَيۡـٔٗا وَلَا يُقۡبَلُ مِنۡهَا
شَفَٰعَةٞ وَلَا يُؤۡخَذُ مِنۡهَا عَدۡلٞ وَلَا هُمۡ يُنصَرُونَ ٤٨

48 ***Have fear of a Day when no self***
will be able to compensate for another in any way.
No intercession will be accepted from it,
no ransom taken from it,
and they will not be helped.

Have fear of a Day

This is a command which is also a threat, and *"yawm"* (Day) here refers to the punishment and terror of the Last Day.

when no self will be able to compensate for another in any way.

This means that no one will be punished for the sin of anyone else nor can he avert it from him. Abū Hurayra reported that the Messenger of Allah, may Allah bless him and grant him peace, said, "Whoever has done an injustice to his brother with regard to his honour or anything else should seek to be absolved by him before the Day when there will be neither dinar nor dirham. If he has some right actions, they will be taken from him to counterbalance any injustice he did and if he does not have any good actions, some of the bad actions of his friend will be taken and he will be made to carry them." (al-Bukhārī)

No intercession will be accepted from it,

The word for intercession is derived from the root "*shaf'a*" (even) which means one of a pair and to make an odd number even. *Shu'fa* (pre-emption) is called that because it is used when someone adds the property of his partner to his own. A camel which is *shāfi'* is one which is pregnant when there is a young foal still with it.

The position of the people who hold to the truth is that intercession is a reality, while the Mu'tazilites deny it and believe that sinful believers who enter the Fire will remain in it for ever. There are mutually supporting reports that sinful rebellious people from the nations of the Prophets who affirm the Unity of Allah will be interceded for by the angels, Prophets, martyrs and righteous. There are two firm grounds for refuting the Mu'tazilites. The first is the numerous *aḥādīth* with multiple transmission which affirm intercession, and the second is the consensus of the *Salaf* in their acceptance of these reports. No one denies them and everyone agrees that they are sound and accepts them as decisive evidence for the soundness of the creed of the people who hold to the truth and the falseness of the claims of the Mu'tazilites.

The Mu'tazilites claim that there are *āyat*s in the Book which refute these traditions, like, *"The wrongdoers will have no close friend or any intercessor who might be heard,"* (40:18) and *"Anyone who does evil will be repaid for it"* (4:123) and here *"no intercession will be accepted from it."* We reply that these *āyat*s are general to every wrongdoer and the general has no definite application and so these *āyat*s do not apply to everyone who does evil and every soul. What is meant by them is the unbelievers rather than the believers which is supported by the evidence of the traditions reported about that.

Allah established intercession for some people and denied it for others. He says about the unbelievers, *"The intercession of the interceders will not help them"* (74:48), *"They only intercede on behalf of those with whom He is pleased"* (21:28), and *"Intercession with Him will be of no benefit except from someone who has His permission."* (34:23) By this we know that intercession will help the believers but not the unbelievers. Commentators agree that what is meant by this *āyat* is the unbelievers, not every self. If we say that there is punishment for every rebellious wrongdoer, we do not say that they will be for ever in the Fire by the evidence of the *aḥādīth* we related and by the words of Allah, *"He forgives whoever He wishes for other than that"* (4:48) and *"No one despairs of solace from Allah except for people who are unbelievers."* (12:87)

In regard to *"those with whom He is pleased"* (21:28), if they point out that the deviant is not pleasing, we reply that He did not say, "those who are not pleasing." Allah is pleased to grant intercession to the unifiers since He says, *"They have no right of intercession. None do but those who have a contract with the All-Merciful."* (19:87) The Prophet was asked, "What is the contract which Allah made with His creation?" He replied, "That they believe in Him and not associate anything with Him."

If they say that the one who is pleasing is the one who repents and has made a contract with Allah by repenting to Him, since the angels ask forgiveness for them and Allah says, *"Forgive those who turn to you and who follow Your Way"* (40:7), and thus the intercession of the Prophets is only for the people of repentance and not the people of wrong actions, our reply is as follows: What you maintain obliges Allah to accept repentance. If Allah accepts the repentance of the wrongdoer, there is no need for intercession or asking forgiveness. The commentators agree that what is meant by, *"forgive those who turn,"* refers to turning away from *shirk* and *"follow Your Way,"* means the Path of the believers. They asked Allah to forgive them for their wrong actions other than *shirk* as He says, *"He forgives whoever He wishes for other than that"* (4:48)

If they say, "All of the Community hopes for the intercession of the Prophet, may Allah bless him and grant him peace. If it was particularly for the people of wrong actions, their request would be invalid," our reply is that every Muslim seeks the intercession of the Messenger and desires that Allah accept it since no one believes himself to be entirely free of wrong actions nor to have performed everything Allah has required of him. Everyone acknowledges their shortcomings and so they fear the punishment and hope for salvation. The Prophet, may Allah bless him and grant him peace, said, "None of you will be saved by what he does." They said, "Not even you, Messenger of Allah?" He said, "Not even me unless Allah covers me with His mercy."

The reason for the revelation of this *āyat* is that the tribe of Israel said, "We are the sons of Allah, beloved of Him and the sons of His Prophets and our fathers will intercede for us." So Allah informed them about the Day of Rising on which day such intercession will not be accepted and no ransom will be taken. He mentioned intercession, ransom and help because they are the things on which human beings rely in this world.

وَإِذْ نَجَّيْنَٰكُم مِّنْ ءَالِ فِرْعَوْنَ يَسُومُونَكُمْ سُوٓءَ ٱلْعَذَابِ
يُذَبِّحُونَ أَبْنَآءَكُمْ وَيَسْتَحْيُونَ نِسَآءَكُمْ ۚ وَفِى ذَٰلِكُم بَلَآءٌ مِّن رَّبِّكُمْ
عَظِيمٌ ٤٩

49 ***Remember when We rescued you***
from the people of Pharaoh.
They were inflicting an evil punishment on you –
slaughtering your sons and letting your women live.
In that there was a terrible trial for you
from your Lord.

Remember when We rescued you from the people of Pharaoh.

The word *"idh"* (when) means "remember My blessing when..." and the following *āyat*s mention some of the blessings which the tribe of Israel enjoyed. It is addressed to those present but refers to their ancestors. Allah says, *"We rescued you"* because the rescue of their forefathers was a reason for the existence of those present. The word "*najā*" (rescue) comes from the root *najwa* which is a raised place on the earth. So a rescued person is someone who emerges out of constriction into expansion. The "*āl*" (people) of Pharaoh means his family, followers and all who follow his *dīn*. Similarly, the *āl* of the Prophet refers to those who follow his *dīn* in his time and at all times, whether related to him or not. Whoever does not follow his *dīn* is not one of his family or his people, even if he is related to him. Evidence for this is in the words of Allah, *"We drowned the people of Pharaoh."* (2:50) and elsewhere.

Pharaoh may have been the name of the king himself but it is more probable that it was the title of the rulers of Egypt, like Caesar and Chosroes were titles of the emperors of Rome and Persia. It is said that this Pharaoh's actual name was Qābūs. Wahb said it was al-Walīd.

They were inflicting an evil punishment on you

The word used for inflicting (*yasūmūna*) indicates a constant punishment because *sawm* means constancy. The evil punishment consisted of making them slaves and chattels. They had to build, till the land, harvest and serve and anyone who did not work had to pay a poll tax. Allah ascribes the action to the people of Pharaoh even though they were acting on his command since it was them who imposed the punishment. This informs us that someone who does something is punished for his action even if he is just following orders. Aṭ-Ṭabarī says that when a tyrant orders someone to kill someone, the one who does the killing is criminally responsible.

In that there was a terrible trial for you from your Lord.

The words "in that" indicate everything which went on. The word used here for trial (*balā*) can also be a blessing as Allah says elsewhere using the same root *"test the believers with this excellent trial."* (8:17). So it can be good or bad but the majority say that, in this instance, it refers to the slaughtering of the male children and so here it is an evil test.

وَإِذْ فَرَقْنَا بِكُمُ ٱلْبَحْرَ فَأَنجَيْنَٰكُمْ وَأَغْرَقْنَآ ءَالَ
فِرْعَوْنَ وَأَنتُمْ تَنظُرُونَ ﴿٥٠﴾

50 ***And when We parted the sea for you and rescued you,***
and drowned the people of Pharaoh
while you watched.

When Allah parted the sea, each side was like a great mountain. The image comes from parting the hair and it is used for separating the truth from falsehood. The word *"baḥr"* (sea) indicates a large expanse of water, usually salty.

and drowned the people of Pharaoh while you watched.

"While you looked on with your own eyes." They saw the drowning of the people of Pharaoh while they had been saved and that was the greatest favour to them. It is also said to mean reflecting with the inner eye because they were too busy to actually watch. The first is more likely because they were in no state to reflect when they emerged from the sea.

وَإِذْ وَٰعَدْنَا مُوسَىٰٓ أَرْبَعِينَ لَيْلَةً ثُمَّ ٱتَّخَذْتُمُ ٱلْعِجْلَ
مِنۢ بَعْدِهِۦ وَأَنتُمْ ظَٰلِمُونَ ﴿٥١﴾

51 ***And when We allotted to Mūsā forty nights.***
Then you adopted the Calf when he had gone
and you were wrongdoers.

And when We allotted to Mūsā forty nights.

Mūsā is a foreign name and so it is not declined. Copts call water "*mū*" and tree *shā*". Mūsā was found in the basket in the water by a tree and so he was called Mūsā because of that. The majority say that the forty nights referred to were the whole of Dhū'l-Qa'da and the first ten days of Dhū'l-Ḥijja. That was after they had crossed the sea and his people asked him to give them a Book from Allah. Mūsā went to Sinai with seventy of the best of the tribe of Israel and climbed the mountain and Allah allotted them forty nights.

Then you adopted the Calf when he had gone and you were wrongdoers

Some commentators say that the tribe of Israel waited twenty days and twenty nights and then said, "Allah has broken His promise," and they adopted the Calf. The Sāmirī told them *"This is your god and the god of Mūsā,"* and they accepted what he said. Hārūn forbade them to do that, saying, *"My people! It is just a trial for you. Your Lord is the All-Merciful, so follow me and obey my command!"* (20:90) but they did not obey him and they all, except for one group of them, insisted on worshipping the Calf. When Mūsā returned, he found them doing that and threw down the Tablets. He recovered six pieces from the broken Tablets. The remaining pieces contained the lawful and unlawful and other things they needed. He destroyed the Calf with fire and threw the ashes into the sea. They repented, but their repentance was not accepted unless they killed one another, as we find in Allah's words below in *āyat* 54. They stood face to face wielding knives and swords from sunrise until full daylight arrived and then killed one another indiscriminately without any consideration of family ties until Mūsā called to Allah, "Lord! The tribe of Israel is annihilated!" Allah had mercy on them and poured out His bounty on them and accepted the repentance of those who remained and made the rest martyrs.

If it is asked why nights rather than days are mentioned, the answer is that it is because the night precedes the day, each month beginning with the sighting of the moon after sunset.

Some take this *āyat* as providing evidence for continuous fasting because if Allah had mentioned the days, it would be possible to believe that Mūsā broke the fast during the night.

ثُمَّ عَفَوْنَا عَنكُم مِّنۢ بَعْدِ ذَٰلِكَ لَعَلَّكُمْ تَشْكُرُونَ ﴿٥٢﴾

52 ***Then We pardoned you after that***
so that perhaps you would show thanks.

Then We pardoned you after that

Allah is able to pardon His creation and this can take place before or after punishment. This differs from forgiveness where there is no punishment at all. Pardon (*'afw*) is the effacement of the wrong action. It means, "We effaced your wrong actions and excused you." The words "after that" refer to the worship of the Calf.

so that perhaps you would show thanks.

This means "Be grateful for Allah's pardoning you. At-Tirmidhī and Abū Dāwūd report from Abū Hurayra from the Prophet, may Allah bless him and grant him peace: "The person who does not thank people does not thank Allah." This has two meanings. One is that the one whose nature is to be ungrateful for what he receives from people and does not thank them for their kindness will also inevitably be ungrateful for Allah's blessings and fail to thank Him. The other is that Allah does not accept the thanks of a slave for His goodness to him when that person does not thank people for their goodness to him and is ungrateful for their kindness since the two are connected.

Scholars have said many things about gratitude to Allah. Sahl ibn 'Abdullāh said, "Thankfulness is striving to obey together with avoiding disobedience secretly and openly." He said on another occasion, "Thankfulness is acknowledgement of your inability to thank the Blesser. That is why Allah says, *'Work, family of Dā'ūd, in thankfulness.'* (34:13) Dā'ūd asked, 'How can I be thankful, O Lord. Thankfulness is a blessing from you!' He said, 'By acknowledging Me and thanking Me even though you recognise that thankfulness is a blessing from Me.' He said, 'O Lord, show me Your most hidden blessing to me!' He said, 'Breathe, Dā'ūd.' Dā'ūd took a breath. Allah said, 'Who counts this blessing night and day?' Mūsā then asked, 'How can I thank You when my actions cannot repay even the smallest blessing which You have given Me?' So Allah revealed to Him, 'Mūsā, now you have truly thanked Me.'"

Al-Junayd said, "The reality of thankfulness is the ability to be thankful." He also said, "Once, when I was a boy of seven, I was playing in front of as-Sarī as-Saqaṭī while a group of people with him were discussing thankfulness. He asked me, 'Boy, what is thankfulness?' I replied, 'Not to disobey Allah in respect of His blessings.' He told me, 'I fear that your portion from Allah lies in your tongue.'" Al-Junayd said, "I still weep on account of what as-Sarī said to me." Ash-Shiblī said, "Thankfulness is humility and continuing to do good actions, opposing appetites, doing acts of obedience, and being always on the watch for the Compeller of the Heavens and the earth."

وَإِذْ ءَاتَيْنَا مُوسَى ٱلْكِتَٰبَ وَٱلْفُرْقَانَ لَعَلَّكُمْ تَهْتَدُونَ ٥٣

53 ***Remember when We gave Mūsā***
the Book and discrimination
so that perhaps you would be guided.

It is generally agreed that the Book mentioned here is the Torah, but there is disagreement about the meaning of the word "*furqān*" (discrimination), which is one of the names of the Qur'ān. Al-Farrā' and Quṭrub said that the meaning is: "We gave Mūsā the Torah and Muḥammad the Furqān." This is considered to be grammatically impossible. The best of what is said about the matter is what Mujāhid said: "It means discrimination between the truth and falsehood, meaning, in other words, what Allah taught him." Ibn Zayd said that it refers to the splitting of the sea so that they could cross. It is said to be separation from grief because they were enslaved under the Egyptians. It is also said to refer to their separation from the people of Pharaoh, who were drowned while they were saved.

وَإِذْ قَالَ مُوسَىٰ لِقَوْمِهِۦ يَٰقَوْمِ إِنَّكُمْ ظَلَمْتُمْ أَنفُسَكُم
بِٱتِّخَاذِكُمُ ٱلْعِجْلَ فَتُوبُوٓا۟ إِلَىٰ بَارِئِكُمْ فَٱقْتُلُوٓا۟ أَنفُسَكُمْ
ذَٰلِكُمْ خَيْرٌ لَّكُمْ عِندَ بَارِئِكُمْ فَتَابَ عَلَيْكُمْ ۚ إِنَّهُۥ هُوَ ٱلتَّوَّابُ
ٱلرَّحِيمُ ٥٤

54 ***And when Mūsā said to his people, 'My people,***
You wronged yourselves by adopting the Calf
so turn towards your Maker and kill yourselves.
That is the best thing for you in your Maker's sight.'
And He turned towards you.
He is the Ever-Returning, the Most Merciful.

And when Mūsā said to his people, 'My people, You wronged yourselves by adopting the Calf

Those with knowledge of the precise use of language say that the Calf represents a person's lower self and whoever abases it and opposes its desires is freed from its tyranny. However, here it clearly refers to the Calf which the tribe of Israel worshipped.

so turn towards your Maker and kill yourselves.

When Allah told them to turn towards Him, they asked how to do that and He told them to kill themselves. Some interpreters who seek out the motivation for actions have said that the meaning of this was that they abased their lower selves by acts of obedience and thus expiated their excesses, but the sound view is that they actually killed one another in the way we saw above in the commentary on *āyat* 51. Sufyān ibn 'Uyayna said, "Accepted repentance is a blessing from Allah which He has bestowed on this Community and not on others. The repentance of the tribe of Israel entailed death." It is agreed that Allah did not command everyone who worshipped the Calf to kill himself. They formed two rows and killed one another until they were told, "Enough!" Some commentators say that He sent tyrants to them who did the killing. Others things are said about the method involved. One point taken from this is that if a community does not actively combat wrongdoing when it occurs among them, they all become liable to punishment.

The Divine Name *al-Bāri'*, "Maker", is a different from *al-Khāliq*, "Creator". *Al-Bāri'* is the innovator who makes something new which never existed before whereas *al-Khāliq* is the one who decrees and moves things from one state to another.

And He turned towards you.

This refers to those who remained after the slaughter.

وَإِذْ قُلْتُمْ يَٰمُوسَىٰ لَن نُّؤْمِنَ لَكَ حَتَّىٰ نَرَى ٱللَّهَ جَهْرَةً
فَأَخَذَتْكُمُ ٱلصَّٰعِقَةُ وَأَنتُمْ تَنظُرُونَ ﴿٥٥﴾ ثُمَّ بَعَثْنَٰكُم
مِّنۢ بَعْدِ مَوْتِكُمْ لَعَلَّكُمْ تَشْكُرُونَ ﴿٥٦﴾

55 ***And when you said, 'Mūsā, we will not believe in you***
until we see Allah with our own eyes.'
So the thunder-bolt struck you dead
while you were looking.
56 ***Then We brought you back to life after your death,***
so that perhaps you would show thanks.

And when you said, 'Mūsā, we will not believe in you until we see Allah with our own eyes.'

It is said that this refers to the seventy men picked out by Mūsā. That is because they said, when they heard what Allah had said, "We will not believe in you..." But belief in the Prophets is mandatory after they have displayed their miracles so Allah sent down lightning from heaven which struck them dead. Then Mūsā prayed to his Lord and He brought them back to life. The full story of this incident will be found later in *Sūrat al-A'rāf*. Ibn Fūrak said that it is possible that their punishment was for asking to see Allah openly which was beyond the power of Mūsā to grant.

There is disagreement about the possibility of seeing Allah. Most innovaters deny its possibility in either this world or the Next. Those who follow the *Sunna* and the *Salaf* say it is possible in both worlds, and say that it will certainly happen in the Next World. This means that what they asked Mūsā for was not an impossibility. This will be disucssed in *Sūrat al-An'ām* and *Sūrat al-A'rāf*.

There are two possible meanings for the expression "with our own eyes" (lit. "openly"). One is that it is connected to their speech, meaning "they openly said". The other is that it describes the way they desired to see Allah, meaning with their own eyes, openly and directly. The use of the word also stresses the difference between seeing in a dream and seeing while awake.

So the thunder-bolt struck you dead while you were looking.

If it is asked how they could die while they were looking, the reply is that the Arabs use this expression when something is very close at hand. It is also said that it refers to what they were doing when the thunder-bolt struck.

Then We brought you back to life after your death, so that perhaps you would show thanks.

Qatāda said that they died and their spirits left them and then were returned to their bodies so that their natural lifespans could be fulfilled. An-Naḥḥās said that it is evidence against those of Quraysh who did not believe in the resurrection and also evidence against the People of the Book. Some people say that it means, "We gave you knowledge after your ignorance."

Al-Māwardī said, "There are two different positions about the continuance of responsibility of those brought back after death. One is that it continues and the other is that it is removed." The first view is the soundest because when the tribe of Israel saw the mountain in the air about to fall to them and the fire surrounding them that was part of what forced them to believe and their legal responsibility continued and so they were like the people of Yūnus. It is impossible that they should cease to be responsible. Allah knows best.

وَظَلَّلْنَا عَلَيْكُمُ الْغَمَامَ وَأَنزَلْنَا عَلَيْكُمُ الْمَنَّ وَالسَّلْوَىٰ كُلُوا مِن طَيِّبَاتِ مَا رَزَقْنَاكُمْ وَمَا ظَلَمُونَا وَلَٰكِن كَانُوا أَنفُسَهُمْ يَظْلِمُونَ ﴿٥٧﴾

57 ***And We shaded you with clouds***
and sent down manna and quails to you:
'Eat of the good things We have provided for you.'
They did not wrong Us;
rather it was themselves they were wronging.

And We shaded you with clouds

Allah caused the clouds to act as an awning above them. Commentators say this was when they were in the desert between Egypt and Palestine after they refused to enter the city of the tyrants and fight them and said to Mūsā, *"You and your Lord go and fight."* (5:24) For that they were punished by having to wander for forty years in a small area of desert. It is related that they walked for the entire day and stopped at night and in the morning they were once more where they had been the previous morning. In the desert, they asked Mūsā, "Who will provide us with food?" and Allah sent down manna and quails for them. They asked, "Who will protect us from the heat of the sun?" And the clouds shaded them. They asked, "What will we have to give us light?" So there was a pillar of light for them wherever they went. Makkī said it was a pillar of fire. They asked, "Where will we find water!" Mūsā was ordered to strike the stone. They asked, "Who will provide us with clothes!" So their garments did not wear out or become ragged and the children's clothes grew as they grew. Allah knows best.

and sent down manna and quails to you:

There is disagreement about the word "*manna*". It is said to be simply manna which is what most commentators say. It is also said to be sweet gum or honey or a sweet drink. It is said to be flat bread. It is said that it is a verbal noun for all that Allah gives as a blessing (*manna*) to His slaves without fatigue or cultivation on their part. We also have the words of the Messenger of Allah, may Allah bless him and grant him peace, "Truffles are the manna which Allah sent down for the tribe of Israel and its juice contains healing for the eye." (Muslim). Our scholars say that this hadith indicates that truffles are part of what Allah sent down to the tribe of Israel which Allah created for them in the desert. It is related that it used to rain down on them from dawn to sunset, like snow, and a man would take enough for the day. If anyone stored any of it, it went bad except on Friday, when they stored it for the Sabbath and it did not go bad because Saturday was their day of worship and nothing came down to them on the Sabbath.

There is also disagreement about the quails, *salwā* in Arabic. It is said to be actual quails as aḍ-Ḍaḥḥāk said. Ibn 'Aṭiyya said that there is consensus that it is birds of some kind. In fact, there is no consensus, because some commentators claim that it is honey.

'Eat of the good things We have provided for you.'

An elision is implied, namely: "We said: 'Eat…'". The words "good things" entail both lawfulness and deliciousness.

They did not wrong Us; rather it was themselves they were wronging.

This means that they were not thankful for the blessings they received but responded with acts of disobedience to Allah.

وَإِذْ قُلْنَا ٱدْخُلُوا۟ هَٰذِهِ ٱلْقَرْيَةَ فَكُلُوا۟ مِنْهَا حَيْثُ
شِئْتُمْ رَغَدًا وَٱدْخُلُوا۟ ٱلْبَابَ سُجَّدًا وَقُولُوا۟ حِطَّةٌ يُغْفَرْ
لَكُمْ خَطَٰيَٰكُمْ وَسَنَزِيدُ ٱلْمُحْسِنِينَ ﴿٥٨﴾

58 ***Remember when We said, 'Go into this town.***
and eat from it wherever you like, freely.
Enter the gate prostrating and say,
"Relieve us of our burdens!"
Your mistakes will be forgiven.
We will grant increase to all good-doers.'

Remember when We said, 'Go into this town and eat from it wherever you like, freely.

A town in Arabic is called a *qarya* because there is a concentration of people in it. The root of the verb from which it is derived describes the act of water collecting in a tank. Another meaning is hospitality (*qirā*) for the guest. *Miqra*, from the same root, means a tank. *Qarī* is a water course. *Maqāri* is a large bowl.

The commentators disagree about where this town was. Most say it was Jerusalem but it is also said to be Jericho. 'Umar ibn Shabba said, "It was the capital and the king's residence." Ibn Kaysān said Syria. Aḍ-Ḍaḥḥāk said Ramla, Jordan, Palestine and Tadmur. The great blessing involved was that, after their wandering, they were allowed to leave the desert and enter this town.

The instruction to eat is one of permission rather than command and the adverb "freely" indicates plenty and the lifting of the restrictions to which they had been subject in the desert.

Enter the gate prostrating and say, "Relieve us of our burdens!"

The gate referred to is said to be the gate of Jerusalem which people know as the Bāb Ḥiṭṭa. It is said to be the Qubba Gate towards which Mūsā and the tribe of Israel pray. The word *"sujjad"* (prostrating), according to Ibn 'Abbās, here means "bent over, bowing". It is said to mean humbling oneself without any particular way of doing it.

There is considerable discussion about the exact significance of the word *"ḥiṭṭa"* translated as "Relieve us of our burdens!" Al-Afkhash says it means, "Relieve us of our wrong actions." An-Naḥḥās said that there was a *ḥadīth* from Ibn 'Abbās: "They were told to say: 'There is no god but Allah.'" Another *ḥadīth* says that they were told to say: "Forgiveness!" In other words: "Say this, and your wrong actions will be removed." Ibn Fāris said that "*ḥiṭṭa*" was a word they were commanded to say so that their wrong actions would be removed.

It is possible that they used to use this expression in their worship, which is apparent from the *ḥadīth* reported from Abū Hurayra that the Messenger of Allah, may Allah bless him and grant him peace, said, "The tribe of Israel were told, 'Enter the gate prostrating and say, *"Relieve us of our burdens." Your mistakes will be forgiven,'* but they altered it and entered sliding on their buttocks, saying, 'That (*ḥiṭṭa*) is a grain of barley!'" (al-Bukhārī). It is also related that they said, "*Ḥinṭa*" (wheat) and "*ḥibba*" (seed).

The upshot of all these various things that are said is that Allah gave them a command but they disobeyed, were insolent and made mockery of it. So Allah punished them. Ibn Zayd said, "The plague destroyed seventy thousand of them."

Scholars use this *āyat* as evidence for changing the wording of expressions in the *Sharī'a* as long as they do not form part of an act of worship which requires that specific wording. When it is a question of an act of worship in which a particular form of wording is specified, it is not permitted to alter it since Allah censures that in His words here. If it is just the idea which is intended, it can be changed to something else which conveys the same meaning. But not all scholars agree about this. It is related from Mālik, ash-Shāfi'ī and Abū Ḥanīfa that a scholar can express the meaning of a text, provided that he conveys the entire meaning. That is the position of the majority. A considerable number of scholars, however, forbid that, including Ibn Sīrīn and Rajā' ibn Ḥawya. Mujāhid said, "One can shorten it but not add to it." Mālik was strict concerning the *aḥādīth* of the Messenger of Allah, may Allah bless him and grant him peace, that they be related with exactitude.

Your mistakes will be forgiven.

There are three readings of the word "forgiven" in this *āyat*: "We will forgive" (***n**aghfir* with *nūn*) which is the Ḥafṣ reading; "they will be forgiven" (***y**ughfar* with *yā'*) which is the Warsh reading; and "He will forgive" (*yaghfir*) also with *yā'*.

We will grant increase to all good-doers.'

Meaning those who did not worship the Calf. It is said that He will forgive the sins of those who store up and increase His goodness to those who do not. It is said that He will forgive the errors of those who disobey and increase His goodness to those who do good. A "good-doer" is someone whose *tawḥīd* is sound, who conducts himself well, performs his obligations and spares the Muslims his evil.

فَبَدَّلَ ٱلذِينَ ظَلَمُواْ قَوْلًا غَيْرَ ٱلذِے قِيلَ لَهُمْ فَأَنزَلْنَا
عَلَى ٱلذِينَ ظَلَمُواْ رِجْزًا مِّنَ ٱلسَّمَآءِ بِمَا كَانُواْ يَفْسُقُونَ ﴿٥٩﴾

59 ***But those who did wrong substituted words***
other than those they had been given.
So We sent down a plague from heaven
on those who did wrong
because they were deviators.

But those who did wrong substituted words other than those they had been given.

They changed the words they had been told to use. That was when they said *ḥinṭa* instead of *ḥiṭṭa*, and they added a letter and so they were punished since adding to the *dīn* and innovating in the *Sharī'a* is a terrible crime and causes great harm. This is due to their changing the word which indicated their repentance. That in itself merits punishment, so how much more must that be the case when the attributes of what is worshipped are altered! Words are less than actions, so what about changing actions! The word "*baddala*" (substituted) means to replace a thing with something else. The *Abdāl* are a category of righteous people who always exist in the world and are so called because, when one of them dies, Allah replaces him with another.

So We sent down a plague from heaven on those who did wrong

"Those who did wrong" is repeated a second time rather than simply using the pronoun "them" because of the gravity of what they did. Repetition is of two types. One is when it is used, as here, in a second phrase after the first has been completed, which intensifies the terribleness of the action done. The second is when there is repetition before the sense of the word is complete, as in *"The Undeniable. What is the Undeniable?"* (69:1) and elsewhere, in which case the result is to honour the thing mentioned. The word "*rijz*" (plague) is a Divine punishment and it also means "filth".

وَإِذِ ٱسْتَسْقَىٰ مُوسَىٰ لِقَوْمِهِۦ فَقُلْنَا ٱضْرِب بِّعَصَاكَ
ٱلْحَجَرَ ۖ فَٱنفَجَرَتْ مِنْهُ ٱثْنَتَا عَشْرَةَ عَيْنًا ۖ قَدْ عَلِمَ كُلُّ
أُنَاسٍ مَّشْرَبَهُمْ ۖ كُلُوا۟ وَٱشْرَبُوا۟ مِن رِّزْقِ ٱللَّهِ وَلَا
تَعْثَوْا۟ فِى ٱلْأَرْضِ مُفْسِدِينَ ۝٦٠

60 ***And when Mūsā was looking for water for his people,***
We said, 'Strike the rock with your staff.'
Then twelve fountains gushed out from it
and all the people knew their drinking place.

'Eat and drink of Allah's provision
and do not go about the earth corrupting it.'

And when Mūsā was looking for water for his people,

The type of "looking for water" referred to here is what you do when there is no water and there has been no rain for some time. Then you display true slavehood, poverty, need, abasement, repentance and integrity. Our Prophet Muḥammad, may Allah bless him and grant him peace, did the same when he asked for rain and went out to the place of prayer, humble, abased and making supplication. If we have no repentance and nothing but obstinacy and opposition to the Lord, how can we ask for rain? The Prophet, may Allah bless him and grant him peace, said in a *ḥadīth* related by Ibn 'Umar: "They do not refuse to pay the *zakāt* due on their property without being denied rain from heaven. Were it not for the animals, they would not have any rain at all."

The *sunna* of the Rain Prayer is to go out to the place of prayer, and for there to be a *khuṭba* and the prayer. That is the position of the majority of scholars. Abū Ḥanīfa believes that this prayer is not *sunna* nor is going out for it. In his view there should only be supplication. Enough for us, however, is the *ḥadīth* of 'Abdullāh ibn Yazīd al-Māzinī: "The Messenger of Allah, may Allah bless him and grant him peace, went out to ask for rain and reversed his cloak and prayed two *rak'at*s." (Muslim) More about the rain prayer will come in *Sūra Hūd, inshā'allāh.*

Then twelve fountains gushed out from it

Something is elided here, implying: "he struck it and it gushed." Allah has the power to make water gush and to split the stone without the blow, but He wanted to connect causes to effects. This is His wisdom for His slaves in respect of their obtaining their desires and to determine their reward and punishment according to that in the Hereafter. The meaning of the verb *infajara* is to burst out by breaking through, as dawn splits the sky. *Fujra* designates the place where water pours out.

When Mūsā asked for water for his people, he was instructed to strike the stone with his staff at the same time as making supplication. The stone in question was cubiform and about the size of a sheep's head. Three springs flowed out from each face.

and all the people knew their drinking place.

Each of the tribes knew its own spring and did not drink from any other. There were twelve tribes, descended from the sons of Ya'qūb. We have heard that there were fifty thousand in each tribe.

'Eat and drink of Allah's provision

Eat the manna and quails and drink of the water issuing from the stone.

and do not go about the earth corrupting it.'

The expression "*ta'thaw*" (go about) already implies extreme corruption which is forbidden and the word "corrupting" (*mufsidīn*) is added for more emphasis.

وَإِذْ قُلْتُمْ يَٰمُوسَىٰ لَن نَّصْبِرَ عَلَىٰ طَعَامٍ وَٰحِدٍ فَادْعُ لَنَا
رَبَّكَ يُخْرِجْ لَنَا مِمَّا تُنۢبِتُ ٱلْأَرْضُ مِنۢ بَقْلِهَا وَقِثَّآئِهَا
وَفُومِهَا وَعَدَسِهَا وَبَصَلِهَا قَالَ أَتَسْتَبْدِلُونَ ٱلَّذِى
هُوَ أَدْنَىٰ بِٱلَّذِى هُوَ خَيْرٌ ٱهْبِطُوا۟ مِصْرًا فَإِنَّ لَكُم مَّا
سَأَلْتُمْ وَضُرِبَتْ عَلَيْهِمُ ٱلذِّلَّةُ وَٱلْمَسْكَنَةُ وَبَآءُو بِغَضَبٍ
مِّنَ ٱللَّهِ ذَٰلِكَ بِأَنَّهُمْ كَانُوا۟ يَكْفُرُونَ بِـَٔايَٰتِ ٱللَّهِ وَيَقْتُلُونَ
ٱلنَّبِيِّۦنَ بِغَيْرِ ٱلْحَقِّ ذَٰلِكَ بِمَا عَصَوا۟ وَّكَانُوا۟ يَعْتَدُونَ ٦١

61 ***And when you said, 'Musa, we will not put up***
with just one kind of food
so ask your Lord to supply to us some of
what the earth produces –
its green vegetables, cucumbers,
grains, lentils and onions,'
he said, 'Do you want to replace what is better
with what is inferior?
Go back to Egypt,
then you will have what you are asking for.'
Abasement and destitution were stamped upon them.
They brought down anger from Allah upon themselves.
That was because they rejected Allah's Signs
and killed the Prophets without any right to do so.
That was because they rebelled
and went beyond the limits.

And when you said, 'Musa, we will not put up with just one kind of food

They said this when they were in the desert and became bored with a diet of manna and quails and remembered their previous life in Egypt. Al-Ḥasan said, "Some people brought with them vegetables and onions and they inclined to their bad old ways. Their natures yearned for their old habits and they spoke these words. They refer to manna and quails as one food because they ate them together or because it was always the same thing.

The word "*ṭa'ām*" (food) can refer both to what is eaten and what is drunk. Allah says, *"Anyone who does not taste it* (yaṭma'hu) *is with me"* (2:249) and *"When you have eaten* (ṭa'imtum) *disperse."* (33:53) The Messenger of Allah, may Allah bless him and grant him peace, said of the water of Zamzam, "It is a food to eat and a healing for illness." If *salwā* is honey, then it was drunk as well. Perhaps what is meant is wheat, as we find the same word used in *aḥādīth* for what can be used for *zakāt al-fiṭr*.

so ask your Lord to supply to us some of what the earth produces – its green vegetables, cucumbers, grains, lentils and onions,'

What is implied here are all those things produced by the earth which are edible. There is disagreement about what *fūm,* translated here as grains, means. It is said to mean garlic, like *thūm*. It is also said that it means grains and that is what is related from Ibn 'Abbās and most commentators.

Scholars disagree about eating onions and garlic with their unpleasant smell. The majority of scholars agree that it is permitted because of firm *aḥādīth* on the topic. One group of literalists who say that the prayer must be performed in a group, forbid it because the eating of them would prevent people going to the prayer.

he said, 'Do you want to replace what is better with what is inferior?

Adnā (inferior), according to az-Zajjāj, is derived from *dunūw*, meaning "of mediocre worth". 'Alī ibn Sulaymān said that it comes from *danā'a*, meaning "lower", and the *hamza* has been removed. It is also said that it is derived from *dūn*, meaning "base", and the original form would be *"adwan"*.

They disagree about what makes manna and quail better than what they asked for. There are five reasons given. One is that vegetables are relatively unimportant compared to manna and quail which are of higher quality. The second is that it is since manna and quail were Allah's gift to them and He had commanded them to eat them and so, by eating them, they were following a divine command, which would ensure them a reward in the Next World. The same did not apply to what they were asking for which was, therefore, inferior. The third reason is that what Allah gave them is in fact better and more delicious than what they were asking for. The fourth is that what they were given entailed no work or fatigue on their part and what they were asking for could only be obtained by tillage, harvesting and hard work. The fifth is that there was no doubt about the lawfulness and purity of what came to them there since it came directly from Allah whereas the produce of the earth can be impaired by unlawful transactions and other corrupt practices.

Go back to Egypt, then you will have what you are asking for.'

This command was an impossibility for them so it was a challenge they could not rise to because they were in the desert and this was their punishment. It is said that they were given what they asked. It is also said that *miṣr* means any city. Mālik said. "I think that it means the city where Pharaoh lived."

Abasement and destitution were stamped upon them.

These qualities stayed with them and were decreed for them. The verb *ḍaraba* (stamp) is used for "striking a tent". There is no Jew, even if he is wealthy, who does not have an air of poverty about him. It is said that the abasement referred to was the obligation of *jizya*. Al-Ḥasan and Qatāda said that their "destitution" (*maskana*) implied humiliation, as taken from *sukūn*.

That was because they rejected Allah's Signs

They denied His Book and the miracles of His Prophets such as 'Īsā, Yaḥyā, Zakariyyā and Muḥammad, peace be upon them.

and killed the Prophets without any right to do so.

The root of Prophet (*nabī'*) is *nabā*, which means to appear. It comes from *nabwa*, meaning something high. The position of a Prophet is high. The words *"without any right to do so"* emphasise the atrocity and the wrong action that they committed.

If it is observed that this is evidence that there might be an occasion on which it might be right to kill a Prophet even though it is known that the Prophets are protected from those who attack them, we reply that that is not the case. When they are killed, it must be wrongly. No Prophet can be killed by right. If they are killed it is in defence of the truth. If it is asked how could it be permitted for the unbelievers to have power over the Prophets, the answer is that it was a mark of honour for them and increased their stations, like those of the believers who are killed in the Way of Allah. Ibn 'Abbās and al-Ḥasan said, "No Prophet was ever killed except for those of them who had been commanded to fight, and everyone commanded to fight is helped."

إِنَّ ٱلَّذِينَ ءَامَنُوا۟ وَٱلَّذِينَ هَادُوا۟ وَٱلنَّصَـٰرَىٰ وَٱلصَّـٰبِـِٔينَ مَنْ ءَامَنَ
بِٱللَّهِ وَٱلْيَوْمِ ٱلْـَٔاخِرِ وَعَمِلَ صَـٰلِحًا فَلَهُمْ أَجْرُهُمْ عِندَ رَبِّهِمْ
وَلَا خَوْفٌ عَلَيْهِمْ وَلَا هُمْ يَحْزَنُونَ ﴿٦٢﴾

62 ***Those who believe, those who are Jews,***
and the Christians and Sabaeans,
all who believe in Allah and the Last Day
and act rightly,
will have their reward with their Lord.
They will feel no fear and will know no sorrow.

Those who believe,

This refers to those who believe in Muḥammad, may Allah bless him and grant him peace. Sufyān said that what is meant are the hypocrites, so it is as if He were saying, "Those who outwardly believe." That is why they are joined with the Jews, Christians and Sabaeans. Then He clarified the judgement by mentioning Allah and the Last Day.

those who are Jews,

The verb *hādū* means "to be Jews," and it is ascribed to Yahūdhā, who was the oldest son of Ya'qūb. It is said that they were called that for their turning away from worshipping the Calf and repenting, and so it means repentance.

and the Christians

The word for Christians, *naṣārā*, is the plural of *naṣrānī*. It is said that the name is derived from Nazareth where ʻĪsā lived. It is also said that it comes from the word *anṣār* which means "helpers" as in 3:52.

and Sabaeans,

Linguistically, the Arabic word *(ṣābi')* means one who inclines from one *dīn* to another *dīn*. The Arabs used it to describe someone who became Muslim.

There is no disagreement that the Jews and Christians are People of the Book and so it is permitted to marry their women and eat their food. *Jizya* is imposed on them. There is disagreement about the Sabaeans. As-Suddī said that they are a sub-group of the People of the Book, as Isḥāq ibn Rāhawayh states. Ibn al-Mundhir and Isḥāq say that there is nothing wrong in eating the animals they slaughter because they are People of the Book. Abu Ḥanīfa says the same. Ibn ʻAbbās, however, says that one should not marry their women. Other things are said about them.

It is reported from Ibn ʻAbbās that this *āyat* is abrogated by *"If anyone desires anything other than Islam as a* dīn, *it will not be accepted from him."* (3:85) Others said that it is not abrogated and that it is about those who believe in the Prophet, peace be upon him, and who are firm in their belief.

وَإِذْ أَخَذْنَا مِيثَٰقَكُمْ وَرَفَعْنَا فَوْقَكُمُ ٱلطُّورَ خُذُوا۟ مَآ
ءَاتَيْنَٰكُم بِقُوَّةٍ وَٱذْكُرُوا۟ مَا فِيهِ لَعَلَّكُمْ تَتَّقُونَ ﴿٦٣﴾
ثُمَّ تَوَلَّيْتُم مِّنۢ بَعْدِ ذَٰلِكَ ۖ فَلَوْلَا فَضْلُ ٱللَّهِ عَلَيْكُمْ
وَرَحْمَتُهُۥ لَكُنتُم مِّنَ ٱلْخَٰسِرِينَ ﴿٦٤﴾

63 ***Remember when We made the covenant with you and lifted up the Mount above your heads:***

'Take hold vigorously of what We have given you
and pay heed to what is in it,
so that hopefully you will be godfearing.'
64 *Then after that you turned away,*
and were it not for Allah's favour to you
and His mercy,
you would have been among the lost.

Remember when We made the covenant with you and lifted up the Mount above your heads:

It is said that a mountain was removed from its place and raised above the surface of the earth. There is disagreement about what "the Mount" (*aṭ-ṭūr*) is. It is said to be the name of the mountain where Allah spoke to Mūsā and where the Torah was revealed to him (Sinai), and this was what Ibn 'Abbās said. Aḍ-Ḍaḥḥāk said that it is a mountain on which plants grow unlike most others on which they do not grow. Mujāhid and Qatāda said it could be any mountain and Mujāhid said that it is simply the Syriac word for mountain.

The Mount was lifted in this way because, when Mūsā brought the Tablets from Allah which contained the Torah to the tribe of Israel, he told them, "Take them and hold fast to them." But they replied, "No! Not unless Allah tells us to do the same as you tell us!" So they were struck dead and then brought back to life. Mūsā again told them to take them and again they refused. So Allah commanded the angels to uproot one of the mountains of Palestine and it was held over them like a cloud. The sea was behind them and a fire in front of them and they were told to take the covenant otherwise the mountain would fall on top of them. They prostrated in repentance and took the Torah and the covenant. Aṭ-Ṭabarī said, "If they had taken it the first time, there would have been no need for a covenant." It is clear that they only submitted by force, not willingly.

'Take hold vigorously of what We have given you

"Bi-quwwa" (vigorously, lit. with strength) means with gravity and striving, as Ibn 'Abbās, Qatāda and as-Suddī stated. It is said that it means with sincerity. Mujāhid said, "'With strength' means 'putting it into action'." It is also said to mean "with a lot of study".

and pay heed to what is in it,

This means "reflect and observe His commands and warnings in it and do not neglect that and waste it". It is thus with all the Divine Books: that you act according to them and not just recite them on the tongue. To do otherwise is to waste them. Abū Sa'īd al-Khudrī reported that the Messenger of Allah, may Allah bless him and grant him peace, said, "The worst of people is an impious man who recites the Qur'ān and pays no heed to any of it." So he explained that the goal is to put it into action. Mālik said, "The Qur'ān can be recited by someone who has no good in him. This was an obligation for those before us just as it is obliged for us."

Allah says, *"Follow the best that has been sent down to you from your Lord."* (39:55) So He commanded us to follow His Book and act by it, but we have abandoned it just as the Jews and Christians did. There remain people with many books and copies of the Qur'ān who do not benefit at all from it because they are dominated by ignorance, desire for power, and the following of appetites. We find in at-Tirmidhī that Abū'd-Dardā' said, "We were with the Prophet, may Allah bless him and grant him peace, and he looked towards heaven and said, 'This is a time in which knowledge will be snatched away from its people until they have none left.' Ziyād ibn Labīd al-Anṣārī asked, 'How can it be snatched away from us when we recite the Qur'ān! By Allah, we recite it and our women and children recite it.' He replied, 'May your mother be bereft, Ziyād! I consider you to be like those in Madina who know the Torah and Gospel which the Jews and Christians have. What help was it to them?'"

In the *Muwaṭṭā'* we read that 'Abdullāh ibn Mas'ūd remarked to someone, "You are in a time when men of understanding (*fuqahā'*) are many and Qur'ān reciters are few, when the *ḥudūd* defined in the Qur'ān are protected and its letters are neglected, when few people ask and many give, when they make the prayer long and the *khuṭba* short, and put their actions before their desires. A time will come for people when their *fuqahā'* are few but their Qur'ān reciters are many, when the letters of the Qur'ān are guarded carefully but its *ḥudūd* are neglected, when many ask but few give, when they make the *khuṭba*s long but the prayer short, and they put their desires before their actions." (*Muwaṭṭā'*, 9.24.91) Yaḥyā said, "I asked Ibn Nāfi' about what is meant by 'put their desires before their actions,' and he replied, 'They follow their desires and abandon the actions prescribed for them.'"

Then after that you turned away,

This is a physical term which is used metaphorically for turning away from commands, religion and faith. *"After that"* means after the evidence you have seen and after your taking of the covenant and the raising of the mountain.

وَلَقَدْ عَلِمْتُمُ ٱلَّذِينَ ٱعْتَدَوْا۟ مِنكُمْ فِى ٱلسَّبْتِ فَقُلْنَا لَهُمْ
كُونُوا۟ قِرَدَةً خَٰسِـِٔينَ ﴿٦٥﴾

65 ***You are well aware of those of you***
who broke the Sabbath.
We said to them, 'Be apes, despised, cast out.'

You are well aware of those of you who broke the Sabbath.

An-Nasā'ī related that Ṣafwān ibn 'Assāl reported that a Jew said to his friend, "Let us go to this Prophet." His friend said, "Do not say 'Prophet'! He might hear you. He has four eyes!" They went to the Messenger of Allah, may Allah bless him and grant him peace, and asked him for seven clear commandments and He told them, "Do not associate anything with Allah; do not steal; do not fornicate; do not kill anyone Allah has made inviolate, unless with a legal right; do not slander an innocent person to a ruler; do not use magic; do not consume usury; do not slander chaste women; and do not turn your backs in retreat when the fighting is fierce. And, as Jews, you have one specially for you: that you do not profane the Sabbath." They kissed his hands and feet and said, "We testify that you are a Prophet!" He asked, "What prevents you from following me, then?" They replied, "Dā'ūd prayed that the line of Prophets would continue to be from his descendants and we fear that if we follow you, the other Jews will kill us." (at-Tirmidhī)

It is possible that the *āyat* refers to rulings about the Sabbath in general or it may just refer to the one on which they caught the fish. The word "*sabt*" (sabbath) is derived from *sabat* which means "cutting off". That is because it was a day of rest, cut off from the rest of the week.

We said to them, 'Be apes, despised, cast out.'

Scholars disagree about the transformation and whether they had offspring. Some people said that apes are descended from them and Qāḍī Abū Bakr ibn al-'Arabī chose that opinion. Most say that they had no offspring and these animals existed before them and that those who were transformed died without progeny because they were struck by Allah's wrath and punishment. They only lasted in that form for three days, unable to eat or drink.

فَجَعَلْنَٰهَا نَكَٰلًا لِّمَا بَيْنَ يَدَيْهَا وَمَا خَلْفَهَا
وَمَوْعِظَةً لِّلْمُتَّقِينَ ٦٦

66 ***We made it an exemplary punishment***
for those there then,
and those coming afterwards,
and a warning to those who are godfearing.

We made it an exemplary punishment

Various things are said about "it". It is said to refer to the punishment and it is said to refer to the town. It is said to be the whole nation which was transformed. It is said to be snakes, but this is unlikely. The word applies to suppression and punishment. *Ankāl* are fetters because they restrain. *Nikl* is used for a heavy bit in a bridle which restrains the animal. *Nakila* is to refrain from a matter. *Tankīl* is to inflict a penalty on enemies which acts as a deterrent to others.

and a warning to those who are godfearing.

It was a warning to everyone with *taqwā*. Ibn 'Aṭiyya says that this includes every godfearing person of every nation. Az-Zajjāj says that it is an admonishment only for the godfearing of the community of Muḥammad, may Allah bless him and grant him peace, to refrain from what Allah has forbidden lest they experience a punishment like that of the people who profaned the Sabbath.

وَإِذْ قَالَ مُوسَىٰ لِقَوْمِهِۦٓ إِنَّ ٱللَّهَ يَأْمُرُكُمْ أَن تَذْبَحُوا۟
بَقَرَةً ۖ قَالُوٓا۟ أَتَتَّخِذُنَا هُزُوًا ۖ قَالَ أَعُوذُ بِٱللَّهِ أَنْ أَكُونَ مِنَ
ٱلْجَٰهِلِينَ ﴿٦٧﴾

67 ***And when Mūsā said to his people,***
'Allah commands you to sacrifice a cow,'
they said, 'What! Are you making a mockery of us?'
He said, 'I seek refuge with Allah
from being one of the ignorant!'

And when Mūsā said to his people, 'Allah commands you to sacrifice a cow,'

There is no disagreement that the *dhabḥ* method (cutting the throat and carotid arteries) is used for slaughtering sheep and the *naḥr* method (stabbing through the throat) for camels, and that one can choose either of them for cattle. It is said that *dhabḥ* is more fitting because Allah mentioned it. Malik and others dislike using the wrong form of slaughter on an animal but did not consider the meat to be *ḥarām* if it happened.

The word "*baqara*" (cow) refers to the female while *thawr* is the word for a male, like *nāqa* and *jamal* in the case of camels. It is said that *baqara* is a single cow. The root means "to split open", since the cattle split the earth open when they plough it.

they said, 'What! Are you making a mockery of us?' He said, 'I seek refuge with Allah from being one of the ignorant!'

They said that to Mūsā when they replied to him. That was because they found someone murdered among them and were uncertain about who the killer was. They disagreed. They said, "Murder takes place while the Messenger of Allah is among us!" They came to him and asked him for clarification. That was before *qasāma* [a collective oath taken by the people about a murder victim] was revealed in the Torah. They asked Mūsā to pray to his Lord and He commanded them to sacrifice a cow. When they heard that from Mūsā, which was not a clear answer, they asked him about it and asked for a decision. He sought refuge with Allah because leaving someone who asks for guidance unanswered and mocking him is ignorance and not one of the qualities of the Prophets. Ignorance is the opposite of knowledge. The form of words indicates the unsound faith of those who said that. It is not possible to believe that of a Prophet who has displayed miracles.

This *āyat* indicates the prohibition against mocking the *dīn* of Allah and the *dīn* of the Muslims and those who must be esteemed, and that to do so is ignorance. The person who does that merits punishment. Joking, however, is not part of mockery. Indeed, the Prophet, may Allah bless him and grant him peace, and the imāms after him used to make jokes. Ibn Khuwayzimdād said, "We heard that a man went to the Qāḍī of Kufa, 'Ubaydullāh ibn al-Ḥasan, and 'Ubaydullah joked with him, asking, 'Is this cloak of yours from the wool of a ewe or that of a ram?' The man exclaimed, 'Don't be ignorant, Qāḍī!' 'Ubaydullāh said to him, 'Where do you find that joking is ignorance?' The man recited this *āyat* to him, and 'Ubaydullāh turned away from him because he saw that the man was ignorant and could not distinguish joking from mockery when they are not the same."

قَالُوا۟ ٱدْعُ لَنَا رَبَّكَ يُبَيِّن لَّنَا مَا هِىَ ۚ قَالَ إِنَّهُۥ يَقُولُ إِنَّهَا
بَقَرَةٌ لَّا فَارِضٌ وَلَا بِكْرٌ عَوَانٌۢ بَيْنَ ذَٰلِكَ ۖ فَٱفْعَلُوا۟
مَا تُؤْمَرُونَ ﴿٦٨﴾

68 ***They said, 'Ask your Lord to make it clear to us***
what it should be like.'
He said, 'He says it should be a cow,
not old or virgin, but somewhere between the two.
So do as you have been told.'

They said, 'Ask your Lord to make it clear to us what it should be like.'

This shows how prone they were to disobedience. If they had obeyed the command and slaughtered any cow, the result would have been obtained, but they made things difficult for themselves so Allah made things difficult for them. Ibn 'Abbās, Abū'l-'Āliyya and others said that.

He said, 'He says it should be a cow, not old or virgin, but somewhere between the two.

This indicates the permission for abrogation before an act takes place because the command to slaughter a cow meant any cow. When they wanted further description, He superseded the first ruling with another one. "*Fāriḍ*" (old) means one which has had many calves and virgin means one which has had none.

So do as you have been told.'

This repeats the command and reinforces it. This indicates that a command of this type is mandatory (*wujūb*) in the language of the *fuqahā'*.

قَالُوا۟ ٱدْعُ لَنَا رَبَّكَ يُبَيِّن لَّنَا مَا لَوْنُهَا ۚ قَالَ إِنَّهُۥ
يَقُولُ إِنَّهَا بَقَرَةٌ صَفْرَآءُ فَاقِعٌ لَّوْنُهَا تَسُرُّ ٱلنَّـٰظِرِينَ ﴿٦٩﴾

69 *They said, 'Ask your Lord to make it clear to us*
what colour it should be.'
He said, 'He says it should be a red cow,
the colour of sorrel,
a pleasure to all who look.'

They said, 'Ask your Lord to make it clear to us what colour it should be.'

In other words, they were asking, "Should it be black, white or red?"

He said, 'He says it should be a red cow, the colour of sorrel,

There is some disagreement among the commentators about the particular colour meant by the word *ṣafrā'* as the word can be used for yellow, red or black. Makkī said that even the horns and hooves were of the same colour. It is said that it was just the horns and hooves. Al-Ḥasan said that it meant black but this is unlikely, because the word only means black when referring to camels.

A pleasure to all who look.'

This means that the colour should be pure with no other colour mixed in with it. Wahb said that the sunlight danced off its hide.

قَالُوا ادْعُ لَنَا رَبَّكَ يُبَيِّن لَّنَا مَا هِيَ إِنَّ الْبَقَرَ تَشَابَهَ عَلَيْنَا
وَإِنَّا إِن شَاءَ اللَّهُ لَمُهْتَدُونَ ﴿٧٠﴾

70 ***They said, 'Ask your Lord to make it clear to us***
what it should be like.
Cows are all much the same to us.
Then, if Allah wills, we will be guided.'

They said, 'Ask your Lord to make it clear to us what it should be like. Cows are all much the same to us.

This was their fourth question so they still did not obey the command even when it had been made abundantly clear to them.

Then, if Allah wills, we will be guided.'

The use of "if Allah wills" in this sentence shows their eventual repentance and obedience. It is an indication that they regretted their lack of acceptance of what they had been commanded to do. It is related that the Prophet, may Allah bless him and grant him peace, said, "If they had not said 'if Allah wills' they would never have been guided to it at all."

قَالَ إِنَّهُ يَقُولُ إِنَّهَا بَقَرَةٌ لَّا ذَلُولٌ تُثِيرُ الْأَرْضَ وَلَا تَسْقِي
الْحَرْثَ مُسَلَّمَةٌ لَّا شِيَةَ فِيهَا قَالُوا الْآنَ جِئْتَ بِالْحَقِّ فَذَبَحُوهَا
وَمَا كَادُوا يَفْعَلُونَ ﴿٧١﴾

71 ***He said, 'He says it should be a cow***
not trained to plough or irrigate the fields –
completely sound, without a blemish on it.'
They said, 'Now you have brought the truth.'
So they sacrificed it – but they almost did not do it.

He said, 'He says it should be a cow not trained to plough or irrigate the fields –

Al-Ḥasan said that the cow was untamed and hence untrained. This *āyat* provides evidence for singling out animals by their description. If they are definitely known, then an advance sale is permitted. That is the position of Mālik and his people, al-Awzā'ī, al-Layth and ash-Shāfi'ī. The same applies to everything which has a clearly defined description.

completely sound, without a blemish on it.'

"Musallama" (sound) means that the cow must have no lameness or other impairments. Al-Ḥasan said that it means free of traces of work. *"Without a blemish on it"* means that nothing mars its colour.

These qualities in the cow were imposed because the tribe of Israel were difficult and so Allah made the matter difficult for them. The *dīn* of Allah is ease. It is blameworthy to go deep into asking the Prophets and others about matters of detail in this way. We ask Allah for well-being.

There are various stories related about this cow. The gist of them is that a man of the tribe of Israel had a son and he had a calf which he released in the woods, saying, "Oh Allah, I entrust this calf to You for this boy." The man died and when the child was grown, his mother told him, "Your father entrusted a calf to Allah for you, so go and fetch it." He went, and when the cow saw him, it came to him and he took it by the horn, even though it was wild. He led it to his mother. The people met him and found that he had the cow which they were commanded to sacrifice. They haggled with him for it. Its price was said to be thirty dinars or its weight in gold.

They said, 'Now you have brought the truth.'

Meaning "made the truth clear". Qatāda said that that is what it means.

So they sacrificed it – but they almost did not do it.

Because of their rebellion and excessive questioning or because of the high price of the cow.

وَإِذْ قَتَلْتُمْ نَفْسًا فَادَّارَأْتُمْ فِيهَا وَاللَّهُ مُخْرِجٌ مَّا كُنتُمْ
تَكْتُمُونَ ﴿٧٢﴾

72 *Remember when you killed someone*
and violently accused each other of it,
and Allah brought out what you were hiding.

Remember when you killed someone and violently accused each other of it.

There are two positions about the reason for the murder. One is that a man wanted to marry a beautiful daughter of his to his uncle's son but the uncle refused, so he killed him and took him to another village and dumped his body there. It is also said that he dumped his body between two villages. The second view is that the man murdered the other out of desire for the inheritance he would receive. He claimed that some tribes had killed him. They then accused one another and then went to Mūsā with their quarrel and he told them to sacrifice a cow. In Islamic *fiqh,* the ruling is that a murderer cannot inherit from his victim, although the heir does inherit in case of accidental killing according to Mālik, al-Awzā'ī, Abū Thawr and ash-Shāfi'ī. That is not the position of ath-Thawrī, Abū Ḥanīfa or ash-Shāfi'ī, according to another position.

فَقُلْنَا اضْرِبُوهُ بِبَعْضِهَا كَذَٰلِكَ يُحْيِ اللَّهُ الْمَوْتَىٰ
وَيُرِيكُمْ آيَاتِهِ لَعَلَّكُمْ تَعْقِلُونَ ﴿٧٣﴾

73 *We said, 'Hit him with part of it!'*
In that way Allah gives life to the dead

and He shows you His Signs
so that hopefully you will understand.

We said, 'Hit him with part of it!'

The part referred to is said to have been the tongue because that is the organ of speech and it is said to have been with the rump end of the tail. It is also said to have been the leg or another of the bones. In any case the corpse was struck with it and then said who his killer was and then reverted back to being a lifeless corpse.

Mālik used this episode as evidence for the validity of applying the *qasāma* oath on the basis of the last words of the dying victim of a homicidal attack when he says, "So-and-so killed me." Ash-Shāfi'ī and most scholars forbid this, claiming that it is contrary to the principle that a suspect is innocent except when there is absolute certainty of his guilt, and in that case there is only probability because the words of the victim may be true or false. They say that the case of the man of the tribe of Israel was a miraculous one and so it does not apply in normal circumstances. Ibn al-'Arabī replies that the miracle consisted of the bringing back to life and that, therefore, what the man said has the same ruling as the words of any person who is alive.

This *āyat* contains evidence that all true aspects of any *Sharī'a* which existed before ours are also binding on us, as many *mutakallimūn* and *fuqahā'* have said.

In that way Allah gives life to the dead

As He gave life to this man after his death, so Allah will revive everyone on the Last Day.

ثُمَّ قَسَتْ قُلُوبُكُم مِّنۢ بَعْدِ ذَٰلِكَ فَهِىَ كَٱلْحِجَارَةِ أَوْ أَشَدُّ قَسْوَةً ۚ
وَإِنَّ مِنَ ٱلْحِجَارَةِ لَمَا يَتَفَجَّرُ مِنْهُ ٱلْأَنْهَٰرُ ۚ وَإِنَّ مِنْهَا لَمَا يَشَّقَّقُ
فَيَخْرُجُ مِنْهُ ٱلْمَآءُ ۚ وَإِنَّ مِنْهَا لَمَا يَهْبِطُ مِنْ خَشْيَةِ ٱللَّهِ ۗ
وَمَا ٱللَّهُ بِغَٰفِلٍ عَمَّا تَعْمَلُونَ ﴿٧٤﴾

74 ***Then your hearts became hardened after that,***
so they were like rocks or even harder still.
There are some rocks from which rivers gush out,
and others which split open and water pours out,
and others which crash down from fear of Allah.
Allah is not unaware of what you do.

Then your hearts became hardened after that,

This refers to the lack of repentance on the part of the Jews and their refusal to submit to the Signs of Allah. Abū'l-'Āliyya, Qatāda and others said that what is meant here are the hearts of all the sons of Israel. Ibn 'Abbās, however, says that what is meant are the hearts of the heirs of the victim because when he was brought to life and named his killer and then became dead again, they denied it and said, "He lied" after seeing this great sign. So their hearts were made blind and they were the most adamant in denying their Prophet.

At-Tirmidhī reported from 'Abdullāh ibn 'Umar that the Messenger of Allah, may Allah bless him and grant him peace, said, "Do not speak a lot without mentioning Allah. A lot of words without mentioning Allah produce hardness of the heart. The furthest of people from Allah are the hard hearted." Anas reported that the Prophet, may Allah bless him and grant him peace, said, "Four things are part of wretchedness: unresponsive eyes, hard hearts, far-reaching hopes and greed for this world."

There are some rocks from which rivers gush out,

This refers to springs which become ever larger until they become rivers or rocks that simply split, even if no water comes out.

and others which split open and water pours out,

Some rocks benefit more than hearts because water emerges from them.

and others which crash down from fear of Allah.

Mujāhid said, "No rock falls from the top of a mountain, nor river gushes from a rock nor water emerges from it, except from fear of Allah. Some *mutakallimūn* say that the rocks, in this instance, mean hail. Ibn Baḥr said that it means, "Some hearts fall down." The first, however, is the soundest. It does not prevent some inanimates from having knowledge as we find in various accounts of the Prophet's miracles.

أَفَتَطْمَعُونَ أَن يُؤْمِنُوا۟ لَكُمْ وَقَدْ كَانَ فَرِيقٌ مِّنْهُمْ
يَسْمَعُونَ كَلَـٰمَ ٱللَّهِ ثُمَّ يُحَرِّفُونَهُۥ مِنۢ بَعْدِ مَا عَقَلُوهُ وَهُمْ
يَعْلَمُونَ ٧٥

75 ***Do you really hope they will follow you in faith***
when a group of them heard Allah's Word
and then, after grasping it, knowingly distorted it?

Do you really hope they will follow you in faith

This question implies a negative response as there was no hope for the faith of a group of Jews because they had already rejected. It is addressed to the Companions of the Prophet. That is because some of the Anṣār wanted the Jews to become Muslim because of their alliance with them and proximity to them. It is said that it is addressed to the Prophet alone. Ibn 'Abbās says that it means: "Do not be sad about their denial of you."

when a group of them heard Allah's Word

What is meant by this are the seventy whom Mūsā chose to hear the Word of Allah, but who then did not obey and altered His words when they told their people. This is what ar-Rabī'a and Ibn Isḥāq said. This interpretation is somewhat weak. As-Suddī said that they were not able to listen and they were confused and wanted Mūsā to repeat it for them. When they left they then altered what they had heard him say.

People disagree about how Mūsā recognised the Speech of Allah when he had not heard it before. Some say that he heard words without letters or voices, with no pause or breath and then knew that it could not be a human voice but must be the voice of the Lord of the worlds. Others said that he heard words which did not come from any direction and so he knew they were not of human origin. It is said that his entire body heard it and so he knew that it was the Word of Allah. It is said that the miracle indicated that it was the Word of Allah when he was told to cast down his staff and it became a serpent. That was proof of the truth of the matter. It is said that he concealed something inside himself which only He who knows the Unseen worlds would know and Allah informed him of that and so he knew that he was addressed by Allah.

and then, after grasping it, knowingly distorted it?

Mujāhid and as-Suddī said that they were the Jewish scholars who altered the Torah and made what was unlawful lawful and what was lawful unlawful, following their own whims and desires. This is to rebuke them because of what their fathers did. It indicates that any scholar who is opinionated regarding the truth is far from right guidance because he knows the promise and threat, and yet still follows his own opinion.

وَإِذَا لَقُوا الَّذِينَ آمَنُوا قَالُوا آمَنَّا وَإِذَا خَلَا
بَعْضُهُمْ إِلَىٰ بَعْضٍ قَالُوا أَتُحَدِّثُونَهُم بِمَا فَتَحَ اللَّهُ
عَلَيْكُمْ لِيُحَاجُّوكُم بِهِ عِندَ رَبِّكُمْ أَفَلَا تَعْقِلُونَ ٧٦
أَوَلَا يَعْلَمُونَ أَنَّ اللَّهَ يَعْلَمُ مَا يُسِرُّونَ وَمَا يُعْلِنُونَ ٧٧

76 *When they meet those who believe, they say,*
'We believe.'
But when they go apart with one another, they say,
'Why do you speak to them about
what Allah has decided about you,
so they can use it as an argument against you
before your Lord?
Will you not use your intellect?'
77 *Do they not know that Allah knows*
what they keep secret and what they make public?

When they meet those who believe, they say, 'We believe.'

This is about the hypocrites.

But when they go apart with one another,

This refers to the Jews because some of them outwardly became Muslim but were actually hypocrites. They would talk to the believers about how their ancestors were being tormented. So the Jews said to them:

'Why do you speak to them about what Allah has decided about you,

"When you speak regarding the punishment which Allah has ordained for you, so that they can say , 'We are more honoured with Allah than you are.'" This is the meaning according to Ibn 'Abbās and as-Suddī. The root of the word used for "*fataḥa*" (decided) means to give a judgement or decision but the word can also indicate help and assistance as well as judgement.

so they can use it as an argument against you before your Lord?

This is generally taken as referring to the Next World but it is also said that it means "when your Lord is mentioned".

Will you not use your intellect?'

This is generally taken to be the words of the rabbis to their followers but it is also possible that it is addressed by Allah to the believers, meaning, "Do you not know that the tribe of Israel do not believe and therefore this is the way they behave?" Then Allah follows that with another rebuke.

وَمِنْهُمْ أُمِّيُّونَ لَا يَعْلَمُونَ ٱلْكِتَٰبَ إِلَّآ أَمَانِيَّ
وَإِنْ هُمْ إِلَّا يَظُنُّونَ ٧٨

78 ***Some of them are illiterate,***
knowing nothing of the Book but wishful thinking.
They only speculate.

Some of them are illiterate,

"Them" may refer to the Jews alone or to both the Jews and the hypocrites. The word "*ummiyyūn*" (illiterate) means that they can neither read nor write. It is derived from *ummiyya*, meaning "to still be in the state in which your mother bore you, without having learned to read or write". Ibn 'Abbās said that they are illiterate because they do not affirm the Mother of the Book. It is said that they are People of the Book who do not know the Book. 'Ikrima and aḍ-Ḍaḥḥāk said that it refers to Christian Arabs. The first explanation is more likely, and Allah knows best.

knowing nothing of the Book but wishful thinking.

"*Amānī*" (wishful thinking) is the plural of *umniya* (recitation) from *amnuya*, as we see in *"without Shaytan insinuating something into his recitation while he was reciting (tamannā)."* (22:52) *Amānī* also means "lies". That is how Ibn 'Abbās and Mujāhid explain it here. It is also what a person wishes for and desires, and so Qatāda said that the meaning is that they desire what they in reality do not have.

They only speculate.

This means that they lie and come up with new things because they have no knowledge about whether what they recite is true or not. They imitate what their rabbis recite. Al-Anbārī says that the Arabs use *ẓann* (speculation) for knowledge, doubt and lies. Here Allah means that they are lying.

Our scholars say that Allah describes the rabbis as changing and altering their Book and Allah says in the next *āyat*, *"Woe to them for what their hands have written!"* (2:79) That is because they studied the matter, but their scholars were bad shepherds, greedy for worldly things and so they looked for things to draw people's attention towards themselves. Therefore they made up new things in their *Sharī'a* and altered it. They added these inventions to the Torah and told their foolish followers, "This is from Allah" so that it would be accepted from them and would establish their power. By so doing they obtained nothing but the rubble and filth of this world.

They said various things. One is: *"We are under no obligation where the Gentiles (lit. illiterate) are concerned"* (3:75) referring to the Arabs, meaning that whatever property of theirs they usurped was lawful for them. Another thing they said was that no sins they committed would harm them because they were the beloved of Allah and His sons. (cf. 5:18) Allah is exalted above that! The Torah has: "My rabbis and sons of My Messengers!'. They changed it to "My loved ones and My sons." They also said, "Allah will not punish us. If He does punish us, it will only be for forty days," (cf. 2:80) the number of days they were worshipping the Calf.

فَوَيْلٌ لِّلَّذِينَ يَكْتُبُونَ ٱلْكِتَٰبَ بِأَيْدِيهِمْ ثُمَّ
يَقُولُونَ هَٰذَا مِنْ عِندِ ٱللَّهِ لِيَشْتَرُوا۟ بِهِۦ ثَمَنًا
قَلِيلًا ۖ فَوَيْلٌ لَّهُم مِّمَّا كَتَبَتْ أَيْدِيهِمْ وَوَيْلٌ لَّهُم
مِّمَّا يَكْسِبُونَ ۖ ٧٩

79 ***Woe to those who write the Book***
with their own hands and then say
'This is from Allah'
to sell it for a paltry price.
Woe to them for what their hands have written!
Woe to them for what they earn!

Woe

There is disagreement about what "*wayl*" (woe) means. 'Uthmān ibn 'Affān related from the Prophet that it is a mountain of fire. Abū Sa'īd al-Khudrī said that *Wayl* is a valley in Hell situated between two mountains whose depth is a fall of forty years. Sufyān and 'Aṭā' ibn Yasār said that *Wayl* is a valley in Hellfire through which flows the pus of the people of the Fire. It is said to be a cistern in the Fire or a gate of Hell. Ibn 'Abbās said that it is harsh punishment. Al-Khalīl says that it is intense evil. It is also said to be extreme sorrow and the expression is used in times of great sorrow and distress. Its root is said to be that destruction which invites woe. Al-Farrā' said that its root is *way*, meaning sorrow.

to those who write the Book

The first to write with the pen was the Prophet Idrīs, as we read in *ḥadīth.*

with their own hands.

This is for emphasis because it is well known that writing is done with the hands. This kind of linguistic usage is often used for stress in the Qur'ān. The fact that they wrote it also indicates that it was not revealed to them, but they are the ones who fabricated it.

This *āyat* and the one before it warn against making any alterations or changes or additions to the *Sharī'a.* Anyone who alters, changes or innovates something in the *dīn* of Allah which is not in it and not permitted in it, is subject to this terrible threat and painful punishment. The Messenger of Allah, may Allah bless him and grant him peace, cautioned his community about what he knew would occur at the end of time. He said, "Those of the People of the Book before you divided into 72 sects and this community will divide into 73, all of whom will be in the Fire except for one."

to sell it for a paltry price.

It is paltry because it will inevitably disappear and have no permanence, or because it is unlawful as there is no blessing in anything unlawful. Their action will have no value or increase with Allah.

وَقَالُوا۟ لَن تَمَسَّنَا ٱلنَّارُ إِلَّآ أَيَّامًا مَّعْدُودَةً ۚ قُلْ أَتَّخَذتُّمْ
عِندَ ٱللَّهِ عَهْدًا فَلَن يُخْلِفَ ٱللَّهُ عَهْدَهُۥٓ ۖ أَمْ تَقُولُونَ
عَلَى ٱللَّهِ مَا لَا تَعْلَمُونَ ﴿٨٠﴾

80 ***They say, 'The Fire will only touch us***
for a number of days.'
Say, 'Have you made a contract with Allah –
then Allah will not break His contract –
or are you rather saying about Allah
what you do not know?'

They say, 'The Fire will only touch us for a number of days.'

As was mentioned above "They" in this *āyat* refers to the Jews. There is disagreement about the reason for its revelation. It is said that the Prophet, may Allah bless him and grant him peace, asked the Jews, "Who are the people of the Fire?" They replied, "We are. Then you will follow us." He said, "You lie. You know that we will not follow you," and this was revealed. Ibn Zayd said that. Ibn 'Abbās said, "When the Messenger of Allah, may Allah bless him and grant him peace, came to Madina, the Jews were saying, 'The duration of this world is seven thousand [years?]. People will be punished in the Fire for one day of the days of the Next World for each thousand years of the days of this world. That is seven days.' Then Allah revealed this *āyat*." This is what Mujāhid said. Others said that the Jews said that the Torah says that Hellfire is a distance of forty years across. They will cross a year's length every day until they have gone right across and then leave Hellfire. Aḍ-Ḍaḥḥāk related that from Ibn 'Abbās. Ibn 'Abbās said that the Jews claim that they found written in the Torah that there is a length of forty years between the sides of Hell until they reach the tree of Zaqqūm. They said, "We will be punished until we reach the Tree of Zaqqūm and then we will leave the Fire."

This *āyat* refutes Abū Ḥanīfa and his people in their conclusion that the words of the Prophet, "leave the prayer during the days of your menstruation" is evidence that the period of menstruation is what can be called "the days of menstruation". For this reason they say that the minimum time for a menstrual period is three days and its maximum ten days because, for any period less than three days, the singular or dual is used and for numbers more than ten the singular is also used and not the plural. The reply to this is that Allah uses the plural "days" in other ways than this way, as when He says about fasting that is for "known days" (2:184) and in that case it is known to mean the entire month of Ramaḍān and here *"The Fire will only touch us for a number of days,"* (3:24) means forty days.

بَلَىٰ مَن كَسَبَ سَيِّئَةً وَأَحَٰطَتۡ بِهِۦ خَطِيٓـَٔتُهُۥ
فَأُوْلَٰٓئِكَ أَصۡحَٰبُ ٱلنَّارِۖ هُمۡ فِيهَا خَٰلِدُونَ ٨١ وَٱلَّذِينَ
ءَامَنُواْ وَعَمِلُواْ ٱلصَّٰلِحَٰتِ أُوْلَٰٓئِكَ أَصۡحَٰبُ ٱلۡجَنَّةِۖ
هُمۡ فِيهَا خَٰلِدُونَ ٨٢

81 ***No indeed! Those who accumulate bad actions***
and are surrounded by their mistakes,
such people are the Companions of the Fire,
remaining in it timelessly, for ever;
82 ***whereas those who believe and do right actions,***
such people are the Companions of the Garden,
remaining in it timelessly, for ever.

This *āyat* is a clear refutation of the claim the Jews make. The bad actions referred to are said to be *shirk.* Ibn Jurayj said, "I asked 'Aṭā' about the expression 'accumulate bad actions' and he said, 'It means *shirk,*' and recited *'Those who perform bad actions will be flung head-first into the Fire.'* (27:90)" Al-Ḥasan and Qatāda said that it means all major wrong actions.

This *āyat* is also important because it indicates that there are two preconditions for salvation and that both are necessary: faith and right action. It is similar to what Allah says: *"Those who say, 'Our Lord is Allah,' and then go straight."* (41:30) When Sufyān ibn 'Abdullāh ath-Thaqafī asked the Prophet, "Messenger of Allah, tell me something about Islam which will preclude my having to ask anyone after you," the Prophet said, "Say, 'I have believed in Allah,' and go straight." (Muslim) This was discussed in *āyat* 35.

وَإِذْ أَخَذْنَا مِيثَٰقَ بَنِىٓ إِسْرَٰٓءِيلَ لَا تَعْبُدُونَ إِلَّا
ٱللَّهَ وَبِٱلْوَٰلِدَيْنِ إِحْسَانًا وَذِى ٱلْقُرْبَىٰ وَٱلْيَتَٰمَىٰ
وَٱلْمَسَٰكِينِ وَقُولُوا۟ لِلنَّاسِ حُسْنًا وَأَقِيمُوا۟ ٱلصَّلَوٰةَ
وَءَاتُوا۟ ٱلزَّكَوٰةَ ثُمَّ تَوَلَّيْتُمْ إِلَّا قَلِيلًا مِّنكُمْ
وَأَنتُم مُّعْرِضُونَ ﴿٨٣﴾

83 ***Remember when We made a covenant***
with the tribe of Israel:
'Worship none but Allah and be good to your parents
and to relatives and orphans and the very poor.
And speak good words to people.
And establish the prayer and pay zakat.'
But then you turned away – except a few of you –
you turned aside.

Remember when We made a covenant with the tribe of Israel: 'Worship none but Allah

There is disagreement about the covenant referred to here. Makkī said that it is the covenant which they made when they were brought out from the loins of Ādam (cf. 7:172) and it is also said that it was the covenant they made to worship none but Allah while they were rational and alive. Worship entails affirming the Unity of Allah, confirming His Messenger and performing what is revealed in His Books.

Al-Farrā', az-Zajjaj and a group said, "It means that Allah's contract with them was conditional on their not worshipping anything other than Allah and being good to their parents, etc."

and be good to your parents

Allah connected being good to one's parents with *tawḥīd* because the first development in the womb came from Allah, and the second, which involves upbringing and teaching, is in the hands of one's parents. That is why Allah Almighty enjoined thankfulness to them, as in His words: *"Give thanks to Me and to your parents."* (31:14) Being good to parents implies keeping them company correctly and courteously, being humble to them, obeying them, praying for forgiveness for them, and maintaining ties with the people they love.

and to relatives

They are commanded to be good to their relatives by maintaining ties with them and giving them gifts.

and orphans

An orphan is a child without a father. This *āyat* commands people to be kind to orphans and encourages caring for them and protecting their property, which will be explained elsewhere. The Messenger of Allah, may Allah bless him and grant him peace, said, "I and an orphan's guardian, whether he is a relative or a non-relative, will be like these two in the Garden," and the transmitter, Mālik ibn Anas, indicated his index and middle fingers. (From Abū Hurayra in Muslim) Abū Mūsā al-Ash'arī reported that the Prophet, may Allah bless him and grant him peace, said, "When an orphan sits with some people at their table, Shayṭān does not come near it." Ibn 'Abbās reported that he said, "If someone includes a Muslim orphan at his table until Allah enriches him, he will be forgiven his wrong actions entirely unless he does something which is unforgivable. And if Allah takes away the two things a person loves most and he remains steadfast and in expectation of the reward, he will be forgiven his wrong actions entirely." They asked, "What are the two things he loves most?" He replied, "His two eyes," and then continued, "and whoever has three daughters or three sisters and supports them and is good to them until they marry or die all his wrong actions will be forgiven unless he does something which is unforgivable." A bedouin man who had emigrated called out, "Messenger of Allah, or two?" The Messenger of Allah, may Allah bless him and grant him peace, said, "Or two." Ibn 'Abbās said that it is an *gharīb ḥadīth.*

and the very poor

They are those who are in need and those who are destitute. This contains encouragement to give *ṣadaqa* and solace to people in need, and to keep an eye on the conditions of the poor and weak. Muslim reported from Abu Hurayra that the Prophet, may Allah bless him and grant him peace, said, "Someone who strives on behalf of widows and the poor is like someone who fights in the way of Allah and like someone who continually stands at night in prayer and like someone who continually fasts."

And speak good words to people.

The sentence implies: "Speak words which contain good for people since *"ḥusn"* (good) is a verbal noun. Ibn 'Abbās said that it means, "Say to them: 'There is no god but Allah' and instruct them to say it." Ibn Jurayj said: "Speak the truth to people about Muḥammad, may Allah bless him and grant him peace, and do not alter his description." Sufyān ath-Thawrī said: "Command them to what is known to be right and forbid them what is recognised as wrong." Abū'l-'Āliyya said that it means: "Speak good words to them and excuse them as you yourself would want to be excused."

All of this encourages noble character. A person should be gentle when he speaks to people and maintain a cheerful face with both the pious and the impious, the one who holds to the *Sunna* and even to the innovator, provided you do not flatter him or say anything which might appear to approve of his position. Allah Almighty said to Mūsā and Hārūn, *"Speak to him with gentle words."* (20:44). No speakers could be better than Mūsā and Hārūn and no one impious could be worse than Pharaoh, and yet Allah commanded them to be gentle with him. Ṭalḥa ibn 'Umar said, "I said to 'Aṭā', 'You are a man with whom people from different sects meet and I am a man who tends to be sharp. I tell them some harsh home truths.' He replied, 'Do not do that! Allah says, *"Speak good words to people."* The Jews and Christians are included in this *āyat*, so what about others?'" It is related that the Prophet, peace be upon him, told 'Ā'isha, "Do not use obscenities. If obscenity had been a man, it would have been a bad man."

It is said that *"an-nās"* (people) in this *āyat* refers to Muḥammad, may Allah bless him and grant him peace, as Allah says, *"Or do they in fact envy people for the bounty Allah has granted them?"* (4:54) So it would mean: "Speak good words to the Prophet."

Al-Mahdawī related that Qatāda said that this verse was abrogated by the *Āyat* of the Sword. Ibn 'Abbās is reported as saying, "This *āyat* was revealed at the beginning and then abrogated by the Sword Verse." Ibn 'Aṭiyya said, "This indicates that our Community was instructed to act like this at the beginning of Islam, but it is not abrogated in respect of the tribe of Israel. Allah knows best.

And establish the prayer and pay zakāt.'

This is directed to the tribe of Israel. Ibn 'Aṭiyya said, "Their *zakāt* used to be burned, so it was not like the *zakāt* of the nation of Muḥammad, may Allah bless him and grant him peace.

But then you turned away – except a few of you – you turned aside.

This is addressed to the Jews who were the contemporaries of Muḥammad, may Allah bless him and grant him peace. The turning away done by their ancestors is ascribed to them since they also continued to do the same thing. The few who did not were men like 'Abdullāh ibn Sallām, who became Muslim. It is said that *"tawallaytum"* (turning away) is with the body and *"mu'riḍūn"* (turning aside) is with the heart.

وَإِذْ أَخَذْنَا مِيثَٰقَكُمْ لَا تَسْفِكُونَ دِمَآءَكُمْ وَلَا تُخْرِجُونَ
أَنفُسَكُم مِّن دِيَٰرِكُمْ ثُمَّ أَقْرَرْتُمْ وَأَنتُمْ تَشْهَدُونَ ﴿٨٤﴾

84 ***And when We made a covenant with you***
not to shed your own blood
and not to expel yourselves from your homes,
you agreed and were all witnesses.

It is the tribe of Israel which is being addressed here, but the meaning includes those after them. The word for self (*nafs*) is derived from *nafāsa* (preciousness), so the self of a person is the dearest thing he has. They agreed to this covenant which was made with them and their ancestors. Their hearts were witnesses to this covenant. Witnessing can also mean being present, so they witnessed the bloodshed and expulsion.

The Jews were a single religious community and so their affairs were unified and they were like a single individual. Therefore one of them killing another was like him killing himself. It is said that retaliation is meant here, commanding them not to kill someone so that they are killed in retaliation, so that it is as if they were shedding their own blood. The same applies to committing fornication or apostasy which would also entail their own deaths. Allah made a covenant with the tribe of Israel in the Torah not to kill each other or expel anyone or enslave him or let him be robbed and other such things. This was all forbidden to us as well but all those things occur in the trials we are experiencing. "We belong to Allah and to Him we return!" The Revelation says, *"Or to confuse you in sects and make you taste one another's violence."* (6:65).

Ibn Khuwayzimdād said that the meaning may be literal, commanding them not to commit suicide nor to be expelled from their houses through their own foolishness, nor for a man to kill himself through overwork or self-imposed affliction, nor to wander in the desert without seeking shelter in people's houses out of ignorance of religion and foolishness. It can be taken to apply to all those things. It is reported that 'Uthmān ibn Maz'ūn gave his allegiance along with ten others of the Prophet's Companions. They decided to wear ragged garments, wander in the desert, not take refuge in houses, or eat meat or go near women. The Prophet, may Allah bless him and grant him peace, heard about that and went to 'Uthmān's house, but did not find him there. He asked his wife, "What is this that we have heard about 'Uthmān?" She disliked to disclose her husband's secrets or to lie to the Prophet, so she said, "Messenger of Allah, if you have heard something, it is as you have heard it." He said, "Say to 'Uthmān from me: 'Are you opposed to my *Sunna* or following a religion other than mine? I pray and sleep, fast and break the fast, have intercourse with women, resort to houses and eat meat. Anyone who dislikes my *Sunna*, is not with me.'" So 'Uthmān and his companions stopped doing what they were doing.

ثُمَّ أَنتُمْ هَٰٓؤُلَآءِ تَقْتُلُونَ أَنفُسَكُمْ وَتُخْرِجُونَ فَرِيقًا
مِّنكُم مِّن دِيَٰرِهِمْ تَظَّٰهَرُونَ عَلَيْهِم بِالْاِثْمِ وَالْعُدْوَٰنِ ۝
وَإِن يَأْتُوكُمُ أُسَٰرَىٰ تُفْدُوهُمْ وَهُوَ مُحَرَّمٌ عَلَيْكُمُ
إِخْرَاجُهُمُ أَفَتُومِنُونَ بِبَعْضِ اِلْكِتَٰبِ وَتَكْفُرُونَ
بِبَعْضٍ فَمَا جَزَآءُ مَن يَفْعَلُ ذَٰلِكَ مِنكُمُ إِلَّا خِزْيٌ فِي
اِلْحَيَوٰةِ اِلدُّنْيَا وَيَوْمَ اَلْقِيَٰمَةِ يُرَدُّونَ إِلَىٰٓ أَشَدِّ اِلْعَذَابِ
وَمَا اَللَّهُ بِغَٰفِلٍ عَمَّا يَعْمَلُونَ ﴿٨٥﴾ أُوْلَٰٓئِكَ اَلذِينَ اَشْتَرَوُاْ
اُلْحَيَوٰةَ اَلدُّنْيَا بِالْاخِرَةِ فَلَا يُخَفَّفُ عَنْهُمُ اُلْعَذَابُ وَلَا هُمْ
يُنصَرُونَ ﴿٨٦﴾

85 ***Then you are the people who are killing yourselves***
and expelling a group of you from their homes,
ganging up against them
in wrongdoing and enmity.
Yet if they are brought to you as captives,
you ransom them, when it was forbidden for you
to expel them in the first place!
Do you, then, believe in one part of the Book
and reject another?
What repayment will there be
for any of you who do that
except disgrace in this world
And on the Day of Rising, they will be returned
to the harshest of punishments.
Allah is not unaware of what they do.

86 Those are the people who trade the Next World for this world. The punishment will not be lightened for them. They will not be helped.

This *āyat* is addressed to some of the Jews who had attacked other Jews. It was revealed about the Jewish tribes of Qaynuqā' and an-Naḍīr. Qaynuqā' were the enemies of the Jewish tribe of Qurayẓa and the Arab tribe of Aws were the allies of Qaynuqā' and the Arab tribe of Khazraj were the allies of Qurayẓa. So An-Naḍīr, Aws and Khazraj formed a brotherhood and Qurayẓa and an-Naḍīr formed a brotherhood. Then they split up and fought. When the war ended, they ransomed their captives and that is what Allah is censuring here.

ganging up against them in wrongdoing and enmity.

"*Taẓẓāharūna*" (ganging up) means helping each other in wrongdoing. It is derived from the word *ẓahr* (back) because they strengthened one another like the back strengthens a person. "*Ithm*" (wrongdoing) is an action for which the one who does it deserves to be blamed. "Enmity" (*'udwān*) is excess in injustice and crossing the limits in it. The Madinans and Makkans read "ganging up" as "*taẓẓāharūna*", from *tataẓāhrūna* and the *tā'* is elided into the *ẓā'*, doubling it, while the Kufans read it as "*taẓāharūna*", without the *shadda*.

Yet if they are brought to you as captives, you ransom them, when it was forbidden for you to expel them in the first place!

The word for "captive" (*asīr*) is derived from *isār* which is the leather thong by which a litter is secured and held in place. It is used for someone who is captured, whether or not he is physically bound.

Our scholars say that there are four clauses in the covenant: not to kill, not to expel, not to gang up against people, and the command to ransom captives. They turned away from all that they agreed to except for ransoming and so Allah rebuked them for that. That is why He asks, *"Do you, then, believe in one part of the Book,"* referring to the Torah, *"and reject another?"* (2:85)

By Allah, we ourselves, the Muslims, have turned from all good in the course of the troubles that have beset us and we too gang up against one another. Would that it was with other Muslims, but in many cases it is with the unbelievers! We leave our brothers in abasement and degradation under the rule of the idolaters when it is an obligation for all Muslims to fight to free them.

وَلَقَدْ ءَاتَيْنَا مُوسَى ٱلْكِتَٰبَ وَقَفَّيْنَا مِنۢ بَعْدِهِۦ
بِٱلرُّسُلِ ۖ وَءَاتَيْنَا عِيسَى ٱبْنَ مَرْيَمَ ٱلْبَيِّنَٰتِ وَأَيَّدْنَٰهُ
بِرُوحِ ٱلْقُدُسِ ۗ أَفَكُلَّمَا جَآءَكُمْ رَسُولٌۢ بِمَا لَا تَهْوَىٰٓ أَنفُسُكُمُ
ٱسْتَكْبَرْتُمْ فَفَرِيقًا كَذَّبْتُمْ وَفَرِيقًا تَقْتُلُونَ ﴿٨٧﴾

87 ***We gave Mūsā the Book***
and sent a succession of Messengers after him.
We gave 'Īsā, son of Maryam, the Clear Signs
and reinforced him with the Purest Rūḥ.
Why then, whenever a Messenger came to you
with something your lower selves did not desire,
did you grow arrogant,
and deny some of them and murder others?

We gave Mūsā the Book and sent a succession of Messengers after him.

The Book here is the Torah. The word used for "sent a succession" is derived from *qafā*, which means to come second, following in the tracks of the first and, in this way, comes to mean following after.

We gave 'Īsā, son of Maryam, the Clear Signs and reinforced him with the Purest Rūḥ.

The "Purest *Rūḥ*" is said by Ibn 'Abbās and Qatāda to be Jibrīl, peace be upon him. An-Naḥḥās said that Jibrīl is called a *rūḥ* and purity is attributed to him because Allah formed him as a *rūḥ* without any parent, which is why 'Īsā is also called a *rūḥ*. Mujāhid said, "The purity is of Allah Almighty, as al-Ḥasan said, and the *rūḥ* is Jibrīl. It is said that what is meant is the Gospel which is here called *rūḥ* in the same way that Allah calls the Qur'ān a *rūḥ* in His words, *"We have revealed to you a Rūḥ by Our command,"* (42:52) The first is more likely, and Allah knows best.

Why then, whenever a Messenger came to you with something your lower selves did not desire, did you grow arrogant,

"Why did you refuse to respond out of disdain for the Messengers and thinking the Message unlikely." The root of *hawā* (desire) means "to incline to something". Al-Jawharī said that it is called that because of the fact that it makes a person incline to the Fire and therefore it is only used for what is not true and has no good in it. This *āyat* shows that aspect of it but it can, in fact, also be used in a good sense, as we find in various *aḥādīth*.

وَقَالُوا۟ قُلُوبُنَا غُلْفٌۢ ۚ بَل لَّعَنَهُمُ ٱللَّهُ بِكُفْرِهِمْ فَقَلِيلًا مَّا يُؤْمِنُونَ ﴿٨٨﴾

88 ***They say, 'Our hearts are uncircumcised.'***
Rather, Allah has cursed them for their disbelief.
What little belief they have!

They say, 'Our hearts are uncircumcised.'

"They" are the Jews again. "Uncircumcised" means that they have a covering over them. It is similar to Allah's words: *"Our hearts are covered up against what you call us to."* (41:5) 'Ikrima said that there was a stamp on them. Linguists use this term for the sheathing of a sword. It means that their hearts are veiled from understanding and discrimination. Ibn 'Abbās said that the meaning is: "Our hearts are filled with knowledge and we have no need of the knowledge of Muḥammad, may Allah bless him and grant him peace, or anyone else."

Rather, Allah has cursed them for their disbelief.

Allah makes it clear that the reason for their aversion to faith is that they have been cursed for their disbelief and defiance in earlier times. This is repaying wrong action with something worse than it. The root of "*la'n*" (curse) has the meaning of "driving away and putting far away". *"La'īn"* is used for a man who is an outcast and is also used for a wolf. This means that Allah has put them far from His mercy, or from His success and guidance, or from every good.

What little belief they have!

It is said that this can also mean, "They believe only a little of what they have and reject most of it."

وَلَمَّا جَآءَهُمْ كِتَٰبٌ مِّنْ عِندِ ٱللَّهِ مُصَدِّقٌ لِّمَا مَعَهُمْ
وَكَانُوا۟ مِن قَبْلُ يَسْتَفْتِحُونَ عَلَى ٱلَّذِينَ كَفَرُوا۟ فَلَمَّا جَآءَهُم
مَّا عَرَفُوا۟ كَفَرُوا۟ بِهِۦ ۚ فَلَعْنَةُ ٱللَّهِ عَلَى ٱلْكَٰفِرِينَ ﴿٨٩﴾

89 *When a Book does come to them from Allah,*
confirming what is with them –
even though before that they were praying
for victory over the unbelievers –
yet when what they recognise does come to them,
they reject it.
Allah's curse is on the unbelievers.

"Them" means the Jews and the "Book" here is the Qur'ān while "what is with them" refers to the Torah and Gospel. The word for "praying for victory" here (*yastaftiḥūn*) comes from the root *fataḥa* and implies the opening of something which is locked, and is used, for instance, for the opening of a door. An-Nasā'ī reports that Abū Sa'īd al-Khudrī said that the Prophet, may Allah bless him and grant him peace, said, "Allah gave victory to this community because of its weak members by means of their supplication, prayer and sincerity." An-Nasā'ī also reports from Abū'd-Dardā' that the Messenger of Allah, peace be upon him, said, "Help me in seeking out the weak. They are supported. You are provided for on account of the weak among you." Ibn 'Abbās reported that the Jews of Khaybar fought the tribe of Ghaṭafān and were defeated and so the Jews used this supplication, saying, "We ask You by the right of the unlettered Prophet whom You promised to send us at the end of time to make us victorious against them." They then defeated the tribe of Ghaṭafān. But when the Prophet was indeed sent, they rejected him and so Allah revealed this.

بِئْسَمَا اشْتَرَوْا بِهِۦٓ أَنفُسَهُمْ أَن يَكْفُرُوا بِمَآ
أَنزَلَ اللَّهُ بَغْيًا أَن يُنَزِّلَ اللَّهُ مِن فَضْلِهِۦ عَلَىٰ مَن يَشَآءُ
مِنْ عِبَادِهِۦ ۖ فَبَآءُو بِغَضَبٍ عَلَىٰ غَضَبٍ ۚ وَلِلْكَٰفِرِينَ عَذَابٌ
مُّهِينٌ ﴿٩٠﴾

90 ***What an evil thing they have sold themselves for***
in rejecting what Allah has sent down,
outraged that Allah should send down His favour
on whichever of His slaves He wills.
They have brought down anger upon anger
on themselves.
The unbelievers will have a humiliating punishment.

outraged that Allah should send down His favour

The word "*baghyan*" (outraged) refers to their envy according to Qatāda and as-Suddī. Al-Asmā'ī said the same verb is used when a wound goes bad. It is said that its root meaning is connected with selling something, which is why a prostitute is called *baghī.*

They have brought down anger upon anger on themselves.

The "anger" referred to here is Divine punishment. It is said that the first anger is on account of their worship of the Calf and the second on account of their rejection of Muḥammad, may Allah bless him and grant him peace. Ibn 'Abbās said that. 'Ikrima said that it is because the Jews first rejected 'Īsā and then rejected Muḥammad. Qatāda also said that their first disbelief was by rejecting the Gospel and the second was by rejecting the Qur'ān. Some people said that the word is repeated twice to stress the severity of what will happen to them.

The unbelievers will have a humiliating punishment.

The word *"muhīn"* (humiliating) is only used when referring to the punishment of unbelievers. The punishments which befall rebellious Muslims in this world and the Next are a purification for them.

وَإِذَا قِيلَ لَهُمْ ءَامِنُوا۟ بِمَآ أَنزَلَ ٱللَّهُ قَالُوا۟ نُؤْمِنُ بِمَآ
أُنزِلَ عَلَيْنَا وَيَكْفُرُونَ بِمَا وَرَآءَهُۥ وَهُوَ ٱلْحَقُّ مُصَدِّقًا
لِّمَا مَعَهُمْ ۗ قُلْ فَلِمَ تَقْتُلُونَ أَنۢبِيَآءَ ٱللَّهِ مِن قَبْلُ إِن
كُنتُم مُّؤْمِنِينَ ﴿٩١﴾

91 ***When they are told,***
'Believe in what Allah has sent down,'

they say, 'We believe in what was sent down to us,'
and they reject anything beyond that,
even though it is the truth, confirming what they have.
Say, 'Why then, if you are believers,
did you previously kill the Prophets of Allah?'

When they are told, 'Believe in what Allah has sent down,' they say, 'We believe in what was sent down to us,'

"What Allah has sent down" refers here to the Qur'ān. What was sent down to them was the Torah.

Why then, if you are believers, did you previously kill the Prophets of Allah?

Allah refutes their claim that they believe in what was revealed to them. He says that they are lying and rebukes them by asking them why, in that case, did they kill the Prophets when that was forbidden in their Book. It is addressed to those Jews who were present with Muḥammad, may Allah bless him and grant him peace, while their ancestors are meant. It is said to their descendants because they have continued on the same path.

وَلَقَدْ جَآءَكُم مُّوسَىٰ بِٱلْبَيِّنَٰتِ ثُمَّ ٱتَّخَذْتُمُ
ٱلْعِجْلَ مِنۢ بَعْدِهِۦ وَأَنتُمْ ظَٰلِمُونَ ﴿٩٢﴾

92 *Mūsā brought you the Clear Signs;*
then, after he left, you adopted the Calf
and were wrongdoers.

Reference to "the Clear Signs" of Mūsā can be found in Allah's words: *"We gave Mūsā seven clear signs."* (17:101) They were: the staff, the drought, the white hand, the blood, the plague, the locusts, the lice, the frogs and the splitting of the sea. It is said that the expression "Clear Signs" refers to the Torah and the evidence it contains. The use of the word "then" indicates that they did this after receiving the Signs, which makes their wrong action all the worse.

وَإِذْ أَخَذْنَا مِيثَٰقَكُمْ وَرَفَعْنَا فَوْقَكُمُ ٱلطُّورَ خُذُوا۟
مَآ ءَاتَيْنَٰكُم بِقُوَّةٍ وَٱسْمَعُوا۟ ۖ قَالُوا۟ سَمِعْنَا وَعَصَيْنَا
وَأُشْرِبُوا۟ فِى قُلُوبِهِمُ ٱلْعِجْلَ بِكُفْرِهِمْ ۚ قُلْ
بِئْسَمَا يَأْمُرُكُم بِهِۦٓ إِيمَٰنُكُمْ إِن كُنتُم مُّؤْمِنِينَ ﴿٩٣﴾

93 ***Remember when We made a covenant with you***
and lifted up the Mount above your heads:
'Take hold vigorously
of what We have given you and listen.'
They said, 'We hear and disobey.'
They were made to drink the Calf into their hearts
because of their disbelief.
Say, 'If you are believers, what an evil thing
your faith has made you do.'

The first part of this *āyat* has been discussed previously in the commentary on 2:63 above.

They said, 'We hear and disobey.'

There is disagreement about whether this was the actual words they used or whether they did an action which took the place of the words, and so it was metaphor.

They were made to drink the Calf into their hearts because of their disbelief.

In other words love of the gold Calf penetrated them. It means that their hearts imbibed it. It is a metaphor because the whole matter of the Calf had become firm in their hearts. We read in a *ḥadīth*, "Seditions will be presented to the hearts like a mat, reed by reed. A black spot is formed in the heart of anyone who is made to drink them." Their love of the Calf is referred to as drinking rather than eating because drinking something makes it penetrate right through the whole of the body.

As-Suddī said that Mūsā filed down the Calf and put it in water and told the tribe of Israel to drink that water. They all drank it and those who loved the Calf had gold filings on their lips. This is extremely unlikely.

Say, 'If you are believers, what an evil thing your faith has made you do.'

The faith referred to is that which they claimed by their words, *"We believe in what was sent down to us."* It is said that these words were addressed to the Prophet, peace be upon him, and he was commanded to rebuke them. So it means, "Muḥammad, tell them that what they were doing is evil."

قُلْ إِن كَانَتْ لَكُمُ ٱلدَّارُ ٱلْآخِرَةُ عِندَ ٱللَّهِ خَالِصَةً
مِّن دُونِ ٱلنَّاسِ فَتَمَنَّوُا ٱلْمَوْتَ إِن كُنتُمْ صَٰدِقِينَ ﴿٩٤﴾
وَلَن يَتَمَنَّوْهُ أَبَدًا بِمَا قَدَّمَتْ أَيْدِيهِمْ ۗ وَٱللَّهُ عَلِيمٌ بِٱلظَّٰلِمِينَ ﴿٩٥﴾

94 ***Say, 'If the abode of the Next World with Allah***
is for you alone, to the exclusion of all others,
then long for death if you are telling the truth.'
95 ***But they will never ever long for it***
because of what they have done.
Allah knows the wrongdoers.

When the Jews made their various false claims, as Allah reports from them in His Book, such as: *"The Fire will only touch us for a number of days,"* (2:80) and *"No one will enter the Garden except for Jews and Christians"* (2:111), Allah told His Prophet what to say to them. They were told to wish for death, because if someone truly believes that he is one of the people of the Garden he will prefer death to life in this world, since he will obtain the bliss of the Garden and the difficulties of this world will be removed from him by it. But they shrank from doing that out of fear of Allah because of the terrible things they had done, thus demonstrating that they did not really believe what they said and indicating their greed for this world. If they had truly longed for death they would have died, as is related from the Prophet, may Allah bless him and grant him peace, when he said, "If the Jews had really longed for death, they would have died and seen their place in the Fire." It is said that Allah kept them from longing for it so as to make that a Sign for His Prophet. These are all aspects of the fact that they did not long for death as they claimed.

The observation may be made that longing can be expressed with the tongue or with the heart, and so how is it known that they did not wish for it in their hearts? The reply to that is that the Qur'ān stated that when Allah says: *"they will never ever long for it."* If they had wished for it in their hearts, it would have appeared on their tongues so that they could refute the Prophet, may Allah bless him and grant him peace, and invalidate his argument. This is clear.

ولتجدنهم أحرص الناس على حيوة ومن الذين أشركوا
يود أحدهم لو يعمر ألف سنة وما هو بمزحزحه
من العذاب أن يعمر والله بصير بما يعملون ﴿٩٦﴾

96 ***Rather you will find them the people***
greediest for life, along with the idolaters.
One of them would love to be allowed
to live a thousand years.
But being allowed to live would not save him

from the punishment.
Allah sees what they do.

It is said that this refers to the Jews and it is said that the words about them stop at "life" and then what is referred to is a group of idolaters, namely the Magians. That is clear in that they say to someone who sneezes, "Live a thousand years!" They believed that to be the extent that their reckoning would last. Al-Ḥasan believes that it refers to the Arab idolaters because they did not believe in the resurrection after death.

Allah sees what they do.

"*Ya'malūn*" (they do) is also read "*ta'malūn*" (you do). The word "*baṣīr*" (see) in Arabic also means "to know something" and "be aware of it". You could use it for someone who has knowledge of medicine (*baṣīr bi'ṭ-ṭibb*) or *fiqh*. It is also said that the phrase means that Allah makes the things we do visible.

قُلْ مَن كَانَ عَدُوًّا لِّجِبْرِيلَ فَإِنَّهُۥ نَزَّلَهُۥ عَلَىٰ قَلْبِكَ بِإِذْنِ ٱللَّهِ مُصَدِّقًا لِّمَا بَيْنَ يَدَيْهِ وَهُدًى وَبُشْرَىٰ لِلْمُؤْمِنِينَ ﴿٩٧﴾

97 *Say, 'Anyone who is the enemy of Jibrīl*
should know that it was he who brought it down
upon your heart, by Allah's authority,
confirming what came before,
and as guidance and good news for the believers.

The reason for the revelation of this *āyat* is that the Jews said to the Prophet, may Allah bless him and grant him peace, "Every Prophet has one of the angels bring him the Message and Revelation from His Lord. Who is your companion so that we can follow you?" "Jibrīl," he replied. They said, "That is the one who brings war and fighting. He is our enemy! If you had said Mikā'īl, who brings down the rain and mercy, we would have followed you." So Allah revealed this. There are two possibilities for the second "it" which might also be read as "he". It might possibly mean: "Allah sent down Jibrīl to your heart" or, more likely, "Jibrīl brought down the Qur'ān to your heart." The heart is mentioned because it is the place of the intellect and knowledge. The *āyat* indicates the nobility of Jibrīl and censures his enemies.

مَن كَانَ عَدُوًّا لِّلَّهِ وَمَلَٰٓئِكَتِهِۦ وَرُسُلِهِۦ وَجِبْرِيلَ
وَمِيكَىٰلَ فَإِنَّ ٱللَّهَ عَدُوٌّ لِّلْكَٰفِرِينَ ﴿٩٨﴾

98 ***Anyone who is the enemy of Allah and of His angels,***
and of His Messengers and of Jibrīl and Mikā'īl,
should know that Allah
is the enemy of the unbelievers.'

This is a threat and rebuke to the enemies of Jibrīl and is an announcement that enmity towards some results in Allah's enmity towards those who show it. The enmity of the slave of Allah is shown by his disobedience to Allah, his failure to obey Him, and enmity towards His friends. Allah's enmity to the slave is shown by punishing him and the effects of enmity on him.

If it is asked why Allah singled out Jibrīl and Mikā'īl for mention when they have already been included under the general category of 'angels', the reply is that they are singled out for mention in order to honour them. It is also said that they are singled out because the Jews had mentioned the two of them and they were the cause of the *āyat* being revealed.

Various things are said by linguists about these two names. The forms given for Jibrīl's name are: Jibrīl, which is the Ḥijāzī form, Jabrīl, Jabrā'īl, Jabra'il, Jibriyil, Jabr'īn, Jibrīn. The forms for Mikā'īl are: Mīkā'il (as Nāfi' has it), Mikā'īl, Mīkāl (Ḥijāzī), Mīk'īl, Mīkāyil, and Mīkā'al.

Ibn 'Abbās says that *jabr* means "slave" and *mīkā* means "owned". *Īl* is the Name of Allah, thus both names mean "slave of Allah".

وَلَقَدْ أَنزَلْنَآ إِلَيْكَ ءَايَٰتٍۭ بَيِّنَٰتٍ ۖ وَمَا يَكْفُرُ بِهَآ إِلَّا
ٱلْفَٰسِقُونَ ﴿٩٩﴾

99 ***We have sent down Clear Signs to you***
and no one rejects them except the deviators.

Ibn 'Abbās said that this is the reply to Ibn Ṣūriyā when he said to the Prophet, may Allah bless him and grant him peace, "Muḥammad, you have not brought us anything which accords with our knowledge and no clear sign has been sent down to you for us to follow." Then this *āyat* was revealed.

أَوَكُلَّمَا عَٰهَدُوا۟ عَهْدًا نَّبَذَهُۥ فَرِيقٌ مِّنْهُم ۚ بَلْ أَكْثَرُهُمْ
لَا يُؤْمِنُونَ ﴿١٠٠﴾

100 ***Why is it that, whenever they make a contract,***
a group of them disdainfully tosses it aside?
No indeed! Most of them do not believe.

The Jews had made a contract that they would believe in Muḥammad when he was sent and would side with him against the Arab idolaters. Then when he was sent, they rejected him. 'Aṭā' says that the *āyat* refers to the agreements which the Prophet, may Allah bless him and grant him peace, made with the Jews which they subsequently broke.

وَلَمَّا جَاءَهُمْ رَسُولٌ مِّنْ عِندِ اللَّهِ مُصَدِّقٌ لِّمَا مَعَهُمْ
نَبَذَ فَرِيقٌ مِّنَ الَّذِينَ أُوتُوا الْكِتَابَ كِتَابَ
اللَّهِ وَرَاءَ ظُهُورِهِمْ كَأَنَّهُمْ لَا يَعْلَمُونَ ۖ ﴿١٠١﴾

101 ***When a Messenger comes to them from Allah***
confirming what is with them,
a group of those who have been given the Book
disdainfully toss the Book of Allah
behind their backs, just as if they did not know.

They tossed it behind them by rejecting the Messenger. As-Suddī said, "They cast aside the Torah and took the book of Āṣaf and the magic of Hārūt and Mārūt." It is said that it can refer to the Qur'ān. Ash-Sha'bī said that they used to read it but rejected acting by it. Sufyān ibn 'Uyayna said, "They covered the Book in silk and brocade and adorned it with gold and silver but did not make lawful what it made lawful or unlawful what it made unlawful."

وَاتَّبَعُوا مَا تَتْلُوا الشَّيَاطِينُ عَلَىٰ مُلْكِ سُلَيْمَانَ ۖ وَمَا كَفَرَ
سُلَيْمَانُ ۖ وَلَٰكِنَّ الشَّيَاطِينَ كَفَرُوا يُعَلِّمُونَ النَّاسَ
السِّحْرَ وَمَا أُنزِلَ عَلَى الْمَلَكَيْنِ بِبَابِلَ هَارُوتَ
وَمَارُوتَ ۖ وَمَا يُعَلِّمَانِ مِنْ أَحَدٍ حَتَّىٰ يَقُولَا إِنَّمَا نَحْنُ فِتْنَةٌ
فَلَا تَكْفُرْ ۖ فَيَتَعَلَّمُونَ مِنْهُمَا مَا يُفَرِّقُونَ بِهِ بَيْنَ الْمَرْءِ
وَزَوْجِهِ ۖ وَمَا هُم بِضَارِّينَ بِهِ مِنْ أَحَدٍ إِلَّا بِإِذْنِ اللَّهِ ۖ
وَيَتَعَلَّمُونَ مَا يَضُرُّهُمْ وَلَا يَنفَعُهُمْ ۖ وَلَقَدْ عَلِمُوا لَمَنِ

ٱشْتَرَىٰهُ مَا لَهُۥ فِى ٱلْـَٔاخِرَةِ مِنْ خَلَـٰقٍ ۚ وَلَبِئْسَ مَا
شَرَوْا۟ بِهِۦٓ أَنفُسَهُمْ ۚ لَوْ كَانُوا۟ يَعْلَمُونَ ﴿١٠٢﴾

102 ***They follow what the shaytans recited***
in the reign of Sulaymān.
Sulaymān did not disbelieve, but the shayṭāns did,
teaching people sorcery
and what had been sent down to Hārūt and Mārūt,
the two angels in Babylon,
who taught no one without first saying to him,
'We are merely a trial and temptation,
so do not disbelieve.'
People learned from them
how to separate a man and his wife
but they cannot harm anyone by it,
except with Allah's permission.
They have learned what will harm them
and will not benefit them.
They know that any who deal in it
will have no share in the Next World.
What an evil thing they have sold themselves for
if they only knew!

They follow what the shayṭāns recited in the reign of Sulaymān.

Allah here reports about the group who discarded the Book by pursuing magic. They were the Jews. As-Suddī said, "The Jews opposed Muḥammad, may Allah bless him and grant him peace, but the Torah and the Qur'ān agreed, so they discarded the Torah and adopted the book of Āṣaf and the magic of Hārūt and Mārūt."

Muḥammad ibn Isḥāq said, "When the Messenger of Allah, may Allah bless him and grant him peace, mentioned Sulaymān as one of the Messengers, some of the rabbis said, 'Muḥammad claims that the son of Dā'ūd was a Prophet! By Allah, he was nothing but a sorcerer!' Then Allah revealed, *'Sulaymān did not disbelieve, but the shayṭāns did.'* This means that the rabbis told people that what Sulaymān did with respect to riding the seas and subjugating the birds and jinn was magic."

Al-Kalbī said, "The shayṭāns wrote magic and necromancy as dictated by Āṣaf, the scribe of Sulaymān during the time when Allah had removed his kingdom from him and buried it in the place where he prayed. Sulaymān was not aware of this. When Sulaymān died, they brought the books out and told people, 'He ruled you by this, so learn it.' The scholars of the tribe of Israel said, 'We seek refuge with Allah from this being the knowledge of Sulaymān!' while the fools accepted that it was and learned it and discarded the books of their Prophets until Muḥammad, may Allah bless him and grant him peace, was sent. Then Allah revealed Sulaymān's innocence of the accusation they made."

'Aṭā' said that *"ittaba'ū"* (follow) in this *āyat* means "read" while Ibn 'Abbās says that it actually means "follow". Aṭ-Ṭabarī said that it means "prefer" since they preferred it to other things.

"In the reign (*mulk*)" means during the time of his *Sharī'a* and Prophethood. Az-Zajjāj said that it means during his reign. It is said that it means during his kingship. The shayṭāns here are said to be shayṭāns of the jinn. When shayṭān is used for a human being, it refers to someone who is obdurate in misguidance.

SulaymÅn did not disbelieve but the shayṭāns did,

This declares his innocence. The Jews accused him of magic and, since magic entails disbelief, they were ascribing disbelief to him. The disbelief of the shayṭāns is established because they taught magic.

teaching people sorcery

The root meaning of *"siḥr"* (sorcery) is distortion and producing illusions. It happens when a sorcerer does something and the person under the spell imagines something to be different from what it is. This resembles a mirage which someone sees and imagines to be water. It is said to be derived from diverting a child when he is tricked. It is said that the root of *siḥr* is "concealment", because a sorcerer does it in concealment. It is also said that its root is "diversion", since it diverts a person from what is really happening. Its root is also said to be "enticement" and all that entices and bewitches you. Al-Jawharī said that spells and charms and anything whose means are subtle can be called sorcery.

There is disagreement about whether it is real or not. The Mu'tazilites say that it is simply deceit and has no real basis. Ash-Shāfi'ī says that it is whispering and illness. He said, "We think that its function is talismanic and is based on the effect of the particular qualities of the stars or by the shayṭāns making things easy which were difficult."

We believe that it is true and that it has a reality and that Allah creates through it whatever He wishes, as will be explained. There is also a kind of magic which is merely sleight of hand and legerdemain. Another aspect is spells. Another aspect is words which are memorised and talismans which use the Names of Allah. That may also be part of the work of shayṭāns, or medicines and fumes and other things.

The Messenger of Allah, may Allah bless him and grant him peace, called eloquence in speech sorcery. He said, "Some kinds of eloquence are sorcery." (Mālik and others) That is because they make the false seem credible so that the listener imagines it to be true. That statement is said, by some, to imply censure and by others to imply praise. Censure is more likely, because a person may obtain something which is not rightfully his by means of it.

Another kind of sorcery is the sort whose perpetration makes the one who does it an unbeliever. This includes such claims as changing the forms of people and transforming them into animals, going on a month's journey in a single night and flying through the air and other such things. If anyone does that so that people will imagine that it is true, that turns him into an unbeliever. Abū 'Amr said. "If anyone claims to be a sorcerer who can change animals from one form to another, or turn a person into a donkey and the like, or to have the power to transform bodies and destroy and alter them, this is someone who should be killed because he rejects the Prophets, laying claim to prophethood himself since he tries, by the use of trickery, to perform the same feats as them. As for the one who admits that his magic is simply deceit, distortion and illusions, he is not killed unless he does something else for which the punishment is death.

Sunnis believe that sorcery is real. Most Mu'tazilites and some Shāfi'īs believe that it is baseless and is only distortion and illusion so that a thing is made to appear other than what it is. They say that it is a sort of legerdemain, as Allah says, *"they appeared to him, by their magic, to be slithering around."* (20:66) He did not say that it was real, but that it appeared so. This is not evidence because we do not deny that illusion-making is part of magic but other matters are confirmed which defy explanation. If magic did not have a reality, it would not be possible to teach it and the fact that Allah mentioned them teaching it indicates that it is real.

Allah says that the sorcerers *"produced an extremely powerful magic"* (7:116) and scholars agree that *Sūrat al-Falaq* was revealed because of the magic of Labīd ibn al-Aṣamm. That is reported in al-Bukhārī and Muslim. When the spell was removed, the Prophet said, "Allah healed me." Healing only occurs by removing an illness. So both Allah and the Prophet have reported that it is real. We find no denial of its existence among the Companions or the *Tābi'ūn*. Ibn 'Abbās said, "Magic was taught in one of the towns of Egypt called Farama." Anyone who denies it is an unbeliever who denies Allah and His Messenger.

Our scholars say that it is not denied that breaking of normal patterns occurs through sorcerers and that, although this is not in the normal power of a human being, it is, nevertheless, a human possibility. It is, however, Allah who creates these things when the magic takes place, just as He creates fullness after eating and quenching of thirst through drinking.

Muslims agree that there was no magic involved in what Allah did in relation to the locusts, lice, frogs, splitting the sea, the transformation of the staff, bringing the dead to life and other such signs of the Prophets. Our scholars said that the difference between magic and a Prophetic miracle is that magic can exist with a sorcerer or someone else and a group of people can know it and can do it at the same time, whereas Allah does not give anyone but His Prophet the power to perform a miracle. A sorcerer cannot claim to be a Prophet and what he does is not a miracle. A miracle must be accompanied by a true claim to Prophethood and the challenge to imitate it.

Fuqahā' differ about the ruling of a Muslim or *dhimmī* sorcerer. Mālik believed that when a Muslim does magic with words which are disbelief, he should be killed and not asked to repent. Even if he were asked to repent, his repentance would not be accepted because he would conceal his sorcery like a heretic or fornicator, and because Allah Himself called sorcery disbelief. Ibn Ḥanbal, Abū Thawr, Isḥāq, ash-Shāfi'ī and Abū Ḥanīfa also said that. The execution of sorcerers is reported from 'Umar, 'Uthmān, Ibn 'Umar, Ḥafṣa, Abū Mūsā, Qays ibn Sa'd and seven *Tābi'ūn*. It is related that the Prophet, may Allah bless him and grant him peace, said, "The *ḥadd* for a sorcerer is to be struck with the sword." (At-Tirmidhī but it is not strong.) It is related that 'Ā'isha sold a witch who had used magic on her and used the price to free slaves.

Ibn al-Mundhir said, "When a man admits that he did magic with words which constitute disbelief, then he must be killed, even if he repents. The same applies if there is clear evidence against him. If the words which he used in his magic are not tantamount to disbelief, it is not permitted to kill him. If he deliberately inflicts an injury on the person who has been subjected to his sorcery, retaliation is obliged. If there is no retaliation for it, there is blood money."

Ibn al-Mundhir also said, "When the Companions of the Messenger of Allah, may Allah bless him and grant him peace, disagree about something, we are obliged to follow the view which is closest to the Book and the *Sunna*. It is possible that the magic for which some of them commanded the sorcerer to be executed did indeed constitute disbelief and this corresponds to the *Sunna* of the Messenger of Allah, may Allah bless him and grant him peace. It is also possible that the magic of the witch whom 'Ā'isha sold did not actually constitute disbelief. If the *ḥadīth* about killing sorcerers is sound, then it is only possible when the magic of the sorcerer amounts to disbelief, and so that is in keeping with what is reported from the Prophet, may Allah bless him and grant him peace: 'A Muslim's blood is only lawful by one of three…'"

This is true. The blood of Muslims is protected and only allowed when there is certainty and when there is disagreement there is no certainty, Allah knows best. Some scholars say that magic is only achieved through disbelief and arrogance or by esteeming Shayṭān and thus sorcery is evidence of disbelief. Allah knows best. It is related that ash-Shāfi'ī said, "The sorcerer is not killed unless he kills by his magic and says that it was deliberate. If he does not say it was deliberate, he is not killed but pays blood money for accidental homicide. If he causes harm, he is disciplined according to the extent of harm he caused." Ibn al-'Arabī said that this is false for two reasons. One is that he does not know the reality of magic which, in fact, consists of formulae which revere things other than Allah to which powers and entities are ascribed. The second is that Allah clearly states in His book that the shayṭāns disbelieved.

The Mālikīs argue that a sorcerer's repentance is not accepted because sorcery is something hidden and not shown and so his repentance cannot be relied on. The person who is asked to repent is someone who openly apostatises. Mālik said that if a sorcerer or heretic repents before there is testimony against him, his repentance is accepted.

Most Mu'tazilites deny the existence of shayṭāns and the jinn. This indicates their weakness because not only is it not logically impossible to affirm their existence but also the texts of the Book and the *Sunna* indicate their existence. An intelligent person who clings to the rope of Allah must accept things which are beyond normal experience when there is a text stating that they exist. Allah said, *"the shayṭāns disbelieved"* and He also mentions them elsewhere and the Prophet, may Allah bless him and grant him peace, mentioned them and therefore they must exist.

and what had been sent down to Hārūt and Mārūt, the two angels in Babylon,

That is mentioned because the Jews said the two angels (*malakayn*) that Allah sent with magic were Jibrīl and Mikā'īl and Allah denies that. Ibn 'Abbās, Ibn Abzā, aḍ-Ḍaḥḥāk and al-Ḥasan read the word as *malikayn*, which means two kings, and take it as referring to Dā'ūd and Sulaymān. This is weak.

'Abdullāh ibn Bishr al-Māzinī related that the Messenger of Allah, may Allah bless him and grant him peace, said, "Fear this world. By the One who has my soul in His hand, it has more sorcery in it than Hārūt and Mārūt." That is because it deceives you and captures your attention.

who taught no one without first saying to him, 'We are merely a trial and temptation, so do not disbelieve.'

'Alī is reported as saying that the angels taught people by warning them against magic, it is not that they were inviting them to it." Az-Zajjāj says, "This is the position held by most of the people with expertise in language and investigation. It means that they taught people the prohibition and said to them, 'Do not do this. Do not use that to come between a man and wife.'"

Anyway it is clear that Allah sent down magic to the angels as a test for people. Allah tests His slaves in whatever way He wishes. This is why the angels said, "*We are merely a trial.* We inform you that the act of sorcery is disbelief. If you obey us, you will be saved. If you disobey, you will be destroyed."

People learned from them how to separate a man and his wife

One group believe that a sorcerer cannot do more than cause separation, as Allah mentions here, because Allah mentioned that when He criticised sorcery and the aim of learning it. If they had been able to do more than that, they say, Allah would have mentioned that. Another group say that separating a man and his wife is the most common application of magic and does not preclude magic of other kinds.

but they cannot harm anyone by it, except with Allah's permission.

It is said that this refers to the Jews and it is said that it is refers to the shayṭāns. "Allah's permission" here means His will and decree, not His command, because Allah does not command the reprehensible and then judge people according to it. Az-Zajjāj said, "It means 'only by the knowledge of Allah.'" An-Naḥḥās said that this is incorrect.

They have learned what will harm them and will not benefit them.

Meaning in the Next World even if they obtain some benefit from it in this world. It is said that it will also harm them in this world because the harms which results from magic and causing disunion rebounds on the sorcerer in this world if he is discovered because he will be disciplined and punished and the ill fame of sorcery is attached to him.

وَلَوْ أَنَّهُمْ ءَامَنُوا۟ وَٱتَّقَوْا۟ لَمَثُوبَةٌ مِّنْ عِندِ ٱللَّهِ خَيْرٌ
لَّوْ كَانُوا۟ يَعْلَمُونَ ۖ ﴿١٠٣﴾

103 ***If only they had believed and been godfearing!***
A reward from Allah is better, if they only knew.

"They" here refers to the sorcerers.

يَٰٓأَيُّهَا ٱلَّذِينَ ءَامَنُوا۟ لَا تَقُولُوا۟ رَٰعِنَا وَقُولُوا۟ ٱنظُرْنَا
وَٱسْمَعُوا۟ ۗ وَلِلْكَٰفِرِينَ عَذَابٌ أَلِيمٌ ۖ ﴿١٠٤﴾

104 ***You who have faith! do not say, 'Rā'inā,'***
say, 'Unẓurnā,' and listen well.
The unbelievers will have a painful punishment.

This is talking about another act of ignorance on the part of the Jews and its object is to forbid Muslims from doing the same thing. The meaning of *"rā'inā"* is "look at us and we will look at you" because the form of the verb dictates that. It further signifies: "protect us and we will protect you; watch us and we will watch you." Using this word, however, entails coarseness and so the believers were commanded to choose a better word with a finer meaning.

Ibn 'Abbās said, "The Muslims used to say to the Prophet, *"rā'inā"* by way of asking and desire, from *murā'ā* (supervision, respect). In Hebrew it was a curse, meaning "Listen, you do not hear." So the Jews took advantage of that and said, "We curse him secretly. Now we will curse him openly!" and they used to use this word to address the Prophet, may Allah bless him and grant him peace, and then laugh about it. Sa'd ibn Mu'ādh overheard them because he knew their language. He told them, "The curse of Allah on you! If I hear a single man of you say it to the Prophet, may Allah bless him and grant him peace, I will lob his head off!" They replied, "But you say it!" Then the *āyat* was revealed and they were forbidden to do it so that the Jews would not imitate them and intend a bad meaning by it.

This *āyat* contains evidence for two rulings. One is that you should avoid ambiguous expressions which could be disparaging or allude to faults. A corollary of this is that slander can be by allusion and we say that doing this obliges the *ḥadd* punishment whereas Abū Ḥanīfa and ash-Shāfi'ī said that the aspect of doubt involved removes the *ḥadd*.

The second ruling to be gained from the *āyat* is that *sadd adh-dharā'i'* (the blocking of the means), and the protection it gives, constitutes a valid legal principle, which is the position of Mālik and also of Aḥmad ibn Ḥanbal in one transmission from him. The Book and *Sunna* provide evidence for this principle. *Dharī'a* (means) is something which is not prohibited in itself but it is feared that someone who does it will fall into the prohibited. In the Qur'ān, this *āyat* demonstrates the principle. The way the principle is applied here is that the Jews used to say this phrase which was a curse in their language. Then Allah informed the Muslims about it and issued the prohibition of the use of this phrase because, although it is all right in itself, it is the means to the evil result. There are also Allah's words, *"Do not curse those they call upon besides Allah, in case that makes them curse Allah in animosity without knowledge."* (6:108) So Allah forbids cursing their gods – something which is not wrong in itself – out of the fear that they would retaliate.

As for the *Sunna*, there are many firm, sound *aḥādīth*, including the *ḥadīth* of 'Ā'isha that Umm Ḥabība and Umm Salama mentioned to the Messenger of Allah a church they had seen in Abyssinia with images, and the Messenger of Allah, may Allah bless him and grant him peace, said, "Among those people, when a righteous man died, they built a place of prayer over his grave and adorned it with those images. Those are the worst of creatures in the sight of Allah." (al-Bukhārī and Muslim) Our scholars have said that those earlier people did that to console themselves by seeing those images and remembering the righteous behaviour of the people buried there and they strove as they had striven and worshipped Allah at their graves. Then time passed and those after them were ignorant of their aims and Shayṭān whispered to them that their fathers and forefathers had worshipped those images and so they started to worship them. The Prophet, may Allah bless him and grant him peace, warned against the same thing happening and strongly objected to people doing that. He blocked the means to that and said, "The anger of Allah is terrible against people who take the graves of their Prophets and righteous men as mosques," and "O Allah, do not make my grave an idol which is worshipped."

The well known *ḥadīth* says: "The *ḥalāl* is clear and the *ḥarām* is clear. But between the two there are doubtful things about which most people have no knowledge. Whoever exercises caution with regard to what is doubtful, shows prudence in respect of his *dīn* and his honour. Whoever involves himself in doubtful things is like a herdsman who grazes his animals near a private preserve (*ḥimā*). He is bound to enter it." So the Prophet forbade doing doubtful things out of the fear of falling into the forbidden. That is *sadd adh-dharā'i'*.

The Prophet, may Allah bless him and grant him peace, said, "The slave will not achieve the status of being one of the godfearing until he leaves what does not concern him out of consideration for what does concern him." He also said, "One of the major wrong actions is for a man to abuse his parents." They said, "O Messenger of Allah, is it possible for a man to abuse his parents?" He said, "Yes. He may curse another man's father who in turn curses his father, or curse his mother and he in turn curses his mother." And there are many more examples in the *aḥādīth* of the use of this principle.

مَّا يَوَدُّ الَّذِينَ كَفَرُوا مِنْ أَهْلِ الْكِتَابِ وَلَا
الْمُشْرِكِينَ أَن يُنَزَّلَ عَلَيْكُم مِّنْ خَيْرٍ مِّن رَّبِّكُمْ ۗ
وَاللَّهُ يَخْتَصُّ بِرَحْمَتِهِ مَن يَشَاءُ ۚ وَاللَّهُ ذُو الْفَضْلِ
الْعَظِيمِ ١٠٥

105 ***Those of the People of the Book who disbelieve***
and the idolaters
do not like anything good to be sent down to you
from your Lord.
But Allah selects for His mercy whomever He wills.
Allah's favour is truly vast.

But Allah selects for His mercy whomever He wills.

'Alī ibn Abī Ṭālib said, that this means for His Prophethood, which He singled out for Muḥammad, may Allah bless him and grant him peace. Some people say that the mercy of the Qur'ān is what is intended and others say that the mercy mentioned here is general to all types of mercy which Allah has given to His slaves, both now and in the past.

مَا نَنسَخْ مِنْ ءَايَةٍ أَوْ نُنسِهَا نَأْتِ بِخَيْرٍ مِّنْهَا أَوْ مِثْلِهَا
أَلَمْ تَعْلَمْ أَنَّ ٱللَّهَ عَلَىٰ كُلِّ شَيْءٍ قَدِيرٌ ﴿١٠٦﴾

106 ***Whenever We abrogate an āyat***
or cause it to be forgotten,
We bring one better than it or equal to it.
Do you not know
that Allah has power over all things?

Whenever We abrogate an āyat or cause it to be forgotten,

This is a very important *āyat* about judgements. Its cause was that the Jews envied the Muslims when they turned away from Jerusalem and faced the Ka'ba, and they attacked Islam for that, saying that Muḥammad commanded his Companions to do one thing and then forbade it and maintained that the Qur'ān was of his own making. They contradicted one another and so Allah revealed, *"If We replace one āyat with another one..."* (16:101) and this *āyat*.

This subject is very important and scholars must be aware of it. Only ignorant fools deny it because of the effect of events on rulings and recognition of the *ḥalāl* and *ḥarām*. Abū'l-Bakhtarī said, "'Alī entered the mosque while a man was causing the people there to become frightened. He asked, 'What is this?' They said, 'A man who is reminding people.' He said, 'He is not a man who reminds people. He says, "I am so-and-so son of so-and-so, so acknowledge me."' He sent for him and asked, 'Do you know the abrogating from the abrogated?' 'No,' he replied. He said, 'Then leave our mosque and do not admonish people in it.'"

There are two aspects to abrogation or supersession (*naskh*). The first is transfer, like from one divine Book to another. According to this, all the Qur'ān is "abrogated" in the sense that it was taken from the Preserved Tablet and sent down to the House of Might in the lowest heaven. This is nothing to do with this *āyat.* The second form of abrogation is invalidation and removal, which is what is meant here. This, in turn, is divided into two types.

The first is supersession which is the invalidation of a thing and its removal and then putting something else in its place. The verb, *nasakha*, is used for the sun replacing the shadow when it takes its place. That is its meaning in this *āyat*. In the *Ṣaḥīḥ* of Muslim we find: "There is no Prophethood at all but that it is superseded by the next (*tanāsakha*)." Ibn Fāris said that *naskh* refers to the Book, and it means to remove a command before it is acted on and then supersede it with something else, like an *āyat* revealed about a matter and then superseded by another. The verb is used for the sun replacing shade, old age replacing youth and the succession of heirs by successive deaths.

The second type of abrogation is the removal of a thing without replacing it with something else, as wind obliterates (*nasakha*) a track. This meaning is seen in the words of Allah, *"Allah revokes (*yansakhu*) what Shayṭān insinuates."* (22:52) i.e. removes it and so it is not recited nor does it have a replacement elsewhere in the Qur'ān.

Pertinent to this matter is what is related from Ubayy and 'Ā'isha to the effect that *Sūrat al-Aḥzāb* (33) was originally the same length as *Sūrat al-Baqara* as will be later clarified. Evidence for this is also found in what Abū Bakr al-Anbārī transmitted that Sahl ibn Ḥunayf said while in the assembly of Sa'īd ibn al-Musayyab. He said that a man stood up in the night to recite a *sūra* of the Qur'ān but was unable to recite any of it. Another man rose and could not recite any of it either. So in the morning they went to the Messenger of Allah, may Allah bless him and grant him peace. One said, "I stood in the night to recite a *sūra* of the Qur'ān and I could not recite any of it." The other stood up and said, "The same happened to me, Messenger of Allah!" Yet a third rose and said,

"And the same thing happened to me, Messenger of Allah." The Messenger of Allah, peace be upon him, said, "It was part of what Allah abrogated yesterday."

Some modern groups of those who are called Muslims deny that such an occurrence is possible. They are veiled from the consensus of the Salaf that it occurs in the *Sharī'a*. Some Jewish groups also reject that and they are veiled from what comes in the Torah since they claim that Allah told Noah when he left the Ark, "I make every animal eatable for you and your descendants." Then He forbade many animals to Mūsā and the tribe of Israel. There is also the fact that Ādam married a brother to a sister, and Allah forbade that to Mūsā and others. Ibrāhīm was ordered to sacrifice his son and then told not to do it. Mūsā commanded the tribe of Israel to kill those of them who worshipped the Calf and then stopped that. There are many examples of this. This is transfer from one act of worship to another and one ruling to another for the sake of best interest. Intelligent people do not disagree that the laws of the Prophets are intended to meet the best interests of people in the *dīn* and this world.

Know that the real abrogator is Allah Almighty. What He says can be called abrogation since abrogation occurs by it, one judgement being replaced by another. It is said that the fast of Ramaḍān superseded the fast of 'Āshūra', replacing one form of worship with another.

The sayings of our scholars differ regarding the definition of *naskh*, That which intelligent people who follow the *Sunna* hold is that it is the removal of an established legal ruling by a further instruction which comes later in time. That is the definition of 'Abdu'l-Wahhāb and Qāḍī Abū Bakr, who added, "If it were not for that, the prior ruling would remain firmly in place." So they retain the linguistic definition which means "removal" while avoiding the logical consequence of taking that literally. That which was abrogated, according to our Imāms, the people of the *Sunna*, constitutes a firm judgement in itself.

Our scholars disagree about whether reports are subject to abrogation. Most say that abrogating is specific to commands and prohibitions and that traditions cannot be affected by abrogation since it is impossible for the Prophet, may Allah bless him and grant him peace, to lie. It is said that if the report contains a legal judgement, then abrogation is permitted.

It might be imagined that making what is general specific is abrogation, but that is not the case because specification does not remove the general (*'āmm*). If something moves the general ruling to something else, then that is abrogation, not specification. If someone refers to it as abrogation, that is metaphorical rather than actual. Know that an unrestricted *ḥadīth* in the *Sharī'a* might be limited in another place, thus removing the unrestricted nature of it. Someone with no intelligence might think that this is abrogation, but that is not the case. It is restriction of the unrestricted.

Our scholars say that abrogation is permitted from what is onerous to that which is easier. A case in point is the abrogation of the ruling on standing firm in *jihād* when the odds are ten to one by standing firm when they are two to one. But it is also permitted to move from the easier to the harder, as happened when the fast of 'Āshūrā' and some other days were exchanged for Ramaḍān as will be mentioned. And like can be abrogated by like, as happened in the case of the *qibla* changing from Jerusalem to the House of Allah in Makka. Matters can be abrogated without being replaced, like giving *ṣadaqa* before conversing with the Prophet, peace be upon him. The Qur'ān can be abrogated by the Qur'ān, the *Sunna* by a *mutawātir ḥadīth,* and a single *ḥadīth* by another single *ḥadīth*.

Astute Imāms also say that the Qur'ān can be abrogated by the *Sunna*. An example of that is the words of the Prophet: "There is no bequest to an heir." It is acknowledged by Mālik, but ash-Shāfi'ī and Abū'l-Faraj al-Mālikī rejected it. The first is a sounder approach by the evidence that all is the judgement of Allah Almighty and from Him, even if the names differ. Flogging was also dropped in the *ḥadd* for the adulterer who is stoned. That was only dropped by the *Sunna* which the Prophet, may Allah bless him and grant him peace, made clear.

They also say that the *Sunna* can be abrogated by the Qur'ān. That happened when the *qibla* was changed. They agree that it is logically permitted for the Qur'ān to be abrogated by a single *ḥadīth*, but they disagree about whether it actually occurs. Some believe that it happened when the people of the Mosque of Qubā' changed their *qibla* but others reject that. It is not proper to abrogate a text through analogy since one of the preconditions of analogy is that it does not differ from a definitive text.

All of this occurred during the lifetime of the Prophet, may Allah bless him and grant him peace. The Community agree that there is no abrogation after his death, once the *Sharī'a* was firmly in place. This is why there is a consensus that there is no abrogation after the end of Revelation. When we find a consensus which is apparently contrary to a text, it is known that the consensus relied on an abrogating text which we do not know. An opposed text is not acted upon, and therefore it must have been abrogated even though it remains a *sunna* which is read and reported. An example of this is the *āyat* of the *'idda* (waiting period of a widow) of a year which is recited in the Qur'ān. Reflect on this. It is something extremely important. This is abrogation of a judgement while leaving its recitation, like the giving of *ṣadaqa* before conversing with the Prophet (58:12). The opposite can also occur when the recitation is abrogated but not the judgement, which happened in the case of the *āyat* of stoning. It is also possible for both recitation and judgement to be abrogated. What astute scholars believe is that if someone has not heard about the abrogation, he continues to worship according to the first ruling. They also permit abrogation of a ruling before it is acted on.

There are means for recognising an abrogating text. One is when the expression indicates it, like the words of the Prophet, "I used to forbid visiting graves. Now you may visit them. I forbade drinking except from skins, now you may drink from every container, but do not drink intoxicants." Another indication is when the transmitter mentions the date, as when he says, "It was the year of the Ditch," when it is known that what was abrogated occurred before it. Another indication is when it is stated: "Such-and-such a ruling is abrogated." Yet another means is when the entire Community agree that the ruling is abrogated.

or cause it to be forgotten,

It is said that this means: "omit it". It is removed from you so that you do not read or remember it. *"Nunsihā"* (forgotten) is also recited with a *hamza* (*nunsi'hā*) meaning "to defer", meaning "We defer its sending down or its abrogation to a later date".

We bring one better than it or equal to it.

This means "more beneficial for people" The benefit is immediate if the abrogating ruling is easier and in the Next World if it is harder. It is also said that it is superior in that it has a greater benefit and reward since there is no disparity in the worth of the Words of Allah.

أَلَمْ تَعْلَمْ أَنَّ ٱللَّهَ لَهُۥ مُلْكُ ٱلسَّمَٰوَٰتِ وَٱلْأَرْضِ
وَمَا لَكُم مِّن دُونِ ٱللَّهِ مِن وَلِيٍّ وَلَا نَصِيرٍ ﴿١٠٧﴾

107 ***Do you not know that Allah is He to Whom***
the kingdom of the heavens and the earth belongs
and that, besides Allah,
you have no protector and no helper?

This means that He brings into existence and originates and has sovereignty and authority over all things and that His will and command is carried out in every instance. The Prophet, may Allah bless him and grant him peace, is addressed while his entire community is meant.

أَمْ تُرِيدُونَ أَن تَسْـَٔلُوا۟ رَسُولَكُمْ كَمَا سُئِلَ مُوسَىٰ
مِن قَبْلُ ۗ وَمَن يَتَبَدَّلِ ٱلْكُفْرَ بِٱلْإِيمَٰنِ فَقَدْ
ضَلَّ سَوَآءَ ٱلسَّبِيلِ ﴿١٠٨﴾

108 ***Or do you want to question your Messenger***
as Mūsā was questioned before?
Anyone who exchanges faith for disbelief
has definitely gone astray from the level way.

"Am" (or) in fact means "indeed" you do want and it is a rebuke. This is said to refer to their demanding proofs of Prophethood, like asking him to bring Allah and the angels. Ibn 'Abbās and Mujāhid said that they asked for Ṣafā to be turned into gold. "Level" (*sawā'*) means the middle way of something. It is said that it means the aim, and so it would be "astray from the goal of the Path," which is obeying Allah. Ibn 'Abbās said that the reason for this *āyat* was that Rāfi' ibn Khuzayma and Wahb ibn Zayd said to the Prophet, may Allah bless him and grant him peace, "Bring us a Book from heaven which we can read and make rivers flow for us and we will follow you."

وَدَّ كَثِيرٌ مِّنْ أَهْلِ الْكِتَابِ لَوْ يَرُدُّونَكُم مِّن بَعْدِ
إِيمَانِكُمْ كُفَّارًا حَسَدًا مِّنْ عِندِ أَنفُسِهِم مِّن بَعْدِ مَا تَبَيَّنَ
لَهُمُ الْحَقُّ فَاعْفُوا وَاصْفَحُوا حَتَّىٰ يَأْتِيَ اللَّهُ بِأَمْرِهِ إِنَّ اللَّهَ عَلَىٰ
كُلِّ شَيْءٍ قَدِيرٌ ﴿١٠٩﴾

109 ***Many of the People of the Book would love it***
if they could make you revert to being unbelievers
after you have become believers,
showing their innate envy
now that the truth is clear to them.
But you should pardon and overlook
until Allah gives His command.
Truly Allah has power over all things.

Many of the People of the Book would love it if they could make you revert to being unbelievers after you have become believers, showing their innate envy now that the truth is clear to them.

They do so simply out of envy without having any legitimate authorisation for it from their Book or anywhere else.

There are two types of envy: blameworthy envy and praiseworthy envy. The blameworthy kind is when you desire Allah's blessing to be removed from your brother Muslim whether you want it to come to you or not. Allah censured this type in His Book when He says, *"Or do they in fact envy people for the bounty Allah has granted them."* (4:54) It is blameworthy because it is tantamount to thinking that Allah is foolish and that He has blessed someone who does not deserve His blessing.

The praiseworthy type is what comes in the sound *ḥadīth* in which the Prophet, may Allah bless him and grant him peace, said, "You may only have envy in two cases: for a man whom Allah has given the Qur'ān and he gets up and recites it throughout the night, and for a man whom Allah has given wealth and he spends it throughout the night and the day." This sort of envy is called *ghibṭa* rather than *ḥasad*, and al-Bukhārī has a chapter on envying people for their knowledge and wisdom. Its reality is that you desire to have the good and blessing which your Muslim brother has, without any good being removed from him. It is possible to call this aspiration, as the Almighty says, *"Let people with aspiration aspire to that!"* (83:26)

But you should pardon and overlook until Allah gives His command.

The root of the word *"'āfu"* (pardon) means not to call to account for wrong action. The root of "*ṣafḥ*" (overlook) is to remove its effect from the heart. This *āyat* is, however, abrogated by Allah's words, *"Fight those who do not believe ... abasement."* (9:29) according to Ibn 'Abbās. It is said that it is abrogated by *"kill the idolaters."* (9:5) Abū 'Ubayda said, "Every *āyat* which obviates fighting is Makkan and abrogated by the command to fight." Ibn 'Aṭiyya said about this, "His ruling that this *āyat* is Makkan is weak because the hostilities with the Jews only occurred in Madina."

Ibn 'Aṭiyya's opinion is sound. Al-Bukhārī and Muslim related from Usāma ibn Zayd that the Messenger of Allah, may Allah bless him and grant him peace, rode a donkey with a saddlecloth made in Fadak and Usāma ibn Zayd was riding behind him. He went to visit Sa'd ibn 'Ubāda in the Banū'l-Ḥārith branch of al-Khazraj before the Battle of Badr. On the way he passed by a gathering which contained 'Abdullāh ibn Ubayy ibn Salūl, and that was before 'Abdullāh ibn Ubayy became Muslim. The gathering contained a mixture of Muslims, idolaters, pagans, and Jews. 'Abdullāh ibn Rawāḥa was also in the gathering.

When the dust from the donkey reached the gathering, 'Abdullāh ibn Ubayy covered his nose with his cloak and then said, "Don't cover us with dust!" The Messenger of Allah, may Allah bless him and grant him peace, greeted them and then stopped. He dismounted and invited them to Allah and recited the Qur'ān to them. 'Abdullāh ibn Ubayy ibn Salūl said, "You! There is nothing better than what you say if it is the truth. So do not annoy us with it in our gatherings. Return to your mount and only recount it to those who come to you." 'Abdullāh ibn Rawāḥa said, "Indeed, Messenger of Allah! Bring it to us in our gatherings. We like that!" So the Muslims, idolaters and Jews abused one another until they were practically fighting. The Prophet kept on calming them down until they were quiet.

Then the Messenger of Allah, may Allah bless him and grant him peace, mounted his animal and went on to visit Sa'd ibn 'Ubāda. The Messenger of Allah said, "Sa'd, did you hear what Abū Ḥubāb (meaning 'Abdullāh ibn Ubayy) said? He said such-and-such." Sa'd ibn 'Ubāda said, "O Messenger of Allah, pardon him and overlook it. By the One who sent down the Book to you with the truth, Allah brought you with the truth which He sent down to you after the people of this little town had already agreed to crown him. When that was prevented on account the truth which Allah gave you, he was vexed because of that. That is why he did what you saw." The Messenger of Allah, may Allah bless him and grant him peace, pardoned him.

The Messenger of Allah, may Allah bless him and grant him peace, and the Companions used to pardon the idolaters and the People of the Book as Allah commanded them to do and they endured much harm from them. Allah says, *"You will hear many abusive words from those given the Book before you and from those who are idolaters,"* (3:186) and "*Many of the People of the Book would love it...*"

The Messenger of Allah, may Allah bless him and grant him peace, continued to pardon them as long as Allah commanded him to do so until the time when Allah gave permission to fight them. When the Messenger of Allah went on the Badr expedition, Allah killed the nobles of Quraysh through him and Ibn Ubayy ibn Salūl and those of the idolaters and pagans with him, said, "This is a business which has proved to be victorious," and they gave allegiance to the Messenger of Allah in Islam, and became Muslim.

وَأَقِيمُوا۟ ٱلصَّلَوٰةَ وَءَاتُوا۟ ٱلزَّكَوٰةَ ۚ وَمَا تُقَدِّمُوا۟
لِأَنفُسِكُم مِّنْ خَيْرٍ تَجِدُوهُ عِندَ ٱللَّهِ ۗ إِنَّ
ٱللَّهَ بِمَا تَعْمَلُونَ بَصِيرٌ ﴿١١٠﴾

110 ***Establish the prayer and pay zakāt.***
Any good you send ahead for yourselves,
you will find with Allah.
Certainly Allah sees what you do.

We read in a *ḥadīth*: "When someone dies, people ask, 'What did he leave behind?' while the angels ask, 'What did he send ahead?'" Al-Bukhārī and an-Nasā'ī transmitted that 'Abdullāh [ibn Mas'ūd] reported that the Messenger of Allah, may Allah bless him and grant him peace, said, "Which of you loves the property of his heir more than his own property?" They said, "Messenger of Allah, there is none of who does not love his own property more than that of his heir?" The Messenger of Allah, may Allah bless him and grant him peace, said, "No, there is none of you who does not love the property of his heir more than his own property. Your own property is what you send ahead and the property of your heir is what you leave behind." 'Umar ibn al-Khaṭṭāb passed by the graveyard of Baqī' al-Gharfad and said, "Peace be upon you, people of the graves. The news with us is that your wives have married, your houses are lived in and your property divided." An invisible voice answered him, "Ibn Khaṭṭāb! The news with us is that we have found what we sent ahead, profited from what we spent, and lost what we left behind."

وَقَالُوا لَن يَدْخُلَ الْجَنَّةَ إِلَّا مَن كَانَ هُودًا أَوْ نَصَارَىٰ ۖ
تِلْكَ أَمَانِيُّهُمْ ۖ قُلْ هَاتُوا بُرْهَانَكُمْ إِن كُنتُمْ
صَادِقِينَ ۖ ﴿١١١﴾ بَلَىٰ مَنْ أَسْلَمَ وَجْهَهُ لِلَّهِ وَهُوَ مُحْسِنٌ فَلَهُ
أَجْرُهُ عِندَ رَبِّهِ وَلَا خَوْفٌ عَلَيْهِمْ وَلَا هُمْ يَحْزَنُونَ ﴿١١٢﴾

111 *They say, 'No one will enter the Garden*
except for Jews and Christians.'
Such is their vain hope.
Say, 'Produce your evidence
if you are telling the truth.'
112 *Not so! All who submit themselves*
completely to Allah and are good-doers
will find their reward with their Lord.
They will feel no fear and will know no sorrow.

They say, "No one will enter the Garden except for Jews and Christians."

This means that the Jews said that none but Jews would enter the Garden and the Christians said that none but Christians would enter it.

Say, 'Produce your evidence, if you are telling the truth.'

The "*burhān*" (evidence) referred to in this *āyat* is the kind which produces certainty. Aṭ-Ṭabarī says that the purpose of demanding evidence here is to confirm the truth and refute those who deny it. Rather than telling the truth, they are, in fact, lying about both their faith and also their statement concerning entering the Garden.

Not so! All who submit themselves completely to Allah

"Aslama" (submit) here means "to be humble and submit" or it is said to mean to be sincere in action. The words "themselves completely" is literally "their faces" and is used because it is the noblest part of the human being and because it is the home of the senses and the place where might and abasement show themselves most clearly. For this reason the Arabs used the word "face" to designate the entire person.

وَقَالَتِ ٱلْيَهُودُ لَيْسَتِ ٱلنَّصَٰرَىٰ عَلَىٰ شَيْءٍ وَقَالَتِ ٱلنَّصَٰرَىٰ
لَيْسَتِ ٱلْيَهُودُ عَلَىٰ شَيْءٍ وَهُمْ يَتْلُونَ ٱلْكِتَٰبَ كَذَٰلِكَ
قَالَ ٱلَّذِينَ لَا يَعْلَمُونَ مِثْلَ قَوْلِهِمْ فَٱللَّهُ يَحْكُمُ بَيْنَهُمْ
يَوْمَ ٱلْقِيَٰمَةِ فِيمَا كَانُوا۟ فِيهِ يَخْتَلِفُونَ ١١٣

113 ***The Jews say, 'The Christians***
have nothing to stand on,'
and the Christians say,
'The Jews have nothing to stand on,'

yet they both recite the Book.
Those who do not know say the same as they say.
Allah will judge between them on the Day of Rising
regarding the things about which they differ.

The Jews say, 'The Christians have nothing to stand on,' and the Christians say, 'The Jews have nothing to stand on,' yet they both recite the Book.

Each of them claim that the other group have nothing and that they are more entitled to mercy than them. "The Book" means the Torah and the Gospel.

Those who do not know say the same as they say.

"Those who do not know" are said by the majority to be the unbelieving Arabs because they had no Book. 'Aṭā' said that what is meant are the nations before the Jews and Christians.

Ibn 'Abbās said that the reason for the revelation of this *āyat* was that some Christians of Najrān came to the Prophet and the Jewish rabbis also came and they argued in the presence of the Prophet and each said this about the other.

وَمَنْ أَظْلَمُ مِمَّن مَّنَعَ مَسَٰجِدَ ٱللَّهِ أَن يُذْكَرَ فِيهَا ٱسْمُهُۥ
وَسَعَىٰ فِى خَرَابِهَآ ۚ أُو۟لَٰٓئِكَ مَا كَانَ لَهُمْ أَن يَدْخُلُوهَآ إِلَّا
خَآئِفِينَ ۚ لَهُمْ فِى ٱلدُّنْيَا خِزْىٌ وَلَهُمْ فِى ٱلْءَاخِرَةِ عَذَابٌ
عَظِيمٌ ﴿١١٤﴾

114 *Who could do greater wrong than someone*
who bars access to the mosques of Allah,
preventing His name from being remembered in them,
and goes about destroying them?
Such people will never be able to enter them
– except in fear.

They will have disgrace in this world
and in the Next World
they will have a terrible punishment.

Who could do greater wrong than someone who bars access to the mosques of Allah, preventing His name from being remembered in them,

By "mosques" here Allah means either Jerusalem and the area around it or the Ka'ba. The plural is used to honour the mosque because it is the *qibla* for all other mosques. It is also said that what is meant are all mosques.

People disagree about what is meant by this *āyat* and about whom it was revealed. Some commentators said that it was revealed about Nebuchadnezzar because he destroyed Jerusalem. Ibn 'Abbās and others say that it was revealed about the Christians and it means, "How, Christians, can you claim to be people of the Garden when you laid waste to Jerusalem and prevented those who pray from praying in it?" In that case the sense of the *āyat* would be astonishment at what the Christians did to Jerusalem, in spite of their esteem for it, and that they did what they did out of their animosity towards the Jews. It is said that it was revealed about the idolaters when they prevented the worshippers and the Prophet, may Allah bless him and grant him peace, from reaching the Sacred Mosque in the year of al-Ḥudaybiyya. It is said that what is meant is anyone who bars access to any mosque until the Day of Rising. That is sound because the expression is general, and Allah knows best.

The destruction of mosques can be actual, like the destruction wrought by Nebuchadnezzar on Jerusalem and also by the Christians when they attacked the tribe of Israel under one of their emperors (possibly Vespasian). They slaughtered the people, looted the city, burned the Torah, and put excrement in the Temple and destroyed it. But it can also have a metaphorical meaning, as the idolaters prevented the Messenger of Allah from reaching the Sacred House. Or in general, it could mean letting mosques fall into disuse.

Our scholars said, "This *āyat* provides the legal basis for our ruling that it is not permitted to forbid a woman from making *ḥajj* if she has not performed it, whether or not she has a *maḥram*, nor should she be prevented from praying in mosques as long as it is not feared that that will be a cause of immoral behaviour. The Prophet, may Allah bless him and grant him peace, said, "Do not bar the female slaves of Allah from the mosques of Allah."

The *āyat* is also why it is said that it is not permitted to demolish a mosque, sell it, or to let it become idle, even if the town in which it is located falls into ruins. One should not forbid the construction of a mosque unless the aim of building it is to cause dissent and schism, as would be the case when people build a mosque beside another mosque or close to it, and their intention is to cause dissension among the people of the first mosque and ruin it. In such a case, the second mosque should be destroyed and its construction forbidden. It is also why it is not permitted to have two Friday mosques in the same city, or two imams in the same mosque, or two group prayers said in the same mosque. This will be further explained in *Sūrat at-Tawba*, Allah willing, and elsewhere. The *āyat* also indicates esteem for the prayer and that it is the best of actions and has the greatest reward and that preventing it is the greatest of wrong actions.

Every place in which Allah is worshipped and prostrated to (*sajada*) is called a mosque (*masjid*). The Messenger of Allah, may Allah bless him and grant him peace, said, "The whole earth was made a mosque and is pure for me (to pray in)." The Community agree that when an area is singled out for the prayer by a declaration, it is no longer private property and becomes public for all Muslims. If a man builds a mosque in his house and screens it off from people and singles it out for himself, it remains his property and does not become a mosque in the true sense of the word. If he opens it to everyone, its judgement is that of general mosques and it is no longer private property.

Such people will never be able to enter them – except in fear.

When the Muslims gain control of them and they are under their authority, then it will not be possible for the unbelievers to enter them, and, if they do enter them, it will be in fear that the Muslims will attack them and punish them for entering them. This is an indication that unbelievers should never be allowed to enter mosques as will come in *Sūrat at-Tawba*, Allah willing. If the *āyat* is about the Christians, it is related that it points ahead to the time of 'Umar's reconstruction of Jerusalem after its conquest by the Muslims and his ruling that no Christian should enter the mosque of Jerusalem without being beaten, when it had previously been their place of worship. If it is considered to be about Quraysh, it is said that it refers to the announcement made after the proclamation of the Prophet, may Allah bless him and grant him peace: "After this year, no idolater should make *ḥajj* nor do *ṭawāf* of the House naked." It is said that what is meant is the command to struggle against them and eradicate them so that none of them enters the Sacred Mosque except in fear.

They will have disgrace in this world and in the Next World they will have a terrible punishment.

Qatāda reports that the word "disgrace" refers to killing in the case of the *ḥarbī* and *jizya* in the case of the *dhimmī*. As-Suddī said that their disgrace in this world will be the coming of the Mahdī, and the conquest of 'Amuriyya, Rumiyya, Constantinople and other cities. If it refers to Quraysh, it is said to refer to their disgrace at the Conquest of Makka and the punishment in the Next World of those of them who died unbelievers.

وَلِلَّهِ ٱلْمَشْرِقُ وَٱلْمَغْرِبُ فَأَيْنَمَا تُوَلُّوا۟ فَثَمَّ وَجْهُ ٱللَّهِ
إِنَّ ٱللَّهَ وَٰسِعٌ عَلِيمٌ ١١٥

115 ***Both East and West belong to Allah,***
so wherever you turn,
the Face of Allah is there.
Allah is All-Encompassing, All-Knowing.

Both East and West belong to Allah,

East is where the sun rises and West is where it sets, so the *āyat* implies that all things are subject to Allah's sovereignty, along with all the directions and creatures contained within them. He is the One who originated them and brought them into existence. These two directions – East and West – are singled out for connection to Him as a mark of honour, like "the House of Allah" and because the reason for the revelation of the *āyat* dictates that, as will be made clear.

so wherever you turn, the Face of Allah is there.

Scholars disagree about the reason for the revelation of this *āyat*. There are several positions. 'Āmir ibn Rabī'a says, "It was revealed about some people who prayed in a direction other than the *qibla* on a dark night as is transmitted by at-Tirmidhī: "We were with the Prophet, may Allah bless him and grant him peace, on a journey during a dark night and we did not know where the *qibla* was. Each of us prayed according to his own devices. In the morning, we mentioned that to the Messenger of Allah, may Allah bless him and grant him peace, and this *āyat* was revealed."

This *ḥadīth* lacks a proper *isnād* and one of its transmitters is weak. But most of the people of knowledge accept the implied judgement and say that if someone prays on a cloudy day in a direction other than the *qibla* and then it later becomes clear to him that he did not pray in the right direction, his prayer is allowed. That was said by Sufyān, Ibn al-Mubārak, Aḥmad and Isḥāq. It is also the position of Abū Ḥanīfa and Mālik, although Mālik says:

> It is preferred that he repeat (the prayer) within the time but that is not an obligation on him because he has performed his obligation as he was commanded to do. Perfection is to seek to correct it within the time, and there is evidence in the *sunna* in the case of someone who prayed alone and then caught that prayer in its time in the group. He repeated it with them. It is only recommended for someone to repeat it if he had his back to the *qibla* or faced a direction very much away from the *qibla*. If, by his *ijtihād*, he was only a little to the right or left, he does not need to repeat it either in the time or after the time.

Al-Mughīra and ash-Shāfi'ī said that such a prayer is invalid because facing the *qibla* is one of the preconditions of the prayer. What Mālik said is sounder because the direction of *qibla* can be abandoned out of necessity in hand-to-hand combat and is also permitted as a dispensation while travelling. Ibn 'Umar said, "It was revealed about travellers who turn wherever their mounts turn." (Muslim) He said, "The Messenger of Allah, may Allah bless him and grant him peace, used to pray on his camel going from Makka to Madina whatever the direction the camel was facing. About that was revealed: *"so wherever you turn, the Face of Allah is there."* There is no disagreement between scholars that it is permitted to pray *nāfila* prayers while mounted, going by this *ḥadīth*. No one, however, is permitted to deliberately abandon *qibla* in a *farḍ* prayer for any other direction unless that is due to intense fear.

Mālik has differing opinions about someone who is ill and prays on his litter. In one opinion he says that he may not pray a *farḍ* prayer on the back of a camel, even if he is very ill. Saḥnūn said, "If he does that, he should repeat the prayer." He said on another occasion, "If he is one of those who can only pray on the ground using gestures, then he can pray on the camel after it has been halted and made to face *qibla*." They agree that it is not valid for anyone who is healthy to pray a *farḍ* prayer except on the ground, unless he is in a state of fear.

Fuqahā' disagree about a traveller on a journey in which the prayer cannot be shortened. Mālik and his people and ath-Thawrī said, "There can be no voluntary prayers on a camel except during a journey on which the prayer may be shortened, because all the journeys which are reported from the Messenger of Allah on which he did *nāfila* prayers were those during which the prayer may be shortened. Ash-Shāfi'ī, Abū Ḥanīfa, al-Ḥasan ibn Ḥayy, al-Layth ibn Sa'd and Dā'ūd ibn 'Alī said that it is permitted to do *nāfila* prayers while mounted outside a city on a journey of any length, whether or not the prayer may be shortened, because the reports do not specify one journey rather than another, so it is permitted on every journey. Abū Yūsuf said that it is even permitted to pray mounted in a city using gestures going by a report in which Anas ibn Mālik prayed on a donkey in an alley in Madina using gestures.

Another position is that stated by Ibn Zayd: "The Jews recommended to the Prophet, may Allah bless him and grant him peace, that he should pray facing Jerusalem. When he did, they said, 'He was only guided by us.' Then, when the *qibla* was changed to the Ka'ba, the Jews said, *'What has turned them from their qibla they used to face?'* and this *āyat* was revealed." According to this position, there is a sequence in the events leading up to it.

A further view is that this *āyat* is abrogated by Allah's words, *"Wherever you come from, turn your face to the Masjid al-Ḥarām."* (2:1498) Ibn 'Abbās said that it seems that in the beginning a man prayed in whatever direction he wished to and then that was abrogated. Qatāda says that the *āyat* which abrogated it was: *"Turn your face, therefore, towards the Masjid al-Ḥaram."* (2:144)

Yet another view related from Mujāhid and aḍ-Ḍaḥḥāk is that it remains a firm ruling. It means: wherever you are in the east or the west, there is the face of Allah which you are commanded to face and that is the direction of the Ka'ba. Mujāhid and Ibn Jubayr said that when *"Call on Me and I will answer you"* (40:60) was revealed, people asked, "Where?" and *"so wherever you turn, the Face of Allah is there"* was revealed. Ibn 'Umar and an-Nakhā'ī said, "Wherever you turn on your journeys and when moving about, the face of Allah is there." It is further said that it is connected to Allah's words in the previous *āyat* (2:114), *"Who could do greater wrong ... "* and means: "O believers, the lands of Allah are vast enough for you, so those who ruin the mosques of Allah cannot prevent you from turning your faces towards Allah's *qibla* no matter where you are on the earth." It is said that when the Prophet, may Allah bless him and grant him peace, was barred from the House in the Year of al-Ḥudaybiyya, the Muslims were saddened by that.

People disagree about the interpretation of the word *"wajh"* (Face) as ascribed to Allah Almighty in the Qur'ān and the *Sunna*. Astute scholars say that it refers to created existence and is used for it as a metaphor, since the face is the most apparent part of the body and the most sublime. Ibn Fūrak said, "The attribute of the thing is mentioned and it is meant to designate the One described by it. The expression 'having a face' means that something has existence." Ibn 'Abbās said, "The Face designates Allah Himself." Some imāms say that this designation should be affirmed when it is heard, even if it contradicts what intellects demand of attributes which are appropriate for the Eternal. Ibn 'Aṭiyya says that this is weak and what is actually meant is Allah's existence. It is also said that it means the direction which one faces, in other words the *qibla*, and it is also said that it means what you aim at.

Another opinion is that the word "*wajh*" (Face) as ascribed to Allah means: "Wherever the pleasure of Allah lies and His reward," going by Allah's words, *"We feed you only out of desire for the Face of Allah."* (76:9), meaning in order to please Him and seek His reward, and by the words of the Prophet, may Allah bless him and grant him peace: "If anyone builds a mosque by which he desires the Face of Allah, Allah will build for him its like in the Garden."

Allah is All-Encompassing, All-Knowing.

He gives His slaves latitude in their *dīn* and does not oblige them to so something which is beyond their capacity. It is said that

"All-Encompassing" means that His knowledge encompasses everything, as in Allah's words, *"He encompasses everything in knowledge."* (20:98) Al-Farrā' said that the name All-Encompassing indicates the Generous whose giving encompasses everything as in Allah's words, *"My mercy encompasses everything"* (7:156) It is said that His forgiveness is all-encompassing. It is said that He is gracious to His slaves and has no need of their actions.

وَقَالُوا۟ ٱتَّخَذَ ٱللَّهُ وَلَدًا ۗ سُبْحَٰنَهُۥ ۖ بَل لَّهُۥ مَا فِى ٱلسَّمَٰوَٰتِ
وَٱلْأَرْضِ ۖ كُلٌّ لَّهُۥ قَٰنِتُونَ ﴿١١٦﴾

116 ***They say, 'Allah has a son.'***
Glory be to Him!
No, everything in the heavens and earth
belongs to Him.
Everything is obedient to Him,

They say, 'Allah has a son.' Glory be to Him!

This refers to what the Christians say about the Messiah being the son of God. It is also said that it refers to the Jews' statement about 'Uzayr being the son of God. It is said that it is about the unbelieving Arabs who say that the angels are the daughters of Allah. These points will be discussed in *Sūrat Maryam* and *Sūrat al-Anbiyā'*.

Al-Bukhāri transmitted from Ibn 'Abbās that the Prophet, may Allah bless him and grant him peace, said, "Allah Almighty says, 'The son of Ādam has denied Me and he has no right to do that. He has abused Me and he has no right to do that. He denies Me by claiming that I cannot bring him back as he was. He abuses Me by saying that I have a child. I am too glorious to take a consort or child.'"

The word "*subḥāna*" (Glory be) mean "to declare free of" and "to disconnect". It declares the impossibility of their statement that

Allah has a son. Allah is unique in His Essence, One in His attributes. He has not begotten obviating the need for him to have a consort. *"How could He have a son when He has no wife?"* (6:101) He was not begotten obviating the need for something to have existed before Him. He is greatly exalted above what the wrongdoers and deniers say.

A child is always of the same genus as his parent and so how could Allah – glory be to Him! – have a son among His creatures when nothing is like Him? The nature of a child is to be of the same species and in-time while timelessness necessitates oneness and stability. He is Timeless, Pre-eternal, One, Unique, Alone, the Everlasting Sustainer of all.

Everything in the heavens and earth belongs to Him

There is nothing which He did not originate and bring into existence.

Everything is obedient to Him.

Qānit (obedient) means submissive and compliant. All creatures are subjected to Allah. The obedience of inanimates is in the manifestation of the work done on them and by them. The word *qunūt* means obedience as well as meaning silence. As-Suddī said that it means that everyone will stand in obedience to Him on the Day of Rising. Al-Ḥasan said that it means that everyone undertakes to testify that he is His slave. *Qunūt* linguistically means standing as az-Zajjāj said. The *āyat* means: creatures are obedient, undertake slavehood, either by conscious admission or, if they do not consciously obey, the effect of Allah's action becomes clear on them. It is also said that the root meaning is "obedience".

بَدِيعُ ٱلسَّمَٰوَٰتِ وَٱلْأَرْضِ ۖ وَإِذَا قَضَىٰٓ أَمْرًا فَإِنَّمَا يَقُولُ
لَهُۥ كُن فَيَكُونُ ﴿١١٧﴾

117 ***the Originator of the heavens and earth.***
When He decides on something,
He just says to it, 'Be!' and it is.

the Originator of the heavens and earth.

The form used for the name "the Originator" is one which gives extra emphasis to the meaning. To originate something is to bring it into existence without any prior model. This means that Allah brought the heavens and the earth into existence and fashioned them without any previous model. Anyone who makes something not previously thought of is called an originator. The verb is the source of the term *bid'a* which means innovation. It is called that because the one who does it innovates something which was not previously done or enunciated by any qualified imām.

No innovation issuing from a creature can have a basis in the *Sharī'a*. If it has any basis at all it may fall under the category of recommended actions. If it is praiseworthy, even if it has no precedent, like some type of generosity or other good deed, it may well be a praiseworthy action, even if no one has done it before. This is supported by the words of 'Umar, regarding the *tarāwīḥ* prayer, "This is an excellent innovation", since it was a good and praiseworthy action. The Prophet, may Allah bless him and grant him peace, had prayed it, and then left it and did not continue doing it and people did not gather for it. 'Umar reinstated it and people gathered for it and he recommended it to them as an innovation, but a praiseworthy one.

Anything which is contrary to what Allah and His Messenger commanded is categorically repudiated and blameworthy and this is what is being referred to by the Messenger of Allah, may Allah bless him and grant him peace, when he said in his *khuṭba*, "The worst of matters are the new ones, and every innovation (*bid'a*) is misguidance," meaning anything which is not in keeping with the Book or the *Sunna* or the practice of the Companions. The matter is made even clearer by the words of the Prophet, may Allah bless him and grant him peace: "Anyone who initiates a good *sunna* in Islam has its reward and the reward of whoever does it after him without that decreasing his reward in any way. Anyone who initiates a bad *sunna* in Islam bears its burden and the burden of whoever acts by it after him without that decreasing his burden in any way." So innovations can be good or bad, and this is the basic principle regarding this matter. Protection and success are by Allah. There is no Lord but Him.

When He decides on something, He just says to it, 'Be!' and it is.

This means that, when He desires to complete something and make it perfect in accordance with His perfect foreknowledge of it, He says to it, "Be!" Ibn 'Arafa said, "Allah's decision on a thing entails perfecting it, carrying it out and finishing it. That is why a judge is called a *qāḍī*, because, when he decides on a judgement, the quarrel is ended. Al-Azharī said that the verb "*qaḍā*" (decide) has various meanings. Its root meaning means to finish something and complete it.

Our scholars say that *qaḍā* is a word with various meanings. It can mean "to create" as in Allah's words: *"In two days He determined them as seven heavens"* (41:12), meaning "created them". It can mean "to inform" as in: *"We decreed for the tribe of Israel in the Book,"* (17:4) and it can mean to force a judgement to be carried out. It can mean to settle a right in full and it can also mean "to will", meaning "to decide or want". Ibn 'Aṭā' says it means "determine". According to the Mu'tazilites, He determined when He created and brought into existence.

The word translated here as "something" (*amr*), which generally means a command or a matter, is used in the Qur'ān in different ways to mean various things:

- **Islam**: *"Until the truth came and Allah's* ***command*** *prevailed"* (9:48), meaning here Islam.
- **Punishment**: *"When the* ***affair*** *is decided"* (14:22) meaning the punishment becomes mandatory.

- **The Prophet 'Īsā**: Allah says, *"When He decides on* ***something,****"* (3:47) meaning, in this instance, 'Īsā, whom He knew would be born without having had a father.

- **The killing of the unbelievers at Badr**: Allah says, *"When Allah's* ***command*** *comes,"* (40:78) meaning the killing which would take place at Badr. And again: *"So that Allah could settle a* ***matter*** *whose result was preordained"* (8:42) referring to the killing of the unbelievers of Makka.

- **The conquest of Makka**: Allah says, *"Wait until Allah brings about His* ***command****"* (9:24), meaning the Conquest of Makka.

- **The killing of the Jewish tribe of Qurayẓa and the nobles of the tribe of an-Naḍīr**: Allah says, *"Pardon and overlook until Allah gives His* ***command****."* (2:109) referring to the Jewish enemies of the Muslims in Madina.

- **The Day of Rising**: Allah says, *"Allah's* ***command*** *is coming."* (16:1)

- **Existence as a whole**: Allah says, *"He directs the whole* ***affair****,"* (10:3) meaning everything He has created.

- **Revelation**: Allah says, *"He directs the whole* ***affair*** *from heaven to earth."* (32:5) Revelation descends from heaven to earth. And He says, *"The* ***Command*** *descending down through all of them"* (65:12), meaning Divine Revelation.

- **Command over creation**: Allah says, *"Indeed all* ***matters*** *return eventually to Him"* (42:53), meaning the affairs of every creature.

- **Victory**: Allah says, *"They say, 'Do we have any say in the* ***affair*** *at all?'"* (3:154), meaning victory. *"The* ***affair*** *belongs entirely to Allah"* (3:154), meaning victory.

- **Wrong action**: Allah says, *"They tasted the evil consequences of* ***what they did****"* (65:9), meaning the repayment for their wrong actions.

- **Action**: Allah says, *"Pharaoh's **command** was not rightly guided"* (11:97). And He says, *"Those who oppose his **command** should beware,"* (24:63), meaning the action of the Prophet, may Allah bless him and grant him peace.

The Divine command *"kun"* (Be!) is what is meant by the words of the Prophet, "I seek refuge in the complete Word (or words) of Allah from the evil of what He created." This is also indicated in what is related by Abū Dharr from the Prophet that Allah said in a *ḥadīth qudsī*: "My gift is words and My punishment is words." (at-Tirmidhī). So "word" can mean "words", but when one word is used for different matters at different times, it becomes words, even if it goes back to one word.

Depending on how the grammar is taken, there are two possible ways of looking at the phrase *"fa-yakūnu"* (and it is). The first is that the thing comes into being after the command. Even if it was non-existent, it has the same status as something existent because Allah already "knew" it as will be explained. According to the second view, the thing comes into being simultaneously with the command, and aṭ-Ṭabarī preferred that. He said, "His command to the thing does not have prior or later existence." The thing commanded to exist only exists by the command, and there is nothing which exists except that it has been commanded to exist as will be explained. He said, "It is like when people rise from their graves. Allah's summons (30:25) is neither earlier nor later, it is at the moment when He calls them." Ibn 'Aṭiyya says this is weak and incorrect in respect of the meaning because it would necessitate the word to be accompanied by bringing into being and existence.

To summarise what is deduced from this *āyat*: Allah Almighty continues to command non-existent things to come into existence. He decrees and can delay decreed things and He is All-Knowing and can delay known things. The entire *āyat* demands futurity, required by the things commanded, since temporal things come into being after they were not. All depends on Allah's power and knowledge. He is timeless and continues forever. The meaning of the Divine command "Be!", however, is timeless and connected to the Essence.

Al-Māwardī says, "It might be asked, 'In what state were the things to which He said *"'Be' and it is"* – non-existence or existence? If it was in a state of non-existence, it is impossible that He command other than what is commanded, as it is impossible for the command to issue from other than the One who commands. If it is the state of its existence, that state cannot have existence or temporality commanded for it because it is already a temporal existent.'" There are three answers to this question:

- It is a report from Allah regarding the carrying out of His commands in His existing creation, as when He commanded the tribe of Israel to become apes, in which case it is not about bringing something non-existent into existence.
- Allah knows every being before it is and so the things which do not yet actually exist are already in His prior knowledge of them. So they are similar to what exists and it is permissible to say, "Be!" to them and to command them to emerge from the state of non-existence to the state of existence since He has conceived of them and has knowledge of them in the state of non-existence.
- It is a general report from Allah about what He brings into being and forms when He desires to create it and bring it into being. It is His Decree which is designated by the word "Be!", even if it is not an actual word.

وَقَالَ ٱلَّذِينَ لَا يَعۡلَمُونَ لَوۡلَا يُكَلِّمُنَا ٱللَّهُ أَوۡ تَأۡتِينَآ
ءَايَةٞۗ كَذَٰلِكَ قَالَ ٱلَّذِينَ مِن قَبۡلِهِم مِّثۡلَ قَوۡلِهِمۡۘ
تَشَٰبَهَتۡ قُلُوبُهُمۡۗ قَدۡ بَيَّنَّا ٱلۡأٓيَٰتِ لِقَوۡمٖ يُوقِنُونَ ١١٨

118 ***Those who do not know say,***
'If only Allah would speak to us,

or some sign come to us!'
just like those before them
who said the same as they say.
Their hearts are much the same.
We have made the Signs clear
for people who have certainty.

Ibn 'Abbās said that *"those who do not know"* are the Jews while Mujāhid said that it is the Christians who are being referred to, which aṭ-Ṭabarī prefers because they are mentioned immediately before this *āyat*. Ar-Rabī', as-Suddī and Qatāda said that it is the Arab idolaters who said these words, claiming that they would become believers if this were to happen. "Their hearts are much the same" as the hearts of those before them in respect of obstinacy, brashness and lack of faith.

إِنَّآ أَرْسَلْنَٰكَ بِالْحَقِّ بَشِيرًا وَنَذِيرًا ۖ
وَلَا تَسْـَٔلْ عَنْ أَصْحَٰبِ الْجَحِيمِ ﴿١١٩﴾

119 ***We have sent you with the Truth,***
bringing good news and giving warning.
Do not ask about the inhabitants of the Blazing Fire.

Do not ask about the inhabitants of the Blazing Fire.

Muqātil said that the Prophet, may Allah bless him and grant him peace, said, "If Allah were to send down His violent force on the Jews, they would have faith," and then Allah revealed this. It is said that the reason for this was that the Prophet was asked about the state of his ancestors and this *āyat* was revealed.

There are two readings of the word "ask". Nāfi' has it as *tas'al*, the apocopate form as a prohibition, meaning "Do not ask". The others have it as *tus'alu*, "You will not be asked".

وَلَن تَرْضَىٰ عَنكَ ٱلْيَهُودُ وَلَا ٱلنَّصَٰرَىٰ حَتَّىٰ تَتَّبِعَ مِلَّتَهُمْ
قُلْ إِنَّ هُدَى ٱللَّهِ هُوَ ٱلْهُدَىٰ وَلَئِنِ ٱتَّبَعْتَ أَهْوَآءَهُم بَعْدَ ٱلَّذِى
جَآءَكَ مِنَ ٱلْعِلْمِ مَا لَكَ مِنَ ٱللَّهِ مِن وَلِىٍّ وَلَا نَصِيرٍ ﴿١٢٠﴾

120 ***The Jews and the Christians will never be pleased with you until you follow their religion.***
Say, 'Allah's guidance is the true guidance.'
If you were to follow their whims and desires, after the knowledge that has come to you, you would find no protector or helper against Allah.

The Jews and the Christians will never be pleased with you until you follow their religion.

Allah is telling His Messenger that it is not the goal of the Jews and Christians are not aiming to gain faith by their queries about the *āyat*s. Even if he were to bring them everything they asked for, they would still not be pleased with him. They will not be pleased until he abandons Islam and follows them. The word "*milla*" (religion) means what Allah, has prescribed for His slaves in His Books and on the tongues of His Messengers and so *milla* and *sharī'a* are very similar in meaning. There is a difference between the words *dīn*, *milla* and *sharī'a*. *Milla* and *sharī'a* designate what Allah orders His slaves to do and *dīn* is what the slaves actually make of Allah's commands to them.

A group of scholars, including Abū Ḥanīfa, ash-Shāfi'ī, Dā'ūd and Aḥmad ibn Ḥanbal, hold the view that, according to this *āyat*, all disbelief constitutes one religion since the Almighty says, *"your religion"*, which is singular, and He says, *"You have your dīn and I have my dīn"* (109:6) and the Prophet, peace be upon him, said, "The people of two religions do not inherit from one another." What is meant is Islam as the Prophet also said, "A

Muslim does not inherit from an unbeliever." Mālik and Aḥmad, in another transmission, believe that disbelief consists of several different religions and so a Jew does not inherit from a Christian and neither of them inherit from a Magian, taking the *ḥadīth* of the Prophet, may Allah bless him and grant him peace, literally. The word *milla* here means a multiplicity of beliefs, even though it is singular.

Say, 'Allah's guidance is the true guidance.'

This means: "O Muḥammad, what you have of the true guidance of Allah, which He places in the heart of whomever He wishes, is the true guidance, not what these people claim."

If you were to follow their whims and desires,

There are two aspects to the use of the second person here. One is that it is addressed to the Messenger and the second is that, while it is addressed to the Messenger, it is his Community which is meant. According to the first aspect, it means to discipline his Community since their position is less than his. The reason for the *āyat* was that the idolaters were asking for a truce while continuing to attack the Prophet, may Allah bless him and grant him peace, and Islam. So Allah informed him that they would not be pleased until he followed their religion and He commanded *jihad* against them.

after the knowledge that has come to you,

Aḥmad ibn Ḥanbal was asked about the one who says that the Qur'an is created. He said, "He is an unbeliever." It was asked, "On what basis is he an unbeliever?" He said, "By the *āyat*s of the Book of Allah: '*If you were to follow their whims and desires after the knowledge that has come to you.*' This shows that the Qur'ān is part of Allah's knowledge and so whoever claims it is created is an unbeliever."

ٱلَّذِينَ ءَاتَيْنَٰهُمُ ٱلْكِتَٰبَ يَتْلُونَهُۥ حَقَّ تِلَاوَتِهِۦٓ أُو۟لَٰٓئِكَ يُؤْمِنُونَ بِهِۦ
وَمَن يَكْفُرْ بِهِۦ فَأُو۟لَٰٓئِكَ هُمُ ٱلْخَٰسِرُونَ ﴿١٢١﴾ يَٰبَنِىٓ إِسْرَٰٓءِيلَ
ٱذْكُرُوا۟ نِعْمَتِىَ ٱلَّتِىٓ أَنْعَمْتُ عَلَيْكُمْ وَأَنِّى فَضَّلْتُكُمْ عَلَى
ٱلْعَٰلَمِينَ ﴿١٢٢﴾ وَٱتَّقُوا۟ يَوْمًا لَّا تَجْزِى نَفْسٌ عَن نَّفْسٍ شَيْـًٔا وَلَا يُقْبَلُ
مِنْهَا عَدْلٌ وَلَا تَنفَعُهَا شَفَٰعَةٌ وَلَا هُمْ يُنصَرُونَ ﴿١٢٣﴾

121 *Those to whom We have given the Book,*
who recite it in the way it should be recited,
such people believe in it.
As for those who reject it, they are the losers.
122 *Tribe of Israel! remember the blessing*
I conferred on you,
and that I preferred you over all other beings.
123 *Have fear of a Day when no self*
will be able to compensate for another in any way,
and no ransom will be accepted from it,
and no intercession benefit it,
and they will not be helped.

Those to whom We have given the Book,

Qatāda said that they are the Companions of the Prophet, may Allah bless him and grant him peace, and the Book is the Qur'ān. Ibn Zayd said, "They are those of the tribe of Israel who became Muslim, and so the Book is the Torah." The *āyat* is, in fact, general.

who recite it in the way it should be recited,

There is disagreement about meaning of the *āyat*. It is said that it means they follow the Book as it should be followed by obeying its commands and avoiding its prohibitions, observing the *ḥalāl* and *ḥarām* and in general acting according to what it contains, as ʻIkrima said. ʻIkrima also said, "In the words of Allah Almighty, *'The moon when it follows it,"* (91:2) the word *talā* – which in this *āyat* means recite – means "to follow", and that is what Ibn ʻAbbās and Ibn Masʻūd said. Ibn ʻUmar said that these words of Allah mean, "They follow it as it should be followed."

ʻUmar ibn al-Khaṭṭāb said, "They are those who, when they read an *āyat* of mercy, ask Allah for it, and when they read an *āyat* of punishment, seek refuge from it." This understanding was reported in connection with the Prophet, may Allah bless him and grant him peace. It was said of him that when, in the course of his recitation, he recited an *āyat* of mercy, he asked for it and when he recited an *āyat* of punishment, he sought refuge from it. Al-Ḥasan said, "They are those who know its *āyat*s of judgement, believe in its ambiguous *āyat*s, and entrust what is unclear in them to its Knower." It is said that it means *"they recite it properly"*, but this is unlikely, unless it means they pronounce its phrases slowly and understand its meanings. One understands meanings by following them.

وَإِذِ ابْتَلَىٰ إِبْرَاهِيمَ رَبُّهُ بِكَلِمَاتٍ فَأَتَمَّهُنَّ ۖ قَالَ إِنِّي جَاعِلُكَ
لِلنَّاسِ إِمَامًا ۖ قَالَ وَمِن ذُرِّيَّتِي ۖ قَالَ لَا يَنَالُ عَهْدِي
الظَّالِمِينَ ﴿١٢٤﴾

124 ***Remember when Ibrāhīm was tested by his Lord***
with certain words
which he carried out completely.
He said, 'I will make you a model for mankind.'
He asked, 'And what of my descendants?'
He said, 'My contract does not
include the wrongdoers.'

Remember when Ibrāhīm was tested by his Lord with certain words which he carried out completely.

Since the Ka'ba and *qibla* are shortly going to be mentioned, this section is linked with Ibrāhīm who is the one who built the House. Part of the duty of the Jews, who are the descendants of Ibrāhīm, is not to turn away from his *dīn*. The "testing" referred to was by commands and acts of worship. Ibrāhīm is a Syriac name, meaning "merciful father". The "words" referred to are, in reality, the words of the Creator but they are considered to be the tasks which He imposed on Ibrāhīm. Since the means of their imposition was through words, they are called words, just as 'Īsā is also called a word since He issued from the word "Be!" A thing can be called metaphorically by what it resulted from.

Scholars disagree about what is meant by these "words" (*kalimāt*). One position is that they are the laws of Islam and that they entail thirty qualities. Ten are in *Sūrat at-Tawba*:

> *"Those who make sincere repentance, those who worship, those who praise, those who fast, those who bow, those who prostrate, those who command what is known to be right, those who forbid what is recognised as wrong, those who preserve the limits of Allah: give good news to the believers."* (9:112)

Ten are in *Sūrat al-Aḥzāb*:

> *"Men and women who are Muslims, men and women who are believers, men and women who are obedient, men and women who are truthful men and women who are steadfast, men and women who are humble, men and women who give* sadaqa, *men and women who fast, men and women who guard their private parts, men and women who remember Allah much: Allah has prepared forgiveness for them and an immense reward."* (33:35)

And ten are in *Sūrat al-Mu'minūn*:

> *"It is the believers who are successful: those who are humble in their prayer; those who turn away from worthless talk; those who pay* zakāt; *those who guard their private parts except from their wives, or those they own as slaves, in which case they are not blameworthy; but those who desire anything more than that are people who have gone beyond the limits; those who honour their trusts and their contracts; those who safeguard their prayer."* (23:1-9)

Ibn 'Abbās said, "Allah did not test any person who fulfilled every one of these qualities except for Ibrāhīm. He was tested by Islam and fulfilled it completely. Allah exonerated him and said, *"Ibrāhīm who paid his dues in full."* (53:37) Some said that it means the command and prohibition. Another said that the test was sacrificing his son. Yet another said it means carrying out the Message. The ideas are close to one another. Mujāhid said, "It refers to the words of the Almighty to Ibrāhīm. Ibrāhīm asked, "Will You make me a model for mankind?" "Yes," He said. He said, "And what of my descendants?" He said, "My contract does not include the wrongdoers." He asked, "Will You make the House a place of return for people?" "Yes," He said. He asked, "And a sanctuary?" "Yes," He said. He said, "Will You show us our rites of worship and turn towards us?" "Yes," He said. He asked, "Will You provide its inhabitants with fruits?" "Yes," He said. So according to this position, Allah Almighty is the one who carried out His own words.

Sounder than this is what Ṭāwūs reported that Ibn 'Abbās said about this matter: "Allah tested him by acts of purification: five connected with the head and five with the body. They are, in respect of the head trimming the moustache, rinsing the mouth, snuffing water up the nose, using the *siwāk*, and parting the hair; and in respect of the body they are clipping the nails, shaving the pubes, circumcision, plucking the underarms, and washing the site of faeces and urine with water." According to this position, the one who carried out the words was Ibrāhīm. It is the literal meaning of the Qur'ān.

Qatāda said that they are the practices of the *Ḥajj*. Al-Ḥasan said that they are six things: rejecting first the planets, then the moon, then the sun, being thrown into the fire, emigration and circumcision. Az-Zajjāj said that these reports are not contradictory because all of them are part of what Ibrāhīm was tested with.

We see in the *Muwaṭṭā'* and elsewhere that Sa'īd ibn al-Musayyab was heard to say, "Ibrāhīm was the first to be circumcised, the first to give hospitality, the first to make a mosque, the first to clip his nails, the first to trim the moustache, and the first to have white hair. When he saw the white hair, he asked, 'What is this?' Allah said, 'Gravity.' He said, 'Lord, increase me in gravity.'" Sa'īd ibn Jubayr reported that his father said: "The first to give a *khuṭba* on a minbar was Ibrāhīm, the Friend of Allah." Someone else said that he was the first to make a meat stew, the first to strike with a sword, the first to use *siwāk*, the first to use water in the lavatory and the first to wear trousers." Mu'ādh ibn Jabal reported that the Prophet, may Allah bless him and grant him peace, said, "If I adopt a minbar, my father Ibrāhīm adopted it. If I take a staff, my father Ibrāhīm used it." All these things will be dealt with in their proper place.

Scholars agree that Ibrāhīm was the first to be circumcised. There is disagreement about the age in which the circumcision took place. In the *Muwaṭṭā'* Abū Hurayra is reported as stating that he was 120 and lived for 80 years after that. This is only an opinion. Others relate that it was done at the age of 80 and was carried out with an adze. Scholars disagree about the legal status of circumcision. The majority say that it is a confirmed *sunna* and part of the natural form of Islam which men should not abandon. A group say that it is obligatory. A boy born with no foreskin is spared circumcision.

With regard to clipping the nails, Mālik said, "It is recommended for women to clip their nails and shave their pubes just as it is for men." Trimming the moustache involves cutting it back a little so that the edge of the lip appears but not removing it completely, which constitutes self-mutilation according to Mālik. Ibn 'Abdi'l-Ḥakam reported that he said, "I think that someone who shaves off his moustache should be disciplined." Ashhab said that Mālik said about shaving it, "It is an innovation and I think that the one who does it should be beaten." This was because he viewed it as self-mutilation. Abū Ḥanīfa, Abū Yūsuf and Muḥammad prefer removing a lot of it to trimming it. Ash-Shāfi'ī took the same view.

Regarding white hair the Prophet, may Allah bless him and grant him peace, said, "Do not pluck out white hair. There is no Muslim who has become white-haired in Islam but that it will be a light for him on the Day of Rising and a good deed will be written for him and an error dropped." It is also disliked to dye it black, but permitted to use other colours as is reported in the *ḥadīth*.

He said, 'I will make you a model for mankind.'

The word *imām* here means a model. It is used for a builder's rule and for a road because it directs the traveller. It means: "We will make you an imām for people whom they will imitate in these qualities and the righteous will follow you." So He made him an imām for the people who obey Him. That is why all the nations agree that he was rightly guided, and Allah knows best.

He asked, 'And what of my descendants?'

This is a kind of supplication which consists of asking for information from Allah, meaning, "Lord, will You place this right guidance among my descendants?" This is asking for information, or a simple question. Allah informed him that the disobedient and wrongdoers among them are not entitled to be models.

He said, 'My contract does not include the wrongdoers.'

There is disagreement about what is meant by *'ahd* (contract) here. Ibn 'Abbās said that it refers to Prophethood as did as-Suddī. Mujāhid said it refers to the imāmate; Qatāda that it refers to faith; 'Aṭā' that it refers to mercy; and aḍ-Ḍaḥḥāk that it refers to the *dīn* of Allah. It is said that Allah's contract is His command and that the usage of *'ahd* is found elsewhere in the Qur'ān, as in *"Allah made a contract with us,"* (3:183) meaning "commanded us". Qatāda also said that it means "My contract does not include the wrongdoers in the Next World. As for in this world, it is possible that wrongdoers may obtain it." Sa'īd ibn Jubayr said that wrongdoer here means idolater.

A group of scholars use this *āyat* as evidence that the imām must be one of the people of justice, good and excellence and have the ability to do the job. It is what the Prophet, may Allah bless him and grant him peace, commanded: "Do not dispute power with its people." The people of iniquity, injustice and wrong cannot be considered its people because of this *āyat*. This was the reason for the rebellion of Ibn az-Zubayr and that of al-Ḥusayn, may Allah be pleased with them, and also the rebellion of the virtuous people and scholars of Iraq against al-Ḥajjāj and the rebellion of the people of Madina against the Umayyads at al-Ḥarra.

Most scholars take the view that perseverance in obedience to an unjust ruler is better than rebellion because the consequences of resisting him and rebelling against him, is to replace security with fear, shed blood, give free rein to foolish people, attack the Muslims and corrupt the earth. The other is a position of a group of Mu'tazilites, and the position of the Kharijites.

Ibn Khuwayzimandād said, "No wrongdoer can be a Prophet or khalif or judge or *muftī* or leader of the prayer. If such a thing occurs then what he relates of the *Sharī'a* is not accepted and his testimony is not accepted in judgement, although he is not dismissed for his iniquity until those entitled to appoint and dismiss do so. His judgements which are in accordance with what is correct are carried out. Mālik stated this about the Khārijites and the rebels: their judgements are not declared void when they entail some form of *ijtihād* and do not violate the consensus or oppose texts and this was the consensus of the Companions. That is because the Khārijites rebelled in their time but it is not transmitted that the imāms criticised their judgements or cancelled any of them or repeated their collection of *zakāt* or objected to their carrying out the *ḥudūd* when they had done it. That indicates that when they use proper *ijtihād*, their judgements are not attacked.

Ibn Khuwayzimandād said, "As for taking stipends from unjust leaders, it falls into three categories. If everything in their possession has been gathered according to the just demands of the *Sharī'a*, it is permitted to take it and the Companions and *Tābi'ūn* took it from al-Ḥajjāj and others. If the *ḥalāl* and unjust are mixed, as is the case of amīrs today, it is scrupulous to forgo it, but it is permitted for the needy to take it. In this case the amīr is like a thief who has both stolen property and lawful property in his possession and gives something as charity to someone. The recipient is permitted to accept it as *ṣadaqa.* If, however, everything that is in his possession is clearly unlawful, then it is not permitted to accept his *ṣadaqa*.

وَإِذْ جَعَلْنَا ٱلْبَيْتَ مَثَابَةً لِّلنَّاسِ وَأَمْنًا وَٱتَّخِذُوا۟ مِن مَّقَامِ
إِبْرَٰهِـۧمَ مُصَلًّى ۖ وَعَهِدْنَآ إِلَىٰٓ إِبْرَٰهِـۧمَ وَإِسْمَـٰعِيلَ أَن
طَهِّرَا بَيْتِىَ لِلطَّآئِفِينَ وَٱلْعَـٰكِفِينَ وَٱلرُّكَّعِ ٱلسُّجُودِ ﴿١٢٥﴾

125 ***And when We made the House a place of return,***
a sanctuary for mankind,
and they took the Maqām of Ibrāhīm
as a place of prayer.
We contracted with Ibrāhīm and Ismā'īl:
'Purify My House for those who circle it,
and those who stay there,
and those who bow and who prostrate.'

And when We made the House a place of return, a sanctuary for mankind,

The House is the Ka'ba. "*Mathāba*" (place of return) is the form of the noun used for a place, derived from the verb *thāba*, "to return". It is called that because people return to it year after year. The use of the word "sanctuary" in this *āyat* was taken by Abū Ḥanīfa and a group of *fuqahā'* as evidence for not imposing the *ḥadd* in the Ḥaram when an adulterer or thief takes refuge there. In making that ruling they also rely on the words of Allah, *"All who enter it are safe."* (3:97) The sound position is that the *ḥudūd* are carried out in the Ḥaram and that this *āyat* is abrogated although there is agreement that the killing does not take place in the House but outside of it. The disagreement is about killing in the Ḥaram. If someone violates a *ḥadd* there, he is punished there. If someone attacks in it, he is fought and killed where he is. Abū Ḥanifa says that the one who seeks refuge in the Ḥaram is not killed or pursued and remains confined in it until he dies or leaves. We kill him with the sword and Allah kills him by hunger and constriction, thus condemning him to a worse death. The fact that it is a sanctuary reinforces the command to face the Ka'ba in the prayer because Jerusalem does not have this virtue and people do not make *ḥajj* to it.

and they took the Maqām of Ibrāhīm as a place of prayer.'

There are two readings of the verb "to take" in this phrase. Nāfi' has *ittakhadhū* rather than *ittakhidhū*, making it a report about those of the followers of Ibrāhīm who prayed there, so it reads: *"they took the Maqām of Ibrāhīm as a place of prayer."* The second reading is in the imperative mood so the meaning is a command and the phrase reads: "Take the Maqām of Ibrāhīm as a place of prayer." According to the first, there is one sentence, and according to the second, there are two sentences. The majority read it with a *kasra* as a command and disconnect it from the first sentence.

Ibn 'Umar reported that 'Umar said, "I coincided with my Lord on three occasions: regarding the Maqām of Ibrāhīm, the *ḥijāb* and the captives of Badr." (Muslim) A similar report comes from al-Bukhārī. He suggested praying behind the Maqām and then this was revealed.

The word *maqām* means a place where you stand. There are various statements about the Maqām. The soundest is that it is the stone which people recognise today and behind which they pray the two *rak'at*s after completing the *Ṭawāf* of Arrival. This is the position of Jābir ibn 'Abdullāh, Ibn 'Abbās, Qatāda and others. In the *Ṣaḥīḥ* of Muslim, in a long *ḥadīth*, Jābir said, "When the Prophet, may Allah bless him and grant him peace, saw the House, he greeted the Corner and then trotted three circuits and walked four. Then he went to the Maqām Ibrāhīm and recited, *'they took the Maqām of Ibrāhīm as a place of prayer.'* and prayed two *rak'ats* in which he recited *Sūrat al-Ikhlāṣ* and *Sūrat al-Kāfirūn*." In al-Bukhārī it states that it is the stone which Ibrāhīm climbed on when he was too weak to lift up the stones which Ismā'īl handed him when they were building the House and his feet sank into it. Anas said, "In the Maqām I saw the trace of his fingers and heels and the hollows of his feet. But that disappeared when people continue to wipe it with their hands." As-Suddī said, "The Maqām is the stone which Ismā'īl's wife placed under Ibrāhīm's feet when she washed his head."

The sound position is the first statement about the Maqām since it is confirmed in the *Ṣaḥīḥ*. Jābir reported, "The Prophet, may Allah bless him and grant him peace, looked at a man between the corner and the Maqām – or the door and the Maqām – making supplication. He was saying, 'O Allah, forgive so-and-so.' The Prophet, may Allah bless him and grant him peace, asked him, 'What is this?' He said, 'A man charged me to supplicate for him in this Maqām.' He said, 'Return. Your companion is forgiven.'"

We contracted with Ibrāhīm and Ismā'īl: Purify My House

"We contracted" (*'ahidnā*) here means "We commanded" or "We revealed to." The Kufans say that "purify" means to clear it of idols, as Mujāhid and az-Zuhrī said. 'Ubayd ibn 'Umayr and Sa'īd ibn Jubayr said that it means to purify it of evil things and doubt. It is said that it means from unbelievers. As-Suddī said, "They built it and founded it on purity and with the intention of purity and so it is like the words of the Almighty, *'Founded on taqwā.'* (9:108) By saying 'My House' Allah ascribes it to Himself to honour it. It is like the connection of a creature to the Creator and a slave to the Master."

When Allah says, *"Purify My House"* He means all mosques, and so its ruling is that of cleanliness and purification. The Ka'ba is mentioned because it was the only mosque at that time or because it is the most respected House. The first view is more likely, and Allah knows best. We read in the Revelation, *"In houses which Allah has permitted to be built."* (24:36)

for those who circle it,

The word used here is *ṭā'ifīn* and its apparent meaning is to circumambulate it, as 'Aṭā' says. Sa'īd ibn Jubayr says that it means "strangers who come to Makka".

and those who stay there,

This is also said to mean those who live in its vicinity, or even, as Ibn 'Abbās states, those who pray there. It is said that it means those who sit there without doing *ṭawāf*.

and those who bow and who prostrate.'

Bowing and prostrating refer to praying towards the Ka'ba in the Ḥaram. These two things are mentioned because they are the states in which the one who prays is closest to Allah.

Ash-Shāfi'ī, Abū Ḥanīfa, ath-Thawrī and a group of the Salaf used this *āyat* as evidence for the permission to pray both the *farḍ* and *nāfila* prayers inside the House. Ash-Shāfi'ī said, that if you pray inside it and face one of its walls, then your prayer is allowed. If you pray towards the open door, your prayer is invalid. That also applies to someone who prays on top of it because he does not face anything. Mālik said, "You may not pray a *farḍ* or *sunna* prayer in it, but you may pray *nāfila* prayers. If someone prays the *farḍ* there, he must repeat it if it is still within the time of that prayer. Aṣbagh said he must always repeat it, even outside the time.

This is sound according to what Muslim related from Ibn 'Abbās. He said, "Usāma ibn Zayd told me that when the Prophet, may Allah bless him and grant him peace, entered the House, he made supplication in all its corners and did not pray in it until he had come out. When he came out, he prayed two *rak'ats* facing the Ka'ba and said, 'This is the *qibla*.'" Abū Ḥanīfa says that the one who prays in it does not owe anything.

They also disagree about which is better: praying at the House or *ṭawāf* of it. Mālik said that *ṭawāf* is better for the people of other places and that prayer is better for the people of Makka. That is mentioned from Ibn 'Abbās, 'Aṭā' and Mujāhid. The majority say that the prayer is better. Allah knows best.

وَإِذْ قَالَ إِبْرَٰهِيمُ رَبِّ ٱجْعَلْ هَٰذَا بَلَدًا ءَامِنًا وَٱرْزُقْ أَهْلَهُۥ مِنَ ٱلثَّمَرَٰتِ مَنْ ءَامَنَ مِنْهُم بِٱللَّهِ وَٱلْيَوْمِ ٱلْءَاخِرِ ۖ قَالَ وَمَن كَفَرَ فَأُمَتِّعُهُۥ قَلِيلًا ثُمَّ أَضْطَرُّهُۥٓ إِلَىٰ عَذَابِ ٱلنَّارِ ۖ وَبِئْسَ ٱلْمَصِيرُ ﴿١٢٦﴾

126 ***And when Ibrāhīm said, 'My Lord,***
make this a place of safety
and provide its inhabitants with fruits –
all of them who believe
in Allah and the Last Day,'
He said, 'I will let anyone who
becomes an unbeliever enjoy himself a little
but then I will drive him
to the punishment of the Fire.
What an evil destination!'

And when Ibrāhīm said, 'My Lord, make this a place of safety and provide its inhabitants with fruits –

This means Makka. He prayed for his descendants and others to have security and ample livelihood there. It is related that when he made this supplication, Allah commanded Jibrīl to uproot the town of Ṭā'if from Syria and he then carried it around the Ka'ba for a week, which is why it is called Ṭā'if. Then he set it down in Tihāma. Makka and what was around it was a desert without water or plants. Allah blessed the area around it like Ṭā'if and other places and plants grew.

Scholars disagree about whether Makka became a Ḥaram by Ibrāhīm's supplication or whether it was one before that. One view is that it has always been a Ḥaram, protected from tyrants, earthquakes and other such things which happen to lands. Rebellious people feel respect for it so that its people alone enjoy security. In it Allah has placed the great symbol of His Unity. Its special status is shown by game which go into it. Dogs and game meet in it and the dogs do not attack the game. But, when the game leave the Ḥaram, the dogs run after them. Ibrāhīm asked his Lord to protect it from drought, famine and attacks and to provide its people with fruits. He did not refer to shedding blood in it. That was not what he intended.

The second view is that it was not a Ḥaram before the prayer of Ibrāhīm and was like any other place and that it only became a Ḥaram when he made his supplication, as Madina became one when the Messenger of Allah, may Allah bless him and grant him peace, made it one. The people of the first position use as evidence the *ḥadīth* of Ibn 'Abbās in which the Messenger of Allah, may Allah bless him and grant him peace, said, on the Day of the Conquest, "This city was made a Ḥaram the day when Allah created the heavens and the earth and so will remain sacred by Allah's making it sacred until the Day of Rising. It was not lawful for anyone to fight in it before me and it was only lawful for me for one hour of one day. It will remain sacred because Allah has made it so until the Day of Rising. Its thorns should not be cut, its game should not be hunted and something dropped should not be picked up except by someone who announces that he has found it."

In the *Ṣaḥīḥ* of Muslim, 'Abdullāh ibn Zayd reported that the Messenger of Allah, may Allah bless him and grant him peace, said, "Ibrāhīm made Makka a Ḥaram and prayed for its people. I made Madina a Ḥaram as Ibrāhīm made Makka a Ḥaram and I prayed for its *ṣā'* and *mudd* in the same way that Ibrāhīm prayed for the people of Makka." Ibn 'Aṭiyya said that the two *ḥadīth*s are not contradictory because the first one reports about the prior knowledge and decree of Allah for it and that it was sacred in the time of Ādam and the time when those with belief lived there. The second reported about Ibrāhīm renewing its inviolability after it had fallen away.

He said, 'I will let anyone who becomes an unbeliever enjoy himself a little ...

Scholars disagree about whether this statement is made by Ibrāhīm or Allah. Ubayy ibn Ka'b, Ibn Isḥāq and others said, "That is from Allah Almighty". Six readings have *"umatti'uhu"* ("I will let enjoy") while Ibn 'Āmir has *"numatti'uhu"* ("We will let enjoy") as well as "We will drive him". Ibn 'Abbās, Mujāhid and Qatāda said that the statement was made by Ibrāhīm. They read it as "*amti'hu*" with the imperative, and so it is a supplication made by Ibrāhīm against them: "Let him enjoy..."

وَإِذْ يَرْفَعُ إِبْرَٰهِيمُ ٱلْقَوَاعِدَ مِنَ ٱلْبَيْتِ وَإِسْمَٰعِيلُ رَبَّنَا تَقَبَّلْ
مِنَّآ إِنَّكَ أَنتَ ٱلسَّمِيعُ ٱلْعَلِيمُ ﴿١٢٧﴾

127 ***And when Ibrāhīm laid***
the foundations of the House with Ismā'īl:
'Our Lord, accept this from us!
You are the All-Hearing, the All-Knowing.

The word "*qawā'id*" (foundations) mentioned here is the subject of some discussion. Abū 'Ubayda and al-Farrā' say it means foundations but al-Kisā'ī says it means walls. Its usual meaning, however, is foundations. In a report we find: "When the House was demolished, huge stones from it were brought, and Ibn Az-Zubayr said, 'These are the foundations which Ibrāhīm laid.'" It is said that the foundations had been demolished and Allah informed Ibrāhīm about them. Ibn 'Abbās said, "The House was set on foundations which existed a thousand years before this world was created."

People disagree about who first built the House and its foundations. It is said that it was the angels. 'Aṭā' and Ibn al-Musayyab reported that Allah revealed to Ādam, "When you go down to the earth, build me a House. Then go around it as you saw the angels going around My Throne in heaven." 'Aṭā' said, "People claim that it was built from five mountains: Ḥirā', Sinai, Lebanon, al-Jūdī and Mt. Zaytā." Many more things are said about its origins.

The name Ismā'īl in Syriac means "Listen, O God!"

رَبَّنَا وَاجْعَلْنَا مُسْلِمَيْنِ لَكَ وَمِن ذُرِّيَّتِنَا أُمَّةً مُّسْلِمَةً لَّكَ وَأَرِنَا مَنَاسِكَنَا وَتُبْ عَلَيْنَا إِنَّكَ أَنتَ التَّوَّابُ الرَّحِيمُ ﴿١٢٨﴾

128 ***Our Lord, make us both Muslims submitted to You,***
and our descendants a Muslim community
submitted to You.
Show us our rites of worship and turn towards Us.
You are the Ever-Returning, the Most Merciful.

Our Lord, make us both Muslims submitted to You,

"Muslims" here means both in terms of faith and in terms of action, as Allah says, *"The dīn with Allah is Islam."* (3:19). Those who say that Islam and faith are one and the same use this as evidence.

and our descendants a Muslim community submitted to You.

It is said that every Prophet only prayed for himself and his own community, except for Ibrāhīm who also prayed for this community. The word "*umma*" (community) means a social grouping. It can refer to a single person since he is imitated in good, as Allah says, *"Ibrāhīm was a community in himself, obedient to Allah"*

(16:120), and it can also be used in other contexts to mean religion, time, or stature or the face.

Show us our rites of worship

The linguistic root of the word *manāsik* (rites of worship) is *nusk* and means "washing". In the Sharī'a it is the term used for an act of worship. Scholars disagree about what rites are meant here. It is said that it means the practices and waymarks of *ḥajj* as Qatāda and as-Suddī said. Mujāhid, 'Aṭā' and Ibn Jurayj held the view that it refers to sacrificing. It is also said to mean all the acts of worship by which Allah is worshipped. *Nāsik* means a worshipper.

It is said that, when Ibrāhīm finished building the House, Allah sent Jibrīl to him and he performed the *ḥajj* for him. After 'Arafa on the Day of Sacrifice, Iblīs appeared and Jibrīl ordered Ibrāhīm to stone him. So Ibrāhīm threw seven pebbles at him, and this happened for the next two days. Then Ibrāhīm went out to Thabīr and called out, "Slaves of Allah, answer!" and his call was heard.

Mujāhid said that it refers to Ṣafā and Marwa, which are the "waymarks of Allah" mentioned in the text of the Qur'ān.

and turn towards Us.

There is disagreement about what this means since both Ibrāhīm and Ismā'īl were Prophets protected from wrong action. A group say that they were asking for constancy and continuance, not for forgiveness from wrong actions. This is good but even better than that is the interpretation which maintains that, when they had learned the practices and built the House, they wanted to make that clear to people and acquaint them with the rites they had to perform and inform them that this place of standing and those places are places for intercession for wrong actions and seeking repentance. It is said that it means: "Turn towards the wrongdoers among our community."

رَبَّنَا وَابْعَثْ فِيهِمْ رَسُولًا مِّنْهُمْ يَتْلُوا عَلَيْهِمْ آيَاتِكَ
وَيُعَلِّمُهُمُ الْكِتَابَ وَالْحِكْمَةَ وَيُزَكِّيهِمْ ۚ إِنَّكَ أَنتَ
الْعَزِيزُ الْحَكِيمُ ﴿١٢٩﴾

129 *Our Lord, raise up among them a Messenger*
from them to recite Your Signs to them
and teach them the Book and Wisdom
and purify them.
You are the Almighty, the All-Wise.'

Our Lord, raise up among them a Messenger from them.

It is related that a group of the Companions of the Prophet, may Allah bless him and grant him peace, said, "Messenger of Allah, tell us about yourself." The Prophet, peace be upon him, replied, "Indeed, I am the supplication of my father Ibrāhīm and the good news of 'Īsā."

The word "*rasūl*" (Messenger) means someone who is sent and comes from the verb *arsala* meaning to send out.

and teach them the Book and Wisdom

The "Book" is the Qur'an and the "Wisdom" (*ḥikma*) is recognition and acceptance of the *dīn,* grasping its interpretation and understanding it, which is by an innate faculty and light from Allah. Mālik stated that, and Ibn Wahb related it from him. Qatāda said that the "Wisdom" is the *Sunna* and clarification of the laws of the *Sharī'a*. It is said that it refers to the judgements and rulings derived from it. The meanings are close. Teaching is ascribed to the Prophet since he gives the commands which are followed and taught us how to look at the Revelation Allah gave him. It is said that the "Book" means the meaning of the words and the "Wisdom" refers to the judgements derived from it. Allah means the unrestricted and restricted, detailed and general, ambivalent and specific.

and purify them

from the filth of idolatry, as Ibn Jurayj and others said.

You are the Almighty, the All-Wise.'

The Almighty (*al-'Azīz*) is the One whom no one can reach or overpower. Ibn Kaysān said that it means the One whose power extends to everything as evinced by Allah's words: *"Allah cannot be withstood in any way, either in the heavens or on earth."* (35:44) It is also said that it means the One who has nothing like Him, the Incomparable.

وَمَن يَرْغَبُ عَن مِّلَّةِ إِبْرَٰهِـۧمَ إِلَّا مَن سَفِهَ نَفْسَهُۥ ۚ وَلَقَدِ
ٱصْطَفَيْنَٰهُ فِى ٱلدُّنْيَا ۖ وَإِنَّهُۥ فِى ٱلْـَٔاخِرَةِ لَمِنَ ٱلصَّـٰلِحِينَ ﴿١٣٠﴾

130 ***Who would deliberately renounce***
the religion of Ibrāhīm
except someone who reveals himself to be a fool?
We chose him in this world
and in the Next World
he will be one of the people of right action.

Who would deliberately renounce the religion of Ibrāhīm except someone who reveals himself to be a fool?

This question is in fact a rebuke, and a negative answer to it is implied such as: "No one would." It is also an expression which tends to distance the reader from doing such a thing. *Milla* means religion and *dīn*. The "someone who reveals himself to be a fool" is said by Qatāda to be the Jews and Christians who renounced the religion of Ibrāhīm and adopted Judaism and Christianity which were innovations which did not come from Allah. "*Safiha*" (to be a fool) means "to be ignorant of a matter because of not thinking about it". Abu 'Ubayda says that it means "destroys himself". Ibn Baḥr says, "It means that it refers to someone having no self-knowledge and no grasp of the evidence and proofs within himself which indicate that he has an incomparable Creator and thus failing to recognise Allah's unity and power."

This *āyat* is used as evidence by those who say that the *Sharī'a* of Ibrāhīm is the same as our *Sharī'a* except for those aspects of it which have been abrogated.

We chose him in this world

This means: "We chose him to bear Our Message and purified him." The word "*iṣtafā*" (chose) is derived from *ṣafwa* which means to be pure and to choose the best.

and in the Next World he will be one of the people of right action.

The "people of right action" in the Next World are those who are successful and will enter the Garden.

إِذْ قَالَ لَهُۥ رَبُّهُۥٓ أَسْلِمْ قَالَ أَسْلَمْتُ لِرَبِّ ٱلْعَٰلَمِينَ ﴿١٣١﴾

131 ***When his Lord said to him, 'Become a Muslim!' he said, 'I am a Muslim who has submitted to the Lord of all the worlds.'***

This *āyat* is connected to the previous one and the implication is, "We chose him when his Lord said to him, 'Become a Muslim and submit.'" This was said by Allah to Ibrāhīm after He had tested him with the stars, the moon and the sun (cf. 6:76-84). Ibn Kaysān and al-Kalbī said it means: "Make your *dīn* sincere for Allah with *tawḥīd.*" It is said that it means: "Be humble and submitted." Ibn 'Abbās said, "Allah said that to him when he left the way of his people." Islam here entails all its various aspects. In Arabic the word "Islam" implies submission and obedience to the one submitted to. Not everyone's Islam entails faith but everyone's faith entails Islam because whoever believes in Allah necessarily submits to and obeys Allah. Not everyone who submits to Allah believes in Him because his submission may be because of fear of the sword and that is not faith. The Qadariyya and Khārijites hold a contrary view saying that Islam is synonymous with faith and that every Muslim is a believer and every believer a Muslim. Success is by Allah.

وَأَوْصَىٰ بِهَآ إِبْرَٰهِـۧمُ بَنِيهِ وَيَعْقُوبُ يَـٰبَنِىَّ إِنَّ ٱللَّهَ
ٱصْطَفَىٰ لَكُمُ ٱلدِّينَ فَلَا تَمُوتُنَّ إِلَّا وَأَنتُم مُّسْلِمُونَ ١٣٢

132 ***Ibrāhīm directed his sons to this, as did Ya'qūb: 'My sons! Allah has chosen this deen for you, so do not die except as Muslims.'***

Ibrāhīm directed his sons to this, as did Ya'qūb:

This may refer to "the religion" or to the words, "I submit to the Lord of the worlds." The latter view is more correct because it was the last thing mentioned. Some readings have *waṣṣā* for "directed" whereas the people of Madina and Syria read *awṣā.*

Ibrāhīm had two sons: Ismā'īl and Isḥāq. The elder was Ismā'īl and his mother was Hājar the Copt. There are three positions regarding the age of Ismā'īl at the time Ibrāhīm took him to Makka: as a baby, as a two year old infant or as a fourteen year old youth. The first is considered the soundest. He was born fourteen years before his brother Isḥāq and died when he was one hundred and thirty-seven or one hundred and thirty years old. He was eighty years old when Ibrāhīm died. According to one statement, he was the son Ibrāhīm was commanded to sacrifice. Isḥāq's mother was Sārah, and he was the sacrifice according to another statement, which seems sounder. We will deal with this when we examine the story in *Sūrat aṣ-Ṣāffāt* (37:102-109). Isḥāq lived to the age of one hundred and eighty and died in the Holy Land. He was buried with his father Ibrāhīm. When Sārah died, Ibrāhīm married Qanṭūrā (Keturah) bint Yaqṭan the Canaanite and she bore him several children. He died about 2600 years before the birth of the Prophet, may Allah bless him and grant him peace.

Ya'qūb gave the same directive to his other sons. Al-Kalbī said, "When Ya'qūb looked at the people in Egypt, he saw them worshipping idols, fire and cows, so he collected his sons and alerted them, asking, "What will you worship after me?"

so do not die except as Muslims.

This means: Cling to Islam and persevere in it and do not part from it until you die. This contains an admonition and a reminder of death. That is because everyone knows that they will die but they do not know when.

أَمْ كُنتُمْ شُهَدَآءَ إِذْ حَضَرَ يَعْقُوبَ ٱلْمَوْتُ إِذْ قَالَ لِبَنِيهِ مَا
تَعْبُدُونَ مِنۢ بَعْدِى قَالُوا۟ نَعْبُدُ إِلَٰهَكَ وَإِلَٰهَ ءَابَآئِكَ
إِبْرَٰهِۦمَ وَإِسْمَٰعِيلَ وَإِسْحَٰقَ إِلَٰهًا وَٰحِدًا وَنَحْنُ لَهُۥ مُسْلِمُونَ ﴿١٣٣﴾

133 *Or were you present when death came to Ya'qūb*
and he said to his sons,
'What will you worship when I have gone?'
They said, 'We will worship your God,
the God of your forefathers,
Ibrāhīm, Ismā'īl and Isḥāq –
one God.
We are Muslims submitted to Him.'

This is addressed to the Jews and Christians who, by following Judaism and Christianity, falsely attribute to Ibrāhīm something for which he gave no authority. Allah refuted their words and rebuked them here. He says that they are forging lies. Ismā'īl is included because the uncle is counted with the father.

تِلْكَ أُمَّةٌ قَدْ خَلَتْ لَهَا مَا كَسَبَتْ وَلَكُم مَّا كَسَبْتُمْ
وَلَا تُسْـَٔلُونَ عَمَّا كَانُوا۟ يَعْمَلُونَ ﴿١٣٤﴾

134 ***That was a community***
which has long since passed away.
It has what it earned.
You have what you have earned.
You will not be questioned about what they did.

This *āyat* indicates that a person's actions and earnings are ascribed to him, even though it is Allah who gives him the power to do what he does. If it is good, it is by Allah's favour. If it is evil, it is by His justice. This is the school of the People of the *Sunna*. There are many *āyat*s in the Qur'ān which express this. A person earns his actions since the power connected to the action was created for him and there is a clear difference between a movement he makes by his own choice and, for instance, an involuntary movement such as a shiver. That capacity is the core of accountability. The Jabrites negate any possibility of personal responsibility and say that people are like plants which move whichever way the wind blows. The Qadarites and Mu'tazilites take the opposite position that a person creates his own actions.

وَقَالُوا۟ كُونُوا۟ هُودًا أَوْ نَصَـٰرَىٰ تَهْتَدُوا۟ ۗ قُلْ بَلْ مِلَّةَ إِبْرَٰهِـۧمَ
حَنِيفًا ۖ وَمَا كَانَ مِنَ ٱلْمُشْرِكِينَ ﴿١٣٥﴾

135 ***They say, 'Be Jews or Christians***
and you will be guided.'
Say, 'Rather adopt the religion of Ibrāhīm,
a man of natural pure belief.
He was not one of the idolaters.'

Each group claims that what it has is the real truth but Allah refuted that. The *āyat* means: "Say, O Muḥammad, 'We follow the true religion.'" This is why the word "*milla*" (religion) is in the accusative case. "A man of natural pure belief" (*ḥanīf*) is one who inclines from disliked religions to the truth, which is the *dīn* of Ibrāhīm. It means that he went straight.

قُولُوٓا۟ ءَامَنَّا بِٱللَّهِ وَمَآ أُنزِلَ إِلَيْنَا وَمَآ أُنزِلَ إِلَىٰٓ إِبْرَٰهِـۧمَ
وَإِسْمَٰعِيلَ وَإِسْحَٰقَ وَيَعْقُوبَ وَٱلْأَسْبَاطِ وَمَآ أُوتِىَ
مُوسَىٰ وَعِيسَىٰ وَمَآ أُوتِىَ ٱلنَّبِيُّونَ مِن رَّبِّهِمْ لَا نُفَرِّقُ بَيْنَ
أَحَدٍ مِّنْهُمْ وَنَحْنُ لَهُۥ مُسْلِمُونَ ﴿١٣٦﴾

136 ***Say, 'We believe in Allah***
and what has been sent down to us
and what was sent down to Ibrāhīim
and Ismā'īl and Isḥāq
and Ya'qūb and the Tribes,
and what Mūsā and 'Īsā were given,
and what all the Prophets were given by their Lord.
We do not differentiate between any of them.
We are Muslims submitted to Him.'

Al-Bukhārī transmitted that Abū Hurayra said, "The People of the Book used to recite the Torah in Hebrew and explain it in Arabic to the people of Islam. The Messenger of Allah, may Allah bless him and grant him peace, said, "Neither believe or deny the People of the Book. Say, 'We believe in Allah and what has been revealed.'" Muḥammad ibn Sīrīn said, "When you are asked, 'Are you a believer?' recite this *āyat*." Many of the *Salaf* disliked anyone saying, "I am truly a believer." The reason for that will be explained in *Sūrat al-Anfāl*, Allah willing. Ibn 'Abbās said, "A group of Jews came to the Prophet, may Allah bless him and grant him peace, and asked him about which of the Prophets he believed in and this *āyat* was revealed. When he mentioned 'Īsā, they said, 'We do not believe in 'Īsā or in anyone who does believe in him.'"

and the Tribes,

"Asbāṭ" (the Tribes) are from the twelve sons of Ya'qūb. A nation sprang from each of them. They are called *asbāṭ*, which comes from *sabṭ*, which means succession, and so it was as if they followed one another. It is also said that the word is derived from *sabaṭ*, which means a tree. Ibn 'Abbās said, "All the Prophets were from the tribe of Israel except for ten: Nūḥ, Shu'ayb, Hūd, Ṣāliḥ, Lūṭ, Ibrāhīm, Isḥāq, Ya'qūb, Ismā'īl and Muḥammad. None of them had two names except for 'Īsā and Ya'qūb. *Sibṭ* denotes a group or tribe who come from a single ancestor.

We do not differentiate between any of them

This means "We do not believe in some and reject others like the Jews and Christians do."

فَإِنْ ءَامَنُوا۟ بِمِثْلِ مَآ ءَامَنتُم بِهِۦ فَقَدِ ٱهْتَدَوا۟ ۖ وَّإِن تَوَلَّوْا۟
فَإِنَّمَا هُمْ فِى شِقَاقٍ ۖ فَسَيَكْفِيكَهُمُ ٱللَّهُ ۚ
وَهُوَ ٱلسَّمِيعُ ٱلْعَلِيمُ ﴿١٣٧﴾

137 ***If their faith is the same as yours***
then they are guided.
But if they turn away,
they are entrenched in hostility.
Allah will be enough for you against them.
He is the All-Hearing, the All-Knowing.

If their faith is the same as yours then they are guided.

This is addressed to Muḥammad and his community. It means that if they believe as you believe and affirm what you affirm, they are guided. So similarity can occur between two faiths. It is also said to mean that if they believe in your Prophet and all the Prophets without differentiating between them, then they are guided.

But if they turn away, they are entrenched in hostility.

Zayd ibn Aslam said that the expression "entrenched in hostility" (*fī shiqāq*) means "in contention". It is said to be quarrelling, opposition and hostility. It is derived from *shaqq,* which is the side of a chasm, so it is as if each was one of two sides. It is said that it is derived from a verb meaning to be difficult and hard and so it is as if it means that each side wants to make things difficult for the other side.

Allah will be enough for you against them.

Allah will protect His Messenger against his enemies. This is a promise from Allah to His Prophet, may Allah bless him and grant him peace, that He would protect him from those who were hostile to him and opposed him. He carried out that promise. That was when the Banū Qaynuqā' and the Banū Qurayẓa were killed and Banū'n-Naḍīr were expelled. It was this *āyat* on which 'Uthmān's blood spilled when he was murdered.

صِبْغَةَ ٱللَّهِ ۖ وَمَنْ أَحْسَنُ مِنَ ٱللَّهِ صِبْغَةً ۖ وَنَحْنُ لَهُۥ عَٰبِدُونَ ١٣٨

138 ***The dye of Allah –***
and what dye could be better than Allah's?
It is Him we worship.

Al-Akhfash said that "the dye of Allah" is the *dīn* of Allah and is an appositive for "*milla*", and so it implies: "Follow it". Qatāda said, "The Jews used to baptise their sons as Jews and the

Christians baptised their sons as Christians. The baptism of Allah is Islam. Mujāhid said that it is the natural form on which people are created. Az-Zajjāj says, "This statement of Mujāhid refers to Islam because the natural form ever since the beginning of creation has been Islam." Mujāhid, al-Ḥasan, Abū'l-'Āliyya and Qatāda said that the "dye" is the *dīn*. This also derives from immersion in water. Ibn 'Abbās said that Christians baptised their children when they were seven days old to replace circumcision, which is purification. When they do this, they say, "Now he is truly a Christian." Allah refuted them by saying that the dye of Islam is better. It is Islam. Calling the *dīn* this is a metaphor since the effect of its actions can be seen in a person in the same way that dye can be seen in a garment. It is said that it refers to the *ghusl* taken by someone who wants to become Muslim which replaces Christian baptism.

Because one meaning of "dye of Allah" is the "washing (*ghusl*) of Allah" it is said that washing when you become Muslim is an obligatory practice. The evidence for this in the *Sunna* is from Qays ibn 'Āṣim and Thumāma ibn Athāl who both had a *ghusl* when they became Muslims.

قُلْ أَتُحَآجُّونَنَا فِى ٱللَّهِ وَهُوَ رَبُّنَا وَرَبُّكُمْ وَلَنَآ أَعْمَٰلُنَا
وَلَكُمْ أَعْمَٰلُكُمْ وَنَحْنُ لَهُۥ مُخْلِصُونَ ﴿١٣٩﴾

139 ***Say, 'Do you argue with us about Allah***
when He is our Lord and your Lord?
We have our actions and you have your actions.
We act for Him alone.'

Al-Ḥasan said, "Their argument is that they say, *'We are more entitled to Allah than you because we are the sons of Allah and those He loves.'*" (cf. 5:18) It is said that it was because of "our ancestors and books and because we did not worship idols." So the meaning of the *āyat* is: "Ask them, Muḥammad," meaning those Jews and Christians who claim that they are the sons of Allah and those He loves and claim that they are more entitled to Allah than you because of their ancestors and Books, "Where is your argument when the Lord is One and everyone will be repaid for his actions? What advantage will precedence in the *dīn* give you?"

We act for Him alone.'

"We are sincere in our worship." This contains a sense of rebuke, implying, "You are not sincere so how can you claim that you are more entitled?" The reality of sincerity (*ikhlāṣ*) is to purify the action in question from taking any account of creatures. The Prophet, may Allah bless him and grant him peace, said, "Allah Almighty says, 'I am the best associate. Anyone who associates a partner with Me, belongs to his associates. O people, make your actions sincere for Allah Almighty. Allah Almighty does not accept other than what is done sincerely for Him alone. Do not say, 'This is for Allah and my relatives.' If it is for your relatives, none of it is for Allah. Do not say, 'This is for Allah and your sakes.' Then it is for your sakes and none of it is for Allah." Aḍ-Ḍaḥḥāk related it and ad-Dāraquṭnī transmitted it.

Ruwaym said, "Sincerity in action is that the person who does something does not want any recompense or return for it in either this world or the Next." Al-Junayd said, "Sincerity is a secret between Allah and the slave. An angel cannot know it so as to record it, nor can a shayṭān corrupt it, nor can passion incline to it." Al-Qushayrī reported that the Prophet, may Allah bless him and grant him peace, said, "I asked Jibrīl about sincerity and what it was. He replied, 'I asked the Lord of Might about what sincerity was and He said, "A secret of Mine which I entrust in the heart of those I love among My slaves."'"

أَمْ يَقُولُونَ إِنَّ إِبْرَٰهِيمَ وَإِسْمَٰعِيلَ وَإِسْحَٰقَ
وَيَعْقُوبَ وَالْأَسْبَاطَ كَانُواْ هُودًا أَوْ نَصَٰرَىٰ قُلْ
ءَآنتُمْ أَعْلَمُ أَمِ اللَّهُ وَمَنْ أَظْلَمُ مِمَّن كَتَمَ شَهَٰدَةً
عِندَهُۥ مِنَ اللَّهِ وَمَا اللَّهُ بِغَٰفِلٍ عَمَّا تَعْمَلُونَ ١٤٠

140 ***Or do they say that Ibrāhīm and Ismā'īl and Isḥāq***
and Ya'qūb and the Tribes were Jews or Christians?
Say, 'Do you know better or does Allah?'
Who could do greater wrong
than someone who hides
the evidence he has been given by Allah?
Allah is not unaware of what you do.

Or do they say that Ibrāhīm and Ismā'īl and Isḥāq and Ya'qūb and the Tribes were Jews or Christians?

Imām Warsh has *"do they say?"* while Ḥafṣ has *"do you say?"* This is, in either case, a rebuke to the claims of both the Jews and the Christians.

Who could do greater wrong than someone who hides the evidence he has been given by Allah?

The word "evidence" (*shahāda*) here refers to the actions they have been commanded to do since the *dīn* of all the Prophets was Islam. It is also said to refer to their concealment of the description of Muḥammad, may Allah bless him and grant him peace, in their Revealed Books, as Qatāda said, but the first explanation is more in keeping with the context.

Allah is not unaware of what you do.

This is a threat that they will not be spared and will have to pay for what they did. A heedless or unaware person (*ghāfil*) is someone who does not grasp things because he ignores them. It is derived from earth which is *ghufl*, which means there is no sign or trace of habitation on it. A camel which is *ghufl* has no markings. A man who is *ghufl* has no experience of matters.

تِلْكَ أُمَّةٌ قَدْ خَلَتْ لَهَا مَا كَسَبَتْ وَلَكُم مَّا كَسَبْتُمْ
وَلَا تُسْـَٔلُونَ عَمَّا كَانُوا يَعْمَلُونَ ١٤١

141 ***That was a community***
which has long since passed away.
It has what it earned.
You have what you have earned.
You will not be questioned about what they did.

This is repeated (cf. 2:134 above) because it contains a threat. Since the Prophets, in spite of their excellence and imamate, will be repaid for their actions, how much more will that be the case with you!

سَيَقُولُ السُّفَهَاءُ مِنَ النَّاسِ مَا وَلَّاهُمْ عَن قِبْلَتِهِمُ الَّتِي كَانُوا
عَلَيْهَا قُل لِّلَّهِ الْمَشْرِقُ وَالْمَغْرِبُ يَهْدِي مَن يَشَاءُ إِلَى صِرَاطٍ
مُّسْتَقِيمٍ ١٤٢

142 ***The fools among the people will ask,***
'What has made them turn round
from the direction they used to face?'
Say, 'Both East and West belong to Allah.
He guides whoever He wills to a straight path.'

The fools among the people will ask,

Allah Almighty is giving advance warning of what some people are going to say about the believers changing the direction they face in prayer from Syria to the Ka'ba. The word "fools" is qualified by "people" because foolishness is also found in animals. The fools are those who say this. A fool is someone with a shallow intellect. A garment which is *safīh*, the root from which the word comes, is loosely woven. Quṭrub says that they are ignorant wrongdoers. What is meant are the Jews in Madina, as Mujāhid says. As-Suddī said that it refers to the hypocrites and az-Zajjāj says that it means the unbelievers of Quraysh when they objected to the change of *qibla*.

'What has made them turn round from the direction they used to face?'

The imāms report that Ibn 'Umar said, "While people were at Qubā' performing the *Ṣubḥ* prayer, someone came to them and said, 'The Messenger of Allah, may Allah bless him and grant him peace, received Revelation in the night and he has been commanded to face the Ka'ba.' They were facing Syria and then turned right round to face the Ka'ba." Al-Bukhārī transmitted from al-Barā' that the Prophet was praying towards Jerusalem for sixteen or seventeen months. He wanted his *qibla* to be towards the Ka'ba. The first prayer he prayed towards it was *'Aṣr* and people prayed it with him. A man who had prayed with the Prophet, may Allah bless him and grant him peace, left and passed by the people of another mosque who were in *rukū'*. He said, "I testify by Allah that I prayed with the Prophet, may Allah bless him and grant him peace, towards Makka." So they turned round so that they were facing the House. There were men who died while they were facing the old *qibla* before the change to the House and they did not know what to say about them. So Allah Almighty revealed, *"Allah would never let your faith go to waste."* (2:143)

This transmission mentions the *'Aṣr* prayer whereas the transmission of Mālik mentioned the *Ṣubḥ* prayer. It is said that it was revealed while the Prophet was in the mosque of the Banū Salama doing *Ẓuhr* and he changed *qibla* after two *rak'at*s of it. For that reason it was called the Mosque of the Two *Qibla*s.

There is disagreement about the length of time the Prophet, may Allah bless him and grant him peace, was in Madina before the *qibla* was changed. It is said that it was changed after sixteen or seventeen months, as we find in al-Bukhārī. Ad-Dāraquṭnī also reported that from al-Barā' who said, "We prayed with the Messenger of Allah after he came to Madina for sixteen months towards Jerusalem. Then Allah informed the Prophet that He was aware of his desire to change *qibla* and the Revelation came: *'We have seen you looking into the heaven, turning this way and that.'* (2:144) It was sixteen months without doubt." Mālik related that Sa'īd ibn al-Musayyab said that the *qibla* was changed two months before Badr. Ibrāhīm ibn Isḥāq said that was in Rajab, 2 AH. Al-Bustī said, "The Muslims prayed towards Jerusalem for seventeen months and three days. He came to Madina on Monday, 15 Rabī' al-Awwal, and Allah commanded him to face the Ka'ba on Tuesday, 15 Sha'bān the following year."

Scholars are of three different opinions concerning the reason why he faced Jerusalem. Al-Ḥasan said, "It was by opinion and *ijtihād*." 'Ikrima and Abū'l-'Āliyya agreed with that view. The second opinion is that he had a choice between it and the Ka'ba and chose Jerusalem because he wanted the Jews to believe. Aṭ-Ṭabarī said that. Az-Zajjāj said that it was to test the idolaters because they were used to the Ka'ba. The third opinion and the one which the majority hold, Ibn 'Abbās and others, is that he was obliged to face it by the command of Allah and His Revelation. Then Allah abrogated that and commanded him to face the Ka'ba in the prayer.

There is also disagreement about when the prayer was first made obligatory for him at Makka and whether the *qibla* was then towards Jerusalem or the Ka'ba. There are two positions. One group say that it was towards Jerusalem and remained that way in Madina for seventeen months and then Allah changed it to the Ka'ba. Ibn 'Abbās said that. Others say that when the prayer was first made obligatory for him he faced towards the Ka'ba and he continued to pray towards it while he was in Makka as Ibrāhīm and Ismā'īl had done. When he went to Madina he prayed toward Jerusalem for sixteen or seventeen months and then Allah changed the *qibla* back to the Ka'ba. Abū 'Umar said, "I consider this to be the sounder of the two positions." Another said, "That was because when the Prophet, may Allah bless him and grant peace, came to Madina, he wanted to court the Jews and turned to their *qibla* so that the Message would be easier for them to accept. When their obstinacy was evident and he despaired of them, he wanted to change back to the Ka'ba and he looked at the sky. His love was for Makka because it was the *qibla* of Ibrāhīm, as Ibn 'Abbās said. It is said that it was to call the Arabs to Islam. It is said that it was to be different from the Jews, as Mujāhid said.

This *āyat* contains clear evidence that the rulings of Allah and His Book can be both abrogating and abrogated, and the *Umma* agree on that except for the rare exception. Scholars agree that the *qibla* was the first ruling to be abrogated in the Book and that it was abrogated twice, according to one of the positions about the matter. It also indicates that it is permissible for the *Sunna* to be abrogated by the Qur'ān. That is because the Prophet, may Allah bless him and grant him peace, prayed towards Jerusalem and there was no Qur'ānic text on that. That was a judgement only from the *Sunna* and then that was abrogated by the Qur'ān.

The *āyat* also contains evidence of the permission to make a ruling based on a single *ḥadīth*. That was because facing Jerusalem was definite in our *Sharī'a*, and then when someone came to the people of Qubā' and told them that the *qibla* had been changed to the Sacred Mosque, they accepted that and turned towards it and abandoned the *mutawātir* in favour of the single report they heard. However it became forbidden after the death of the Prophet, may Allah bless him and grant him peace, by the consensus of the Companions and the position then was that the Qur'ān and the *mutawātir* are well-known and may not be abrogated by a single *ḥadīth*, and no one believes that possible.

It also makes it very clear that the Qur'ān was revealed to the Messenger of Allah, may Allah bless him and grant him peace, piece by piece and circumstance after circumstance, according to need, until the *dīn* was complete.

Say: 'Both East and West belong to Allah.

Since He owns them both, He is entitled to command any direction He wishes.

He guides whoever He wills to a straight path.'

This indicates Allah's guidance of this Community to the *qibla* of Ibrāhīm and Allah knows best.

وَكَذَٰلِكَ جَعَلْنَٰكُمْ أُمَّةً وَسَطًا لِّتَكُونُوا۟ شُهَدَآءَ عَلَى ٱلنَّاسِ
وَيَكُونَ ٱلرَّسُولُ عَلَيْكُمْ شَهِيدًا ۗ وَمَا جَعَلْنَا ٱلْقِبْلَةَ ٱلَّتِى
كُنتَ عَلَيْهَآ إِلَّا لِنَعْلَمَ مَن يَتَّبِعُ ٱلرَّسُولَ مِمَّن يَنقَلِبُ عَلَىٰ عَقِبَيْهِ ۚ
وَإِن كَانَتْ لَكَبِيرَةً إِلَّا عَلَى ٱلَّذِينَ هَدَى ٱللَّهُ ۗ وَمَا كَانَ ٱللَّهُ
لِيُضِيعَ إِيمَٰنَكُمْ ۚ إِنَّ ٱللَّهَ بِٱلنَّاسِ لَرَءُوفٌ رَّحِيمٌ ﴿١٤٣﴾

143 ***In this way We have made you***
a middlemost community,
so that you may act as witnesses against mankind
and the Messenger as a witness against you.
We only appointed the direction you used to face
in order to know those who follow the Messenger
from those who turn round on their heels.
Though in truth it is a very hard thing –
except for those Allah has guided.
Allah would never let your faith go to waste.
Allah is All-Gentle, Most Merciful to mankind.

In this way We have made you a middlemost community,

As the Ka'ba is in the middle of the earth, so We made you a middlemost nation, meaning that we made you inferior to the Prophets but superior to other communities. The word "*wasaṭ*" (middlemost) implies being just and balanced. The basis of this is the expression: "The most praised of things is the middlemost of them." The middle part of a valley is the best place in it and has the most plants and water. The middle avoids excess and falling short and is praiseworthy, so this community does not go to excess in elevating their Prophet nor fall short as the Jews do in respect of their Prophets. In a *ḥadīth* we find, "The best of matters is the middlemost of them." 'Alī said, "You must take the middle way. The high descend to it and the low rise to it." Someone who is from the middlemost of his people is one of the best of them.

so that you may act as witnesses against mankind

This is referring to the Gathering, when the Prophets are joined with their nations, as is established in the *Ṣaḥīḥ* al-Bukhārī when Abū Sa'īd al-Khudrī reported that the Messenger of Allah, may Allah bless him and grant him peace, said, "Nūḥ will be summoned on the Day of Rising and he will say, 'At your service and obedience, O Lord!' Allah will say, 'Did you convey it?' He will say, 'Yes.' It will be said to his community, 'Did he convey it to you?' They will say, 'No warner came to us.' Allah will ask Nūḥ, 'Who will then testify on your behalf?' He will say, 'Muḥammad and his community.' They will testify that he conveyed it."

'Ubāda ibn aṣ-Ṣāmit said that he heard the Messenger of Allah, may Allah bless him and grant him peace, say, "My Community was given three things which no other Prophets were given. Whenever Allah sent a Prophet, He said to him, 'Call on Me and I will answer you.' He said to this Community, 'All of you call on Me and I will answer you.' When He sent a Prophet, He said to him, 'I have not imposed any hardship on you in the *dīn*.' He said to this Community, 'I have not imposed any hardship on any of you in the *dīn*.' When He sent a Prophet, He made him a witness against his people but He made this Community witnesses against the whole of mankind." (at-Tirmidhī)

Our scholars say that, in His Book, our Lord has informed us of the preference He has given us by describing us as just and by entrusting us with the important task of bearing witness against all creation. He has given us the first place even if we are the last in time; as the Prophet said, "We are the first who came last." This is also evidence that only the just may be witnesses, which will be discussed later.

This *āyat* also contains evidence for the soundness of the consensus of the community and the obligation to judge by it because they have been considered just enough to testify against all mankind. Every generation is a witness for those who come after them. The position of the Companions is evidence and testimony for the *Tābi'ūn* and that of the *Tābi'ūn* for those after them. Since the Community have been made witnesses, it is mandatory to accept what they say.

and the Messenger as a witness against you.

meaning about your actions on the Day of Rising. It is also said that this can mean, "for you," bearing witness that you have faith.

We only appointed the direction you used to face in order to know those who follow the Messenger

What is meant is the first *qibla*. 'Alī said that "know" in this context means "see". The Arabs used knowledge to mean seeing and seeing to mean knowledge. It is also said to mean, "So that you know that We know." The hypocrites had doubts about Allah's knowledge of things before they took place. It is said that this distinguishes the people of certainty from the people of doubt, as Ibn Fūrak said. Aṭ-Ṭabarī mentioned the same view from Ibn 'Abbās. It is said that it means: "so that the Prophet and his followers will know." The best view is that the meaning is that there is direct witnessing of that which makes repayment mandatory. Allah knows the unseen and the visible and He knows what will be before it takes place. The circumstances of known things vary but His knowledge does not vary. His knowledge is the same in every instance. "Follow the Messenger" here means in respect of his command to change the *qibla* to the Ka'ba.

from those who turn round on their heels

This is referring to those who apostatised from the *dīn*, because when the *qibla* was changed some of the Muslims reverted to disbelief and some became hypocrites.

Though in truth it is a very hard thing –

Meaning the change of *qibla* as Ibn 'Abbās, Mujāhid and Qatāda said.

Allah would never let your faith go to waste.

The scholars agree that this was revealed about those who died having prayed toward Jerusalem as we see in al-Bukhārī. In at-Tirmidhī, Ibn 'Abbās said, "When the Prophet, may Allah bless him and grant him peace, turned towards the Ka'ba, they asked, 'Messenger of Allah, what about our brothers who died while they were praying towards Jerusalem?' and Allah revealed this." The prayer is called "faith" here because it contains intention, word and action. Mālik said, "I mention this *āyat* to refute the position of the Murji'ites that the prayer is not part of faith."

قَدْ نَرَىٰ تَقَلُّبَ وَجْهِكَ فِى ٱلسَّمَآءِ فَلَنُوَلِّيَنَّكَ قِبْلَةً تَرْضَىٰهَا
فَوَلِّ وَجْهَكَ شَطْرَ ٱلْمَسْجِدِ ٱلْحَرَامِ وَحَيْثُ مَا كُنتُمْ
فَوَلُّوا۟ وُجُوهَكُمْ شَطْرَهُۥ وَإِنَّ ٱلَّذِينَ أُوتُوا۟ ٱلْكِتَـٰبَ
لَيَعْلَمُونَ أَنَّهُ ٱلْحَقُّ مِن رَّبِّهِمْ وَمَا ٱللَّهُ بِغَـٰفِلٍ عَمَّا
يَعْمَلُونَ ﴿١٤٤﴾

144 ***We have seen you looking up into heaven,***
turning this way and that,
so We will turn you towards
a direction which will please you.
Turn your face, therefore,
towards the Masjid al-Ḥarām.
Wherever you all are, turn your faces towards it.
Those given the Book know
it is the truth from their Lord.
Allah is not unaware of what they do.

We have seen you looking up into heaven,

Aṭ-Ṭabarī said that he was turning his eyes in the heaven. "Heaven" is mentioned because it was the main direction he looked in and is the source of things like rain, mercy and revelation.

Turn your face, therefore, towards the Masjid al-Ḥarām.

It is said to be towards any part of the House as Ibn 'Abbās said. Ibn 'Umar said toward the Mīzāb of the Ka'ba as Ibn 'Aṭiyya said. The Mīzāb is the *qibla* of Madina and the people of Syria and of Andalusia. Ibn 'Abbās reported that the Messenger of Allah said, "The House is the *qibla* for the people who can see it and the mosque is the *qibla* for the people of Makka and Makka is the *qibla* for the rest of the people of my community, wherever they are on the earth, east or west." The word "towards" (*shaṭr*) here means "in the direction of" although the word can mean "half".

There is no disagreement among scholars that the Ka'ba itself is the actual *qibla* of everyone. They agree that it is mandatory for it to be faced by someone who can actually see it and if he does not do that, his prayer is invalid and he must repeat it.

There is disagreement about whether someone not at the Ka'ba must face it exactly or just face in the direction of it. Facing in the direction of it is sound for three reasons. We are only responsible for doing what is possible for us. That is what we are commanded to do in the Qur'ān by this *āyat*. The third reason is that scholars use the long line in the prayer as evidence, since clearly if the line is longer than the side of the Ka'ba not everyone can be facing it directly.

The *āyat* also contains clear evidence in support of what Mālik and those who agree with him hold, which is the ruling that someone praying should only look at the place where he is going to prostrate.

Those given the Book know it is the truth from their Lord.

This means that the Jews and Christians know the change of direction has come from Allah. If it is asked, "How can they know this when it is not part of their *dīn* or in their Book?" there are two answers. One is that since they know from their Book that Muḥammad, may Allah bless him and grant him peace, is a Prophet, they know that it follows that he only speaks the truth and only commands it. The second is that they know from their *dīn* that abrogation is permitted, even if some deny it, and so they know that abrogation is permitted in respect of the *qibla*.

وَلَئِنْ أَتَيْتَ ٱلَّذِينَ أُوتُوا۟ ٱلْكِتَٰبَ بِكُلِّ ءَايَةٍ مَّا
تَبِعُوا۟ قِبْلَتَكَ ۚ وَمَآ أَنتَ بِتَابِعٍ قِبْلَتَهُمْ ۚ وَمَا بَعْضُهُم
بِتَابِعٍ قِبْلَةَ بَعْضٍ ۚ وَلَئِنِ ٱتَّبَعْتَ أَهْوَآءَهُم مِّنۢ بَعْدِ
مَا جَآءَكَ مِنَ ٱلْعِلْمِ ۙ إِنَّكَ إِذًا لَّمِنَ ٱلظَّٰلِمِينَ ﴿١٤٥﴾

145 ***If you were to bring every Sign***
to those given the Book,
they still would not follow your direction.
You do not follow their direction.
They do not follow each other's direction.
If you followed their whims and desires,
after the knowledge that has come to you,
you would then be one of the wrongdoers.

If you were to bring every Sign to those given the Book, they still would not follow your direction.

This is because they disbelieve even when the truth is clear to them and signs do not help them.

You do not follow their direction. They do not follow each other's direction.

You do not incline to anything they face. Then Allah tells us that the Jews do not follow the *qibla* of the Christians nor the Christians that of the Jews. As-Suddī and Ibn Zayd said that this tells us about their disunity and misguidance. Some people say that it means that those of them who have become Muslim and follow you do not follow the *qibla* of those who are not Muslim nor do those who are not Muslim follow the *qibla* of those who are. The first view is more likely, and Allah knows best.

If you followed their whims and desires,

This is addressed to the Prophet but it is his Community that is meant because it is not permitted for the Prophet to do anything that would entail wrongdoing. It is possible that it means those who disobey the Prophet. The Prophet is addressed to give the command more emphasis.

ٱلَّذِينَ ءَاتَيْنَٰهُمُ ٱلْكِتَٰبَ يَعْرِفُونَهُۥ كَمَا يَعْرِفُونَ أَبْنَآءَهُمْ
وَإِنَّ فَرِيقًا مِّنْهُمْ لَيَكْتُمُونَ ٱلْحَقَّ وَهُمْ يَعْلَمُونَ ﴿١٤٦﴾

146 ***Those We have given the Book recognise it***
as they recognise their own sons.
Yet a group of them knowingly conceal the truth.

Those We have given the Book recognise it

The third person pronoun "it" referring back to the Book can also be read as "him" referring to the Prophet, may Allah bless him and grant him peace, in which case it means they recognise his Prophethood and affirm his Message, as Mujāhid, Qatāda and others said. It is also said that what they recognise is that the change of the *qibla* is true, as Ibn 'Abbās, Ibn Jurayj, ar-Rabī' and Qatāda said.

as they recognise their own sons.

'Abdullāh ibn Sallām said, "I recognised the Prophet, may Allah bless him and grant him peace, more readily than I recognise my own son because I have doubts about my son."

Yet a group of them knowingly conceal the truth.

The "truth" they conceal can be their recognition of Muḥammad, may Allah bless him and grant him peace, or the change of the *qibla* and is the result of their obstinacy.

ٱلْحَقُّ مِن رَّبِّكَ فَلَا تَكُونَنَّ مِنَ ٱلْمُمْتَرِينَ ١٤٧

147 ***The truth is from your Lord,***
so on no account be among the doubters.

The truth is from your Lord,

This refers to the change of *qibla* not what the Jews say about their *qibla*. According to 'Alī, this is connected to "they know" in the previous *āyat* and so it means, "They know the truth from your Lord." Or it implies: "Hold to the truth."

so on no account be among the doubters.

Again, although the Prophet, may Allah bless him and grant him peace, is addressed, it is his Community that is meant.

وَلِكُلٍّ وِجْهَةٌ هُوَ مُوَلِّيهَا فَٱسْتَبِقُوا۟ ٱلْخَيْرَٰتِ أَيْنَ مَا
تَكُونُوا۟ يَأْتِ بِكُمُ ٱللَّهُ جَمِيعًا إِنَّ ٱللَّهَ عَلَىٰ كُلِّ شَىْءٍ قَدِيرٌ ١٤٨

148 ***Each person faces a particular direction***
so race each other to the good.
Wherever you are, Allah will bring you all together.
Truly Allah has power over all things.

Each person faces a particular direction

What is meant is the *qibla*. They do not face your *qibla* and you do not face theirs. Each has a *qibla*, either by the truth or by his own whims and desires. The word "faces" implies that each person with a religion has a *qibla* to which he turns.

so race each other to the good.

The primary meaning of the *āyat* is to hasten to what Allah has commanded regarding the facing of the Masjid al-Ḥarām, although the phrase, in fact, contains encouragement to hasten to all acts of obedience in general. What is meant here is facing the *qibla* because of the context. What is meant by "racing" is to do the prayer at the beginning of its time, and Allah knows best. An-Nasā'ī reported from Abū Hurayra that the Prophet, may Allah bless him and grant him peace, said, "The metaphor of the one who goes early to the prayer is that of someone who sacrifices a camel. The one after him is like someone who sacrifices a cow. The one after him is like someone who sacrifices a ram. Then the one after him is like someone who sacrifices a chicken and the one after him is like someone who sacrifices an egg." Ad-Dāraquṭnī reports from Abū Hurayra that the Messenger of Allah, may Allah bless him and grant him peace, said, "Each of you should pray the prayer at its time. What is at the beginning of the time is better for him than his family and wealth." Ad-Dāraquṭnī also transmits that the Prophet, peace be upon him, said, "The best of actions is the prayer at the beginning of its time." He also said, "The beginning of the time is the pleasure of Allah, the middle of the time is the mercy of Allah, and the end of the time is the pardon of Allah."

Ibn 'Arabī said about this, "Abū Bakr said, 'I prefer Allah's pleasure to His pardon. His pleasure is for the good-doers and His pardon is for those who fall short.'" That is what ash-Shāfi'ī preferred. Abū Hanīfa said, "The end of the time is better because it is the time of the obligation."

Mālik made a distinction, saying that, in the case of *Ṣubḥ* and *Maghrib*, the beginning of the time is better. In respect of *Ṣubḥ*, he goes by the *ḥadīth* of 'Ā'isha, "The Messenger of Allah, may Allah bless him and grant him peace, used to pray *Ṣubḥ* when it was dark and the women would leave wrapped in their mantles and could not be recognised due to the darkness." And in the case of *Maghrib*, he goes by the *ḥadīth* of Salama ibn al-Akwa' that the Messenger of Allah prayed *Maghrib* when the sun set. In the case of *'Ishā'*, it is better to delay it if one is able to do so. Ibn 'Umar related, "We remained that night waiting for the *'Ishā'* prayer with the Messenger of Allah, may Allah bless him and grant him peace. He came out to us when a third of the night or more had passed and we did not know whether he was doing something with his family or something else. When he came out, he said, "You are waiting for a prayer when none of the people of the *dīn* except you are waiting for it. If it had not been that it would be onerous for this Community, I would always pray at this time with them." Abū Barza said, "The Prophet, may Allah bless him and grant him peace, preferred to delay it."

As for *Ẓuhr*, it arrives at a time when people are inattentive and so it is recommended to delay it a little so that people can prepare and gather together. Abū'l-Faraj said that Mālik said, "The beginning of the time is better for every prayer except for *Ẓuhr* when it is very hot." Ibn Abī Uways said, "Mālik disliked praying *Ẓuhr* at midday but did it a little later." He said that praying exactly at midday is the prayer of the Khārijites.

Wherever you are, Allah will bring you all together.

This is a reference to the Day of Rising. Then Allah describes Himself as having power over all things since that attribute is appropriate for what was mentioned of being brought back to life after death.

وَمِنْ حَيْثُ خَرَجْتَ فَوَلِّ وَجْهَكَ شَطْرَ ٱلْمَسْجِدِ ٱلْحَرَامِ ۖ وَإِنَّهُۥ
لَلْحَقُّ مِن رَّبِّكَ ۗ وَمَا ٱللَّهُ بِغَٰفِلٍ عَمَّا تَعْمَلُونَ ﴿١٤٩﴾ وَمِنْ حَيْثُ خَرَجْتَ
فَوَلِّ وَجْهَكَ شَطْرَ ٱلْمَسْجِدِ ٱلْحَرَامِ ۚ وَحَيْثُ مَا كُنتُمْ فَوَلُّوا۟
وُجُوهَكُمْ شَطْرَهُۥ لِئَلَّا يَكُونَ لِلنَّاسِ عَلَيْكُمْ حُجَّةٌ
إِلَّا ٱلَّذِينَ ظَلَمُوا۟ مِنْهُمْ فَلَا تَخْشَوْهُمْ وَٱخْشَوْنِى
وَلِأُتِمَّ نِعْمَتِى عَلَيْكُمْ وَلَعَلَّكُمْ تَهْتَدُونَ ﴿١٥٠﴾

149 *Wherever you come from,*
turn your face to the Masjid al-Haram.
This is certainly the truth from your Lord.
Allah is not unaware of what you do.
150 *Wherever you come from,*
turn your face to the Masjid al-Ḥaram.
Wherever you are, turn your faces towards it
so that people will have
no argument against you –
except for those among them who do wrong
and then you should not fear them
but rather fear Me –
and so that I can complete My blessing to you
so that hopefully you will be guided.

This is stressing the command to face the *qibla* and the importance of that because the change was very difficult for them. So this command is repeated so that people will see the importance of it and it will be easier for them. It is said that the first command to turn the face is to look at the Ka'ba when you are praying in front of it. Then "wherever you are" is for the Muslims in all the mosques in Madina and elsewhere. This is a command to face it everywhere.

This statement is better than the first one because it gives a benefit to each *āyat.* Ad-Dāraquṭnī related that Anas ibn Mālik said, "When the Prophet, may Allah bless him and grant him peace, was on a journey and wanted to pray on his camel, he faced *qibla* and said the *takbīr* and then prayed in whatever direction it turned." Ash-Shāfi'ī, Abū Thawr and Aḥmad said that. Mālik believed that you are not obliged to face Makka, going by the *ḥadīth* of Ibn 'Umar, "The Messenger of Allah, may Allah bless him and grant him peace, used to pray facing from Makka towards Madina on his camel."

There is no contradiction between the two *aḥādīth* because this is part of the legal area of texts which are unrestricted or restricted, so the position of ash-Shāfi'ī is more fitting and the *ḥadīth* of Anas is sound. It is related that Ja'far ibn Muḥammad was asked about the meaning of the repetition of stories in the Qur'ān. He said, "Allah knows that all people do not know the Qur'ān by heart. If there was no story repeated, then it would be possible that only some people would know the story. It is repeated so that everyone will know it."

so that people will have no argument against you –

Mujāhid said that the "people" referred to here are the Arab idolaters and their argument is what they said about the *qibla*. Aṭ-Ṭabarī said, "Allah made it clear that no one has evidence against the Prophet, may Allah bless him and grant him peace, and his Companions regarding their facing the *qibla*."

and then you should not fear them but rather fear Me –

"*Khashya*" (fear) derives from the lack of peace of mind in the heart about what to expect while *khawf* is the alarm of the heart which makes the limbs tremble. The *āyat* calls attention to the fact that all that is other than Allah is insignificant. The command is for people to cast aside their own affairs and to obey the command of Allah.

and so that I can complete My blessing to you

According to az-Zajjāj, this refers to Allah making his chosen *qibla* known to them. The completion of guidance is being guided to the *qibla*. It is said that it is admitting them to the Garden.

كَمَآ أَرْسَلْنَا فِيكُمْ رَسُولًا مِّنكُمْ يَتْلُوا۟ عَلَيْكُمْ ءَايَٰتِنَا
وَيُزَكِّيكُمْ وَيُعَلِّمُكُمُ ٱلْكِتَٰبَ وَٱلْحِكْمَةَ وَيُعَلِّمُكُم
مَّا لَمْ تَكُونُوا۟ تَعْلَمُونَ ﴿١٥١﴾

151 ***For this We sent a Messenger***
to you from among you
to recite Our Signs to you and purify you
and teach you the Book and Wisdom
and teach you things you did not know before.

This is connected to His words, *"to complete"* or to His words, *"Remember Me."* The first is most likely. The blessing in respect of the *qibla* is like the blessing in respect of the Message itself.

فَٱذْكُرُونِىٓ أَذْكُرْكُمْ وَٱشْكُرُوا۟ لِى وَلَا تَكْفُرُونِ ﴿١٥٢﴾
يَٰٓأَيُّهَا ٱلَّذِينَ ءَامَنُوا۟ ٱسْتَعِينُوا۟ بِٱلصَّبْرِ وَٱلصَّلَوٰةِ
إِنَّ ٱللَّهَ مَعَ ٱلصَّٰبِرِينَ ﴿١٥٣﴾

152 ***Remember Me – I will remember you.***
Give thanks to Me and do not be ungrateful.
153 ***You who believe!***
seek help in steadfastness and the prayer.
Allah is with the steadfast.

Remember Me – I will remember you.

Allah's remembering of us signifies reward. The root meaning of the word for remembering (*dhikr*) is to be aware with the heart of what is remembered and awake to it. *Dhikr* with the tongue is called *dhikr* because it indicates the remembrance of the heart. It is often used, however, with reference to the spoken words and phrases employed in its performance.

The *āyat* means: "Remember Me by obeying Me and I will remember you with the reward and forgiveness", as Sa'īd ibn Jubayr said. He also said, "*Dhikr* is obeying Allah. Anyone who does not obey Him, does not remember Him, even if he does a lot of glorification, *shahāda* and recitation of the Qur'ān." It is related that the Prophet, may Allah bless him and grant him peace, said, "Anyone who obeys Allah has remembered Allah, even if he has not done much prayer, fasting or good action. Anyone who disobeys Allah has forgotten Allah, even if he has done a lot of prayer, fasting and good action." As-Suddī said, "A person does not remember Allah without Allah remembering Him. A believer does not remember Allah without Allah remembering him with mercy. An unbeliever does not remember Allah without Allah remembering him with the punishment."

Someone said to Abū 'Uthmān an-Nahdī, "We remember Allah but we do not experience any sweetness in our hearts." He said, "Praise Allah Almighty for the fact that He has adorned one of your limbs with obedience!" Dhū'n-Nūn al-Miṣrī said, "Anyone who really remembers Allah, forgets everything except His remembrance and Allah preserves him from every bad thing and is His redress for everything." Mu'ādh ibn Jabal said, "The son of Ādam does not do any action which will be more effective in saving him from the punishment of Allah than *dhikr* of Allah."

There are many *aḥādīth* on the virtue of *dhikr* and its reward. Ibn Mājah reports from 'Abdullāh ibn Yūsuf that a bedouin told the Messenger of Allah, may Allah bless him and grant him peace, "The laws of Islam are a lot for me. Tell me something on which I can really concentrate my efforts." He said, "Let your tongue remain moist with the remembrance of Allah Almighty." It is transmitted that Abū Hurayra reported that the Prophet, may Allah bless him and grant him peace, said, "Allah Almighty says, 'I am with My slave when he remembers Me and moves his lips with My Name.'" This subject will be discussed in greater depth elsewhere.

Give thanks to Me

Thankfulness (*shukr*) is to acknowledge kindness received and to speak of it. The linguistic root of *shukr* means "to display". So Allah's slave shows his thankfulness by mentioning Allah's goodness to him and the Real thanks the slave by praising him for obeying Him.

and do not be ungrateful.

Do not be ungrateful for Allah's blessings. The word *kufr* here means to cover up the blessing, not total disbelief.

وَلَا تَقُولُوا لِمَن يُقْتَلُ فِي سَبِيلِ اللَّهِ أَمْوَاتٌ بَلْ أَحْيَاءٌ وَلَٰكِن
لَّا تَشْعُرُونَ ﴿١٥٤﴾

154 ***Do not say that those who are killed***
in the Way of Allah are dead.
On the contrary, they are alive
but you are not aware of it.

This is like another verse: *"Do not suppose those killed in the Way of Allah are dead. No indeed! They are alive and well provided for in the very presence of their Lord."* (3:169) There we will discuss martyrs and the rulings that apply in their case, Allah willing. Allah will bring them to life after death so as to provide for them and so it is equally possible for the unbelievers to be brought to life so that they can be punished. This is evidence for the punishment in the grave. The martyrs are alive, as Allah says. It does not mean that they will be brought to life later, since in that case there would be no difference between them and anyone else because everyone will be brought back to life on the Last Day. The evidence for this is found in His words, "but you are not aware of it", and the believers are certainly aware that they will be brought to life.

وَلَنَبْلُوَنَّكُم بِشَيْءٍ مِّنَ الْخَوْفِ وَالْجُوعِ وَنَقْصٍ مِّنَ
الْأَمْوَالِ وَالْأَنفُسِ وَالثَّمَرَاتِ وَبَشِّرِ الصَّابِرِينَ ﴿١٥٥﴾

155 ***We will test you***
with a certain amount of fear and hunger
and loss of wealth and life and fruits.
But give good news to the steadfast:

We will test you with a certain amount of fear and hunger and loss of wealth and life and fruits.

We will test you so that We know who are the fighters and the steadfast by direct evidence in order that they may be rewarded. It is said that they will be tested as a sign for those after them and so they know that if they too are steadfast in this, then truth will be clear to them. It is said that they will inform them of this so that they will have certainty that it will befall them as well.

The word "fear" here refers to fear of the enemy and alarm when fighting as Ibn 'Abbās said. Ash-Shāfi'ī said that it is fear of Allah that is meant. "Hunger" means by drought and famine according to Ibn 'Abbās. Ash-Shāfi'ī said that it refers to the hunger felt in the month of Ramaḍān. "Loss of wealth" comes through being occupied with fighting the unbelievers. It is said that it refers to damage to crops. Ash-Shāfi'ī said that it is what occurs through the obligatory *zakāt*. "Loss of life", according to Ibn 'Abbās, is by killing and death in *jihād*. Ash-Shāfi'ī said that it is through illnesses. "Loss of fruits", according to ash-Shāfi'ī means the death of children. Ibn 'Abbās says that it means plants.

But give good news to the steadfast:

Give them the news of the reward for their steadfastness. The root of the word "steadfast" (*ṣabr*) means to confine and restrict and its reward is without limit, but that only refers to steadfastness at the first blow, as al-Bukhārī transmitted from Anas that the Prophet, may Allah bless him and grant him peace, said, "Steadfastness is at the first blow." The steadfastness which is difficult for the self and which has such an immense reward is that shown when the affliction first strikes since it indicates the strength of the heart and its firmness in the station of steadfastness. When an affliction lessens with time, anyone can be steadfast. That is why it is said, "In affliction, every intelligent person must withstand what a fool can only withstand after three." Sahl ibn 'Abdullāh at-Tustarī said, "When the Almighty said, *'give good news to the steadfast',* steadfastness became a way of life."

There are two types of steadfastness: steadfastness in not disobeying Allah and this is the *mujāhid*, and steadfastness in obeying Allah, and this is the worshipper. If someone is steadfast in not disobeying Allah and steadfast in obeying Allah, Allah will grant him complete satisfaction with His decree. The sign of this satisfaction is tranquillity in the heart with everything which occurs to you, whether disliked or liked. Al-Khawwāṣ said, "Steadfastness is firmness in holding to the rulings of the Book and *Sunna*." Ruwaym said "Steadfastness is abandoning complaint." Dhū'n-Nūn al-Miṣrī said, "Steadfastness is seeking the help of Allah Almighty."

ٱلَّذِينَ إِذَآ أَصَٰبَتۡهُم مُّصِيبَةٞ قَالُوٓاْ إِنَّا لِلَّهِ وَإِنَّآ إِلَيۡهِ
رَٰجِعُونَ ١٥٦ أُوْلَٰٓئِكَ عَلَيۡهِمۡ صَلَوَٰتٞ مِّن رَّبِّهِمۡ وَرَحۡمَةٞۖ وَأُوْلَٰٓئِكَ
هُمُ ٱلۡمُهۡتَدُونَ ١٥٧

156 ***Those who, when disaster strikes them, say,***
'We belong to Allah and to Him we will return.'
157 ***Those are the people who will have***
blessings and mercy from their Lord;
they are the ones who are guided.

Those who, when disaster strikes them,

The word "disaster" (*muṣība*) means everything that harms and afflicts the believer. In the *Ṣaḥīḥ* of Muslim there is a *ḥadīth* transmitted from Abū Sa'īd and Abu Hurayra in which they heard the Messenger of Allah say, "Whatever afflicts the believer – discomfort, fatigue, illness or sorrow, even a care that concerns him – expiates his evil deeds." Ibn Mājah transmitted in the *Sunan* that al-Ḥusayn said that the Messenger of Allah, may Allah bless him and grant him peace, said, "If someone suffers an affliction and remembers his affliction and says, 'We belong to Allah and to Him we will return,' even after a long time, Allah will write for him a reward the same as if he had said it on the day he was afflicted."

One of the worse afflictions is affliction which affects ones *dīn*. 'Aṭā' ibn Rabāḥ reported that the Messenger of Allah, may Allah bless him and grant him peace, said, "When someone suffers an affliction, he should remember his loss of me. That is one of the greatest afflictions." Abū 'Umar said, "The Messenger of Allah, may Allah bless him and grant him peace, spoke the truth because the affliction of losing him is greater than any other affliction which a Muslim might suffer after that until the Day of Rising. The Revelation has come to an end and Prophethood died out." The first evil to appear was the apostasy of the Arabs. His death was the beginning of loss. Abū Sa'īd al-Khudrī said, "Our hands had not brushed off the dust of the grave of the Messenger of Allah when we found that we did not know our hearts."

We belong to Allah and to Him we will return.

Allah has made these words the refuge of all those overcome by affliction and the resort of all those undergoing trial since it contains many blessed meanings. "We belong to Allah" is *tawḥīd*, and affirmation of our slavehood and Allah's mastership. "And to Him we will return" is affirmation of the inevitability of death and resurrection from the grave and certainty that the entire business will return to Allah as it belongs to Him. Sa'īd ibn Jubayr said, "These words were not given to any Prophet before our Prophet. If Ya'qūb had known them, he would not have said, *'My sorrow for Yūsuf!'*" (12:84)

Abū Sinān said, "When I buried my son Sinān, Abū Ṭalha al-Khawlānī was standing at the edge of the grave. When I was about to leave, he took my hand and tried to cheer me up. He said, 'Shall I give you good news, Abū Sinān? Aḍ-Ḍaḥḥāk reported to me from Abū Mūsā that the Prophet, may Allah bless him and grant him peace, said, "When someone's child dies, Allah says to the angels, 'You have taken the child of My slave?' 'Yes,' they reply. He says, 'You took the apple of his eye?' 'Yes,' they reply. He asks, 'What did My slave say?' They reply, 'He praised You and said, "We belong to Allah and to Him we will return."' Allah Almighty will say, 'Build My slave a house in the Garden and name it the House of Praise.'"'"

Muslim reported from Umm Salama that the Messenger of Allah said, "There is no Muslim who is afflicted by a calamity and then says, 'We belong to Allah and to Him we return. O Allah, give me a reward for my calamity and give me something better to replace it,' without Allah granting him something better in its place." This is indicated by the words of Allah Almighty, *"Give good news to the steadfast."* (2:155). The replacement which Allah gave Umm Salama was the Messenger of Allah, may Allah bless him and grant him peace. He married her when her husband, Abū Salama, died. Otherwise there is an ample reward in the Next World, as in the *ḥadīth* of Abū Mūsā.

Those are the people who will have blessings and mercy from their Lord.

The blessings (*ṣalawāt*) of Allah on His slave are His pardon, mercy, blessing and honour for him in this world and the Next. Az-

Zajjāj said, "*Ṣalawāt* from Allah means forgiveness and good praise." One element of this is the funeral prayer for the dead person which entails praise for him and supplication for him. The word "mercy" is repeated, when the phrase varies, for emphasis and to expand the meaning. It is said that by "mercy" Allah means removing grief and fulfilling every need. In al-Bukhārī, 'Umar said, "The two sides of the baggage and what is put on it."[1]

إِنَّ ٱلصَّفَا وَٱلۡمَرۡوَةَ مِن شَعَآئِرِ ٱللَّهِۖ فَمَنۡ حَجَّ ٱلۡبَيۡتَ أَوِ ٱعۡتَمَرَ
فَلَا جُنَاحَ عَلَيۡهِ أَن يَطَّوَّفَ بِهِمَاۚ وَمَن تَطَوَّعَ خَيۡرٗا فَإِنَّ ٱللَّهَ
شَاكِرٌ عَلِيمٌ ١٥٨

158 ***Ṣafā and Marwa are among the Landmarks of Allah,***
so anyone who goes on ḥajj to the House
or does 'umra incurs no wrong
in going back and forth between them.
If anyone spontaneously does good,
Allah is All-Thankful, All-Knowing.

Ṣafā and Marwa are among the Landmarks of Allah,

Al-Bukhārī related that 'Āṣim ibn Sulaymān said, "I asked Anas ibn Mālik about Ṣafā and Marwa and he said, 'We used to think that the observance connected with them was part of the *Jāhiliyya*. When Islam came, we kept back from them and then Allah revealed this.'" In at-Tirmidhī we find that 'Urwa said, "I said to 'Ā'isha, 'I do not think that someone who does not go between Ṣafā and Marwa owes any sacrifice and I do not care if I go between them or not.' She said, 'My nephew, what you say is wrong. The Messenger of Allah, may Allah bless him and grant him peace, went between them and so did all the Muslims. Those

1. The two sides are the carriers on the animal and what is put on it is something like a waterskin, etc. The commentators say that the sides are blessing and mercy, and what is on top is "those are the guided."

who previously used to go into *iḥrām* for the idol Manāt which they used to worship at al-Mushallal considered it wrong to go between Ṣafā and Marwa, so Allah revealed, *"anyone who goes on ḥajj to the House or does 'umra incurs no wrong in going back and forth between them."* If it was as you say, it would have been: "incurs no wrong if he does not go between them."''' Az-Zuhrī said, "I mentioned that to Abū Bakr ibn 'Abdu'r-Raḥmān and he liked it and remarked, 'There is something. I heard men of knowledge say, "Those Arabs who do not go between Ṣafā and Marwa said that our *ṭawāf* between these two stones is part of the *Jāhiliyya*," and others among the Anṣār said, "We are commanded to do *ṭawāf* of the House and go between Ṣafā and Marwa." So Allah revealed, *"Ṣafa and Marwa are among the Landmarks of Allah."*''' Abū Bakr said, "I think it was revealed about these groups. Al-Bukhārī transmitted something to that effect."

Also in al-Bukhārī there is a *ḥadīth* in which 'Ā'isha said, "The Messenger of Allah, may Allah bless him and grant him peace, made a *sunna* of going between them. No one should abandon going between them." Then she told Abū Bakr ibn 'Abdu'r-Raḥmān and he said, "This is a piece of knowledge I have not heard. I did hear some of the people of knowledge saying that the people – except for those 'Ā'isha mentioned who went into *iḥrām* for Manāt – all used to go between Ṣafā and Marwa. When Allah Almighty mentioned *ṭawāf* of the House and did not mention Ṣafā and Marwa in the Qur'ān, they said, 'Messenger of Allah, we used also to do *ṭawāf* around Ṣafā and Marwa and Allah has revealed *ṭawāf* of the House without mentioning Ṣafā. Is it a sin for us to do *ṭawāf* of Ṣafā and Marwa?' Allah Almighty then revealed, *'Ṣafā and Marwa are among the Landmarks of Allah.'*" Abu Bakr said, "I heard that this *āyat* was revealed about both groups, those who used to consider it a sin to do *ṭawāf* of Ṣafā and Marwa in the time of *Jāhiliyya*, and those who had done *ṭawāf* of them and then considered it a sin to do so in the time of Islam because Allah Almighty had commanded *ṭawāf* of the House without mentioning Ṣafā, only speaking of it after what He said about *ṭawāf* of the House."

Ibn 'Abbās said, "In the time of *Jāhiliyya* some shayṭāns used to play music the entire night between Ṣafā and Marwa and there were idols between them. When Islam came, the Muslims said, 'Messenger of Allah, we do not go between Ṣafā and Marwa. To do so is *shirk*.' Then this was revealed." Ash-Sha'bī said, "In the *Jāhiliyya*, there was an idol called Isāf on Ṣafā and an idol called Nā'ila on Marwa. They used to wipe their hands on the idols when they went between them. So the Muslims refused to go between them. It was because of that that the *āyat* was revealed."

The root meaning of the name Ṣafā is smooth stone. It is a high rock at Makka and Marwa is another high rock. That is why they take the definite article. Ṣafā gets its name because Ādam, the chosen (*muṣṭafā*), stopped there, and so it was named after him. Ḥawwā' stopped on Marwa and it was named after the word for "woman" (*mar'a*). Allah knows best.

"The Landmarks (*sha'ā'ir*) of Allah" are one of His signs and the places of His worship. These are the site of acts of worship which Allah informs us about, thereby making them signs for people: the standing, *sa'y*, and sacrifice. *Shi'ār* is an identification mark of the kind put on the hump of camels to be sacrificed.

so anyone who goes on ḥajj to the House or does 'umra

He heads for it. The root meaning of the word "*ḥajj*" means to aim for something. *'Umra* means a visit.

incurs no wrong in going back and forth between them.

They do not commit any sin by doing that. The root of the word for "*junāḥ*" (wrong) is *junūḥ*, which means bending and is used for the limbs because they bend. To use this expression means to permit the action. 'Urwa thought that it meant that it is permissible to abandon *ṭawāf* and then he saw that the *Sharī'a* confirmed the fact that there is no allowance to abandon it.

At-Tirmidhī transmitted from Jābir that, when the Prophet, may Allah bless him and grant him peace, came to Makka, he went around the House seven times, and recited, *"Take the Maqām of Ibrāhīm as a place of prayer,"* (2:125) and he prayed behind the

Maqām. Then he went to the Stone and kissed it and then said, "We begin with what Allah began with." So he began with Ṣafā. The correct practice, therefore, according to the people of knowledge, is that you begin with Ṣafā.

Scholars disagree about the obligation of *sa'y* between Ṣafā and Marwa. Ash-Shāfi'ī and Ibn Ḥanbal said that it is a pillar of the *Ḥajj*. This is the well-known position in the school of Mālik since the Prophet, may Allah bless him and grant him peace, said, "Do *sa'y*. Allah has written *sa'y* for you." (ad-Dāraquṭnī) Mālik said that *sa'y* is the same in *ḥajj* or *'umra*, although it is not *farḍ* in *'umra*. If someone has sexual contact with a woman, he must do *'umra* and sacrifice according to Mālik, but he completes his practices. Ash-Shāfi'ī said that he owes a sacrifice and there is no point in doing *'umra* if he has gone back and performed *ṭawāf* and *sa'y*. Abū Ḥanīfa and his people, ath-Thawrī and ash-Sha'bī said that *sa'y* is not mandatory.

If anyone spontaneously does good, Allah is All-Thankful, All-Knowing.

This refers to any good action someone does which is not imposed on them, whether *ṭawāf* or anything else. Allah will show gratitude for the action by rewarding them.

It is not permitted for anyone to do *ṭawāf* of the House or go between Ṣafā and Marwa while riding unless he has an excuse. If he does this with a valid excuse, then he owes a sacrifice. If he does it without an excuse, he must repeat the action if he is still at the House. Otherwise he must sacrifice. We say that because the Prophet, may Allah bless him and grant him peace, did *ṭawāf* himself and he said, "Take your practices from me." We are allowed to do that with an excuse because the Prophet, may Allah bless him and grant him peace, did *ṭawāf* on his camel and greeted the Corner with his whip and when 'Ā'isha asked him about it, he said, "I am unwell."

إِنَّ الَّذِينَ يَكْتُمُونَ مَا أَنزَلْنَا مِنَ الْبَيِّنَاتِ وَالْهُدَىٰ مِن
بَعْدِ مَا بَيَّنَّاهُ لِلنَّاسِ فِي الْكِتَابِ ۙ أُولَٰئِكَ يَلْعَنُهُمُ اللَّهُ
وَيَلْعَنُهُمُ اللَّاعِنُونَ ﴿١٥٩﴾

159 ***Those who hide the Clear Signs and Guidance***
We have sent down,
after We have made it clear to people in the Book,
Allah curses them, and the cursers curse them –

Those who hide the Clear Signs and Guidance We have sent down,

Allah reports that anyone who hides the Clear Signs and Guidance is cursed. Scholars disagree about what is meant by that. It is said that the Jewish rabbis and Christian monks are the ones who concealed their knowledge of the coming of Muḥammad, may Allah bless him and grant him peace, and the Jews concealed the command about stoning. It is said that it means everyone who conceals the truth, and so it is general to all who conceal any knowledge of the *dīn* of Allah which should be made known. That is explained by the words of the Prophet, "If anyone is asked about knowledge which he knows and conceals it, Allah will bridle him with a bridle of Fire on the Day of Rising." (Ibn Mājah)

That is counterbalanced by the statement of 'Abdullāh ibn Mas'ūd, "You should not tell people a *ḥadīth* which is beyond the grasp of their intellects lest it be as a trial for some of them." He also said, "Relate to people according to their ability to understand. Do you want Allah and His Messenger to be denied?" This applies to some areas of knowledge, like *kalām* and the like which not everyone can grasp.

This *āyat* is the one which Abū Hurayra was referring to when he said, "If it had not been for an *āyat* in the Book of Allah Almighty, I would not have told you a single *ḥadīth*." Scholars use it as evidence for the obligation of conveying true knowledge and making knowledge clear in general without taking a wage for it since no wage is received for what it is mandatory to do, just as there is no wage for simply being a Muslim. This has already been discussed in the commentary on *āyat* 41.

The meaning of the *āyat* is that, when a scholar intends to conceal knowledge, he disobeys Allah. When that is not his intention, he is not obliged to convey something if he knows that other people know it. When he is asked, he is obliged to convey what he knows by this *āyat* and the *ḥadīth*. He is not, however, permitted to teach an unbeliever the Qur'ān and knowledge of the *dīn* until he becomes Muslim. Similarly he is not permitted to teach an innovator proofs and arguments which he might then use to argue against the people who possess the truth. He should not instruct a litigant techniques of legal advocacy so that he can use it against his opponent to take his money, nor should he teach a ruler a particular interpretation which he can then use to harm his subjects. He should not inform fools of permissive opinions which they might then use as a justification for committing forbidden acts or abandoning their obligations or other such things. It is related that the Messenger of Allah said, "Do not deny wisdom to those entitled to it so that you do not wrong them and do not give it to those not entitled to it so that you do not wrong them." It is also reported that he said, "Do not hang pearls from the necks of swine," meaning teach *fiqh* to someone who is not able to grasp it.

The *"Clear Signs and Guidance"* mentioned in the *āyat* are not specific things. On the contrary, rather it is a general statement since guidance includes all knowledge of the *dīn*. The *āyat* is evidence for the obligation to act by the statement of one person because clarification would only be mandatory for him if it was mandatory to accept what he says. Allah says, *"except for those who sincerely repent and put things right and make things clear."* (2:160) So its ruling is that clarification occurs simply by virtue of them reporting it.

If it is said that it is possible that every person is forbidden to conceal the matter, and commanded to make it clear so that there will be a great number of people who report it, we reply to those who say this that it is a mistake. That is because they were only forbidden to conceal things because they were among those who might collude in concealing knowledge. If someone is one of those who might collude in concealment, their report is not mandatory, and Allah knows best.

The use of the words "Clear Signs and Guidance" also indicates that it is permitted to conceal anything other than that, especially when there is fear of what its misunderstanding might provoke, in which case its concealment is even more emphatically encouraged. Fear of the consequences involved led Abū Hurayra to do precisely that. He said, "I preserved two vessels from the Messenger of Allah, may Allah bless him and grant him peace. I have disseminated one of them. If I were to disseminate the other one, my throat would be cut." (al-Bukhārī) Our scholars say that the part which Abū Hurayra did not disseminate and on account of which he feared dissension or that he himself might be killed was knowledge which was connected to seditions, information about apostates and hypocrites, and other such things which are not connected to Clear Signs and guidance. And Allah knows best.

after We have made it clear to people in the Book,

This alludes to the Clear Signs and Guidance which Allah has revealed to the human race. "The Book" is generic, meaning all the Revealed Books.

Allah curses them,

He declares Himself free of them and puts them far from His reward, telling them they are cursed. The root meaning of curse is to put away and drive away.

and the cursers curse them.

Qatāda and ar-Rabīʿ said that the "cursers" are the angels and the believers. Mujāhid and ʿIkrima say that they are the insects and beasts who curse them because they are afflicted by drought on account of the wrong actions of those evil scholars who conceal knowledge. Az-Zajjāj said that the correct view is that it is the angels and believers. He says that the truth of the assertion that it is the beasts of the earth would necessarily depend on a text or a report to that effect and none has been found to back it up. There is, however, a *ḥadīth* from al-Barā' ibn 'Āzib in which the Prophet, may Allah bless him and grant him peace, said in reference to this *āyat* that it is the beasts of the earth. This *ḥadīth* can be found in Ibn Mājah.

If it is asked, "How can the plural reserved for things which have intelligence be used for creatures without intelligence?", the reply is that it is because the action of intelligent beings is ascribed to them. An example of this is when Allah says in *Sūrat Yūsuf*, "I saw them [the stars] prostrating to me" (12:4), using the masculine plural. There are many other instances of this and it is something which will be discussed later, Allah willing. Al-Barā' and Ibn 'Abbās said that the "cursers" are all creatures except for men and jinn. That is because the Prophet, may Allah bless him and grant him peace, said, "When the unbeliever is put in his grave and shouts, everything hears him except for men and jinn. All who hear him curse him."

إِلَّا ٱلَّذِينَ تَابُوا۟ وَأَصْلَحُوا۟ وَبَيَّنُوا۟ فَأُو۟لَـٰٓئِكَ أَتُوبُ
عَلَيْهِمْ وَأَنَا ٱلتَّوَّابُ ٱلرَّحِيمُ ١٦٠

160 ***except for those who sincerely repent***
and put things right and make things clear.
I turn towards them.
I am the Ever-Returning, the Most Merciful.

except for those who sincerely repent

Those who repent are righteous in their actions and do deeds which make their repentance clear. Simple repentance is not enough according to our scholars; it is necessary for the opposite of someone's original condition to be clearly manifest in him. If he is an apostate and then returns to Islam, he has to be manifestly obeying its laws. If he is one of the people of disobedience, he must become one of the people who perform righteous actions and avoid people immersed in corruption and his former life. If he is an idolater, he must shun the company of other idolaters and mix with the people of Islam. Repentance and its rulings will be explained in *Sūrat an-Nisā',* Allah willing.

and put things right and make things clear.

Some scholars say that "make things clear" means by breaking wine containers and spilling out their contents and other clear actions connected with breaking with past patterns of behaviour. It is said that it means make clear what is in the Torah about the Prophethood of Muḥammad, may Allah bless him and grant him peace, and the obligation to follow him. It is better to take it in the more general sense of displaying the opposite of what people were doing previously. Allah knows best.

إِنَّ ٱلَّذِينَ كَفَرُواْ وَمَاتُواْ وَهُمْ كُفَّارٌ أُوْلَٰٓئِكَ عَلَيْهِمْ
لَعْنَةُ ٱللَّهِ وَٱلْمَلَٰٓئِكَةِ وَٱلنَّاسِ أَجْمَعِينَ ﴿١٦١﴾ خَٰلِدِينَ فِيهَا
لَا يُخَفَّفُ عَنْهُمُ ٱلْعَذَابُ وَلَا هُمْ يُنظَرُونَ ﴿١٦٢﴾

161 ***But as for those who are unbelievers***
and die unbelievers,
the curse of Allah is upon them
and that of the angels and all mankind.
162 ***They will be under it for ever.***
The punishment will not be lightened for them.
They will be granted no reprieve.

Ibn al-'Arabī said, "Many of my shaykhs told me that it is not permitted to curse a particular unbeliever because his state at the time of his death is not known. Allah Almighty stipulated in this *āyat* that the application of the curse depends on someone actually dying as an unbeliever. As for what is related about the Prophet, may Allah bless him and grant him peace, cursing specific unbelievers, that was only because he knew what their fate would be." Ibn al-'Arabī also said, "I consider it valid, however, to curse an unbeliever on the basis of his outward state and it is permitted to fight and kill him. It is related that the Prophet said, 'O Allah, 'Amr ibn al-'Āṣ has satirised me and he knows that I am not a poet, so curse him and satirise him to the extent that he has satirised me.' So he cursed him, even though faith, the *dīn* and Islam were to be his end. He was fair when he said, 'To the extent that he has satirised me,' and no more."

As for cursing unbelievers in general, without specifying anyone, there is no disagreement about doing that since Mālik reported a statement with an *isnād* going back to al-A'raj who said, "People definitely used to curse the unbelievers in Ramaḍān." Our scholars add, "Whether or not they are *dhimmī*s." This is not mandatory but it is permitted if someone does it because they deny the truth and are hostile towards the *dīn* and its people. The same applies to anyone who commits acts of disobedience openly like drinking wine and consuming usury, and other such things.

The point of cursing an unbeliever is not to drive him away from disbelief. It is repayment for his disbelief and his display of it. Some of the *Salaf* said, "There is no point in cursing those who are mad or dead among them, either by way of repayment or as a rebuke. It has no effect."

What is meant by the *āyat*, according to this understanding, is that people will curse them on the Day of Rising so that it has an effect and harms and pains their hearts. That is the repayment for their disbelief as the Almighty says, *"Then on the Day of Rising, they will reject one another and curse one another."* (29:25) This position inclines to the view that the *āyat* is a simple report from Allah and not a command. Ibn al-'Arabī mentioned that it is not permitted to curse an individual rebel because it is reported that a man who had drunk wine several times was brought before the Prophet and one of those present said, "Allah curse him! How often he is brought!" The Prophet, may Allah bless him and grant him peace, said, "Do not help Shayṭān against your brother," and he called him a brother, which obliges compassion for him. This is a *ṣaḥīḥ ḥadīth.*

Cursed people are far from Allah's mercy. The intent of a curse made by people is to drive someone away, and Allah's curse is punishment.

If it is observed that not all mankind curse them because their own people do not, there are three answers to this objection. One is that the curse of most people is applied to them, since it denotes the majority. The second is what as-Suddī said which is that everyone curses a wrongdoer and a wrongdoing unbeliever even curses himself. The third is Abū'l-'Āliyya's statement that what is meant is the Day of Rising when his own people will curse him along with everyone else.

وَإِلَٰهُكُمْ إِلَٰهٌ وَاحِدٌ ۖ لَّا إِلَٰهَ إِلَّا هُوَ الرَّحْمَٰنُ الرَّحِيمُ ﴿١٦٣﴾

163 ***Your God is One God.***
There is no god but Him,
the All-Merciful, the Most Merciful.

Your God is One God.

When Allah warned against concealing the truth, He made it clear that the first thing which must be made clear and which it is not permitted to conceal is knowledge of Allah's unity. He connected the proof to that and instructed people on how to examine that: one should reflect on the wonders of creation so as to know that there must be a Unique Doer who is not like anything else.

There is no god but Him,

This means that there is nothing worthy of worship except Allah. It is reported that ash-Shiblī used to say the name *'Allah'* alone and omit the words *'lā ilāha'* – 'there is no god'. He was asked about that and said, "I fear that I might die on the word of denial and not reach the word of affirmation." This is one of the very refined areas of knowledge which has no real substance. Allah mentions this phrase in His Book with both negation and affirmation and repeats it many times and promised, on the tongue of His Prophet, an ample reward for whoever says it. He said, may Allah bless him and grant him peace, "If someone's last words are 'There is no god but Allah', he will enter the Garden." (Muslim) What is meant is with the heart, not the tongue alone. If someone says, "There is no god" and dies before completing the formula but his belief and conscience affirm Allah's unity and His necessary attributes, he is one of the people of the Garden by the agreement of the people of the *Sunna*.

إِنَّ فِے خَلْقِ اِ۬لسَّمَٰوَٰتِ وَالْأَرْضِ وَاخْتِلَٰفِ اِ۬ليْلِ وَالنَّهَارِ
وَالْفُلْكِ اِ۬لتِے تَجْرِے فِے اِ۬لْبَحْرِ بِمَا يَنفَعُ اُ۬لنَّاسَ وَمَآ أَنزَلَ اَ۬للَّهُ مِنَ
اَ۬لسَّمَآءِ مِن مَّآءٖ فَأَحْيَا بِهِ اِ۬لْأَرْضَ بَعْدَ مَوْتِهَا وَبَثَّ فِيهَا مِن
كُلِّ دَآبَّةٖ وَتَصْرِيفِ اِ۬لرِّيَٰحِ وَالسَّحَابِ اِ۬لْمُسَخَّرِ بَيْنَ اَ۬لسَّمَآءِ
وَالْأَرْضِ لَأٓيَٰتٖ لِّقَوْمٖ يَعْقِلُونَ ﴿١٦٤﴾

164 *In the creation of the heavens and earth,*
and the alternation of the night and day,
and the ships which sail the seas
to people's benefit,
and the water which Allah sends down
from the sky –
by which He brings the earth to life
when it was dead
and scatters about in it creatures of every kind –
and the varying direction of the winds,

and the clouds subservient
between heaven and earth,
there are Signs for people who use their intellect.

When the previous *āyat* was revealed, the unbelievers of Quraysh said, "How can One God be enough for people!" And then this *āyat* was revealed. Abū'ḍ-Ḍuḥā said that, when the previous *āyat* was revealed, they said, "What proof is there of this?" And so Allah revealed this *āyat*. It is as if they were asking for a sign to make the oneness of Allah clear to them: this universe and wondrous structure must have a Builder and Maker. *"Samāwāt"* (heavens) is in the plural because there are different types of heaven. Each heaven is different from all the other heavens. *"Arḍ"* (earth) is singular because there is only one earth. Allah knows best. The sign of the heavens is that they are elevated without support under them or above them. That indicates incomprehensible power. Then there are the sun, moon and stars which rise and set in them which are yet another sign of Allah's power.

and the alternation of the night and day,

as they come and go from where it is not known. It is said that their differentiation is in respect of the variable intensity of the light and darkness, and the variation in the length and shortness of each. "*Nahār*" (day) denotes the time of light between dawn and sunset.

and the ships which sail the seas to people's benefit,

"*Fulk*" (ships) is a generic term for all water craft. The meaning of the *āyat* is that Allah controls them so that they move on the surface of the water and float in spite of their weight. The first person to make one was Nūḥ, as Allah reports.

This *āyat* and those like it indicate the permission to travel on the sea in general, for commerce or for acts of worship such as the *Ḥajj* and *jihād*. In the *Sunna* we find the *ḥadīth* of Abū Hurayra, "A man came to the Messenger of Allah, may Allah bless him and grant him peace, and said, 'Messenger of Allah, we travel on the sea and carry a little water with us.'" And there are other *aḥādīth* to the same effect. When the sea is rough, however, it is not permitted for anyone to embark on it nor to do so at times when it is generally unsafe.

The words "to people's benefit" in this phrase refer to benefit they might have in trade or anything else which is proper for them. If people criticise the Qur'ān, saying, "Allah revealed in the Book, *'We have not omitted anything from the Book,'* (6:38) so where do we find food seasonings like salt, pepper and the like?", the reply is, "They can be found in Allah's words 'to people's benefit.'"

and the water which Allah sends down from the sky –

This, of course, means the rain which brings the world to life and makes the plants grow and is conserved in it for use at other times, as Allah says, *"We lodged it firmly in the earth."* (23:18)

and scatters about in it creatures of every kind –

This means separates them and spreads them out. The word "*dābba*" (creatures) includes all animals. Some people say that this *āyat* excludes birds, but this is rejected because they too have feet for walking on the earth.

and the varying direction of the winds,

Sending them as sometimes barren, sometimes fertilising, sometimes as freezing gales, sometimes helping, sometimes destroying, sometimes hot and sometimes cold, sometimes gentle and sometimes tempestuous. It is said that the expression refers just to their direction – north, south, east or west and the way they veer from one to the other. It is said that it means that it moves large ships with full loads as well as small ships and averts what will harm them. It is said to refer to their variation from season to season.

Abū Hurayra reported that the Messenger of Allah, may Allah bless him and grant him peace, said, "The wind (*rīḥ*) is part of the solace (*rawḥ*) given by Allah. It brings mercy and brings punishment. When you see it, do not curse it. Ask Allah for its good and seek refuge with Allah from its evil." It is also related that the Prophet, may Allah bless him and grant him peace, said, "Do not curse the wind. It is from the breath of the All-Merciful." That means that Allah Almighty puts relief, refreshment and comfort in it.

and the clouds subservient between heaven and earth,

"*Saḥāb*" (clouds) takes that name because they are dragged (*insiḥāb*) along in the air. *Saḥaba* means to drag along. *Saḥb*, from the same root, means vigorous eating and drinking. They are "subservient" because they are moved without resistance from one place to another. It is said that their subservience lies in their remaining poised between heaven and earth without any support. The first is more likely. They can bring water or punishment. In Muslim, Abū Hurayra reported that the Prophet, may Allah bless him and grant him peace, said, "Once, while a man was walking in the desert, he heard a voice in a cloud saying, 'Water the garden of so-and-so.' And that cloud went and poured out its water into a rocky area. There was a certain water channel which held all the water and he followed it and found a man standing in his garden directing the water with his spade. He said to him. 'Slave of Allah, what is your name?' He said, 'So-and-so,' giving the same name he had heard from the cloud. The man then said to him, 'O slave of Allah, why did you ask me my name?' The first man said, 'I heard a voice in the cloud from which this water came say, "Water the garden of so-and-so" giving your name. What are you doing with it?' He said, 'Since you have asked this, I will [reply]. I wait and see what it produces and give a third of it away as *ṣadaqa*, and my family and I eat from a third, and I reinvest a third back into it.'" In one version, "I devote a third of it to the poor, beggars and travellers."

In the Qur'ān we also find, *"It is Allah who sends the winds which raise the clouds which We then drive to a dead land."* (35:9) and there are many other similar *āyat*s. 'Ā'isha said, "When the Prophet, may Allah bless him and grant him peace, saw a cloud coming on the horizon, he left what he was doing, even if he was in the prayer, to salute it. He would say, 'O Allah, we seek refuge with You from the evil of what You have sent.' If it rained, he would say, 'O Allah, a useful watering.' two or three times. If Allah moved it on and it did not rain, he would praise Allah for that." 'A'isha also said, "When it was a day of wind and clouds, that could be seen in the face of the Messenger of Allah, may Allah bless him and grant him peace. He paced back and forth. If it rained, he was happy and that state left him." She said. "I asked him and he said, 'I fear that it will be a punishment sent on My community.'"

Ka'b al-Aḥbar said, "The clouds are sieves for the rain. Were it nor for the clouds, when water descended from heaven, it would ruin the earth on which it fell." Ibn 'Abbās related that from him.

there are Signs for people who use their intellect.

Allah's Signs are evidence of His oneness and power. That is why these matters are mentioned after the previous *āyat* which begins *"Your God is One God…"* in order to demonstrate the truth of that statement. The Prophet, may Allah bless him and grant him peace, said, "Woe to the person who reads this *āyat* and dismisses it," i.e. does not reflect on it or ponder it.

وَمِنَ ٱلنَّاسِ مَن يَتَّخِذُ مِن دُونِ ٱللَّهِ أَندَادًا يُحِبُّونَهُمْ كَحُبِّ
ٱللَّهِ ۖ وَٱلَّذِينَ ءَامَنُوٓا۟ أَشَدُّ حُبًّا لِّلَّهِ ۗ وَلَوْ تَرَى ٱلَّذِينَ
ظَلَمُوٓا۟ إِذْ يَرَوْنَ ٱلْعَذَابَ أَنَّ ٱلْقُوَّةَ لِلَّهِ جَمِيعًا
وَأَنَّ ٱللَّهَ شَدِيدُ ٱلْعَذَابِ ۗ ﴿١٦٥﴾

165 ***Some people set up equals to Allah,***
loving them as they should love Allah.
But those who believe have greater love for Allah.
If only you could see those who do wrong
at the time when they see the punishment,

and that truly all strength belongs to Allah, and that Allah is severe in punishment.

Some people set up equals to Allah,

In the previous *āyat*, Allah gave evidence of His oneness, power and the immensity of His authority and He now adds these cogent *āyat*s, for those with intelligence, about people who set up equals to Him. Mujāhid says that what is meant are the idols which they worshipped in the same way that they worshipped Allah, giving them equal value.

loving them as they should love Allah.

They love their false idols as much as the believers love the Truly Real. Al-Mubarrad said that. Az-Zajjāj said, "In spite of the lack of power of the idols, they love them as the believers love Allah with His real power." Ibn 'Abbās and as-Suddī said that it refers to their leaders whom they follow in disobeying Allah.

If only you could see those who do wrong at the time when they see the punishment,

The reading of the people of Madina and Syria is "you could see" whereas the people of Makka and Kufa read it as "they could see". Abū 'Ubayd said, "The meaning is, that if those who do wrong in this world were to see the punishment of the Next World, they would know when they see it that all strength belongs to Allah." "See" then would mean actual vision. An-Naḥḥās says in his book, *The Meanings of the Qur'ān*, "This position is the one generally held by the people of *tafsīr*." Muḥammad ibn Yazīd said that this explanation of Abū 'Ubayd is unlikely and it is not well expressed because it implies "if those who did wrong had seen the punishment." So it is as if he considers it uncertain when Allah has made it mandatory.

and that truly all strength belongs to Allah,

Al-Akhfash said that the verb "see" continues so that the meaning is, "If those who do wrong could see that strength belongs to

Allah...," and that the word "see" means "know" in this context so it really means if they knew the reality of the strength of Allah and the severity of His punishment.

Taking the Madinan reading, it is a threat: "If you, Muḥammad, could see those who do wrong when they see the punishment and are terrified of it, they would affirm that all strength belongs to Allah." The Prophet, may Allah bless him and grant him peace, knew that, but he was addressed when his whole community was intended, as is often the case. It may also mean: "Say, Muḥammad, to the wrongdoer..."

إِذْ تَبَرَّأَ ٱلَّذِينَ ٱتُّبِعُوا۟ مِنَ ٱلَّذِينَ ٱتَّبَعُوا۟
وَرَأَوُا۟ ٱلْعَذَابَ وَتَقَطَّعَتْ بِهِمُ ٱلْأَسْبَابُ ﴿١٦٦﴾

166 ***When those who were followed***
disown those who followed them,
and they see the punishment,
and the connection between them is cut,

When those who were followed disown those who followed them,

"Those who were followed" are the masters and leaders of the unbelievers. They will declare themselves free of those who followed them in disbelief, as Qatāda, 'Aṭā' and ar-Rabī' said. Qatāda also said, as did as-Suddī, that they were the shayṭāns who misguide mankind and who will declare themselves free of them on the Last Day. It is said that it is general to all who are followed in disbelief.

and they see the punishment,

"They" are both the followers and the followed. It is said to be through the certainty they will have in this world at the time of their death about the inevitability of punishment and it is said to refer to their being presented before Allah and questioned in the

Next World. Both may be true: it can mean at the time of death and it can mean in the Next World when they actually experience the pain of the punishment.

and the connection between them is cut,

This refers to their connection in this world through kinship and in other ways, as Mujāhid and others said. The root of the word for "connection" (*sabab*) is a rope which is tied to a thing so that it can be pulled. So what pulls a thing into existence is a *sabab*, which gives the word its usual meaning of means or cause. As-Suddī and Ibn Zayd said, "The means are their actions."

وَقَالَ ٱلَّذِينَ ٱتَّبَعُوا۟ لَوْ أَنَّ لَنَا كَرَّةً فَنَتَبَرَّأَ مِنْهُمْ كَمَا
تَبَرَّءُوا۟ مِنَّا ۗ كَذَٰلِكَ يُرِيهِمُ ٱللَّهُ أَعْمَٰلَهُمْ حَسَرَٰتٍ عَلَيْهِمْ ۖ
وَمَا هُم بِخَٰرِجِينَ مِنَ ٱلنَّارِ ۝١٦٧

167 ***those who followed will say,***
'If only we could have another chance,
we would disown them
just as they have disowned us.'
In that way Allah will show them their actions
as a cause of anguish and remorse for them.
They will never emerge from the Fire.

those who followed will say, 'If only we could have another chance,

The followers claim that they would act righteously if they were given another opportunity.

In that way Allah will show them their actions as a cause of anguish and remorse for them.

As Allah will show them the Fire, so He will also show them their actions which are the cause of their entering it. This is actual seeing with the eye. Ar-Rabīʿ said that these are the corrupt actions which they committed which made the Fire mandatory for them. Ibn Masʿūd and as-Suddī said that it refers to the righteous actions which they abandoned and thereby forfeited the Garden. There are many *aḥādīth* to this effect. As-Suddī said, "They will be shown the Garden and will look at it and at their houses there which they would have had if they had obeyed Allah. Those houses will be divided between the believers. They are called "their" actions because they were commanded to do them. "*Ḥasara*" (anguish) is the highest degree of regret for something forfeited. It is derived from *ḥasīr* (exhausted), which is when something is cut off and its strength gone, like a camel which is completely exhausted. It also means to uncover.

They will never emerge from the Fire.

An indication that the unbelievers will be in the Fire forever and never leave it. This is the position of the people of the *Sunna*.

يَٰٓأَيُّهَا ٱلنَّاسُ كُلُوا۟ مِمَّا فِى ٱلْأَرْضِ حَلَٰلًا طَيِّبًا وَلَا
تَتَّبِعُوا۟ خُطُوَٰتِ ٱلشَّيْطَٰنِ إِنَّهُۥ لَكُمْ عَدُوٌّ مُّبِينٌ ١٦٨

168 ***Mankind! eat what is good and lawful on the earth.***
And do not follow in the footsteps of Shayṭān.
He truly is an outright enemy to you.

Mankind!

It is said that this was revealed about the tribes of Thaqīf, Khuzāʿa and Banū Mudlij about the blessings which they denied themselves, but the words bear a general meaning.

eat what is good and lawful on the earth.

"Ṭayyib" (good) here means "lawful" and this is emphasised by the use of the actual legal term (*ḥalāl*) immediately after it. This is the position of Mālik about "good". Ash-Shāfiʿī said that it means

"pleasant and wholesome" which is why he forbade feeding animals filth. Allah willing, this will be dealt with in greater depth in *Sūrat al-An'ām* and *Sūrat al-A'rāf.*

The term "*ḥalāl*" (lawful) is called that because the bond of prohibition has been released (*inḥilāl*) from it. Sahl ibn 'Abdullāh said, "Salvation lies in three things: consuming the *ḥalāl*, performing the obligations and imitation of the Prophet, may Allah bless him and grant him peace." Abū 'Abdullāh as-Sājī, Sa'īd ibn Yazīd, said, "There are five qualities which complete knowledge: gnosis of Allah Almighty, recognition of the truth, sincere action for Allah, acting according to the *Sunna* and consuming the *ḥalāl*. If even one of them is lacking, the action is not complete." Sahl said, "Eating the *ḥalāl* is only valid with knowledge, and wealth is not *ḥalāl* until it is free of six things: usury, the *ḥarām*, theft, usurpation, the disliked and the doubtful."

And do not follow in the footsteps of Shaytan.

It is possible that the word "*khuṭuwāt*" (footsteps) comes from *khaṭī'a* (error). The majority say that the phrase means: Do not follow the actions of Shayṭān. As-Suddī said that it means: do not obey him. The sound position is that it is general to all customs and laws stemming from innovations and acts of disobedience.

He truly is an outright enemy to you.

An intelligent person must be cautious about this enemy whose enmity has been clear from the time of Ādam and who has devoted his energy to corrupting the states of mankind. For this reason Allah commanded us to be on our guard against him in many places in the Qur'ān. 'Abdullāh ibn 'Umar said, "Iblīs is confined to the lower earth. When he moves, every evil in the earth between two or more people is set in motion."

إِنَّمَا يَأْمُرُكُم بِالسُّوٓءِ وَالْفَحْشَآءِ وَأَن
تَقُولُوا۟ عَلَى ٱللَّهِ مَا لَا تَعْلَمُونَ ١٦٩

169 ***He only commands you to do evil and indecent acts and to say about Allah what you do not know.***

He only commands you to do evil and indecent acts

The word for evil is *sū'* because it is bad for the person who does it and brings evil consequences in its wake. The root of the word for indecent acts (*faḥshā'*) means something which is ugly to look at. The *Sharī'a* is what makes something good or ugly. All that the *Sharī'a* forbids is ugly and so it is part of the indecent. Muqātil said, "Everywhere the Qur'ān mentions "indecency" it implies fornication except where He says, *"Shayṭān promises you poverty and commands you to avarice (faḥshā')," *(2:268) where it means to refuse to pay *zakāt*.

According to this, there is no *ḥadd* for "evil", but there is for "indecency." That is related from Ibn 'Abbās and others, and Allah knows best.

and to say about Allah what you do not know.

Aṭ-Ṭabarī says that this refers to various animals, like *baḥīra*, *sā'iba* and other such animals[1] which the idolaters made unlawful without any basis for doing so.

وَإِذَا قِيلَ لَهُمُ ٱتَّبِعُوا۟ مَآ أَنزَلَ ٱللَّهُ قَالُوا۟ بَلْ نَتَّبِعُ مَآ أَلْفَيْنَا عَلَيْهِ
ءَابَآءَنَآ ۗ أَوَلَوْ كَانَ ءَابَآؤُهُمْ لَا يَعْقِلُونَ شَيْـًٔا وَلَا يَهْتَدُونَ ﴿١٧٠﴾

170 ***When they are told,***
'Follow what Allah has sent down to you,'
They say, 'We are following
what we found our fathers doing.'
What, even though their fathers did not understand
a thing and were not guided!

1. See 5:103. This refers to pagan superstitions about animals. A she-camel which had produced many young, had its ear split and was called *baḥīra.* A camel consecrated to a deity and left to freely graze was called *sā'iba*.

When they are told, 'Follow what Allah has sent down to you,'

It is generally held that it is the unbelieving Arabs who are being addressed here but Ibn 'Abbās said that it was revealed about the Jews. Aṭ-Ṭabarī said that the pronoun refers back to 'mankind' in the last-but-one *āyat*. Following implies both acceptance and action.

They say, 'We are following what we found our fathers doing.'

The strength of the expression of this *āyat* would seem, on the surface, to challenge the whole matter of *taqlīd*, which is the acceptance of an inherited position without calling it into question, and there are other *āyat*s which have the same import. This *āyat* and the ones like it, however, are connected to what came before them. That is because Allah informs us about the ignorance of the Arabs in judging by their superstitious customs concerning animals like *baḥīra*, *sā'iba* and *waṣīla*, using as evidence the fact that their fathers did that, and the command to abandon such customs was revealed by Allah to His Messenger.

Some people, however, believe that this *āyat* censures taking the position of *taqlīd* since Allah Almighty censures the unbelievers for following their fathers in falsehood and imitating them in disbelief and disobedience. This is sound where falsehood is concerned. As for *taqlīd* in respect of the truth, it is one of the principles of the *dīn* and is a protection for the Muslims to which unlearned people who are unqualified to make rulings about matters of the *dīn* should have recourse. Scholars disagree about the permissibility of *taqlīd* in matters of *uṣūl* (basic principles), as will be discussed, but it is universally permitted in respect of secondary rulings.

According to scholars, the reality of *taqlīd* is to accept a position without evidence. Accordingly, someone who accepts the Prophet, may Allah bless him and grant him peace, without looking at his miracles would be a *muqallid*. Someone who looks into them would not be. It is said that it is believing in the soundness of the *fatwās* of someone when the soundness of his position is not known. It is derived from the *qilāda* or halter of the camel, which is when a rope is placed around its neck so that it can be led anywhere.

Taqlīd is not a means to knowledge nor does it reach it, either in respect of basic principles or secondary rulings. That is the position of the majority of intelligent people and scholars, as opposed to what is related from the ignorant Ḥashwiyya and Tha'alibiyya who claim that *taqlīd* is the sole means to recognise the truth and that it is mandatory, and that investigation and consideration are *ḥarām*.

The obligation for the common person who is not able to deduce rulings from basic principles because he is not qualified to do so on account of his lack of knowledge of the *dīn* is to head for the person with the most knowledge in his time and his land and ask him about his problem and follow his *fatwā* since Allah says, *"Ask the people of the Reminder if you do not know."* (16:43) He uses *ijtihād* in finding the most knowledgeable of the people of his time by investigating until he satisfied that he has found the man whom most people agree to be the most learned. A scholar must also imitate a scholar who has a similar standing to him in a case in which he does not find the solution through evidence and his own investigation. Qāḍī Abū Bakr and a group of established scholars believed that.

Ibn 'Aṭiyya said, "The Community agrees that *taqlīd* in respect of articles of faith is invalid." Others, however, stated that there is disagreement about that, like Qāḍī Abū Bakr ibn 'Arabī and Abū 'Amr 'Uthmān Ibn Darbās. In *al-Intiṣār*, Ibn Darbās said, "Some people permit *taqlīd* in respect of *tawḥīd*, but this is shown to be wrong by the words of Allah: *'We found our fathers following a religion'* (43:23), so He censured their imitation of their fathers and not following the Messenger, and this is just what the followers of sects do when they imitate their great men and do not follow the *dīn* of Muhammad, may Allah bless him and grant him peace. It is an obligation for every responsible person to learn *tawḥīd* and proper understanding of it. That can only be obtained through the

Book and the *Sunna* as we made clear. Allah guides whomever He wills."

Ibn Darbās also said, "Many of the people who follow sects say that those who cling to the Book and *Sunna* are imitators. This is an error on their part. This designation is more applicable to them and their scholars are less able since they turn to the position of their masters and great men in their deviation from the Book of Allah and the *Sunna* of His Messenger and the consensus of the Companions. So they are included among those whom Allah censures when He says, *'Our Lord, we obeyed our masters and great men...'* (33:67)"

وَمَثَلُ الَّذِينَ كَفَرُوا كَمَثَلِ الَّذِي يَنْعِقُ بِمَا لَا يَسْمَعُ إِلَّا
دُعَاءً وَنِدَاءً صُمٌّ بُكْمٌ عُمْيٌ فَهُمْ لَا يَعْقِلُونَ ﴿١٧١﴾

171 ***The likeness of those who disbelieve***
is that of someone
who yells out to something which cannot hear –
it is nothing but a cry and a call.
Deaf – dumb – blind.
They do not use their intellect.

One understanding of this *āyat* is that Allah is making a metaphorical allusion to Muḥammad, may Allah bless him and grant him peace, who is the warner of the unbelievers and the one who calls them to faith. He is saying that he is like a shepherd who calls out to his sheep and camels, but they only hear his call but do not understand what he says. Ibn 'Abbās, 'Ikrima, as-Suddī, az-Zajjāj, al-Farrā' and Sibuwayh explained it like that, saying that the unbeliever is not the one who calls out but the one called out to. The call is like someone shouting out in the night and being answered by an echo without receiving any meaningful response.

Quṭrub, however, said, "The metaphor refers to the unbelievers calling out to something which cannot possibly respond, meaning their idols, likening them to a shepherd who calls out to his sheep when he has no idea where they are. Aṭ-Ṭabarī says it means that the unbelievers, in calling on their idols, are like people who call out to something which is distant and cannot hear. In these latter interpretations those calling out are the unbelievers and the idols are what they are calling out to.

يَٰٓأَيُّهَا ٱلَّذِينَ ءَامَنُوا۟ كُلُوا۟ مِن طَيِّبَٰتِ مَا رَزَقْنَٰكُمْ وَٱشْكُرُوا۟
لِلَّهِ إِن كُنتُمْ إِيَّاهُ تَعْبُدُونَ ﴿١٧٢﴾

172 ***You who believe! eat of the good things***
We have provided for you
and give thanks to Allah if you worship Him alone.

This confirms the first command (2:168) which was to mankind in general. The believers are mentioned here out of preference and what is meant by "eating" is consuming things and using them in any way. It is also said that it is eating in the usual sense of the word. In the *Ṣaḥīḥ* Collection of Muslim, the Messenger of Allah, may Allah bless him and grant him peace, said, "People! Allah is good and only accepts the good. Allah gives the same command to the believers that He gives the Messengers. Allah Almighty says, *'O Messengers, eat of the good things and act rightly. I most certainly know what you do'* (23:51) and He says, *'You who believe! eat of the good things We have provided for you...'* (this *āyat*)" Then he mentioned a man who goes on a long journey, is dishevelled and dusty and stretches out his hands to heaven saying, "O Lord! O Lord!" and said, "When his food is unlawful, his drink is unlawful, his clothes are unlawful, and his whole sustenance is unlawful. How could such a man be responded to?"

إِنَّمَا حَرَّمَ عَلَيْكُمُ الْمَيْتَةَ وَالدَّمَ وَلَحْمَ الْخِنزِيرِ وَمَآ أُهِلَّ بِهِۦ لِغَيْرِ اللَّهِ فَمَنِ اضْطُرَّ غَيْرَ بَاغٍ وَلَا عَادٍ فَلَآ إِثْمَ عَلَيْهِ إِنَّ اللَّهَ غَفُورٌ رَّحِيمٌ ١٧٣

173 ***He has only forbidden you carrion, blood and pork***
and what has been consecrated to other than Allah.
But anyone who is forced to eat it –
without desiring it or going to excess in it –
commits no crime.
Allah is Ever-Forgiving, Most Merciful.

He has only forbidden you

The Arabic expression used here implies limitation and restriction, and so Allah moves from the general permission in the previous *āyat* to what is forbidden in this one. There is no food forbidden beyond this. This is a Madinan *āyat* and it is reinforced by another *āyat* revealed at 'Arafa, *"I do not find in what has been revealed to me, any food it is* ḥarām *to eat except for..."* (6:145) So it is completely clear.

carrion,

This applies to animals which are normally slaughtered but which have died without being slaughtered, and to animals which may not be eaten even if they have been slaughtered, such as beasts of prey. This will be examined in more detail when we reach the relevant passage in *Sūrat al-An'ām.*

This *āyat* is general and is qualified by the words of the Prophet, "Two kinds of carrion are lawful for us: fish and locusts; and the blood of the liver and spleen is also lawful." (ad-Dāraquṭnī). This is an instance of a *ḥadīth* qualifying a general text in the Qur'ān. Most of the people of knowledge permit the eating of all the animals of the sea, alive or dead, and this is the school of Mālik. He hesitated about "sea pigs" (dolphins) and said, "You said 'pig'!" Ibn al-Qāsim said, "I am cautious about it but do not think that it is *ḥarām*."

People disagree about the possibility of the Book of Allah being qualified by the *Sunna* and they agree that it is not permitted for this to take place if the *ḥadīth* is weak. Ibn al-'Arabī said that. There is evidence that this verse has been qualified by a number of *aḥādīth*. In the *Ṣaḥīḥ* Collection of Muslim, 'Abdullāh ibn Abī Wafā said, "We went on seven expeditions with the Messenger of Allah, may Allah bless him and grant him peace, during which we ate locusts." It is clear that they ate them even though they had died. This is what most scholars including ash-Shāfi'ī and Abū Ḥanīfa say. The Mālikīs say that they are not eaten if they have been smothered because they are land creatures.

Scholars disagree about using carrion or anything which is impure for purposes other than eating. There are different positions related from Mālik regarding that as well. Once he said that their use was permitted because it is recorded that the Prophet, peace be upon him, passed by a dead sheep and said, "Why didn't you take its skin?" Another time he said, "It is all forbidden and it is not permitted to use any of it nor any other impurity in any way," so that he did not permit watering crops or animals with impure water or feeding animals things which are impure or even giving them to dogs and wild animals. The reason for that is the words of Allah, *"Ḥarām for you are carrion and blood."* (5:3). And the Prophet, peace be upon him, said in another *ḥadīth*, "Do not use any part of carrion."

When a camel, cow or sheep is slaughtered, and there is a foetus inside it, it is permitted to eat the foetus without slaughtering it unless it emerges alive in which case it should be slaughtered. If the foetus emerges dead after the mother has been slaughtered it is considered as one of its limbs. That is clear because it is not permitted to sell an animal excluding her unborn foetus.

The transmissions from Mālik vary about whether the skin of carrion is made pure by tanning or not. It is related that it is not and that is the well-known position of his school, and it is related that it is pure, based on the words of the Prophet, may Allah bless him and grant him peace, "Any skin which is tanned is pure." It is possible that it means that tanning removes external impurities and so it can be used for dry things and for sitting on or for holding water, because water is pure as long as it is not changed in colour, taste or smell.

The hair of carrion and wool is pure since it is related from Umm Salama that the Prophet, may Allah bless him and grant him peace, said, "There is no harm in keeping carrion when it is tanned and its wool and hair are washed." That is because it is pure if it is taken from it while alive, and so the same applies after death, while the flesh is impure, alive or dead.

blood

Scholars agree that blood is *ḥarām* and impure and may not be eaten or used. What is forbidden is blood that is spilled. 'Ā'isha said, "We used to cook a dish in the time of the Messenger of Allah, may Allah bless him and grant him peace, and it had a yellow colour from the blood but we ate it without dislike." Otherwise that would entail undue hardship.

In this *āyat* Allah forbids blood without qualification and then He qualifies it in *al-An'ām* (6:145) by the word "spilled" (*masfūḥ*). Scholars agree that this qualifies the unqualified and the blood meant is that which is spilled out and not that which is mixed with the flesh which, by consensus, is not forbidden. There is disagreement about fish blood which is separated from it. It is related that it is pure and that is said by Ibn al-'Arabī. Abū Ḥanīfa takes the same view and they argue against the Shāfi'īs.

and pork

Allah mentioned the meat of pigs to indicate that it is forbidden, whether slaughtered or not. It includes the fat, gristle and all other parts. The community agree that the fat of pigs is forbidden. Mālik and his people used as evidence that if someone who swears not to eat fat eats meat, he has not broken his oath but if he swears not to eat meat and then eats fat, he has broken it because fat is included with meat.

There is no disagreement that all of the pig is forbidden except for the bristle which can be used for stitching. It is reported that a man asked the Messenger of Allah, may Allah bless him and grant him peace, about stitching with pig bristle and he said, "There is no harm in it."

and what has been consecrated to other than Allah.

This is something over which other than the Name of Allah was mentioned when it was slaughtered. It refers to the slaughtering done by Magians, idol worshippers and atheists. The idol worshipper sacrifices to an idol, the Magian to the fire, and the atheist, who does not believe anything, slaughters for himself. There is no disagreement among the scholars that whatever a Magian or idol-worshipper slaughters to their idol or fire may not be eaten. According to Mālik, ash-Shāfi'ī and others, what such people sacrifice to the fire or idol may not be eaten at all. Ibn al-Musayyab and Abū Thawr, however, permit that meat to be eaten if it is slaughtered for a Muslim at his order. This will explained in more detail in *Sūrat al-Mā'ida*. The word "consecration" (*uhilla*) means "to raise the voice". Ibn 'Abbās said, "What is meant is what is sacrificed to idols and stones." The custom of the Arabs was to shout the name of the one intended by the sacrifice. That was their usual practice and so it is considered to be tantamount to the intention.

But anyone who is forced to eat it –

Forcing can be either by physical force exerted by a wrongdoer or compulsion due to extreme hunger. If someone is physically forced by someone to eat something unlawful, that renders it lawful for him for the duration of the time that the force is being applied. Hunger can be either persistent or not. If it is persistent, there is no disagreement that it is permitted to eat one's fill of carrion. If someone is suffering from hunger and finds the property of a Muslim whose value is not sufficient to cause his hand to be cut off for theft and will cause no annoyance to the owner, like some dates hanging from a tree, a sheep astray in the mountains and the like, it is not lawful for him to then eat carrion. There is no disagreement about this because of the *ḥadīth* reported by Abū Hurayra who said, "Once, when we were with the Messenger of Allah, may Allah bless him and grant him peace, on a journey we saw some camels tied to the branches of some trees. We went to them but the Messenger of Allah called to us and we returned to him. He said, 'These camels belong to people from a Muslim house. After Allah, it is their strength and fortune. Would you like to return to your bags of provisions and find them gone? Do you think that that would be fair?' 'No,' we replied. He said, 'This is the same situation.' We asked, 'And if we need food and drink?' He said, 'Eat but do not take anything away with you. Drink but do not take anything away with you.'" (Ibn Mājah)

Ibn Mājah said, "I believe this to be the basic principle." Ibn al-Mundhir said, "We asked, 'Messenger of Allah, what is lawful for someone to take from his brother's property if he is compelled (by hunger).' He replied, 'He should eat but not take anything away and drink but not take anything away.'" Abū 'Umar said, "The predominant position is that it is incumbent on a Muslim to preserve the life of another Muslim. It is an individual obligation for him unless someone else takes care of it."

In Ibn Mājah, we read that a man of the Banu Ghubar said, "We suffered in the year of the famine and I came to Madina and went to one of its gardens and took an ear of corn, ground it, and ate some and put some in my garment. The owner came and beat me and took the garment. I went to the Messenger of Allah, may Allah bless him and grant him peace, and told him. He told the man, 'Why did you not feed him when he was hungry or starving? Why did you not teach him since he was ignorant?'" He commanded him to return the man's garment to him and ordered a *wasq* or half a *wasq* of food for him. And there are more *aḥādīth* to the same effect. Abū Dāwūd transmitted from Samura that the Prophet, may Allah bless him and grant him peace, said, "When one of you comes to a flock and the owner is there, he should ask his permission to milk and drink. If no one is there, he should shout three times. If the person comes, he asks permission. If not, he may milk a ewe and drink but may not take anything with him." It is reported that the Prophet, may Allah bless him and grant him peace, said, "If someone takes what he needs (from hanging fruit) and does not take any away, he has done nothing wrong."

If someone is physically forced to drink wine, he may drink it but if it is on account of hunger or thirst, he should not do so. That is what Mālik said according to *al-'Utbiyya*. It is the position of ash-Shāfi'ī. Allah completely forbade wine and forbade carrion provided that there is no dire necessity. Al-Abharī says, "If wine will remove hunger or thirst from him, he should drink it because Allah says that pigs are impure but then permits them in case of necessity. Allah calls wine an impurity and it should be included under the same permission as that of pigs in necessity according to the apparent meaning which is stronger than using analogy. Aṣbagh related that Ibn al-Qāsim said, "Someone in dire need may drink blood but not wine. He may eat carrion but not take advantage of lost camels." Ibn Wahb also said that. He may drink urine but should not go near wine because the *ḥadd* is obliged for it, and because of this the prohibition is stronger.

If someone chokes on food, is wine allowed or not to relieve it? It is said that it is not, out of the fear that people will simply use that as an excuse. Ibn Ḥabīb claims that it is permitted in that instance because it is a case of necessity. Ibn al-'Arabī said, "Someone who chokes on something is permitted it in respect of what is between him and Allah. As for what is between him and us, if we see him, the circumstances are not hidden from us in that he is choking on something and so he is believed if he shows that. If he does not show it, he is given the *ḥadd* outwardly but is safe from the punishment of Allah inwardly if it really is the case."

If someone who is in dire need finds carrion, pork and human flesh, he may eat carrion because it is *ḥalāl* for him in that one situation whereas pork and human flesh never are, and so it is better to go for the lesser prohibition. Similarly, if someone is forced to have intercourse with his sister or an unrelated woman, he should choose the unrelated woman. This is the rule in these judgements. He should not eat human flesh, even if that results in his death. Our scholars said that and Aḥmad ibn Ḥanbal and Dā'ud relate that. Ash-Shāfi'ī says that he should.

As for using these things for medical treatment, either in their original form or burned, Ibn Ḥabīb says that they are permitted for medicinal use if they are changed by burning. Ibn al-Mājishūn said that burning purifies since it changes the character of the substance (as in burned bones). Saḥnūn said that carrion or pig should never be used for medicinal purposes since something else can be used. Wine may not be used for medicinal use either, as Mālik stated, and that is also the main position of ash-Shāfi'ī. Some people forbid using anything unlawful for medicine, quoting the Prophet's words, "Allah did not put the treatment of my community in something He made forbidden for them." He also said to Ṭāriq ibn Suwayd when he wanted to use wine for medicine, "It is not a remedy; it is an illness." (Muslim). It is possible that this is limited to necessity. It is permitted to use poison for medicine, but not to drink it.

without desiring it

This means without having an appetite for it or taking pleasure in it.

or going to excess in it –

This means by eating beyond taking what is necessary to satisfy one's hunger. The basic meaning of the word for going to excess, *baghī*, is to aim for and intend corruption.

The basic ruling in this matter, as we have made clear, is that Allah permits, in the case of necessity, the consumption of all forbidden things if there is no possibility of obtaining permitted things.

Scholars disagree about what the ruling is if criminal acts of disobedience leads to a such state of necessity, like as highway robbery or causing alarm to people in other ways. Mālik, and ash-Shāfi'ī in one of his positions, forbade using the general permission to cover such acts because Allah made the allowance to help us and it is not lawful to help a rebel. If he wants to eat, let him repent and eat. Abū Ḥanīfa and ash-Shāfi'ī in another position, allow it. They consider the permission to be the same.

The sound position is that it is not forbidden for a criminal to take such food because the destruction of a man in disobedience is worse than the disobedience he is involved in. Allah says, *"Do not kill yourselves."* (4:29) This is general. Perhaps he might repent later and his repentance will efface what went before. Masrūq said, "If someone needs to eat carrion, blood, and pork, and then does not eat and dies as a consequence, he will enter the Fire unless Allah pardons him. Eating carrion in necessity is an allowance but in his case becomes mandatory.

Allah is Ever-Forgiving, Most Merciful.

Allah forgives acts of disobedience and so He is more likely to forgive something He has given permission for.

إِنَّ ٱلَّذِينَ يَكْتُمُونَ مَآ أَنزَلَ ٱللَّهُ مِنَ ٱلْكِتَٰبِ وَيَشْتَرُونَ
بِهِۦ ثَمَنًا قَلِيلًا ۙ أُو۟لَٰٓئِكَ مَا يَأْكُلُونَ فِى بُطُونِهِمْ إِلَّا ٱلنَّارَ
وَلَا يُكَلِّمُهُمُ ٱللَّهُ يَوْمَ ٱلْقِيَٰمَةِ وَلَا يُزَكِّيهِمْ وَلَهُمْ
عَذَابٌ أَلِيمٌ ﴿١٧٤﴾

174 ***Those who conceal***
what Allah has sent down of the Book
and sell it cheap,
take nothing into their bellies but the Fire.
On the Day of Rising Allah will not speak to them
or purify them.
They will have a painful punishment.

Those who conceal what Allah has sent down of the Book

These are the Jewish scholars who concealed the part of the Torah Allah revealed dealing with the description of Muḥammad, may Allah bless him and grant him peace, and the truth of his Message. The word *"anzala"* (sent down) here means "disclosed". It is also said that it means "revealed", which is its usual meaning.

and sell it cheap,

They do this by accepting bribes. The word "cheap" is used because what they receive will soon disappear and its result is evil. It is also said to mean that the amount of the bribe was small.

take nothing into their bellies but the Fire.

This indicates the reality of consuming since the metaphor of actual eating is used. The use of the word "bellies" also alludes to their greed and the fact that they have sold the Next World for their portion of food in this one. The fact that they will go to the Fire is because they consumed something which is unlawful and for which Allah will, therefore, punish them. Consuming the bribe is called "fire" because it leads to the Fire. It is said that it is also literally fire in their bellies.

On the Day of Rising Allah will not speak to them

This denotes Allah's anger with them and the removal of His pleasure from them. It is said that it means He will not send them angels with greeting.

or purify them.

This means that Allah will not rectify their wrong actions and purify them. Az-Zajjāj says, "He will not praise them or call them pure." In *Ṣaḥīḥ* Muslim, Abū Hurayra reported that the Messenger of Allah, may Allah bless him and grant him peace, said, "There are three people that Allah will not speak to on the Day of Rising, or purify, or look at, and they will have a painful punishment: an aged adulterer, a lying ruler and a poor person who is arrogant." These are singled out for painful punishment and intense torment for pure obstinacy in wrong action and making light of the things which move them to commit these acts of disobedience since need did not instigate them to do these things nor did necessity bring them to do them as might be the case with others.

أُو۟لَـٰٓئِكَ ٱلَّذِينَ ٱشْتَرَوُا۟ ٱلضَّلَـٰلَةَ بِٱلْهُدَىٰ
وَٱلْعَذَابَ بِٱلْمَغْفِرَةِ ۚ فَمَآ أَصْبَرَهُمْ عَلَى ٱلنَّارِ ۝١٧٥

175 ***Those are the ones who have sold guidance***
for misguidance
and forgiveness for punishment.
How steadfastly they will endure the Fire!

Punishment follows misguidance as forgiveness follows guidance.

How steadfastly they will endure the Fire!

Most commentators, including al-Ḥasan and Mujāhid, say that the particle *mā* in this phrase is used to connote wonder and refers to creatures. It is as if Allah were saying, "They wonder at how steadfast they are in remaining in the Fire!" This is the meaning which Abū 'Alī accepts. Al-Ḥasan, Qatāda, Ibn Jubayr and ar-Rabī' said, "They do not have, by Allah, any steadfastness, but how bold they are towards people!" It is a known Yemeni dialectical form. It is said that it means "How bold they are in actions which bring them to the Fire!" since they do actions which lead them to the Fire. Az-Zajjāj says that it refers to the great length of time they will remain in the Fire.

ذَٰلِكَ بِأَنَّ ٱللَّهَ نَزَّلَ ٱلْكِتَـٰبَ بِٱلْحَقِّ ۗ وَإِنَّ ٱلَّذِينَ
ٱخْتَلَفُوا۟ فِى ٱلْكِتَـٰبِ لَفِى شِقَاقٍۭ بَعِيدٍ ۝١٧٦

176 ***That is because Allah has sent down the Book***
with truth
and those who differ from the Book
are entrenched in hostility.

That is because Allah has sent down the Book with truth

"That" means "that judgement," or it can mean "that punishment" or "that command." "Truth" here means evidence or truthfulness.

and those who differ from the Book

The "Book" referred to here is the Torah. The Christians claim that it mentioned 'Īsā and the Jews denied him. It is said that their ancestors disagreed about holding to it. It is said that they disagree about what was in the Torah regarding the description of Muḥammad, may Allah bless him and grant him peace, and differed about that. It is said that the Qur'ān is meant and those who differed from it were the unbelievers of Quraysh when some of them said that it was magic, others said that it was nothing but ancient myths, and still others said that it was forged.

are entrenched in hostility.

See 2:137.

لَّيْسَ ٱلْبِرَّ أَن تُوَلُّوا۟ وُجُوهَكُمْ قِبَلَ ٱلْمَشْرِقِ وَٱلْمَغْرِبِ
وَلَٰكِنِ ٱلْبِرُّ مَنْ ءَامَنَ بِٱللَّهِ وَٱلْيَوْمِ ٱلْءَاخِرِ وَٱلْمَلَٰٓئِكَةِ وَٱلْكِتَٰبِ
وَٱلنَّبِيٓـِٕينَ وَءَاتَى ٱلْمَالَ عَلَىٰ حُبِّهِۦ ذَوِى ٱلْقُرْبَىٰ وَٱلْيَتَٰمَىٰ
وَٱلْمَسَٰكِينَ وَٱبْنَ ٱلسَّبِيلِ وَٱلسَّآئِلِينَ وَفِى ٱلرِّقَابِ وَأَقَامَ
ٱلصَّلَوٰةَ وَءَاتَى ٱلزَّكَوٰةَ وَٱلْمُوفُونَ بِعَهْدِهِمْ إِذَا عَٰهَدُوا۟

وَالصَّٰبِرِينَ فِي الْبَأْسَآءِ وَالضَّرَّآءِ وَحِينَ الْبَأْسِ أُوْلَٰٓئِكَ الَّذِينَ
صَدَقُواْ وَأُوْلَٰٓئِكَ هُمُ الْمُتَّقُونَ ﴿١٧٧﴾

177 *True goodness does not lie in turning your faces*
to the East or to the West.
Rather, those with true goodness are those
who believe in Allah and the Last Day,
the Angels, the Book and the Prophets,
and who, despite their love for it,
give away their wealth to their relatives
and to orphans and the very poor,
and to travellers and beggars
and to set slaves free,
and who establish the prayer and pay zakat;
those who honour their contracts
when they make them,
and are steadfast in poverty
and illness and in battle.
Those are the people who are true.
They are the people who are godfearing.

True goodness does not lie in turning your faces to the East or to the West.

There is disagreement about who is being addressed by these words. Qatāda said, "It was mentioned to us that a man asked the Messenger of Allah, may Allah bless him and grant him peace, about true goodness (*birr*) and then Allah revealed this *āyat*." Qatāda continued, "Before the obligatory acts of worship were prescribed, when a man testified that there is no god but Allah and Muḥammad is His slave and Messenger and then died affirming that, that was sufficient to assure him of the Garden, and so this *āyat* was revealed to redress the balance." Qatāda and ar-Rabī' said that it is the Jews and Christians who are being addressed because they disagreed about which direction they should turn towards. The Jews faced west towards Jerusalem and the Christians east towards where the sun rose. They spoke about the change of *qibla* and each group preferred its own direction. They were told that that was not where true goodness lay.

Rather, those with true goodness are those who believe

Here "*birr*" (true goodness) is a word which includes all good. Its use on its own here implies: "But true goodness is the goodness of the one who believes ..." but there is an elision. It is said that the meaning is, "But those with true goodness..." That is because when the Prophet, may Allah bless him and grant him peace, emigrated to Madina and the obligations were prescribed, the *qibla* redirected towards the Ka'ba, and the statutory punishments (*ḥudūd*) were established, Allah revealed this in order to say that true goodness does not lie in praying or doing any other particular action, but rather that a person who is truly good is someone who believes in Allah, and all the other things mentioned in the *āyat*. Ibn 'Abbās, Mujāhid, aḍ-Ḍaḥḥāk, Aṭā', Sufyān and az-Zajjāj held that view. It is possible for *birr* to mean *bārr* and *barr*. *Barr* means kind and benign and filial, while *bārr* also has that meaning, but is a little more restricted.

Our scholars point out that this is an immense *āyat*, one of the matrices of judgement because it contains sixteen different elements:

- the requirement to have faith in Allah and His Names and Attributes
- the Resurrection
- the Gathering
- the Balance
- the *Sirāṭ*
- the Basin
- the Intercession
- the Garden and the Fire
- the Angels
- the Books revealed by Allah
- the Prophets

- the duty to spend one's wealth in ways that are both mandatory and recommended
- maintaining ties of kinship and not severing them
- looking after orphans and the poor and not neglecting them
- caring for travellers (or guests) and beggars
- setting slaves free

All these things will be clarified elsewhere. Also included are safeguarding the prayer, paying *zakāt*, fulfilling contracts and showing steadfastness in afflictions. Each of these items would require an entire book to do it justice.

and who, despite their love for it, give away their wealth

This is used as evidence by those who say that there are legal rights on wealth other than just *zakāt* and they are the means by which true goodness is achieved. It is said that what is meant here is obligatory *zakāt*. The first is sounder since ad-Dāraquṭnī transmitted from Fāṭima bint Qays that the Prophet, may Allah bless him and grant him peace, said, "There is a right on wealth over and above *zakāt*," and he mentioned this *āyat* in full. Ibn Mājah and at-Tirmidhī transmit it as well.

The soundness of this *ḥadīth*, even if there is something to be said about the *isnād*, is indicated by the words of Allah later in the same *āyat*, *"establish the prayer and pay zakāt"*. That indicates that what is meant by this phrase is not obligatory *zakāt* because otherwise that would entail an unnecessary repetition, and Allah knows best. Scholars agree that, when an urgent need for the Muslims exists after the payment of *zakāt*, there is a communal obligation to spend money on it. Mālik obliged people to ransom captives, even if it used up all their wealth. There is also consensus on this, and that strengthens what we prefer concerning this matter.

It is said the phrase refers to their love for what they give but the pronoun can also be made to refer to Allah, in which case the meaning becomes "for love of Him". Yet another possibility is that the pronoun refers to the person being given the gift when the meaning would be "out of love for him" with a small "h". The same applies to Allah's words in *Sūrat al-Insān*, *"They give food, despite their love for it, to the poor."* (76:8) in which the same three possible meanings exist.

those who honour their contracts when they make them,

Contracts between themselves and Allah and between themselves and other people.

and are steadfast in poverty and illness and in battle.

Bāsā' is hardship and poverty, and *ḍarrā'* is illness. Ibn Mas'ūd said that. *Ba's* is the time of war.

Those are the people who are true. They are the people who are godfearing.

They are described as having integrity and *taqwā* in their affairs and fulfilling them. They are serious regarding the *dīn*. This is great praise. In a *ḥadīth* we find: "You must have integrity. Integrity guides to goodness and goodness guides to the Garden. A man continues to be true and takes care to remain truthful until he is written with Allah as a true man (*ṣiddīq*)."

يَٰٓأَيُّهَا ٱلَّذِينَ ءَامَنُوا۟ كُتِبَ عَلَيْكُمُ ٱلْقِصَاصُ فِى ٱلْقَتْلَى ۖ ٱلْحُرُّ
بِٱلْحُرِّ وَٱلْعَبْدُ بِٱلْعَبْدِ وَٱلْأُنثَىٰ بِٱلْأُنثَىٰ ۚ فَمَنْ عُفِىَ لَهُۥ مِنْ أَخِيهِ
شَىْءٌ فَٱتِّبَاعٌۢ بِٱلْمَعْرُوفِ وَأَدَآءٌ إِلَيْهِ بِإِحْسَٰنٍ ۗ ذَٰلِكَ تَخْفِيفٌ
مِّن رَّبِّكُمْ وَرَحْمَةٌ ۗ فَمَنِ ٱعْتَدَىٰ بَعْدَ ذَٰلِكَ فَلَهُۥ عَذَابٌ
أَلِيمٌ ۝١٧٨

178 ***You who believe! retaliation is prescribed for you***
in the case of people killed:
free man for free man,

slave for slave,
female for female.
But if someone is absolved the thing by his brother,
blood-money should be claimed with correctness
and paid with good will.
That is an easement and a mercy from your Lord.
Anyone who goes beyond the limits after this
will receive a painful punishment.

You who believe! retaliation is prescribed for you in the case of people killed:

Al-Bukhārī and ad-Dāraquṭnī related that Ibn 'Abbās said, "There was retaliation among the tribe of Israel but no blood money. In this *āyat* Allah revealed the possibility of absolution which is to accept blood money in cases of homicide. That should be claimed with correctness and paid with good will. He made this easier for us than what was imposed on those before us. "Going beyond the limits" refers to killing after having accepted blood money.

The word "*kutiba*" (prescribed) means "established and made obligatory", and "*qiṣāṣ*" (retaliation) is from a root meaning someone who follows a trail which has been blazed. A *qāṣṣ* is a storyteller who follows traditions and reports. *Qaṣṣ* also means cutting the hair by following its line. It is as if the killer takes a path in killing and retaliation is to follow after him and proceed along the same path in that. It is said that *qaṣṣ* is cutting and that is the source of *qiṣāṣ* because the retaliator wounds with the same type of wound or kills in the same way. The verb is also used for mutilation.

The form that retaliation takes is that when the relative (*walī*) wants to kill, the killer is obliged to submit to the command of Allah and to accept the prescribed retaliation. The relative of the murdered man is obliged to stop at the killer of his relative and not to go beyond him and kill someone else as well, which is what the Arabs used to do before Islam. That is the meaning of the words of the Prophet, may Allah bless him and grant him peace, "On the

Day of Rising, the most insolent of people towards Allah will be three men: someone who killed other than the killer, someone who kills in the Ḥaram, and someone who acts by the blood feuds of the *Jāhiliyya*."

Ash-Sha'bī, Qatāda and others said, "The people of the *Jāhiliyya* were excessive and obeyed Shayṭān. When a tribe possessed might and power and a slave of theirs was killed by the slave of another person, they said, "We will only kill a free person for him." If a woman of theirs was killed, they said, "We will only kill a man for her." When a base person among them was killed, they said, "We will only kill a noble for them." They said, "Killing safeguards against killing." Allah forbade them transgression in this *āyat* and others.

There is no disagreement that retaliation in killing is only adjudged by those in authority. It is the ruler who imposes on them retaliation, establishes the *ḥudūd* and other things because, although Allah Almighty gives all believers the possibility of retaliation, not all believers are ready to agree to it. Therefore the ruler represents them in the matter of carrying out retaliation and imposing other *ḥudūd*. Retaliation itself is not obligatory. What is obligatory is not to exceed in retaliation or other *ḥudūd*. If there is consent to forgo retaliation and to accept blood money or to pardon, that is permitted.

If it is said that "prescribed for you" means it is obligatory and necessary, so how, in that case, can *qiṣāṣ* not be mandatory? The reply is that it implies "if you desire it." Know that *qiṣāṣ* is the limit for those who want blood.

free man for free man, slave for slave, female for female.

There is disagreement about the interpretation of this. One group say that the *āyat* was revealed to clarify the judgement of the category of those whose blood is forfeit when someone of the same category is killed. So when a free person is killed, someone free is killed in retaliation for him, and when a slave is killed, a slave is killed in retaliation, and a woman is killed in retaliation for a woman. The *āyat* is a firm judgement which is general and explained by the words of Allah, *"life for life"* (5:45) and explained by the Prophet in his *Sunna* when he killed a Jew in retaliation for a woman. Mujāhid said that. Ibn 'Abbās said the same, although it is related from him that it is abrogated by the *āyat* in *Sūrat al-Mā'ida*. That is the position of the people of Iraq.

The Kufans and ath-Thawrī say that a free man is killed if he has killed a slave and a Muslim if he has killed a *dhimmī*. Their evidence is the words of Allah here which are general and the *āyat* in *Sūrat al-Mā'ida* (5.45). Mentioned in the previous paragraph). They said that the blood of a *dhimmī* has the same inviolability as that of a Muslim and should be satisfied by retaliation. It is the inviolability of blood which is the principle. Both the Muslim and the *dhimmī* are the people of the Abode of Islam. The thing which verifies that is the fact that a Muslim's hand is cut off for stealing the property of a *dhimmī* which indicates that the property of a *dhimmī* is the same as that of a Muslim. It follows that their blood must be the same since property is respected by respect for its owner. Abu Ḥanīfa and his people, ath-Thawrī, and Ibn Abī Laylā agree that a free man is killed in retaliation for a slave just as a slave is killed in retaliation for him. That is the position of Dā'ūd. The same is related from 'Alī and Ibn Mas'ūd and is the position of Sa'īd ibn al-Musayyab, Qatāda, Ibrāhīm an-Nakhā'ī, and al-Ḥakam ibn 'Uyayna.

The majority of scholars do not accept killing a free man in retaliation for a slave because of the categories and divisions shown in the *āyat*. Abū Thawr said, "Since everyone agrees that there is no retaliation between slaves and free people in cases less than homicide, it is even more likely to be the case where homicide is concerned. Those who make a distinction in respect of that are wrong." Furthermore the consensus is that if someone accidentally kills a slave, he only owes the price of that slave. Since slaves do not resemble free men where accidental killing is concerned, the same should hold true in cases of intentional homicide. Moreover, a slave is a commodity who is bought and sold and can be disposed of by a free person and so there is no equality between them.

The majority also agree that a Muslim is not killed in retaliation for an unbeliever since the Prophet, may Allah bless him and grant him peace, said, "A Muslim is not killed in retaliation for an unbeliever." (al-Bukhārī) They do not consider as sound what is related from Rabī'a about the Prophet killing a Muslim in retaliation for an unbeliever at Khaybar because its *isnād* is broken.

It is related from 'Alī and al-Ḥasan al-Baṣrī that the *āyat* was revealed to explain the judgement of those mentioned in the *āyat* and to indicate the difference between them and those who would kill a free person in retaliation for a slave or a slave in retaliation for a free person, or male in retaliation for a female or a female in retaliation for a male. They said, "When a man kills a woman and her relatives want to kill him, they do so and his relatives are paid half of the blood price. If they want to let him live, they accept a woman's blood money from him. If a woman kills a man and his relatives want to kill her, they can kill her and take half the blood money or alternatively they can take the full blood money and let her live." Ash-Sha'bī related this from 'Alī, but it is not sound because ash-Sha'bī did not meet 'Alī. Al-Ḥakam related that 'Alī and 'Abdullāh said, "When a man murders a woman with premeditation, he is her retaliation." This is contrary to the transmission of ash-Sha'bī from 'Alī.

Scholars agree that a man is killed in retaliation for killing a woman and a woman in retaliation for killing a man and the majority do not think anything is repaid. One group think that the difference in the blood money is repaid. Mālik, ash-Shāfi'ī, Aḥmad, Isḥāq, ath-Thawrī and Abū Thawr said that is how retaliation proceeds between a man and a woman in respect of what is less than a life. Ḥammād ibn Abī Sulaymān and Abū Ḥanīfa said that there is no retaliation between them in injuries which fall short of killing, in which there is life for life.

Ibn al-'Arabī said, "Ignorance leads some people to say that a free man should be killed in retaliation for killing his own slave," and a *ḥadīth* is related regarding that from Samura where the Messenger of Allah, may Allah bless him and grant him peace, said, "We kill the one who kills his slave," but it is a weak *ḥadīth*.

Our evidence is the words of Allah, *"If someone is wrongly killed, We have given authority to his next of kin. But he should not be excessive in taking life."* (17:33) In this case this refers to his master. All the scholars agree that if a master kills his slave accidentally, the price of the slave is not taken from him for the treasury. ‘Amr ibn Shu‘ayb related that a man murdered his slave and the Prophet, may Allah bless him and grant him peace, flogged him and exiled him for a year and removed his share as a Muslim and did not help him to pay it.

It might be asked, "If a man kills his wife, why do you not say that marriage sets up a doubt which would avert retaliation from the husband since marriage is a type of slavery?" Al-Layth ibn Ṣa‘d said that. Our reply is that marriage is a contract between him and her with implied restrictions on both sides: he cannot marry her sister or four additional wives (making the total five), and she can demand her right of intercourse from him just as he can demand it from her. He, however, has the merit of guardianship over her which Allah gave him because he supports her from his wealth, according to what is obligatory for him in terms of the bride-price and maintenance. If a doubt had existed, it would exist for both parties.

Imām Aḥmad ibn Ḥanbal used this *āyat* as evidence that a group should not be killed in retaliation for the death of one person. He said, "Because Allah stipulated equality, and there is no equality between a group and one individual." The answer to this is that retaliation in this *āyat* entails killing the one who did the killing, whoever that may be. This was to refute the Arabs who wanted to kill someone who was not the killer for someone who had been killed and to kill a hundred innocent people in retaliation for one or to take advantage of rank and power. Therefore Allah commanded fairness and equality so that only those who kill are killed. ‘Umar killed seven men in Sana', and said, "If all the people of Sana‘ had participated in the murder, I would have killed them all."

‘Alī killed the Kharijites for killing ‘Abdullāh ibn Khabbāb. When they were merely guilty of innovation, he held back from killing them, but when they murdered 'Abdullāh ibn Khabbāb as a sheep would be slaughtered and 'Alī was informed about that, he said, "Allah is greater!" He called them to bring out the murderers of 'Abdullāh ibn Khabbāb to him. They said, "All of us killed him," three times. 'Alī told his companions, "There are the people." 'Alī and his people did not hesitate to kill them all. Ad-Dāraquṭnī transmits both reports.

In at-Tirmidhī we find, "If the people of the heaven and the people of the earth had participated in shedding the blood of a believer, Allah would throw them all into the Fire." It is said that this is a *gharīb ḥadīth.* Furthermore if a group knew that if they were to kill a person, they would not be killed, then enemies would help one another to kill their enemies by participating in their killing and achieving their desire for revenge. So it is more fitting to follow this rule than the literal words, and Allah knows best. Ibn al-Mundhir said, "Az-Zuhrī, Ḥabīb ibn Abī Thābit and Ibn Sīrīn said, 'Two are not killed in retaliation for one.'" That is related from Mu'ādh ibn Jabal, Ibn az-Zubayr and 'Abdu'l-Mālik.

The Imāms related from Abū Shurayḥ al-Ka'bī that the Messenger of Allah, may Allah bless him and grant him peace, said, "You company of Khuzā'a killed this man from Hudhayl and I am responsible for him. Whoever has a relative killed after these words of mine, is entitled to one of two things: taking the blood money or killing in retaliation." (Abū Dāwūd) Another transmission says, "The relative of the one killed can kill in retaliation, pardon or take blood money." This is the position of some of the people of knowledge. It is the position of Aḥmad and Isḥāq.

The people of knowledge disagree about taking blood money from the murderer. One group say that the relative of the murdered man has a choice. If he wishes, he takes retaliation, and if he wishes he takes blood money, even if the killer does not consent. This is related from Sa'īd ibn al-Musayyab, 'Aṭā' and al-Ḥasan. Ashhab relates this position from Mālik and it is also the position of al-Layth, al-Awzā'ī, ash-Shāfi'ī, Aḥmad, Isḥāq and Abū Thawr. Their proof is the *ḥadīth* of Abū Shurayḥ above and it is a legal text (*naṣṣ*) sufficient to resolve the dispute. It is also deduced by analysis since blood money is imposed on him without his consent because it is an obligation on him to save his own life as Allah says, *"Do not kill yourselves."* (4:29) He says in this *āyat*, *"But if someone is absolved by his brother,"* in other words, he forgoes his right to retaliation in one interpretation and is satisfied with blood money, *"blood-money should be claimed with correctneṣs",* meaning that the one with right to retaliation follows it by correctly demanding blood money, the killer must pay it with good will without delay.

But if someone is absolved the thing by his brother, blood-money should be claimed with correctness and paid with good will.

Scholars disagree about the interpretation of the words "someone", "absolved" and "thing" in this *āyat*.

One view is that "someone" means the killer and "absolved" refers to what the relative of the deceased does. The "brother" is the brother of the deceased. "The thing" is his right to retaliation which is absolved and for which he takes blood money. This is the position of Ibn 'Abbās, Qatāda, Mujāhid and a group of scholars. So absolving, in this case, means abandoning the right to retaliation. It means: When the killer is absolved by the relative of the deceased of his right to retaliation and forgoes it, he takes blood money and follows it with correctness, and the killer pays it with good will.

Another position is that of Mālik which is that "someone" refers to the relative and "absolved" is to make easy, not to pardon, and the "brother" is the killer and "thing" is the blood money, so the meaning in this case would be that when the relative inclines to foregoing retaliation and taking blood money, the killer can choose between giving it or surrendering himself. Sometimes it is eased and sometimes not. People other than Mālik say that if the relatives are satisfied with blood money, the killer has no choice: he has to give it. This is also related from Mālik. Abu Ḥanīfa said that "absolve" means to spend. So it is as if the meaning was, "Whoever is paid some of the blood money should accept it and pursue it with correctness." Some people say that the killer should pay it with good will and Allah recommends that the relative of the murder victim should take the money when that is easy for the killer. It is a lightening and a mercy.

Some people say that these expressions deal with particular people about whom the entire *āyat* was revealed, and they paid the blood money to one another in respect of the injuries outstanding between them. The meaning of the *āyat* is that when one group received more than the other group, and so "absolved" rather means "has more than". Ash-Sha'bī said explaining this, "There was fighting between two tribes of Arabs and several people were killed. One of the tribes said, "We will not be content until a man is killed for a woman and a woman for a man." They went to the Prophet, may Allah bless him and grant him peace, and he said, "Killing is the same. They made peace on the basis of the payment of blood money and one of the two tribes received more than the other. That is what this *āyat* refers to. Whoever has more than his brother should pay it correctly." Ash-Sha'bī said that this was the reason the *āyat* was revealed.

Finally there is the statement of 'Alī about the difference between the blood money of a man and a woman, free person and slave, so the meaning is that the one who has more, should demand it correctly.

This *āyat* is encouragement from Allah Almighty for correctness on the part of the person seeking payment and good will on the part of the payer. Is that obligatory or recommended? The recitation in the nominative indicates that it is obligatory because the meaning is that it must be pursued with correctness.

That is an easement and a mercy from your Lord.

This alludes to the fact that Allah did not give those before us any choice in the matter and they had to take a life for a life whereas Allah has given this Community the advantage of being able to accept blood money when the relative of the deceased is satisfied by it. Others said that the relative of the dead person can only take retaliation and may not take blood money if the killer agrees to that. Ibn al-Qāsim related that from Mālik, and it is well known from him. Ath-Thawrī and the Kufans also said that. Their evidence is the *ḥadīth* of Anas in the story about ar-Rubayya' who broke a woman's tooth. They stated, "When the Prophet, may Allah bless him and grant him peace, judged that there should be retaliation, he said, 'Retaliation is the Book of Allah. Retaliation is the Book of Allah.'" He did not give the injured woman a choice between retaliation and blood money, and so the judgement of the Book of Allah and the *Sunna* of Messenger is that there is retaliation for a deliberate injury. The first position is sounder because of the *ḥadīth* of Abū Shurayḥ.

Anyone who goes beyond the limits after this will receive a painful punishment.

This refers to someone who kills after taking blood money and forgoing the blood of the killer. Al-Ḥasan said, "In the *Jāhiliyya* when someone killed a person he would flee to his own people and the people of the victim would come and negotiate the blood money. The relative of the victim would say, "I will take the blood money," and then when the killer was made secure by this and left the victim's relative would kill him and throw the blood money back at the killer's family.

Scholars disagree about someone who kills after taking blood money. A group of scholars, including Mālik and ash-Shāfi'ī said that he is the same as the one who kills in the first place. If the relative wishes, he kills him, and if he wishes, he pardons him and he will be punished in the Next World. Qatāda, 'Ikrima, as-Suddī and others said that his punishment is to be killed and it is not possible for the relative to pardon him. Abū Dāwūd related from Jābir ibn 'Abdullāh that the Messenger of Allah, may Allah bless him and grant him peace, said, "I will not pardon someone who kills after having taken blood money." Al-Ḥasan said that his punishment is to return the blood money and his wrong action remains to be dealt with in the Next World. ‘Umar ibn ‘Abdu’l-‘Azīz said that his business is left up to the ruler who does whatever he thinks best.

وَلَكُمْ فِي ٱلْقِصَاصِ حَيَوٰةٌ يَٰٓأُو۟لِي ٱلْأَلْبَٰبِ
لَعَلَّكُمْ تَتَّقُونَ ﴿١٧٩﴾

179 ***There is life for you in retaliation,***
people of intelligence,
so that hopefully you will be godfearing.

There is life for you in retaliation, people of intelligence,

These are succinct and eloquent words which mean: “You should not kill one another.” Sufyān related that from as-Suddī from Abū Mālik. It means that when retaliation is established and achieved, it will deter the one who wants to kill another, out of the fear that retaliation will be taken from him, and so both remain alive. It had previously been the case that, when one man killed another, their two tribes would fight and that would lead to many deaths. When Allah prescribed retaliation, it was a deterrent and they stopped fighting.

The imāms who give *fatwā* agree that it is not permitted for anyone to take retaliation from someone without the involvement of the ruler. People cannot do it on their own. Scholars agree that the ruler can take retaliation from himself if he transgresses against one of his flock since he is one of them and has the prerogative of looking after them, like a guardian or trustee. That does not preclude retaliation and so there is no difference between him and anyone else regarding the judgements of Allah in this *āyat*.

It is confirmed that Abū Bakr aṣ-Ṣiddīq said to a man who complained to him about a governor who had cut off his hand, “If you are telling the truth, I will take retaliation for you from him.” An-Nasā’ī reported that Abū Sa‘īd al-Khudrī said, “Once, while the Messenger of Allah, may Allah bless him and grant him peace, was distributing something a man bent over him and the

Messenger of Allah jabbed him with a stick he had and the man yelled. The Messenger of Allah, may Allah bless him and grant him peace, said to him, 'Come, take your retaliation.' He said, 'I absolve you, Messenger of Allah.'" Abū Dāwūd reported that 'Umar gave a speech in which he said, "Whoever is wronged by an *amīr* (governor, commander) should present his case to me and I will take retaliation from him." 'Amr ibn al-'Āṣ stood up and said, "Amīr al-Mu'minīn, if one of us disciplines a man who is subject to his authority, will you take retaliation from him?" He replied, "How could I not take retaliation from him when I saw the Messenger of Allah take retaliation from himself!"

so that hopefully you will be godfearing.

So that you will be careful to avoid killing and submit to retaliation. That obedience leads to other types of obedience. Allah makes one firm in obedience through obedience.

كُتِبَ عَلَيْكُمْ إِذَا حَضَرَ أَحَدَكُمُ الْمَوْتُ إِن تَرَكَ خَيْرًا الْوَصِيَّةُ
لِلْوَالِدَيْنِ وَالْأَقْرَبِينَ بِالْمَعْرُوفِ حَقًّا عَلَى الْمُتَّقِينَ ١٨٠

180 ***It is prescribed for you,***
when death approaches one of you
and if he has some goods to leave,
to make a will in favour of his parents and relatives,
correctly and fairly:
a duty for all those who are godfearing.

This is the "*Āyat* of the Will". The only *āyat*s in the Qur'ān that deal with wills are this one, and the ones we find in 4:12 and 5:106. This *āyat* is the most comprehensive of them. It was revealed before the revelation of the statutory shares of inheritance and their laws, as will be explained. There is an "and" elided in the words: *"And it is prescribed,"* because it follows on from the previous *āyat* about retaliation and may well be directed to the one who is about to have retaliation inflicted on him which will clearly cause his death. So he is someone who knows that death is near him, and that this is the time when making a will becomes absolutely imperative.

If it is asked why the word *"kutiba"* (prescribed) is in the masculine when the word for will (*waṣiya*) is feminine, the reply to this is that the act of making a will (*īṣā'*) is what is meant and that is masculine. It is also said that it is because the verb is considerably separated from its subject.

and if he has some goods to leave,

Here "*khayr*" (goods) means wealth. There is no dispute about this, but there is disagreement about the amount involved. It is said that it means a lot of wealth, and that is related from 'Alī, 'Ā'isha and Ibn 'Abbās. They said that seven hundred dinars is little. Qatāda and al-Ḥasan said that it means a thousand dinars or more. Ash-Sha'bī said that the amount intended is from five hundred to a thousand dinars. The word "*waṣiya*" (will) can designate anything which someone instructs to be done whether during his lifetime or after his death. Custom, however, has designated it to be a declaration of what is to be done after death.

Scholars disagree about whether it is obligatory for those who leave property to make a will, although they agree that it is mandatory for those who hold deposits and have debts. Most scholars believe that a will is not mandatory for those who have neither of these. That is the position of Mālik, ash-Shāfi'ī and ath-Thawrī, whether a person is rich or poor. Another group including az-Zuhrī and Abū Mijlaz say that making a will is mandatory, judging by the literal text of the Qur'ān, whether a person has a little or a lot of wealth. Abū Thawr said that a will is only mandatory for a man who has a debt or wealth belonging to others and then it is obligatory for him to write a will, saying what he owes. As for someone who has no debts or deposits, it is not mandatory for him to make one unless he wishes to do so.

Ibn al-Mundhir said, "This is good because Allah has made it obligatory to return trusts to their owners but it is not mandatory for someone who holds goods on trust to make a will." The people with the first view use what is related from Ibn 'Umar as evidence. He said that the Messenger of Allah, may Allah bless him and grant him peace, said, "It is not right for a Muslim man who owes something which he should specify in a will to spend two nights without making a written will." One variant says three nights. Those who argue the opposite say that, if it was mandatory, it would not have been left to the discretion of the one making the will.

If it is said that Allah's use of the words, "prescribed for you" means that it is mandatory, the answer to that is in the previous *āyat*. It is only when you want to make a will, and Allah knows best. An-Nakhā'ī said, "The Messenger of Allah, may Allah bless him and grant him peace, died without making a will. Abū Bakr made a will. It is good to make a will but there is nothing wrong in not making one."

to make a will in favour of his parents and relatives,

The majority of scholars believe that it is not permitted for anyone to will away more than a third of his property, except for Abū Ḥanīfa and his followers who said: "If a person does not have any statutory heirs, he is permitted to will away all his wealth." They said that on the basis that limiting the legacy to a third is in order to leave the statutory heirs with sufficient property since the Prophet said, "It is better for you to leave your heirs well provided for than to leave them needy, begging from other people."

Scholars agree that people who die with statutory heirs should not will away all of their wealth. It is related that when he was dying 'Amr ibn al-'Āṣ said to his son 'Abdullāh, "I want to make a bequest," and his son said to him, "Go ahead and make a bequest and what you will can be paid from my property." He called for a paper and dictated. 'Abdullāh said, "I said to him, 'I think that you have exhausted both my property and your property. I will summon my brothers and ask them to permit it.'"

They agree that anyone can change his will and retract any part of it if he wishes. They disagree about doing that in respect of a slave who has a specific contract by which he is to be freed after his owner's death (*mudabbar*). Mālik said, "The business agreed upon among us is that when someone makes a will, whether he is healthy or ill, in which he frees a slave or something else, he can change whatever of it he wants to and add or delete whatever he likes until he dies. If he wants to cancel that will, he can do so – with the exception of a *tadbīr* contract." The other imāms say that he can even retract a *tadbīr* contract if he wishes.

Scholars disagree about whether this *āyat* is abrogated or is one which contains an active legal judgement. It is said to be the latter. Its literal expression is general and its meaning is only specific in respect of someone whose parents do not inherit automatically, because they are unbelievers or slaves, for instance, and in respect of relatives other than a person's statutory heirs. Aḍ-Ḍaḥḥāk, Ṭāwūs and al-Ḥasan held that view and aṭ-Ṭabarī preferred it. Az-Zuhrī said that a will is mandatory whether someone has a little or a lot of property. Ibn al-Mundhir said that they all agree that the will mentioned in the *āyat* is general and the specific judgement it contains was binding for a period of time and then abrogated in respect of all those who automatically inherit by virtue of the *āyat*s specifying the statutory shares of inheritance.

It is said that the *āyat*s specifying the statutory shares of inheritance are not the only thing which abrogates this *āyat* and are supplemented by the words of the Prophet, may Allah bless him and grant him peace, "Allah has given everyone entitled to a right his right, and so there is no legacy in favour of an heir." (at-Tirmidhī) So the abrogation of the *āyat* is by the firm *Sunna*, not only by the *āyat*s explaining the shares of inheritance, according to the sound position of scholars. If it were not for this *ḥadīth*, it would be possible to combine this *āyat* with the *āyat*s specifying the statutory shares of inheritance by receiving property from the legator both by statutory inheritance and by bequest. This *ḥadīth* and the consensus derived from it prevent that happening.

Ibn 'Abbās and al-Ḥasan say that the bequest to parents is abrogated by their statutory shares in *Sūrat an-Nisā'*, and is confirmed for relatives who do not inherit automatically. That is the position of ash-Shāfi'ī, most Mālikīs and a group of the people of knowledge. In al-Bukhārī, Ibn 'Abbās said, "It used to be that property belonged to the child and the parents only inherited through a will, so Allah abrogated what He wished in respect of that."

Ibn 'Umar, Ibn 'Abbās and Ibn Zayd said that the *āyat* is abrogated while the recommendation to make a bequest remains. That is similar to Mālik's position and an-Naḥḥās mentioned it from ash-Sha'bī and an-Nakhā'ī.

Some people say that it is better to make a will in favour of your relatives rather than non-relatives because of this text from Allah regarding them, so that aḍ-Ḍaḥḥāk says, "A person who makes a bequest to other than his relatives ends his actions with disobedience. It is related that Ibn 'Umar willed each of his slave-girls who bore him children four hundred thousand (dirhams)." It is related that 'Ā'isha willed her household utensils to a freed slave of hers. Various scholars hold that bequests to non-relatives should be rescinded and made over to his relatives. Mālik, ash-Shāfi'ī, Abū Ḥanīfa, al-Awzā'ī, and Aḥmad ibn Ḥanbal said that, if someone leaves a bequest to non-relatives and leaves his relatives in need, he has committed a wrong action. If he does that, however, his bequest stands and is carried out.

The majority of scholars believe that a very sick person is legally barred from disposing of his property. Sa'd said, "The Messenger of Allah, may Allah bless him and grant him peace, visited me during the Farewell *Ḥajj* when I was ill and expecting to die and I said, 'Messenger of Allah, my illness has reached what you see. I have wealth but only have one daughter as an heir. Can I give two-thirds of my wealth away as *ṣadaqa*?' 'No,' he said. I said, 'A half?' and he said, 'No.' He then added, 'No, but (give) a third, and a third is a lot. It is better for you to leave your heirs wealthy than to leave them in need, begging from people.'"

correctly and fairly:

This means with justice. It is entrusted to the discretion and opinion of the one making the will, but it cannot be more than a third.

a duty for all those who are godfearing.

In other words it is a confirmed and established practice but it is not an obligation to do so since Allah says it is for the godfearing. This indicates that making a will is recommended because if it were obligatory, Allah would have said that it was a duty for all Muslims, not just the godfearing.

Scholars have said that the exhortation to hasten to make a will is not taken from this *āyat* but from the *ḥadīth* of Ibn 'Umar.

Anas ibn Mālik said, "They used to write at the beginning of their wills, 'This is the will of so-and-so son of so-and-so who testifies that there is no god but Allah alone with no partner and that Muḥammad is His slave and Messenger. The Hour is coming. There is no doubt about it and Allah will raise up those in the graves.'" A man would command those who survived him to fear Allah as He should be feared, act correctly towards one another and to obey Allah and His Messenger, and would advise them as Ibrāhīm and Ya'qūb had advised their sons: *"My sons! Allah has chosen this dīn for you, so do not die except as Muslims."* (2:132)

فَمَنۢ بَدَّلَهُۥ بَعۡدَ مَا سَمِعَهُۥ فَإِنَّمَآ إِثۡمُهُۥ عَلَى
ٱلَّذِينَ يُبَدِّلُونَهُۥٓۚ إِنَّ ٱللَّهَ سَمِيعٌ عَلِيمٞ ١٨١

181 ***Then if anyone alters it after hearing it,***
the crime is on the part of those who alter it.
Allah is All-Hearing, All-Knowing.

Alters the wording of the will. "Hearing it" can mean hearing the testator himself or alternatively hearing what is confirmed from him by two witnesses. "The crime" refers to the alteration.

This *āyat* indicates that when a person mentions a debt in his will, it should be paid immediately since it is his first responsibility and the executor must produce what is demanded and has a wage for carrying it out. It is a sin for him to delay paying it.

There is no disagreement that when a person wills something which is not permitted, like wine, pigs or any act of disobedience, it is permitted to change the will and it is not permitted to carry it out in the same way that it is not permitted to carry out bequests of more than a third.

فَمَنْ خَافَ مِن مُّوصٍ جَنَفًا أَوْ إِثْمًا فَأَصْلَحَ بَيْنَهُمْ فَلَآ إِثْمَ عَلَيْهِ
إِنَّ ٱللَّهَ غَفُورٌ رَّحِيمٌ ﴿١٨٢﴾

182 ***But if someone fears bias or wrongdoing***
on the part of the person making the will,
and puts things right between the people involved,
in that case he has not committed any crime.
Allah is Ever-Forgiving, Most Merciful.

The word *"khāfa"* (fear) can also mean "know of" in this instance. "*Janaf*" (bias) means "inclining towards something". Mujāhid said that this *āyat* means "whoever fears that the testator will be biased and cut off the inheritance of some people and deliberately cause harm, or even bring it about without doing it deliberately". This kind of bias is not necessarily a wrong action, although it is definitely a wrong action if it is deliberate. The *āyat* means that someone who warns a testator about that and averts him from doing it, thereby putting things right between him and his heirs and between the heirs themselves, does nothing wrong. Allah is "Ever-Forgiving" to the testator when he acts on the warning and retracts the injury he intended.

Ibn 'Abbās, Qatāda, ar-Rabī' and others say that the meaning of the *āyat* is that anyone who knows the testator was biased and intended injury to some of his heirs should act after his death and put right the disturbance and schism which then arises between the heirs. He does nothing wrong by doing this when the change is in the best interests of the people concerned.

The *āyat* is addressed to all Muslims. They are told: if you fear that a testator will be biased in his bequest, turn from what is the right, fall into wrong action and not do what is correct by inclining to his daughter's husband, for instance, or his daughter's child so that the money will go to his daughter, or to the son of his son when he wants it to go to his son, or he wills it to someone distant and neglects his nearer relatives, then they should hasten to put things right. Putting things right will remove the wrong action from the one who does it. It is a *farḍ kifāya* so if no one does it, everyone is guilty of wrong action.

The *āyat* provides evidence for judging by opinion because, if someone thinks that corruption is intended, he is obliged to strive to put things right. If the corruption is verified, it is no longer considered in the category of putting things right because it becomes a different kind of judgement: one concerned with averting and putting an end to corruption.

There is no disagreement that giving *ṣadaqa* is better when one is alive and healthy than when one is dead since, when the Prophet, may Allah bless him and grant him peace, was asked, "Which *ṣadaqa* is better?" he said, "That you give *ṣadaqa* when you are desirous of money and healthy." He also said, "It is better for a man to give one dirham while he is alive than a hundred when he is dead," and he said, "The example of someone who spends or gives *ṣadaqa* after his death is like someone who gives food after he is full."

Provided it does not harm anyone, it is permitted for someone to pay any *zakāt* he neglected to pay during his lifetime through his will.

Ad-Dāraquṭnī related from Ibn 'Abbās that the Messenger of Allah, may Allah bless him and grant him peace, said, "Harming people through a bequest is one of the major wrong actions." Abū Hurayra reported that the Messenger of Allah, may Allah bless him and grant him peace, said, "A man or woman can work to obey Allah for sixty years and then when they are about to die harm someone in their will and they end up in the Fire because of it." (Abū Dāwūd) 'Imrān ibn Ḥusayn says that a man freed six slaves he had when he died and that was the only property he possessed. The Prophet, peace be upon him, heard about that and was angry and stated, "I wish that I had not prayed over him." Then he brought the man's slaves and divided them into three parts and then drew lots and freed two and left four as slaves. (Muslim)

يَٰٓأَيُّهَا ٱلَّذِينَ ءَامَنُوا۟ كُتِبَ عَلَيْكُمُ ٱلصِّيَامُ كَمَا كُتِبَ عَلَى
ٱلَّذِينَ مِن قَبْلِكُمْ لَعَلَّكُمْ تَتَّقُونَ ﴿١٨٣﴾ أَيَّامًا مَّعْدُودَٰتٍ
فَمَن كَانَ مِنكُم مَّرِيضًا أَوْ عَلَىٰ سَفَرٍ فَعِدَّةٌ مِّنْ
أَيَّامٍ أُخَرَ وَعَلَى ٱلَّذِينَ يُطِيقُونَهُۥ فِدْيَةٌ طَعَامُ مِسْكِينٍ
فَمَن تَطَوَّعَ خَيْرًا فَهُوَ خَيْرٌ لَّهُۥ وَأَن تَصُومُوا۟
خَيْرٌ لَّكُمْ إِن كُنتُمْ تَعْلَمُونَ ﴿١٨٤﴾

183 *You who believe! fasting is prescribed for you,*
as it was prescribed for those before you –
so that hopefully you will become godfearing –
184 *for a specified number of days.*
But any of you who are ill or on a journey
should fast a number of other days.
For those who are able to fast,
their fidya is to feed the poor.
And if someone does good of his own accord,
it is better for him.
But that you should fast is better for you,
if you only knew.

You who believe! fasting is prescribed for you,

Allah mentions two injunctions for Muslims, retaliation and making a will, and then mentions a third, saying that fasting is also prescribed for them and obligatory and mandatory for all. There is no disagreement about this. The Prophet, may Allah bless him and grant him peace, said "Islam is based on five: the testimony that there is no god but Allah and Muḥammad is the Messenger of Allah, establishing the prayer, paying *zakāt*, fasting Ramaḍān and *ḥajj*." (Ibn 'Umar) Linguistically "*ṣiyām*" (fasting) means refraining from something and not moving from one state to another. Silence is called fasting because it is refraining from speaking, as Allah says in *Sūrat Maryam*, *"I have made a vow of silence (*ṣawm*) to the All-Merciful."* (19:26) The verb is also used to refer to the wind being still, and to an animal when it goes off its food, and to the day when it reaches its midpoint. In terms of the *Sharī'a*, fasting means to refrain from things which break the fast, having made the intention to do so, between dawn and sunset, and it is completed and perfected by avoiding all forbidden things and not falling into any prohibited actions, as the Prophet, peace be upon him, said, "If anyone does not abandon lying and acting by it, Allah has no need of him abandoning food and drink."

The excellence of fasting is immense and its reward enormous. There are many good and excellent reports attesting to that. It is sufficient evidence of the excellence of fasting that Allah singled it out for ascription to Himself as is confirmed in the *ḥadīth* in which the Prophet reports his Lord as saying, "Allah Almighty says: 'Every action of the son of Ādam is his except for fasting. It is Mine and I reward it.'" He singled out fasting as being His, even though all acts of worship are in fact His, for two reasons which make fasting different from other acts of worship. The first is that fasting curtails the enjoyment and appetites of the self which other acts of worship do not do. The second is that fasting is a secret between the slave and his Lord which only He knows. That is why it is particular to Him. All other acts of worship are outward and may contain some artifice and showing off, which is not the case with fasting.

as it was prescribed for those before you –

Ash-Sha'bī, Qatāda and others said that the comparison refers to the time of fasting and amount of fasting. Allah had prescribed fasting Ramaḍān for the people of Mūsā and 'Īsā but they altered it. The priests added ten days due to a vow made by one of the priests and eventually, due to further oaths, the Christian fast became fifty days and that was too arduous in the heat so it was moved to the spring. It is said that the comparison applies to the fact of the obligation to fast, not to the time or amount of fasting. It is said that the comparison is in respect of the description of fasting, as it is denial of food, drink and intercourse.

Some say, including Ibn 'Abbās, that this phrase refers to what happened when the fast was first prescribed for the Muslims when it was three days of every month and the Day of 'Āshūrā' and *"those before you"* refers to the Jews who had the same prescription. This was then abrogated for the Muslims by prescription of the month of Ramaḍān in the second *āyat*.

so that hopefully you will become godfearing –

You are weak. When you eat little, your appetites are weakened. When the appetites are weakened, acts of disobedience are lessened. It is said it means so that you will be wary of acts of disobedience. It is said that it is general because fasting, as the Prophet, may Allah bless him and grant him peace, said, "is a covering and hope" and this is a means to becoming godfearing.

for a specified number of days

This refers to the month of Ramaḍān.

But any of you who are ill or on a journey should fast a number of other days.

There are two possibilities for someone who is ill. One is that he cannot fast at all and it is obligatory for him to break it. The second is that he is able to fast but only with difficulty. This person is recommended to break his fast and only an ignorant person fasts in that condition. Ibn Sīrīn said, "When a person is in a state which can be called illness, he can break the fast, analogous with the traveller who does so by reason of travelling, even if he does not have to." Ṭarīf ibn Tammām said, "I visited Muḥammad ibn Sīrīn in Ramaḍān and he was eating, When he finished he said, 'I have something wrong with this finger.'"

Most scholars, however, say that when someone has an illness which pains or harms him or when he fears that it will last longer or increase if he fasts, then he can break the fast. Ibn 'Aṭiyya said, "This is the position of the people of Mālik who possess extensive knowledge." Ibn Khuwayzimandād said that there were different transmissions from Mālik about the kind of illness which permits breaking the fast. One view was that the illness was one in which there was fear of someone dying if they fasted. Another was that it was a serious illness and there was fear of it getting worse and causing hardship and this is the sound position of his school. But the fairest thing concerning this topic, Allah willing, is what Ibn Sīrīn said, and al-Bukhārī reports a similar position from Isḥāq ibn Rāhawayh, because the term "illness" is unspecified.

or on a journey

Scholars disagree about the length of journey on which it is permitted to break the fast and shorten the prayer although there is consensus about the journey being one which is in obedience to Allah, such as *ḥajj* or *jihād*, or a journey to visit relatives or seeking necessary livelihood. As for journeys for trade and other permitted things, there is disagreement about whether it is forbidden or permitted on these. That it is permitted is more likely. As for a journey for the sake of disobedience, there is also disagreement about whether it is permitted or prohibited to break the fast during it, and prohibited is more likely.

Ibn 'Aṭiyya said, "The distance which must be travelled to break the fast according to Mālik is the same as that for which the prayer can be shortened." Scholars disagree about exactly what that is. Mālik said, "A day and a night," and then he retracted that and said, "Forty-eight miles."[1] He is once reported as saying forty-two miles, or thirty-six miles, or a day and night, or two days, which is the position of ash-Shāfi'ī. There is a difference between land and sea journeys. It is said that the sea journey is a day and a night and on land it is forty-eight miles. Other things are also said.

Scholars agree that someone travelling in Ramaḍān is not permitted to break the fast at home before setting out because a traveller is not a traveller by intention as opposed to a resident who is. He becomes a traveller by action and setting out. A resident does not need an intention for residence when he is resident since residency does not need any other action. They say that there is no disagreement about someone who intends to travel: he is not permitted to break the fast before he leaves. If he does break it, Ibn Ḥabīb says that, if he has made preparations to travel and has begun the process, he owes nothing provided that the journey takes place. That is also related from Aṣbagh and Ibn al-Mājishūn. If he is then prevented from travelling, he owes *kaffāra*. It is related from Ibn al-Qāsim that he only has to make up that day. Ashhab says he owes nothing whether he travels or not. Saḥnūn says that he owes *kaffāra* whether he travels or not and he is like a woman expecting her period.

The position of Ibn al-Qāsim and Ashhab about not owing *kaffāra* is good because it is an action which he is permitted to do and he has no responsibility. Nothing is established about it except by certainty and there is no certainty when there is a disagreement.

Scholars disagree about which is better: breaking the fast or fasting on a journey. Mālik and ash-Shāfi'ī said that fasting is better for the one who is strong enough to do it. The majority opinion in the school of Mālik is that there is a choice, which is also the position in the school of ash-Shāfi'ī. Anas and others also said that the fasting is better for those who are strong enough and that is the position of Abū Ḥanīfa and his people. Ibn 'Umar and Ibn 'Abbās said, "Taking advantage of the dispensation is better," as did others.

1. The calculation of this distance varies according to how far you consider to be the distance of one mail stage (*barīd*), and there is more than one view about that. The Arab mile is also slightly shorter than an English mile.

should fast a number of other days.

There is an elision here, i.e. "whoever among you is ill or on a journey should break the fast and then make up..." The majority of scholars say that when the people of the land fast twenty-nine days and a man is ill, when he recovers, he makes up twenty-nine days. He makes up the days he missed.

People disagree about whether it is obligatory for the days to be continuous or not. 'Ā'isha says that originally the *āyat* said "fast a continuous number" and then "continuous" was dropped. Abū Hurayra reported that the Messenger of Allah, may Allah bless him and grant him peace, said, "Anyone who owes a fast or Ramaḍān, should do it continuously and not break it." Ibn 'Abbās, however, says about making up Ramaḍān, "Fast it however you wish." The majority of scholars say that it is permitted to break up the days and Mālik and ash-Shāfi'ī said that. Allah did not specify in this *āyat* that they should be continuous.

When Allah says, "a number of other days", it indicates the obligation to make it up without specifying a time for doing it because the phrase applies to times, which are not distinct.

If someone must make up days of Ramaḍān and enough days pass after Ramaḍān in which he could make them up and he delays until something prevents him from making them until the following Ramaḍan, he does not have to feed anyone because he was not negligent since he was permitted to delay. This is the position of the Baghdādī Mālikīs and they relate the position of Ibn al-Qāsim in the *Mudawwana*.

If someone delays making up the fast until Sha'bān has ended, which is the usual time for making it up, does he owe *fidya*? Mālik, Aḥmad, ash-Shāfi'ī and Isḥāq said that he does but Abū Ḥanīfa and his people said he does not. There is a *ḥadīth* from Abū Hurayra about the one who neglects to make up the days he owes of Ramaḍān until the next Ramaḍān. He said that he fasts it with the people and then fasts what he missed and feeds a poor person for every day.

For those who are able to fast, their *fidya* is to feed the poor.

The people of Madina and Syria read *masākīn* in the plural rather than *miskīn* in the singular but the meaning is the same: one poor person must be fed for each day.

Scholars disagree about exactly what is meant by this phrase. It is said that it is abrogated and that it was revealed about those for whom fasting was difficult, and was abrogated by "*But that you should fast is better for you*". It used to be that the obligation was either to fast or to feed. Ibn 'Abbās said that this was revealed about the allowance for old people and the infirm who do not fast when they are able to do so, which was abrogated by *"Any of you who are resident for the month should fast it."* So the dispensation is now only for those who are unable to fast. It is also possible that the words, "those who are able to" apply, not to fasting, but to paying *fidya*, in which case this instruction has clearly not been abrogated and remains the judgement applicable to old people who cannot fast, telling them to feed a poor person for every day they do not fast. Abrogation can mean qualifying an earlier judgement and a lot of earlier people used that meaning for the word *naskh*. Allah knows best.

This can also refer to those who are physically able to fast but for whom fasting might entail undue hardship, and so includes pregnant and nursing women. They can fast or feed. If they fear for the child, they do not fast and pay *fidya* instead. Some scholars put them in the position of those who are ill, and say that they simply have to make up the fast and need not feed. Others say that they must both make it up and pay *fidya* as well.

There is disagreement about the amount owed by people who have to pay *fidya*. Mālik said it is a *mudd* of the Prophet for every day and ash-Shāfi'ī also said that. Abū Ḥanīfa said that it is a *ṣā'* of dates or half a *ṣā'* of grain.

And if someone does good of his own accord, it is better for him.

Ibn Shihāb said that this refers to anyone who wants to feed as well as fast. Mujāhid said that it is about giving more than a *mudd* when paying *fidya*. Ibn 'Abbās said that it is to feed another poor person.

But that you should fast is better for you if you only knew.
Fasting is better than breaking the fast. This is before the abrogation. It is said that it refers to travelling and any illness which is not serious. Allah knows best.

شَهْرُ رَمَضَانَ ٱلَّذِىٓ أُنزِلَ فِيهِ ٱلْقُرْءَانُ هُدًى
لِّلنَّاسِ وَبَيِّنَٰتٍ مِّنَ ٱلْهُدَىٰ وَٱلْفُرْقَانِ ۚ فَمَن شَهِدَ
مِنكُمُ ٱلشَّهْرَ فَلْيَصُمْهُ ۖ وَمَن كَانَ مَرِيضًا أَوْ عَلَىٰ
سَفَرٍ فَعِدَّةٌ مِّنْ أَيَّامٍ أُخَرَ ۗ يُرِيدُ ٱللَّهُ بِكُمُ ٱلْيُسْرَ
وَلَا يُرِيدُ بِكُمُ ٱلْعُسْرَ وَلِتُكْمِلُوا۟ ٱلْعِدَّةَ وَلِتُكَبِّرُوا۟
ٱللَّهَ عَلَىٰ مَا هَدَىٰكُمْ وَلَعَلَّكُمْ تَشْكُرُونَ ﴿١٨٥﴾

185 ***The month of Ramaḍān***
is the one in which the Qur'an
was sent down as guidance for mankind,
with Clear Signs
containing guidance and discrimination.
Any of you who are resident for the month
should fast it.
But any of you who are ill or on a journey
should fast a number of other days.
Allah desires ease for you;
He does not desire difficulty for you.
You should complete the number of days
and proclaim Allah's greatness
for the guidance He has given you
so that hopefully you will be thankful.

The month of Ramaḍān

Historians state that the first person to fast Ramaḍān was the Prophet Nūḥ when he left the Ark. We have already mentioned that Mujāhid said that Allah made fasting the month of Ramaḍān obligatory for every nation and it is known that there were nations before Nūḥ, and Allah knows best. The word for month, *shahr*, is derived from *ishhār* which means to make something known in such a way that it is not difficult for anyone to know it. The verb is also used for a sword being unsheathed. The name "Ramaḍān" is derived from *ramaḍ*, which is burning, because the belly of the faster is burning from thirst. *Ramḍā'* is intense heat. It is said that the month was named because it was the time of intense heat. It is said that it is called that because it burns up wrong actions by righteous actions. It is said that it is because, in it, the hearts take the heat of admonition and reflection about the Next World as the sand and stones are burned from the heat of the sun.

The statement implies: "Obligatory for you is the fasting of the month of Ramaḍān" or "part of what has been prescribed for you is the month of Ramaḍān." It is also said that this phrase is just descriptive.

Allah imposed fasting from the start of the month of Ramaḍān, which is when its new moon appears, and that is why the moon is called month, as in the *ḥadīth*, "When the month is clouded over for you," meaning the new moon. If it is cloudy, Sha'bān is counted as thirty days, or if the end of Ramaḍān is cloudy, it is counted as thirty days so that there will be certainty in worship and certainty that it has ended. Allah says in His Book, *"We have sent down the Reminder to you so that you can make clear to people what has been sent down to them."* (16:44)

Reliable imāms relate that the Prophet, may Allah bless him and grant him peace, said, "Fast by seeing it and break the fast by seeing the moon. If it is cloudy, calculate it." Muṭarrif ibn 'Abdullāh, one of the great *Tabi'ūn*, and Ibn Qutayba, the linguist, said, "One can rely on reckoning when it is cloudy by observing the stages of the moon, taking the *ḥadīth* of the Prophet, may Allah bless him and grant him peace, "If it is cloudy, calculate it," to mean to use its stages as evidence and complete the month accordingly. The majority, however, say that "calculate" means to complete the number which is elucidated by the *ḥadīth* reported by Abū Hurayra which says specifically, "Complete the number." Most Shāfiʻīs take the position that one can consider the statement of astronomers regarding this matter but the overwhelming consensus is the argument against them. Ibn Nāfiʻ related from Mālik that, if a ruler does not fast by sighting the moon or break it by sighting it and fasts and breaks it by calculation, you should not follow him or imitate him.

Mālik and ash-Shāfiʻī disagree about whether the new moon of Ramaḍān is confirmed by a single witness or whether it needs two. Mālik says, "A single testimony is not accepted for it because it is the testimony of a new moon, and not less than two is accepted for it." Ash-Shāfiʻī and Abū Ḥanīfa say that one witness is accepted.

They disagree about someone who sees the new moon of Ramaḍān or that of Shawwāl when he is alone. Ash-Shāfiʻī is reported as saying, "If someone sees the new moon of Ramaḍān on his own, he should fast, and if someone sees the new moon of Shawwāl on his own he should break the fast but conceal it." Ibn Wahb reported from Mālik that someone who sees the new moon of Ramaḍān alone should fast because he should not eat knowing that it is one of the days of Ramaḍān. If someone sees the new moon of Shawwāl on his own, he should not eat on it because the people would suspect anyone among them who broke the fast and he would not be safe.

They disagree about what happens when someone reports about the sighting of the moon in another land. If it is near, their ruling should be followed; if it is far away, then the people of each land should sight it separately. This is related from ʻIkrima, al-Qāsim and Sālim. It is related from Ibn ʻAbbās and Isḥāq also said it. Al-Bukhārī indicated it in a chapter entitled: "The people of each land sight it." Others said that, when it is established among people that the people of a land have sighted it earlier, then they must make up any days they did not fast. That is what al-Layth and ash-Shāfiʻī said. Ibn al-Mundhir said, "I only know that to be the position of al-Muzanī and al-Kūfī."

The Ḥanafīs agree that when the people of one country fast thirty days by sighting and the people of another land fast only twenty-nine days, those who fasted twenty-nine have to make up one day. The Shāfi'īs do not think that since the moon rising in different places can vary. The evidence of the Ḥanafīs is the words of the Almighty, *"Complete the number."* It is established by the sighting of the people of a land that the number is thirty and so those people must complete it.

Those who differ from them argue by the words of the Prophet, may Allah bless him and grant him peace, "Fast by sighting it and break the fast by sighting it." That necessitates considering the custom of every people in their land. Abū 'Umar reported the consensus that one does not pay attention to sighting in distant lands, like Andalusia in relation to Khorasan. He said, "Each land sights it, except for those areas neighbouring large cities."

Kurayb mentioned that Umm al-Faḍl bint al-Ḥārith sent him on a mission to Mu'āwiya in Syria. He said, "I came to Syria and did what she asked me to do. Ramaḍān began while I was in Syria and I saw the new moon on a Friday night. Then I came to Madina at the end of the month and 'Abdullāh ibn 'Abbās asked me about when I had seen the new moon. 'Friday night,' I replied.' You yourself saw it?' he asked. 'Yes.' I said, 'and the people saw it and fasted and Mu'āwiya fasted.' He said, 'But we saw it on Saturday night. We will continue to fast until it is the full thirty days or we see it.' I said, 'Isn't it enough that Mu'āwiya saw the moon and fasted?' 'No,' he said, 'that is what the Messenger of Allah, may Allah bless him and grant him peace, commanded us to do.'"

Our scholars said, "The statement of Ibn 'Abbās, 'That is what the Messenger of Allah, may Allah bless him and grant him peace, commanded us to do', is a clear statement that goes back to the command of the Prophet, may Allah bless him and grant him peace, and that is evidence that when the lands are far from each other as Syria is far from the Ḥijāz, the people of each land must act according to their own sighting. If that is confirmed with the overall leader [i.e. the Khalif], he cannot impel people to follow him in that. But if he does, it is not permitted to oppose him."

The position of school of Mālik regarding this question related by Ibn Wahb and Ibn al-Qāsim in *al-Majmū'a* is that when the people of Baṣra saw the new moon of Ramaḍān and then news of it reached the people of Kūfa, Madina and Yemen, they had to fast or make it up. Qāḍī Abū Isḥāq related from Ibn al-Mājishūn that if it was confirmed at Baṣra as a generally known fact which does not require testimony and witnesses (because of the large number of people who had seen it) then it was obligatory for the people of other lands to make it up. If it was confirmed with the ruler only by the testimony of two witnesses then it was not obliged for other countries. It is only obliged for those under that ruler's rule. But if it was confirmed with the *Amīr al-Mu'minīn*, then the whole community of Muslims must make it up. That is the position of Mālik.

is the one in which the Qur'an was sent down as guidance for mankind

This provides textual evidence that the Qur'ān was revealed during the month of Ramaḍān. It explains the words of the Almighty, *"Ḥa Mim, by the Book which makes things clear. We sent it down on a blessed night."* (44:1-3), meaning the Night of Power, and *"We sent it down on the Night of Power."* (97:1) This also indicates that the Night of Power is only in Ramaḍān. There is no disagreement that the Qur'ān was sent down from the Preserved Tablet on the Night of Power all at once. It was then lodged in the House of Might in the lowest heaven. Then Jibrīl brought it down, bit by bit, with commands and prohibitions brought about by different situations over the course of the following twenty-three years.

The word "Qur'ān" designates the Words of Allah Almighty and means recited. This is a common linguistic usage in Arabic. So the Qur'ān which is recited is not created. Sometimes the word is also used for the bound book (*muṣḥaf*) in which the words of the Qur'ān are written down.

as guidance for mankind, with Clear Signs containing guidance and discrimination.

The Qur'ān guides them. It is also clarification, as it makes things clear to them. This refers to the entire Qur'ān, its firm judgements and ambiguous expressions, its abrogating and abrogated *āyat*s, and Allah here lays emphasis on the Clear Signs in it, meaning by that the *ḥalāl* and *ḥarām,* and its warnings and rulings. Its "discrimination" is that it distinguishes truth from falsehood.

Any of you who are resident for the month should fast it.

This qualifies the command to fast. Whoever is present at the beginning and end of the month should fast as long he is resident. If he travels, he may break the fast. This is sound and is backed up by firm *aḥādīth*. Al-Bukhārī has a chapter entitled: "Whoever fasts some days of Ramaḍān and then travels." Ibn 'Abbās reported that the Messenger of Allah, may Allah bless him and grant him peace, went to Makka in Ramaḍān and fasted until he reached al-Kadīd and then broke the fast and the people broke it with him.

It is confirmed that the obligation of fasting is made binding by being Muslim, adulthood, and having knowledge of the month. When an unbeliever becomes Muslim or a child becomes an adult before dawn, they must fast the following day. If it is already dawn, then it is recommended for them not to eat, but they do not have to make up the past days of the month, only the day they became adult or Muslim.

Allah desires ease for you; He does not desire difficulty for you.

Mujāhid and aḍ-Ḍaḥḥāk said that the word "ease" refers to not fasting on a journey and the word "difficulty" to fasting on it. The meaning, however, can be general to all matters of the *dīn* because the Almighty says, *"He has not placed any constraint upon you in the dīn."* (22:78) The Prophet, may Allah bless him and grant him peace, said, "The *dīn* is ease," and he further said, "Make things easy and do not make things difficult."

The *āyat* indicates that Allah wills by His pre-eternal timeless Will which is distinct from His Essence. This is the position of the people of the *Sunna*, as He knows by knowledge, has power by power, lives by life, hears by hearing, sees by sight and speaks by speech. These are all attributes which exist before time and are distinct from the Essence. The philosophers and Shi'a believe that these attributes are negated.

You should complete the number of days

There are two interpretations of this. One is that someone who breaks the fast on a journey or due to illness must complete the number by fasting the days he missed. The second is that it refers to the number of days in the month, whether it is twenty-nine or thirty. Jābir ibn 'Abdullāh said that the Prophet said, "The month is twenty-nine." There is, however, a contrary report as well.

There is no consideration given to a claimed sighting of the new moon of Shawwāl on the 30th of Ramaḍān during the daytime. That moon belongs to the coming night. This is the sound position.

and proclaim Allah's greatness

This is encouragement to say the *takbīr* at the end of Ramaḍān according to the position of the majority of interpreters. People disagree about its definition. Ash-Shāfi'ī says that it is reported that Sa'īd ibn al-Musayyab, 'Urwa, and Abū Salama used to say the *takbīr* on the Night of the *'Īd* and praise Allah. He said that that night resembles the Night of Sacrifice. Ibn 'Abbās said, "It is a duty for the Muslims, when they see the new moon of Shawwāl, to say the *takbīr*."

The form of the *takbīr* according to Mālik and a group of scholars is to say: *"Allāhu akbar. Allāhu akbar. Allāhu akbar"* three times. It is related from Jābir ibn 'Abdullāh. Some scholars say the *takbīr*, *shahāda* and glorification are all included here in the *takbīr*. Some people say, *"Allāhu akbar kabīran wa'l-ḥamdu lillāhi kathīran wa subḥāna'llahi bukratan wa aṣīla."* (Allah is much very greater. Praise belongs to Allah and glory be to Allah morning and evening.) Ibn al-Mundhir reported that Mālik did not specify any particular form. Aḥmad ibn Ḥanbal said that there is scope. Ibn al-'Arabī said, "Our scholars prefer the simple *takbīr.* It is the literal text of the Qur'ān, and I incline to that view."

for the guidance He has given you

It is said that this is mentioned because the Christians went astray by altering their fast and it is said that it refers to replacing what was done in the past because the practice of the *Jāhiliyya* involved boasting about ancestors and rivalry based on lineage and titles. It is also said that it means to esteem Allah for the laws He has guided us to, in which case the phrase has a general significance.

وَإِذَا سَأَلَكَ عِبَادِي عَنِّي فَإِنِّي قَرِيبٌ أُجِيبُ دَعْوَةَ
الدَّاعِ إِذَا دَعَانِ فَلْيَسْتَجِيبُوا لِي وَلْيُؤْمِنُوا بِي
لَعَلَّهُمْ يَرْشُدُونَ ﴿١٨٦﴾

186 ***If My slaves ask you about Me, I am near.***
I answer the call of the caller when he calls on Me.
They should therefore respond to Me and believe in Me
so that hopefully they will be rightly guided.

If My slaves ask you about Me,

"If they ask you Who it is that they worship, then tell them that I am near and I reward obedience and answer the one who makes supplication to Me." Allah knows what His slaves do in respect of fasting, prayer and other things. The commentators disagree about the reason this *āyat* was revealed. Muqātil said that 'Umar had sexual intercourse with his wife after he had prayed *'Ishā'* and regretted that and wept. He went to the Messenger of Allah and informed him and returned deeply upset. That was before the permission to do so was revealed. Then this *āyat* was revealed.

It is said that when it was obligatory for them to refrain from eating after going to sleep, one of the Companions ate and regretted that and this *āyat* was sent down about accepting his repentance and abrogating that judgement as will be clarified. Ibn 'Abbās reported that the Jews said, "How can our Lord hear our call when you claim that there is five hundred years between Him and heaven?" This was then revealed. Al-Ḥasan said, "The reason for its revelation was that some people said to the Prophet, "Is your Lord near so that we can speak to Him or far so that we must call to Him?" Then this was revealed.

I am near.

This is in respect to the response. It is said to mean near by My knowledge, and it is said to mean near to My friends through My favour and blessing to them.

I answer the call of the caller when he calls on Me.

This means: "I accept the worship of the one who worships Me." The calling means worship and the answer means acceptance. An-Nu'mān ibn Bashīr reported that the Prophet, may Allah bless him and grant him peace, said, "Supplication is worship. Your Lord says, 'Call on Me and I will answer you.' So calling (*du'ā'*) is the same as worship. Evidence for that can be found in the words of the Almighty, *'Those who are too proud for My worship will enter Hell abject.'* (40:60) Here it means supplication."

So Allah Almighty commanded *du'ā'* and encouraged it and called it worship and promised that He would answer it. 'Ubāda ibn aṣ-Ṣāmit reported that the Prophet, may Allah bless him and grant him peace, said, "My Community have been given three things that only the Prophets were given previously. Whenever Allah sent a Prophet, he said, 'Call on Me and I will answer you.' He told this whole community, 'Call on Me and I will answer you.' When Allah sent a Prophet, he said to him, 'I have not placed any constraint on you in the *dīn*.' He told this whole community, 'I have not placed any constraint on you in the *dīn*.' When

Allah sent a Prophet, He made him a witness against his people, and He made this entire community witnesses against mankind."

If it is asked, "Why would a caller call if he did not expect to be answered?", the reply is that the words of Allah in the two *āyat*s, "answer" and "respond" do not absolutely necessitate an answer for every supplicator in detail nor every seeker in detail. Allah says in another *āyat*, *"Call on your Lord humbly and secretly. He does not love those who overstep the limits."* (7:55) Everyone who persists in a major wrong action, knowingly or ignorantly, is a transgressor and Allah reports that He does not love transgressors and so how could He answer such a one? The categories of transgression are numerous and Allah, willing, they will be mentioned in *Sūrat al-A'rāf*. Some scholars say: "He can answer if He wishes as He says, *"If He wills, He will deliver you from whatever it was that made you call on Him."* (6:41) This is general and limited. The Prophet, may Allah bless him and grant him peace, made three supplications and was granted two and denied one as will be made clear in *Sūrat al-An'ām*, Allah willing.

It is said that what is intended by this report is to acquaint all believers with the fact that their Lord answers the call of those who call in general, and that He is close to the slave and hears his supplication and knows his need and responds to whatever He wishes and in whatever way He wishes. *"Who is further astray that the one who calls other things besides Allah, which will not respond to them?"* (46:5) The master answers his slave and the father his child but may not give them the thing they are asking for. So it is not inevitable that what is asked for will be granted.

It is related through Ibn 'Umar from the Prophet, may Allah bless him and grant him peace, "Whoever has supplication opened to him, has the doors of the answer opened to him as well." Allah revealed to Dā'ūd, "Tell My wrongdoing slaves not to call on Me for I have made it incumbent on Myself to answer those who call on Me and when I answer wrongdoers, I afflict them." People have said that Allah answers every supplication and that the answer either appears in this world or takes the form of expiation of sins or is stored up in the Next World. Abū Sa'īd al-Khudrī reported that the Prophet, may Allah bless him and grant him peace, said, "There is no Muslim who supplicates to Allah Almighty with a supplication which does not contain a request for anything wrong or severance from his kin without Allah giving him one of three things: He either hastens it to him, or stores it up for him or turns away the like of it in evil from him." They asked, "When we do a lot of supplication?" "Allah has more," he replied.

They should therefore respond to Me

They should call on Me. Ibn 'Aṭiyya said that this means: They should seek for My response. Mujāhid and others said that the meaning is: "They should respond to Me regarding what I call them to in respect of faith," in other word they should obey Allah and act on His commands.

أُحِلَّ لَكُمْ لَيْلَةَ ٱلصِّيَامِ ٱلرَّفَثُ إِلَىٰ نِسَآئِكُمْ هُنَّ لِبَاسٌ لَّكُمْ
وَأَنتُمْ لِبَاسٌ لَّهُنَّ عَلِمَ ٱللَّهُ أَنَّكُمْ كُنتُمْ تَخْتَانُونَ أَنفُسَكُمْ
فَتَابَ عَلَيْكُمْ وَعَفَا عَنكُمْ فَٱلْـَٰٔنَ بَٰشِرُوهُنَّ وَٱبْتَغُوا۟
مَا كَتَبَ ٱللَّهُ لَكُمْ وَكُلُوا۟ وَٱشْرَبُوا۟ حَتَّىٰ يَتَبَيَّنَ
لَكُمُ ٱلْخَيْطُ ٱلْأَبْيَضُ مِنَ ٱلْخَيْطِ ٱلْأَسْوَدِ مِنَ ٱلْفَجْرِ ثُمَّ
أَتِمُّوا۟ ٱلصِّيَامَ إِلَى ٱلَّيْلِ وَلَا تُبَٰشِرُوهُنَّ وَأَنتُمْ عَٰكِفُونَ
فِى ٱلْمَسَٰجِدِ تِلْكَ حُدُودُ ٱللَّهِ فَلَا تَقْرَبُوهَا كَذَٰلِكَ
يُبَيِّنُ ٱللَّهُ ءَايَٰتِهِۦ لِلنَّاسِ لَعَلَّهُمْ يَتَّقُونَ ١٨٧

187 *On the night of the fast it is lawful for you*
to have sexual relations with your wives.
They are clothing for you and you for them.

Allah knows that you have been betraying yourselves
and He has turned towards you and excused you.
Now you may have sexual intercourse with them
and seek what Allah has written for you.
Eat and drink until you can clearly discern
the white thread from the black thread of the dawn,
then fulfil the fast until the night appears.
But do not have sexual intercourse with them
while you are in retreat in the mosques.
These are Allah's limits, so do not go near them.
In this way does Allah make
His Signs clear to people
so that hopefully they will be godfearing.

On the night of the fast it is lawful for you to have sexual relations with your wives.

The way this is expressed indicates that it was first forbidden and then that prohibition was abrogated. Abū Dāwūd reported from Ibn Abī Laylā that, when a man broke the fast and then went to sleep before eating again, he would not break his fast until the following *Maghrib*. One day 'Umar came home and went to his wife and she told him she had already slept. He thought she was making an excuse and had intercourse with her. In another incident a man of the Anṣār wanted to eat and they said, "We will heat something up for you," and he fell asleep. In the morning, this *āyat* was revealed.

Al-Bukhārī related that al-Barā' said, "Among the Companions of Muḥammad, if ever a man was fasting and the time of fast-breaking came but he went to sleep before he had broken his fast, he would not eat that night or the following day until evening. Qays ibn Ṣirma al-Anṣārī was fasting and when the time of fast-breaking came, he went to his wife and said to her, 'Do you have any food?' She said, 'No, but I will go and look for something for you.' He worked during the day and sleep overcame him. His wife returned to him and when she saw him she said, 'You are disappointed.' In the middle of the day, he fainted and it was mentioned to the Prophet, peace be upon him. Then this *āyat* was sent down: *'On the night of the fast it is lawful for you to have sexual relations with your wives.'* Then they were very happy."

They also used not to approach their wives in Ramaḍān but some of them betrayed themselves by having intercourse at night. Whoever disobeys Allah has betrayed himself since he has brought down punishment on himself. Al-Qutaybī said, "The root meaning of betrayal is that a man is entrusted with something and does not convey his trust.

The word "*rafath*" (sexual relations) is an allusion to sexual intercourse because Allah is noble and prefers to use an allusion. Ibn 'Abbās, as-Suddī and az-Zajjāj said, "*Rafath* is a word which denotes all that a man does with a woman."

They are clothing for you and you for them.

The metaphor of clothing is used because a married couple are close to one another like garments and garments cling to the body. Someone said that it is because they cover and protect a thing and so each of them protects the other from what is not *ḥalāl*. It is also said that it is because each of them protects the other from the eyes of other people in respect of what occurs between them.

Allah knows that you have been betraying yourselves and He has turned towards you and excused you.

Betraying yourselves by having forbidden sexual intercourse and eating after sleeping during the nights of fasting. Allah's turning towards them has two possible meanings. One is that He accepts their repentance for having betrayed themselves and the other is that it refers to Him making it easier for them through His indulgence and His allowing them to do what had previously been forbidden. So the words "excused you" can refer to the wrong action or it can mean making things wide and easy as the Prophet, may Allah bless him and grant him peace, said, "The beginning of the time is the pleasure of Allah and the end of it is the pardon of Allah."

Now you may have sexual intercourse with them

It is lawful for you now to do what it was forbidden before. "*Mubāshara*" (sexual intercourse) is so called because of the contact of skin to skin. This is the literal meaning of the word.

and seek what Allah has written for you.

Ibn 'Abbās, Mujāhid, al-Ḥakam ibn 'Uyayna, al-Ḥasan, as-Suddī, ar-Rabī' and aḍ-Ḍaḥḥāk said that this refers to seeking to have a child, indicating that it refers directly back to the previous statement about having sexual intercourse. Ibn 'Abbās said, "What Allah has written for you is the Qur'ān." Az-Zajjāj says, "It means: 'Seek in the Qur'ān for what is permitted to you and for what you have been commanded to do.'" Ibn 'Abbās and Mu'ādh ibn Jabal reported that it refers to looking for the Night of Power. It is also said that it means: "Take advantage of the allowance and dispensation Allah has granted you," and this was what Qatāda and Ibn 'Aṭiyya said. It is said that it means to seek slavegirls and wives.

Eat and drink until you can clearly discern the white thread from the black thread of the dawn,

When it is clear that dawn has arrived it is not lawful for anyone to eat, even if there is still some time until sunrise. There is disagreement about the point at which it becomes clear that one must abstain from things which break the fast. The majority say that dawn is the light which spreads right and left on the horizon and there are *aḥādīth* to that effect. Samura reported that the Prophet said, "Do not be deluded from your *saḥūr* by the *adhān* of Bilāl nor by the whiteness of the false dawn on the horizon. It is like that until the dawn spreads like that." Ḥammād related it with his hand open. Ibn 'Abbās reported that the Messenger of Allah said, "There are two dawns. The one that is like the wolf's tail does not permit or forbid anything. As for the one which spreads on the horizon, it makes the prayer permitted and forbids food." One group say that it refers to the time after dawn when it becomes clear in the streets and houses that dawn has arrived. That is related from 'Umar, Ḥudhayfa, Ibn 'Abbās, Ṭalq ibn 'Alī, and others. Abstaining becomes obligatory when it is clearly dawn in the streets and on the tops of the mountains. Ḥudhayfa was asked, "When did you have *saḥūr* with the Messenger of Allah?" He replied, "It was day, although the sun had not yet risen."

Fasting is one of the acts of worship which is only valid with an intention, and the time to make the intention is before dawn *(fajr)*. It is related that 'Adī ibn Abī Ḥātim said, "I said, 'Messenger of Allah, what is the white thread from the black thread? Are they two threads?' He said, 'You are a thick-head if you look at the two threads.' Then he said, 'No, rather it is the blackness of night and the whiteness of day.'" So what is meant by "white thread" is the white thread of daylight. Al-Bukhārī said that dawn is called a thread because what appears is a distinct line of white like a thread.

The root of the word *"fajr"* (dawn) is used for water which gushes up and spreads out. It is used for dawn because when the light of the sun begins to appear, it spreads out along the horizon. One also says that "dawn breaks".

Abū Ḥanīfa has an opinion which differs from the majority regarding the necessity of the intention being made before dawn. The majority position is that fasting is one of the acts of worship and is only valid with an intention and its time, set by the Lawgiver, is before dawn.

then fulfil the fast until the night appears.

All agree that this is a command which embodies an obligatory injunction. Eating, drinking and sexual intercourse describe the night and fasting describes the day. So the judgements of the two times are clear and distinct from each other. What is allowed in the night is not permitted in the day except for travellers or ill people. In any other case, if someone breaks the fast he either does it intentionally or out of forgetfulness. If it is the first case, Mālik said, "Whoever breaks the fast in Ramaḍān by eating, drinking, or sexual intercourse, must make it up and owes *kaffāra*," as is reported in the *Muwatta'* and also the in *Ṣaḥīḥ* Muslim where the

Prophet ordered a man who broke the fast to free a slave, or fast two consecutive months or feed sixty poor people. Ash-Shāfi'ī and others say that this *kaffāra* is specific to someone who breaks the fast through sexual intercourse based on another *ḥadīth*.

When Allah mentions the things forbidden by fasting, such as eating, drinking and sexual intercourse, He does not mention direct physical contact like kissing, touching and other such things. That indicates the soundness of the fast of someone who kisses or touches because the mention of what is allowed at night entails its prohibition during the day, and only three things are mentioned. This is why there is disagreement about this matter and indeed the *Salaf* disagreed. Our scholars say that it is disliked for the one who cannot control himself since it might lead to invalidating the fast.

The injunction "to fast until the night appears" contains an implicit prohibition against continuous fasting since night marks the end of the fast. 'Ā'isha said that. It is a subject of dispute as people like 'Abdullāh ibn az-Zubayr, Ibrāhīm at-Taymī and others fasted continuously. Ibn az-Zubayr used to fast for seven days at a time.

Breaking the fast with dates is recommended. Anas said, "The Messenger of Allah, may Allah bless him and grant him peace, used to break the fast with fresh dates before he prayed, and if there were no fresh dates, then with small dry dates. If there were no dry dates, then with a few sips of water."

But do not have sexual intercourse with them while you are in retreat (*i'tikāf*) in the mosques.

Allah makes it clear that sexual intercourse invalidates *i'tikāf*. The people of knowledge agree that if someone has sexual intercourse with his wife while he is in *i'tikāf*, that violates his *i'tikāf*. Pleasures other than intercourse are disliked, even though they were not intended. Touching without lust is not forbidden, because 'Ā'isha combed the Prophet's hair while he was in *i'tikāf* and that entails touching.

The word for "retreat", *i'tikāf*, linguistically means "to cling to" and someone doing *i'tikāf* clings to good action by obedience to

Allah during the period of his *i'tikāf*. In the usage of the *Sharī'a* it denotes clinging to a particular act of obedience at a particular time with particular conditions in a particular place. Scholars agree that it is not obligatory but is a supererogatory act of devotion which the Messenger of Allah, his Companions and wives obliged on themselves. It is disliked for someone to begin it if he fears that he will not be able to complete it.

Scholars agree that *i'tikāf* can only be done in mosques in view of the words of Allah, "in mosques." They disagree about exactly what is meant by mosques in this instance. Some people believe that the *āyat* was confined to those mosques which were built by a Prophet, like the Masjid al-Ḥarām and Jerusalem. Ḥudhayfa, for example, said that *i'tikāf* can only be done in them. Others say that it can only be done in a mosque in which the *Jumu'a* prayer is held. That is one of the positions of Mālik. Still others say that it is permitted in any mosque. That is the position of ash-Shāfi'ī and Abū Ḥanīfa. They say that it is because the *āyat* is general. It is also one of the positions of Mālik.

According to Mālik and Abū Ḥanīfa, the minimum time of *i'tikāf* is a day and a night. If someone vows to do it for a night, he must do it for a day and a night. Ash-Shāfi'ī says that he must do what he vowed, and its minimum is an instant.

These are Allah's limits, so do not go near them.

"These judgements are the limits of Allah, so do not oppose them." This indicates commands and prohibitions. "*Ḥudūd*" (limits) are barriers. Iron is called *ḥadīd* because it prevents the weapon from reaching the body. The doorman and jailer are called *ḥaddād* because they prevent people from entering or going out. The *ḥudūd* are so called because they prevent the one who commits the crimes from returning to their like.

In this way does Allah make His Signs clear to people

Just as He clarifies these limits, He clarifies all the judgements so that people will be careful not to exceed them. The Signs are the *āyat*s which guide to the truth.

وَلَا تَأْكُلُوٓاْ أَمْوَٰلَكُم بَيْنَكُم بِٱلْبَٰطِلِ وَتُدْلُواْ
بِهَآ إِلَى ٱلْحُكَّامِ لِتَأْكُلُواْ فَرِيقًا مِّنْ أَمْوَٰلِ ٱلنَّاسِ
بِٱلْإِثْمِ وَأَنتُمْ تَعْلَمُونَ ١٨٨

188 ***Do not devour one another's property by false means***
nor offer it to the judges as a bribe,
trying through crime to knowingly usurp
a portion of other people's property.

Do not devour one another's property by false means

This was revealed about 'Abdān ibn Ashwa' al-Ḥadramī. He claimed some property from Imru'l-Qays al-Kindī and they went to the Prophet, may Allah bless him and grant him peace, where 'Imru'l-Qays denied 'Abdān's claim and wanted to make an oath. This was revealed and he refrained from making the oath and the Prophet gave judgement to 'Abdān in respect of the disputed property and 'Imru'l-Qays did not contend against him. But despite the specific cause of the revelation, the *āyat* embraces the entire community of Muḥammad, may Allah bless him and grant him peace. It means: you should not consume one another's property without having the legal right to do so. Things included in this judgement are gambling, fraud, usurpation, denying someone's just rights and anything the owner is not happy about or things which the *Sharī'a* forbids, even if the owner is happy about them, such as money from prostitution, fees for soothsaying and money from wine and pigs and other such things.

Whoever obtains someone else's property in a manner other than that permitted by the *Sharī'a* has consumed it by false means. One such occasion is if a *qāḍī* judges in your favour when you know that you are in the wrong. The *ḥarām* does not become *ḥalāl* by the verdict of a judge, because he judges by the outward. It does not change the inner reality. Umm Salama transmitted that the Prophet, may Allah bless him and grant him peace, said, "I am but a man to whom you bring your disputes. Perhaps one of you is more eloquent in his evidence than the other and so I give judgement according to what I have heard from him. If I make a judgement in his favour about something which is rightfully his brother's, he should not take any of it for I am awarding him a portion of the Fire." This is a clear text expressing the fact that the judgement of the judge by the outward does not change the inward judgement.

The root of the word for "by false means" (*bāṭil*) means literally to go and depart. One form of it means to follow a diversion. In Allah's words: *"The **false** cannot reach it"* (41:42) Qatāda says that it refers to Iblīs. He is not able to add anything or remove anything. In *"Allah wipes out the **false**"* (42:24), it means *shirk*. *Baṭala* means sorcerers.

nor offer it to the judges as a bribe,

It is said that this refers to deposits and things about which there is no evidence, as Ibn 'Abbās and al-Ḥasan said. It is said that it is property belonging to orphans in the possession of their trustees which is presented to the judges when it is demanded. It is said that it means "Do not give bribes (*tarshaw*) to judges so that they judge in your favour because judges are rarely free of this." The root of the word normally used for bribe (*rashwa*) is *rashā'*, a rope, since people use rope to get what they need.

trying through crime to knowingly usurp a portion of other people's property.

The words "through crime" mean through injustice and transgression. It is called a "crime" (*ithm*) because of the wrong action of the doer. "Knowingly" means that you know that it is false and a wrong action and this is astonishing audacity and disobedience.

The people of the *Sunna* agree that whoever takes any kind of property in this way, no matter whether it is a little or a lot, becomes legally iniquitous by doing that. It is forbidden for him to take it.

يَسْـَٔلُونَكَ عَنِ ٱلْأَهِلَّةِ ۖ قُلْ هِىَ مَوَٰقِيتُ لِلنَّاسِ وَٱلْحَجِّ ۗ وَلَيْسَ
ٱلْبِرُّ بِأَن تَأْتُوا۟ ٱلْبُيُوتَ مِن ظُهُورِهَا وَلَـٰكِنَّ ٱلْبِرَّ مَنِ
ٱتَّقَىٰ ۗ وَأْتُوا۟ ٱلْبُيُوتَ مِنْ أَبْوَٰبِهَا ۚ وَٱتَّقُوا۟ ٱللَّهَ لَعَلَّكُمْ
تُفْلِحُونَ ﴿١٨٩﴾

189 ***They will ask you about the crescent moons.***
Say, 'They are set times for mankind
and for the ḥajj.'
It is not devoutness for you
to enter houses by the back.
Rather devoutness is possessed
by those who are godfearing.
So come to houses by their doors
and have fear of Allah,
so that hopefully you will be successful.

They will ask you about the crescent moons.

The Jews asked the Prophet, may Allah bless him and grant him peace, about this when Mu'ādh was with him and Mu'ādh said, "Messenger of Allah, the Jews overwhelm us and ask us a lot of questions about the crescent moons. Why does the moon first appear fine and then increase in size until it is round and then get smaller again until it looks like it did at the beginning?" Then Allah revealed this *āyat*. It is also said that the reason for the revelation of this *āyat* was that the Muslims asked the Prophet, may Allah bless him and grant him peace, about the new moon and the reason for its waning and fullness and its difference from the sun. Ibn 'Abbās, Qatāda, ar-Rabī' and others said that.

"Crescent moons" (*ahilla*) is a reference to the passing months and the term is used to designate months because the month begins with a crescent moon. The term is used for the two days at the end of the month and the two at the beginning. It is also said to apply to the three at the beginning. Al-Aṣmā'ī says it is called a crescent (*hilāl*) when it is curved like a thin thread. It is also said that it is called *hilāl* until its light is clear in the sky, which is the seventh night. Abū'l-'Abbās said that it is called *hilāl* because the word means to raise the voice and people raise their voices when reporting its sighting. One form of the verb is used for the cry of a newborn baby. Another use is for a face shining with joy.

Say, 'They are set times for mankind and for the ḥajj.'

This explains the legal judgement applied to the waxing and waning of the moon. It removes doubt about the length of set terms and transactions, oaths, *ḥajj*, *'idda*, fasting and breaking the fast and the extent of pregnancy, wages and hire and other things.

The expression "set times" (*mawāqīt*) is said to refer to the end of a period. The word is not declined and has no singular form. *Ḥajj* is only mentioned because it is something whose time needs to be known and it is not permitted to delay it beyond its time which differs from what the pre-Islamic Arabs thought because they used to alter the months.

Mālik and Abū Ḥanīfa used this *āyat* as evidence that *iḥrām* for *ḥajj* can be validly adopted outside the months of *ḥajj* because Allah Almighty here makes all the crescent moons apply to it. This is contrary to the position taken by ash-Shāfi'ī in view of the words of Allah: *"The ḥajj takes place during certain well-known months,"* (2:197) as we will discover when we come to that *āyat*. The meaning of this *āyat,* then, is that some crescent moons are times for people (in general) and some are times for *ḥajj* (specifically).

It is not devoutness for you to enter houses by the back.

This is mentioned together with talking about the time of the *ḥajj* because the questions about the crescent moons and entering houses from their backs were asked together and the *āyat* was revealed in answer to both of them.

If the Anṣār set out on *ḥajj* and then returned for something they would not enter the doors of their houses. After they had adopted *iḥrām* for *ḥajj* or *'umra*, they were not allowed to have anything come between them and the sky, so if one of them returned to get something, he would not go inside his house because the ceiling would come between him and the sky. Instead, he would climb up the outside walls onto the roof and then stand by his room and ask for whatever he needed which would be brought out to him. They used to think that this was piety and devoutness and Allah refuted that, making it clear that piety consists in obeying Him.

Ibn 'Abbās said, "During the time of the *Jāhiliyya* and also at the beginning of Islam when someone adopted *iḥrām* for the *ḥajj* and was one of the people who live in houses, he would make a hole in the back of his house and enter and leave through it or put a ladder up and climb up and descend by it. If he lived in a tent, he would enter by the back of the tent unless he was one of the *ḥums*." Az-Zuhri related that the Prophet adopted *iḥrām* for *'umra* in the time of Ḥudaybiyya and entered his room and one of the Anṣār entered after him and made a hole in the wall as was his custom. They asked him, "Why did you go inside when you are in *iḥrām*?" The man replied, "You entered and so I entered." The Prophet said, "I am one of the *ḥums*," meaning those who do not follow that as a *dīn*." The man said to him, "I have the same *dīn* as you do," and the *āyat* was revealed. *Ḥums* means Quraysh, Kināna, Khuzā'a, Thaqīf, and other tribes. It derives from their zealousness (*ḥamāsa*) in their *dīn*.

Whatever the case, this *āyat* clarifies what devoutness is, and it is doing what Allah has commanded. When Allah says to "come to houses by their doors", He is telling people to do things in the manner which Allah has recommended. This *āyat* also makes clear that anything Allah has not prescribed or recommended as an act of devotion is not an act of devotion.

وَقَٰتِلُوا۟ فِى سَبِيلِ ٱللَّهِ ٱلَّذِينَ يُقَٰتِلُونَكُمْ
وَلَا تَعْتَدُوٓا۟ ۚ إِنَّ ٱللَّهَ لَا يُحِبُّ ٱلْمُعْتَدِينَ ﴿١٩٠﴾

190 ***Fight in the Way of Allah***
against those who fight you,
but do not go beyond the limits.
Allah does not love those who go beyond the limits.

Fight in the Way of Allah against those who fight you,

This was the first *āyat* to be revealed with the command to fight. There is no disagreement that fighting was forbidden before the *Hijra* by the words of Allah, *"Repel the bad with something better"* (41:34) and several other similar *āyat*s which were revealed in Makka. When the Prophet emigrated to Madina, he was commanded to fight and this *āyat* was revealed. Ar-Rabīʻ ibn Anas and others said this. Abū Bakr aṣ-Ṣīddiq, however, said that the first *āyat* revealed about fighting was the *āyat* in *Sūrat al-Ḥajj*: *"Permission is given to those who are fought against because they have been wronged."* (22:39). The one in this *sūra* is more frequently cited as being the first.

The *āyat* for the permission to fight was revealed about fighting in general and the instruction is to fight not only those idolaters who fight the Muslims but also those who do not fight. The command refers to the time when the Prophet, may Allah bless him and grant him peace, went out with his Companions to Makka for *'umra*. When he camped at al-Ḥudaybiyya near Makka, the idolaters prevented him from continuing on into Makka and he remained there for a month. They made a treaty stipulating that he could return the following year for three days and that there would be no fighting between them. After concluding this treaty, he returned to Madina. The following year he made preparations for *ḥajj* and the Muslims feared the treachery of the unbelievers and did not like the idea of fighting in the sacred months and in the Ḥaram.

Then this *āyat* was revealed, meaning that it is lawful for you to fight if the unbelievers fight you. So the *āyat* is connected to the prior mention of *ḥajj* and entering houses by the back door. After this the Prophet fought those who fought him and refrained from those who refrained from fighting him until the *āyat* in *Sūrat at-*

Tawba (9:5) was revealed, "Fight the idolaters," and this *āyat* was abrogated. This is the position of the majority of scholars.

Ibn Zayd and ar-Rabī', however, say that this *āyat* was abrogated by Allah's words: *"Fight the idolaters totally,"* (9:36) in which he was commanded to fight all the unbelievers. Ibn 'Abbās, 'Umar ibn 'Abdu'l-'Azīz, and Mujāhid said that it is an *āyat* whose judgement remains operative and means: "Fight those who fight you and do not transgress by killing women, children, monks and the like," as will be explained. An-Naḥḥās said that this is the sounder position in terms of both the *Sunna* and in terms of logic. As for the *Sunna*, there is a *ḥadīth* reported by Ibn 'Umar that, during one of his expeditions the Messenger of Allah, may Allah bless him and grant him peace, saw a woman who had been killed and he abhorred that and forbade the killing of women and children. As for logic, it applies to children and those like them, like monks, the chronically ill, old men and hirelings who clearly should not be killed. When Abū Bakr sent Yazīd ibn Abī Sufyān to Syria, he commanded that he should not do harm to certain groups. Mālik and others transmitted this. Scholars put those who should not be killed into six categories.

- **Women.** But if they fight, they should be fought. Saḥnūn said, "In battle and out of it because of the general nature of Allah's words, 'Fight against those who fight you.' A woman can have an immense effect on the fighting, including supplying assistance and encouraging fighting. Women go out with their hair undone, shouting encouragement and censuring flight. So it is permitted to kill them. If they are captured, however, then enslavement is more beneficial since they more easily convert and it is difficult for them to run away."

- **Children** should not be killed and that is a firm prohibition. If a child fights, however, then he can be killed.

- **Monks** should be neither killed nor enslaved. They are left to live on the property which they own. This is when they live apart from the people of disbelief because of the command which Abū Bakr gave to Yazīd ibn Abī Sufyān, "You will find some people who claim that they have confined themselves for the sake of Allah. Leave them with what they claim." If, however, they are with the unbelievers in churches, they can be killed. As for nuns, Ashhab thinks that they should not be killed. Saḥnūn said, "Being a nun does not alter the basic judgement about her as a woman." Qāḍī Abū Bakr ibn al-'Arabī said, "I think that the sound view is that of Ashhab and nuns are included in the directive of Abū Bakr."

- **The chronically ill.** Saḥnun says that they should be killed. Ibn Ḥabīb says that they should not be killed. The sound position is that we consider their states. If there is potential harm in them, they should be killed. Otherwise, they should be left alone.

- **Old men.** Mālik says that they should not be killed and that is the position of the majority of *fuqahā'*. If an old man is senile and unable to fight and not consulted for his opinion or taking part in defence, he should not be killed. Mālik and Abū Ḥanīfa say that. Ash-Shāfi'ī has two positions: one is that of the majority and the second is that old men and monks should be killed. The sound position is the first because of what Abū Bakr said to Yazīd. No one opposes it and there is a consensus to back it up. Also it is not permitted to kill anyone who does not fight or help the enemy, like women. As for those whose harm is feared in respect of planning, advice or monetary support, if they are captured, the ruler can choose between five options: killing, an act of good will, ransom, enslavement or agreeing to become a *dhimmī* in return for the payment of *jizya*.

- **Hirelings and agricultural workers.** Mālik says that they should not be killed. Ash-Shāfi'ī says that agricultural workers, hirelings, and old men should be killed unless they agree to pay the *jizya*. The first is sounder because of what the Prophet said in the *ḥadīth* reported by Rabāḥ ibn ar-Rabī', "Join Khālid ibn al-Walīd. He is not to kill children or hirelings." 'Umar ibn al-Khaṭṭāb said, "Fear Allah regarding children and agricultural workers who do not fight you."

but do not go beyond the limits.

This is a firm judgement. As for the apostates, the only options available concerning them are execution or repentance. The same applies to people involved in deviation and misguidance: the only options afforded them are execution or repentance. If someone conceals a false belief and then it appears in him, such as a *zindīq*, he should be killed and is not asked to repent. As for those who rebel against just rulers, they must be fought until they return to the truth.

Some people have said that this phrase means: "Do not go beyond the limits by fighting for other than the Face of Allah, for instance, out of fanaticism or to gain fame. Fight in the Way of Allah against those who fight you. Fight in support of the *dīn* so that Allah's Word is uppermost. It is said that it means: do not fight those who do not fight. In that case it would be abrogated by the command to fight all the unbelievers, and Allah knows best.

وَاقْتُلُوهُمْ حَيْثُ ثَقِفْتُمُوهُمْ وَأَخْرِجُوهُم مِّنْ حَيْثُ أَخْرَجُوكُمْ وَالْفِتْنَةُ
أَشَدُّ مِنَ الْقَتْلِ وَلَا تُقَٰتِلُوهُمْ عِندَ الْمَسْجِدِ الْحَرَامِ حَتَّىٰ يُقَٰتِلُوكُمْ فِيهِ
فَإِن قَٰتَلُوكُمْ فَاقْتُلُوهُمْ كَذَٰلِكَ جَزَآءُ الْكَٰفِرِينَ ﴿١٩١﴾ فَإِنِ انتَهَوْا فَإِنَّ
اللَّهَ غَفُورٌ رَّحِيمٌ ﴿١٩٢﴾

191 ***Kill them wherever you come across them***
and expel them from where they expelled you.
Fitna is worse than killing.
Do not fight them in the Masjid al-Ḥarām
until they fight you there.

But if they do fight you, then kill them.
That is how the unbelievers should be repaid.
192 *But if they cease,*
Allah is Ever-Forgiving, Most Merciful.

Kill them wherever you come across them

This is evidence for killing captives, and that topic will be explained in *Sūrat al-Anfāl*, Allah willing.

and expel them from where they expelled you.

According to aṭ-Ṭabarī this is addressed to the Muhājirūn and "they" refers to the unbelievers of Quraysh.

Fitna is worse than killing.

The *fitna* to which they are subjecting you, trying to make you return to disbelief, is worse than killing. Mujāhid said it is referring to the believers, so the meaning is that being killed is better for a believer than being subjected to *fitna*. Others said that *fitna* here means their association of others with Allah and their disbelief in Him and it is a great crime and worse than the killing which they criticise you for. There is evidence that the *āyat* was revealed about 'Amr ibn al-Ḥadramī when he was killed by Wāqid ibn 'Abdullāh at-Tamīmī at the end of the sacred month of Rajab, an incident which will be explained later.

Do not fight them in the Masjid al-Ḥarām until they fight you there.

Scholars take two positions concerning this *āyat*. One is that it is abrogated. The second is that it is an *āyat* containing a firm judgement. Mujāhid says that it is an *āyat* of judgement and that it is not permitted to fight anyone in the Masjid al-Ḥarām unless they fight you there. Ṭāwūs said that as well, and indeed it is what is intimated by the text of the *āyat*. It is a sound position and Abū Ḥanīfa and his people took it. In the *Ṣaḥīḥ* Collection, Ibn 'Abbās reported that the Messenger of Allah, may Allah bless him and grant him peace, said on the day when Makka was conquered, "This land was made sacred on the day Allah created the heavens and the earth and it will remain sacred as Allah has decreed until the Day of Rising. Fighting was not lawful in it for anyone before me and it was only lawful for me for one hour of one day and it will remain sacred until the Day of Rising."

Qatāda said that the *āyat* is abrogated by Allah's words, *"When the sacred months are over, kill the idolaters wherever you find them."* (9:5). Muqātil said the same. So this means it is possible to initiate killing in the Ḥaram and evidence for that position can be found in the fact that *Sūrat at-Tawba*, where this *āyat* occurs, was revealed about two years after *Sūrat al-Baqara* and after the Prophet entered Makka and had Ibn Khaṭal, who was clinging to the drapes of the Ka'ba, killed there.

Ibn Khuwayzimandād said that *"Do not fight them in the Masjid al-Ḥarām"* is abrogated because the consensus is that people should be fought if they attack, even if they occupy Makka. If they stop people from performing *ḥajj*, then it is obliged to fight them, even if they do not start the fighting. Makka is the same as everywhere else in that respect.

Some scholars say that this *āyat* applies in the case of someone who rebels against the ruler but does not apply to unbelievers. Unbelievers are killed in every case when they fight. Rebels are only fought with defence in mind and should not be pursued if they retreat or finished off if they are wounded. This will be discussed in *Sūrat al-Ḥujurāt*.

But if they cease,

If they stop fighting you because they believe and become Muslims, then Allah will forgive them all that they did before and show mercy to all of them by pardoning them.

وَقَٰتِلُوهُمْ حَتَّىٰ لَا تَكُونَ فِتْنَةٌ وَيَكُونَ ٱلدِّينُ لِلَّهِ
فَإِنِ ٱنتَهَوْا۟ فَلَا عُدْوَٰنَ إِلَّا عَلَى ٱلظَّٰلِمِينَ ١٩٣

193 ***Fight them until there is no more fitna***
and the dīn belongs to Allah alone.
If they cease, there should be no enmity
towards any but wrongdoers.

Fight them until there is no more *fitna* and the *deen* belongs to Allah alone.

This is a command to fight every idolater in every place according to those who say that it abrogates the previous *āyat*s. According to those who say that it does not abrogate other *āyat*s, it means: fight those about whom Allah says, "if they fight you". The former is the more likely meaning. It is an unqualified command to fight without any precondition of hostilities being initiated by the unbelievers. The evidence for that is in the words of Allah, "and the *dīn* belongs to Allah alone." The Prophet said, "I was commanded to fight people until they say, 'There is no god but Allah.' The *āyat* and *ḥadīth* both indicate that the reason for fighting is disbelief because Allah says, "until there is no more *fitna*," meaning disbelief in this case. So the goal is to abolish disbelief and that is clear.

Ibn 'Abbās, Qatāda, ar-Rabī', as-Suddī and others said that *fitna* here means *shirk* and the subsequent injury to the believers caused by it. The root of *fitna* is testing and trial, derived from the term for testing silver when it is put in the fire to separate the impurities from the pure metal.

If they cease, there should be no enmity towards any but wrongdoers.

If they stop and become Muslim or submit by paying *jizya* in the case of the people of the Book. Otherwise they should be fought and they are wrongdoers and only transgress against themselves. What is done to the wrongdoers is called enmity since it is the repayment of enmity. Wrongdoing and injustice involve enmity and the repayment of enmity is also called enmity. The wrongdoers are either those who initiate fighting or those who remain entrenched in disbelief and *fitna*.

ٱلشَّهْرُ ٱلْحَرَامُ بِٱلشَّهْرِ ٱلْحَرَامِ وَٱلْحُرُمَٰتُ قِصَاصٌ فَمَنِ ٱعْتَدَىٰ
عَلَيْكُمْ فَٱعْتَدُوا۟ عَلَيْهِ بِمِثْلِ مَا ٱعْتَدَىٰ عَلَيْكُمْ وَٱتَّقُوا۟ ٱللَّهَ وَٱعْلَمُوٓا۟
أَنَّ ٱللَّهَ مَعَ ٱلْمُتَّقِينَ ﴿١٩٤﴾

194 ***Sacred month in return for sacred month –***
sacred things are subject to retaliation.
So if anyone oversteps the limits against you,
overstep against him the same as he did to you.
But have fear of Allah.
Know that Allah is with those who are godfearing.

Sacred month in return for sacred month –

The reason for this being revealed was reported by Ibn 'Abbās, Qatāda, Mujāhid, Miqsam, as-Suddī, ar-Rabī', aḍ-Ḍaḥḥāk and others. They said that it was revealed during the *'Umra* of Fulfilment. When the idolaters prevented the Prophet, may Allah bless him and grant him peace, from completing the *Ḥajj* in the Year of al-Ḥudaybiyya, Allah promised him that he would enter Makka, and he did so in 7 AH and completed the *ḥajj* practices and the *āyat* was revealed. Al-Ḥasan related that the idolaters said to the Prophet, "Have you ceased fighting in the sacred month, Muḥammad?" "Yes" he replied. They wanted to fight and the *āyat* was revealed by which Allah allowed him to fight against them. The first interpretation, however, is better known.

sacred things are subject to retaliation.

Allah means the sacredness of the sacred month, sacred land and the sacredness of *iḥrām*. Retaliation (*qiṣāṣ*) is to make things equal, so in this instance the compensation for you for when they stopped you in 6 AH is to make up the *'umra* in 7 AH. So this is connected to what precedes it. It is said that it is separate and that it refers to the state of affairs at the beginning in Islam which was that, if something sacred was violated, they were entitled to the like of the transgression against them. Then this was abrogated by the *āyat*s of fighting.

One group say that the *āyat* deals with enmity within the community of Muḥammad, may Allah bless him and grant him peace, and crimes and so it is not abrogated. This is between creatures. Ash-Shāfi'ī and others say that, and there is one transmission to that effect from Mālik. A group of Mālikīs say that matters of retaliation are up to the judges, and that is the well known position of their school. Abū Ḥanīfa held that view as well.

So if anyone oversteps the limits against you, overstep against him the same as he did to you.

It is agreed that this *āyat* is general, and retaliation can either be done directly if that is possible, or by obtaining legal judgements. People disagree about whether ordinary compensation is included under this and whether it can be called "overstepping" or not. Some say that there are no metaphors in the Qur'ān and that this is overstepping, but permitted overstepping (*'udwān)*. If that is the case this principle should be applied to all things, even broken bowls since the Prophet, may Allah bless him and grant him peace, said, "A vessel for a vessel and food for food" regarding an incident when one of his wives broke a bowl of food belonging to another wife.

There is no disagreement between scholars that this *āyat* is the basis for parity in retaliation. If someone kills someone, he is killed by the same method he used when he killed, and that is the position of the majority.

The upshot of the *āyat* is that, if anyone wrongs you, you may take your right according to how you were wronged, and if someone insults you, you may respond with what he said but may not go beyond what he said. But you are not permitted to lie about him even if he lies about you. Disobedience may not be countered by disobedience. For instance, if someone says to you, "You unbeliever!" you are permitted to say, "You are the unbeliever." But if he says, "Adulterer!" then your retaliation is to say, "You liar!"

وَأَنفِقُوا۟ فِى سَبِيلِ ٱللَّهِ وَلَا تُلْقُوا۟ بِأَيْدِيكُمْ إِلَى ٱلتَّهْلُكَةِ ۛ وَأَحْسِنُوٓا۟ ۛ إِنَّ
ٱللَّهَ يُحِبُّ ٱلْمُحْسِنِينَ ﴿١٩٥﴾

195 ***Spend in the Way of Allah.***
Do not cast yourselves into destruction.
And do good: Allah loves good-doers.

Spend in the Way of Allah. Do not cast yourselves into destruction.

Al-Bukhārī related from Ḥudhayfa that this whole *āyat* was revealed about spending. Aslam Abī 'Imrān said, "We raided Constantinople and 'Abdu'r-Raḥmān ibn al-Walīd was in charge of the group. The Byzantines were keeping their backs to the wall of the city. A man attacked the enemy and the people said, "Easy! Easy! Do not cast yourselves into destruction." Abū Ayyūb said, "Glory be to Allah! This *āyat* was revealed about us, the Anṣār. When Allah gave His Prophet, may Allah bless him and grant him peace, victory and made His *dīn* victorious, we said, 'We will stay in our property and put it right,' and then Allah revealed, *'Spend in the Way of Allah.'* The expression 'Do not cast yourselves into destruction' referred to staying at home to tend to one's property and abandoning *jihād*." Abū Ayyūb continued to do *jihād* in the Way of Allah until he was buried in Constantinople.

Ḥudhayfa ibn al-Yamān, Ibn 'Abbās, 'Ikrima, 'Aṭā', Mujāhid and the majority of people say that *"do not cast yourselves into destruction"* refers to not spending in the Way of Allah and fearing poverty.

The "Way of Allah" (*sabīli'llāh*) here means *jihād* and refers to all the ways of doing it. Al-Mubarrad says that "your hands" [the Arabic is *"bi-aydīkum"*, lit. "your hands"] means "yourselves". The part designates the whole. It is also said that this is a sort of metaphor. A person puts his hand to something when he undertakes to do it personally, and someone involved in fighting has his weapons in his hand. It is also said that it means: do not hold on to your property as others are certainly going to inherit it and you will be "destroyed" by being deprived of the use of your property. Another meaning is: do not hold on to your property because, by doing so,[1] you will miss out on its restitution in this world and the reward for giving it away in the Next World.

Scholars disagree about a man attacking another man in battle and about attacking the enemy alone. Some say that there is no harm in a man attacking a large army alone when he is strong and has a sincere intention. If he is not strong, that is tantamount to suicide. It is said that, when someone seeks martyrdom and has a sincere intention, he is permitted to attack because his aim is to attack the enemy. Ibn Khuwayzimandād said, "If a man attacks a hundred, or an entire army, or a group of thieves and bandits, there are two possibilities. If he knows and thinks it is probable that he will kill the one he attacks and survive, that is good. If he knows and thinks it probable that he will be killed, but will cause great harm or open a path which the Muslims can use, then it is also permitted."

Muḥammad ibn al-Ḥasan said, "If one man attacks a thousand idolaters on his own, there is no harm in that if he hopes to survive or inflict great damage on the enemy. If that is not the case, then it is disliked because he exposes himself to destruction without any benefit for the Muslims. If his intention is to encourage other Muslims to follow him, it may be permitted because of the benefit for the Muslims involved. If he intends to terrify the enemy and show them the resolve of the Muslims, it may also be permitted."

If that will help the Muslims, strengthen the *dīn* of Allah and weaken the unbelievers, then it is the noble station which Allah praises when He says, *"Allah has bought from the believers their selves and their wealth in return for them having the Garden. They fight in the way of Allah, and they kill and are killed."* (9:111) The same applies to the ruling of commanding what is correct and forbidding what is bad when one hopes that it will help the *dīn* and a person strives to achieve that until he is killed. Ibn 'Abbās reported

1. As Allah says, *"Anything you expend will be replaced by Him."* (34:39)

that the Prophet, may Allah bless him and grant him peace, said, "The best of martyrs is Ḥamza ibn 'Abdu'l-Muṭṭalib and a man who speaks the truth in the presence of a tyrannical ruler who kills him."

And do good: Allah loves good-doers.

Spend in obedience and have a good opinion of Allah that He will repay you for doing it.

وَأَتِمُّوا۟ ٱلْحَجَّ وَٱلْعُمْرَةَ لِلَّهِ ۚ فَإِنْ أُحْصِرْتُمْ فَمَا ٱسْتَيْسَرَ مِنَ ٱلْهَدْىِ ۖ
وَلَا تَحْلِقُوا۟ رُءُوسَكُمْ حَتَّىٰ يَبْلُغَ ٱلْهَدْىُ مَحِلَّهُۥ ۚ فَمَن كَانَ مِنكُم مَّرِيضًا
أَوْ بِهِۦٓ أَذًى مِّن رَّأْسِهِۦ فَفِدْيَةٌ مِّن صِيَامٍ أَوْ صَدَقَةٍ أَوْ نُسُكٍ ۚ فَإِذَآ
أَمِنتُمْ فَمَن تَمَتَّعَ بِٱلْعُمْرَةِ إِلَى ٱلْحَجِّ فَمَا ٱسْتَيْسَرَ مِنَ ٱلْهَدْىِ ۚ
فَمَن لَّمْ يَجِدْ فَصِيَامُ ثَلَٰثَةِ أَيَّامٍ فِى ٱلْحَجِّ وَسَبْعَةٍ إِذَا رَجَعْتُمْ ۗ
تِلْكَ عَشَرَةٌ كَامِلَةٌ ۗ ذَٰلِكَ لِمَن لَّمْ يَكُنْ أَهْلُهُۥ حَاضِرِى
ٱلْمَسْجِدِ ٱلْحَرَامِ ۚ وَٱتَّقُوا۟ ٱللَّهَ وَٱعْلَمُوٓا۟ أَنَّ ٱللَّهَ شَدِيدُ ٱلْعِقَابِ ﴿١٩٦﴾

196 ***Perform the Ḥajj and 'umra for Allah.***
If you are forcibly prevented,
make whatever sacrifice is feasible.
But do not shave your heads
until the sacrificial animal
has reached the place of sacrifice.
If any of you are ill or have a head injury,
the expiation is fasting or ṣadaqa or sacrifice
when you are safe and well again.
Anyone who comes out of iḥrām
between 'umra and ḥajj
should make whatever sacrifice is feasible.

For any one who cannot,
there is three days' fast on ḥajj
and seven on your return – that is ten in all.
That is for anyone whose family does not live near
the Masjid al-Ḥarām.
Be fearful of Allah and know
that Allah is fierce in retribution.

Perform the ḥajj and 'umra for Allah.

Scholars disagree about what this means. It is said that it means: perform them, doing both of them, as the verb is used elsewhere to mean this. This is according to the position of those who consider *'umra* to be obligatory. Those who do not consider it to be obligatory say that it means complete them once you have begun them. When someone assumes *iḥrām*, he is obliged to complete the act for which he has entered it.

This *āyat* is evidence for *'umra* being obligatory because Allah commands it to be completed as He commands the *ḥajj* to be completed. Aṣ-Ṣubayy ibn Ma'bad said, "I went to 'Umar and said, 'I was a Christian and became Muslim. I find that *ḥajj* and *'umra* are prescribed for me and so I assumed *iḥrām* for both of them"' 'Umar said to him, "You have been guided to the *Sunna* of your Prophet, may Allah bless him and grant him peace." Ibn al-Mundhir observed that he did not object to what he said and the fact that they were obligatory for him. 'Alī, Ibn 'Umar and Ibn 'Abbās all said that they were both obligatory.

Mālik, however, said, "*'Umra* is *sunna*. But we do not know of anyone who made an allowance for abandoning it." That is also the position of an-Nakhā'ī and the People of Opinion (*ra'y*). Some people of Qazwin and Baghdad report from Abū Ḥanīfa that he considered it obligatory (*wājib*) like the *ḥajj*, and that it is a firm *sunna*. Ibn Mas'ūd and Jābir ibn 'Abdullāh also said that.

Scholars do not disagree that someone who attends the *ḥajj* or *'umra* practices must make an intention to do so. Part of the completion of the act of worship is the presence of the intention, which is an obligation in itself.

If you are forcibly prevented,

Ibn al-'Arabī says that this *āyat* is problematical but in fact, there is nothing problematic about it as we will explain. Being prevented refers to any obstacle which stops you doing what you intended, whatever that obstacle might be, whether an enemy, the injustice of a ruler, illness, highway robbers or whatever else might stop a person from fulfilling his intention. Scholars disagree about the actual obstacle referred to in the *āyat* and have two views. One is stated by 'Alqama, 'Urwa ibn az-Zubayr and others which is that it refers to illness and not to an enemy. But it is also said that it is only an enemy which is meant, and that is the view of Ibn 'Abbās, Ibn 'Umar, Anas and ash-Shāfi'ī. Ibn al-'Arabī said that that is the opinion our scholars prefer, while linguists prefer illness.

make whatever sacrifice is feasible.

According to most scholars, this means a sheep. Ibn 'Umar, 'Ā'isha, and Ibn az-Zubayr said that it is whatever camel or whatever cow is available. Al-Ḥasan said, "The greatest sacrifice is the camel, the medium one the cow and the lowest the sheep." This phrase provides evidence for what Mālik believes, which is that someone stopped by enemy forces does not have to make up his *ḥajj*, because only the sacrifice is mentioned. Allah knows best.

This word for "sacrifice" (*hadī*) is used because it refers to camels which are led (*hadā*) to the House of Allah. Abū Bakr said that they are called this because they are given (*yuhdā*) to the House of Allah.

But do not shave your heads until the sacrificial animal has reached the place of sacrifice.

This is addressed to all Muslims performing the *ḥajj*, not just those who are prevented from completing their *ḥajj*. Some scholars think, however, that it only refers to those who have been stopped. The "place of sacrifice" (*maḥillahu*) referred to is the place where it is lawful to slaughter the sacrificial animals. For Mālik and ash-Shāfi'ī, the place to sacrifice is the place where people have been stopped, to imitate the Messenger of Allah, may Allah bless him and grant him peace, at Ḥudaybiyya. Abū Ḥanīfa says that it means the Ḥaram of Makka.

Scholars disagree about whether someone who is prevented from continuing should shave his head and the way in which he should come out of *iḥrām* before sacrificing. Mālik said: "The firm *sunna* about which there is no disagreement with us is that it is not permitted for someone to take off any of his hair until he has sacrificed." Abū Ḥanīfa and his people say that if he comes out of *iḥrām* before he sacrifices he owes another sacrifice. There is disagreement about whether someone forced to stop can shave his head or not once he has sacrificed. One group say that he does not have to shave because his rites have ended and the other position is that he should shave.

Abū Hurayra reported that the Messenger of Allah, may Allah bless him and grant him peace, said, "O Allah, forgive those who shave their heads." They said, "And those who cut their hair short!" He said, "O Allah, forgive those who shave their heads." They said, "And those who cut their hair short!" He said it a third time and added, "and those who cut the hair short." (Agreed upon) It is agreed that shortening the hair is permitted for men.

Women do not shave their heads. Their *sunna* is to shorten the hair since the Prophet, may Allah bless him and grant him peace, said, "Women do not have to shave their hair. They shorten it." (Abū Dāwūd). There is disagreement about the amount which should be cut. 'Aṭā' says it is three fingers. Qatāda says a third or a quarter. Ḥafsa bint Sīrīn says that a woman who is older cuts a quarter and a young woman only cuts a little. Mālik say that it should be cut all round but whatever she removes is adequate, but all her locks must be trimmed.

If any of you are ill or have a head injury, the expiation is fasting or ṣadaqa or sacrifice when you are safe and well again.

"If any of you": some Shāfi'ī scholars say that this phrase definitely indicates that the one who is "prevented" at the beginning of

the *āyat* is by an enemy and not by illness since there would be no need for the repetition here. This does not necessarily follow in the context. It was revealed about Ka'b ibn 'Ujra when the Prophet, may Allah bless him and grant him peace, saw lice dropping from his hair onto his face and said, "Perhaps your head is causing you harm?" He commanded him to shave his head at Ḥudaybiyya while they were still hoping to enter Makka. Then Allah revealed *fidya* (expiation) and the Prophet, may Allah bless him and grant him peace, commanded him to feed six poor people, sacrifice a sheep or fast three days.

Ibn 'Abdu'l-Barr says, "The sacrifice, in this case, is a sheep and there is no disagreement about it. There is disagreement about the amount of fasting and feeding. Most Muslim scholars believe that the fast is for three days, as in the *ḥadīth* from Ka'b. Al-Ḥasan, 'Ikrima, and Nāfi' say that it is ten days. The *ḥadīth* would give the impression that there is an order in the three alternatives, but that is not the case. There is a simple choice. Most say that the feeding required is two *mudd*s by the *mudd* of the Prophet, may Allah bless him and grant him peace.

It is said that the words *"when you are safe"* means when you have recovered from your illness. It is said that it means safe from fear of the enemy, as Ibn 'Abbās and Qatāda said. That is more in keeping with the expression used, because no one can ever be free from fear of illness to the extent that it is possible to feel entirely safe from it, and Allah knows best.

Anyone who comes out of iḥrām between 'umra and ḥajj should make whatever sacrifice is feasible.

Scholars disagree about who is being referred to in this phrase. 'Abdullāh ibn az-Zubayr, 'Alqama and Ibrāhīm say that the *āyat* is about those who are forcibly prevented and cannot go on. According to Ibn az-Zubayr the situation referred to is when someone is held up until he misses the *ḥajj* and then reaches the House after it has passed and assumes *iḥrām* for *'umra* and then performs *ḥajj* in the following year to make up for the one he missed. This joins his *'umra* to the *ḥajj* of making up. Others say that the situation referred to is when someone is detained and then delays *'umra* until the following year and does it in the months of *ḥajj* and performs *ḥajj* in the same year.

There is no disagreement among scholars that *ḥajj* involving a temporary removal of *iḥrām* (*tamattu'*), *ḥajj* on its own (*ifrād*) and *ḥajj* and *'umra* combined (*qirān*) are all permitted because the Prophet, may Allah bless him and grant him peace, declared himself happy with all of them. Scholars do, however, disagree about which of them the Messenger of Allah, may Allah bless him and grant him peace, adopted when performing his own *ḥajj* and which is the best, all based on different *aḥādīth* which have been reported. Some, including Mālik, said that *ifrād* is better the *qirān* and *qirān* is better than *tamattu'* because the Prophet, may Allah bless him and grant him peace, did *ifrād*. The preference of *ifrād* is one of two positions reported from ash-Shāfi'ī. Others prefer *tamattu'* because it is mentioned in the Book. Yet others prefer *qirān*, and they include Abū Ḥanīfa and ath-Thawrī because the Prophet did it.

For any one who cannot, there is three days' fast on ḥajj and seven on your return – that is ten in all.

Anyone who should sacrifice but is unable to do so due to lack of money or lack of animals, must fast for three days during the *ḥajj* and seven when he returns home. The three days are the three days up to and including the Day of 'Arafa. This is the position of Ṭāwus and it is related from a number of scholars. Abū Thawr reports that Abū Ḥanīfa says that a person may also fast them during the time he is in *iḥrām* for *'umra* because it is one of the two *iḥrām*s of *tamattu'* and so it is permitted to fast these days in the *iḥrām* for *'umra* as it is in the *iḥrām* for *ḥajj*. It is also reported from Abū Ḥanīfa and his people that the day before the day of Tarwiya (7th Dhū'l-Ḥijja) should be fasted, then the Day of Tarwiya and then the Day of 'Arafa.

Ibn 'Abbās and Mālik ibn Anas say that the three days may be fasted at any time from the time someone assumes *iḥrām* for *ḥajj* until the Day of Sacrifice because Allah says, *"three days fast on ḥajj"*. If they are fasted on *'umra*, it is before the time and so it is not allowed. Ash-Shāfi'ī and Ibn Ḥanbal say that the days may be fasted at any time between assuming *iḥrām* for *ḥajj* up until the day of 'Arafa, which is the position of Ibn 'Umar and 'Ā'isha. This is also related from Mālik and is stated in the *Muwaṭṭā'* and it is in order to avoid fasting on the Day of 'Arafa. That is following the *Sunna* and stronger for worship. Aḥmad also said that it is possible to fast for three days before assuming *iḥrām* (but in Dhū'l-Ḥijja). 'Urwa said that the days may be fasted as long as one remains in Makka and during the days of Mina, and Mālik and a group of the people of Madina also took that view.

The words *"your return"* mean when you return to your country although some linguists say that it means when you leave *iḥrām* and return to the state you were in.

The words *"that is ten in all"* are to eliminate any possibility that someone might assume that there is a choice between three on *ḥajj* and seven when one returns.

That is for anyone whose family does not live near the Masjid al-Ḥarām.

A sacrifice is required from anyone not resident in the Ḥaram who performs *tamattu'*. It is related that Ibn 'Abbās was asked about *ḥajj at-tamattu'* and said, "The Muhājirūn and the Anṣār and the wives of the Prophet went into *iḥrām* for the Farewell *Ḥajj* and we went into *iḥrām* too. When we reached Makka, the Messenger of Allah, may Allah bless him and grant him peace, said, 'Make your *iḥrām* for *ḥajj* an *iḥrām* for *'umra* – except for those who have garlanded sacrificial animals.' We did *ṭawāf* of the House and went between Ṣafā and Marwa, and then went to our wives and put on our (normal) clothes. He said, 'Anyone who has garlanded his sacrificial animal should not come out of *iḥrām* until the sacrifice reaches its place.' Then, on the eve of Tarwiya, he told us to go into *iḥrām* for *ḥajj*. When we had finished the rites, we came and did *ṭawāf* of the House and went between Ṣafā and Marwa. Our *ḥajj* was complete and we had to sacrifice, in compliance with the words of Allah Almighty: *'He should make whatever sacrifice is feasible. For any one who cannot, there is three days' fast on ḥajj and seven on your return'* to your cities, a sheep being sufficient. So we combined two practices – *ḥajj* and *'umra* – in the same year. Allah Almighty sent it down in His Book and it was the *Sunna* of His Prophet, may Allah bless him and grant him peace. It was allowed to people other than the people of Makka. Allah says, *'that is for anyone whose family does not live near the Masjid al-Ḥaram.'* The months of *ḥajj* which Allah Almighty mentioned are Shawwāl, Dhū'l-Qa'da and Dhū'l-Ḥijja. Whoever performs *tamattu'* in these months must sacrifice or fast."

"Be fearful of Allah."

Fear Him in respect of what He has made obligatory for you. This is a general command to be godfearing.

ٱلْحَجُّ أَشْهُرٌ مَّعْلُومَٰتٌ ۚ فَمَن فَرَضَ فِيهِنَّ ٱلْحَجَّ فَلَا
رَفَثَ وَلَا فُسُوقَ وَلَا جِدَالَ فِى ٱلْحَجِّ ۗ وَمَا تَفْعَلُوا۟
مِنْ خَيْرٍ يَعْلَمْهُ ٱللَّهُ ۗ وَتَزَوَّدُوا۟ فَإِنَّ خَيْرَ ٱلزَّادِ
ٱلتَّقْوَىٰ ۚ وَٱتَّقُونِ يَٰٓأُو۟لِى ٱلْأَلْبَٰبِ ﴿١٩٧﴾

197 ***The Ḥajj takes place***
during certain well-known months.
If anyone undertakes the obligation of ḥajj in them,
there must be no sexual intercourse, no wrongdoing,
nor any quarrelling during ḥajj.
Whatever good you do, Allah knows it.
Take provision;
but the best provision
is fearful awareness of Allah.
So be fearful of Me, people of intelligence!

The Ḥajj takes place during certain well-known months.

Allah now explains the difference between the times of *'umra* and *ḥajj*. The period during which *iḥrām* may be assumed for *'umra* is any time throughout the entire year, but *ḥajj* is only at one particular time each year. So the *āyat* means that the months when the *ḥajj* takes place are well-known months, or the time of the *ḥajj* falls during well-known months, or the time when the actions of the *ḥajj* take place is well-known, or it may mean simply that the *ḥajj* occurs in certain months.

There is disagreement about exactly which months are referred to as "well-known". Ibn Mas'ūd, Ibn 'Umar, 'Aṭā', ar-Rabī', Mujāhid and az-Zuhrī said that the months of *ḥajj* are all of Shawwāl, Dhū'l-Qa'da, and Dhū'l-Ḥijja. Ibn 'Abbās, as-Suddī, ash-Sha'bī and an-Nakhā'ī say that it is Shawwāl, Dhū'l-Qa'da, and only the first ten days of Dhū'l-Ḥijja. Both are transmitted from Mālik. Allah does not name the months of *ḥajj* in His Book since they were well-known to the people addressed. It is possible in Arabic for the plural "months" to be applied to two months and part of a third month.

They disagree about assuming *iḥrām* for *ḥajj* outside the months of *ḥajj*. Ibn 'Abbās says that part of the Sunna is to assume it during the months of *ḥajj*. 'Aṭā', Mujāhid, Ṭāwūs and al-Awzā'ī said that if someone assumes *iḥrām* for *ḥajj* before the months of *ḥajj,* it can only be considered an *'umra* and not *ḥajj*. He is like someone who prays before the time of the prayer. Ash-Shāfi'ī says that. Mālik, however, says that *iḥrām* for *ḥajj* can be assumed at any time during the entire year and that is also the position of Abū Ḥanīfa.

If anyone undertakes the obligation of ḥajj in them.

This means if someone obliges himself to do *ḥajj* by making the inward intention and performing the outward action of setting off and vocalising the *talbīya* in words. Ibn Ḥabīb and Abū Ḥanīfa say that the *talbīya* is the definitive action of setting off on *ḥajj* but ash-Shāfi'ī said that that is not the case because the *talbīya* is not one of the pillars of *ḥajj*. He says that the intention and the assumption of *iḥrām* is enough.

Linguistically the root of the word for "undertakes the obligation" (*faraḍa*) means to make a notch or cut. From that is derived *furḍa*, the notch in an arrow, an inlet in the bank of a river or a crevice in a mountain. So *ḥajj* is obligatory for the slave of Allah in the same way that the notch is necessary for an arrow. It is also said that *faraḍa* means to make clear, and this goes back to cutting because cutting something makes it distinct from other things.

there must be no sexual intercourse,

The word for sexual intercourse here is *rafath*. Ibn 'Abbās, Ibn Jubayr, as-Suddī, Qatāda, al-Ḥasan, 'Ikrima, az-Zuhrī, Mujāhid and Mālik said that *rafath* means sexual intercourse and that sexual intercourse invalidates the *ḥajj*. Scholars agree that sexual intercourse before 'Arafa invalidates the *ḥajj* and obliges a new *ḥajj* and a sacrifice. It is also said to mean obscene speech. It is also said, by some, to apply to all sexual activity which might take place between a man and his wife.

no wrongdoing,

Fusūq (wrongdoing) in this context means all acts of disobedience according to Ibn 'Abbās, 'Aṭā' and al-Ḥasan. Ibn 'Umar and a group said that, in this context, it means committing those acts of disobedience to Allah which are specific to the state of *iḥrām* for *ḥajj*, such as killing game, paring nails, cutting hair and the like. Ibn Zayd and Mālik said that it means sacrificing to idols, as Allah says, "*Or some deviance (*fisq*) consecrated to other than Allah.*" (6:145) Aḍ-Ḍaḥḥāk said it means exchanging obscene epithets. Ibn 'Umar also said that it is cursing. The first position is the soundest since it includes all the other possibilities. The Prophet, may Allah bless him and grant him peace, said, "Anyone who makes *ḥajj* and does not engage in sexual intercourse or wrongdoing returns as he was on the day his mother bore him." And: "An accepted *ḥajj* has no repayment except the Garden." He also said, "By the One who has my soul in His hand, there is no action between heaven and earth better than *jihād* in the Way of Allah or an accepted *ḥajj* in which there is no sexual intercourse, wrongdoing or quarrelling." The *fuqahā'* state that the accepted *ḥajj* is one in which one does not disobey Allah while performing it.

nor any quarrelling during ḥajj.

Jidāl (quarrelling) is argumentation and is derived from the word *jadl* which means twisting. A rein which is braided (*majdūl*) is derived from the same root. It is also possible that *jidāl* comes from the word *jadāla* which means the earth. It is as if each of the opponents stands against the other person and one overcomes the other.

Scholars disagree about its exact meaning here and offer several possibilities. Ibn Mas'ūd, Ibn 'Abbās and 'Aṭā' say that *jidāl* here means to argue with a Muslim until you make him angry to the extent that that leads to insults. As for discussing points of knowledge, that is not forbidden. Qatāda said that it means abuse. Ibn Zayd and Mālik ibn Anas said that here it means the disagreements people used to have about which of them was in the authentic places of Ibrāhīm, which used to happen in the *Jāhiliyya*, and so it means that there must be no quarrelling about that. One group say that it refers to when one group say, "The *ḥajj* is today" and another group say, "The *ḥajj* is tomorrow." Mujāhid and a group said, "It is to argue about the months according to the Arab reckoning. It used to happen that some would be at 'Arafa while others were at Muzdalifa and they would quarrel about who was in the right." According to these two last interpretations, it means that there must be no quarrelling about the time and place of *ḥajj*. These two positions are the soundest of what is said regarding the interpretation.

Whatever good you do, Allah knows it.

This means that Allah will repay you for your actions because repayment is only made by the one who has knowledge of the matter concerned. It is also said that this is encouragement to use good words instead of obscenities and to be pious and godfearing rather than wrongdoing and argumentative. It is said that the word "good" refers to people restraining themselves so that they do not do what is forbidden.

Take provision;

Ibn 'Umar, 'Ikrima, Mujāhid, Qatāda and Ibn Zayd said, "The *āyat* was revealed about a group of Arabs who used to come to *ḥajj* with no provision. One of them would say, "How could we make *ḥajj* to the House of Allah and He not feed us?" So they were dependent on other people for their needs. They were forbidden to do that and commanded to take provisions. 'Abdullāh ibn az-Zubayr said, "People used to rely on one another and not take provisions, and so they were commanded to take provision." Some people say that it means a righteous companion, but this is said to be weak. It is also said that the meaning of the *āyat* is to store up provision for the Next World in the form of righteous actions.

The first position is sounder because what is meant is provision for the *ḥajj* journey. It is as al-Bukhārī related from Ibn 'Abbās, "The people of Yemen used to go on *ḥajj* and not take provision. They would say, 'We are relying on Allah.' When they came to Makka, they begged from people, so Allah Almighty sent down, *"Take provision, but the best provision is fearful awareness (*taqwā*) of Allah."'"* This is what the text suggests and is the position of most commentators. Ash-Sha'bī says that it means specifically dates and *sawīq* (barley mush). Ibn Jubayr says biscuits and *sawīq*. Ibn al-'Arabī says that Allah commands the people of wealth to take provision. Those who have no money and have a craft by which they support themselves and those who beg are not addressed. Those addressed are people who have wealth but who leave their wealth and go out without provision.

but the best provision is fearful awareness of Allah.

The best provision is avoiding what is forbidden and so Allah commands us here to add fearful awareness to taking provision. It means to fear Allah by following His command to take provision. It is said that it can mean that the best provision is that by which the traveller is kept safe from destruction or from the need to beg. It is said that it makes it clear that this world is not the abode of permanence. The people with knowledge of subtle indications (*ishārāt*) say that Allah is reminding us of the journey to the Next World and commands us to take fearful awareness of Him as provision. Fearful awareness is the provision of the Next World.

So be fearful of Me, people of intelligence!

Those with intelligence are singled out, even though the command is to everyone because they are those through whom the proof of Allah is established. They receive His commands and undertake to carry them out. The word used for intelligent people is the plural of *lubb*, which refers to the core of anything.

لَيْسَ عَلَيْكُمْ جُنَاحٌ أَن تَبْتَغُوا فَضْلًا مِّن رَّبِّكُمْ
فَإِذَا أَفَضْتُم مِّنْ عَرَفَاتٍ فَاذْكُرُوا اللَّهَ عِندَ
الْمَشْعَرِ الْحَرَامِ وَاذْكُرُوهُ كَمَا هَدَاكُمْ
وَإِن كُنتُم مِّن قَبْلِهِ لَمِنَ الضَّالِّينَ ﴿١٩٨﴾

198 ***There is nothing wrong***
in seeking bounty from your Lord.
When you pour down from Arafat,
remember Allah at the Sacred Landmark.
Remember Him because He has guided you,
even though before this you were astray.

There is nothing wrong in seeking bounty from your Lord.

The word for "wrong" (*junāḥ*) means wrong action. After mentioning the things prohibited during *ḥajj,* Allah mentions that trade is allowed. In the Qur'ān, the phrase *"seeking bounty"* is used for engaging in trade. In al-Bukhārī, Ibn 'Abbās is reported as observing: "'Ukāẓ, Majinna and Dhū'l-Majāz were markets in the time of the *Jāhiliyya* and people thought it sinful to trade during the festivals and then this was revealed about the *ḥajj* festival." So this *āyat* is evidence that it is permitted for someone on *ḥajj* to trade during it while performing the rites of *ḥajj*. Intending to do so is not *shirk* and does not detract from the sincerity of the person concerned.

When you pour down from 'Arafat,

"*Afāḍa*" (pour down) means to rush on. The verb is used for when you pour liquid into a vessel until it overflows down the sides. A man who is *fayyāḍ* is very munificent. A *ḥadīth* which is *mustafīḍ* is extensively known.

It is said that the plain is called 'Arafāt because people know it (*'arafahū*). It is said that when Ādam descended in India and Ḥawwā' at Jadda, after a long search, they met at 'Arafāt on the Day of 'Arafa, and so the day is called 'Arafa and the place 'Arafāt. Aḍ-Ḍaḥḥāk said that. It is said that it is derived from *'arf,* which means scent. Some say that the name is derived from steadfastness because they are steadfast in supplication, trial and enduring hardships to perform this act of worship, and the meaning of *'ārif* is someone who is steadfast and humble.

The literal text of the Qur'ān and the *Sunna* indicates that all of the plain of 'Arafāt is a standing place.

The excellence of the Day of 'Arafa is immense. In it Allah expiates the worst wrong actions and multiplies good actions. The Prophet, may Allah bless him and grant him peace, said, "The best supplication is supplication on the Day of 'Arafa and the best of what I and the Prophets before have said is, 'There is no god but Allah alone with no partner.'" The people of knowledge recommend fasting on the Day of 'Arafa, except for the people who are actually there.

remember Allah at the Sacred Landmark.

Remember Him by making supplication and reciting the *talbiya* at the Sacred Landmark. The place is called *Jam'* because the prayers of *Maghrib* and *'Ishā'* are joined together (*jumi'a*) there. Qatāda said that it is because Ādam met Ḥawwā' there and they joined each other (*jama'a*) there and that is also why it is called Muzdalifa (*izdalafa*, to draw near). It is said that it is called that on account of the actions of the people there, because they draw near (*izdalafa*) to Allah by standing there. The word for Sacred Landmark (*mash'ar*) comes from *shi'ār* which means a sign or landmark, and it is called that because it is a landmark of the *ḥajj* due to the fact that people are required to pray there and spend the night there in supplication to Allah.

Spending the night at Muzdalifa is one of the pillars of the *ḥajj* according to the majority of scholars, but there is disagreement about whether someone who does not spend the night there is obliged to sacrifice.

Remember Him because He has guided you, even though before this you were astray.

The command to remember is repeated for emphasis. It is said that the first is a command to remember at the *Mash'ar al-Ḥarām* and the second is to remember with sincerity. It is said that the second time it means to acknowledge the blessing and show gratitude for it and then to remind them about the time when they were misguided. Remember Him as He has taught you to do and do not turn from it. *"Before this"* refers to before the guidance of Islam came or before the Qur'ān. Allah knows best.

ثُمَّ أَفِيضُوا مِنْ حَيْثُ أَفَاضَ النَّاسُ
وَاسْتَغْفِرُوا اللَّهَ إِنَّ اللَّهَ غَفُورٌ رَّحِيمٌ ﴿١٩٩﴾

199 ***Then press on from where the people press on***
and ask Allah's forgiveness.
Allah is Ever-Forgiving, Most Merciful.

Then press on from where the people press on

The "people" referred to here are those called *Ḥums* (Quraysh and others), who did not stop with the people at 'Arafāt, but stopped at Muzdalifa, which is part of the Ḥaram, claiming that they were its people and must venerate only it. Despite the fact that they knew that 'Arafāt was where Ibrāhīm had stood, they did not leave the Ḥaram and stood instead at Jam' while the people were at 'Arafāt. Aḍ-Ḍaḥḥāk says that the entire community is addressed and "people" means Ibrāhīm. It is, however, possible that the pressing on here means the pressing on from Muzdalifa.

This is evidence to support those who oblige stopping at Muzdalifa since there is a command to press on from it, and Allah knows best. The sound position in the interpretation of this *āyat* is the first position.

فَإِذَا قَضَيْتُم مَّنَاسِكَكُمْ فَاذْكُرُوا اللَّهَ كَذِكْرِكُمْ
آبَاءَكُمْ أَوْ أَشَدَّ ذِكْرًا ۗ فَمِنَ النَّاسِ مَن يَقُولُ
رَبَّنَا آتِنَا فِي الدُّنْيَا وَمَا لَهُ فِي الْآخِرَةِ مِنْ خَلَاقٍ ﴿٢٠٠﴾

200 ***When you have completed your rites,***
remember Allah
as you used to remember your forefathers
– or even more.
There are some people who say,
'Our Lord, give us good in this world.'
They will have no share in the Next World.

When you have completed your rites, remember Allah

Mujāhid says that the "*manāsik*" (rites) referred to here are the sacrifices and it means the spilling of blood. It is said that it refers to the pillars of *Ḥajj* since the Prophet said, "Take your rites from me." So the meaning is: "When you perform the rites of *Ḥajj*, remember Allah, and also remember him and praise Him for His blessings to you."

as you used to remember your forefathers – or even more.

The custom of the Arabs was that, when they completed the *ḥajj,* they would stand at the *Jamra* and boast of their forefathers and mention the glorious feats of their ancestors and this *āyat* was revealed commanding them to remember Allah more than they used to remember their forefathers in the time of the *Jāhiliyya*. This is the position of most commentators. Ibn 'Abbās, 'Aṭā', aḍ-Ḍaḥḥāk and ar-Rabī' said that the meaning of the *āyat* is, "Remember Allah as children remember their fathers and mothers. Seek help from Him and seek refuge with Him as you did with your parents when you were a child." Another group say that the *āyat* means: "Remember Allah and esteem Him, defend His sanctity and repel those who desire to introduce *shirk* into His *dīn* and rites just as you would speak well of your parents when someone criticised them, and protect and defend them."

Abu'l-Jawzā' said to Ibn 'Abbās, "These days no one mentions his forefathers. So what does the *āyat* mean?" He replied, "It is not like that. Allah is angrier when someone disobeys Him than your parents are angry with you when you abuse them."

There are some people who say, 'Our Lord, give us good in this world.'

This refers to the idolaters. As-Suddī and Ibn Zayd said, "In the time of the *Jāhiliyya*, the Arabs used only to pray for the good things of this world. They would ask for camels, sheep and victory over their enemies. They would not ask for the Next World since they did not acknowledge it or believe in it. Here they are being forbidden to ask for only this world. The prohibition comes in the form of a report about what they do. It is also possible that this threat refers to the believers when their supplication is confined to this world. They will have no portion in the Next World because they do not ask for it.

وَمِنْهُم مَّن يَقُولُ رَبَّنَآ ءَاتِنَا فِى ٱلدُّنْيَا حَسَنَةً
وَفِى ٱلْءَاخِرَةِ حَسَنَةً وَقِنَا عَذَابَ ٱلنَّارِ ﴿٢٠١﴾

201 ***And there are others who say,***
'Our Lord, give us good in this world,
and good in the Next World,
and safeguard us from the punishment of the Fire.'

The "others" referred to here are the Muslims who ask for the good of this world and the Next World. There is disagreement about exactly what the two kinds of good entail and there are many things said about this. It is related from 'Alī ibn Abī Ṭālib that the good in this world is a good woman and in the Next World it is the houris and the *"punishment of the Fire"* refers to a bad woman. This, however, is unlikely and is not a sound transmission from 'Alī because the Fire is, in reality, a burning fire and interpreting it to be a woman would only be metaphorical.

Qatāda said the good of this ephemeral world takes the form of health and adequate wealth. Al-Ḥasan said that the good of this world is knowledge and worship. Other things are said. But what most of the people of knowledge believe is that what is meant by the two kinds of good are the blessings of this world and the Next World. This is sound and the expression entails all of that because the word "good" in both cases has no definite article and so it can be applied to all sorts of good. The good of the Next World is the Garden by consensus. It is also said that it does not mean one particular good, but rather "Give us the good of this world."

and safeguard us from the punishment of the Fire.'

What is meant here is a supplication that the person will not enter the Fire because of his acts of disobedience and that he should be brought out if it by intercession. It is possible that it is a supplication confirming the request to enter the Garden so that it expresses the desire for salvation and success on both fronts. It is like what one of the Companions said to the Prophet, "I say in my supplication, 'O Allah, make me enter the Garden and protect me from the Fire.' I do not know what it is that you and Mu'ādh mumble." The Messenger of Allah, may Allah bless him and grant him peace, said to him, "We say that in a low voice."

This *āyat* is one of the comprehensive supplications, asking for both this world and the Next. Anas was asked, "Make supplication for us." He said, "Give them good in this world and good in the Next World and protect them from the punishment of the Fire." They said, "More." He said, "What more do you want? I have asked for this world and the Next World!" In the *Ṣaḥīḥ* collections Anas is reported as saying that the Prophet, may Allah bless him and grant him peace, frequently used this supplication, "Give them good in this world and good in the Next World and protect them from the punishment of the Fire." Anas used to use this supplication regularly. It is reported that while 'Umar was doing *ṭawāf*, he said, "Our Lord, give us good in this world and good in the Next World and protect us from the punishment of the Fire," and that he said nothing else. Ibn Jurayj said that he heard that the most frequent supplication of the Muslim when standing at 'Arafat should be this.

أُوْلَٰٓئِكَ لَهُمْ نَصِيبٌ مِّمَّا كَسَبُواْۚ وَٱللَّهُ سَرِيعُ ٱلْحِسَابِ ۝٢٠٢

202 ***They will have a good share***
from what they have earned.
Allah is swift at reckoning.

They will have a good share from what they have earned.
This refers to the second group, the party of Islam, and informs them that they will have the reward for the *hajj* or the reward for the supplication. A believer's supplication is worship in itself. It is also said that the word "they" refers to both groups. The believer will receive the reward for his action and his supplication, and the unbeliever will have the punishment for his *shirk* and his confining his outlook to this world. That is like the words of Allah, *"All have ranks according to what they did."* (6:132)

Allah is swift at reckoning.

"*Ḥisāb*" (reckoning) means the same as what is counted (*muḥāsaba*) and so what is counted consitutes the reckoning. *Ḥasab*, meaning noble descent, is what a man counts as one of his glories. One can say, his glory (*ḥasab*) is his *dīn* or his wealth. In a *ḥadīth* we find, "*Ḥasab* is wealth and nobility is piety." (Ibn Mājah)

The *āyat* means that Allah is swift in calculating the reckoning and has no need of counting, addition or the action of thought as a human reckoner would. That is why He says, *"We are enough as Reckoner."* (21:47) The Messenger of Allah, may Allah bless him and grant him peace, said, "O Allah, Sender down of the Book, Swift at Reckoning." Allah knows His slaves and what they do and has no need of memory or reflection since He knows everything to be reckoned for or against them. The purpose of reckoning is ascertaining the truth.

It is said that the phrase means that Allah is swift at repaying people for their actions. It is said that it means that one thing does not distract Him from other things. He reckons them all at the same time as we find in His words: "*Your creation and rising is only like that of a single self.*" (31:28) Al-Ḥasan said, "His reckoning is swifter than the blink of a eye." One report says: "Allah reckons in the amount of time it takes to milk a sheep." 'Alī was asked, "How can Allah reckon His slaves in a single day?" He replied, "In the same way that He provides for them in a single day!" Another possible meaning of reckoning is that Allah acquaints His slaves with the exact repayment they will receive for their actions and reminds them of what they forgot. It is said that it means that He is swift at bringing about the Day of Reckoning and so the meaning of the *āyat* is to warn about the Day of Rising.

All of these interpretations are possible. The slave of Allah should make the reckoning light for himself through righteous actions. The reckoning will be lighter in the Next World for the one who calls himself to account in this world.

Ibn 'Abbās said, "The words 'They will have a good share…' refer to a man who takes money to perform *ḥajj* for someone else and has a reward." A *ḥadīth* is reported about that in which a man said, "O Messenger of Allah, my father died without making *ḥajj*. Can I perform *ḥajj* on his behalf?" The Prophet, peace be upon him, replied, "If your father had a debt, would you not pay it?" He said, "Yes." He said, "A debt owed to Allah is more entitled to receive settlement." He asked, "Will I have a reward?" and then Allah revealed, "*"They will have a good share from what they have earned."* So the meaning is that the reward for the *ḥajj* for the dead person is shared between him and the dead person.

Ibn Khuwayzimandād stated in *al-Aḥkām*, "The position of Ibn 'Abbās is like that of Mālik because the final position of Mālik is that the one for whom the *ḥajj* is done has the reward for paying for it and the *ḥajj* belongs to the one who does it. So it is as if the person doing the *ḥajj* has the reward of his body and actions and the one who pays for it has the reward of his spending."

وَاذْكُرُوا اللَّهَ فِي أَيَّامٍ مَّعْدُودَاتٍ ۚ فَمَن تَعَجَّلَ فِي يَوْمَيْنِ
فَلَا إِثْمَ عَلَيْهِ وَمَن تَأَخَّرَ فَلَا إِثْمَ عَلَيْهِ ۚ لِمَنِ اتَّقَىٰ ۗ وَاتَّقُوا
اللَّهَ وَاعْلَمُوا أَنَّكُمْ إِلَيْهِ تُحْشَرُونَ ٢٠٣

203 ***Remember Allah on the designated days.***
Those who hurry on in two days
have done no wrong,
and those who stay another day
have done no wrong –
those of them who are fearful of Allah.
So be fearful of Allah.
And know that you will be gathered back to Him.

Remember Allah on the designated days.

There is no disagreement among scholars that the designated days here refer to the days of Mina. They are the days of *tashrīq*. These three days have various names. They are the days of the stoning of the *jamra*s which takes place over three days but then it is permitted for someone on *ḥajj* to hurry and do it in two days after the Day of Sacrifice. Ath-Tha'labī and Ibrāhīm [an-Nakhā'ī] said that the "designated days" are the *'ushar* (10th, 11th and 12th) and the "particular days" (22:28) are the days of sacrifice. Makkī and al-Mahdawī also said that the "designated days" are the *'ushar*.

Allah commands His slaves to remember Him on designated days which are the days after the Day of Sacrifice. The Day of Sacrifice itself is not one of them by the consensus of the people that no one can hurry and leave the second day. The days of stoning are "designated" and the days of sacrifice are "known". Ibn 'Umar related that the "designated" days and "known" days together add up to four days: the Day of Sacrifice and the three days after it. The Day of Sacrifice is "known", and not "designated"; the next two days are both "known" and "designated", and the fourth day is "designated" and not "known". This is the position in the school of Mālik and others.

That is the case because the first day, the Day of Sacrifice, is not one of the days particular to Mina nor one of those which the Prophet, may Allah bless him and grant him peace, specified when he said, "The days of Mina are three." The Day of Sacrifice is "known".

There is no disagreement that the person addressed here is the person on *ḥajj* who says the *takbīr* while stoning the *jamra*s, over the animals he intends to sacrifice during the known days, and after the prayers. Does it include other than those on *ḥajj*? The *fuqahā'* of all the regions and the famous Companions and *Tābi'ūn* agree that everyone is meant to do the *takbīr*, especially at the times of the prayer, and so it is recited whether you pray alone or in a group to imitate the Salaf. The *Mukhtaṣar* of Khalīl states that women should not do it but the first position is better known since women follow the rules of *iḥrām* in the same way that men do and the *Mudawwana* says that.

If someone forgets the *takbīr* after the prayer and not much time has passed since he completed it, he should say it. If, however, a long time has passed, he owes nothing. Mālik is reported in the *Mukhtaṣar* as saying that you should say it as long as you are still sitting. If you rise before saying it, you owe nothing.

Scholars disagree about the end of the time of saying the *takbīr*. 'Umar, 'Alī and Ibn 'Abbās said that it is said from the *Ṣubḥ* prayer on the Day of 'Arafa up until *'Aṣr* on the last of the days of *Tashrīq*. Ibn Mas'ūd and Abū Ḥanīfa say that it is from the morning of the Day of 'Arafa up until *'Aṣr* of the Day of Sacrifice. His two companions disagree and take the first position. So they agree about its beginning, but not its end. Mālik says that the *takbīr* should be said from *Ẓuhr* on the Day of Sacrifice to the *Ṣubḥ* prayer on the last of the days of *Tashrīq*. Ash-Shāfi'ī agrees with that, and it is also the position of Ibn 'Umar and another position of Ibn 'Abbās. Ibn al-'Arabī says that those who say that the *takbīr* is said from the Day of 'Arafa and stopped at *'Aṣr* on the Day of Sacrifice have abandoned the evident text.

There is disagreement about the words of the *takbīr*. The well-known position in the school of Mālik is that the *takbīr* is said three times after each prayer. One transmission is that one says after the three *takbīr*s: "There is no god but Allah. Allah is greater and praise be to Allah." (*"Lā ilaha illā'llāh, wa'llāhu akbar, wa lillāhi'l-ḥamd."*) In the *Mukhtaṣar* Mālik is reported as saying, "Allah is greater. Allah is greater. There is no god but Allah and Allah is greater. Allah is greater and praise be to Allah." (*"Allāḥu akbar. Allāḥu akbar. Lā ilaha illā'llāh, wa'llāhu akbar. Allāḥu akbar, wa lillāhi'l-ḥamd."*)

Those who hurry on in two days have done no wrong,

Hurrying on is only permitted at the end of the second day. The same applies to the third day because the time of stoning during those days is after midday. All agree that on the Day of Sacrifice you only stone the *Jamrat al-'Aqaba* because the Messenger of Allah, may Allah bless him and grant him peace, did not stone the other *jamra*s on the Day of Sacrifice. The time for stoning on that day is from sunrise to midday. They agree that the time for stoning the *jamra*s on the days of *tashrīq* is after midday until sunset. They disagree about someone who stones the *Jamrat al-'Aqaba* before dawn or after dawn but before sunrise. Mālik, Abū Hanifa, Aḥmad and Ismā'īl said that it is allowed if it was after dawn, but not before dawn.

Ibn al-Mundhir said that scholars agree that if someone wants to leave Mina to return to his country and come out of *iḥrām* without staying at Makka in the first departure, he can depart after midday when he has stoned during the day after the Day of Sacrifice. That is because Allah says, *"Those who hurry on in two days have done no wrong."* He can go as long as there is some of the day left.

those of them who are fearful of Allah.

This statement is connected to forgiveness. It implies that there is forgiveness for those who are fearful of Allah. This is the interpretation of Ibn Mas'ūd and 'Ali. Qatāda said, "Ibn Mas'ūd mentioned to us that forgiveness is reserved for those who remain fearful of Allah after finishing the *ḥajj* and avoid all acts of disobedience." Al-Akhfash said that it implies: "Forgiveness is for those who are fearful of Allah." One of them said that it refers to not killing game in *iḥrām* or in the Ḥaram. It is said that there is safety for whoever is fearful of Allah. It is also said that it is connected to the remembrance in the words, *"Remember,"* meaning that remembrance is confined to those who are fearful of Allah. Allah commands us to be fearful of Him and reminds us of the Gathering and Standing.

وَمِنَ ٱلنَّاسِ مَن يُعْجِبُكَ قَوْلُهُۥ فِى ٱلْحَيَوٰةِ ٱلدُّنْيَا
وَيُشْهِدُ ٱللَّهَ عَلَىٰ مَا فِى قَلْبِهِۦ وَهُوَ أَلَدُّ ٱلْخِصَامِ ٢٠٤

204 ***Among the people there is someone whose words about the life of this world excite your admiration, and he calls Allah to witness what is in his heart, while he is in fact the most hostile of adversaries.***

Among the people there is someone whose words about the life of this world excite your admiration,

This *āyat* is here because Allah has just mentioned that the aspiration of some people is confined to this world in His words a little earlier: *"Our Lord, give us good in this world."* The believers are those who ask for the good of both the worlds. A hypocrite is mentioned because hypocrites display faith while concealing disbelief. As-Suddī and other commentators say that it was revealed about al-Akhnas ibn Sharīq. He was a man of sweet words and good appearance. He came to the Prophet and made a display of Islam and said, "Allah knows that I am telling the truth," and then after that he ran away. On his way he passed some crops and animals belonging to some Muslims and burned the crops and hamstrung the donkeys. Al-Mahdawī said that Allah's words: *'But do not obey any vile swearer of oaths, and backbiter, slandermonger,'* (68:10-11) were revealed about him as were: *'Woe to every fault-finding slanderer.'* (104:1)

Ibn 'Aṭiyya said, "It is not established that al-Akhnas became Muslim." Ibn 'Abbās says that it was revealed about some hypocrites who spoke about those killed in the Rajī' expedition, saying that they should have stayed at home. Then this was revealed to describe the hypocrites while those who were martyred in Rajī' are referred to in the words: *"And among the people there are some who give up everything."* (2:207).

Qatāda, Mujāhid and a group of scholars said that the *āyat* was revealed about anyone who conceals disbelief, hypocrisy, lying or vindictiveness while showing the opposite of that in his words. This is like what is related in at-Tirmidhī as being contained in one of the books of Allah which goes: "There are some slaves of Allah whose tongues are sweeter than honey while their hearts are more bitter than aloes. They appear to people like gentle sheep while they use the *dīn* to buy this world."

and he calls Allah to witness what is in his heart,

He does this by saying, "Allah knows that I am telling the truth," whereas Allah knows that he is different to what He says, as Allah says, *"Allah bears witness that the hypocrites are certainly liars."* (63:1).

Our scholars say that this *āyat* calls attention to the necessity of caution in dealing with both matters of the *dīn* and matters of the material world, and the need to verify the states of witnesses and *qāḍī*s. It points out that a judge should not base his judgement merely on the outward states of people and any display of faith and rectitude they make without investigating their inward because Allah will make the inward states of people clear. Some people can speak sweetly while intending evil.

If it is said that this is contradicted by the words of the Prophet, "I was commanded to fight people until they say, 'There is no god but Allah'..." the answer is that that was at the beginning of Islam when people's Islam was sound, before corruption became widespread. That is what Ibn al-'Arabī said. The sound position, however, is that a judge should judge by the outward until something contrary to it becomes clear, going by the statement of 'Umar ibn al-Khaṭṭāb in al-Bukhārī, "O people. Revelation has come to an end. We now judge according to what appears to us of your actions. If someone exhibits good, we consider him trustworthy and bring him near. We know nothing of what is concealed within him, Allah will call him to account for what is in his heart. If someone exhibits bad to us, we do not consider him trustworthy or believe him, even if it happens to be that his heart is good."

while he is in fact the most hostile of adversaries.

The word "*aladd*" (hostile) is derived from the word *ladīdān*, meaning both sides of the neck so that the implication is that his hostility is deeply rooted. The word "*khiṣām*" (adversaries) is a verbal noun from *khāṣama*, and it is also said to be the plural of *khaṣm*. It means that he is the strongest in argumentation when he speaks to you, even though it is inwardly false. We read in the *Ṣaḥih* Collection of Muslim that 'Ā'isha reported that the Messenger of Allah, may Allah bless him and grant him peace, said. "The man Allah most hates is the most hostile of adversaries."

وَإِذَا تَوَلَّىٰ سَعَىٰ فِي الْأَرْضِ لِيُفْسِدَ فِيهَا وَيُهْلِكَ
الْحَرْثَ وَالنَّسْلَ ۗ وَاللَّهُ لَا يُحِبُّ الْفَسَادَ ﴿٢٠٥﴾

205 ***When he leaves you, he goes about the earth corrupting it,***
destroying crops and animals
Allah does not love corruption.

When he leaves you, he goes about the earth corrupting it,

The verb "*tawallā*" (leaves) is said to imply being misguided, angry and arrogant and "*sa'y*" (goes about) to imply scheming and striving to bring about reverses for Islam and its people, as Ibn Jurayj and others have said. It is also said that *tawallā* simply means to turn his back and leave and *sa'y* is just to travel about, as Ibn 'Abbās and others say.

destroying

This is added to "corrupting." Although the *āyat* is held to refer specifically to al-Akhnas burning crops and killing camels, aṭ-Ṭabarī said that its meaning is general and should be extended to all who fit its description. Mujāhid said, "What is meant is that wrongdoers work corruption in the earth so that Allah withholds the rain from it, causing crops and animals to die.

crops and animals.

The root of the word "*ḥarth*" (crops) linguistically means splitting and the word for plough (*miḥrāth*) comes from it since it splits the earth. By extension *ḥarth* comes to mean gaining and amassing wealth. In a *ḥadīth*, "Cultivate (*aḥrith*) for this world as if you are going to live forever." *Ḥarth* is agriculture. *Ḥarrāth* is a ploughman. Other uses of the verb are *aḥratha*, to study thoroughly, and to ride an animal until it is exhausted, and to stir the fire. *Miḥrāth* is also a poker.

The word "*nasl*" (animals) denotes any progeny of a female. Its root meaning is "to leave and fall". The verb is used for hair falling out and feathers moulting. So the words in the *āyat* indicate planting and cultivating the earth and putting in trees to bear fruit and seeking increase in livestock which provide livelihood for a person.

It is also said that the word "crops" designates women and "animals" sons. The reason for this is because hypocrisy leads to disunion and fighting and that causes people to be killed. Az-Zajjāj said something to that effect. This means that the *āyat* is a metaphor about striving to cause sedition and make people fight.

Allah does not love corruption.

Al-'Abbās ibn al-Faḍl said that "*fasād" (*corruption) means ruin. Sa'īd ibn al-Musayyab said that clipping dirhams forms part of corruption in the land. The *āyat* is general to all kinds of corruption in the land, in respect of either property or the *dīn*, and that is the sound position, Allah willing.

وَإِذَا قِيلَ لَهُ اتَّقِ اللَّهَ أَخَذَتْهُ الْعِزَّةُ بِالْإِثْمِ
فَحَسْبُهُ جَهَنَّمُ وَلَبِئْسَ الْمِهَادُ ٢٠٦

206 ***When he is told to be fearful of Allah,***
he is seized by a feeling of might
which drives him to wrongdoing.
Hell will be enough for him!
What an evil resting-place!

This describes the chief attribute of the unbeliever and the hypocrite: arrogance. It is disliked for a believer to fall into this. 'Abdullāh said, "It is enough wrong action for a man that he says to his brother, 'Fear Allah,' and he retorts, 'Mind your own business! Someone like you advises me!'" The word "*'izza*" (might) denotes strength and dominance. It is also said to mean unapproachableness. It means that his pride leads him to commit wrong action, so that he commits disbelief for the sake of might and the zeal of the *Jāhiliyya*. The usual meaning of the word "resting place" (*mihād*) is a place prepared for sleep. *Jahannam* (Hell) is referred to as one because it is where the unbelievers will remain.

وَمِنَ ٱلنَّاسِ مَن يَشْرِى نَفْسَهُ ٱبْتِغَآءَ مَرْضَاتِ ٱللَّهِ ۗ وَٱللَّهُ رَءُوفٌۢ بِٱلْعِبَادِ ﴿٢٠٧﴾

207 ***And among the people***
there are some who give up everything,
desiring the good pleasure of Allah.
Allah is Ever-Gentle with His slaves.

After speaking of the actions of the hypocrites, Allah talks about the behaviour of the believers. It is said that the *āyat* was actually revealed about Ṣuhayb. He emigrated to the Messenger of Allah and some people of Quraysh followed him. He descended from his mount, took out what was in his quiver and took up his bow and said, "You know that I am the best shot among you. By Allah you will not reach me until I have shot what is in my quiver and struck with my sword until nothing remains in my hands and then do what you wish." They said, "We will not let you leave us a wealthy man when you came to us with nothing. Direct us to your property in Makka and we will let you go." They made an agreement with him to that effect and he did that. When he came to the Messenger of Allah, may Allah bless him and grant him peace, this *āyat* was revealed and the Prophet said to him, "A profitable sale, Abū Yaḥyā!" and recited it to him.

Commentators say that the idolaters took Ṣuhayb and tortured him and Ṣuhayb said to them, "I am an old man. Your security will not be prejudiced if I am with other than you. Will you not take my wealth and leave me with my *dīn*?" They did that and he stipulated a camel and provision for himself and went to Madina where Abū Bakr, 'Umar and some men met him. Abū Bakr told him, "A profitable sale, Abū Yaḥyā!" Ṣuhayb asked what he meant and he told him about the revelation of the *āyat*.

Al-Ḥasan said, "Do you know about whom this *āyat* was revealed? It was revealed about a Muslim who met a unbeliever and told him, 'Say: There is no god but Allah'. If you say it, your property and life are safe. He refused to say it. The Muslim said, 'By Allah, I will sell my self to Allah' and he advanced and fought until he was killed." It is said that it was revealed about all those who command what is known to be right and forbid what is recognised to be wrong and that is the way it was interpreted by 'Umar, 'Ali and Ibn 'Abbās. It is also said that it was revealed about those marytred in the Rajī' expedition. Qatāda said that it refers to the Muhājirūn and Anṣār. It is said that it was revealed about 'Alī when the Prophet left him on his bed on the night he went out to the cave. It is said that the *āyat* is general and applies to everyone striving in the way of martyrdom for Allah's sake or changing something wrong.

يا أيها الذين ءامنوا ادخلوا في السلم كافة
ولا تتبعوا خطوات الشيطان إنه لكم عدو
مبين ٢٠٨

208 ***You who believe! enter Islam totally.***
Do not follow in the footsteps of Shayṭān.
He is an outright enemy to you.

You who believe! enter Islam totally.

After Allah has made it clear that people are either believers, unbelievers or hypocrites, He says, "Follow only one religion and agree on Islam and remain firm in it." Here the word *salm* means Islam as Mujāhid said and as is related from Ibn 'Abbās. It cannot mean "truce or a peace treaty", because the Muslims were never commanded to enter into a truce in this way. Rather the Prophet, peace be upon him, was told to incline to peace if the enemy inclined to it, but not to initiate it. Aṭ-Ṭabarī said that. It is said that Allah commands those who articulate belief with their tongues to enter into it with their hearts. Ṭāwūs and Mujāhid said that it means, "Enter under the authority of the *dīn*." Sufyān ath-Thawrī says that it refers to all types of piety.

It is read both as *salm* (Warsh) and *silm* (Ḥafs) and they mean the same and both are used to signify Islam and to signify truce, although some say that *salm* means truce and *silm* means Islam. Aṭ-Ṭabarī says that it means Islam. Regarding this *āyat*, Ḥudhayfa ibn al-Yamān said, "Islam is divided into eight parts. The prayer is one part, *zakāt* is one part, fasting is one part, *ḥajj* is one part, *'umra* is one part, *jihād* is one part, commanding what is known to be right is one part, and forbidding what is recognised as wrong is one part. Disappointed is he who has no part of Islam."

Ibn 'Abbās said that it was revealed about the people of the Book and the meaning is: "You who believe in Mūsā and 'Īsā, enter into Islam totally through Muḥammad, may Allah bless him and grant him peace." Abū Hurayra reported that the Prophet, may Allah bless him and grant him peace, said, "By the One who has the soul of Muḥammad in His hand, no Jew or Christian will hear this and then die without believing in what I was sent with but that he will be one of the people of the Fire."

Do not follow in the footsteps of Shaytan.

Muqātil said, "'Abdullāh ibn Salām and his people asked for permission to recite the Torah in the prayer and to do some of what is in the Torah and this was revealed. It means: "It is better to follow the *Sunna* now that Muḥammad, may Allah bless him and grant him peace, has been sent than to follow the footsteps of Shayṭān." It is said that it means: "Do not follow the path which Shayṭān calls you to."

فَإِن زَلَلْتُم مِّنۢ بَعْدِ مَا جَآءَتْكُمُ ٱلْبَيِّنَـٰتُ
فَٱعْلَمُوٓا۟ أَنَّ ٱللَّهَ عَزِيزٌ حَكِيمٌ ٢٠٩

209 ***If you backslide after the Clear Signs***
have come to you,
know that Allah is Almighty, All-Wise.

If you backslide

In other words, if you turn aside from the path of righteousness. The root of "*zalal*" (backslide) relates to the foot slipping and so it is used metaphorically for reverting from beliefs, opinions and other such things.

after the Clear Signs have come to you,

This may refer to the miracles of the Prophet, may Allah bless him and grant him peace, or to the *āyat*s of the Qur'an if it is addressed to the believers. If it is addressed to the people of the Book, the Clear Signs are what came in their Books telling them about Muhammad, may Allah bless him and grant him peace. The *āyat* contains evidence that the punishment of a man of knowledge for a wrong action is greater than the punishment of someone ignorant, and is also evidence that someone who has not heard the call of Islam is not an unbeliever by the fact that he does not observe its laws.

هَلْ يَنظُرُونَ إِلَّآ أَن يَأْتِيَهُمُ ٱللَّهُ فِى ظُلَلٍ مِّنَ ٱلْغَمَامِ
وَٱلْمَلَٰٓئِكَةُ وَقُضِىَ ٱلْأَمْرُ وَإِلَى ٱللَّهِ تُرْجَعُ ٱلْأُمُورُ ﴿٢١٠﴾

210 ***What are they waiting for***
but for Allah to come to them
in the shadows of the clouds,
together with the angels,
in which case the matter will have been settled?
All matters return to Allah.

What are they waiting for

This is referring to those who do not enter into Islam and implies obstinacy on their part. Qatāda says that it refers to the angels coming to take their souls. It is also said to refer to the Day of Rising, and that is more likely.

but for Allah to come to them in the shadows of the clouds

"For Allah to come" means for the command and judgement of Allah to come to them. It is said that it means that the reckoning and punishment that Allah has promised them is lying in wait for them in the shadows, as we find in *"Then Allah came upon them from where they least expected it."* (59:2) This is what az-Zajjāj said. The first is the view of al-Akhfash. It is also possible that what is being referred to is the repayment they will receive for their wrong actions, and that this particular usage is employed to intensify the threat and to convey alarm. The word "coming" can entail all these ideas because its root linguistically means to aim for something and so the *āyat* means: "What are they waiting for but for Allah to show them something by means of one of His created forms, with the aim of repaying them and judging their affairs?"

Allah also has the capability to originate an event without any cause or instrument which He refers to here by the word "coming". Glory be to Him! Ibn 'Abbās said, "This is part of what is unknowable and should not be explained." So some people were silent about its interpretation. It is not possible to consider that this and similar things in the Qur'ān and the *aḥādīth* apply to actual movement because that is one of the attributes of physical bodies and Allah is too majestic to be likened to any physical body!

The word for "clouds" (*ghamām*) in this *āyat* means "thin fine white clouds". They are called that because they cover, for the verb *ghamma* means "to cover".

in which case the matter will have been settled

The matter being settled is a reference to the repayment and the punishment of the people of disobedience. Although most readings have *"turja'u'l-'umūr"* ("All matters return to Allah), Ibn 'Āmir, Ḥamza and al-Kisā'i have *"tarji'u'l-'umūr"*.

سَلْ بَنِيٓ إِسْرَٰٓءِيلَ كَمْ ءَاتَيْنَٰهُم مِّنْ ءَايَةٍۭ بَيِّنَةٍ ۗ وَمَن يُبَدِّلْ
نِعْمَةَ ٱللَّهِ مِنۢ بَعْدِ مَا جَآءَتْهُ فَإِنَّ ٱللَّهَ شَدِيدُ ٱلْعِقَابِ ﴿٢١١﴾

211 *Ask the tribe of Israel*
how many Clear Signs We gave to them.
If anyone alters Allah's blessing
after it has come to him,
Allah is fierce in retribution.

Ask the tribe of Israel how many Clear Signs We gave to them.

What is being referred to by this *āyat* is the great number of signs which came to them making the coming Prophethood of Muḥammad, may Allah bless him and grant him peace, clear to them and directing them to him. Mujāhid, al-Ḥasan and others said that it refers to the miraculous signs which Mūsā manifested such as the splitting of the sea, the shading by the clouds, his staff turning into a snake, his hand turning white and other things. The command present in the *āyat* is to His Prophet to ask them by way of rebuking them.

If anyone alters Allah's blessing after it has come to him,

This is a general expression applying to everyone, even if it is the Tribe of Israel who are mentioned in this instance. They changed things in their Books and denied the Prophethood of Muḥammad, may Allah bless him and grant him peace. But the expression applies to all those who alter the blessing of Allah. Aṭ-Ṭabarī said that the blessing here is Islam and this is close to the first statement. The expression also includes the unbelievers of Quraysh since the fact that the Prophet was sent to them was a blessing to them andinstead of being thankful they rejected him.

Allah is fierce in retribution.

This is a threat. *'Iqāb* (retribution) is derived from *'aqib* which means the last part or heel of something and so it is as if the one being punished has retribution following at his heels. Also from the same root is *'uqba,* used for the "turn of the person riding" (when people taking it in turns to ride an animal) and someone's turn to get water (when a water source is being shared). *'Iqāb* and *'uqūba* are punishment, because they follow after the wrong action and punishment is a consequence of a wrong action.

زُيِّنَ لِلَّذِينَ كَفَرُواْ ٱلْحَيَوٰةُ ٱلدُّنْيَا وَيَسْخَرُونَ مِنَ ٱلَّذِينَ ءَامَنُواْۖ
وَٱلَّذِينَ ٱتَّقَوْاْ فَوْقَهُمْ يَوْمَ ٱلْقِيَٰمَةِۗ وَٱللَّهُ يَرْزُقُ مَن يَشَآءُ
بِغَيْرِ حِسَابٍۖ ٢١٢

212 ***To those who disbelieve, the life of this world***
is painted in glowing colours
and they laugh at those who believe.
But on the Day of Rising
those who fear Allah will be over them.
Allah provides for whoever He wills
without any reckoning.

To those who disbelieve, the life of this world is painted in glowing colours.

Although no one is named, those intended here are the leaders of Quraysh. Those who disbelieve are singled out for mention because they are totally taken in by the adornment of this world and turn to it and turn away from the Next World because of it. Allah has made what is on the earth its adornment in order to test His creatures to see who will perform the best actions. The believers who follow the norms of the *Sharī'a* are not tempted by worldly adornment but it dominates the minds of the unbelievers because they do not believe in anything but it. Abū Bakr aṣ-Ṣiddiq said when he was offered wealth, "O Allah we cannot do other than rejoice in what You have made seem attractive to us."

and they laugh at those who believe.

So it is as if the unbelievers of Quraysh thought highly of their state in this world and delighted in it and scoffed at the followers of Muḥammad, may Allah bless him and grant him peace. Ibn Jurayj said that they scoffed at their seeking the Next World. It is said that they mocked their poverty and those who were poor among them like Bilāl, Ṣuhayb, Ibn Mas'ūd and others.

But on the Day of Rising those who fear Allah will be over them.

Allah calls attention to the lowering of their position because of their ugly behaviour. 'Alī reported that the Prophet, may Allah bless him and grant him peace, said, "If anyone demeans a believing man or woman, or disdains them on account of their poverty and lack of possessions, Allah will make him known on the Day of Rising and will disgrace him. If anyone slanders a believing man or woman or says something about him that is not true, Allah Almighty will make him stand on a hill of fire on the Day of Rising until he produces what he said about him. If someone esteems a believer, Allah will esteem and honour him more than one of the angels near to Him. There is nothing which Allah loves better than a repentant believing man or repentant believing woman. A believer is acknowledged in heaven as a man is acknowledged among his family and children."

It is said that this expresssion refers to their ranks because they will be in the Garden while the unbelievers are in the Fire. It is possible that "over" actually does have a kind of spatial meaning since heaven is high and the Fire is the lowest of the low. It is also possible that it means that what they will have is better than what the unbelievers claim to have.

Allah provides for whoever He wills without any reckoning.

Aḍ-Ḍaḥḥāk says that this means without being subject to accountability in the Next World. It is said that it refers to those who are being victimised, meaning that Allah will provide them with a high station. The *āyat* calls attention to the great blessing they will receive and says their provision is without reckoning because it will last for ever and never end and so the amount of it cannot be calculated. It is said that "without any reckoning" refers to Allah's provision which He dispenses as He wishes and His bounty is beyond reckoning.

كَانَ ٱلنَّاسُ أُمَّةً وَٰحِدَةً فَبَعَثَ ٱللَّهُ ٱلنَّبِيِّـۧنَ مُبَشِّرِينَ وَمُنذِرِينَ
وَأَنزَلَ مَعَهُمُ ٱلْكِتَٰبَ بِٱلْحَقِّ لِيَحْكُمَ بَيْنَ ٱلنَّاسِ فِيمَا ٱخْتَلَفُوا۟ فِيهِ ۚ
وَمَا ٱخْتَلَفَ فِيهِ إِلَّا ٱلَّذِينَ أُوتُوهُ مِنۢ بَعْدِ مَا جَآءَتْهُمُ ٱلْبَيِّنَٰتُ
بَغْيًۢا بَيْنَهُمْ ۖ فَهَدَى ٱللَّهُ ٱلَّذِينَ ءَامَنُوا۟ لِمَا ٱخْتَلَفُوا۟ فِيهِ مِنَ ٱلْحَقِّ
بِإِذْنِهِۦ ۗ وَٱللَّهُ يَهْدِى مَن يَشَآءُ إِلَىٰ صِرَٰطٍ مُّسْتَقِيمٍ ﴿٢١٣﴾

213 ***Mankind was a single community.***
Then Allah sent out Prophets
bringing good news and giving warning,
and with them He sent down the Book with truth
to decide between people
regarding their differences.
Only those who were given it differed about it,
after the Clear Signs had come to them,
envying one another.
Then, by His permission,
Allah guided those who believed
to the truth of that about which they had differed.
Allah guides whoever He wills to a straight path.

Mankind was a single community.

This means that they had one *dīn*. Ubayy ibn Ka'b and Ibn Zayd said that what is meant by "mankind" are all the sons of Ādam when Allah brought out their souls from the back of Ādam and they affirmed His oneness. Muhājid said that "mankind" refers to Ādam alone. The term is used for him because he is the source of his offspring. It is said that it means Ādam and Ḥawwā'. Ibn 'Abbās and Qatāda said that what is meant are the generations between Ādam and Nūḥ, which were ten, who followed the truth until they differed, and then Allah sent Nūḥ and the Prophets after him. Ibn Abī Khaythama said that the length of time which passed from the time Allah created Ādam until He sent Muḥammad, may Allah bless him and grant him peace, is fifteen thousand eight hundred years. It is said that it is more than that. There were twelve hundred years between him and Nūḥ and Ādam lived to the age of nine hundred and sixty. People in his time had one religion and held to the *dīn* and the angels shook hands with them. They remained like that until Idrīs was taken up and then they differed.

This is unclear because it is known that Idrīs came after Nūḥ. Some people, including al-Kalbī, say that what is meant is Nūḥ and those with him in the Ark. They were Muslims and then after the death of Nūḥ they differed. Ibn 'Abbās said, "They were one community in disbelief, meaning in the time of Nūḥ until Allah sent Nūḥ." He also said, "People in the time of Ibrāhīm were one community: all unbelievers. Ibrāhīm was born in a time of ignorance and then Allah sent Ibrāhīm and other Prophets."

According to these statements, the verb "*kāna*" (was) actually means the past. So mankind were believers for the time mentioned and then they disagreed and then the Prophets came. This indicates a reversal of order so that the phrase "Only those who were given it differed about it" refers to the time before the Prophets were sent. In other words people were following the true *dīn* and then differed and then the Prophets were sent to give good news to those who obey and warn those who disobey. Prophets were sent to all of those whom Allah decreed would become unbelievers. But it is also possible that *kāna* has a continuous meaning and that what is meant is to inform us that mankind as a species would all be one community in respect of their failure to follow Allah's laws and their ignorance of the truth if it were not for Allah's grace to them and His favour in granting them Messengers. In this case *kāna* does not actually refer to the past.

The word "*umma*" (community) is taken from *amma*, meaning to aim for. So an *umma* has one focus. One person can be called an *umma*, when what is meant is that his aim is not the same as that of other people. An example of that is what the Prophet, may Allah bless him and grant him peace, said about Quss ibn Sā'ida, "He will be gathered on the Day of Rising as a whole *umma*." *Imma* means blessing because people aim for it. *Imām* is used because people aim in the same direction as him.

Then Allah sent out Prophets

There were twenty-four thousand Prophets and three hundred and thirteen of them were Messengers. There are eighteen mentioned by name in the Qur'ān. The first Messenger was Ādam as we find in the *ḥadīth* of Abū Dharr. It is also said that it was Nūḥ going by the *ḥadīth* of intercession where people say to him, "You are the first of the Messengers." It is also said that the first was Idrīs. This will be dealt with in *Sūrat al-A'rāf*, Allah willing.

and with them He sent down the Book with truth

Here "Book" is generic and means all the Books. Aṭ-Ṭabarī says that it means the Torah.

to decide between people regarding their differences.

Most scholars say that it is "the Book" which is the deciding factor since every Prophet judges according to his Book. When he judges by the Book it is as if the Book itself does the judging. It is said that the meaning is that Allah judges, and so it means that Allah Himself is the decider.

Only those who were given it differed about it,

The "it" can also be understood as "him" in which case it refers to the one it has been revealed to, meaning Muḥammad, may Allah bless him and grant him peace. Az-Zajjāj said that. They disagreed about the Prophet, peace be upon him, only after they were given knowledge of him.

envying one another.

Their failure to accept him was only due to envy. This calls attention to the foolishness of what they did and its ugliness.

Then, by His permission, Allah guided those who believed

Allah guided the community of Muḥammad, may Allah bless him and grant him peace, to the truth since He clarified the matters about which those before them had disagreed. One group says that it means that the previous communities denied each other's Books and so Allah guided the community of Muḥammad, may Allah bless him and grant him peace, to what was true in all of them. Another group says that Allah guided the believers to the truth regarding the disagreements of the People of the Book about whether Ibrāhīm was a Jew or a Christian. Ibn Zayd and Zayd ibn Aslam said that it is about their *qibla*: the Jews faced Jerusalem and the Christians the east. Or it may be about the Day of *Jumu'a.* The Prophet, may Allah bless him and grant him peace, said, "This is the day about which they differed and Allah guided us to it. The Jews have tomorrow and the Christians the day after it." It is also said to be about fasting or about all their differences. Ibn Zayd said, "They disagree about 'Īsā, the Jews say he was a fraud and the Christian say he was a Lord. So Allah guided the believers to consider him to be a slave of Allah."

At-Ṭabarī says that there is an inversion here and the meaning is: "So Allah guided those who believe to the truth regarding that about which they differed." This is necessary, according to Ibn 'Aṭiyya, so that it is not imagined that they disagreed about the truth.

The words "by His permission" mean "by His knowledge" according to az-Zajjāj. An-Naḥḥās says that this is not correct and that it means "by His command". When He gives permission for something, it is commanded. Allah guided those who believe by commanding them to do what they were obliged to do.

Allah guides whoever He wills to a straight path.

This is another refutation of the rationalist Mu'tazilite position that maintains that the human being is his own guide.

أَمْ حَسِبْتُمْ أَن تَدْخُلُوا۟ ٱلْجَنَّةَ وَلَمَّا يَأْتِكُم مَّثَلُ ٱلَّذِينَ خَلَوْا۟
مِن قَبْلِكُم ۖ مَّسَّتْهُمُ ٱلْبَأْسَآءُ وَٱلضَّرَّآءُ وَزُلْزِلُوا۟ حَتَّىٰ
يَقُولَ ٱلرَّسُولُ وَٱلَّذِينَ ءَامَنُوا۟ مَعَهُۥ مَتَىٰ نَصْرُ ٱللَّهِ ۗ أَلَآ
إِنَّ نَصْرَ ٱللَّهِ قَرِيبٌ ﴿٢١٤﴾

214 ***Or did you suppose that you would enter the Garden***
without facing the same
as those who came before you?
Poverty and illness afflicted them
and they were shaken to the point
that the Messenger
and those who believed with him said,
'When is Allah's help coming?'
Be assured that Allah's help is very near.

Or did you suppose that you would enter the Garden

Qatāda, as-Suddī and most commentators say that this *āyat* was revealed about the Battle of the Ditch [in 5/627] when the Muslims suffered from overtiredness, stress, heat and cold, poor food and various other difficulties. As Allah says, it was a time when: *"your hearts rose to your throats"* (33:10). It is also said that it was revealed about the Battle of Uḥud and is similar to what Allah says in *Āl 'Imrān*: *"Or did you reckon that you were going to enter the Garden without Allah knowing those among you who had struggled?"* (3:142) One group say that it was revealed to console the Muhājirūn when they were forced to leave their homes and wealth in the hands of the idolaters in Makka, preferring the pleasure of Allah and His Messenger, and then the Jews showed animosity to the Prophet, may Allah bless him and grant him peace, and some of the wealthy Madinans concealed hypocrisy in their hearts. This was revealed to cheer the hearts of the Muhājirūn.

without facing the same as those who came before you?

Meaning that they would be tried to the same degree that those before them were tried so that they could be steadfast in the same way as those before them had been steadfast. Allah calls on them to be steadfast and promises them that they will be helped if they are.

Poverty and illness afflicted them and they were shaken to the point

The word "shaken" (*zulzilū*) refers to the great turbulence. It can be applied to both individuals and situations. The noun *zalzala* means "earthquake" and its plural *zalāzil* is used for hardships. Az-Zajjāj said the root of the word is *zalla*, which is used when a thing slips from its place.

that the Messenger and those who believed with him said, 'When is Allah's help coming?' Be assured that Allah's help is very near.

This is part of the words of the Prophet, may Allah bless him and grant him peace, in which he asks for help to come quickly, without expressing doubt or uncertainty about its arrival in any way. The word *"rasūl"* (Messenger) is generic here. One group said that there is a reversal of normal order here. The implied meaning is that those who believed said, "When is Allah's help coming?" and the Messenger said, "Be assured that Allah's help is very near." The Messenger, may Allah bless him and grant him peace, is mentioned first because of his high rank. The words of the believers are put first because they occurred earlier in time. Ibn 'Aṭiyya said this is an arbitrary interpretation and it is probable that the words *"Be assured that Allah's help is very near"* is simply a report from Allah.

يَسْـَٔلُونَكَ مَاذَا يُنفِقُونَ ۖ قُلْ مَآ أَنفَقْتُم مِّنْ خَيْرٍ
فَلِلْوَٰلِدَيْنِ وَٱلْأَقْرَبِينَ وَٱلْيَتَٰمَىٰ وَٱلْمَسَٰكِينِ وَٱبْنِ ٱلسَّبِيلِ ۗ
وَمَا تَفْعَلُوا۟ مِنْ خَيْرٍ فَإِنَّ ٱللَّهَ بِهِۦ عَلِيمٌ ﴿٢١٥﴾

215 ***They will ask you what they should give away.***
Say, 'Any wealth you give away should go
to your parents and relatives
and to orphans and the very poor and travellers.'
Whatever good you do, Allah knows it.

This was revealed about 'Amr ibn al-Jamūḥ who was a very old man. He said, "Messenger of Allah, I have a lot of wealth. What *ṣadaqa* should I give and to whom should I give it?" and this was revealed.

It is said that the askers are the believers, and it means: they will ask you about the ways in which to spend and whether to spend. As-Suddī said that this *āyat* was revealed before *zakāt* became obligatory and that the imposition of *zakāt* abrogated it. Ibn 'Aṭiyya said that al-Mahawī thinks this statement to be weak. He stated that the *āyat* was about the obligatory *zakāt.* It was at a later time that parents ceased to be recipients of it. Ibn Jurayj and others said that it refers to recommended spending and that *zakāt* is something else and so this *āyat* is not abrogated.

It clarifies the channels of voluntary *ṣadaqa.* A rich man must spend on his needy parents to the point that their standard of living is brought up to the level of his own in respect of food, clothing and other such things. Mālik said that a son is not obliged to go as far as procuring a wife for his father but he should spend on his father's wife, whether she is his mother or not. Mālik said that he does not have to procure a wife for his father because he thinks that, in general, there is no real need for him to marry. If, however, his father does really need a wife, then he should procure one for him. As for expenses connected to worship, the son does not have to pay for his father to perform *ḥajj* or go on *jihād* but he does have to pay his *zakāt al-fiṭr*. The other channels – orphans, the poor and travellers – have already been discussed.

كُتِبَ عَلَيْكُمُ الْقِتَالُ وَهُوَ كُرْهٌ لَّكُمْ وَعَسَىٰٓ أَن تَكْرَهُوا۟ شَيْـًٔا وَهُوَ خَيْرٌ
لَّكُمْ وَعَسَىٰٓ أَن تُحِبُّوا۟ شَيْـًٔا وَهُوَ شَرٌّ لَّكُمْ وَاللَّهُ يَعْلَمُ وَأَنتُمْ لَا
تَعْلَمُونَ ﴿٢١٦﴾

216 ***Fighting is prescribed for you***
even if it is hateful to you.
It may be that you hate something
when it is good for you
and it may be that you love something
when it is bad for you.
Allah knows and you do not know.

Fighting is prescribed for you

This means that fighting is obligatory and refers to the obligation of *jihād*. Allah makes it clear that He has made the trial of fighting a means to reach the Garden. What is meant by fighting is fighting enemies among the unbelievers. This is known from the context. The Prophet, may Allah bless him and grant him peace, was not given permission to fight while he was in Makka. When he emigrated, he was given permission to fight those idolaters who fought him and then he was given permission to fight idolaters in general.

There is disagreement about who is meant by the *āyat*. It is said that it refers to the Companions of the Prophet in particular, and so fighting with the Prophet is an obligation for each of them individually. When the *Sharī'a* was established, it became a *farḍ kifāya*, an obligation for the community as a whole but not for every individual in it. 'Aṭā' and al-Awzā'ī stated that. Ibn Jurayj said, "I asked 'Aṭā', 'Is *jihād* made obligatory for everyone by this *āyat*?' He replied, 'No, it was prescribed for those people in particular.'"

The majority say that, at first, it was a *kifāya* obligation, not specific to all of them, but when the Prophet, may Allah bless him and grant him peace, called them out, it was incumbent on them to obey him. Sa'īd ibn al-Musayyab said, *"Jihād* will remain an obligation forever for every single Muslim." Al-Māwardī related that. Ibn 'Aṭiyya said, "That on which there is consensus is that *jihād* is a *farḍ kifāya* for the entire community of Muhammad, may Allah bless him and grant him peace. If some undertake it, the obligation falls from the rest, unless the enemy arrives in a Muslim land and then it is an obligation for every individual." This will be explained in *Sūrat at-Tawba*, Allah willing. Ath-Thawrī said that *jihād* is voluntary. Ibn 'Aṭiyya remarked that he thought that what ath-Thawrī said was in response to a question put by someone who had already performed *jihād*.

even if it is hateful to you.

It is natural to dislike it. Ibn 'Arafa said about the word "*kurh*" (hateful) that, when it is pronounced with a *ḍamma*, ***kurh***, as it is here, it means hardship and when it is pronounced with a *fatḥa*, ***karh,*** it means hateful. It is also possible that ***kurh*** has the same meaning as ***karh***. *Jihād* is hateful because it involves spending money, leaving one's homeland and family, exposing one's body to head fractures and wounds, loss of limbs and death. So people find that aspect of it hateful, not the fact that it is an obligation from Allah. 'Ikrima mentioned that they first hated it and then came to love it because even though obeying the command entails hardship, the knowledge of the reward made it easy.

It is similar to the removal of things which cause people pain and which they fear, like the amputation of limbs, the extraction of teeth, venesection, cupping and other such things which people undergo to improve their health. Knowledge of the eventual benefit makes people keen to undergo these things in spite of the temporary hardship they entail. There could be no benefit greater than everlasting life in the Abode of Eternity and *"on seats of honour in the Presence of an all-powerful King"*(54:55).

It may be that you hate something when it is good for you and it may be that you love something when it is bad for you.

The word "*'asā*" (may be) can mean that it is actually the case, in other words: "You do hate the hardship in *jihād* but it is good for you in that you conquer, have victory, take booty and are rewarded and whoever dies dies a martyr. You do love peace and not fighting but it is evil for you since you will be overcome and abased and your authority lost." This is absolutely true and it happened in Andalusia when they abandoned *jihād* and avoided fighting and many fled. The enemy took the land and captured, killed and enslaved the Muslims. We belong to Allah and to Him we return!

يَسْـَٔلُونَكَ عَنِ ٱلشَّهْرِ ٱلْحَرَامِ قِتَالٍ فِيهِ قُلْ قِتَالٌ فِيهِ كَبِيرٌ
وَصَدٌّ عَن سَبِيلِ ٱللَّهِ وَكُفْرٌۢ بِهِۦ وَٱلْمَسْجِدِ ٱلْحَرَامِ وَإِخْرَاجُ
أَهْلِهِۦ مِنْهُ أَكْبَرُ عِندَ ٱللَّهِ وَٱلْفِتْنَةُ أَكْبَرُ مِنَ ٱلْقَتْلِ وَلَا يَزَالُونَ
يُقَٰتِلُونَكُمْ حَتَّىٰ يَرُدُّوكُمْ عَن دِينِكُمْ إِنِ ٱسْتَطَٰعُوا۟ وَمَن يَرْتَدِدْ
مِنكُمْ عَن دِينِهِۦ فَيَمُتْ وَهُوَ كَافِرٌ فَأُو۟لَٰٓئِكَ حَبِطَتْ أَعْمَٰلُهُمْ
فِى ٱلدُّنْيَا وَٱلْـَٔاخِرَةِ وَأُو۟لَٰٓئِكَ أَصْحَٰبُ ٱلنَّارِ هُمْ فِيهَا خَٰلِدُونَ ٢١٧
إِنَّ ٱلَّذِينَ ءَامَنُوا۟ وَٱلَّذِينَ هَاجَرُوا۟ وَجَٰهَدُوا۟ فِى سَبِيلِ ٱللَّهِ أُو۟لَٰٓئِكَ
يَرْجُونَ رَحْمَتَ ٱللَّهِ وَٱللَّهُ غَفُورٌ رَّحِيمٌ ٢١٨

217 *They will ask you about the Sacred Month*
and fighting in it.
Say, 'Fighting in it is a serious matter;
but barring access to the Way of Allah
and rejecting Him

and barring access to the Masjid al-Ḥarām
and expelling its people from it
are far more serious in the sight of Allah.
Fitna is worse than killing.'
They will not stop fighting you until
they make you revert from your dīn,
if they are able.
As for any of you who revert from their dīn
and die unbelievers,
their actions will come to nothing
in this world and the Next.
They are the Companions of the Fire,
remaining in it timelessly, for ever.
218 *Those who believe and make hijra*
and do jihād in the Way of Allah
can expect Allah's mercy.
Allah is Ever-Forgiving, Most Merciful.

They will ask you about the Sacred Month

Ibn 'Abbās said, "I have not seen any people better than the Companions of Muḥammad, may Allah bless him and grant him peace. They only asked him about thirteen matters, all of which are in the Qur'ān. 'They will ask you about menstruation,' 'they will ask you about the Sacred Month,' 'they will ask you about orphans.' They only asked him about what would benefit them." Ibn 'Abdu'l-Barr said, "There are only three of the thirteen in the *ḥadīth*."

Jundub ibn 'Abdullāh reported that the Prophet sent out a party of which 'Abdullāh ibn Jaḥsh was the leader and wrote a letter for him and instructed him not to read the letter until he reached a certain place. He said, "Do not force your companions to go." When he reached the place, he read the letter and said, "We belong to Allah and return to Him. We hear and obey His Messenger." Two men returned and the rest continued. They met Ibn al-Ḥadramī and killed him, not knowing that it was Rajab. The idolaters said, "You have killed in the Sacred month!" and Allah revealed this.

It is related that the reason for its revelation was that two men of the Banū Kilāb met 'Amr ibn Umayya aḍ-Ḍamrī. That was on the first day of Rajab and he killed them. Quraysh said, "You killed them during the Sacred Month," and Allah revealed the *āyat*. The most commonly accepted version, however, is that of 'Abdullāh ibn Jaḥsh.

Scholars disagree about whether the *āyat* was abrogated. The majority say that it was abrogated and that it is permitted to fight the idolaters in the Sacred Months. They disagree about what abrogated it. Az-Zuhrī said that it is *"fight the idolaters totally."* (9:36). It is said that it was abrogated by the expedition of the Prophet against Thaqīf in the Sacred month and his sending 'Āmir against Awṭās in the Sacred Month.

The word *"Shahr"* (Month) here is generic and applies to all the Sacred Months which are Rajab, Dhū'l-Qa'da, Dhū'l-Ḥijja and Muḥarram.

and fighting in it.

The unbelievers will ask you in wonder at the violation of the sanctity of the month and the reason they asked was because of the fighting in it. Az-Zajjāj said they ask you about fighting in the month. Al-Qutaybī said, "They are asking whether it is permitted to fight in the sacred month."

Say, 'Fighting in it is a serious matter;

It was objectionable because the prohibition against fighting in the Sacred Month was still in place at that time.

but barring access to the Way of Allah and rejecting Him

This is a greater wrong action than fighting in the Sacred Month. Al-Mubarrad and others said that and it is sound since they prevented people from doing *ṭawāf* of the Ka'ba. The words *"kufrun bihi"* (rejecting Him) are generally taken to be referring to rejecting Allah though it is also said that they refer to the *ḥajj* and the Sacred Months.

and expelling its people from it are far more serious in the sight of Allah.

This means that these things merit a far greater punishment with Allah than fighting in the Sacred Month.

***Fitna* is worse than killing.**

Mujāhid and others said that *fitna* in this instance means disbelief so their disbelief is worse than our killing them. Most say that *fitna* here means their tempting the Muslims away from their *dīn* so that they would be destroyed. That is a worse crime than killing people in the Sacred Month.

They will not stop fighting you until they make you revert from your *dīn*,

This warns the believers of the nature of the evil of the unbelievers. Mujāhid said that it is the unbelievers of Quraysh who are meant.

As for any of you who revert from their *dīn* and die unbelievers, their actions will come to nothing in this world and the Next.

So if anyone apostasises and returns to disbelief their actions are nullified and useless. The root of the word for "come to nothing" is *ḥabaṭ*, which is a word denoting what happens to livestock when they eat too much herbage and their bellies swell. This sometimes causes them to die. This is a threat to the Muslims, warning them to stay firm in Islam.

Scholars disagree about whether or not apostates are asked to repent. One group say that they are asked to repent and, if they do not, they are killed. Some say they are given an hour and others a month. Others say that they are asked to repent three times, and that is the view of Mālik. Al-Ḥasan said they are asked a hundred times. It is also said that they are killed without being asked to repent.

There is also discussion about whether people's actions are considered to have been invalidated by apostasy or not if they later return to the *dīn*. Ash-Shāfi'ī says that an apostate who returns to Islam does not have his actions or *ḥajj* invalidated. His actions come to nothing if he dies in disbelief. Mālik says that they are invalidated by apostasy. There is disagreement about a Muslim's *ḥajj* when he apostatises and then returns to Islam. Mālik said that he must make *ḥajj* again because the first was cancelled by apostasy. Ash-Shāfi'ī says that he does not have to repeat it because the action remains.

Another question is whether apostates are inherited from and there is disagreement about that. 'Alī, al-Ḥasan, ash-Shāfi'ī, al-Ḥakam, al-Layth, Abū Ḥanīfa and Isḥāq ibn Rāhawayh said that their property reverts to their Muslim heirs. Mālik, Rabī'a, Ibn Abī Laylā, ash-Shāfi'ī and Abū Thawr said that their property goes to the treasury.

Those who believe and make *hijra*

Jundub ibn 'Abdullāh, 'Urwa ibn az-Zubayr and others said that when Wāqid ibn 'Abdullāh at-Tamīmī killed 'Amr ibn al-Ḥadramī in the sacred month, the Messenger of Allah, may Allah bless him and grant him peace, hesitated to take the *khums*, which was his rightful share of the booty, from 'Abdullāh ibn Jaḥsh and the captives. The Muslims rebuked 'Abdullāh ibn Jaḥsh and his companions until it became hard for them and then Allah revealed this *āyat* about the sacred month and relieved them and informed them that they had the reward of those who emigrated and fought.

To make *hijra* means to move from one place to another, and the aim is to leave one out of preference for the other. *Hajr* means separation, the opposite of connection. A *muhājir* is someone who emigrates from one land to another, leaving the first for the second. *Tahājur* is mutual severance. Some say that *muhājara* is to move from the desert to the city. This is weak because that was normal among the Arabs and also because the people of Makka would, in that case, not be *Muhājirūn*.

and do *jihād* in the Way of Allah can expect Allah's mercy.

Doing *jihād* involves the expenditure of both effort and money. *Jahād* means "hard land". The word "expect" implies hope and also trying to bring near. It is said that this is praise of them because no one in this world knows if he will go to the Garden, no matter how many good works he does. There are two reasons for this. The first is that he does not know what his seal will be and the second is that he should not rely on his actions. Hope delights and hope is always accompanied by fear and fear is always accompanied by hope. Hope derives from a desire for a good outcome.

يَسْـَٔلُونَكَ عَنِ ٱلْخَمْرِ وَٱلْمَيْسِرِ ۖ قُلْ فِيهِمَآ إِثْمٌ كَبِيرٌ وَمَنَٰفِعُ
لِلنَّاسِ وَإِثْمُهُمَآ أَكْبَرُ مِن نَّفْعِهِمَا ۗ وَيَسْـَٔلُونَكَ مَاذَا
يُنفِقُونَ قُلِ ٱلْعَفْوَ ۗ كَذَٰلِكَ يُبَيِّنُ ٱللَّهُ لَكُمُ ٱلْءَايَٰتِ لَعَلَّكُمْ
تَتَفَكَّرُونَ ﴿٢١٩﴾

219 ***They will ask you***
about alcoholic drinks and gambling.
Say, 'There is great wrong in both of them
and also certain benefits for mankind.
But the wrong in them is greater than the benefit.'
They will ask you what they should give away.
Say, 'Whatever is surplus to your needs.'
In this way Allah makes the Signs clear to you,
so that hopefully you will reflect.

They will ask you about alcoholic drinks and gambling

Those who ask are the believers. The word for "alcoholic drinks" (*khamr*) comes from *khamara*, to cover, and the *khimār* (veil) of a woman comes from the same root. The verb is used for anything that covers something, as in the expression, "Cover your vessels." So wine covers the intellect and obscures it. *Khamar* is also used for a covert of trees because it conceals what is under it, so that wolves and other animals are able to conceal themselves there. It is also used for hiding oneself in a crowd when a person is in a situation which causes him to feel alarm. The verb is used for withholding an opinion until the matter involved becomes clear. It is said that wine is called *khamr* because it muddles the intellect. The meanings are close together, but the true linguistic root means covering.

The word *khamr* is generally used for the juice of grapes which has become fermented. However any other substance which intoxicates the mind carries the same ruling, just as there is a consensus among scholars that all types of gambling are *ḥarām* even though only *maysir* is mentioned here. All other kinds of types of gambling follow the same ruling by analogy. *Maysir* is, in fact, the act of drawing arrows to determine the distribution of meat. By the same process every alcoholic drink that intoxicates like wine falls under the same ruling.

The majority of the Community believe that when a lot of something intoxicates, then drinking either a little or a lot of it is *ḥarām* and the *ḥadd* punishment is obliged for doing it. Abū Ḥanīfa, ath-Thawrī, Ibn Abī Laylā, Ibn Shubruma and a group of scholars of Kufa say that when a lot of something, other than actual wine made from grapes, intoxicates, it is lawful and if someone becomes intoxicated by it without intending to then the *ḥadd* punishment is not applicable. This is weak and refuted both by logic and by reports as will come in the commentary about it in *Sūrat al-Mā'ida* and *Sūrat an-Naḥl*, Allah willing.

Some commentators say that there is no honour or kindness which Allah failed to bestow on this Community. Part of His generosity and kindness was that He did not impose laws on them all at once, but little by little. This was the case with the prohibition of wine. This is the first *āyat* revealed about it, and then after it comes 4:43, then 5:91 and finally 5:90 as will be explained in those places, Allah willing.

The "gambling" (*maysir*) referred to here, as mentioned above, is a particular type of gambling which the Arabs did with arrows. Ibn 'Abbās said, "In the *Jāhiliyya*, a man would stake his wealth and family with another man and then this *āyat* was revealed." Mujāhid, Ibn Sīrīn, al-Ḥasan, Ibn al-Musayyab, 'Aṭā', Mu'āwiya ibn Ṣāliḥ, Ṭāwūs, 'Alī and Ibn 'Abbās say that everything in which there is an element of gambling, such as backgammon and chess, is considered to be *maysir*, even children playing with walnuts and dice. An exception is made in the case of permitted wagers in respect of horses and drawing lots to sort out rights. Mālik said that there are two types of *maysir*: one constitutes simple amusement and the other is gambling. The kind which constitutes amusement includes chess, backgammon and other games. Gambling is when people bet against one another. 'Alī said that chess is the *maysir* of the non-Arabs. This will be further clarified in *Sūrat Yūnus*.

The word *maysir* is derived from *yasar*, which is when something is imposed on a person. *Yāsir* is the person who casts the divining arrows. Al-Azharī said that *maysir* is the slaughtered camel for which they are betting. It is called *maysir* because it is divided into parts and the *yāsir* is the slaughterer because he divides the meat into portions. He said that this is the original root of *yāsir* and then it was used for those who cast arrows and gamble for animals.

Mālik related in the *Muwaṭṭā'* that Sa'īd ibn al-Musayyab said, "One form of the gambling of the people of *Jāhiliyya* was bartering live animals for slaughtered meat, for instance, one live sheep for two slaughtered sheep." This is applied by Mālik and most of his people to the same category, i.e. selling an animal in exchange for meat of the same type. He considered it part of *muzābana*, chance and gambling because it is not known whether the live animal will have the same amount of meat or not. It is not permitted to sell meat for meat when there is a disparity, and selling a live animal for meat is like selling meat for other meat which is still in its skin.

Say, 'There is great wrong in both of them

The wrong in wine is the evil which issues from the drinker: quarrelling, cursing, foul language, lies, loss of the intellect and, therefore, of the obligations owed to the Creator, the invalidation of the prayer, turning from remembering Allah and other such things. In an-Nasā'ī, 'Uthmān is reported as saying, "Avoid wine. It is the mother of all foul things." And he said, "Allah does not combine faith and inveterate drinking without one being on the point of expelling the other."

It is related that when al-A'shā went to Madina to become Muslim, some idolaters met him on the road and asked him, "Where are you going?" He said that he was going to Muḥammad, may Allah bless him and grant him peace. They said, "Do not go to him. He will command you to pray." He replied, "It is obligatory to worship the Lord" They said, "He will command you to give wealth to the poor." He answered, "Giving charity is also obligatory." He was told, "He forbids fornication." He replied, "It is foul and ugly and, in any case, I have become old and have no need of it." He was then told, "He forbids drinking wine." He said, "This is something I cannot endure!" So he went back. He said, "I will drink wine for a year and then go back to him." Before reaching his house, he fell from his camel, broke his neck and died.

'Umar flogged Abu Miḥjan several times for drinking and exiled him to an island in the sea. Sa'd met him and 'Umar wrote, telling him to imprison him and he did so. He was a bold and brave warrior. Sa'd released his chains in the Battle of al-Qādisiyya and said, "We will never flog you again for drinking wine." Abū Miḥjan said, "And I, by Allah, will never drink again!" and he never drank after that. One version adds, "I used to drink and then the *ḥadd* would be imposed on me and so I would be purified of it. Since you have granted me immunity, by Allah, I will never drink again!"

Someone who drinks becomes a laughing-stock for those who are sober. He may play with his urine and filth and may wipe his face with his urine. Gambling brings about enmity and hatred because it is consuming someone's property falsely.

and also certain benefits for mankind.

Wine has the benefit of producing profitable trade. They used to bring it from Syria for a cheap price and sell it in the Ḥijaz for a profit. They could not store it and the wine sold for a high price. This is the soundest of what is related about its benefit. It is said that it helps to digest food, strengthens the weak, increases sexual energy, makes the miser generous, the coward brave, brightens colour and gives other kinds of pleasure.

The benefit of gambling is that a man obtains something without toil or work. They used to buy the camel carcass and divide it into shares. Whoever had a share drawn took his share of the meat without paying anything, whereas the others would pay the full price and not get any of the meat.

But the wrong in them is greater than the benefit.'

Allah tells us that the wrong is greater than the benefit and will incur harm in the Next World and so the great wrong action is after the prohibition and the benefits before it.

Some people say that this *āyat* prohibits wine because of the use of the word "wrong" (*ithm*) in it. This is not correct, because Allah does not call wine "wrong" in itself in this *āyat*. He says that there is wrong in these two things. The other *āyat*s which will be mentioned prohibit it.

They will ask you what they should give away. Say, 'Whatever is surplus to your needs.'

Scholars say that since the first question mentioned previously in *āyat* 215 above is a question of who to spend on, as we made clear, the answer is appropriate to the question. The second question here is about the amount to give, and it is still connected with the question asked by 'Amr ibn al-Jamūḥ. He asked, "How much?" and was told, "Your surplus," (*'afw*), which means what is easy, feasible and superfluous and is not hard to give." It means spend what is surplus to your needs so that you will not harm yourselves by it and thus become needy. This is the most fitting of what is said regarding the interpretation of this phrase, and it is what al-Ḥasan, Qatāda, 'Aṭā', as-Suddī, al-Quraẓī, Ibn Abī Laylā and others said. They said "surplus to poverty", and Ibn 'Abbās said the same. Mujāhid said, "Giving *ṣadaqa* when you are wealthy." The Prophet, may Allah bless him and grant him peace, said, "The best *ṣadaqa* is what you give when you are wealthy."

Qays ibn Sa'd said, "This means obligatory *zakāt*." But the majority of scholars said that it refers to voluntary spending. It is said that it is abrogated. Al-Kalbī said, "After the revelation of this *āyat*, when a man had gold, silver, crops or animals, he would work out what would satisfy him and his dependants for a year and keep that and give the rest as *ṣadaqa*. If he was someone who earned his living from manual work, he kept what was adequate for the day and gave the rest away. This was the case until the *āyat* of obligatory *zakāt* was revealed and this was abrogated." Some people say that this *āyat* is one of judgement and that there is a right on property over and above *zakāt*. The first position is the most evident.

In this way Allah makes the Signs clear to you,

By the command to spend.

so that hopefully you will reflect.

and work out how much of your property is needed for you in the life of this world and spend the rest on what will benefit you in the Next World.

فِي الدُّنْيَا وَالْآخِرَةِ ۗ وَيَسْأَلُونَكَ عَنِ الْيَتَامَىٰ ۖ قُلْ إِصْلَاحٌ لَّهُمْ خَيْرٌ ۖ
وَإِن تُخَالِطُوهُمْ فَإِخْوَانُكُمْ ۚ وَاللَّهُ يَعْلَمُ الْمُفْسِدَ مِنَ الْمُصْلِحِ ۚ وَلَوْ شَاءَ
اللَّهُ لَأَعْنَتَكُمْ ۚ إِنَّ اللَّهَ عَزِيزٌ حَكِيمٌ ﴿٢٢٠﴾

220 ***on this world and the Next.***
They will ask you about the property of orphans.
Say, 'Managing it in their best interests is best.'

If you mix your property with theirs,
they are your brothers.
Allah knows a squanderer from a good manager.
If Allah had wanted,
He could have been hard on you.
Allah is Almighty, All-Wise.

They will ask you about the property of orphans.

Abū Dāwud and an-Nasā'ī related that Ibn 'Abbās said: "When Allah revealed, *'Do not go near the property of orphans except in a good way'* (6:152) and *'those who consume the property of orphans wrongfully'* (4:10), everyone who had an orphan in his care separated his food and drink from that of any orphans in their care and began to keep their food aside for them until they ate or it went bad. That was hard for people. They mentioned that to the Messenger of Allah, may Allah bless him and grant him peace, and then Allah revealed this. So they mixed their food and drink."

This *āyat* is connected to what came before it because the command to preserve the property of orphans is connected to the discussion about property. It is said that the asker was 'Abdullāh ibn Rawāḥa and it is said that it was the Arabs who thought it bad luck to touch the property of orphans in what they ate. When Allah gave permission for dealing with orphans with the intention of making things right for them, that indicated the permission to use the property of orphans. The executor deals with selling, division and other things since this *āyat* is general.

There are many *aḥādīth* about making use of an orphan's property in *mudāraba* and trade. The permission for a guardian to mix his property with that of the orphan is evidence that it is permitted to dispose of the orphan's property by buying and selling and other such things when that is beneficial. They disagree about using an orphan's money for a *qirāḍ*. Ashhab forbade it, based on analogy with the guardian being forbidden to buy or sell from them for himself. Someone else said that, if the guardian takes a share of the profit of the *qirāḍ*, then the *qirāḍ* is acceptable, it being comparable to the guardian selling something on behalf of an orphan, subject to investigation. Muḥammad ibn 'Abdu'l-Ḥakam said, "If the guardian of an orphan buys something on credit, that is questionable."

Ibn Kināna says that a guardian can spend on an orphan's wedding and perfume and things required for it and other matters which are in his best interests. That depends on the orphan's social standing as well as that of the person he marries and the extent of his wealth. The same applies to his circumcision. If he fears that he might fall under suspicion of misusing the orphan's wealth, he should tell the ruler what he wants to do. He can then command him according what is intended. It is, however, permitted for him to do that if he thinks that correct. The exchange of gifts to curry favour is not permitted nor is bad management of the orphan's wealth. The literal meaning of the *āyat* indicates that guardians should teach the orphans in their care about this world and the Next and pay for someone to teach them a craft. When an orphan is given something, the guardian can take it and use it in the orphan's best interests.

Say, 'Managing it in their best interests is best.'

No specifics are mentioned. Abū Ḥanīfa said, "Since welfare is good, it is permitted to arrange his marriage. Ash-Shāfi'ī does not think that marriage should be considered a best interest unless there is a real need for it and there is no real need before puberty. Ibn Ḥanbal permits marrying because it may be in someone's best interest.

If you mix your property with theirs, they are your brothers. Allah knows a squanderer from a good manager.

If it is said that the property of an orphan should be left alone because dealing with it might lead to suspicion, Allah here permits a certain level of mixing the orphan's property with that of his guardian, and enjoins the guardians to be true to their trusts in that, saying, "*Allah knows a squanderer from a good manager.*" It is not said about other risky matters which Allah has entrusted to people that they are a means to something unlawful and so must be forbidden. For instance, Allah has entrusted Muslim women with protecting their private parts, even though there are immense judgements that arise from sexual behaviour which are connected to lawfulness, unlawfulness and lineage, and even though it is possible that the women concerned may lie. When Ṭāwūs was asked about orphans, he would recite, *"Allah knows a squanderer from a good manager."* Ibn Sīrīn said that it is preferable concerning the property of orphans that their advisors meet and see what would be best for the orphans concerned.

This mixing of property is like mixing like with like, like dates with dates. Abū 'Ubayd said, "This mixing is when an orphan has money and it is difficult for his guardian to isolate his food. Thus he finds no alternative to mixing the orphan's property with that of his dependants, and so he takes what is adequate from the orphan's property by investigation and puts it with his family's maintenance. This may increase and decrease. This abrogating *āyat* brought the allowance to do this." Abū 'Ubayd also said, "I consider this to be the basis for what fellow travellers do in a journey. They distribute their provisions equally between them although they may vary in the amount of food they bring. Not everyone who eats a little food is happy about giving the surplus to his companion. Since there is leeway in the property of orphans, that applies even more to others."

The second phrase is a warning. Allah knows those who squander the property of orphans from those who look after it and will repay each of them.

If Allah had wanted, He could have been hard on you.

Ibn 'Abbās said, "If He had wanted to He could have made what you took of the property of orphans a crime." The expression "hard on you" means: "He could have destroyed you" according to az-Zajjāj and Abū 'Ubayda. Al-Qutaybī says that it means: "He could have constricted things for you and been harsh, but He only desired ease for you." It is said that it means that Allah could have obliged you to repay what you used when you mixed your property with theirs as was the case with those before you, but He made things easier for you.

"*'Anat*" (hardship) is a word used for the breaking of a bone when it has been previously broken and then mended. It is used for an animal which rebreaks a bone so that it cannot walk. *'Anūt* is used for a mountain which is hard to climb. Ibn al-Anbārī says that the root of the word means to make something hard and difficult, to force someone to do something which is difficult to perform and the meaning is extended to the sense of destruction.

Allah is Almighty, All-Wise.

There is nothing impossible for Him. He is "Wise" in disposing of His kingdom as He wishes and nothing can stop Him doing so.

وَلَا تَنكِحُوا۟ اُ۬لْمُشْرِكَٰتِ حَتَّىٰ يُومِنَّ وَلَأَمَةٌ مُّومِنَةٌ خَيْرٌ
مِّن مُّشْرِكَةٍ وَلَوَ اَعْجَبَتْكُمْ وَلَا تُنكِحُوا۟ اُ۬لْمُشْرِكِينَ
حَتَّىٰ يُومِنُوا۟ وَلَعَبْدٌ مُّومِنٌ خَيْرٌ مِّن مُّشْرِكٍ وَلَوَ اَعْجَبَكُمْ
أُو۟لَٰٓئِكَ يَدْعُونَ إِلَى اَ۬لنَّارِ وَاللَّهُ يَدْعُوٓا۟ إِلَى اَ۬لْجَنَّةِ وَالْمَغْفِرَةِ
بِإِذْنِهِۦ وَيُبَيِّنُ ءَايَٰتِهِۦ لِلنَّاسِ لَعَلَّهُمْ يَتَذَكَّرُونَ ﴿٢٢١﴾

221 ***Do not marry women of the idolaters***
until they believe.
A slavegirl who is one of the believers is better
for you than a woman of the idolaters,
even though she may attract you.
And do not give [your women] in marriage
to men of the idolaters until they believe.
A slave who is one of the believers is better for you
than a man of the idolaters,
even though he may attract you.

Such people call you to the Fire
whereas Allah calls you, with His permission,
to the Garden and forgiveness.
He makes His Signs clear to people
so that hopefully they will pay heed.

Do not marry women of the idolaters until they believe.

The root of the word used for "marry" here – *nakaḥa* – means to have sexual intercourse and it is used metaphorically to mean marriage.

After Allah has given permission for using an orphan's property in a beneficial manner and for arranging their marriage, He makes it clear that marriage with the idolaters is not permitted. Muqātil said, "This *āyat* was revealed about Abū Mirthad al-Ghanawī or Kannāz ibn Ḥuṣayn. The Messenger of Allah sent him secretly to Makka to bring out one of his Companions. There was a woman in Makka called 'Anāq whom he had loved in the time of *Jāhiliyya.* She came to him and he told her, 'Islam forbids what used to happen in the time of *Jāhiliyya.*' 'So marry me,' she said. He replied, 'Not until I ask permission from the Prophet, may Allah bless him and grant him peace.' He asked for permission and he forbade him to marry her because he was a Muslim and she was an idolater."

Scholars disagree about the interpretation of this *āyat*. One group says that Allah forbade marrying all women idolaters in *Sūrat al-Baqara*, including women of the Book (Jews and Christians), and then allowed marriage with them in *Sūrat al-Mā'ida.* This position is related from Ibn 'Abbās and was related by Mālik ibn Anas, Sufyān ath-Thawrī and al-Awzā'ī. Qatāda and Sa'īd ibn Jubayr said that the *āyat* is general to every woman unbeliever and there is a special case for women of the Book, which is explained in *Sūrat al-Mā'ida,* and so the general statement never included women of the Book. This is the position of ash-Shāfi'ī. The first position is that of Mālik; and Ibn Ḥabīb mentioned it and said, "Marrying a Jewish or Christian woman, even though it is allowed by Allah Almighty, is disliked and blameworthy."

Isḥāq ibn Ibrāhīm al-Ḥarbī said: "Some people say that the *āyat* in *Sūrat al-Baqara* is the abrogating one and the one in *Sūrat al-Mā'ida* is abrogated, and so they forbid any woman idolater, whether she is of the Book or not." An-Naḥḥās observes that the prohibition against marrying Christian or Jewish women is outside the position of the majority because some of the Companions and *Tābi'ūn* married women of the Book, including, among the Companions, 'Uthmān, Ṭalḥa, Ibn 'Abbās, Jābir and Ḥudhayfa, and among the *Tābi'ūn*, Sa'īd ibn al-Musayyab, Sa'īd ibn Jubayr, al-Ḥasan, Mujāhid, Ṭāwūs, 'Ikrima, ash-Sha'bī, and aḍ-Ḍaḥḥāk. It is also impossible for this *āyat* to abrogate the one in *Sūrat al-Mā'ida* because *Sūrat al-Baqara* was one of the first *sūra*s to be revealed in Madina and *Sūrat al-Mā'ida* was one of the last, and the later clearly abrogates the earlier. In any case, there is no dispute that a Muslim is better than an unbeliever. This is clear.

It is not lawful to marry the people of the Book when they are people who are fighting the Muslims and Mālik disliked marrying such women because of leaving children in the *Dār al-Ḥarb* and because of their consumption of wine and pork.

A slavegirl who is one of the believers is better for you than a woman of the idolaters, even though she may attract you.

She may attract you by her lineage, wealth or beauty. This is what aṭ-Ṭabarī and others said. It was revealed about Khansā', a black girl who belonged to Ḥudhayfa ibn al-Yamān. Ḥudhayfa said, to her, "Khansā', you were mentioned in the Highest Assembly in spite of the fact that you are black and ugly. Allah mentioned you in His Book." So Ḥudhayfa freed her and married her.

As-Suddī said that it was revealed about 'Abdullāh ibn Rawāḥa. He had a black slavegirl whom he slapped in anger and then regretted doing so. He went to the Prophet, may Allah bless him and grant him peace, and told him and the Prophet asked, "What kind of girl is she, 'Abdullāh?" He replied, "She fasts, prays, does *wuḍū'* well, and testifies to the *shahāda*." The

Messenger of Allah, may Allah bless him and grant him peace, said, "She is a believer." Ibn Rawāḥa said, "I will free her and marry her." He did so and he was attacked by some of the Muslims who said, "He has married a slavegirl!" They thought that they could marry idolatrous women out of the desire for their lineage, and so this *āyat* was revealed. Allah knows best.

Scholars disagree about the permissiblity of marrying Christian or Jewish slavegirls and also about the permissiblity of marrying Magian women. Mālik, ash-Shāfi'ī, Abū Ḥanīfa, al-Awzā'ī and Isḥāq forbid it. Ibn Ḥanbal says, "I do not like it."

And do not give [your women] in marriage to men of the idolaters until they believe. A slave who is one of the believers is better for you than a man of the idolaters, even though he may attract you.

A Muslim woman may not marry an idolatrous man. The Community agree that an idolater may not marry a believing woman in any case.

This *āyat* provides textual evidence of the fact that marriage is only possible with a *walī*. Muḥammad ibn 'Alī said, "That marriage with a *walī* is found in the Book," and he recited this *āyat*. Ibn al-Mundhir said, "It is confirmed that the Messenger of Allah said, 'There is no marriage except by a *walī*,' and most scholars transmit this." This is the position of Mālik and others. Other *āyat*s in the Qur'ān indicate this as well, like *"do not prevent them from marrying their first husbands."* (2:232) and *"Marry off those among you who are unmarried..."* (24:32) Both the Book and the *Sunna* confirm that there is no marriage without a *walī*.

Having witnesses to the marriage is not one of the pillars of marriage in the view of Mālik and his people. It is enough that it be made known and announced and not be kept secret. As for keeping a marriage secret, Ibn al-Qāsim reports that Mālik stated, "If someone marries with witnesses and then orders them to keep that secret, the marriage is not allowed because it is a secret marriage." Abū Ḥanīfa and ash-Shāfi'ī say that it is permitted if there were two witnesses. Ash-Shāfi'ī says that any marriage without two or more male witnesses is invalid. This is based on the *ḥadīth* transmitted by Ibn 'Abbās: "There is no marriage without two witnesses and a sensible *walī*."

Such people call you to the Fire

meaning the men and women who are idolaters. They call you to actions which make the Fire inevitable. Keeping their company and being intimate with them means that you yourself are bound to participate in many of their deviances quite apart from what they will teach your children.

وَيَسْـَٔلُونَكَ عَنِ ٱلْمَحِيضِ ۖ قُلْ هُوَ أَذًى فَٱعْتَزِلُوا۟ ٱلنِّسَآءَ فِى
ٱلْمَحِيضِ ۖ وَلَا تَقْرَبُوهُنَّ حَتَّىٰ يَطْهُرْنَ ۖ فَإِذَا تَطَهَّرْنَ فَأْتُوهُنَّ
مِنْ حَيْثُ أَمَرَكُمُ ٱللَّهُ ۚ إِنَّ ٱللَّهَ يُحِبُّ ٱلتَّوَّٰبِينَ وَيُحِبُّ
ٱلْمُتَطَهِّرِينَ ﴿٢٢٢﴾

222 ***They will ask you about menstruation.***
Say, 'It is an impurity,
so keep apart from women during menstruation
and do not approach them
until they have purified themselves.
But once they have purified themselves,
then go to them in the way
that Allah has enjoined on you.'
Allah loves those who turn back from wrongdoing
and He loves those who purify themselves.

They will ask you about menstruation.

Aṭ-Ṭabarī mentioned from as-Suddī that the askers referred to in this *āyat* were Thābit ibn ad-Daḥdāḥ or Usayd ibn Ḥuḍayr and 'Abbād ibn Bishr, which is the position of the majority. The reason for the question, according to Qatāda and others, was that the Arabs in Madina and around it had adopted the custom of the Jews with respect to avoiding menstruating women and this was revealed. Mujāhid said, "They used to avoid normal intercourse with women when they were menstruating and they would have anal intercourse with them during their period of menstruation and then this was revealed."

We find in the *Ṣaḥīḥ* Muslim that Anas said, "When Jewish women menstruated, the Jews would not eat with them or go to them in their rooms. The Companions asked the Prophet about this and Allah revealed, *'They will ask you about menstruation.'*" The Messenger of Allah, may Allah bless him and grant him peace, said, "Do everything short of intercourse." The Jews heard this and they said, "This man will not leave any practice we do without opposing us in it!" Usayd and 'Abbād told the Prophet, may Allah bless him and grant him peace, what they were saying and asked, "Messenger of Allah, the Jews say such-and-such. Should we not have sex with women?" They said, "The face of the Messenger of Allah, may Allah bless him and grant him peace, changed colour until we thought that he was angry with them. They left. The Messenger of Allah had been given a gift of buttermilk and so he sent for those two men and gave them it to drink. So they knew that he was not angry with them." Our scholars say that Jews and Magians shunned menstruating women while the Christians did not avoid them at all, and this was a middle way.

The root of the word for menstruation (*maḥīḍ*) means to flow and overflow. It is used for a torrent which overflows or a tree whose sap or gum flows out. *Ḥawḍ* which means a basin or reservoir is from the same root because water flows into it. Scholars agree that menstruating women do not pray or fast and that they must make up days of fasting missed but not missed prayers.

Say, 'It is an impurity,

It is something by which women and others are bothered, referring to the smell of menstrual blood. The word "*adhā*" (impurity) alludes to impurity in general and is also applied to disliked words.

This *āyat* is used as evidence by those who forbid sexual intercourse with a woman experiencing *"istiḥāḍa"* (false menstruation) when blood is flowing since all blood is impurity and must be washed from the clothes and body. All such blood, whether menstrual or resulting from *istiḥāḍa* is still an impurity. Permission to pray is an allowance brought by the *Sunna* just as someone with incontinence can also pray. This is the position of Ibrāhīm an-Nakhā'ī, Sulaymān ibn Yasār, al-Ḥakam ibn 'Uyayna, 'Āmir ash-Sha'bī, Ibn Sīrīn and az-Zuhrī. 'Ā'isha also said that a woman's husband should not come to her at that time.

The majority of scholars, however, say that a woman experiencing *istiḥāḍa* can pray, fast, do *ṭawāf* and recite Qur'ān. Her husband can come to her as well. Mālik said, "The position of the people of *fiqh* and knowledge is this, even if the bleeding is considerable." Aḥmad said, "I prefer that a husband should not have intercourse with such a woman unless her condition persists for a long time."

so keep apart from women during menstruation

This can either mean "during" the time of menstruation or it may refer to the place of menstruation itself in which case it would merely mean avoiding the actual act of sexual intercourse. Scholars disagree about other kinds of sexual contact with a menstruating woman and what is permitted in that respect. Ibn 'Abbās and 'Abīda as-Salmānī said that a man must leave his wife's bed. This is an aberrant position, outside the position of most scholars. Even if the general words of the *āyat* may suggest that, the *Sunna* is contrary to it. Ibn 'Abbās' aunt, Maymūna went to him and said, "Do you turn from the *Sunna* of the Messenger of Allah, may Allah bless him and grant him peace!"

Mālik, ash-Shāfi'ī, al-Awzā'ī, Abū Ḥanīfa, Abū Yūsuf and the vast majority of scholars say that a man can enjoy everything above the waist-wrapper because that is what the Prophet said about this matter in a number of *aḥādīth*. Ath-Thawrī, ash-Shaybānī and some Shāfi'īs say that he should avoid the actual site of the blood, since the Prophet said, "Do everything except sexual intercourse," and there is another report from 'Ā'isha in which she says, "Everything except the genitals." Scholars say that the reason a woman wears a waist wrapper is to cut off the means because a man might otherwise exceed what is allowed.

They disagree about what someone who does have sexual intercourse with his wife while she is menstruating should do. Mālik, ash-Shāfi'ī and Abū Ḥanīfa say that he should ask for Allah's forgiveness and owes nothing. That is the position of Rabī'a and Yaḥyā ibn Sa'īd. Ash-Shaybānī says that he should give half a dinar as *ṣadaqa*. Ibn Ḥanbal quotes a *ḥadīth* of the Prophet, peace be upon him, in which he commanded the giving of a dinar or half a dinar as *ṣadaqa*. Aṭ-Ṭabarī recommended that, but if someone does not do it, he owes nothing.

and do not approach them until they have purified themselves.

This means until they have performed *ghusl* by the consensus of all. It is *ḥarām* for a man to go near his wife after the blood stops until she has purified herself. The disagreement is about the type of purification required. Some say it is *ghusl*, some say it is *wuḍū'* and some say it is merely washing the genitals.

But once they have purified themselves,

This is generally understood to refer to a full *ghusl* with water. That is the position of Mālik and most scholars. They say that the purification by which intercourse with a menstruating woman becomes lawful is by washing the whole body with water like you do for *janāba*. Neither *tayammum* nor anything else is adequate. That is the position of Mālik, ash-Shāfi'ī, aṭ-Ṭabarī, Muḥammad ibn Maslama, the people of Madina and others. Yaḥyā ibn Bukayr and Muḥammad ibn Ka'b al-Qurtubī said, "When the period of a menstruating woman has completely finished and she does *tayammum* in a situation when there is no water, she is lawful for her husband without doing *ghusl*. Abū Ḥanīfa, Abū Yūsuf and ash-Shaybānī said that when the blood has stopped for ten days, he can have intercourse with her before she does *ghusl*. If it is before that time, he is not permitted to do so unless she has a *ghusl*. The *ghusl* is the same type as is done for *janāba*.

Scholars disagree about whether a woman of the Book should be forced to have a *ghusl* or not. In the transmission of Ibn al-Qāsim, Mālik said that she is compelled to have one in order to make intercourse with her husband lawful. Ashhab, however, relates from Mālik that she is not compelled to do so because she does not believe in that. The instruction is addressed to believing women.

then go to them in the way that Allah has enjoined on you.'

Have sexual intercourse with them. It is a command which gives permission. "Go to" is a euphemism for sexual intercourse.

Allah loves those who turn back from wrongdoing and He loves those who purify themselves.

There is disagreement about what this means. It is said that it refers to those who turn back from wrong action and *shirk* and those who purify themselves with water from *janāba* and minor impurities. 'Aṭā' and others said that. Mujāhid said that it is turning back from wrong actions and also from anal intercourse with women. Ibn 'Aṭiyya said, "It appears he is thinking about the words about the people of Lūṭ in 7:82." It is said that those who purify themselves are those who have not committed wrong actions. Someone who repents is someone who does not despair of gaining Allah's mercy and is not arrogant.

نِسَآؤُكُمْ حَرْثٌ لَّكُمْ فَأْتُوا۟ حَرْثَكُمْ أَنَّىٰ
شِئْتُمْ ۖ وَقَدِّمُوا۟ لِأَنفُسِكُمْ ۚ وَاتَّقُوا۟ ٱللَّهَ وَٱعْلَمُوٓا۟
أَنَّكُم مُّلَٰقُوهُ ۗ وَبَشِّرِ ٱلْمُؤْمِنِينَ ﴿٢٢٣﴾

223 ***Your women are fertile fields for you,***
so come to your fertile fields however you like.
Send good ahead for yourselves
and be fearful of Allah.
Know that you are going to meet Him.
And give good news to the believers.

Your women are fertile fields for you.

It is related in Muslim from Jābir ibn 'Abdullāh, "The Jews used to say, 'If a man has intercourse with a woman from the rear, the child will be squint-eyed?'" Then this *āyat* was revealed. Al-Ḥumaydī says that the word refers to the vagina. The Anṣār had adopted the Jewish practice of sexual intercourse while the Quraysh did not confine themselves to any particular position. When the Muhājirūn came to Madina and one of them married an Anṣārī woman and started to do that, she disliked that. Then this was revealed, meaning "use whatever position you want".

The *āyat* uses the word *"ḥarth"* (fields) and so this must apply to the vagina, because that entails fertility.

so come to your fertile fields however you like.

The majority of the Companions, the *Tābi'ūn* and the imāms qualified to give *fatwā* say that it means whatever direction, front or back. The word for "however" (*annā*) has various meanings in Arabic: however, whenever, and wherever. "However" refers to the manner of joining. One group who say it means "wherever" say that it is permitted to penetrate the anus and various Mālikī scholars say that, while the astute Mālikīs say that that position is not correct.

When Mālik was informed that some people in Egypt claimed that he allowed anal intercourse, he objected to that and rebuked the one who told him. "They have lied about me! They have lied about me! They have lied about me!" Then he asked, "Are they not an Arab people? Did not Allah say, *'come to your fertile fields'*? Is a fertile field other than a place capable of growth!"

There are also numerous *aḥādīth* which are excellent, sound and well-known, related from twelve Companions with different texts, all of which forbid anal intercourse with women. The Prophet referred to it as "the lesser sodomy".

Send good ahead for yourselves and be fearful of Allah.
Do what will be of benefit to you on the Last Day. Allah says elsewhere, "*Any good you send ahead for yourselves you will find with Allah.*" (2:110) So it means obedience and righteous actions. It is also said that it means seeking children and progeny since a child is good for this world and the Next. He may be an intercessor and protection for you. It is said it means marriage with a chaste woman so that the ensuing child will be pure and righteous.

Know that you are going to meet Him.
This is a far-reaching threat, because Allah will repay them both for their piety and for any wrong actions they commit.

وَلَا تَجْعَلُوا اللَّهَ عُرْضَةً لِأَيْمَانِكُمْ أَنْ تَبَرُّوا وَتَتَّقُوا
وَتُصْلِحُوا بَيْنَ النَّاسِ وَاللَّهُ سَمِيعٌ عَلِيمٌ ﴿٢٢٤﴾

224 ***Do not, by your oaths, make Allah a pretext***
to avoid good action and being fearful of Him
and putting things right between people.
Allah is All-Hearing, All-Knowing.

Do not, by your oaths, make Allah a pretext
Scholars say that Allah commands spending and behaving well towards orphans and women and, as a corollary, He is saying, "Do not reject anything of noble character, using as an excuse, 'I took an oath that I would not do such-and-such a thing.'" That is what Ibn 'Abbās, an-Nakhā'ī, Mujāhid, ar-Rabī' and others said the *āyat* means. Sa'īd ibn Jubayr said, "It is about a man refusing to be pious, or to maintain contact with his kin, or to put things right

between people, all of which constitute goodness, saying that he took an oath not to." Some commentators say that it means "Do not swear falsely by Allah if you truly desire good and that things be put right." It is said that it simply means to make an excessive number of oaths by Allah because such oaths are more likely to convince and move people.

The word "*'urḍa*" (pretext) means a target, intention, obstacle, or something which strengthens and supports something, in this case, the oath.

to avoid good action and being fearful of Him

Doing this means that you have little real piety and fear of Allah because if there is a lot of oath-taking, it means there will be a lot of breaking of oaths and little concern for Allah. This is an excellent interpretation. Mālik ibn Anas said, "I heard that people make oaths about everything." It is said that this means do not use an oath about everything, true or false.

It is said that it was revealed about when Abū Bakr made an oath not to give any more money to Misṭaḥ, his kinsman who was poor, when he gossiped about 'Ā'isha as we shall read in the story of the Lie which will be discussed in *Sūrat an-Nūr* (24). It is said that it was revealed about Abū Bakr when he swore not to eat with guests. It is said that it was revealed about 'Abdullāh ibn Rawāḥa when he swore not to speak to Bashīr ibn an-Nu'mān. Allah knows best.

No oath you make should ever prevent you from doing good and being godfearing and putting things right.

لَا يُؤَاخِذُكُمُ اللَّهُ بِاللَّغْوِ فِي أَيْمَانِكُمْ وَلَٰكِن
يُؤَاخِذُكُم بِمَا كَسَبَتْ قُلُوبُكُمْ ۗ وَاللَّهُ
غَفُورٌ حَلِيمٌ ﴿٢٢٥﴾

225 ***Allah will not take you to task for***
careless statements in your oaths,
but He will take you to task for
the intention your hearts have made.
Allah is Ever-Forgiving, All-Forbearing.

Allah will not take you to task for careless statements in your oaths,

The expression "*laghw*" (careless statements) means making use of unnecessary words or things which are not good or which do not involve wrongdoing. It is used in a *ḥadith* to describe someone else speaking while the imām is speaking on the minbar.

Scholars disagree about exactly what is meant by a careless oath. Ibn 'Abbās said that it refers to those that people make while speaking or arguing when they say, "No, by Allah" and "Yes, by Allah" without really intending to make an oath. Al-Marwazī says: "The careless oath about which scholars agree are the careless words of a man, 'No, by Allah' and 'Yes, by Allah' when an actual oath is not intended." 'Ā'isha said, "A careless oath is one made when arguing or joking and words which the heart does not intend." It is said that a careless oath is one which is based on speculation and so the truth may turn out to be different. Mālik said that, as did a group of the *Salaf.* He stated in the *Muwaṭṭā',* "The best of what I have heard on the matter is that carelessness in oaths is when a man takes an oath on something which he feels certain is like he said, only to find that it is other than what he said." There is no *kaffāra* owed for it.

The word used for oath is *"yamīn",* which literally means "right hand, and the basis for that is that among the Arabs, when they made a contract or alliance, they would shake each other's right hands and so an oath became termed *yamīn.* It is said that it is because it contains blessing (*yumn*).

but He will take you to task for the intention your hearts have made.

Because then, of course, the oath ceases to be merely careless and becomes fully intentional.

لِّلذِينَ يُولُونَ مِن نِّسَآيِهِمْ تَرَبُّصُ أَرْبَعَةِ أَشْهُرٍ فَإِن
فَآءُو فَإِنَّ اَللَّهَ غَفُورٌ رَّحِيمٌ ﴿٢٢٦﴾ وَإِنْ عَزَمُوا الطَّلَٰقَ
فَإِنَّ اَللَّهَ سَمِيعٌ عَلِيمٌ ﴿٢٢٧﴾

226 ***Those who swear to abstain from***
sexual relations with their wives
can wait for a period of up to four months.
If they then retract their oath,
Allah is Ever-Forgiving, Most Merciful.

227 ***If they are determined to divorce,***
Allah is All-Hearing, All-Knowing.

Those who swear to abstain from sexual relations with their wives

This kind of oath is called *īla'* in Arabic. 'Abdullāh ibn 'Abbās said that the *īlā'* in the days of *Jāhiliyya* could be for one, two or even more years. Men intended by that to harm their wives and so a maximum time of four months was set for it. If someone vows less than that it is not considered an *īlā'*. It is said that the Prophet , may Allah bless him and grant him peace, pronounced an *īlā'* because his wives asked him for maintenance which he did not have, according to the *Ṣaḥīḥ* Collection of Muslim. It is said that it is because Zaynab returned his gift to him and he became angry and divorced his wives. This is what we find in Ibn Mājah.

Īlā' brings about the same legal conditions as a pronouncement of divorce, and a free person, slave or drunk person can invoke it, as can a simpleton. Scholars disagree about the kind of oath by which *īlā'* occurs. Some say it only occurs with an oath by Allah alone. Ash-Shāfi'ī said that in his new school.[1] Ibn 'Abbās says that any oath is sufficient for it. That is what is said by Mālik, the people of Ḥijāz, the people of Iraq and ash-Shāfi'ī in his first view.

If a man makes an oath not to have intercourse and says "*inshā'llāh*", it can still be an *īlā'*, but if he has intercourse with his wife, he owes no *kaffāra* in the transmission of Ibn al-Qāsim from Mālik. Ibn al-Mājishūn said in *al-Mabsūṭ* that in that case it is not an *īlā'*, and that is sounder because of the "*inshā'llāh*" which undoes the oath. That is the position of the people of all regions. If a man swears by the Prophet, the angels, or the Ka'ba not to have intercourse or says that he is a Jew or a Christian or fornicator if he does, this is not an *īlā'*. Mālik and others said that. If a man refuses to have intercourse with his wife without making an oath in order to harm her, he is ordered to have intercourse with her. If he refuses to do so, then they are divorced without a term being set.

The words *"their wives"* include free women, *dhimmī* women and slave girls when they are married, and slaves when they are husbands. The *āyat* is general to all. It includes all marriages whether they have been consummated or not, except if the wife is a girl who has not yet reached puberty. A *dhimmī* man cannot pronounce an *īlā'*, and since *dhimmīs* are not bound by the *Sharī'a*, they owe no *kaffāra*. They are sent to their own judges.

can wait for a period of up to four months.

The reason for this period of time, according to Ibn 'Abbās, has already been mentioned. It is said that this is the maximum which a woman can endure. Regarding the length of time, 'Umar once heard a woman reciting a poem complaining about her situation and sent for her the following day. He asked her where her husband was and she replied that he had sent him to Iraq. He summoned the women and asked them about the length of time a wife could endure being without her husband. "Two months," they replied. "Her patience becomes stretched after three months, and disappears after four." Therefore 'Umar made four months the

1. Ash-Shāfi'ī had two schools of *fiqh*: "the old school", based on the school of Madina, and the "new school", which he developed after moving to Cairo.

maximum length of time for a man to be absent on a military expedition. Then they would be replaced by another. Allah knows best, but this makes it clearer why four months is singled out here.

If they then retract their oath,

This means retract it or go back on it. Scholars agree that retraction consists in having sexual intercourse unless he has an excuse. If he has an excuse in the form of illness or imprisonment or the like, his simple statement of retraction is valid. If the excuse ends and he still refuses to have sexual intercourse, the couple are separated if the end of the time has been reached. Mālik says that in the *Mudawwana* and the *Mabsūṭ*. Mālik, ash-Shāfi'ī, Abū Ḥanīfa and his people, and most scholars say that a man must do *kaffāra* if he retracts his oath. Al-Ḥasan said that there is no *kaffāra*.

If they are determined to divorce,

Determination (*'azima*) means to conclude a contract on something and the root meaning of "*ṭalāq*" (divorce) is to release and let go. This is evidence that the wife is not divorced simply by the conclusion of the time. As Mālik says, "The divorce does not occur automatically after the time is up."

Allah is All-Hearing, All-Knowing.

Allah is referred to as "All-Hearing" meaning that the pronouncement is heard after the time. Abū Ḥanīfa said that "He hears" the *īlā'* and "knows" the resolve.

وَالْمُطَلَّقَاتُ يَتَرَبَّصْنَ بِأَنفُسِهِنَّ ثَلَاثَةَ قُرُوءٍ ۚ وَلَا يَحِلُّ
لَهُنَّ أَن يَكْتُمْنَ مَا خَلَقَ اللَّهُ فِي أَرْحَامِهِنَّ إِن كُنَّ يُؤْمِنَّ
بِاللَّهِ وَالْيَوْمِ الْآخِرِ ۚ وَبُعُولَتُهُنَّ أَحَقُّ بِرَدِّهِنَّ فِي ذَٰلِكَ
إِنْ أَرَادُوا إِصْلَاحًا ۚ وَلَهُنَّ مِثْلُ الَّذِي عَلَيْهِنَّ بِالْمَعْرُوفِ ۚ
وَلِلرِّجَالِ عَلَيْهِنَّ دَرَجَةٌ ۗ وَاللَّهُ عَزِيزٌ حَكِيمٌ ٢٢٨

228 *Divorced women should wait by themselves*
for three menstrual cycles;
and it is not lawful for them to conceal
what Allah has created in their wombs
if they believe in Allah and the Last Day.
Their husbands have the right
to take them back within that time,
if they desire to be reconciled.
Women possess rights
similar to those held over them
to be honoured with fairness;
but men have a degree above them.
Allah is Almighty, All-Wise.

Divorced women should wait by themselves for three menstrual cycles;

Allah follows the mention of *īlā'* by talking about women who have been divorced and clarifies the rulings applying to women after divorce has taken place. The husband can take his wife back within the waiting period (*'idda*) unless he has divorced her three times. This applies to consummated marriages. The purpose of the waiting period, in this instance, is to ascertain whether or not the woman is pregnant, whereas the waiting period at the time of bereavement is for worship. If the woman does not menstruate due to youth or age, then it is counted in months rather than menstrual cycles.

The waiting referred to here is a command rather than a suggestion. The term "menstrual cycles" (*qurū'*) can refer to the actual time of menstruation or to the period of purity between them. Scholars disagree about which of them is meant here. The people of Kūfa say that it is the time of menstruation which is meant, based on what 'Umar, 'Alī, Ibn Mas'ūd, Abū Mūsā, Mujāhid, Qatāda, aḍ-Ḍaḥḥāk, 'Ikrima and as-Suddī said, while the people of the Ḥijāz say that it is the period of purity which is meant, which is the position of 'Ā'isha, Ibn 'Umar, Zayd ibn Thābit, az-Zuhrī, Abān ibn 'Uthmān, and ash-Shāfi'ī. Those who consider it to be menstruation do so because the blood collects (*qara'a*) in the womb and those who consider it to be purity do so because the blood collects in the body.

and it is not lawful for them to conceal what Allah has created in their wombs

'Ikrima, az-Zuhrī, and an-Nakhā'ī, among others, said that this refers to the concealment of menstruation, whereas others, including 'Umar and Ibn 'Abbās and Mujāhid, said that it is the concealment of pregnancy which is meant and still others said that it is about both menstruation and pregnancy. This is because the length of the waiting period (*'idda*) depends on the statement of the women concerned and their word is accepted. The reason for prohibiting concealment is to prevent harming the husband and taking away his right. Qatāda also mentions that it was the custom in the time of *Jāhiliyya* for women to conceal their pregnancy so that the child could be ascribed to a new husband and that is the reason that the *āyat* was revealed.

Ibn al-Mundhir said, "All that I remember from scholars is that when a woman well within her waiting period says, 'I have had three periods and my waiting period is over,' her words are not believed or accepted." They disagree about the time when the woman's statement is accepted. Mālik says that what she says is accepted if the period of time is reasonable for someone like her. We find in the *Mudawanna*: "If she says she has had three periods in a single month and other women confirm it, she is believed." Other things are also said.

if they believe in Allah and the Last Day.

This is a strong threat to emphasise the prohibition against concealment and to encourage women to fulfil the trust placed in them by telling the truth about what is in their wombs. It makes concealment tantamount to not believing in Allah.

Their husbands have the right to take them back within that time, if they desire to be reconciled.

The word used for "husbands" here is the plural of the word *ba'l*. This word is used because of a husband's position with regard to his wife. We find in 37:125, *"Do you call on Baal?"* Baal means a lord or someone in a high position. The word *ba'l* can in fact be used for husband or wife.

The *"right to take them back"* can be exercised in two ways: one is during the waiting period and the other is after the waiting period has come to an end, because the *āyat* is not specific. If the waiting period has finished, the man has to propose a new marriage with a *walī* and witnesses. This is the consensus of the scholars.

Taking back is either by sexual intercourse or verbal declaration. If the man has not made his intention clear, the woman should refuse intercourse until he declares that he has taken her back according to Isḥāq since "actions are by intentions." If someone else marries her during the waiting period, the marriage is invalid.

The word "right" is used in the comparative form here, *"aḥaqq"* (lit. "more right") because there are two rights in any conflict and one has to be preferred. So the husband has the right during the waiting period to take his wife back, which is not the case when the waiting period has ended. The husband is recommended to take his wife back but that is provided that he puts things right between himself and her. If he just desires to harm her more and to prolong her waiting period, it is forbidden and the person does wrong.

Women possess rights similar to those held over them

Women have rights over men just as men have rights over women. This is why Ibn 'Abbās said, "I adorn myself for my wife as she adorns herself for me. I do not want to take from her all the rights she owes me for then I would be obliged to give her all her rights I owe her because the Almighty says, *'Women possess rights similar to those held over them to be honoured with fairness,'* i.e.

for their husbands to make themselves attractive as long as it does not involve something wrongful." He also said, "They are entitled to good company and intimate relations with their husbands and they must obey their husbands." It is said that their right is that their husbands should not cause them harm and in return they should not cause harm to their husbands. Aṭ-Ṭabarī said that. Ibn Zayd said, "Fear Allah in respect of them as they should fear Allah in respect of you." The meanings are close and the *āyat* is general to all marital rights.

Ibn 'Abbās said, "I adorn myself for my wife." Scholars say that a man's adornment is dependent on his state. Men do that according to what is seemly and appropriate. Sometimes adornment is proper at one time but not at another, and some adornment suits young men but not old men, and some suits old men but not young men. Do you not see that when old men and mature men trim their moustaches, it is seemly and adorns them, but when young men do that, it is ugly and unseemly because their beard is not yet full. If someone trims his moustache as soon as the hair appears on his face, it is silly. If his beard is full and he trims his moustache, that adorns him. It is related that the Prophet, may Allah bless him and grant him peace, said, "My Lord commanded me to leave my beard and trim my moustache." The same principle applies to dress.

This applies to all seeking of rights. A man acts according to what is seemly and appropriate with his wife in respect of adornment so that it delights her and makes her abstain from other men. The same is true of mature men: one type of adornment may be appropriate for some but not others. As for wearing perfume, using siwak and toothpicks, removing dirt, excess hair, washing and clipping the nails, that is clearly appropriate for everyone. Henna is for old men, and rings are adornment for all, young and old. That is the adornment of men, as will be made clear in *Sūrat an-Naḥl*. A husband must bear in mind the times when a wife needs a man to satisfy her so that she has no need to look elsewhere. If a man sees that he is unable to carry out his wife's right to sexual satisfaction from him, he should take medicines to increase his potency.

but men have a degree above them.

The root of the word "*daraja*" (degree) means "to roll up". A *daraja* is a step which one steps on to ascend. The extra degree of a man is on account of intelligence, power to spend and maintain, paying blood money, larger shares of inheritance, and *jihād*. Ḥumayd said that the degree referred to is the beard, but this is weak because it is not implied by the *āyat* nor does the *āyat* mean it. Ibn al-'Arabī said, "Bliss to the slave who refrains from what he does not know, especially when it concerns the Book of Allah!"

Furthermore woman is created from man, and so he is her root. He can prevent her going out without his permission and she may only fast with his permission and only make *ḥajj* with him. It is said that the degree is the bride-price as ash-Sha'bī said. It is said that it is the permission to discipline. Thus the degree entails preference. Ibn 'Abbās said, "The degree indicates encouragement for men to be good company and expansive to women in money and character, because the one preferred must make greater efforts." Ibn 'Aṭiyya said that this is an outstanding and excellent position. Al-Māwardī said that it is because he can initiate divorce but she cannot.

ٱلطَّلَٰقُ مَرَّتَانِ فَإِمْسَاكٌۢ بِمَعْرُوفٍ أَوْ تَسْرِيحٌۢ بِإِحْسَٰنٍ وَلَا يَحِلُّ
لَكُمْ أَن تَأْخُذُوا۟ مِمَّآ ءَاتَيْتُمُوهُنَّ شَيْـًٔا إِلَّآ أَن يَخَافَآ أَلَّا
يُقِيمَا حُدُودَ ٱللَّهِ فَإِنْ خِفْتُمْ أَلَّا يُقِيمَا حُدُودَ ٱللَّهِ فَلَا
جُنَاحَ عَلَيْهِمَا فِيمَا ٱفْتَدَتْ بِهِۦ تِلْكَ حُدُودُ ٱللَّهِ فَلَا
تَعْتَدُوهَا وَمَن يَتَعَدَّ حُدُودَ ٱللَّهِ فَأُو۟لَٰٓئِكَ هُمُ ٱلظَّٰلِمُونَ ٢٢٩

229 ***Divorce can be pronounced two times;***
in which case wives may be retained
with correctness and courtesy
or released with good will.

It is not lawful for you to keep
anything you have given them
unless a couple fear that they will not remain
within Allah's limits.
If you fear that they will not remain
within Allah's limits,
there is nothing wrong in the wife ransoming herself
with some of what she received.
These are Allah's limits so do not overstep them.
Those who overstep Allah's limits are wrongdoers.

Divorce can be pronounced two times;

It is confirmed that the people in the time of *Jāhiliyya* had no limit to the number of divorces they could pronounce although they did have a known waiting period (*'idda*). It was like that at the beginning of Islam: a man would divorce his wife as often as he wished. Then when she was almost free he would take her back. Then during the time of the Prophet a man said to his wife, "I will not house you nor will I let you go." "How can you do that?" she asked. He said, "I will divorce you and when your *'idda* is almost up, take you back." The woman complained about that to 'Ā'isha and she mentioned it to the Prophet and then Allah revealed this *āyat*, which clarifies the number of divorces a man can pronounce. This was said by 'Urwa ibn az-Zubayr, Qatāda, Ibn Zayd and others. Ibn Mas'ūd, Ibn 'Abbās, Mujāhid and others said that the *āyat* is simply meant to establish the *sunna* of divorce.

Divorce is accomplished by the removal of the contractual bond between a husband and wife by means of the pronouncement of certain words. It is permitted by this *āyat* and others and by the words of the Prophet in the *ḥadīth* of Ibn 'Umar, "If he wishes, he may keep her, and if he wishes, he may divorce her." The Prophet, may Allah bless him and grant him peace, divorced Ḥafsa and then took her back. (Ibn Mājah) Scholars agree that it is *sunna* to divorce when the woman concerned is free of menstruation.

Mu'ādh ibn Jabal said, "The Messenger of Allah, may Allah bless him and grant him peace, said, 'Mu'ādh, Allah has not created on the face of the earth anything dearer to Him than setting free a slave and Allah has not created anything on the face of the earth more hateful to Him than divorce."

in which case wives may be retained with correctness and courtesy or released with good will.

This means that you must do that or that it is obligatory for you to retain them correctly. The releasing referred to here either means to leave the woman until the waiting period of the second divorce has ended or to divorce her a third time and let her go. The latter is more likely for three reasons. One is a *ḥadīth* in ad-Dāraquṭnī, reported by a man who said, "Messenger of Allah, Allah says, 'Divorce is twice.' Why does it become three?" He replied, "Retaining with correctness or releasing with good will is the third." The second possibility is that the word "release" is one of the expressions used for divorce. The third is that it is allowed by the verbal form of "release" which is causative.

"Divorce can be pronounced two times" means that that is the maximum number after which there must be either retaining with correctness during the waiting period or releasing. Releasing means to leave her without returning to her until the end of the waiting period. That is being good to her if there is regret between them. Allah says, *"You never know, it may well be that after that Allah will cause a new situation to develop,"* (65:1), meaning regret about separation and the desire to return. The pronouncement of three in one go is not good because it is abandoning what is recommended in that which Allah has allowed.

The same verb is used in 33:49, *"Let them go."* So this is explicit divorce, according to ash-Shāfi'ī. The scholars disagree about the meaning of this and whether it is tantamount to divorce.

It is not lawful for you to keep anything you have given them

This is addressed to husbands. They are forbidden to take anything from their wives which might cause them harm. The *khul'* divorce is only valid when it is the man alone who has not done anything which would be grounds for divorce. Husbands are mentioned because the custom among people is that, in separation, a man seeks what he has given his wife as a dower and support.

The majority agree that taking a payment for divorce is allowed and they agree that it is forbidden to take anything belonging to the wife unless it is a case of disobedience and bad behaviour on her part. It is related that Ibn al-Mundhir said that an-Nu'mān said, "If the disobedience or injustice comes from him and she asks for a *khul'*, it is allowed and he is a wrongdoer. What he did is not lawful but he cannot be forced to return what he has taken." Ibn al-Mundhir says that this is contrary to the text of the Book of Allah and contrary to a firm report from the Prophet, and contrary to what scholars agree on, since the Book forbids something and he has no proof that it is permitted.

unless a couple fear that they will not remain within Allah's limits.

In this *āyat* Allah forbids a man to take anything unless there is fear that they will not establish the limits of Allah and he stresses the prohibition by a threat issued to the one who exceeds the limits. It means that each of them thinks that he will not be able to endure giving the obligatory rights to his or her companion due to the dislike she has for him or vice versa. This is not an objection to her ransoming herself, nor is there any objection to the husband taking what she pays. The *āyat* is addressed to the couple and the dual is used. "Fear" here implies knowledge, so the inference is that they know that they will not be able to remain within the limits, and that is true fear. It is apprehension that something disliked is bound to happen.

If you fear that they will not remain within Allah's limits,

The words "if you fear" here are taken as evidence of the need for taking the *khul'* divorce to the ruler. That is the position of Sa'īd ibn Jubayr, al-Ḥasan and Ibn Sīrīn. Shu'ba said, "I asked Qatāda, 'From whom did al-Ḥasan derive the fact that the *khul'* case should be taken to the ruler?' 'From Zayd,' he replied. He was the governor for 'Umar and 'Alī." But this position does not make sense because when a man gives a *khul'* to his wife, it is according to what they agree and the ruler cannot impose that. There is no sense in the position that it is up to the ruler to decide the matter. There is no doubt that 'Umar, 'Uthmān and Ibn 'Umar allowed *khul'* divorce to take place without the involvement of the ruler, as is the case with marriage and other kinds of divorce. That is the position of the majority of scholars.

The limits obliged for them are good company and affectionate fellowship. This directive is addressed to judges and mediators, even if the husband is not a judge. Not establishing the limits of Allah on the part of a wife is making light of the rights of her husband and not obeying him. Ibn 'Abbās, Mālik and most of the scholars said that. Al-Ḥasan and others say that it is when she says, "I will not obey you at all and I will not have a *ghusl* for *janāba* and will not observe any oaths you make," then *khul'* is lawful." Ash-Sha'bī says that it means that they will not obey Allah. That is because mutual anger leads to abandoning obedience. 'Aṭā' ibn Abī Rabāḥ said, "The *khul'* is lawful as is taking the property in cases where the woman tells her husband, by way of asking for her freedom, 'I hate you and do not love you,' and other such things."

there is nothing wrong in the wife ransoming herself

Al-Bukhārī reports a *ḥadīth* from Ibn 'Abbās that the wife of Thābit ibn Qays came to the Prophet, may Allah bless him and grant him peace, and said, "Messenger of Allah, I do not fault him in respect of the *dīn* or his character, but I will not obey him!" The Messenger of Allah, may Allah bless him and grant him peace, said, "Will you return his garden to him?" "Yes," she replied. In Ibn Mājah we read that Jamīla bint Salūl came to the Prophet and said, "By Allah, I do not fault Thābit in respect of his *dīn* or his character, but I dislike ingratitude in Islam and I will not obey him due to my hatred of him." The Prophet, peace be upon him, asked, "Will you return his garden to him?" "Yes," she replied, and he commanded him to take his garden from her and no more. She absolutely hated him while he was very much in love with her. The Messenger of Allah, may Allah bless him and grant him peace, separated them by means of the *khul'* divorce and it was the first *khul'* divorce in Islam.

Ibn 'Abbās is also reported as saying that the first person to have a *khul'* divorce in Islam was the sister of 'Abdullāh ibn Ubayy. She came to the Prophet, may Allah bless him and grant him peace, and said, "Messenger of Allah, my head and his head will never be joined. I lifted the side of the tent and saw him in a group and he was the ugliest and shortest of them and had the ugliest face." He asked, "Will you return his garden to him?" "Yes," she replied, "and if he wishes, I will give more." He separated them. This is the basis of the *khul'* divorce and it is accepted by the majority of *fuqahā'*. Mālik said, "That is what I have heard from those who possess knowledge, and it is what is done among us. If a man does not harm his wife and is not bad to her and she wants to leave him, it is lawful for him to take whatever she pays to ransom herself as the Prophet did with the wife of Thābit ibn Qays.

If the recalcitrance is on his side, as it is when he oppresses her and harms her, he should return to her anything he has taken from her. 'Uqba ibn Abi'ṣ-Ṣahbā' said, "I asked Bakr ibn 'Abdullāh al-Muzanī about a man who wanted his wife to pronounce a *khul'* divorce and he said, "It is not lawful for him to take anything from her." I asked, "So where are the words of Allah, '*If you fear that they will not remain within Allah's limits. there is nothing wrong in the wife ransoming herself.*' 'It was abrogated,' he replied. 'Where?' I asked. He said, 'In *Sūrat an-Nisā'*: "*If you desire to exchange one wife for another, and have given your original wife a large amount, do not take any of it. Would you take it by means of slander and downright crime?"* (4:20)'" An-Naḥḥās said, "This is an aberrant view outside of the general consensus. Neither of the two contradicts the other so that there is abrogation because 'If you fear…' does not cancel the other *āyat* because when they fear this, the husband does not fall into the category designated by the words *'If you desire to exchange…'* because the latter is addressed to men alone." Aṭ-Ṭabarī said, "This *āyat* is one of judgement and what Bakr said is nonsense."

Those who think that *khul'* is specific to the state of schism and harm use this *āyat*, and say that it is a precondition for *khul'*. They support this by what Abū Dāwūd related from 'Ā'isha to the effect that Ḥabība bint Sahl was married to Thābit ibn Qays and he hit her and broke her jaw. She went to the Messenger of Allah after the *Ṣubḥ* prayer and complained to him. The Prophet summoned Thābit and said, "Take some of her property and separate from her." He asked, "Is that proper, Messenger of Allah?" "Yes," he said. He said, "I gave her the two gardens she has as a dowry." The Prophet said, "Take them and separate from her." He took them and separated from her. The position of the majority is that *khul'* is permitted without any complaint of harm as we see in other *aḥādīth*.

The *āyat* also indicates the permission for taking more in a *khul'* divorce than what a husband gave to his wife. Scholars disagree about this. Mālik, ash-Shāfi'ī, Abū Ḥanīfa and his people and Abū Thawr say that it is permitted to do whatever they agree on, whether it is less or more. This is reported from 'Uthmān ibn 'Affān, Ibn 'Umar, Qabīṣa and an-Nakhā'ī. Mālik said, "Doing that is not part of noble character, but I have not seen any of the people of knowledge express dislike of it."

These are Allah's limits so do not overstep them.

When Allah has clarified the judgements of marriage and divorce, He says, *"These are Allah's limits"* which you are commanded to obey, just as He explains those matters which are prohibited during the fast in another *āyat* and says, *"Those are Allah's limits, so do not go near them."* (2:187) So He divided the limits into two categaries: limits which one is commanded to obey and limits which one is commanded to avoid. Then He ends with the threat, *"Those who overstep Allah's limits are wrongdoers."*

فَإِن طَلَّقَهَا فَلَا تَحِلُّ لَهُۥ مِنۢ بَعْدُ حَتَّىٰ تَنكِحَ زَوْجًا غَيْرَهُۥ ۗ فَإِن
طَلَّقَهَا فَلَا جُنَاحَ عَلَيْهِمَآ أَن يَتَرَاجَعَآ إِن ظَنَّآ أَن يُقِيمَا
حُدُودَ ٱللَّهِ ۗ وَتِلْكَ حُدُودُ ٱللَّهِ يُبَيِّنُهَا لِقَوْمٍ يَعْلَمُونَ ﴿٢٣٠﴾

230 ***But if a man divorces his wife a third time,***
she is not lawful for him after that
until she has married another husband.
Then if he divorces her, there is nothing wrong
in the original couple getting back together
provided they think
they will remain within Allah's limits.
These are Allah's limits
which he has made clear to people who know.

But if a man divorces his wife a third time,

Some of the Khorasani Ḥanafī shaykhs used this *āyat* as evidence that the *khul'* should be followed by normal divorce. They said, "Allah prescribed an explicit divorce after she has ransomed herself through *khul'* because the use of the particle *fā'* here is sequential."

Scholars disagree about the divorce after the *khul'* during the *'idda*. One group say that if a wife frees herself from her husband by *khul'* and then he divorces her again during the waiting period, the new divorce applies rather than the *khul'*. That was stated by Sa'īd ibn al-Musayyab, Shurayḥ, Ṭāwūs, an-Nakhā'ī, az-Zuhrī, al-Ḥakam, Ḥammād, ath-Thawrī and the People of Opinion. There is a second view and that is that the second divorce bears no legal weight and is not considered. Ibn 'Abbās, Ibn az-Zubayr, 'Ikrima, al-Ḥasan, Jābir ibn Zayd, ash-Shāfi'ī, Aḥmad, Isḥāq and Abū Thawr take this position. It is also the position of Mālik, although Mālik says, "If she ransoms herself from him on the condition that he gives her a triple divorce consecutively, when he pronounces the divorce, then the full divorce has taken place.

she is not lawful for him after that until she has married another husband.

This is agreed upon and there is no disagreement about it. But there is disagreement about exactly what constitutes an intervening marriage and what it is permitted to be. Sa'īd ibn al-Musayyab and those who agree with him said that the contract itself is enough. Al-Ḥasan said that there must be ejaculation and sexual intercourse. A group of scholars and *fuqahā'* agree that sexual intercourse is enough, and that consists of the meeting of the private parts in the manner which would necessitate the *ḥadd* and *ghusl*, would invalidate fasting and *ḥajj*, and would make the payment of a full dowry obligatory. Ibn al-'Arabī said, "I have not come across a question in *fiqh* more difficult than this one. That is because the basis of the legal position is contingent on what the judgement is connected to: the minimum to which it is possible to apply the term 'marriage' or the full meaning of the term 'marriage'. If we say the minimum, then we take the position of Sa'īd ibn al-Musayyab. If it is connected to the latter, then there must be ejaculation and penetration, as al-Ḥasan said."

An-Nasā'ī related that the Messenger of Allah, may Allah bless him and grant him peace, cursed those women who tattoo and are tattooed, those who add hairpieces and those to whose hair they are added, those who consume and pay usury and those who facilitate re-marriage and those for whom the facilitation is done." There are other similar *aḥādīth*. This is the position of the knowledgeable Companions of the Prophet, including 'Umar, 'Uthmān, Ibn 'Umar and others, and the position of the *fuqahā'* among the *Tābi'ūn*.

An invalid marriage does not permit a woman who has been divorced three times to remarry her first husband according to the majority position. Mālik, ath-Thawrī, ash-Shāfi'ī, al-Awzā'ī, the People of Opinion, Aḥmad, Isḥāq and Abū 'Ubayd said that she is only lawful for the first husband if she has entered into a valid intervening marriage. 'Umar strongly condemned this practice of false marriage and Ibn 'Umar said, "False marriage to legalise re-marriage (*taḥlīl*) is fornication and people who do it are fornicators, even if they remain together for twenty years."

Then if he divorces her, there is nothing wrong in the original couple getting back together

The word "he" here refers to the second husband. If he divorces the woman concerned there is nothing wrong if she and her first husband remarry. Ibn 'Abbās said that there is no disagreement on this. Ibn al-Mundhir said that scholars agree that when a free man divorces his wife three times, her waiting period ends and she marries another husband who is free and the marriage is consummated and then he divorces her and her waiting period for that divorce ends, then she can re-marry the first husband.

They disagree about what happens when a man divorces his wife once or twice and then she marries someone else and then later returns to her first husband. One group say that she only has the number of divorces which remain from the time she was previously married to the man, as was stated by the great Companions of the Messenger of Allah: 'Umar, 'Alī, Ubayy ibn Ka'b, 'Imrān ibn Ḥuṣayn and Abū Hurayra. That is also related from Zayd ibn Thābit, Mu'ādh ibn Jabal and 'Abdullāh ibn 'Amr. It is also the position of 'Abīda as-Sulmānī, Sa'īd ibn al-Musayyab, al-Ḥasan al-Baṣrī, Mālik, Sufyān ath-Thawrī, Ibn Abī Laylā, ash-Shāfi'ī, Aḥmad, Isḥāq, Abū 'Ubayd, Abū Thawr, Muḥammad ibn al-Ḥasan and Ibn Naṣr. There is a second position that the marriage is new and divorce starts afresh. That was the position of Ibn 'Umar and Ibn 'Abbās.

provided they think they will remain within Allah's limits.

If they think that each of them will treat the other well. It is said that the limits of Allah refer to what He has made obligatory, so it means when they know that there will be correctness between them in the second marriage. If the husband knows that he is unable to support his wife or provide her dowry or any of her obligatory rights, it is not lawful for him to marry her until he makes that clear to her and knows that he will, in fact, be able to fulfil her rights. It is the same if he has a defect which prevents sexual enjoyment. This is so that he does not deceive the woman regarding himself. Similarly he must not deceive her about his lineage or wealth or work by lying about that. Similarly if the woman knows that she will be unable to carry out the duties owed by her to the husband or has a defect which prevents sexual intercourse such as insanity, leprosy or genital defects, she is not permitted to deceive him and must make that clear to him. This same principle applies to those who sell goods: they must make any faults clear.

Ibn Khuwayzimandād said, "Our companions disagree about whether the wife has to serve or not. Some say that a man cannot oblige his wife to serve and that is because the contract specifies enjoyment, not service. Do you not see that it is not a contract of hire or slavery? It is a contract of pleasure and what is entailed by the contract is enjoyment and nothing more and so more than that may not be demanded of her. Do you not see the words of Allah Almighty, *'But if they obey you do not look for a way to punish them'* (4:34)? Others among our companions say that she owes the service of a woman of her standing. If she is noble due to the wealth or lineage of her parents, she must manage the house and direct the servants. If she is middle-class, she must make the bed and the like. If she is less than that, she attends to the house, cooking and washing. If she is a woman from the Kurds, Daylam and the mountains, she is obliged to do what their women are normally obliged to do. That is because Allah says, *"Women possess rights similar to those held over them to be honoured with fairness."* (2:228) The custom of Muslims in their lands, ancient and modern, is as we have mentioned it."

These are Allah's limits which he has made clear to people who know.

The "*ḥudūd*" (limits) are what He has forbidden. The root of the verb is used for confining and denying good. A man who is *maḥdūd* is confined. The verb is used for a woman in mourning who is forbidden adornment. A doorkeeper can be called *ḥaddād*, because he prevents people from entering. The words *"a people who know"* are used because when someone ignorant is subject to a lot of commands and prohibitions, he will not observe them or abide by them. The one who knows will do so. This is why those who know are addressed and not the ignorant.

وَإِذَا طَلَّقْتُمُ ٱلنِّسَآءَ فَبَلَغْنَ أَجَلَهُنَّ فَأَمْسِكُوهُنَّ بِمَعْرُوفٍ
أَوْ سَرِّحُوهُنَّ بِمَعْرُوفٍ ۖ وَلَا تُمْسِكُوهُنَّ ضِرَارًا لِّتَعْتَدُوا۟ ۖ وَمَن يَفْعَلْ
ذَٰلِكَ فَقَدْ ظَلَمَ نَفْسَهُۥ ۖ وَلَا تَتَّخِذُوٓا۟ ءَايَٰتِ ٱللَّهِ هُزُؤًا ۖ وَٱذْكُرُوا۟ نِعْمَتَ
ٱللَّهِ عَلَيْكُمْ وَمَآ أَنزَلَ عَلَيْكُم مِّنَ ٱلْكِتَٰبِ وَٱلْحِكْمَةِ يَعِظُكُم بِهِۦ ۖ وَٱتَّقُوا۟
ٱللَّهَ وَٱعْلَمُوٓا۟ أَنَّ ٱللَّهَ بِكُلِّ شَىْءٍ عَلِيمٌ ﴿٢٣١﴾

231 *When you divorce women*
and they reach the end of their waiting period,
then either retain them
with correctness and courtesy
or release them with correctness and courtesy.
Do not retain them by force,
thus overstepping the limits.
Anyone who does that has wronged himself.
Do not make a mockery of Allah's Signs.
Remember Allah's blessing to you
and the Book and Wisdom
He has sent down to you to admonish you.
Be fearful of Allah
and know that Allah has knowledge of all things.

When you divorce women and they reach the end of their waiting period,

The word *"balagha"* (reach) here means "to draw near to" according to the consensus of scholars, because, if she actually reaches the end, her husband no longer has a choice about keeping her.

then either retain them with correctness and courtesy

This means the husband must undertake to fulfil his legal obligations towards his wife. That is why a group of scholars said that an aspect of retaining with correctness is that if the husband does not have what is necessary for the maintenance of his wife, he must divorce her. If he does not do so, he is no longer in the right and the divorce can be forced upon him by the judge due to the harm she would suffer by remaining with someone who cannot support her. That was the position of Mālik, ash-Shāfi'ī, Aḥmad, Isḥāq, Abū Thawr, Abū 'Ubayd, Yaḥyā al-Qaṭṭān, and 'Abdu'r-Raḥmān ibn Mahdī. It was stated by 'Umar, 'Alī and Abū Hurayra among the Companions, and Sa'īd ibn al-Musayyab among the *Tābi'ūn.* He said that it is *sunna.* Abū Hurayra related that from the Prophet, may Allah bless him and grant him peace.

Another group say that the couple are not separated in that situation and she must put up with that. Maintenance is made his responsibility by the ruling of a judge. That is the position of 'Aṭā' and az-Zuhrī and it is the position which is taken by the Kufans and ath-Thawrī. Their evidence is found in the *āyat, "If someone is in difficult circumstances, there should be a deferral until things are easier"* (2:280) and *"Marry off those among you who are unmarried."* (24:32). So Allah recommends poor people to marry and so poverty cannot be a reason for separation. Also marriage between a couple is established by consensus and there is no separation except by consensus or an irrefutable *sunna* from the Prophet, may Allah bless him and grant him peace. The evidence for the first position is in the *Ṣaḥīḥ* of al-Bukhārī. We consider the separation due to hardship to be a revocable divorce, differing from ash-Shāfi'ī who thinks it is final.

or release them with correctness and courtesy.

This means to divorce them.

Do not retain them by force, thus overstepping the limits.

Mālik related from Thawr ibn Zayd ad-Dīlī that a man would divorce his wife and then take her back, having no need for her and not intending to keep her, but simply to make the waiting period longer for her and to thereby hurt her more, and so Allah revealed this.

Anyone who does that has wronged himself.

Az-Zajjāj says that "wrongs himself," means that he exposes himself to punishment by doing what Allah has forbidden.

Do not make a mockery of Allah's Signs.

This means "Do not mock Allah's judgements". Abū'd-Dardā' said that in the time of *Jāhiliyya* a man used to pronounce a divorce by saying, "You are divorced and I am joking," as he would do in marriage and emancipation. So Allah revealed this *āyat* and the Prophet, may Allah bless him and grant him peace, said, "If anyone divorces, emancipates, marries or gives in marriage and then says, 'I was only joking,' what he said is taken seriously." All such expressions are included in what is said in this *āyat*. The Signs of Allah are His proofs, commands and prohibitions.

There is no disagreement between scholars that, if someone divorces in jest, the divorce is binding but they disagree about other matters as will be dealt with in *Sūrat al-Tawba*, Allah willing. Abū Hurayra reported that the Messenger of Allah, may Allah bless him and grant him peace, said, "Three matters are serious and jests about them are taken seriously: marriage, divorce and taking back in marriage."

Remember Allah's blessing to you and the Book and Wisdom He has sent down to you to admonish you.

The blessing is Islam and Allah making His judgements clear. "Wisdom" refers to the *Sunna* which makes things clear on the tongue of the Messenger of Allah in respect of things about which there is no text in the Qur'ān.

وَإِذَا طَلَّقْتُمُ ٱلنِّسَآءَ فَبَلَغْنَ أَجَلَهُنَّ فَلَا تَعْضُلُوهُنَّ أَن يَنكِحْنَ
أَزْوَٰجَهُنَّ إِذَا تَرَٰضَوْا۟ بَيْنَهُم بِٱلْمَعْرُوفِ ۗ ذَٰلِكَ يُوعَظُ بِهِۦ
مَن كَانَ مِنكُمْ يُؤْمِنُ بِٱللَّهِ وَٱلْيَوْمِ ٱلْءَاخِرِ ۗ ذَٰلِكُمْ أَزْكَىٰ لَكُمْ
وَأَطْهَرُ ۚ وَٱللَّهُ يَعْلَمُ وَأَنتُمْ لَا تَعْلَمُونَ ﴿٢٣٢﴾

232 ***When you divorce women***
and they reach the end of their waiting period,
do not prevent them
from marrying their first husbands
if they have mutually agreed to it
with correctness and courtesy.
This is an admonition for those of you
who believe in Allah and the Last Day.
That is better and purer for you.
Allah knows and you do not know.

When you divorce women and they reach the end of their waiting period, do not prevent them from marrying their first husbands

Ma'qil ibn Yasār related that his sister was married to Abu'l-Baddāḥ and he divorced her and left her until the end of her waiting period and then regretted it and proposed and she agreed to remarry him. Her brother refused to marry her. He said, "It will be unlawful for us to see one another if you marry him," and the *āyat* was revealed. The Prophet summoned Ma'qil and said, "If you are a believer, you will not prevent your sister from remarrying Abū'l-Baddāḥ." He said, "I believe in Allah and give her in marriage to him." This account is reported in al-Bukhārī and ad-Dāraquṭnī. He expiated his oath. It is also said that the individual concerned was Ma'qil ibn Sinān.

If this is true it indicates that it is not permitted for any woman to marry without a *walī* because the sister of Ma'qil had previously been married. If the matter had been left to her and not to her guardian, she would have married herself and would have had no need of Ma'qil. So the words *"do not prevent"* are addressed to guardians. They are commanded to give the women concerned in marriage with their consent. It is also said that it is addressed to the husbands, because taking the woman back to cause her harm keeps her from marrying another and makes her waiting period longer.

The word *"reach"* in this instance really means that it has ended. The verb for "prevent" is *'aḍala.* A *mu'ḍil* is a hen which cannot lay eggs. It is said that *'aḍl* is to constrict and prevent, from the meaning of confinement.

That is better and purer for you.

If you do that you will be righteous.

وَٱلْوَٰلِدَٰتُ يُرْضِعْنَ أَوْلَٰدَهُنَّ حَوْلَيْنِ كَامِلَيْنِ ۖ لِمَنْ أَرَادَ أَن يُتِمَّ
ٱلرَّضَاعَةَ ۚ وَعَلَى ٱلْمَوْلُودِ لَهُۥ رِزْقُهُنَّ وَكِسْوَتُهُنَّ بِٱلْمَعْرُوفِ ۚ
لَا تُكَلَّفُ نَفْسٌ إِلَّا وُسْعَهَا ۚ لَا تُضَآرَّ وَٰلِدَةٌۢ بِوَلَدِهَا
وَلَا مَوْلُودٌ لَّهُۥ بِوَلَدِهِۦ ۚ وَعَلَى ٱلْوَارِثِ مِثْلُ ذَٰلِكَ ۗ فَإِنْ
أَرَادَا فِصَالًا عَن تَرَاضٍ مِّنْهُمَا وَتَشَاوُرٍ فَلَا جُنَاحَ
عَلَيْهِمَا ۗ وَإِنْ أَرَدتُّمْ أَن تَسْتَرْضِعُوٓا۟ أَوْلَٰدَكُمْ
فَلَا جُنَاحَ عَلَيْكُمْ إِذَا سَلَّمْتُم مَّآ ءَاتَيْتُم بِٱلْمَعْرُوفِ ۗ
وَٱتَّقُوا۟ ٱللَّهَ وَٱعْلَمُوٓا۟ أَنَّ ٱللَّهَ بِمَا تَعْمَلُونَ بَصِيرٌ ﴿٢٣٣﴾

233 ***Mothers should nurse their children***
for two full years –
those who wish to complete the full term of nursing.
It is the duty of the fathers to feed and clothe them
with correctness and courtesy –
no self is charged with more than it can bear.
No mother should be put under pressure
in respect of her child
nor any father in respect of his child.
The same duty is incumbent on the heir.
If the couple both wish weaning to take place
after mutual agreement and consultation,
there is nothing wrong in their doing that.
If you wish to find wet-nurses for your children,
there is nothing wrong in your doing that
provided you hand over to them
what you have agreed to give
with correctness and courtesy.
Be fearful of Allah
and know that Allah sees what you do.

Mothers should nurse their children for two full years – those who wish to complete the full term of nursing.

When Allah has mentioned marriage and divorce He then speaks about children since a couple may separate when they have children. So the *āyat* is about divorced women who have children by their ex-husbands. As-Suddī, aḍ-Ḍaḥḥāk and others said that, meaning that they are more entitled to nurse their children than other women because they will be more compassionate towards them and it is harmful to both mother and child to remove a small child from her. This also indicates that even if the child is weaned, the mother is still more entitled to custody because of her compassion for him. She remains more entitled unless she remarries as will be mentioned.

This renders problematic the words, *"It is the duty of the fathers to feed and clothe them"* because divorced women are not entitled to clothing if it is not a revocable divorce. They are entitled to a wage. Noble character, however, would ensure that the wage was adequate for both her food and her clothing. It is said that the *āyat* is general to both divorced women who have children and to wives. The most evident position is that it is about wives while the marriage remains because they are entitled to maintenance and clothing, whether they nurse or not. Maintenance and clothing are according to the man's ability.

Nursing is mandatory for some and recommended for some. People disagree about whether nursing is a right for or against the mother. The expression can mean either because, taken literally, it means that it is obligatory for mothers to nurse their children just as fathers are obliged to maintain them. But that is only while she is married and also only when custom demands it. If she is noble and wealthy, the custom is for her not to nurse. If the child will not, however, accept another woman, then nursing becomes mandatory for her. This is also the case if no one else is available. If the father dies and the child has no property, the position of Mālik in the *Mudawwana* is that the mother is still obliged to nurse without being paid a wage. Ibn al-Jallāb said that the wage should be paid from the Treasury. 'Abdu'l-Wahhāb said that that only applies when the father is one of the poor Muslims.

When a woman has been trebly divorced, she does not have to nurse and only does so if she wishes to. If she does so, she is entitled to a suitable wage if the husband is wealthy. If he does not have wealth, he cannot oblige her to nurse unless she is the only one the child will accept. If she is obliged to nurse and some excuse arises which prevents her from doing so, nursing then becomes the father's responsibility. It is related from Mālik that if he is poor and the child has no property the mother must nurse. If she has no milk and has wealth, the child is nursed at her expense. Ash-Shāfi'ī said that paying for nursing is only mandatory for the father or grandfather.

The words *"two full years"* denote a measure of time which revolves in a full cycle. The word "full" is added because the word "year" by itself can be used for less than a complete year. Allah's words *"those who wish to complete the full term of nursing"* indicates that the two full years is not a definitive term. Weaning can take place before the two years are up. A limit is set merely to eliminate any dispute between the couple about the length of nursing. The father does not have to pay for more than two years and if the father wants the child to be weaned before two years and the mother does not consent, he cannot enforce that. An increase or decrease in the two years can be made provided that the child is not harmed and that the parents agree.

Mālik and those who follow him and another group of scholars deduce from this *āyat* that the nursing which creates a milk relationship[1] only occurs within this first two year period and ends when those two years end, so that any nursing after that is not considered.

A group of commentators say that the period is two years for each child. It is related from Ibn Abbās that that is when the child is in the womb for six months. If it remains for seven months, the nursing period is twenty-three months. If it is nine months, the nursing is twenty-one months going by Allah's words, *"His bearing and weaning is thirty months."* (46:15)

It is the duty of the fathers to feed and clothe them with correctness and courtesy – no self is charged with more than it can bear.

This is evidence for the obligation of the father to maintain the child since he is weak. The feeding referred to is the nourishment which reaches the child by means of the mother through nursing. Scholars agree that a man must support all his children who have no money. When Hind bint 'Utba said to the Prophet, may Allah bless him and grant him peace, "Abū Sufyān is miserly and does not give me adequate maintenance and what is enough for my son. If I take from his property without his knowledge, do I do anything wrong?" he told her, "Take what is adequate for you and your child in a correct manner." *"Ma'rūf"* (correctness) means what is customary in the usage of the *Sharī'a* without excess or negli-

1. Nursing creates the same barriers to marriage as does actual lineage.

gence. Then Allah made it clear that a man's duty of maintenance is according to his wealth and position and no specific amount is stipulated by His words "no self is charged with more than it can bear." This will be clarified later.

Mālik thought that this *āyat* indicates that a mother should have custody of her sons until puberty and of her daughters until marriage. That is her right, and Abū Ḥanīfa stated the same. Ash-Shāfi'ī said that when the child is eight years old, which is the age of discrimination, he is given a choice between his parents. At that stage his interest and desire should be stimulated to learn the Qur'ān, *adab* and the duties of worship. That is the same for both boys and girls. An-Nasā'ī and others reported from Abū Hurayra that a woman came to the Prophet, peace be upon him, and said, "My husband wants to take my son." The Prophet said to him, "This is your father and this is your mother: take whichever of them you wish," and he took his mother's hand.

Abū 'Umar said, "I do not know of any disagreement among scholars that a divorced woman, as long as she does not marry again, is more entitled to her child while he is still young than the father." They disagree about the child being given a choice when he understands the situation and who is most entitled to look after the child then. Ibn al-Mundhir said, "It is confirmed that the Prophet, may Allah bless him and grant him peace, judged that the daughter of Ḥamza should go to her maternal aunt." The Prophet did not give Ḥamza's daughter a choice. Abū Dāwūd reports that when Zayd ibn Ḥāritha went to Makka and brought Ḥamza's daughter, Ja'far said, "I am more entitled to her. She is my uncle's daughter and her maternal aunt is married to me, and the maternal aunt is a mother." 'Alī said, "I am more entitled to care for her. She is my uncle's daughter and I am married to the daughter of the Messenger of Allah, may Allah bless him and grant him peace, and she is more entitled to her." Zayd said, "I am more entitled to her. I went and travelled to her and brought her!" The Prophet said, "I judge the girl to go to Ja'far so she can be with her maternal aunt. The maternal aunt is in the position of the mother."

When a mother forgoes the right to custody and she is not married to another man and then later wants to take the child, she can only take him if she left him with a legitimate excuse. If she left him out of dislike for the child, then she cannot take him.

They disagree about what happens to a couple who are divorced if the wife is a *dhimmī*. One group say that there is no difference between a *dhimmī* and Muslim mother: they are both entitled to the child. This is the position of Abū Thawr, the People of Opinion, and Ibn al-Qāsim. Ibn al-Mundhir says that there is a *marfū' ḥadīth* which states this, although there is some dispute about its *isnād*. The other position is that the child is with the Muslim. This is the position of Mālik, Sawwār, and 'Abdullāh ibn al-Ḥasan, and is reported from ash-Shāfi'ī. There is the same disagreement when one of the couple is free and the other a slave.

No mother should be put under pressure in respect of her child nor any father in respect of his child.

The mother should not refuse to nurse her child in order to harm the father or ask for more than a suitable wage and it is not lawful for the father to refuse to let the mother nurse when she wants to. This is the position of the majority of commentators. The form of the verb *"tuḍārra"* ("put under pressure") is jussive because it is a firm prohibition. Al-Ḥasan said, "She may not harm the husband by refusing to nurse nor may he harm her by removing the child from her if she says that she will nurse him."

The same duty is incumbent on the heir.

There is disagreement about the interpretation of this phrase. Qatāda, as-Suddī, al-Hasan, and 'Umar ibn al-Khaṭṭāb said that the heir referred to is the heir of the child if he dies. Some said that it is only the male heirs who must pay the nurse, as the father of the child would have that duty if he were alive. Mujāhid and 'Aṭā' said that. Qatāda and others said that the heirs of the child can be both men and women and they must have him nursed paying in proportion with their shares of inheritance. Aḥmad and Isḥāq said that. Qāḍī Ismā'īl said in his book, *Meanings of the Qur'ān*, "Abū

Ḥanīfa said that the maintenance and nursing of the child is encumbent on every relative. For instance, in the case of the young son of a sister who is needy and the young son of an uncle when he is his heir: maintenance is encumbent on the maternal uncle if his sister's son becomes fatherless even though he does not inherit from him. The responsiblity is removed from the son of an uncle if there is another son of an uncle who is an heir. Abū Isḥāq said that those who say this are taking a position which is not in the Book of Allah and we do not know of anyone who says it.

Aṭ-Ṭabarī reported that Abū Ḥanīfa and his adherents said that the heir who must pay for the nurse is the child's heir who is a close relative. As for nephews and those who are not close relatives, they are free of responsiblity. It is said that what is meant is that the paternal relatives of the father must maintain and clothe the child.

It is said that the heir meant is the child itself when his father dies, meaning that his nursing is paid for from his own property. Ibn Khuwayzimandād said, "If an orphan is poor and has no money, the ruler must support him from the Treasury. If the ruler does not do it, then the Muslims must do it."

Nursing is mandatory and maintenance is recommended. Husbands are obliged to maintain the women who nurse their children. If the husband is unable to pay what is due because of death or hardship, the duty is not cancelled for the mothers. A waiting period is mandatory for them, as is maintenance and lodging by their husbands. If maintenance is impossible, their waiting period is not thereby cancelled. In *al-Asadiyya* 'Abdu'r-Raḥmān ibn al-Qāsim reported that Mālik ibn Anas said, "A man is not obliged to maintain a sister or a relative. He said that Allah's words *'The same duty is incumbent on the heir'* are abrogated." An-Naḥḥās said that neither Ibn al-Qāsim nor Mālik clarified what it is abrogated by. Allah knows best. According to this, the child is obliged to pay for his upkeep from his property, and not his heir.

Regarding the statement that it is abrogated, Ibn al-'Arabī pointed out that among earlier scholars, specification (*takhṣīṣ*) was referred to as abrogation because it removes part of that which was entailed by the generality of the *āyat*. They used that language and what they meant became unclear to later people.

If the couple both wish weaning to take place...

It is called weaning (*fiṣāl*) because the child is separated from the mother. The root meaning of the noun means "separation". This *āyat* refers to it happening before the two years are up. This indicates that Allah has allowed *ijtihād* in the rulings on that when the parents consult one another about the course which will be in the best interests of the child.

If you wish to find wet-nurses for your children,

This means other than the mother. This is evidence for hiring a wet-nurse when the parents agree to that. Ibn 'Aṭiyya says that the basic position is that every mother is obliged to nurse her child as Allah mentions and their husbands are obliged to give them maintenance and clothing while they are married. If it had been a requirement of the father, Allah would have mentioned it. Mālik, however, excepted noble women and said that they are not obliged to nurse. He removed them from the general category by the legal principle of custom.

provided you hand over to them what you have agreed to give

This means that the father is responsible for paying the wages of the wet-nurse.

وَالَّذِينَ يُتَوَفَّوْنَ مِنكُمْ وَيَذَرُونَ أَزْوَاجًا يَتَرَبَّصْنَ بِأَنفُسِهِنَّ
أَرْبَعَةَ أَشْهُرٍ وَعَشْرًا فَإِذَا بَلَغْنَ أَجَلَهُنَّ فَلَا جُنَاحَ عَلَيْكُمْ فِيمَا
فَعَلْنَ فِي أَنفُسِهِنَّ بِالْمَعْرُوفِ وَاللَّهُ بِمَا تَعْمَلُونَ خَبِيرٌ ٢٣٤

234 ***Those of you who die leaving wives behind:***
they should wait by themselves
for four months and ten nights.

When their waiting period comes to an end,
you are not to blame for anything
they do with themselves
with correctness and courtesy.
Allah is aware of what you do.

Those of you who die leaving wives behind: they should wait by themselves for four months and ten nights.

After Allah has mentioned divorce and then nursing, He speaks about the waiting period for widowhood as well so that it is not assumed that the waiting period for widows is the same as the waiting period for divorce. The words *"those of you"* refer to husbands.

This *āyat* is about the waiting period of widows. Its literal meaning is general while its actual meaning is specific. Al-Mahdī related from one scholar that the *āyat* concerned pregnant women and that it was abrogated by *"The time for those who are pregnant is when they give birth."* (65:4) Most scholars say that this *āyat* abrogates, *"Those of you who die leaving wives behind should make a bequest to their wives..."* (2:240) because, in the beginning of Islam, when a man died and left a pregnant wife, he would make a bequest for her of maintenance for a year and provide lodging for her until she left and remarried. Then this was abrogated by four months and ten days and a share of inheritance. Other people have said that there is no abrogation in this and that it constitutes a reduction from the original year in the same way that the travelling prayer was reduced from four to two *rak'at*s.

This view is a clear error because the ruling was a waiting period for a year provided the widow did not go out. If she went out, she was not prevented from doing so but the maintenance would thereby be brought to an end. Then this was removed and a waiting period of four months and ten days was imposed. This is an abrogation and it has nothing to do with the travelling prayer. In any case 'Ā'isha said, "The prayer was prescribed as two *rak'at*s each, and then the resident prayer was increased and the travel prayer remained the same." That will be dealt with in due course.

The waiting period of a pregnant widow lasts until she gives birth according to the majority of scholars. It is related from 'Alī and Ibn 'Abbās that the end of the waiting period is whichever of the two terms is longer. Among our scholars Saḥnūn chose this view. It is also related that Ibn 'Abbās retracted his statement. Their reasoning is that they prefer to combine both *āyat*s and maintain them by taking the longer term. This view would be good were it not for the fact that it is overturned by the *ḥadīth* of Subay'a al-Aslamiyya. She gave birth some days after the death of her husband and she mentioned that to the Messenger of Allah, may Allah bless him and grant him peace, and he told her to marry. So this makes it clear that this ruling applies both to widows and divorced women when they are pregnant.

The incident involving Subay'a took place after the revelation of the *āyat* about the waiting period of widowhood because it occurred after the Farewell *Ḥajj*. Her husband was Sa'd ibn Khawla, who had been present at the Battle of Badr. He died in Makka while she was pregnant and she gave birth thirty or forty days afterwards. There is some disagreement between scholars about whether a woman can marry during the period of lochia or not. There is no disagreement that the end of the waiting period of every pregnant divorced woman is when she gives birth. The disagreement is only about widows.

The word *"wait"* here means to refrain from remarrying and leaving the marital home. That means not leaving it at night. Allah did not mention the residence of widows in His Book as He did that of divorced woman. The *Sunna* clarifies that and there are many *aḥādīth* from the Prophet which indicate that the waiting period of widowhood is a period of mourning, which should be marked by not wearing jewelry, beautiful dyed garments, perfume and the like. This is the statement of the majority of scholars. Al-Ḥasan said that it is only about not marrying and that a widow is free to adorn herself and use perfume. This is weak because it is contrary to the *Sunna* as we will make clear.

It is confirmed that the Prophet said to Furay'a bint Mālik when she was widowed, "Remain in your house until the term is reached." She said, "My waiting period was for four months and ten days." This *ḥadīth* is transmitted from a great many people. Abu 'Umar says that it contains the judgement for the widow spending the waiting period in her house. The *fuqahā'* agree on this, except for Dā'ūd, who said that a widow may spend the waiting period wherever she wishes because, in the Qur'ān, lodging is only mentioned in the case of divorced women, and he questions the *ḥadīth* of Furay'a. Abū 'Umar points out that this position is confirmed by the *Sunna*. What has come from 'Alī, Ibn 'Abbās, Jābir, and 'Ā'isha supports the opinion of Dā'ūd and that position was taken by Jābir ibn Zayd, 'Aṭā' and al-Ḥasan al-Baṣrī. It is also reported from Abū Ḥanīfa.

'Urwa reported that when 'Ā'isha's sister, Umm Kulthūm, was widowed when her husband, Ṭalha ibn 'Ubaydullāh, was killed, 'Ā'isha took her to Makka on *'umra*. Her judgement was that a widow could go out during her waiting period. Al-Qāsim ibn Muḥammad was heard to remark that some people rejected that position of hers. Az-Zuhrī said, "Those who make allowances for widows take the position of 'Ā'isha and those who are scrupulous and firm take that of Ibn 'Umar." It states in the *Muwaṭṭā'* that 'Umar ibn al-Khaṭṭāb sent back some widows from the desert when they were on their way to *ḥajj* and prevented them from doing it. This was based on his *ijtihād*.

If the husband owned the dwelling, his widow observes her waiting period in it according to most *fuqahā'*, Mālik, Abū Ḥanīfa, ash-Shāfi'ī, and Aḥmad among them. But can the house then be sold if it belonged to the deceased and the heirs want to sell it? Most of our people say that the sale is permitted but a precondition of the sale must be that the widow can observe her waiting period there. Ibn al-Qāsim said that is because she is entitled to her lodging as a creditor. Muḥammad ibn al-Ḥakam said that the sale is invalid until the end of the widow's waiting period.

A widow should stay in a rented house if her deceased husband has paid the rent. If he has not paid it, the *Mudawwana* states that she has no right of lodging from the property of the deceased, even if he was wealthy, because her right was contingent on what he owned completely. She has only what she receives by inheritance and that is property and not lodging. Muḥammad reported that Mālik said that renting a lodging for the widow is an obligation and must be paid for from the property of the decreased.

The words of the Prophet, may Allah bless him and grant him peace, to Furay'a, "Stay in your house until the term is reached" may mean that he commanded her to do that since her husband had paid the rent or had provided for her lodging in his will or that the owner of the house allowed her to spend her waiting period there with or without rent. It is whatever Allah meant by that in view of the fact that it is necessary for her to have somewhere to live until the end of her waiting period.

They disagree about a woman who is informed of her husband's death while she is in a house other than that of her husband. Some relate that she should return to his house and some say that she has a choice. Ibn al-Mundhir says that the sound position of Mālik is that she should return to his house unless he himself had moved her to her current location. She is permitted to go out for her needs and her work at the time when people normally go out for such things up until the time of the *'Ishā'* prayer. She should, however, only spend the night in that house.

Umm 'Aṭiyya said, "People should not mourn for a dead person more than three days, except in the case of a husband, when the mourning period is four months and ten days. A widow should not wear a dyed garment except for one made of pre-dyed yarn. She should not wear eye make-up (koḥl) or perfume until her waiting period has ended, except for *costus* or *aẓfār* (types of aromatic wood)." (al-Bukhārī and Muslim) Umm Ḥabība said, "It is not lawful for a woman who believes in Allah and the Last Day to mourn for a dead person more than three days unless it is her husband. She should mourn him for four months and ten days." (al-Bukhārī) Mourning consists of abandoning all adornment in respect of clothing, perfume, jewellery, make-up and henna during the waiting period, because adornment is a sign of seeking a husband and so it is forbidden as a protection and in order to make sure that that does not happen. Oiling the hair is not considered as adornment but henna is.

The people agree that Muslim widows should go into mourning – with the exception of al-Ḥasan who says that it is not mandatory. He based that on the *ḥadīth* about Asmā' bint 'Umays when Ja'far ibn Abī Ṭālib was killed. She said that the Messenger of Allah, may Allah bless him and grant him peace, told her, "Withdraw for three and then do what you wish." He thought it referred to the period she should observe. According to one view, a woman of the People of the Book does not have to observe this waiting period, while another view says that she does.

There is some discussion about the period of "four months and ten nights" which Allah set for the waiting period of a widow and whether it requires menstruation to take place in it or not. Some say that the widow must be certain that she is not pregnant and some say that she does not owe more than the four months and ten days in any circumstance. Abū'l-'Āliyya was asked why the ten were added. He said, "Because the spirit is breathed in during that time."

When their waiting period comes to an end, you are not to blame for anything they do with themselves with correctness and courtesy.

The waiting period referred to is that of the women whose husbands have died. The words *"you are not to blame"* are addressed to people in general, but particularly to judges and relatives. What widows do once they leave mourning is their own business. "Correctness" refers to what is permitted of choosing husbands and determining dowry without actually making a contract, because it is the guardian who makes the contract. But this does provide evidence that relatives have the right to prevent widows from adorning themselves and seeking a husband during the time of their waiting period. This refutes Isḥāq's view that a divorced woman can do that once she starts her third menstrual period. She is not completely free until she has had a *ghusl*. This may, however, simply be a recommendation.

وَلَا جُنَاحَ عَلَيْكُمْ فِيمَا عَرَّضْتُم بِهِۦ مِنْ خِطْبَةِ ٱلنِّسَآءِ
أَوَ اَكْنَنتُمْ فِي أَنفُسِكُمْ عَلِمَ ٱللَّهُ أَنَّكُمْ سَتَذْكُرُونَهُنَّ
وَلَٰكِن لَّا تُوَاعِدُوهُنَّ سِرًّا إِلَّآ أَن تَقُولُواْ قَوْلًا مَّعْرُوفًا
وَلَا تَعْزِمُواْ عُقْدَةَ ٱلنِّكَاحِ حَتَّىٰ يَبْلُغَ ٱلْكِتَٰبُ أَجَلَهُۥ
وَاعْلَمُوٓاْ أَنَّ ٱللَّهَ يَعْلَمُ مَا فِي أَنفُسِكُمْ فَاحْذَرُوهُ
وَاعْلَمُوٓاْ أَنَّ ٱللَّهَ غَفُورٌ حَلِيمٌ ٢٣٥

235 ***Nor is there anything wrong in any allusion***
to marriage you make to a woman,
nor for any you keep to yourself.
Allah knows that you will say things to them.
But do not make secret arrangements with them,
rather only speak with correctness and courtesy.
Do not finally decide on the marriage contract
until the prescribed period has come to its end.
Know that Allah knows what is in your selves,
so beware of Him!
And know that Allah
is Ever-Forgiving, All-Forbearing.

Nor is there anything wrong in any allusion to marriage you make to a woman,

"Wrong" (*junāḥ*) in this context means sin. The *āyat* is addressed in particular to any man who wants to marry a woman who is still in her waiting period, saying that there is no sin in alluding to marriage during that time. An allusion is not an explicit statement. It produces understanding of what is alluded to words whose expression is not explicit.

Ibn 'Aṭiyya said that the Community is agreed that speaking to a woman in her waiting period about marriage in an explicit way is not permitted. Other than that is permitted. There is a consensus that it is not permitted to allude to marriage with a woman who is in her waiting period following a revocable divorce, because, in that case, she is still in fact a wife. It is, however, permitted in the case of a woman who is in her waiting period after a final divorce. Allah knows best. An allusion may be made through words, intention or intimation using some action or words. In words, he may say something like, "I'm intending to marry" or "You're very beautiful." In actions, he may give her a gift.

nor for any (allusion) you keep to yourself.

This means what you conceal during a woman's waiting period when you want to marry her after it has finished. So Allah removed any wrong action from a man who wants to marry a woman who is still in her waiting period and conceals it. He forbade any arrangements which involve a clear statement of desire for marriage, such as a proposal. Allah made this indulgence because He knows the desire people have and human weaknesses.

Shāfi'īs use this as evidence that the *ḥadd* punishment is not required in the case of a slanderous allusion. They say that, since Allah said that allusion is not wrong in this case, an allusion implying slander should not incur the *ḥadd* because Allah makes it clear here that an allusion is not the same as an explicit statement. We disagree and say that this is an invalid analogy because Allah did not allow explicit marriage proposals, but an allusion by which marriage is understood. An allusion to slander acts in the same way and so the *ḥadd* is required because the slander is in fact clearly understood just as the allusion to marriage was.

Allah knows that you will say things to them.

He knows, whether that is secretly or openly, in yourselves and on your tongues.

But do not make secret arrangements with them,

Scholars disagree about what is meant by "secret" here. It is said that it means to actually marry, in other words a man should not say to a woman during her waiting period, "Will you marry me?" He should merely allude to what he intends and not make an agreement whereby she will not marry someone else. This is the position of Ibn 'Abbās, Ibn Jubayr, Mālik and his people, Mujāhid, 'Ikrima, as-Suddī and most of the people of knowledge. It is also said that "secret" in this context implies fornication, in other words "do not agree to fornicate during the waiting period". Jābir ibn Zayd and Abū Miljaz said that as did others. Ibn Zayd says that it means to not marry them secretly.

Abū Muḥammad ibn 'Aṭiyya said, "The Community agree that it is disliked to arrange a marriage with a woman during her waiting period or for her father to do so." Mālik said, "If they make an arrangement during the waiting period and then marry afterwards, I prefer them to separate, whether or not the marriage has been consummated, and it is one divorce." Ashhab related from Mālik that it is mandatory to separate them and Ibn al-Qāsim said that as well. Ibn al-Mājishūn also said that and added that they cannot then ever marry. Ash-Shāfi'ī said, "If someone makes an explicit proposal and the woman explicitly consents but the marriage does not take place until after the waiting period has ended, the marriage is valid and it was the explicit proposal which was disliked.

rather only speak with correctness and courtesy.

This refers to those allusions which are permitted.

Do not finally decide on the marriage contract until the prescribed period has come to its end.

"*Kitāb*" (prescribed period) literally means book and here denotes the limit which is set and the length of the period. It is called a "book" since it is defined and imposed in the Book of Allah. The same word is used elsewhere in reference to the prayer, as in 4:103.

Allah has definitively forbidden marriage during the waiting period. This is agreed on. According to Mālik and Ibn al-Qāsim marriage during the waiting period creates a perpetual ban against marriage so that any who do marry during it are separated and may never marry one another again. Some say that only a marriage actually consummated during the waiting period creates a perpetual ban and some say that it is not perpetual even then.

لَّا جُنَاحَ عَلَيْكُمْ إِن طَلَّقْتُمُ ٱلنِّسَآءَ مَا لَمْ تَمَسُّوهُنَّ أَوْ
تَفْرِضُوا۟ لَهُنَّ فَرِيضَةً ۚ وَمَتِّعُوهُنَّ عَلَى ٱلْمُوسِعِ قَدَرُهُۥ
وَعَلَى ٱلْمُقْتِرِ قَدَرُهُۥ مَتَٰعًا بِٱلْمَعْرُوفِ ۖ حَقًّا عَلَى ٱلْمُحْسِنِينَ ﴿٢٣٦﴾

236 ***There is nothing wrong in your divorcing women***
before you have touched them
or allotted a dowry to them.
But give them a gift –
he who is wealthy according to his means
and he who is less well off
according to his means –
a gift to be given with correctness and courtesy:
a duty for all good-doers.

There is nothing wrong in your divorcing women before you have touched them or allotted a dowry to them.

This is another of the rulings which deal with divorced women. It deals with removing any aspersion of wrongdoing from a man who divorces before the consummation of a marriage, whether or not a dowry has been stipulated. So the Messenger of Allah, may Allah bless him and grant him peace, forbade marriage merely for the sake of gratification and sexual indulgence and instructed people to marry for the sake of protection and in order to obtain Allah's reward, and with the intention of having a constant companion. The believers did not like divorcing before a marriage had been consummated as they believed that it was disliked and so this *āyat* was revealed to remove their prejudice against it since the basis of marriage lies in the good intention behind it. Some people said that *"nothing wrong"* means that you should not ask for the return of all the dowry. You are only entitled to get back half of what has been allotted to her and you should give a gift to the woman if the amount of the dowry has not been stipulated. It is said that when the command to pay the dowry was confirmed in the *Sharī'a*, it was thought that a dowry was obligatory, either stipulated or appropriate. In this *āyat* the wrong was removed from someone who divorces before any dowry has been stipulated. Some people have said that it refers to those who pronounce divorce during menstruation.

There are four types of divorced women:

- Women in a consummated marriage with an allotted dowry and Allah has mentioned that the ruling in respect of their waiting period is three menstrual periods.
- Women without an allotted dowry whose marriage has not been consummated and this *āyat* is about them. They are not allotted a dowry but Allah says that they should be given a gift. And it is made clear in *Sūrat al-Aḥzāb* (33) that a woman whose marriage has not been consummated and who is divorced has no waiting period.
- Women who have been allotted a dowry whose marriage has not been consummated who will be mentioned after this *āyat*.
- Women without a dowry whose marriage has been consummated. They will be mentioned in *Sūrat an-Nisā'* (4:24).

This *āyat* is about women divorced before either consummation or the allotment of a dowry, and the next is about women who are divorced before consummation but after the allotment of a dowry. The first receives a gift and the second receives half of the dowry.

Allah divided divorced women into two groups: those with an allotted dowry and those without. He indicated that *tafwīḍ* marriage is permitted. This is a marriage in which the dowry is not mentioned and in which the woman is allotted a dowry after the contract.

But give them a gift –

This means give them something they will enjoy having. Some take it as being mandatory, and others, like Mālik and others, as merely being a recommendation. The evidence for the second position is the words, "a duty for good-doers". If it had been mandatory, it would have been made general to all Muslims. The first group say that it is general.

There is disagreement about the pronoun "them" and which women are meant. Ibn 'Abbās, Ibn 'Umar, Jābir ibn Zayd, al-Ḥasan, ash-Shāfi'ī, Aḥmad, 'Aṭā', Isḥāq and the People of Opinion say that a gift is mandatory for a woman divorced before consummation or the allotment of a dowry and recommended for others. Mālik and his people said that it is recommended in every divorce even if the marriage was consummated. In the case of a woman whose marriage has been consummated and who has an allotted dowry, she should receive her dowry but no extra gift. Abū Thawr says that she should receive a gift as well, as should every divorced woman. The people of knowledge say that in the case of a woman who has not been allotted a dowry and whose marriage has not been consummated, she should only receive a gift.

Mālik says that it is not specified whether the gift should be a little or a lot. People disagree about this. Ibn 'Umar said that the minimum is about thirty dirhams. Ibn 'Abbās said, "The largest gift is a servant, then clothes, then maintenance." 'Aṭā' said that a medium-sized gift is a dress, veil (*khimār*) and mantle. Abū Ḥanīfa said, "That is the minimum it should be." Ibn Muḥayriz said that anyone receiving a state pension should give thirty dinars. Al-Ḥasan says that it is according to ability and continued, "One gives a servant, another gives clothes, another a garment and another money." That is what Mālik said because the *āyat* says *"according to his means"*.

If someone is ignorant about the need to give a gift until years have passed, he should still give it to his divorced wife, even if she has since married someone else, or to her heirs if she has died. Ibn al-Mawwāz related that from Ibn al-Qāsim. Aṣbagh said that he does not owe anything if she has died because it is solace for the wife on account of being divorced. Allah knows best.

he who is wealthy according to his means and he who is less well off according to his means –

This is taken as evidence of the mandatory nature of the gift.

a gift to be given with correctness and courtesy:

The words *"with correctness and courtesy"* here mean with moderation according to the *Sharī'a.*

a duty for all good-doers.

This is also evidence for the mandatory nature of the gift. The word *"duty"* stresses it. It is also said that this means that it is for the believers because only they can be called 'godfearing' and 'good-doers'.

وَإِن طَلَّقْتُمُوهُنَّ مِن قَبْلِ أَن تَمَسُّوهُنَّ وَقَدْ فَرَضْتُمْ لَهُنَّ
فَرِيضَةً فَنِصْفُ مَا فَرَضْتُمْ إِلَّا أَن يَعْفُونَ أَوْ يَعْفُوَا الَّذِي
بِيَدِهِۦ عُقْدَةُ النِّكَاحِ وَأَن تَعْفُوا أَقْرَبُ لِلتَّقْوَىٰ
وَلَا تَنسَوُا الْفَضْلَ بَيْنَكُمْ إِنَّ اللَّهَ بِمَا تَعْمَلُونَ بَصِيرٌ ٢٣٧

237 ***If you divorce them before you have touched them***
but have already allotted them a dowry,
they should have half the amount
which you allotted,
unless they forgo it

or the one in charge of the marriage contract forgoes it.
To forgo it is closer to taqwā.
Do not forget to show generosity to one another.
Allah sees what you do.

If you divorce them before you have touched them but have already allotted them a dowry,

People disagree about this *āyat*. One group, including Mālik and others, says that it removes the ruling of the gift in the previous *āyat* from any woman who is divorced after a dowry has been allotted. Sa'īd ibn al-Musayyab said that this *āyat* abrogates the *āyat* in *Sūrat al-Aḥzāb* (33:49). Qatāda says that it abrogates the *āyat* preceding it. I say that the positions of Sa'īd and Qatāda are debatable since the preconditions for abrogation do not exist and it is possible for it to coexist with the other *āyat*s. Ibn al-Qāsim said in the *Mudawwana*, "The gift is for every divorced woman in 2:241 and for any woman whose marriage has not been consummated in the *āyat* in *Sūrat al-Aḥzab* ."

they should have half the amount which you allotted,

This is mandatory. The consensus is that the allotted dowry is divided equally between the man and the woman.

unless they forgo it

This is forgoing the half they are due. This refers to women who have charge of their own affairs. Allah allowed them to forgo it and they can do what they like.

or the one in charge of the marriage contract forgoes it.

People disagree about who is meant by this. In a *ḥadīth* reported by ad-Dāraquṭnī, Jubayr ibn Muṭ'im gave a woman he divorced her full dowry and said that he was the one in charge of the marriage contract since he could act on it or not. That position is taken by many, including Nāfi', Sa'īd ibn al-Musayyab, Ibn 'Abbās, 'Alī, ash-Sha'bī and Abū Ḥanīfa, and it is the sound view from ash-Shāfi'ī. They all say that a guardian has no control over any of his ward's dowry as there is a consensus that it would not be permitted for him to absolve the husband of all the dowry if there were no divorce. So the same applies if there is. They agree that a guardian does not have the power to give away any of his ward's property and the dowry is her property. They agree that guardians cannot absolve the husband, no matter whether they are uncles or fathers. Allah knows best.

Some of them say that a guardian has that right. Ad-Dāraquṭnī also has a report from Ibn 'Abbās regarding that, and it is the position of Ibrāhīm, 'Alqama and al-Ḥasan, and others, as well as Mālik, and it was the old position of ash-Shāfi'ī. According to them it is permitted for a father to forgo half of the dowry of his virgin daughter if she is divorced before the consummation of her marriage. A minor girl is not in a position to forgo. Only a guardian who has good character can do this on her behalf. A simpleton is not permitted to do so either.

To forgo it is closer to *taqwā*.

This is addressed to both men and women according to Ibn 'Abbās.

Do not forget to show generosity to one another.

It is said that "generosity" here may refer either to the man giving her the full dowry or to the woman forgoing half.

Allah sees what you do.

This is a promise to the good-doer and warning for the one who does not do good. What you do is not hidden from Him,

حَٰفِظُواْ عَلَى ٱلصَّلَوَٰتِ وَٱلصَّلَوٰةِ ٱلۡوُسۡطَىٰ وَقُومُواْ لِلَّهِ
قَٰنِتِينَ ﴿٢٣٨﴾

238 ***Safeguard the prayer – especially the middle one. Stand in obedience to Allah.***

Safeguard the prayer – especially the middle one.

The command is in the plural, directed at the entire Community. The *āyat* is a command to persevere in performing the prayers at their correct times with all their preconditions. Safeguarding implies constancy in a thing and perseverance in it. The "middle" of something is the best and most balanced part of it. Allah uses the term in another place in the same way when He says: *"In this way We have made you a middlemost community."* (2:143). The middle prayer is singled out for mention because it is in the middle of all the prayers, to honour it.

There are various positions regarding what constitutes the middle prayer.

- One is that it is *Ẓuhr* because it is in the middle of day, if you understand the day as starting from daybreak. We begin with *Ẓuhr* because it is the first prayer prayed in Islam. That is reported from 'Ā'isha. It is related that it is harder for the Muslims because it comes at a time of heat and they are distracted from it by work. Abū Dāwūd reports from Zayd, "The Prophet, may Allah bless him and grant him peace, used to pray *Ẓuhr* at midday and he did not pray any prayer which was harder for the Companions of the Prophet. Then *'Safeguard the prayer – especially the middle one'* was revealed." Mālik related in the *Muwaṭṭā'* that the middle prayer is *Ẓuhr.*

- It is said to be *'Aṣr* because the two prayers of the day are before it and the two prayers of the night after it. Among those who said this were 'Alī, Ibn 'Abbās, Ibn 'Umar, Abū Hurayra, and Abū Sa'īd al-Khudrī. This view is the one preferred by Abū Ḥanīfa and his people and ash-Shāfi'ī and most of the traditionists. It was the view of 'Abdu'l-Mālik ibn Ḥabīb and preferred by Ibn al-'Arabī. In his *tafsīr,* Ibn 'Aṭiyya said, "It is the position of the majority of people, and I say that. *Aḥādīth* are offered as evidence for this position. Ibn Mas'ūd reported that the Messenger of Allah, may Allah bless him and grant him peace, said, 'The middle prayer is the *'Aṣr* prayer.'"

• It is said to be *Maghrib*. Qubayṣa ibn Abī Dhu'ayb said that as well as others. Their evidence is that it is middle in the number of *rak'ats*, neither more nor less and is not shortened on a journey, and the Prophet, peace be upon him, did not delay it or bring it forward. Prayers are aloud after it and silent before it. 'Ā'isha reported that he said, may Allah bless him and grant him peace, "The best of prayers in the sight of Allah is the *Maghrib* prayer."

• It is said to be *'Ishā'* because it is between two prayers which may not be shortened and it comes at the time of sleep and it is recommended to delay it, so that makes it difficult to safeguard.

• It is said to be *Ṣubḥ*, because the two night prayers before it are those in which the prayer is said out loud and the two daytime prayers after it are silent, and because it is a time when people are asleep and rising for it is hard in the winter because of the cold and in the summer because the night is short. Those who said that it was *Ṣubḥ* include 'Alī and 'Abdullāh ibn 'Abbās. It is also transmitted in the *Muwaṭṭā'* and at-Tirmidhī reports it from Ibn 'Umar. It is the position of Mālik and his people and ash-Shāfi'ī inclined to it according to al-Qushayrī. The sound report from 'Alī is that it is *'Aṣr*. For evidence that it is *Ṣubḥ*, they cite, *"Stand in obedience to Him,"* i.e. in it, and there is no prayer in which *al-qunūt* (standing in obedience) is prescribed except *Ṣubḥ*. There is a report from Ibn 'Abbās saying that *Ṣubḥ* is the middle prayer.

• Some say that it refers to the *Jumu'a* prayer because one is encouraged to go to it and listen to the *khuṭba* in it and it is made a festival. Ibn Ḥabīb and Makkī mentioned that.

• *Ṣubḥ* and *'Aṣr* together. Shaykh Abū Bakr al-Abharī said that his evidence for that was the words of the Messenger of Allah, may Allah bless him and grant him peace. "The angels of the night and the angels of the day succeed one another in overseeing you..." This *ḥadīth* mentions *Ṣubḥ* and *'Aṣr*.

- *'Ishā'* and *Ṣubḥ*. Abū'd-Dardā' said in his final illness, "Listen and convey to your descendants: safeguard these two prayers (i.e. in the group): *'Ishā'* and *Ṣubḥ*. If you had known what was in them, you would have come to them, even crawling on your hands and knees."

- The five prayers as a group. Mu'ādh ibn Jabal said that.

- It is unspecified. Nāfi' quoted Ibn 'Umar as saying that. Ar-Rabī' said that Allah concealed it among the five prayers as He concealed the Night of Power in Ramaḍān and the time of acceptance on the day of *Jumu'a* and the times of the night when supplication is accepted. The wisdom behind its concealment is so that man will persevere in all of them in the same way that happens with the Night of Power which is hidden in the rest of the nights so that people stay up for all those nights. The moment that supplication is answered on Fridays is hidden for the same reason.

This disagreement about the middle prayer indicates the falseness of the position of those who claim that the words "and the *'Aṣr* prayer" were actually part of the Qur'ān.[1]

Stand in obedience to Allah.

This means in the prayer. People disagree about the meaning of the word *qānitīn*. Ash-Sha'bī said that it means "in obedience". Jābir ibn Zayd, 'Aṭā' and Sa'īd ibn Jubayr said that. Aḍ-Ḍaḥḥāk said, "Every use of the word *qanūt* in the Qur'ān refers to obedience." Abū Sa'īd said, quoting the Prophet, may Allah bless him and grant him peace, that the people of every *dīn* will stand as rebels on the Day of Rising, but this Community will be told, "Stand in obedience to Allah." *Qanūt* means long bowing, humility, and lowering the eye. Ar-Rabī' said that *qanūt* means long bowing.

1. As reported in Muslim from al-Barā' ibn 'Āzib.

Ibn 'Abbās said that *qānitīn* means calling or supplicating, and it is used with that meaning in the *ḥadīth*. Some people said that it means to stand for a long time. As-Suddī said that it means to be silent. It is reported that in the early period of Islam, people used to greet the Prophet while he was praying and he would reply. When this *āyat* was revealed, the command was to be silent. It is said that the linguistic root means to be constant in a thing.

Muslims agree that deliberately speaking in the prayer when it is not to put the prayer right, invalidates the prayer. This ruling is based on this *āyat*. They disagree about the one who speaks out of forgetfulness.

If *qanūt* means standing, the community agrees that standing in the obligatory prayer is mandatory for everyone who is sound and able to do so, whether alone or acting as imām.

فَإِنْ خِفْتُمْ فَرِجَالًا أَوْ رُكْبَانًا ۖ فَإِذَا أَمِنتُمْ
فَاذْكُرُوا اللَّهَ كَمَا عَلَّمَكُم مَّا لَمْ تَكُونُوا تَعْلَمُونَ ﴿٢٣٩﴾

239 ***If you are afraid,***
then do the prayer on foot or mounted.
But when you are safe,
remember Allah in the way He taught you
when previously you did not know.

If you are afraid, then do the prayer on foot or mounted.

Allah commanded standing in the prayer with gravity and stillness and with the limbs at rest and this applies when there is security and peace of mind. Then Allah mentions the occasional state of fear and makes it clear that this act of worship is not cancelled for His slave in any circumstances, but in certain situations people are allowed to do the prayer while walking or on the backs of horses, camels and the like, and are permitted to pray with nods and gestures in any direction. This is the position of the scholars. This is the prayer done by someone on his own when he is facing the enemy. There is a consensus of the scholars on this allowance.

They disagree about what constitutes the fear in which it is permitted to pray like this. Ash-Shāfi'ī said that it applies to the situation when the Muslims are actually in sight of the enemy and are not in a fortified position protecting them from being hit by arrows, or when the enemy is so close that they can strike at any time, or when someone whose information is trusted comes and tells them that the enemy is close and making for them. Otherwise it is not permitted to pray the fear prayer. If people pray it based on a report and then the enemy leaves, they do not have to repeat the prayer. Some say that they should, which is the position of Abū Ḥanīfa. The fear prayer behind an imām will be dealt with in *Sūrat an-Nisā'*. Mālik differentiated between fear of the enemy and fear of wild beasts and the like which might attack and bring about death. When it is on account of other than the enemy, it is recommended to repeat the prayer within the time if one is safe. Most scholars view fear as having the same ruling in either instance.

Abu Ḥanīfa said that fighting invalidates the prayer but the *ḥadīth* of Ibn 'Umar refutes that and the evidence of the *āyat* reinforces Ibn 'Umar's position. Ash-Shāfi'ī said that fighting does not invalidate the prayer.

The number of *rak'at*s is not reduced in the fear prayer to below that of the travel prayer according to Mālik, ash-Shāfi'ī and a group of scholars.

But when you are safe, remember Allah in the way He taught you

This means return to what you are commanded to do of the full pillars of the prayer. Mujāhid said that it means when you are resident, and aṭ-Ṭabarī also reported this position. One group say that it means when the fear you were subject to which made you resort to the fear prayer is removed.

Scholars disagree about whether the person in fear builds on the prayer to complete it if the situation becomes safe. Mālik said that if someone prays one *rak'at* in a safe situation and then fear occurs, he should mount and complete the prayer while mounted. This is also one of the positions of ash-Shāfi'ī. Abū Ḥanīfa says that he should not.

The words *"remember Allah"* here mean to thank Him for the blessing of teaching you the form of the fear prayer which satisfies the obligation of prayer imposed on us.

Our scholars say that the basis of the prayer is supplication and a state of fear is one in which supplication is most appropriate which is why the prayer is not cancelled by fear. If the prayer were to be cancelled by fear, it would be more likely to be cancelled by other things, like illness or the like. Allah commanded us to safeguard the prayers in every situation: health or illness, at home or on a journey, in strength or weakness, fear or security. The obligation of prayer is never removed from the responsible person. It means perform the prayer as best you can. This is why the prayer differs from other acts of worship, all of which can be cancelled by excuses. Ibn al-'Arabī says, "Our scholars say that this is an immense matter and the one who abandons the prayer is killed because it resembles faith in that it is never removed."

وَالَّذِينَ يُتَوَفَّوْنَ مِنكُمْ وَيَذَرُونَ أَزْوَاجًا وَصِيَّةً
لِّأَزْوَاجِهِم مَّتَاعًا إِلَى الْحَوْلِ غَيْرَ إِخْرَاجٍ فَإِنْ خَرَجْنَ
فَلَا جُنَاحَ عَلَيْكُمْ فِي مَا فَعَلْنَ فِي أَنفُسِهِنَّ مِن
مَّعْرُوفٍ وَاللَّهُ عَزِيزٌ حَكِيمٌ ﴿٢٤٠﴾

240 *Those of you who die leaving wives behind*
should make a bequest to their wives
of maintenance for a year
without them having to leave their homes
But if they do leave you are not to blame
for anything they do with themselves

with correctness and courtesy.
Allah is Almighty, All-Wise.

Those of you who die leaving wives behind should make a bequest to their wives of maintenance for a year without them having to leave their homes

A group of commentators have said that this means that a widow should stay in the house of her husband for a year and that she is entitled to maintenance from his estate as long as she does not leave the house. If she leaves, the heirs can stop the maintenance. The period of a year was later abrogated by the prescription of the waiting period of four months and ten days and the maintenance was abrogated by the shares of inheritance in *Sūrat an-Nisā'*. Ibn 'Abbās, Qatāda, aḍ-Ḍaḥḥāk, Ibn Zayd and ar-Rabī' followed this opinion. There is disagreement about lodging as was discussed earlier in the comments on *āyat* 234. Mujāhid says that this *āyat* is not abrogated and that the waiting period is confirmed as being four months and ten days but then Allah gives widows a further bequest of lodging for seven months and twenty days during which they may continue to live in their husband's house if they wish or leave if they wish. Ibn 'Aṭiyya says that all this is removed by abrogation, which is agreed upon by everyone except for aṭ-Ṭabarī.

It does mean that the relatives of the deceased and his heirs who inherit the house should not expel his widow from it. This is part of their maintenance.

But if they do leave you are not to blame for anything they do with themselves with correctness and courtesy.

This refers to leaving before the year is up. Then there is nothing held against the guardian, judge or anyone else because the widow does not have to stay in the house for a whole year. It is said that it means that there is nothing wrong in cutting off their maintenance or for them to look for new husbands. Widows may remarry after their waiting period is finished. The words *"with correctness and courtesy"* here mean in accordance with the *Sharī'a.*

وَلِلْمُطَلَّقَاتِ مَتَاعٌ بِالْمَعْرُوفِ حَقًّا عَلَى الْمُتَّقِينَ ﴿٢٤١﴾ كَذَٰلِكَ
يُبَيِّنُ اللَّهُ لَكُمْ آيَاتِهِ لَعَلَّكُمْ تَعْقِلُونَ ﴿٢٤٢﴾

241 ***Divorced women should receive maintenance***
given with correctness and courtesy:
a duty for all who are godfearing.
242 ***In this way Allah makes His Signs clear to you,***
so that hopefully you will use your intellect.

People disagree about this *āyat*. Abū Thawr says that it is one of the *āyat*s of judgement, and every divorced woman is owed maintenance. That is what az-Zuhrī said, adding that it even applies to divorced slavegirls. Sa'īd ibn Jubayr said that every divorced woman receives maintenance. That is one of the positions of ash-Shāfi'ī. Mālik says that every woman divorced once or twice receives it, except in the case of a woman divorced before consummation whose dowry has been allotted; she simply receives half her dowry. If it has not been allotted, then she receives maintenance not exceeding the dowry of a woman of her status. There is no definition of the amount of maintenance, as Ibn al-Qāsim said.

أَلَمْ تَرَ إِلَى الَّذِينَ خَرَجُوا مِن دِيَارِهِمْ وَهُمْ
أُلُوفٌ حَذَرَ الْمَوْتِ فَقَالَ لَهُمُ اللَّهُ مُوتُوا ثُمَّ
أَحْيَاهُمْ إِنَّ اللَّهَ لَذُو فَضْلٍ عَلَى النَّاسِ وَلَٰكِنَّ
أَكْثَرَ النَّاسِ لَا يَشْكُرُونَ ﴿٢٤٣﴾

243 ***What do you think about those who left***
their homes in thousands in fear of death?
Allah said to them, 'Die!'
and then brought them back to life.
Allah shows great favour to mankind,
but most people are not grateful.

The literal meaning of the words *"What do you think... ?"* is "Do you not see?" but in this usage it refers to the vision of the heart and means "Do you not know?" Sibuwayh says that the phrase is used to call attention to the story of those people.

The story behind the *āyat* is that some of the tribe of Israel suffered a plague in a town called Dāwardān and fled from it. They went into a valley and Allah made them die there. Ibn 'Abbās said that there were four thousand of them and they said, "We will go to a land where there is no death," but Allah made them die anyway. A Prophet passed by them and prayed to Allah and He brought them back to life. It is said that they were dead for seven or eight days, and Allah knows best. Al-Ḥasan said that Allah made them die before their time was up as a punishment for them and then brought them back for the rest of their lifespans. It is said that he did that to them as a miracle for one of the Prophets whose name is said to be Sham'ūn.

It is also related that they fled from fighting or from *jihād*. When Allah commanded them to fight through Ezekiel and they feared death in *jihād*, they left their homes and fled from it and Allah made them die to teach them that nothing could save them from death. Then He brought them back to life and commanded them to fight.

Ibn 'Aṭiyya says that all these stories have weak *isnād*s. The important point about the *āyat* is that, in it, Allah informs his Prophet Muḥammad, may Allah bless him and grant him peace, about the importance of taking note of the mistakes of the people of the past and to acquaint him with some people who left their homes in flight from death and how Allah made them die and then brought them to life to show them and all those after them that death is in the hand of Allah and no one else and so there is no sense in having fear of it or in the delusion of being able to escape from it. Allah revealed this *āyat* before commanding the believers of the Community of Muḥammad to fight *jihād*. This is the position of aṭ-Ṭabarī.

The number referred to by the word "thousands" is said to be 60,000 or 80,000. Ibn 'Abbās said 40,000. Abū Mālik said 30,000. As-Suddī said 37,000. It is said to be 70,000. 8,000 is said as well as 4000 and other figures. The sound position is that it was more than 10,000 because of the plural used for "thousands".

The expression "in fear of death" means in order to avoid death. It is said that two angels shouted the word "Die!" at them, meaning that Allah said this by means of the angels, and Allah knows best.

The soundest of these positions and best known is that they fled from the plague, as Ibn 'Abbās said, and then a Prophet asked Allah to bring them back to life so that they could worship Allah, and Allah brought them back to life. Al-Ḥasan said that they all died at the same moment, including their animals.

The Prophet, may Allah bless him and grant him peace, said, "When the plague alights in a land where you are, do not leave it, fleeing from it." This indicates that it is permitted to leave a plague land if one is not fleeing from it.

As for the excellence of steadfastness in the plague, scholars say that Allah sends the plague as a punishment to whomever he wishes among the rebels and unbelievers of His slaves and sends it as means to martyrdom and mercy for the righteous. Mu'ādh said about the 'Amwas Plague, "It is martyrdom and mercy for them and the supplication of your Prophet: 'O Allah, give Mu'ādh and his family a portion of Your mercy.'" Abū Qilāba said, "I knew what martyrdom and mercy are, but I did not know what the supplication of your Prophet meant. I asked and was told that he asked for the obliteration of his community to be by stabbing and the plague." Jābir reported that the Prophet, may Allah bless him and grant him peace, said about the plague, "The one who flees from it is like the one who flees from battle. Whoever is patient is like the one who is steadfast in battle." It is reported that when 'Ā'isha asked him about the plague, the Prophet, peace be upon him, said, "It is a punishment which Allah sent to those before you. He made it a mercy for the believers. There is no one who comes into contact with the plague and then remains where he is with fortitude and in expectation of the reward, knowing that only what Allah has written for him will befall him, who will receive any other reward than that of a martyr."

وَقَـٰتِلُوا۟ فِى سَبِيلِ ٱللَّهِ وَٱعْلَمُوٓا۟
أَنَّ ٱللَّهَ سَمِيعٌ عَلِيمٌ ﴿٢٤٤﴾

244 ***Fight in the Way of Allah.***
Know that Allah is All-Hearing, All-Knowing.

This is addressed to the Community of Muḥammad, may Allah bless him and grant him peace, ordering them to fight in the Way of Allah. The goal of this fighting is to make the word of Allah uppermost. The ways of Allah are many and varied, and the *āyat* applies to all of them. Allah says, *"Say: this is My way."* (12:108) Mālik said, "The ways of Allah are many and there is not one of them which should not be fought on, in or for. The greatest of them is the *dīn* of Islam. There is no disagreement about this."

It also is said that the people addressed are those of the tribe of Israel who were brought to life. That is related from Ibn 'Abbās and aḍ-Ḍaḥḥāk, who say that the *wa* (and) which comes at the beginning of the *āyat* connects it to the previous matter and if this is the case then something is elided and what is intended is: "He said to them, 'Fight…'"

An-Naḥḥās said that the *āyat* is a command to the believers not to flee in the face of fighting. It means, "Know that Allah hears your words if you say the like of what those people said and He knows your intention." Aṭ-Ṭabarī said that those who say that it is those who were brought to life who were commanded to fight have no basis for what they say. Allah knows best.

مَّن ذَا ٱلَّذِى يُقْرِضُ ٱللَّهَ قَرْضًا حَسَنًا فَيُضَٰعِفَهُۥ لَهُۥٓ
أَضْعَافًا كَثِيرَةً وَٱللَّهُ يَقْبِضُ وَيَبْصُۜطُ وَإِلَيْهِ تُرْجَعُونَ ﴿٢٤٥﴾

245 ***Is there anyone who will make Allah a generous loan***
so that He can multiply it
for him many times over?
Allah both restricts and expands.
And you will be returned to Him.

Is there anyone who will make Allah a generous loan

Allah commanded *jihād* and fighting for the truth and there is nothing in the *Sharī'a* which it is not permitted to fight for, the greatest object being the *dīn* of Islam as Mālik said. Then Allah encouraged people to spend to that end and included this in this passage about fighting in the Way of Allah. So a person spends hoping for the reward for fighting, as 'Uthmān ibn 'Affān did in the case of the Army of Hardship.[1]

When this *āyat* was revealed, Abū'd-Daḥdāḥ set out to give all his wealth as *ṣadaqa*, seeking the reward of his Lord. It is reported that when it was revealed, Abū'd-Daḥdāḥ said, "Messenger of Allah, does Allah desire a loan from us?" He replied, "Yes, Abū'd-Daḥdāḥ ." Abū'd-Daḥdāḥ said, "Give me your hand." He gave it to him and he said, "I have lent Allah a garden with six hundred palm trees in it." Then he walked to the garden where Umm ad-Daḥdāḥ was with his family. He called her, "Umm ad-Daḥdāḥ!" "At your service!" she replied. He said, "Come out. I have lent my Lord a garden with six hundred palm trees in it." In another variant, he had two gardens and when he offered them both, the Prophet, may Allah bless him and grant him peace, told him to give one and

1. This was the expedition to Tabūk in 9/631. 'Uthmān gave 1000 dinars to help equip people so they could participate. See pp. 677-678.

keep the other to live on. He gave the best of them and the Prophet said, "Allah will repay you with the Garden for them."

Ibn al-'Arabī said, "By the judgement, wisdom, power, will and decree of the Creator, when people heard this *āyat*, they were separated into categories and divided into three groups. The first group are base. They said, "The Lord of Muḥammad is poor and in need of us and we are rich and independent." This is unconcealed ignorance. They are refuted by His words, *"Allah has heard the words of those who say, 'Allah is poor and we are rich.'"* (3:181) The second group preferred avarice and miserliness and desired wealth and did not spend in the way of Allah or ransom captives or help anyone, being too lazy to obey and relying on this world. The third group set out to obey Allah, choosing to respond to what they heard with haste like Abū'd-Daḥdāḥ and others, and Allah knows best.

The word used for "loan" here is *qarḍ. Aqraḍa* means to advance money to someone. *Qirḍ* is used in another dialect. The word *miqrāḍ,* meaning scissors, comes from it, because *aqraḍa* implies cutting out a piece of one's wealth. Another form of the word is used for when the traces of a people are cut off and they are destroyed. The word is used to make it familiar to people in a way that they will understand. Allah is Rich-beyond-need and Praiseworthy but He likens the giving of the believer in this world in exchange for what he hopes for of reward in the Next World to a loan, as He likens the giving of lives and property in order to obtain the Garden to buying and selling, as will be discussed in *Sūrat at-Tawba* (9), Allah willing.

It is said that the aim of this *āyat* is to encourage *ṣadaqa* and spending wealth in the Way of Allah to help the poor and needy and to be generous with them. Allah alludes to the poor by mentioning Himself, even though He is sublime and beyond need of anything, to encourage *ṣadaqa*, as He alludes to the sick, hungry and thirsty by mentioning Himself in the famous *ḥadīth*: "Son of Ādam, I was ill and You did not visit Me; I asked you for food and you did not feed Me; I asked you for water and you did not give it to Me." The reply was, "O Lord, how could I give you water when

You are the Lord of the worlds?" He said, "My slave asked you for water and you did not give it to him. If you had given it to him, you would have found that with Me." This *ḥadīth* can be found in both al-Bukhārī and Muslim.

Someone who asks for a loan is duty-bound to repay the loan and Allah has made it clear that those who spend in the Way of Allah certainly do not lose by doing so. In a *ḥadīth* we read, "Spending in the Way of Allah is multiplied seven hundred times or more." The reward for a loan is so large because it gives expansion to the Muslim and relieves him. Ibn Mājah related in the *Sunan* from Anas ibn Mālik that the Messenger of Allah, may Allah bless him and grant him peace, said, "On the Night Journey I saw written on the gate of the Garden, '*Ṣadaqa* is rewarded ten times over and a loan eighteen times.' I asked Jibrīl, 'Why is a loan better than *ṣadaqa*?' He replied, 'Because the beggar may ask when he has something but the one who asks for a loan only does so out of real need.'"

A loan in the *Sharī'a* is one to one, in other words, a person returns what has been lent him. Scholars agree that it is permitted to lend dinars, dirhams, wheat, barley, dates and all similar goods. The Muslims agree that stipulating an increase over and above what has been lent is usury, even if it is only a handful of fodder. It is, however, permitted to give more when repaying provided that it was not a precondition because that is courtesy and the *ḥadīth* transmitted by Abū Hurayra, may Allah be pleased with him, reports, "The best of you is the best of you in repayment." It is not permitted for someone who takes a loan to give a gift to the one who gave him the loan while it is still outstanding nor is it permitted for the lender to accept it unless that is their normal custom, and the *Sunna* has brought this.

The word "generous" (*ḥasan*, literally "good") means what is reckoned as good by the lender and in addition implies not entailing obligation or harm.

so that He can multiply it for him many times over?

This stresses the idea of great increase. Al-Ḥasan and as-Suddī say that only Allah knows what this multiplication entails. Abū Hurayra said that this is about money given to help in *jihād*.

Allah both restricts and expands.
This is general to everything.

أَلَمْ تَرَ إِلَى الْمَلَإِ مِنْ بَنِي إِسْرَآءِيلَ مِنْ بَعْدِ مُوسَىٰٓ إِذْ
قَالُواْ لِنَبِيٓءٍ لَّهُمُ ابْعَثْ لَنَا مَلِكًا نُّقَاتِلْ فِي سَبِيلِ
اللَّهِ ۖ قَالَ هَلْ عَسِيتُمُۥٓ إِن كُتِبَ عَلَيْكُمُ الْقِتَالُ
أَلَّا تُقَاتِلُواْ ۖ قَالُواْ وَمَا لَنَآ أَلَّا نُقَاتِلَ فِي سَبِيلِ اللَّهِ
وَقَدُ اخْرِجْنَا مِن دِيَٰرِنَا وَأَبْنَآئِنَا ۖ فَلَمَّا كُتِبَ عَلَيْهِمُ
الْقِتَالُ تَوَلَّوْاْ إِلَّا قَلِيلًا مِّنْهُمْ ۗ وَاللَّهُ عَلِيمٌۢ بِالظَّالِمِينَ ۖ ٢٤٦

246 *What do you think about the council*
of the tribe of Israel after Mūsā's time
when they said to one of their Prophets,
'Give us a king and we will fight
in the Way of Allah!'?
He said, 'Is it not possible that if fighting
were prescribed for you, you would not fight?'
They said, 'How could we not fight
in the way of Allah when we have been driven
from our homes and children?'
But then when fighting was prescribed for them,
they turned their backs – except for a few of them.
Allah knows the wrongdoers.

What do you think about the council of the tribe of Israel

In order to encourage fighting, Allah mentions another story which concerns the tribe of Israel. The "council" (*mala'*) are the nobles among a people. Az-Zajjāj said that they are called this because they are filled (*mala'a*) with everything they need. Here the "council" means representatives of the people, and *mala'* can be used as the name for a group, like *qawm* and *rahṭ*. The word also means good character.

after Mūsā's time

After his death.

When they said to one of their Prophets, 'Give us a king and we will fight in the Way of Allah!'?

It is said that the Prophet referred to was Shamwīl or Sham'ūn [Samuel]. Other things are said as well. This tells us that at that time the tribe of Israel were abased and defeated by their enemies and asked for permission to fight and were commanded to do so. When the command came many were faint-hearted. A few, however, were steadfast and so Allah gave them victory.

He said, 'Is it not possible that if fighting were prescribed for you, you would not fight?'

Ḥafs and the others read "*'asaytum*" whereas Warsh has "*'asītum*". The word *kutiba* (lit. written) here means "prescribed". When they saw the reality of fighting and thought about actually taking part in the battle, their resolve weakened.

But then when fighting was prescribed for them, they turned their backs –

The words "turned their backs" means that their intentions became muddled and the resolve failed. This happens with wealthy nations who incline to comfort and an easy life. When war occurs, they are reluctant to fight.

وَقَالَ لَهُمْ نَبِيُّهُمْ إِنَّ ٱللَّهَ قَدْ بَعَثَ لَكُمْ طَالُوتَ مَلِكًا
قَالُوٓا۟ أَنَّىٰ يَكُونُ لَهُ ٱلْمُلْكُ عَلَيْنَا وَنَحْنُ أَحَقُّ بِٱلْمُلْكِ
مِنْهُ وَلَمْ يُؤْتَ سَعَةً مِّنَ ٱلْمَالِ قَالَ إِنَّ ٱللَّهَ ٱصْطَفَىٰهُ
عَلَيْكُمْ وَزَادَهُۥ بَسْطَةً فِى ٱلْعِلْمِ وَٱلْجِسْمِ وَٱللَّهُ
يُؤْتِى مُلْكَهُۥ مَن يَشَآءُ وَٱللَّهُ وَٰسِعٌ عَلِيمٌ ٢٤٧

247 ***Their Prophet said to them,***
'Allah has appointed Ṭālūt to be your king.'
They said, 'How can he have kingship over us
when we have much more right
to kingship than he does?
He has not even got much wealth!'
He said, 'Allah has chosen him over you
and increased him greatly
in knowledge and physical strength.
Allah gives kingship to anyone He wills.
Allah is All-Encompassing, All-Knowing.'

Their Prophet said to them, 'Allah has appointed Ṭālūt to be your king.'

Their Prophet responded to their request. Ṭālūt (Saul) was a water-bearer, or tanner, or a mule driver but he was a man of knowledge and so Allah elevated him. He was from the tribe of Benjamin and not from the tribe of either prophethood or kingship. Prophethood was in the descendants of Levi and kingship in the tribes of Yahūdhā. That is why they objected. Wahb ibn Munabbih said, "When the Council of the tribe of Israel said this to Samuel, he asked Allah to send them a king and to show him who he was. Allah said to him, 'Keep an observant eye on the horn in your house. When a man comes to you at the time when the oil is bubbling up in the horn, he is the king of the tribe of Israel. Then anoint his head with it and make him their king.'" He said, "Ṭālūt was a tanner and went out looking for an animal he had lost. He went to Samuel to ask him to pray for him to find the animal or to find some relief and the oil bubbled up. So Samuel took him and anointed his head and told him, 'You are the king of the tribe of Israel whom Allah has commanded to be advanced to kingship.' Then he told the tribe of Israel, 'Allah has appointed Ṭālūt to be your king.'"

They said, 'How can he have kingship over us

"How can he rule us when we are more entitled to be kings than he is?" They also pointed out that he was poor, completely ignoring the strongest reason, which was the prior decree of Allah and their Prophet pointed out this conclusive argument against them: "Allah has chosen him over you." He made it clear to them that that was the reason why Ṭālūt was chosen.

He said, 'Allah has chosen him over you and increased him greatly in knowledge and physical strength.

He also possessed knowledge, which is the basis of a person's character, and physical strength which helped him in war and fighting. This *āyat,* therefore, provides the description of what a ruler should be like and the conditions governing rulership. A ruler merits his authority on the basis of knowledge, piety and strength, not on the basis of lineage. Lineage has no real say in the matter as knowledge and virtue supersede it as Allah makes clear by informing us that He chose Ṭālūt over them on account of his knowledge and strength. Ibn 'Abbās said, "At the time, Ṭālūt was the most knowledgeable man among the tribe of Israel, and the most complete. His physical stature alarmed the enemy." It is said that he was called Ṭālūt because of his height (*ṭawl*). It is also said that the increased strength took the form of great charity and courage, not actual physical strength.

This is the meaning of the words of the Prophet, may Allah bless him and grant him peace, to his wives: "The first of you to join me will be the one with the longest hand." It was Zaynab who died first because she used to work with her hands and give *ṣadaqa*. One of the interpreters said that what is meant by knowledge here is knowledge of war. This is making the general particular without any evidence for doing so. It is said that "increased knowledge" refers to the fact that Allah gave him revelation, but this would mean that Ṭālūt was a Prophet.

Allah gives kingship to anyone He wills.

Some commentators believe that these words are part of what Allah said to Muḥammad, may Allah bless him and grant him peace. It is said these are part of the words of Samuel and that is more likely. He said that to them when he saw their obstinacy and argumentativeness. He wanted to conclude his words with some definitive statement which could not be gainsaid, and so he said this. The ascription of a worldly kingdom to Allah is because He owns it.

وَقَالَ لَهُمْ نَبِيُّهُمْ إِنَّ ءَايَةَ مُلْكِهِۦٓ أَن يَأْتِيَكُمُ
ٱلتَّابُوتُ فِيهِ سَكِينَةٌ مِّن رَّبِّكُمْ وَبَقِيَّةٌ مِّمَّا تَرَكَ
ءَالُ مُوسَىٰ وَءَالُ هَٰرُونَ تَحْمِلُهُ ٱلْمَلَٰٓئِكَةُ إِنَّ
فِى ذَٰلِكَ لَءَايَةً لَّكُمْ إِن كُنتُم مُّؤْمِنِينَ ﴿٢٤٨﴾

248 *Their Prophet said to them,*
'The sign of his kingship
is that the Ark will come to you,
containing serenity from your Lord
and certain relics left
by the families of Mūsā and Hārūn.
It will be borne by angels.
There is a sign for you in that if you are believers.'

Their Prophet said to them, 'The sign of his kingship is that the Ark will come to you.

It is said that the Ark (*tābūt*) was sent down to Ādam. From him it reached Ya'qūb and from then on remained with the tribe of Israel. Those who fought with it were victorious until they disobeyed Allah and the Ark was seized and then the Amelekites defeated them: Jālūt (Goliath) and his people according to as-Suddī. So the tribe of Israel were forced to surrender the Ark to them. This is the strongest evidence that disobedience is the cause of failure, and this is clear.

An-Naḥḥās said that it is related that the sign in the Ark was that a groan was heard coming from it. When they heard that, they went out to fight. When there was no groan, they did not go out. It is said that they used to place it at a critical place on the battlefield and they would have victory. This continued until they disobeyed Allah and were defeated and the Ark was taken from them and they were abased. When they saw this, some of them arranged for a Council and they asked the Prophet of the time for a king and then rejected him as Allah tells us. When He gave them the decisive argument, they then asked for a clear sign of that.

We read in aṭ-Ṭabarī, "When they asked their Prophet for the clear sign regarding what he said, he called on his Lord and, because of that, affliction descended on the people who had taken the Ark. It was said that they put it in a temple of theirs in which there were idols and the idols were overturned. They said, 'Put it in the temple of the idols under the great idol,' and in the morning it was on top of the idol. They tied it to its feet and in the morning the hands and feet of the idol were cut off and cast under the Ark. So they took it and put it in a village and those people experienced pains in their necks. When the affliction was great, they said, 'It is this Ark which is the problem,' and they returned it to the tribe of Israel."

containing serenity from your Lord and certain relics left by the families of Musa and Harun.

People disagree about the "*sakīna*" (serenity) and the "*baqiyya*" (relics). The word *sakīna* is derived from *sukūn*, meaning tranquillity, gravity and serenity. So it means that the Ark was a reason for the serenity in their hearts despite their disagreement over Ṭālūt. We find a similar use of the word when Allah says, *"Allah sent down His serenity on him."* (9:40), meaning something which made his heart tranquil. They relied on it and did not abandon it when it accompanied them in war.

Wahb ibn Munabbih said, "The *sakīna* is a *rūḥ* (spirit) from Allah which spoke. When they disagreed about something, it clarified the matter for them, and when it shouted in war, they had victory." 'Alī ibn Abī Ṭālib said, "It was a wind which blew and had a face like a human being." It is said that it was a gale with two heads." Mujāhid said, "It was an animal like a cat with two wings, a tail and shining eyes. When it looked at an army, that army was defeated." Ibn 'Abbās said that it was a gold basin from the Garden in which the hearts of the Prophets were washed. As-Suddī said that. Ibn 'Aṭiyya said, "The sound view is that the Ark contained some excellent objects left by the Prophets and the hearts of the people were strengthened by that."

We read in *Ṣaḥīḥ* of Muslim that al-Barā' said, "A man was reciting *Sūrat al-Kahf* and he had a horse with him tethered by two ropes. Then a cloud came over him and began to draw near and his horse began to shy away from it. In the morning he went to the Prophet and mentioned that to him and he said, 'That was the *Sakīna* which descended on account of the Qur'ān.'"

Several things are said about the relics (*baqiyya*). It is said that they consisted of the staff of Mūsā, the staff of Hārūn, and fragments of the tablets because they were broken when Mūṣā threw them down. Ibn 'Abbās said that. 'Ikrima added the Torah to the list. Abū Ṣāliḥ said that it was the staff and garment of Mūsā and the garment of Hārūn and two tablets of the Torah. Other things along these lines are said. Ath-Thawrī said that some people said it was a measure of manna in a gold basin, the staff of Mūsā, the turban of Hārūn and fragments of the tablets. Aḍ-Ḍaḥḥāk said that the word refers to *jihād* and fighting the enemy. Ibn 'Aṭiyya said the command to do that was in the Ark, either written or by the mere fact of it being brought.

فَلَمَّا فَصَلَ طَالُوتُ بِالْجُنُودِ قَالَ إِنَّ اللَّهَ مُبْتَلِيكُم
بِنَهَرٍ فَمَن شَرِبَ مِنْهُ فَلَيْسَ مِنِّي وَمَن لَّمْ يَطْعَمْهُ
فَإِنَّهُ مِنِّي إِلَّا مَنِ اغْتَرَفَ غُرْفَةً بِيَدِهِ فَشَرِبُوا
مِنْهُ إِلَّا قَلِيلًا مِّنْهُمْ فَلَمَّا جَاوَزَهُ هُوَ وَالَّذِينَ ءَامَنُوا
مَعَهُ قَالُوا لَا طَاقَةَ لَنَا الْيَوْمَ بِجَالُوتَ وَجُنُودِهِ
قَالَ الَّذِينَ يَظُنُّونَ أَنَّهُم مُّلَاقُوا اللَّهِ كَم مِّن
فِئَةٍ قَلِيلَةٍ غَلَبَتْ فِئَةً كَثِيرَةً بِإِذْنِ اللَّهِ
وَاللَّهُ مَعَ الصَّابِرِينَ ﴿٢٤٩﴾

249 ***When Ṭālūt marched out with the army, he said,***
'Allah will test you with a river.
Anyone who drinks from it is not with me.
But anyone who does not taste it is with me –
except for him who merely scoops up
a little in his hand.'
But they drank from it – except for a few of them.
Then when he and those who believed with him
had crossed it, they said,
'We do not have the strength
to face Jālūt and his troops today.'
But those who were sure that
they were going to meet Allah
said, 'How many a small force has triumphed over
a much greater one by Allah's permission!
Allah is with the steadfast.

When Ṭālūt marched out with the army,

The word for march out (*faṣala*) means to go out with them but the verb also means "to separate from". Wahb ibn Munabbih said, "When Ṭālūt set out, they said to him, 'The water will not be enough for us, so ask Allah to make a river flow for us.' He said, 'Allah will test you with a river.'" According to as-Suddī, there were eighty thousand soldiers. Wahb continued, "No one stayed behind the army except for those excused by youth, age or illness." Qatāda said, "The river with which Allah tested them was a river between Jordan and Palestine. The reason for the test was so that Ṭālūt would know that those who left the water alone would obey him in respect of other things and those who were overcome by desire for water and disobeyed his command would disobey him in more important matters. It is related that they reached the river and were thirsty and the water was very sweet. That is why those who obeyed had an allowance of scooping up a handful to remove the pain of thirst from themselves. This was enough to relieve it.

he said, 'Allah will test you with a river.

Those who say that Ṭālūt was a Prophet take these words as a proof, since it is clear that Allah had revealed to him that this was a test from Allah for them. Those who say that he was not a Prophet say that it was Samuel who informed him of the revelation and then he informed the people. The test was to distinguish the sincere people from the falsehearted.

Anyone who drinks from it is not with me.

"He will not be one of my companions in this battle." It was not a test of their faith so they did not become unbelievers by doing that. As-Suddī said that they were eighty thousand and so they inevitably included believers, hypocrites, serious and lazy people.

But anyone who does not taste it is with me –

He uses *ṭama'a* rather than *shariba*. Allah does not repeat the same word, because the best style in Arabic is to avoid repetition and the style of the Qur'ān is the most eloquent possible. This is a part of that eloquence.

Our scholars use this as evidence for the principle of *sadd adh-dharā'i'* because the least taste is included in the word "taste". When "tasting" is forbidden, there is no way for someone to drink from what is forbidden.

The use of the word "taste" indicates that water is considered to be food. If it is food, it means that it nourishes and supports the body

except for him who merely scoops up a little in his hand.'

Scooping is taking something with the hand or a ladle. This usage means to do it once. Some say that when the word *gharfa* (Warsh) is used it means with one hand and when *ghurfa* (Ḥafs) is used it means with two, and some say that they both mean the same thing.

But they drank from it – except for a few of them.

Ibn 'Abbās said that they drank according to the degree of their certainty. The unbelievers drank eagerly, and those who were merely disobedient less than that. Seventy-six thousand of the people failed the test and only the believers remained, some of whom did not drink at all and some of whom took a handful. Those who drank were not quenched, but remained intensely thirsty.

Then when he and those who believed with him had crossed it,

This means that they crossed the river. Ibn 'Abbās and as-Suddī said, "Four thousand men crossed the river with him, including those who drank from it. When they saw Jālūt and his armies, which numbered one hundred thousand, all of them heavily armed, three thousand six hundred and eighty of his army left." If this is so, the believers who had certainty in the resurrection and the return to Allah and who said, *"How many a small force has triumphed over a much greater one by Allah's permission!"* were the same number as the people of Badr. Most commentators say that those who did not drink crossed the river with him and some of them said, "How can we face the enemy when they are so many!" and those with true resolve made the other statement. Al-Barā' ibn 'Āzib says that they were the same number as the people of Badr.

But those who were sure that they were going to meet Allah

Here *ẓann* means certainty. The word can also mean doubt.

said, 'How many a small force has triumphed over a much greater one by Allah's permission!'

A *"fi'a"* (force) is a group of people and section of them. It also comes from a root meaning to cut. This statement was to encourage fighting, being steadfast and obeying. This is how it is mandatory for us to behave. But ugly actions and false intentions have prevented that until we have reached the stage where a large number of us can be defeated by a small number of the enemy as we have seen happen more than once. That is what we have brought on ourselves!

In al-Bukhārī, Abū'd-Dardā' said, "We fight with our actions." In the *Musnad*, the Prophet, may Allah bless him and grant him peace, said, "Are you given provision and victory except on account of your weak ones?" Now actions are false and the weak are neglected. Steadfastness is scarce, reliance on Allah is weak and *taqwā* has completely disappeared! Allah says, *"Be steadfast, be supreme in steadfastness; be firm on the battlefield; and show fear of Allah"* (3:200); *"Put your trust in Allah"* (5:23); *"Allah is with those who show fear of Him and with those who are good-doers"* (16:128); *"Allah will certainly help those who help Him"* (22:40); and *"When you meet a troop, stand firm and remember Allah repeatedly so that perhaps you will be successful."* (8:45)

These are the reasons for victory and its preconditions. They are lacking and do not exist with us. We belong to Allah and to Him we return! Only the mention of the word Islam remains and only the merest trace of the *dīn* due to the appearance of corruption, excessive transgression and lack of guidance so that the enemy has conquered the lands of the east and west, land and sea. Seditions have become widespread, and the trials are terrible. There is no protection except with the All-Merciful!

وَلَمَّا بَرَزُوا۟ لِجَالُوتَ وَجُنُودِهِۦ قَالُوا۟ رَبَّنَآ
أَفْرِغْ عَلَيْنَا صَبْرًا وَثَبِّتْ أَقْدَامَنَا وَٱنصُرْنَا
عَلَى ٱلْقَوْمِ ٱلْكَٰفِرِينَ ﴿٢٥٠﴾

250 ***When they came out against Jālūt and his troops,***
they said, 'Our Lord, pour down
steadfastness upon us, and make our feet firm,
and help us against this unbelieving people.'

They went forth onto the field of battle. Jālūt was the ruler of the Amelekites and their king. His shadow extended for a mile. It is said that the Berbers are descended from him. It is said that he had three hundred thousand warriors. 'Ikrima said seventy thousand. When the believers saw their numbers, they prayed to their Lord, as the Prophet, may Allah bless him and grant him peace, prayed to Allah at the Battle of Badr.

فَهَزَمُوهُم بِإِذْنِ ٱللَّهِ وَقَتَلَ دَاوُۥدُ جَالُوتَ وَءَاتَىٰهُ
ٱللَّهُ ٱلْمُلْكَ وَٱلْحِكْمَةَ وَعَلَّمَهُۥ مِمَّا يَشَآءُ ۗ وَلَوْلَا
دَفْعُ ٱللَّهِ ٱلنَّاسَ بَعْضَهُم بِبَعْضٍ لَّفَسَدَتِ ٱلْأَرْضُ
وَلَٰكِنَّ ٱللَّهَ ذُو فَضْلٍ عَلَى ٱلْعَٰلَمِينَ ﴿٢٥١﴾

251 ***And with Allah's permission they routed them.***
Dā'ūd killed Jālūt

and Allah gave him kingship and wisdom
and taught him whatever He willed.
If it were not for Allah's driving some people back
by means of others,
the earth would have been corrupted.
But Allah shows favour to all the worlds.

And with Allah's permission they routed them.

Allah sent down victory on them. The root of the verb "*hazamū*" (they routed) literally means to break. It also means to sink a well. Zamzam is called "the Hazma of Jibrīl," meaning that he sunk it with his foot and water came out. Another form of the word means kindling.

Dā'ūd killed Jālūt

That was because King Ṭālūt selected him from his people to fight Jālūt. He was a short young man, sallow and sickly. Jālūt was one of the strongest and most powerful of men. He used to defeat entire armies on his own. Yet Jālūt was killed at Dā'ūd's hand. His full name was Dā'ud ibn Ishā [Jesse] or Dā'ūd ibn Zakariyyā and he was descended from Yahudhā ibn Ya'qūb in whose line was both prophethood and kingship. He was a shepherd and the youngest of his brothers and looked after the sheep while his seven brothers accompanied Ṭālūt. When war came, he said to himself, "I will go and see this fight." When he started on the way, he passed by a stone and it called out to him, "Dā'ud! Take me. It is through me that you will kill Jālūt." Then another stone called him and then another. So he took them and put them in his bag and went along.

Jālūt came forward seeking single combat. People backed away from him until Tālūt said, "If someone goes out and kills him, I will marry my daughter to him and give him authority over my property." Dā'ūd came forward and said, "I will go and kill him." Tālūt thought little of him when he saw him because of his youth and small size and rejected him. Jālūt called out a second and third time and Dā'ūd came out once more. Tālūt asked him, "Have you had any experience of fighting?" "Yes," he replied. "What was it?," he asked. He said, "A wolf attacked my sheep and I hit it and then cut off its head." Tālūt said, "Wolves are weak. Have you tested yourself against anything else?" "Yes," he said, "A lion came and I hit it and then took its jaws and split them. Do you think this man is stronger than a lion?" Tālūt had armour intended only for the person who was to fight Jālūt. He told him about it and it was brought and he put it on. Tālūt said, "Ride my horse and take my weapons," which he did.

When he had gone a short distance, people said, "The youth is a coward!" Dā'ūd said, "If Allah does not kill him for me and help me against him, this horse and armour will be of no use to me. I will fight him in the way I am used to fighting." Dā'ūd was extremely skilful with a slingshot. He dismounted and took his bag and tied it round him and took his sling and went out to Jālūt who was bristling in his armour. Jālūt said to him, "You, lad, come out against me!" "Yes," he replied. "You are scarcely even a match for a dog!" Tālūt said. "That may be so," replied Dā'ūd, "but you are less than that." He said, "I will feed your flesh to the birds and wild beasts today!" They approached one another. Jālūt went to seize Dā'ūd with his hand since he thought little of him. Dā'ud took the stone, put it in the sling, said the name of Allah and slung it and it hit him on the head and killed him. He removed his head and put it in his bag. The army was defeated in the subsequent confusion.

and Allah gave him kingship and wisdom.

As-Suddī said, "Allah made him the inheritor of both the kingdom of Tālūt and the prophethood of Samuel. He taught him how to make chain mail, speak the language of the birds and other forms of knowledge.

If it were not for Allah's driving some people back by means of others, the earth would have been corrupted.

For the word "driving" Nāfi' reads *difā'* while the rest read *daf'*. They are both verbal nouns.

Scholars disagree about the people by whom corruption is driven back. It is said that they are the *Abdāl*, who are forty men. Whenever one of them dies, Allah replaces him with another. They will all die on the Last Day. Twelve of them are in Syria, eight in Iraq. It is related that 'Alī said, "I heard the Messenger of Allah, may Allah bless him and grant him peace, say, 'The *Abdāl* are in Syria and they are forty men. When one of them dies, Allah replaces him with another man. By them succour is poured forth and by them He helps the believers against their enemies and removes affliction from the people of trials." (at-Tirmidhī al-Ḥākim, *Nawādir al-Uṣūl*)

The following is also transmitted from Abū'd-Dardā': "The Prophets are the pegs which hold the earth in place. When Prophethood was brought to an end, Allah replaced the Prophets with some of the people from the Community of Muḥammad, may Allah bless him and grant him peace, called the *Abdāl*. They are not superior to other people in respect of fasting or prayer, but on account of their good character, true scrupulousness, good intention, sound hearts and good counsel for all the Muslims, seeking Allah's pleasure by steadfastness, forbearance, intelligence, and humility without abasement. They are the khalifs of the Prophets, the people Allah has chosen for Himself and whom He has selected for Himself by His knowledge. They are forty true men. Thirty of them have a similar certainty to that of Ibrāhīm, the Friend of the All-Merciful. By them Allah drives away disliked things from the people of the earth and innovations which people have introduced. It is because of them that people have rain and provision. None of them dies without Allah putting someone else in his place."

Ibn 'Abbās said, "If it were not for Allah's driving back the enemy by the armies of the Muslims, the idolaters would have triumphed and killed the believers and ruined their towns and mosques." Sufyān ath-Thawrī said, "They are the martyrs who are the means by which the *dīn* is established." Makkī related that most of the commentators said, "If it were not that Allah has defended those who do not pray by those who do and those who are not fearful of Allah by those who are, people would have been destroyed for their wrong actions." Ath-Tha'labī and the rest of the commentators say, "If it were not for Allah's driving back the impious unbelievers by the pious believers, the earth would have been corrupted."

The Prophet, may Allah bless him and grant him peace, is reported as saying in a *ḥadīth*, "Allah drives the punishment away from those of my community who do not pray by those who do, from those who do not give *zakāt* by those who do, from those who do not perform *ḥajj* by those who do, and from those who do not do *jihād* by those who do. If they had all agreed to abandon these things, Allah would not put off their destruction for the blink of an eye." Then the Messenger of Allah, may Allah bless him and grant him peace, recited, *"If it were not for Allah's driving some people back by means of others, the earth would have been corrupted."*

The Prophet also said, "The angels call out every day: 'Were it not for Allah's slaves who pray, suckling children and grazing animals, the punishment would already have fallen upon you.'" (Abū Bakr al-Khaṭīb) It is also related from 'Abdullāh that the Messenger of Allah, may Allah bless him and grant him peace, said, "Were it not for humble men, grazing animals and suckling children, the punishment would already have fallen upon the believers."

Jābir reported that the Messenger of Allah, may Allah bless him and grant him peace, said, "By a man's rectitude, Allah puts right his children and grandchildren and the people of his house and the houses around him and they will remain in Allah's protection as long as he is among them." Qatāda said, "The believers experience trials on account of the unbelievers and the unbelievers experience well-being on account of the believers." Ibn 'Umar reported from the Prophet, may Allah bless him and grant him peace, "On account of a righteous believer Allah will drive away affliction from a hundred of the people of his household and his neighbours." Then he recited this *āyat*.

It is also said that this driving back is by means of the laws prescribed on the tongues of the Messengers. If it were not for that, people would plunder and loot one another and be destroyed. This is an excellent statement as it is general to restraining, defence and other things. Reflect on it. *"But Allah shows favour to all the worlds"* indicates that the fact that the believers avert the evil of the unbelievers is a favour and blessing from Him.

تِلْكَ ءَايَٰتُ ٱللَّهِ نَتْلُوهَا عَلَيْكَ
بِٱلْحَقِّ ۚ وَإِنَّكَ لَمِنَ ٱلْمُرْسَلِينَ ﴿٢٥٢﴾

252 ***Those are Allah's Signs***
which We recite to you with truth.
You are indeed one of the Messengers.

Allah is informing his Messenger, may Allah bless him and grant him peace, that only a sent Prophet will have knowledge of these signs which He mentions.

تِلْكَ ٱلرُّسُلُ فَضَّلْنَا بَعْضَهُمْ عَلَىٰ بَعْضٍ ۘ مِّنْهُم مَّن كَلَّمَ
ٱللَّهُ ۖ وَرَفَعَ بَعْضَهُمْ دَرَجَٰتٍ ۚ وَءَاتَيْنَا عِيسَى ٱبْنَ مَرْيَمَ
ٱلْبَيِّنَٰتِ وَأَيَّدْنَٰهُ بِرُوحِ ٱلْقُدُسِ ۗ وَلَوْ شَآءَ ٱللَّهُ مَا ٱقْتَتَلَ
ٱلَّذِينَ مِنۢ بَعْدِهِم مِّنۢ بَعْدِ مَا جَآءَتْهُمُ ٱلْبَيِّنَٰتُ وَلَٰكِنِ ٱخْتَلَفُوا۟
فَمِنْهُم مَّنْ ءَامَنَ وَمِنْهُم مَّن كَفَرَ ۚ وَلَوْ شَآءَ ٱللَّهُ مَا ٱقْتَتَلُوا۟ وَلَٰكِنَّ
ٱللَّهَ يَفْعَلُ مَا يُرِيدُ ﴿٢٥٣﴾

253 ***These Messengers:***
We favoured some of them over others.
Allah spoke directly to some of them
and raised up some of them in rank.
We gave Clear Signs to 'Īsā, son of Maryam,
and reinforced him with the Purest Rūḥ.
If Allah had willed, those who came after them
would not have fought each other
after the Clear Signs came to them,
but they differed.
Among them there are those who believe
and among them there are those who disbelieve.
If Allah had willed,
they would not have fought each other.
But Allah does whatever He desires.

These Messengers: We favoured some of them over others.

This *āyat* is confusing. There are firm *aḥādīth* in which the Prophet, may Allah bless him and grant him peace, stated, "Do not choose between the Messengers," and "Do not give preference to any of the Prophets of Allah," meaning "Do not say that this one is better than that one." Scholars disagree about this, some saying that these statements were made before there was revelation of his superiority and before he knew that he was the master of the children of Ādam and that the Qur'ān abrogated the prohibition of preference with this *āyat.*

Ibn Qutayba said that by his words, "I am the master of the children of Ādam" he meant on the Day of Rising because he will intercede on that day and he will have the banner of praise and the Basin. His words, "Do not prefer me to Mūsā" is a mark of his humility, as is the case with "No one should say that I am better than Yūnus ibn Mattā." The words of Allah, *"Do not be like the companion of the fish"* (68:48) indicate that the Messenger of Allah, peace be upon him, was better than him.

The leadership and excellence which Allah has given His Prophet on the Day of Rising over all the Prophets was not because of his actions, but rather because Allah preferred him and singled him out for this distinction. This is the interpretation which al-Muhallab preferred. One of them said, "It is forbidden to delve into that because delving into that is a means leading to argumentation and that would lead to mentioning the Prophets in a way which is not appropriate and might lessen the respect due to them. Our shaykhs said that it means that one does not say, "The Prophet is better than all the Prophets," which is the literal prohibition because that might lead to deprecation of the other Prophets. Allah is the One who knows the realities of things.

The best that is said is that the prohibition of preference is in respect of the reality of prophethood itself which is one trait in which there is no rivalry. Rivalry exists in increased states, election, miracles, and kindnesses, not in the fact of prophethood itself. That is why there are Messengers and "those with resolve", the one Allah took as a Friend, the one He spoke to, and those He raised in rank. This is excellent and combines the *aḥādīth* without the need for any abrogation.

Allah spoke directly to some of them.

The one to whom Allah spoke was Mūsā. The Messenger of Allah was asked about Ādam and whether he was a sent Prophet. He said, "He was a Prophet who was spoken to." Ibn 'Aṭiyya said, "The interpretation of people regarding this is that Ādam was spoken to in the Garden and so the special quality of Mūsā remains."

and raised up some of them in rank.

An-Naḥḥās said, "Some of the commentators, including Ibn 'Abbās, ash-Sha'bī and Mujāhid, said that this refers to Muḥammad, may Allah bless him and grant him peace. He said, 'I was sent to the red and black (i.e. all mankind), the earth was made a mosque for me, I was helped by terror at the distance of a month's travel, booty was made lawful for me, and I was given intercession.'" His marks of distiction include the Qur'ān, the splitting of the moon, the tree speaking to him, his feeding a lot of people from a few dates, and his obtaining milk from the sheep of

Umm Ma'bad after its milk had dried up. Ibn 'Aṭiyya said this and added, "He is the person with the largest community and by Him all the Prophets are sealed, not to mention other aspects of the great and noble character which Allah granted him." It is possible that it means both Muḥammad, may Allah bless him and grant him peace, and others whose signs are great. It is possible that it refers to His statement that He raised Idrīs up to a high place and to the ranks of the Prophets in the heavens as reported in the *ḥadīth* of the Night Journey.

We gave Clear Signs to 'Īsā, son of Maryam,

The clear signs of 'Īsā were bringing the dead to life, healing the blind and lepers, and creating a bird of clay as we read in the Qur'ān.

and reinforced him with the Purest Rūḥ.

"The Purest *Rūḥ*" is Jibrīl as already stated.

If Allah had willed, those who came after them would not have fought each other

By "them" Allah means the Messengers. It is said that the pronoun "them" refers specifically to Mūsā and 'Īsā. It is said that it is all the Messengers after them, which is the literal meaning of the *āyat*. It is said that fighting refers to what was done by people after they had all passed away but this is not the meaning. What is meant is people fighting one another after the time of each Prophet. People fell into disagreement after each Prophet. Some believed and some rejected out of rebellion, envy and desire for worldly goods. All of that is by the decree and will of Allah. If He had willed differently, whatever He had willed would have happened, but the secret in this matter is that He did not will other than what occurred.

يَٰٓأَيُّهَا ٱلَّذِينَ ءَامَنُوٓا۟ أَنفِقُوا۟ مِمَّا رَزَقْنَٰكُم مِّن قَبْلِ أَن
يَأْتِىَ يَوْمٌ لَّا بَيْعٌ فِيهِ وَلَا خُلَّةٌ وَلَا شَفَٰعَةٌ وَٱلْكَٰفِرُونَ
هُمُ ٱلظَّٰلِمُونَ ﴿٢٥٤﴾

254 ***You who believe! give away***
some of what We have provided for you
before a Day arrives on which
there is no trading,
no close friendship
and no intercession.
It is the unbelievers who are the wrongdoers.

Al-Ḥasan said that this *āyat* refers to obligatory *zakāt*. Ibn Jurayj and Sa'īd ibn Jubayr said that it includes both obligatory *zakāt* and *ṣadaqa*. Ibn 'Aṭiyya says that this is sound, but the previous *āyat*s which mention fighting and tell us that Allah drives back the unbelievers by means of the believers makes it probable that this is a recommendation rather than an explicit command. It is in the Way of Allah. That is reinforced by the words at the end, *"It is the unbelievers who are the wrongdoers,"* meaning: "Fight with your lives and also by spending your wealth."

According to this interpretation, spending wealth is sometimes mandatory and sometimes recommended according to whether *jihād* is obligatory individually or not. Allah commands His slaves to spend from what He has provided them with and blessed them by and warned them against withholding from spending until a day comes in which it is not possible to buy or sell or obtain maintenance.

"*Khulla*" (close friendship) means sincere mutual love. It is derived from the word *takhallala*, which refers to the interpenetration of secrets between friends. *Khilāla*, *khulāla* and *khalāla* are all words for true friendship and love. *Khulla* can also mean land without thorny trees. *Khalla* is need and poverty. More will be said about the derivation of *Khalīl* (friend) in *Sūrat an-Nisā'*. *Khilla* is a scabbard. Allah tells us that there will no friendship or intercession in the Next World except by the permission of Allah. Its reality is mercy from Him to honour the one who is permitted to intercede.

It is the unbelievers who are the wrongdoers.

'Aṭā' ibn Dīnār said, "Praise be to Allah who said this, and did not say that the wrongdoers are the unbelievers!"

ٱللَّهُ لَآ إِلَٰهَ إِلَّا هُوَ ٱلۡحَيُّ ٱلۡقَيُّومُۚ لَا تَأۡخُذُهُۥ سِنَةٞ وَلَا نَوۡمٞۚ
لَّهُۥ مَا فِي ٱلسَّمَٰوَٰتِ وَمَا فِي ٱلۡأَرۡضِۗ مَن ذَا ٱلَّذِي يَشۡفَعُ
عِندَهُۥٓ إِلَّا بِإِذۡنِهِۦۚ يَعۡلَمُ مَا بَيۡنَ أَيۡدِيهِمۡ وَمَا خَلۡفَهُمۡۖ وَلَا يُحِيطُونَ
بِشَيۡءٖ مِّنۡ عِلۡمِهِۦٓ إِلَّا بِمَا شَآءَۚ وَسِعَ كُرۡسِيُّهُ ٱلسَّمَٰوَٰتِ
وَٱلۡأَرۡضَۖ وَلَا يَـُٔودُهُۥ حِفۡظُهُمَاۚ وَهُوَ ٱلۡعَلِيُّ ٱلۡعَظِيمُ ٢٥٥

255 ***Allah,***
there is no god but Him,
the Living, the Self-Sustaining.
He is not subject to drowsiness or sleep.
Everything in the heavens and the earth belongs to Him.
Who can intercede with Him except by His permission?
He knows what is before them and what is behind them
but they cannot grasp any of His knowledge
save what He wills.
His Footstool encompasses the heavens and the earth
and their preservation does not tire Him
He is the Most High, the Magnificent.

Allah, there is no god but Him,

This is the Throne Verse,[1] the Master of the *Āyat*s of the Qur'an and the greatest *āyat*. It was revealed at night and the Prophet, may Allah bless him and grant him peace, summoned Zayd and he wrote it down. It is related that Muḥammad ibn al-Ḥanafiyya said, "When the *Āyat al-Kursī* was revealed, every idol in this world prostrated, every king in this world prostrated and the crowns fell from their heads. The shayṭāns fled, hitting one another, and went to Iblīs and told him what was happening among them. He commanded them to investigate what had occurred and they went to Madina and heard that the Throne Verse had been revealed."

The Imāms report from Ubayy ibn Ka'b, "The Messenger of Allah, may Allah bless him and grant him peace, said, 'Abū'l-Mundhir! Do you know which verse of the Book of Allah is the greatest?' I said, 'Allah and His Messenger know best.' He said, *'Allah, there is no god but Him, the Living, the Self-Sustaining.'*" Abū 'Abdullāh said, "Allah revealed this *āyat* and made the reward for its reciter both immediate and later. The immediate reward is that it protects the one who recites it from disasters." When 'Abdu'r-Raḥmān ibn 'Awf entered his house, he would recite the *Āyat al-Kursī* in the four corners of his house. He intended by that to guard the four sides and to expel *Shayṭān* from the house.

We read in a tradition, "If someone recites the *Āyat al-Kursī* after every prayer, the Master of Majesty and Nobility will take his spirit directly and he will be like one who fights alongside the Prophets of Allah until he is martyred." 'Alī said, "I heard your Prophet, may Allah bless him and grant him peace, say on the *minbar*, "If someone recites the *Āyat al-Kursī* after every prayer, only death keeps him from entering the Garden, and only someone who is true or a worshipper will persist in it. If someone recites it when he goes to bed, Allah will protect him, his neighbour, his neighbour's neighbour and the houses around him."

1. *Āyat al-Kursī*. Literally translated, this should be the "Verse of the Footstool", but the term "Throne Verse" is maintained here as it is more commonly used. The "Throne" is actually *"al-'arsh"*, and the difference between the two can be seen on page 657.

It is reported from Ubayy ibn Ka'b that Allah Almighty said to Mūsā, "Mūsā, anyone who recites the *Āyat al-Kursī* after every prayer will be given the reward of the Prophets." Abū 'Abdullāh said, "I think that it means that he will be given the reward of the action of the Prophets. None but the Prophets have the reward of Prophethood." This *āyat* contains the truth of *tawḥīd* and the lofty attributes. It is fifty words long, and each word contains fifty blessings. It is equal to a third of the Qur'ān, as a *ḥadīth* reports.

the Living, the Self-Sustaining.

These are combined attributes of Allah. "*Al-Ḥayy*" (The Living) is one of His Beautiful Names. It is said that when 'Īsā wanted to bring the dead to life, he made this supplication, "O Living, O Self-Sustaining." It is said that it was used by Āṣaf when he wanted to bring the throne of Bilqīs to Sulaymān. It is said that it is the supplication people at sea should make when they fear drowning. Qatāda says that it is the Living who does not die. As-Suddī says that it means the One who goes on for ever.

It is said that His greatest name is "*al-Qayyūm*" (The Self-Sustaining), meaning the One who undertakes to uphold everything He has created, as Qatāda said. Al-Ḥasan said that it means the One who attends to every self in respect of what it earns until He has repaid it for its actions, as He knows them, and nothing is hidden from Him. Ibn 'Abbās said, "It means: the One who does not change or vanish."

Al-Bayhaqī said that he saw in the *'Uyūn at-Tafsīr* that Ismā'īl aḍ-Ḍarīr said, "It means the One who does not sleep," which is taken from the verse after it. Al-Kalbī said, "*Al-Qayyūm* is the One with no beginning." Al-Anbārī mentioned that.

He is not subject to drowsiness or sleep.

Then Allah denies that He is subject to drowsiness or sleep. Drowsiness is what affects the eyes and sleep affects the heart. Ibn Zayd said that it is when someone rises from sleep confused. Generally speaking, it is fatigue which affects a person. What is meant by the *āyat* is that He is not affected by lapses or weariness in any way.

People mention what Abū Hurayra reported about a story which the Messenger of Allah, may Allah bless him and grant him peace, recounted on the *minbar*: "Once Mūsā wondered about whether Allah slept and so Allah sent an angel to him to keep him awake for three nights and then gave him two bottles, one in each hand, and commanded him to look after them. He began to fall asleep and his hands almost released them. Then he moved them apart. When he fell asleep, his hands banged together and bottles broke." He said that Allah made an example by that illustrating the fact that if He were to sleep, the heavens and the earth would not be maintained. (al-Bayhaqī)

Everything in the heavens and the earth belongs to Him.

He owns them, so He is the King and Lord of all.

Who can intercede with Him except by His permission?

It is affirmed in this *āyat* that Allah gives permission to whomever He wishes to be an intercessor. They are the Prophets, the scholars, those who strive, angels and others whom Allah has honoured and ennobled. Then they only intercede for those Allah is pleased with as we know from His words: *"They do not intercede except on behalf of those with whom He is pleased."* (21:28)

Ibn 'Aṭiyya said, "It appears that the scholars and righteous intercede for those who have not reached the Fire and are between the two stages, or have arrived there, but have righteous deeds to their credit." In the *Ṣaḥīḥ* Collection of al-Bukhari in the *"Chapter on the rest of the gates of the Vision"* we find: "The believers will say, 'Our Lord, our brothers used to pray with us and fast with us.'" This is intercession for those who are borderline cases. As for the intercession of miscarried children at the gate of the Garden, it is for their parents. The Prophets intercede for the rebels of their community who are in the Fire for their wrong actions. It is not on account of kinship or acquaintance, but on account of faith alone. There then remains the intercession of the Most Merciful of the

Merciful for those who were immersed in errors and wrong actions for which the intercession of the Prophets does not prevail. As for the intercession of Muḥammad, may Allah bless him and grant him peace, to hasten the reckoning, that is his alone.

In his *Ṣaḥīḥ*, Muslim adequately explains how intercession takes place. The intercessors will enter the Fire and bring people out who deserve to be punished. So it is not unlikely that the believers have two intercessions: intercession for those who have not reached the Fire and the intercession of those who have reached it and entered it. May Allah protect us from it!

These *aḥādīth* indicate that the intercession of the believers and others is for those who enter the Fire. May Allah protect us from it! As for those who have not reached it, we read in another *ḥadīth*. transmitted by Ibn Mājah from Anas ibn Mālik, that the Messenger of Allah, may Allah bless him and grant him peace, said, "People will be lined up in rows on the Day or Rising. (Ibn Numayr said "the people of the Garden") and a man from the people of the Fire will pass by a man and say, 'Do you not remember me? Do you not remember the day you asked me for water and I gave you a drink?' The man will intercede for him. A man will pass another man and say, 'Do you not remember the day I brought you water for purification?' and he will intercede for him."

As for the intercession of our Prophet Muḥammad, may Allah bless him and grant him peace, there is disagreement about it. It is said that it will occur three times, or two or five times. It will be dealt with elsewhere.

He knows what is before them and what is behind them

"Them" in this phrase refers to everyone who has sentience. They are all included in *"everything in the heavens and the earth."* Mujāhid said that *"what is before them"* is this world and *"what is behind them"* is the Next World. Ibn 'Aṭiyya said, "All this is valid and there is nothing wrong with it."

but they cannot grasp any of His knowledge save what He wills.

Knowledge here means what is known, meaning that people do not encompass any of what He knows. This is like the statement of al-Khiḍr to Mūsā when the sparrow dipped its beak in the sea, "My knowledge and your knowledge does not diminish the knowledge of Allah except as this sparrow would diminish this sea." This and examples like it refer to known things because the knowledge of Allah is an attribute of His Essence which cannot be separated from it. The meaning is that no one knows other than what Allah wishes him to know.

His Footstool encompasses the heavens and the earth

In his *History*, Ibn 'Asākir mentioned from 'Alī that the Messenger of Allah, may Allah bless him and grant him peace, said, "The Footstool is made of pearl and the Pen is made of pearl and the length of the pen is seven thousand years and the height of the Footstool is only known by Allah." Ibn Mas'ūd is reported as saying, "There is a distance of five hundred years between every heaven and five hundred years between the seventh heaven and the Footstool, and between the Footstool and the Throne is a distance of five hundred years. The Throne is above the water and Allah is above the Throne. He knows what you are in and what you are on." Ibn 'Abbās said that His Footstool is His knowledge, and aṭ-Ṭabarī preferred that. It is said that it is His power by which He sustains the heavens and the earth, as the word *kursī* can be used for the underpinning of a thing.

Regarding this, as-Suddī reported that Abū Mālik said, "It is the rock on which the seventh earth stands and is the whole extent of creation in all its vastness. Four angels are over it. Each of them has four faces: a human face, a lion's face, an ox's face and an eagle's face. They attend to it and encompass the earths and heavens. Their heads are under the Footstool, and the Footstool is under the Throne. Allah has placed His Footstool above the Throne." Al-Bayhaqī said, "This statement indicates that there are two Footstools. One is under the Throne and one is above the Throne." Ibn Mas'ūd reported that some Companions said that the heavens and earth are inside the Footstool and the Footstool is in front of the Throne. The power of Allah is vast, and one must believe in it.

Al-Ḥasan said that the Footstool is the Throne itself, but this is not acceptable. The *aḥādīth* clearly state that the Footstool is a creation which is in front of the Throne and the Throne is greater than it. It is reported from Abū Dharr, "I said, 'Messenger of Allah, what is the greatest *āyat* revealed to you?' He replied, 'The *Āyat al-Kursī*.' Then he said, 'Abū Dharr, the heavens and the Footstool are only like a ring cast in the desert, and the size of the Throne compared to that of the Footstool is like the size of the desert compared to the ring.'" (al-Ajurri, al-Bayhaqī) Mujāhid said, "The heavens and the earth in comparison to the Throne are like a ring cast into the desert."

their preservation does not tire Him

This *āyat* tells us about the immensity of what Allah has created and one should deduce the immensity of Allah from the fact that it requires no effort for Him to preserve it all.

The word "tire" means to find something burdensome and hard. This is how Ibn 'Abbās, al-Ḥasan, Qatāda and others explained it. Az-Zajjāj says that the "him" can refer to Allah or it can refer to the Throne.

He is the Most High, the Magnificent.

"Al-'Alī" (The Most High) refers to height of power and position, not place, because Allah is free of being confined by space. *"Al-'Aẓīm"* (The Magnificent) describes His immense power, importance and nobility, not His physical size.

لَآ إِكْرَاهَ فِي ٱلدِّينِ قَد تَّبَيَّنَ ٱلرُّشْدُ مِنَ ٱلْغَيِّ فَمَن يَكْفُرْ
بِٱلطَّٰغُوتِ وَيُؤْمِنۢ بِٱللَّهِ فَقَدِ ٱسْتَمْسَكَ بِٱلْعُرْوَةِ
ٱلْوُثْقَىٰ لَا ٱنفِصَامَ لَهَا وَٱللَّهُ سَمِيعٌ عَلِيمٌ ٢٥٦

256 ***There is no compulsion where the dīn is concerned.***
Right guidance has become
clearly distinct from error.
Anyone who rejects false gods and believes in Allah
has grasped the Firmest Handhold,
which will never give way.
Allah is All-Hearing, All-Knowing.

There is no compulsion where the *dīn* is concerned.

The word *"dīn"* in this *āyat* means what is believed and religion since it is followed by *"Right guidance has become clearly distinct from error."* Compulsion can take place in judgements regarding oaths, sales, gifts and other things. This will be explained in *Sūrat an-Naḥl* (16:106), since this is not the place for it. To be rightly guided means to reach what is loved and to err is the opposite of that. An-Naḥḥās said that. The root of *"ghayy"* (error) refers to when someone is misguided in what he believes or thinks. One does not say that "error" (*ghayy*) is complete misguidance.

Scholars disagree and hold various positions regarding the legal status and meaning of this *āyat.*

- It is said that it is abrogated because the Prophet, may Allah bless him and grant him peace, forced the Arabs to adopt the *dīn* of Islam and fought them and was only pleased with Islam for them. Sulaymān ibn Mūsā took that view, saying, "It is abrogated by *'O Prophet! Do jihād against the unbelievers and the hypocrites.'* (9:73)" That is related from Ibn Mas'ūd and many commentators.

- It is not abrogated and was sent down about the people of the Book in particular and means that they are not forced to adopt Islam when they pay *jizya*. Those who are forced are the idolaters. Only Islam is accepted from them, and they are the ones about whom *'O Prophet! Do jihād against the unbelievers and the hypocrites'* (9:73) was revealed. This is the position of ash-Sha'bī, Qatāda, al-Ḥasan and aḍ-Ḍaḥḥāk. The evidence for this position is related by Zayd ibn Aslam from his father, "I heard 'Umar ibn al-Khaṭṭāb say to an old Christian woman, 'Become Muslim, old woman, become Muslim. Allah sent Muḥammad with the Truth.' She replied, 'I am an old woman and close to death.' 'Umar said, 'O Allah, witness!' and he recited, *'There is no compulsion where the dīn is concerned.'*"

- Abū Dāwūd reported from Ibn 'Abbās that this was revealed about the *Anṣār*. There was a woman, all of whose children had died. She made a vow that if she had a child who lived she would become a Jew. When the Banū'n-Naḍīr were exiled, among them were many of the children of the *Anṣār*. They said, "We will not leave our sons!" Then Allah revealed this. One variant has, "We did what we did and we think that their *dīn* is better than what we have." When Allah brought Islam, they denied it and this was revealed. Whoever wished remained with them and whoever wished, entered Islam. This is the position of Sa'īd ibn Jubayr, ash-Sha'bī and Mujāhid, but he added that the reason that they were with the Banū'n-Naḍīr was through suckling. An-Naḥḥās said, "The position of Ibn 'Abbās regarding this *āyat* is the best position since its *isnād* is sound."

- As-Suddī said that the *āyat* was revealed about a man of the *Anṣār* called Abū Ḥuṣayn who had two sons. Some merchants came from Syria to Madina with oil and when they wanted to leave, his sons went to them. They invited the two sons to become Christians and they did so and went back with them to Syria. Their father went to the Messenger of Allah, may Allah bless him and grant him peace, to complain about this and asked the Messenger of Allah to send someone to bring them back. Then *"There is no compulsion where the dīn is concerned"* was revealed. He had not then been commanded to fight the People of the Book. He said, "Allah has put them far. They are the first to disbelieve." Abū'l-Ḥuṣayn felt annoyed that the Prophet did not send someone after them. Then Allah revealed, *"No, by your Lord, they are not believers until they make you their judge in the disputes that break out between them"* (4:65). Then *"No compulsion"* was abrogated and he was commanded to fight the People of the Book in *Sūrat at-Tawba*. The sound view for the reason behind the words, *"No, by your Lord, they are not believers ..."* is the *ḥadīth* of az-Zubayr with his Christian neighbour about water as will be dealt with in *Sūra at-Tawba*, Allah willing.

- It is said that it means "do not call those who have submitted through the sword compelled and forced".
- It is said that it was related about captives who were People of the Book. They are not compelled when they are adults. If they are Magians, young or old, or idolaters, they are compelled to adopt Islam because their captivity does not help them when they are idolaters. Do you not see that their sacrifices are not eaten nor their women married. That is what Ibn al-Qāsim reported from Mālik. Ashhab said that children are considered to have the *dīn* of those who captured them. If they refuse that, they are compelled to become Muslim. Children have no *dīn* and that is why they are compelled to enter Islam so that they do not go to a false *dīn*. When other types of unbelievers pay the *jizya*, they are forced to become Muslim, whether they are Arabs or non-Arabs, Quraysh or otherwise. This will be dealt with in *Sūrat at-Tawba*.

Anyone who rejects false gods and believes in Allah

The word for "false gods" (*ṭāghūt*) comes from the root *ṭaghā* which means "to exceed the bounds". The word can indicate the plural or singular. It is said that the root of *ṭāghūt* is *ṭughyān* which means "overstepping the limits". Al-Jawharī said that the word *ṭāghūt* refers to soothsayers, shayṭāns and every leader in misguidance.

has grasped the Firmest Handhold,

This phrase is a metaphor. Commentators disagree about metaphorical usage (*tashbīh*). Mujāhid says that "the Firmest Handhold" is true belief and as-Suddī says that it means Islam. Ibn

'Abbās, Sa'īd ibn Jubayr and aḍ-Ḍaḥḥāk said, "It is *'lā ilāha illā'llāh'*." All these understandings actually amount to the same thing.

which will never give way.

Mujāhid said, "This should be understood alongside Allah's statement that *'He never changes a people's state unless they change what is in themselves'*. (13:11)" In other words He will not remove the designation of believer from them until they actually disbelieve. The word for "give way" (*infiṣām*) means to break, but not completely. When rejection of falsehood and faith in Allah are part of what the tongue articulates and the heart believes, Allah hears what is said and knows what is believed.

ٱللَّهُ وَلِىُّ ٱلَّذِينَ ءَامَنُوا۟ يُخْرِجُهُم مِّنَ ٱلظُّلُمَٰتِ إِلَى ٱلنُّورِ ۖ
وَٱلَّذِينَ كَفَرُوٓا۟ أَوْلِيَآؤُهُمُ ٱلطَّٰغُوتُ يُخْرِجُونَهُم مِّنَ ٱلنُّورِ
إِلَى ٱلظُّلُمَٰتِ ۗ أُو۟لَٰٓئِكَ أَصْحَٰبُ ٱلنَّارِ ۖ هُمْ فِيهَا خَٰلِدُونَ ٢٥٧

257 ***Allah is the Protector of those who believe.***
He brings them out of the darkness into the light.
But those who disbelieve
have false gods as protectors.
They take them from the light into the darkness.
Those are the Companions of the Fire
remaining in it timelessly, for ever.

The word "*Walī*" (Protector) signifies the One who helps His believing slaves. Qatāda said that the darkness mentioned in the *āyat* refers to misguidance and light to guidance. Aḍ-Ḍaḥḥāk and ar-Rabī' said much the same thing. Mujāhid and 'Abda ibn Abi Lubāba said that this was revealed about some people who believed in 'Īsā, upon him be peace. When Muḥammad, may Allah bless him and grant him peace, came, they also rejected him. That was their being brought out from the light into the darkness. The *āyat*, however, cannot be limited to that but rather applies to every disbelieving nation who had partial belief, like the Arabs had. That is because Allah is the Protector of those of them who believed and He brought them out of the darkness of disbelief into the light of belief. Those who disbelieved after the coming of the sent Prophet, may Allah bless him and grant him peace, were misguided by their shayṭāns. It is as if Shayṭān brought them out of faith when they were ready to enter it and so they will enter the Fire for their disbelief. That is justice and Allah is not asked about what He does. Al-Ḥasan said that "false gods" (*tāghūt*) here means shayṭāns. Allah knows best.

أَلَمْ تَرَ إِلَى اَلذِے حَآجَّ إِبْرَٰهِيمَ فِے رَبِّهِۦٓ أَنَ اٰتٰيٰهُ اُللَّهُ
اُلْمُلْكَ إِذْ قَالَ إِبْرَٰهِيمُ رَبِّيَ اَلذِے يُحْيِۦ وَيُمِيتُ قَالَ
أَنَآ أُحْيِۦ وَأُمِيتُ قَالَ إِبْرَٰهِيمُ فَإِنَّ اَللَّهَ يَأْتِے بِالشَّمْسِ
مِنَ اَلْمَشْرِقِ فَأْتِ بِهَا مِنَ اَلْمَغْرِبِ فَبُهِتَ اَلذِے كَفَرَ
وَاللَّهُ لَا يَهْدِے اِلْقَوْمَ اَلظَّٰلِمِينَ ﴿٢٥٨﴾

258 ***What about the one who argued with Ibrāhīm***
about his Lord,
on the basis that Allah had given him sovereignty?
Ibrāhīm said, 'My Lord is He
who gives life and causes to die.'
He said, 'I too give life and cause to die.'
Ibrāhīm said, 'Allah makes the sun
come from the East.
Make it come from the West.'
And the one who was an unbeliever
was dumbfounded.
Allah does not guide wrongdoing people.

The expression "What about?" (*ā lam tarā*) literally means "Have you seen?" and is frequently used in Arabic to introduce something surprising or astonishing. The "one" referred to in the *āyat* is generally taken to be Nimrod, the king of his time and the one who built the fire in which Ibrāhīm was put and was killed by a gnat. This is the position of Ibn 'Abbās, Mujāhid, Qatāda, ar-Rabī', as-Suddī, Ibn Isḥāq, Zayd ibn Aslam and others. He was destroyed when he tried to fight Allah. Allah sent a great cloud of gnats against him and they covered the sun and consumed his army until only their bones were left. One entered his brain and ate it until it became the size of a mouse. The dearest of people to him after that was the one who hit his head with a hammer! He suffered for forty days.

There are two versions of how the debate present in this *āyat* occurred. One is that the people went out to a festival they used to observe and Ibrāhīm went to their idols and broke them. When they returned, he said to them, "Do you worship something you have carved?" They said, "Who do you worship?" He said, "I worship my Lord who gives life and causes to die." It is also said that Nimrod had complete control of the foodstores of his people and when they wanted to eat, they had to buy food from him. When they went to him, they prostrated to him. Ibrāhīm entered and did not prostrate. He asked him, "Why do you not prostrate to me?" He replied, "I prostrate only to my Lord." Nimrod demanded, "Who is your Lord?" Ibrāhīm answered, "My Lord is He who gives life and causes to die."

Zayd ibn Aslam said, "This Nimrod had control of all the provisions of his people. When people came, he said, 'Who is your Lord and God?' 'You,' they said. 'Give them provision,' he said. Ibrāhīm came to seek provision and he asked him the same question. Ibrāhīm replied, 'My Lord is He who gives life and causes to die.' When he heard this, Nimrod said, 'I give life and cause to die.' Then Ibrāhīm asked him the question about the sun and he was dumbfounded. He said, 'Do not give him provision.' Ibrāhīm returned to his people with nothing. He passed by a heap of fine sand and said to himself. 'If I fill my sacks with this, when I enter the children will be happy until I can see to them.' He did that and when he reached his house, the children were happy and began to play on the sacks. He fell asleep from exhaustion and his wife said, 'I will prepare some food for him and he will find it ready when he wakes up.' She opened one of the sacks and found it to be the finest flour and baked it. When he rose, she put it before him. He asked, 'Where is this from?' She said, 'From the flour you brought.' Ibrāhīm knew that Allah had done that."

Ar-Rabī' said about this story that, when Nimrod said, "I give life and cause to die," he summoned two men. He killed one and released the other. He said, "I gave life to that one and made that one die." Then Ibrāhīm countered that with the question about the sun which dumbfounded him. It is related in a *ḥadīth* that Allah said, "The Final Hour will not come until I bring the sun from the West so that I know that I have the power to do that." Then Nimrod commanded Ibrāhīm to be thrown into the fire. That is what tyrants do. When they are opposed in something and unable to offer proof, they inflict punishment. Allah saved Ibrāhīm from the fire as we will see later.

As-Suddī said, "When Ibrāhīm emerged from the Fire, they brought him to the King. He had not been in his presence before that time. He spoke to him and asked, 'Who is your Lord?' He replied, 'My Lord is the One who gives life and causes to die.' Nimrod said, 'I give life and cause to die. I will take four people and put them in a room and will not give them food or water until they are starving. I will bring them out and feed two and they will live and not feed two who will die.' Then Ibrāhīm countered with the question about the sun and he was dumbfounded."

It should be pointed out that Ibrāhīm meant essential qualities in the first instance while Nimrod took what he said metaphorically. So Ibrāhīm left the argument and moved to an example which cannot be made metaphorical. *"And the one who was an unbeliever was dumbfounded."* The king could not argue and refute the second example.

This *āyat* indicates the permissibility of giving an unbeliever the title of "king" when he has kingdom, might and elevation in this world. It also is an affirmation of the use of debate and argument in establishing the proof of a matter and this is often found in the *Sunna* and Qur'ān. Allah says, *"Produce your evidence if you speak the truth,"* (2:111) and *"Have you authority to say this,"* (10:68), meaning evidence. Allah also described how Ibrāhīm argued with his people. Debate shows the difference between truth and falsehood only by the appearance of the proof of the truth and demonstration of the invalidity of false proof. The Prophet, may Allah bless him and grant him peace, debated with the People of the Book. The word "dumbfounded" (*buhita*) is when someone is stopped and falls silent out of confusion.

أَوْ كَالَّذِي مَرَّ عَلَىٰ قَرْيَةٍ وَهِيَ خَاوِيَةٌ عَلَىٰ عُرُوشِهَا
قَالَ أَنَّىٰ يُحْيِي هَٰذِهِ اللَّهُ بَعْدَ مَوْتِهَا فَأَمَاتَهُ اللَّهُ مِائَةَ
عَامٍ ثُمَّ بَعَثَهُ قَالَ كَمْ لَبِثْتَ قَالَ لَبِثْتُ يَوْمًا أَوْ بَعْضَ
يَوْمٍ قَالَ بَل لَّبِثْتَ مِائَةَ عَامٍ فَانظُرْ إِلَىٰ طَعَامِكَ
وَشَرَابِكَ لَمْ يَتَسَنَّهْ وَانظُرْ إِلَىٰ حِمَارِكَ وَلِنَجْعَلَكَ
ءَايَةً لِّلنَّاسِ وَانظُرْ إِلَى الْعِظَامِ كَيْفَ نُنشِرُهَا ثُمَّ
نَكْسُوهَا لَحْمًا فَلَمَّا تَبَيَّنَ لَهُ قَالَ أَعْلَمُ أَنَّ اللَّهَ عَلَىٰ
كُلِّ شَيْءٍ قَدِيرٌ ﴿٢٥٩﴾

259 ***Or the one who passed by a town***
which had fallen into ruin?
He asked, 'How can Allah restore this to life
when it has died?'
Allah caused him to die a hundred years
then brought him back to life.
Then He asked, 'How long have you been here?'

He replied, 'I have been here a day or part of a day.'
He said, 'Not so! You have been here a hundred years.
Look at your food and drink – it has not gone bad –
and look at your donkey
so We can make you a Sign for all mankind.
Look at the bones –
how We raise them up and clothe them in flesh.'
When it had become clear to him, he said,
'Now I know that Allah has power over all things.'

Or the one who passed by a town which had fallen into ruin?

"*Aw*" (or) is a conjunction which has its normal meaning here. According to al-Kasā'ī and al-Farrā' it refers back to the *"What about...?"* in the previous *āyat*. A *"qarya"* (town) is called that because people gather (*qarā*) in it.

Nājiyya ibn Ka'b, Qatāda, Ibn 'Abbās, ar-Rabī', 'Ikrima and aḍ-Ḍaḥḥāk said, "The one who passed by the town was 'Uzayr." Wahb ibn Munabbih, 'Abdullāh ibn 'Ubayd and 'Abdullāh ibn Bakr said that it was Irmiyā', who was a Prophet. Ibn Isḥāq said that Irmiyā' is al-Khiḍr. Ibn 'Aṭiyya said that that was also his position. If al-Khiḍr is Irmiyā', it is not improbable since al-Khiḍr has been alive from the time of Mūsā until now according to the sound position on that which will be talked about in *Sūrat al-Kahf*. Mujāhid said that he was an unnamed man of the tribe of Israel. An-Naqqāsh said that it is said that he was the servant of Lūṭ. Al-Qutaybī has one statement saying that it is Shu'ayb and the one who restored it to life after it was ruined was Kushik al-Farisi and that the town is Jerusalem as stated by Wahb ibn Munabbih, Qatāda, ar-Rabī' ibn Anas and others.

The story goes that Jerusalem had been destroyed by Nebuchadnezzar and the Israelites taken in captivity to Babylon. 'Uzayr was one of them. He was one of the scholars of the Israelites. He went out one day for something he needed to Dayr Hizqal on the banks of the Tigris. He stopped under the shade of a tree. He tied his donkey up in the shade of the tree and then went around the town and did not see anyone living there. It was fallen down and deserted. He said, "How can Allah restore this to life when it has died?"

It is said that it was the town from which thousands fled out of fear of death referred to earlier in 2:243. Ibn Zayd said that. Ibn Zayd said that it was those people who left their homes in thousands in fear of death and Allah told them, "Die!" A man passed by their decayed bones and stopped to look and said. "How can Allah restore this to life when it has died?" Allah caused him to die a hundred years. Ibn 'Aṭiyya, however, says that this position of Ibn Zayd is contrary to the words of the *āyat* since the *āyat* mentions a town fallen into ruin.

In the expression "fallen into ruin" (*khāwiyatun 'alā 'urūshihā*) the word *'urūsh* means roofs of houses and what is set up for the sake of shade or shelter. The expression means that the roofs fell in and then the walls fell in on top of them. That is what as-Suddī says and aṭ-Ṭabarī prefers it. Others said that it simply means that the place was uninhabited while the houses were still standing and the expression simply means "empty".

He asked, 'How can Allah restore this to life when it has died?'

This means: "by what means and method?" The literal meaning of the expression is about bringing the town back to life by restoring its inhabitants and prosperity, as one uses the expression today for the cities which are unlikely to be re-inhabited. Allah made a greater example than what the asker had intended by his question: actually bringing the dead to life. Ibn 'Aṭiyya said that the question does not imply doubt about the power of Allah Almighty to bring the town to life. It is ignorance of the way in which it could occur.

Allah caused him to die a hundred years then brought him back to life.

A year (*'ām*) is called that because it is the amount of time it takes for the sun to "swim" (*'āma*) around the celestial sphere. The literal meaning of this *āyat* is to make someone die by removing their *rūḥ* from their body. In the story behind this *āyat*, it is related that Allah sent a king to refurbish it and renew it so that it was complete when the speaker was revived. It is said that seventy years after his death Allah sent a Persian king called Kushk who refurbished it in thirty years.

Then He asked, 'How long have you been here?'

There is disagreement about the one who asked this. It is said that it was Allah Almighty. It is said that the man heard an unseen voice. It is said that it was Jibrīl or a Prophet or a believing man of the people who saw him. The most apparent position is that it was Allah because of the rest of the *āyat*. Allah knows best.

He replied, 'I have been here a day or part of a day.'

This is what he thought and so he was not lying when he said it. Ibn Jurayj, Qatāda and ar-Rabī' said that Allah made him die in the morning and then raised him up before sunset so that he thought that it was the same day. When he saw the remaining sun, he was afraid that he had lied in saying, "a day," so he added "or part of a day." He was told that he had been there a hundred years and he saw how the town was flourishing and its trees and buildings as evidence of that.

Look at your food and drink – it has not gone bad –

It is said that his food and drink consisted of green figs and grapes, which he had gathered from the trees of the town he passed by, and a skin of wine. The words *"it has not gone bad"* mean that it had not changed over the years. A lot is said about the derivation of this word *"gone bad"* and it comes down to either "your food has not been changed by drying up" or "it has not been changed by the passage of years," and so has remained fresh.

and look at your donkey

Wahb ibn Munabbih said, "Look at how we re-connect its bones and bring it to life bit by bit." It is related that Allah brought it to life by re-connecting its bones and then clothing them in flesh. Then an angel came and breathed the spirit into it and the donkey stood up and brayed. This is what most commentators say. Wahb and aḍ-Ḍaḥḥāk also said that it can mean: look at your donkey standing, untouched after a hundred years.

so We can make you a Sign for all mankind.

A sign of resurrection after death. He was still the age he had been when he died and his sons and grandsons were old men. 'Ikrima said that he was forty when he died. 'Alī said that his wife was pregnant when he left and that he was fifty. He returned to his family after his resurrection. Ibn 'Abbās related, "When Allah brought 'Uzayr to life and he mounted his donkey and rode to his home, he did not recognise people nor did they recognise him. He found an old blind woman in his house who was the mother of the household. This woman had been 20 when 'Uzayr left. He asked her, 'Is this Uzayr's house?' She said, 'Yes!' and wept and then said, ''Uzayr left us in such and such a year.' He said, 'I am 'Uzayr.' She said, ''Uzayr has been gone for a hundred years.' He replied, 'Allah made me die for a hundred years and then brought me to life again.' She said, ''Uzayr was someone whose supplication for the sick and afflicted was answered. Ask Allah to restore my sight to me.' He prayed to Allah and wiped her eyes with his hand and she was healed where she was as if she had been released. She said, 'I testify that you are 'Uzayr!' She went to the assembly of the tribe of Israel, which included a son of 'Uzayr's, who was one hundred and twenty-eight years old, and his grandsons who were old men. She said, 'People! By Allah, this is 'Uzayr!' His son went to him with the people and his son said, 'My father had a black mole like the crescent moon between his shoulders.' He saw it and knew that it was 'Uzayr."

Look at the bones – how We raise them up and clothe them in flesh.'

"Raise them up" is read as *nunshizuhā* by the Kufans and Ibn 'Āmir and *nunshiruhā* by everyone else. In either case it means to bring to life. It is as if death rolls up the bones and limbs and revivification and joining the limbs together is like spreading them out and opening them up (*nashara*) again. If it is read *nashaza* it means an elevated place and the verb means to raise. Makkī says that this gives the picture of the bones rising to one another.

When it had become clear to him, he said, 'Now I know that Allah has power over all things.'

Some say that he meant that he saw it with his own eyes and some say that it means that he understood it. Makkī said that he reported that he had witnessed the power of Allah to bring the dead to life and had certainty of that by witnessing its occurrence.

وَإِذْ قَالَ إِبْرَٰهِيمُ رَبِّ أَرِنِي كَيْفَ تُحْيِ ٱلْمَوْتَىٰ قَالَ أَوَلَمْ تُؤْمِن
قَالَ بَلَىٰ وَلَٰكِن لِّيَطْمَئِنَّ قَلْبِي قَالَ فَخُذْ أَرْبَعَةً مِّنَ ٱلطَّيْرِ فَصُرْهُنَّ
إِلَيْكَ ثُمَّ ٱجْعَلْ عَلَىٰ كُلِّ جَبَلٍ مِّنْهُنَّ جُزْءًا ثُمَّ ٱدْعُهُنَّ يَأْتِينَكَ
سَعْيًا وَٱعْلَمْ أَنَّ ٱللَّهَ عَزِيزٌ حَكِيمٌ ٢٦٠

260 *When Ibrāhīm said, 'My Lord, show me*
how You bring the dead to life.'
He asked, 'Do you not then believe?'
He replied, 'Indeed I do!
But so that my heart may be at peace.'
He said, 'Take four birds
and train them to yourself.
Then put a part of them on each mountain
and call to them;
they will come rushing to you.
Know that Allah is Almighty, All-Wise.'

When Ibrāhīm said, 'My Lord, show me how You bring the dead to life.' He asked, 'Do you not then believe?'

People disagree about Ibrāhīm's request and whether it arose out of doubt or not. The majority say that Ibrāhīm did not doubt that Allah could bring the dead to life but that he simply wanted to see it happen with his own eyes. That is because people have a natural desire for direct proof of what they are told. That is why the Prophet, may Allah bless him and grant him peace, said, "A report about something is not the same as actually seeing it." (Ibn 'Abbās) Al-Akhfash said, "He did not mean the seeing of the heart. He meant the seeing of the eye." Al-Ḥasan, Qatāda, Sa'īd ibn Jubayr and ar-Rabī' said that Ibrāhīm was asking in order to add certainty to his certainty. Some say that Ibrāhīm asked his Lord because he doubted the power of Allah and say that is what is meant by Ibn 'Abbās's words, "I consider this the most hopeful of *āyat*s." 'Aṭā' said. "Something of what enters the hearts of ordinary people entered Ibrāhīm's heart and he said, 'My Lord, show me how You bring the dead to life.'"

There is a *ḥadīth* from Abū Hurayra transmitted by al-Bukhārī and Muslim that the Messenger of Allah said, "We are more entitled to doubt than Ibrāhīm. He said, 'Lord, show me how You bring the dead to life,' and He asked, 'Do you not then believe.' He said, 'Yes, but so that my heart will be at rest.' Allah had mercy on Lūṭ. He took refuge in a strong pillar. If I had remained imprisoned for as long as Yūsuf, I would have answered the invitation.'" This is mentioned by aṭ-Ṭabarī, but Ibn 'Aṭiyya says that his interpretation [about the permissibility of doubt] is rejected.

As for what Ibn 'Abbās said, "I consider this the most hopeful of *āyat*s," that is because it contains boldness (*idlāl*) to Allah Almighty and asking for revivification in this world and there is no suspicion concerning it. It is permitted to say, "I consider this the most hopeful of *āyat*s" since Allah asked, "Do you not believe?" which shows that faith is enough and there is no need for delving and investigation. 'Aṭā's statement can refer to direct witnessing of bringing the dead to life, and the meaning of the *ḥadīth* is: "If he had doubted, then we would have been more entitled to doubt. We do not doubt, and so it is more likely that Ibrāhīm did not doubt either."

The *ḥadīth* is, in fact, negating any doubt on the part of Ibrāhīm. It is related that the Prophet, may Allah bless him and grant him peace, said about it, "That is pure faith." It concerns thoughts which do not last. Doubt means to hesitate between two matters without preferring one to the other. The *Khalīl* did not have that. Bringing the dead to life was affirmed when he heard it. Ibrāhīm knew it, as he said, "My Lord gives life and causes to die," earlier in this *sūra.* Doubt is far from someone whose feet are firm in faith, so how much more must that be the case with someone whose rank is that of a Prophet and Friend. It is agreed that Prophets are protected from major wrong actions and minor ones which are vile by consensus.

If you reflect on the request he made and all the words of the *āyat,* you will find that they do not imply doubt. It is a question of "how". It is a matter of the manner of the occurrence of a phenomenon which exists and is affirmed by the asker. It is like the questions, "How does Zayd know?", "How is cloth woven?" and other such things. "How" is a question about a state and here it asks about the manner of bringing to life. It is not sound to say that it implies doubt about the thing, although the expression can sometimes be used metaphorically with the aim of denial. Ibrāhīm affirmed that he believed.

Doubt of this sort is not permissible for the Prophets. It constitutes disbelief. The Prophets agree on Resurrection. Allah reported that Shayṭān has no way against His Prophets and *awliyā'*. He said, *"You have no authority over any of My slaves."* (15:42) If he has no power over them, how could he make them doubt? He was asking about how the parts of the dead are gathered together after they have been separated and how their sinews and skins are reconstituted after they have fallen apart. Some say that Ibrāhīm meant that he wanted to know how his Lord brings the hearts to life but this is false and rejected.

He replied, 'Indeed I do! But so that my heart may be at peace.'

"I make this request to You so that my heart will be at peace through seeing the difference between what is known by intellectual proof and what is known by direct experience. The peace of the heart is balance and stillness. The peace of the limbs is known, as in *rukū'* when they are still. The peace of the heart is that his thoughts have been stilled about the thing believed. Reflecting about the manner of revivification is not forbidden, just as we still reflect on it today when there are lessons to be learned from it. The *Khalīl* wanted to actually see it take place. Aṭ-Ṭabarī said that this means that he wanted to have certainty. It is also related that it was to increase his certainty. Ibn 'Aṭiyya points out that this is nonsensical since certainty is indivisible.

There is disagreement about what moved him to do this. It is said that Allah promised to make him His *Khalīl* and he wanted a sign of that. As-Sā'ib ibn Yazīd said that. It is said that it was the words of Nimrod, "I give life and cause to die," which made him ask. Al-Ḥasan said that he saw a riding animal which wild beasts and snakes had eaten and asked the question. It was half on the land and half in the sea. When he saw how it was split up, he wanted to know how it would be gathered back together so that his heart would be at peace by seeing how the parts would be rejoined when he saw how they were separated.

He said, 'Take four birds and train them to yourself. Then put a part of them on each mountain and call to them; they will come rushing to you.

It is said that they were a cock, a peacock, a dove and a crow. Ibn Isḥāq mentioned that from some scholars. Mujāhid, Ibn Jurayj 'Aṭā' ibn Yasār and Ibn Zayd said that. Ibn 'Abbās said it was a crane instead of a crow, and elsewhere an eagle in place of the dove.

Ibrāhīm took these birds as he was commanded and slaughtered them and then cut them into small pieces. He mixed their flesh together with the blood and feathers so that they were all jumbled together and then put parts of that mixture on each mountain. He stood where he could see those pieces while he kept the heads of the birds in his hand. Then he said, "Come by Allah's permission," and those parts flew and the blood flew to the blood and feathers to feathers until they were as they had been at first but headless. Then he repeated the call and they ran to him until their heads were placed on their bodies and they flew away by Allah's permission. Az-Zajjāj said that it means: "put a piece of each on each mountain."

The words "*ṣurhunna ilayka*" (train them to yourself) may mean make them incline to you but are also said to mean "cut them up". Ibn 'Abbās, Mujāhid, Abū 'Abīda and al-Anbarī said that. Ibn Isḥāq said that the expression comes from Syriac. Aḍ-Ḍaḥḥāk, 'Ikrima, and Ibn 'Abbās in another transmission said that it means "cut" in Nabatean. It is said that it means "to make them incline to you". It is said that there is something elided and the sense is: make them incline to you and then cut them up.

مَّثَلُ ٱلَّذِينَ يُنفِقُونَ أَمْوَٰلَهُمْ فِى سَبِيلِ ٱللَّهِ كَمَثَلِ
حَبَّةٍ أَنۢبَتَتْ سَبْعَ سَنَابِلَ فِى كُلِّ سُنۢبُلَةٍ مِّاْئَةُ حَبَّةٍ وَٱللَّهُ
يُضَٰعِفُ لِمَن يَشَآءُ وَٱللَّهُ وَٰسِعٌ عَلِيمٌ ﴿٢٦١﴾

261 ***The metaphor of those who spend their wealth***
in the Way of Allah
is that of a grain which produces seven ears;
in every ear there are a hundred grains.
Allah gives such multiplied increase
to whoever He wills.
Allah is All-Encompassing, All-Knowing.

After Allah related the evidence in support of fighting in the Way of Allah, He encouraged *jihād* and confirmed that those who do *jihād* after this without a Prophet having come to them will have an immense reward for their *jihād*. It is reported by al-Bustī from Ibn 'Umar, "When this *āyat* was revealed, the Messenger of Allah, may Allah bless him and grant him peace, said, 'Lord, give my community even more,' and then Allah revealed: *'Is there anyone who will make Allah a generous loan so that He can multiply it for him many times over?'* (2:245) The Messenger of Allah said, 'Lord, give my community even more than that,' and Allah revealed: *'The steadfast will be paid their wages in full without any reckoning.'* (39:10)."

This *āyat* stresses the nobility of spending in the Way of Allah and its excellence and encourages people to do that. There is an elision in the Arabic, which would be "The metaphor of the 'spending' of those who spend..." or "The metaphor of those who spend their wealth is like a farmer who plants his crop of grain in the earth..." The metaphor makes it clear that a good action is worth seven hundred good deeds. *"Allah gives such multiplied increase to whoever He wills."* means that it can be even more than seven hundred. The one who gives *ṣadaqa* is like a farmer. If he is intelligent in his work and the seed is good and the earth is fertile, the crop will be abundant. The same applies if the one who gives *ṣadaqa* is righteous and the wealth is good and he spends it in a place where the reward will be great. Some say that seven hundred fold is the maximum possible increase.

It is related that this *āyat* was revealed about 'Uthmān ibn 'Affān and 'Abdu'r-Raḥmān ibn 'Awf on the occasion when the Messenger of Allah encouraged people to give *ṣadaqa* when he was going on the Tabuk expedition. 'Abdu'r-Rahman brought him four thousand and said, "Messenger of Allah, I have eight thousand. I have kept four thousand for myself and my dependants and I am lending four thousand to my Lord." The Messenger of Allah said, "May Allah bless you in what you have kept and what you have given." 'Uthman said, "Messenger of Allah, I will kit out all those who have no equipment," and this was revealed about them. It is said that it was revealed about voluntary *ṣadaqa*. It is said that it was revealed before the *āyat* of *zakāt* and then abrogated by the *āyat* of *zakāt*. There is no need to claim abrogation because spending in the Way of Allah is recommended at every time. The ways of spending are numerous, and the greatest of them is *jihād* to raise high the word of Allah.

The type of grain referred to is not specified. The word used is *ḥabba* and can designate all grains that are cultivated and stored as food. Wheat, however, is the most famous of them.

The Qur'ān reports that a good action of any type is worth ten like it. This *āyat* tells us that spending in *jihād* is worth seven hundred. Scholars disagree about the meanings of *"Allah gives such multiplied increase to whoever He wills."* One group say that it explains what was mentioned about the seven hundred and does not indicate a greater increase than that. Another group says that it is to inform us that Allah can multiply it more than seven hundred times if He wishes. I consider this to be the soundest because of *aḥādīth* which mention that.

This *āyat* contains evidence that agriculture is a profession adopted by people which is a legitimate way of earning a living. This is why Allah uses it for metaphors. We read in *Ṣaḥīḥ* Muslim that the Prophet said, "There is no Muslim who plants a seedling or cultivates a crop from which birds, humans or animals eat without that being *ṣadaqa* for them," and 'Ā'isha reported that the Messenger of Allah, may Allah bless him and grant him peace, said, "Cling to cultivation in the hidden places of the earth."

الَّذِينَ يُنفِقُونَ أَمْوَالَهُمْ فِي سَبِيلِ اللَّهِ ثُمَّ لَا يُتْبِعُونَ
مَا أَنفَقُوا مَنًّا وَلَا أَذًى لَّهُمْ أَجْرُهُمْ عِندَ رَبِّهِمْ
وَلَا خَوْفٌ عَلَيْهِمْ وَلَا هُمْ يَحْزَنُونَ ٢٦٢

262 ***Those who spend their wealth in the Way of Allah,***
and then do not follow what they have spent
by demands for gratitude or insulting words
will have their reward with their Lord.
They will feel no fear and will know no sorrow.

Those who spend their wealth in the Way of Allah,

This was revealed about 'Uthmān ibn 'Affān. 'Abdu'r-Raḥmān ibn Samura said, "'Uthman brought a thousand dinars for the Army of Hardship and put it in the lap of the Messenger of Allah. I saw him put his hand in it and turn it about. He said, "It does not matter what 'Uthmān does after today. O Allah, do not forget this day for 'Uthmān." Abu Sa'īd al-Khudrī said, "I saw the Prophet raise his hands to pray for 'Uthmān, saying, 'My Lord, 'Uthmān! I am pleased with 'Uthmān, so be pleased with him. After dawn, this *āyat* was revealed."

Spending in the Way of Allah in general was mentioned in the previous *āyat* and then it is made clear in this *āyat* that judgement and reward is for the one who does not follow up what he gives with demands for gratitude or annoyance. For such an action would invalidate the *ṣadaqa* as Allah tells us in the next *āyat*. You must desire the face of Allah and His reward by spending and not hope for any kind of return for it from the one to whom you give it. If you desire something in exchange for it from the person then it is not for the Face of Allah.

and then do not follow what they have spent by demands for gratitude or insulting words

The expression "demands for gratitude" (*mann*) means to mention the blessing by enumerating it and rebuking the person by it, as when you say "I was good to you" and "I restored you" and "After all I have done for you" and other such things. Some say that *manna* means to speak about what you gave so that the recipient hears about it and to insult him. *Mann* is one of the great wrong actions. That is confirmed in *Ṣaḥīḥ* Muslim and elsewhere. Someone who does that is one of the three at whom Allah will not look and whom He will not purify on the Day of Rising, and they will have a painful punishment. Ibn 'Umar related that the Messenger of Allah, may Allah bless him and grant him peace, said, "There are three who will not enter the Garden: the one who disobeys his parents, a habitual drinker, and someone who demands gratitude for his gift."

The expression "*adhā*" (insulting words) means insulting and complaining, and is more general than *mann* which is mentioned because it frequently occurs. Ibn Zayd said, "If you think that your greeting will be onerous for someone on whom you have spent, desiring the Face of Allah, then do not greet him." A woman asked him, "Abu Usāma, show me a man who will truly go out in the Way of Allah. They only go out to consume fruits. I have arrows and a quiver." He said, "May Allah not bless your arrows and quiver! You have harmed them even before giving to them!"

They will feel no fear and will know no sorrow.

They will feel no fear for the future after death and no sorrow for what has passed of this world because they will delight in the Next World. This *āyat* also contains evidence for the excellence of the rich over the poor as will come later, Allah willing.

قَوْلٌ مَّعْرُوفٌ وَمَغْفِرَةٌ خَيْرٌ مِّن صَدَقَةٍ
يَتْبَعُهَآ أَذًى ۗ وَاللَّهُ غَنِيٌّ حَلِيمٌ ﴿٢٦٣﴾

263 ***Correct and courteous words***
accompanied by forgiveness
are better than ṣadaqa
followed by insulting words.
Allah is Rich Beyond Need, All-Forbearing.

Correct and courteous words

This includes making supplication, putting people at their ease and giving them hope for what is with Allah. That is better than *ṣadaqa* which is merely outward with no inward dimension, because correct words will have a reward while outward *ṣadaqa* may have no reward. The Prophet, may Allah bless him and grant him peace, said, "A good word is *ṣadaqa*, and it is part of correct behaviour to meet your brother with a cheerful face." (Muslim) One should meet the beggar with a smile and welcome him so that he will be thankful if you give to him and excuse you if you do not. One of the sages said, "Meet the one with a need with a smile. Even if you miss his gratitude you will not miss his pardon." In the *ḥadīth* of 'Umar we find that the Messenger of Allah, may Allah bless him and grant him peace, said, "When a beggar asks of you, do not interrupt his request until he finishes. Then turn to him with gravity and leniency, or spend a little, or give a good reply. One who is neither human nor jinn will come to you to look at what you do with what Allah has given you."

Its proof is the *ḥadīth* about the leper, the person with scabies and the blind man which Muslim and others transmitted. In that account an angel took the form of a leper, a bald man and a blind man to test the individual concerned.[1]

accompanied by forgiveness

This can refer to disregarding the defect and bad state of the needy and it is also said that its meaning is that to excuse a beggar when he is insistent and rude and harsh is better than giving him *ṣadaqa* with demands of gratitude and insults.

1. Abu Hurayra heard the Prophet, may Allah bless him and grant him peace, say, "Three of the Children of Isra'il were respectively leprous, suffering from scabies and blind. Allah wanted to put them to the test and so he sent an angel to them. He came to the leper and said, 'What would you like best?' He said, 'A good complexion and clear skin and the thing that I have which makes people find me unclean to be taken from me.' He wiped him and his impurity left him and he gave him a good complexion. He said, 'What property do you like best?' He said, 'Camels' and he gave him a pregnant she-camel.' He said, 'May Allah bless you in it.'" The same happened with the bald man and the blind man.

The *ḥadīth* continues: "Then he went to the leper in his own form and appearance and said, 'I am a poor man who has lost his means on his journey. Today I can seek none but Allah and then you. I ask you, by the One who gave you a good complexion and good skin and property, for a camel so that I can complete my journey.' He replied, 'I have many obligations.' He said, 'I seem to recognise you. Were you not a leper, that people found unclean, and poor and then Allah was generous to you?' He said, 'I inherited this property, elder son from elder son.' He said, 'If you are a liar in your claim, may Allah return you as you were!'" The same thing happened with the other two.

Allah is Rich Beyond Need, All-Forbearing.

Allah is Rich beyond need of the *ṣadaqa* of his slaves. He orders them to do it so that He can reward them for it. Part of His forbearance is that He does not hasten the punishment to the one who insults when he gives *ṣadaqa.*

يَٰٓأَيُّهَا ٱلَّذِينَ ءَامَنُوا۟ لَا تُبْطِلُوا۟ صَدَقَٰتِكُم بِٱلْمَنِّ وَٱلْأَذَىٰ
كَٱلَّذِى يُنفِقُ مَالَهُۥ رِئَآءَ ٱلنَّاسِ وَلَا يُؤْمِنُ بِٱللَّهِ
وَٱلْيَوْمِ ٱلْءَاخِرِ ۖ فَمَثَلُهُۥ كَمَثَلِ صَفْوَانٍ عَلَيْهِ تُرَابٌ
فَأَصَابَهُۥ وَابِلٌ فَتَرَكَهُۥ صَلْدًا ۖ لَّا يَقْدِرُونَ عَلَىٰ شَىْءٍ
مِّمَّا كَسَبُوا۟ ۗ وَٱللَّهُ لَا يَهْدِى ٱلْقَوْمَ ٱلْكَٰفِرِينَ ﴿٢٦٤﴾

264 *You who believe! do not nullify your ṣadaqa*
by demands for gratitude or insulting words,
like him who spends his wealth,
showing off to people
and not believing in Allah and the Last Day.
His likeness is that of a smooth rock
coated with soil, which,
when heavy rain falls on it, is left stripped bare.
They have no power over anything they have earned.
Allah does not guide disbelieving people.

You who believe! do not nullify your *ṣadaqa* by demands for gratitude or insulting words,

This tells us that Allah does not accept *ṣadaqa* which is marred in this way and that the reward for it is made null and void. It is an article of faith that, in general, evil deeds do not invalidate good deeds or cancel them out. Demands for gratitude and insults do not invalidate other *ṣadaqa* which has been made without them. The majority of scholars say that it is only the *ṣadaqa* which Allah knows has been used to impose gratitude or used as an insult which is not accepted. It is said that Allah appoints an angel over the giver who does not record that. This is good.

The Arabs say of someone who demands gratitude, that he has "a black hand." When he gives without asking, he has "a white hand." If someone gives after being asked, he has "a green hand". Ibn Sīrīn heard one man say to another man, "I did this and this for you!" He told him, "Be quiet! There is no good in charity when it is counted." The Prophet, may Allah bless him and grant him peace, said, "Beware of demanding gratitude for charity. It invalidates thankfulness and erases the reward." Then he recited this *āyat*.

Our scholars say that, on the basis of this *āyat*, Mālik disliked a man giving his obligatory *zakāt* to his relatives in case he might be praised in return for it or they should show gratitude towards him and recompense him for it. Then it would not be sincerely for the Face of Allah. He preferred it to be given to non-relatives and also preferred that someone other than the giver should undertake to distribute it, if there is no ruler to do so, to prevent the danger of demands for gratitude or insults, and that of praise, or recompense by service from the recipient. This is not the case with *ṣadaqa* because even its if reward is nullified, he is safe from any threat and is just like someone who has not done anything. When the obligatory is nullified, he is threatened about something he has failed to do.

like him who spends his wealth, showing off to people and not believing in Allah and the Last Day.

Allah likens someone who demands gratitude and inflicts insults through his *ṣadaqa* to someone who spends to show off to people, not for the Face of Allah and to an unbeliever who spends so that people will say that he is generous and praise him for it.

His likeness is that of a smooth rock coated with soil, which, when heavy rain falls on it, is left stripped bare.

Then this person is also likened to a smooth rock covered with soil. One would think to look at it that it is fertile, good earth but then the rain comes and washes it away and all that is left is bare rock. That is the metaphor for someone who gives to show off. The intention of seeking gratitude, insult and showing off will be disclosed in the Next World and the act of *ṣadaqa* will be null and void, in the same way that the heavy rain exposes the smooth stone. What is meant is that any person who spends to show off is not rewarded, like an unbeliever, because he does not intend the Face of Allah by his act so as to merit the reward. It is said that the reward is nullified from the moment he demands gratitude or insults. What is before that is written for him and multiplied. Then the insult stops the multiplication because *ṣadaqa* grows and grows until it is as big as a mountain. The first position, however, is most evident, and Allah knows best.

They have no power
This refers to those who show off, unbelievers and those who demand gratitude.

over anything they have earned.
This means that they will not reap the reward of their spending. What they give is simply considered as something they spend for their own needs since it is for other than Allah.

وَمَثَلُ الَّذِينَ يُنفِقُونَ أَمْوَٰلَهُمُ ابْتِغَآءَ مَرْضَاتِ اللَّهِ وَتَثْبِيتًا
مِّنْ أَنفُسِهِمْ كَمَثَلِ جَنَّةٍ بِرُبْوَةٍ أَصَابَهَا وَابِلٌ فَـَٔاتَتْ
أُكْلَهَا ضِعْفَيْنِ فَإِن لَّمْ يُصِبْهَا وَابِلٌ فَطَلٌّ وَاللَّهُ بِمَا
تَعْمَلُونَ بَصِيرٌ ﴿٢٦٥﴾

265 ***The metaphor of those who spend their wealth, desiring the pleasure of Allah***

and firmness for themselves,
is that of a garden on a hillside.
When heavy rain falls on it, it doubles its produce;
and if heavy rain does not fall, there is dew.
Allah sees what you do.

The metaphor of those who spend their wealth, desiring the pleasure of Allah and firmness for themselves,

There is some discussion about the word "*tathbīt*" (firmness) and whether it is a causative object. Ibn 'Aṭiyya says that it is not because spending does not "make firm" and so *tathbīt* cannot be a causative object and, in fact, *"ibtighā'"* (desiring) is a verbal noun. Allah mentions the *ṣadaqa* of those who gain nothing from their *ṣadaqa* and forbade the believers to vitiate their *ṣadaqa* like that in any way. He mentions the spending of the people whose *ṣadaqa* is pure since it is given in keeping with the commands of the *Sharī'a*.

It is said that the word *tathbīt* means that they confirm where they should give their *ṣadaqa*. Mujāhid and al-Ḥasan said that. Al-Ḥasan said, "When a man wants to give *ṣadaqa*, he 'confirms' it by examining himself. If it is truly for Allah, he should give it. If it is mixed with doubt, he should refrain from doing so. It is said that it means to confirm it and be certain about it, as Ibn 'Abbās said. Ibn 'Abbās and Qatāda also said that it means examining their own motives. Ash-Sha'bī, as-Suddī, Qatāda, Ibn Zayd, Abū Ṣāliḥ and others said that it means to make certain, in other words they look into themselves and confirm that their spending is out of obedience to Allah. These three positions are more correct than that of al-Ḥasan and Mujāhid.

is that of a garden on a hillside.

A *"janna"* (garden) is a piece of land with trees which shade it, taken from the linguistic root which means "to cover and conceal". The word *"rubwa"* (hillside) indicates a slightly elevated place which usually has a thick layer of good earth and is very fertile, which is why it is mentioned. Al-Khalīl also says that the water does not flood such a place as frequently happens with flashfloods in Arab lands. *"Rubwa"* (hillside) has various forms in dialects and in the different readings. *"Rubwa"* is the *qirā'a* of Ibn Kathīr. Ḥamza, al-Kisā'ī, Nāfi' and Abū 'Amr. 'Āṣim, Ibn 'Āmir and al-Hasan have *"rabwa"*.

When heavy rain falls on it, it doubles its produce; and if heavy rain does not fall, there is dew.

This continues the praise of the land because dew is enough moisture for it on account of its excellent soil. The word for "dew" (*ṭall*) can mean drizzle or light rain which is very fine. Ibn 'Abbās and others said that and it is a well-known meaning for the word. Others, including Mujāhid, said that it means dew here.

Allah sees what you do.

This is both a promise and a threat.

أَيَوَدُّ أَحَدُكُمْ أَن تَكُونَ لَهُۥ جَنَّةٌ مِّن نَّخِيلٍ وَأَعْنَابٍ
تَجْرِي مِن تَحْتِهَا الْأَنْهَارُ لَهُۥ فِيهَا مِن كُلِّ الثَّمَرَاتِ وَأَصَابَهُ
الْكِبَرُ وَلَهُۥ ذُرِّيَّةٌ ضُعَفَاءُ فَأَصَابَهَا إِعْصَارٌ فِيهِ نَارٌ
فَاحْتَرَقَتْ كَذَٰلِكَ يُبَيِّنُ اللَّهُ لَكُمُ الْآيَاتِ لَعَلَّكُمْ
تَتَفَكَّرُونَ ٢٦٦

266 ***Would any of you like to have***
a garden of dates and grapes,
with rivers flowing underneath
and containing all kinds of fruits,
then to be stricken with old age
and have children who are weak,
and then for a fierce whirlwind containing fire
to come and strike it
so that it goes up in flames?

In this way Allah makes His Signs clear to you, so that hopefully you will reflect.

Would any of you like to have a garden of dates and grapes, with rivers flowing underneath

As-Suddī says that this *āyat* is a metaphor of spending for the sake of showing off to others. It is related from Ibn 'Abbās: "This is an example Allah made of those who show off by their actions which will be nullified on the Day of Rising when they will be most in need of them. They are like a man who has a garden and children who cannot help him. He becomes old and then a firestorm strikes his garden and burns it up, leaving him absolutely destitute."

Ibn 'Aṭiyya says that the words *"Would any of you like"* show that this is not another example of spending to show off because of the context in which it occurs. He says it is a metaphor of the state of every hypocrite or unbeliever who does an action which he supposes to be good. Then comes the moment of need and he finds it was nothing.

It is related from Ibn 'Abbās that it is a metaphor for those who act for other than Allah, and the hypocrites and unbelievers, as will come, even though we find something else confirmed in the *Ṣaḥīḥ* al-Bukhārī. He reports that one day 'Umar ibn al-Khaṭṭāb asked the Companions of the Prophet, quoting this *āyat*, "About what was this *āyat* related?" They replied, "Allah and His Messenger know best." 'Umar became angry and said, "Say: 'We know' or 'We do not know!'" Ibn 'Abbās said, "I know something about it, Amīr al-Mu'minīn." He said, "Nephew, speak and do not undervalue yourself." Ibn 'Abbās said, "It is a metaphor for action." 'Umar asked, "What action?" Ibn 'Abbās replied, "The action of a rich man who works in obedience to Allah and then Allah sends a shayṭān to him and he does acts of disobedience until his good actions are burned up."

One variant has, "When his life is over and term is near, he seals it with the actions of the wretched." 'Umar was pleased with that interpretation. Ibn 'Aṭiyya said, "This is speculative. The *āyat* can be taken to mean all that its words convey." Palm trees and grapes are mentioned because of their honour and excellence over other trees.

containing all kinds of fruits

This means that it does not lack any kind of fruit.

and then for a fierce whirlwind containing fire to come and strike it

Al-Ḥasan says that this means a wind which is intensely cold. Az-Zajjāj said that it is the strong wind which throws the soil into the sky like pillars, which is called a whirlwind. Al-Jawharī said that a "whirlwind" is one of the leaders of the jinn.

يَٰٓأَيُّهَا ٱلَّذِينَ ءَامَنُوٓا۟ أَنفِقُوا۟ مِن طَيِّبَٰتِ مَا كَسَبْتُمْ
وَمِمَّآ أَخْرَجْنَا لَكُم مِّنَ ٱلْأَرْضِ ۖ وَلَا تَيَمَّمُوا۟ ٱلْخَبِيثَ مِنْهُ
تُنفِقُونَ وَلَسْتُم بِـَٔاخِذِيهِ إِلَّآ أَن تُغْمِضُوا۟ فِيهِ ۚ
وَٱعْلَمُوٓا۟ أَنَّ ٱللَّهَ غَنِىٌّ حَمِيدٌ ﴿٢٦٧﴾

267 *You who believe! give away*
some of the good things you have earned
and some of what the earth produces for you.
Do not have recourse to bad things when you give,
things you would only take
with your eyes tight shut!
Know that Allah is Rich Beyond Need, Praiseworthy.

You who believe! give away some of the good things you have earned

This is addressed to the entire Community of Muḥammad, may Allah bless him and grant him peace. Scholars disagree about what is meant by giving here. 'Alī, 'Abīda as-Salmānī and Ibn Sīrīn said that it refers to the obligatory *zakāt.* In the *āyat* Allah forbids people to use bad things to pay it rather than good. Ibn 'Aṭiyya stated that the position of al-Barā' ibn 'Āzib, al-Ḥasan and Qatāda is that the *āyat* is about voluntary *ṣadaqa.* They recommended that people should only give good property. The *āyat* is general to both ideas, but in the case of *zakāt*, it is connected to an actual command, and, as the command is mandatory, it means that it is forbidden to pay *zakāt* with bad property. That command is particular to the obligatory duty.

As for the voluntary a person can give a little, and so he can give what is less in value. A dirham is better than a date. Al-Barā' related that a man hung up a bunch of poor quality dates and the Messenger of Allah, may Allah bless him and grant him peace, saw it and said, "An evil hanging," and the *āyat* was revealed. (at-Tirmidhī) The command, according to this, is a recommendation to only give what is good. Most commentators state that "good things" means things of high quality and which are favoured by people.

Earning can be by physical toil, which is working for a wage, the rulings governing which will be dealt with later, or by trade, which is buying and selling. Inheritance is included in this because, although the heir did not earn it, someone else did. Sahl ibn 'Abdullāh mentioned that Ibn al-Mubārak was asked about a man who wants to earn and intends by his earning to maintain his ties of kinship, do *jihād*, do good deeds and to engage in the pitfalls of earning for this reason. He said, "If he has enough livelihood to spare himself from asking people, then leaving this is better because when he seeks the lawful and spends it in a lawful way, he will be asked about his earning and his spending. Leaving that is *zuhd*."

Ibn Khuwayzimandād said, "According to this *āyat*, it is permitted for a parent to consume some of their child's earnings. That is because the Prophet, may Allah bless him and grant him peace, said, "Your children are part of your good earning. Eat from the property of your children with good cheer."

and some of what the earth produces for you.

This includes plants, mineral wealth and treasure. These three categories are included in this phrase. As for plants, ad-Dāraquṭnī related that 'Ā'isha said, "The *Sunna* of the Messenger of Allah, may Allah bless him and grant him peace, is that there is no *zakāt* on less than five *wasqs*." A *wasq* is sixty *ṣā'*s, so that makes three hundred *ṣā'*s of wheat, barley, dates and raisins. There is no *zakāt* on vegetables produced by the earth. Some of the Ḥanafīs argue by the words here that the ruling is general to both a little and a lot of all varieties of what the earth produces and believe, by the literal understanding, that *zakāt* on vegetables is, therefore, mandatory. This will be fully dealt with in *Sūrat al-An'ām* (6).

As for minerals, the Imāms related from Abū Hurayra that the Messenger of Allah, may Allah bless him and grant him peace, said, "There is no penalty for a wound inflicted by a dumb beast. There is no penalty for an injury due to a well and no penalty for an injury due to a mineral mine. There is a fifth due on treasure." Our scholars say that since the Prophet, may Allah bless him and grant him peace, said, "A fifth on treasure," that indicates that the ruling for minerals is not the same as that for treasure because the Prophet, may Allah bless him and grant him peace, distinguished between minerals and treasure. Allah knows best.

The linguistic root of "*rikāz*" (buried treasure) is something which is "placed" (*irtakaza*) in the earth: like gold, silver and gems. That is what most of the *fuqahā'* say because they maintain that it is rare that minerals found embedded in the earth are obtained without work, effort or toil. There is a fifth due on it because it is *rikāz*. It is related from Mālik that the judgement of the rare case when minerals are extacted without work is the same as that when work is required to extract minerals in the form of buried treasure. The first view mentioned is his final position, and the majority of *fuqahā'* give that judgement. It is related that Abū Hurayra said, "The Messenger of Allah, may Allah bless him and grant him peace, was asked about *rikāz* and said, 'It is the gold which Allah created in the earth on the day when He created the heavens and the earth.'" 'Abdullāh ibn Sa'īd said that the *ḥadīth* is *matrūk* (not acted upon). There is no disagreement that things buried in the time of *Jāhiliyya* are considered as treasure. If it was buried during the time of Islam, it is classified as a find.

Do not have recourse to bad things when you give,

The *āyat* indicates that earnings can be good or bad. In an-Nasā'ī it is related from Abu Umāma that these words refer to bad quality dates. The Messenger of Allah, may Allah bless him and grant him peace, forbade that this type of dates be taken in payment of *zakāt*.

things you would only take with your eyes tight shut!

This refers to things you would only take in payment from people if you were making things easy for them and forgoing your rights: things you dislike and are not pleased with. So when a debt to Allah is involved do not give what you would not be pleased to take for yourselves. Al-Barā', Ibn 'Abbās and aḍ-Ḍaḥḥāk stated that. Al-Ḥasan said that the meaning is things you would not take, if you found them being sold in the market, unless their price was reduced. Something similar is also related from 'Alī. Ibn 'Aṭiyya said, "These two statements are similar inasmuch as they are both about *zakāt*." Ibn al-'Arabī said, "If the *āyat* had been about obligatory *zakāt*, Allah would not say, *'you would only take'*, because bad or defective things are not permitted to be taken in *zakāt* in any case, not with the eyes shut or by overlooking them. Such things can be taken while lowering the eyes in supererogatory *ṣadaqa*."

Know that Allah is Rich Beyond Need, Praiseworthy.

Allah tells us about His attribute of absolute wealth, meaning that He has no need of our *ṣadaqa*. He is praiseworthy in every state. Az-Zajjāj points out that He does not command people to give *ṣadaqa* when they are poor.

ٱلشَّيْطَٰنُ يَعِدُكُمُ ٱلْفَقْرَ وَيَأْمُرُكُم بِٱلْفَحْشَآءِ ۖ وَٱللَّهُ يَعِدُكُم
مَّغْفِرَةً مِّنْهُ وَفَضْلًا ۗ وَٱللَّهُ وَٰسِعٌ عَلِيمٌ ﴿٢٦٨﴾

268 ***Shayṭān promises you poverty***
and commands you to greediness.
Allah promises you forgiveness from Him
and abundance.
Allah is All-Encompassing, All-Knowing.

Shayṭān promises you poverty and commands you to greediness.

The derivation of the word Shayṭān has already been mentioned in the commentary on 2:14. The expression *"promises you poverty"* here means "threatens you with poverty", making you afraid of it so that you do not spend. This *āyat* is connected to the one before it. Shayṭān has a way of hindering someone from spending in the Way of Allah. He also commands "greediness" *(faḥshā')*, which refers to acts of self-gratification and spending on them. It is said that is means: "Do not give *ṣadaqa*; rather disobey and cut people off."

Allah promises you forgiveness from Him and abundance.

The verb *wa'ada* can mean to promise or to threaten. This *āyat* contains both meanings. At-Tirmidhī reports from Ibn Mas'ūd that the Messenger of Allah said, "Shayṭān has a touch he uses on the son of Ādam and the angel has a touch. The touch of Shayṭān has the effect of threatening evil and denying the truth. The touch of the angel has the effect of promising good and confirming the truth. Anyone who experiences that, should know that it is from Allah. Anyone who experiences other than that, should seek refuge with Allah from Shayṭān." Then he recited this *āyat*. (a *ḥasan ṣaḥīḥ ḥadīth*) The word "forgiveness" (*maghfira*) indicates Allah's veiling of the wrong actions of His slaves in this world and the

Next. *"Fadl"* (abundance) here means provision in this world and expansion and blessing in the Next. Both are promised by Allah.

An-Naqqāsh mentioned that some people use this *āyat* to claim that poverty is better than wealth because Shayṭān distances the human being from what is good and does that by alarming them about poverty. Ibn 'Aṭiyya said, "There is no definitive evidence in the *āyat*. In fact, this idea is strongly contradicted." The Qur'ān says, *"Anything you expend will be replaced by Him. He is the best of Providers."* (34:39). Allah gives from His vast wealth and knows where to bestow it.

يُؤْتِي الْحِكْمَةَ مَن يَشَاءُ ۚ وَمَن يُؤْتَ الْحِكْمَةَ
فَقَدْ أُوتِيَ خَيْرًا كَثِيرًا ۗ وَمَا يَذَّكَّرُ إِلَّا أُولُو
الْأَلْبَابِ ﴿٢٦٩﴾

269 ***He gives wisdom to whoever He wills***
and he who has been given wisdom
has been given great good.
But no one pays heed but people of intelligence.

He gives wisdom to whoever He wills.

Allah gives it to whomever He wishes of His slaves. Scholars disagree about the meaning of the word "*ḥikma*" (wisdom) here. As-Suddī said that it refers to Prophethood. Ibn 'Abbās said that it means understanding of the Qur'ān: its *fiqh*, abrogations, *āyat*s of judgement, ambiguous *āyat*s, unusual expressions, and changes in the normal order of words. Qatāda and Mujāhid also said that it means understanding of the Qur'ān. Mujāhid said that it means being correct in word and deed. Ibn Zayd said, "Wisdom is understanding the *dīn*." Mālik ibn Anas said, "Wisdom is recognition of the *dīn* of Allah, understanding it, and putting it into practice." Ibn al-Qāsim related that and said, "Wisdom is reflecting on the commands of Allah and following them." He also said, "Wisdom is obeying Allah and understanding the *dīn* and acting on it." Ar-

Rabī‘ ibn Anas said, "Wisdom is humility." Ibrāhīm an-Nakhā‘ī said, "Wisdom is understanding the Qur'ān." Zayd ibn Aslam also said that. Al-Ḥasan said, "Wisdom is scrupulousness."

Most of these ideas are close in meaning as *ḥikma* (wisdom) is a verbal noun which comes from *iḥkām*, which means perfection in word or deed. All the things mentioned above are wisdom. The Book of Allah is wisdom. The *Sunna* of His Prophet, may Allah bless him and grant him peace, is wisdom. The basic meaning of *ḥikma* is something which prevents foolishness. It is said that it is knowledge because it prevents foolishness and, by it, one knows how to prevent foolishness, which is every ugly action. The same is true for the Qur'ān, intelligence and understanding. Al-Bukhārī has the *ḥadīth*: "When Allah desires good for a person, He gives him understanding in the *dīn*."

and he who has been given wisdom has been given great good.

The word "wisdom" is repeated rather than using a pronoun the second time to indicate its honour and excellence. Anyone who is given wisdom and the Qur'ān has been given the best of what can be given of all the knowledge of the books of the early ones and others because He said about those, *"You have only been given a little knowledge."* (17:85) This is called *"great good"* because the Qur'ān is the all-inclusive Book. One of the sages said, "Whoever is given knowledge and the Qur'an should value himself properly and not humble himself to the people of this world for the sake of worldly things. What he has been given is better than what the people of this world have been given because Allah called this world "a little good" and called knowledge and the Qur'ān "great good"."

وَمَآ أَنفَقْتُم مِّن نَّفَقَةٍ أَوْ نَذَرْتُم مِّن نَّذْرٍ فَإِنَّ ٱللَّهَ يَعْلَمُهُۥ ۗ وَمَا لِلظَّٰلِمِينَ مِنْ أَنصَارٍ ﴿٢٧٠﴾

270 ***Whatever amount you spend or vow you make,***
Allah knows it.
The wrongdoers have no helpers.

Vows were part of the culture of the Arabs and they used to make them a lot. Allah mentions two types of vows: those a man makes voluntarily, and those he makes after obliging himself to do so. This *āyat* is both a promise and threat, telling us that those with sincere intention will be rewarded. Anyone who spends to show off or for any other reason like inducing gratitude or as an insult is a wrongdoer. His action is worthless and he finds no benefit from it. The phrase *"knows it"* means that He takes account of it, according to Mujāhid.

إِن تُبْدُوا۟ ٱلصَّدَقَٰتِ فَنِعِمَّا هِىَ ۖ وَإِن
تُخْفُوهَا وَتُؤْتُوهَا ٱلْفُقَرَآءَ فَهُوَ خَيْرٌ لَّكُمْ
وَنُكَفِّرُ عَنكُم مِّن سَيِّـَٔاتِكُمْ ۗ وَٱللَّهُ
بِمَا تَعْمَلُونَ خَبِيرٌ ﴿٢٧١﴾

271 ***If you make your sadaqa public, that is good.***
But if you conceal it and give it to the poor,
that is better for you,
and We will erase
some of your bad actions from you.
Allah is aware of what you do.

The commentators believe that this *āyat* is about voluntary *ṣadaqa* because concealment of it is better than making it public. This is the case with the rest of the acts of worship: concealment is better in respect of voluntary acts because it precludes showing off. That does not apply to obligatory *zakāt*. Al-Hasan said that making *zakāt* public is better but that concealing voluntary acts of giving is better because it is closer to what Allah desires in that. Ibn 'Abbās said, "Secret giving when it is voluntary is seventy times better than public giving." In the case of obligatory *zakāt*, its public payment is better than paying it secretly, up to twenty-five times according to some. It is the same with all obligations and supererogatory actions.

Such a position is not taken on the basis of mere opinion. In the *Ṣaḥīḥ* of Muslim, the Prophet, may Allah bless him and grant him peace, said. "The best prayer of a man is the one he does in his house except for the obligatory prayer." That is because there is no showing off in the obligatory, while *nāfila* prayers are subject to that. An-Nasā'ī reported from 'Uqba ibn 'Āmir that the Messenger of Allah, may Allah bless him and grant him peace, said, "Someone who recites the Qur'ān aloud is like the one who gives *ṣadaqa* publicly. Someone who recites the Qur'ān silently is like someone who gives secret *ṣadaqa*." In a *ḥadīth*, "Secret *ṣadaqa* extinguishes the wrath of the Lord."

Ibn al-'Arabī said, "There is no preference of public *zakāt* over that done secretly nor of secret *zakāt* over that which is public in sound *ḥadīth*, but there is a firm consensus regarding that. As for voluntary *ṣadaqa*, the Qur'ān clearly states that it is better given secretly than publicly. Our scholars say that this is generally the case. The truth about this matter is that the state of giving *ṣadaqa* varies according to the circumstances of the giver, the recipient and those who witness it. The public giver has the benefit of demonstrating the *Sunna* and the reward for acting as a model for others."

This refers to one whose state is strong and intention good and who is safe from showing off. As for the one whose state falls below this, doing it secretly is better for him. As for the recipient, when giving is done secretly, he is kept safe from people's disdain or from the claim that he took what he did not need and failed to be abstinent. Generally speaking, keeping *ṣadaqa* secret from people is better than making it known to them since they might attack the giver for showing off and the taker for being able to do without it. On the positive side, doing it publicly encourages people to give *ṣadaqa*. But this is rare today.

Yazīd ibn Abī Ḥabīb said, "This *āyat* was revealed about the giving of *ṣadaqa* to the Jews and Christians. It was as if Allah was commanding that a portion of *zakāt* be secret." Ibn 'Aṭiyya said that this position is rejected, especially by the righteous *Salaf*. Aṭ-Ṭabarī said that the consensus is that doing what is obligatory publicly is better.

Aṭ-Ṭabarī mentioned that this *āyat* indicates that it is generally better to conceal *zakāt*. It is the right of the poor and it is better for the owner of property to distribute it himself. This is one of the two positions of ash-Shāfi'ī. In his other position, he stated that what is meant by *ṣadaqa* here is the voluntary *ṣadaqa* rather than obligatory *zakāt*. It is more appropriate to perform the obligatory publicly so that there will be no suspicion. That is why it is said, "It is better to do the *nāfila* prayers alone, but praying in the group removes suspicion about whether someone is fulfilling the *farḍ* prayer."

Al-Mahdawī said, "What is meant by the *āyat* is both the obligation of *zakāt* and what is voluntary. Concealment was better in the time of the Prophet, may Allah bless him and grant him peace. Then people's suspicions arose after that, and therefore scholars recommended making what is obligatory public so that no suspicion would remain." Ibn 'Aṭiyya remarked, "This position is contrary to the traditions (*āthār*). In our time it seems that it is recommended to conceal obligatory *zakāt*. Those who refuse to do it are numerous and paying it publicly opens a person to the accusation of showing off." Ibn Khuwayzimandād said, "It is permitted for the *āyat* to mean obligatory and voluntary *ṣadaqa* because He mentioned the hidden and praises it, and the public and praises it, and so it can be directed to both of them." An-Naqqāsh said that this *āyat* was abrogated by *"Those who give away their wealth by night and day, secretly and openly."* (2:274)

So, in the *āyat* public *ṣadaqa* is praised and then the ruling is given that when it is given secretly it is better. That is why one of the sages said, "When you give charity, conceal it. When you are given it, then make it known." Al-'Abbās said, "The charitable act is only complete when it has three characteristics: hastening it, thinking it small, and concealing it. When you hasten it, you make it more welcome. When you consider it small, you make it great. When you conceal it, you perfect it."

The word "erase" is subject to various readings. Ḥafs has *yukaffiru* (it will erase) whereas Warsh has *nukaffir* (We will erase) with a *sukūn* on the *rā'*. Other readings exist. The meaning is, however, that if you conceal it and give it to the poor, that is better for you and Allah will erase bad actions from you. Abū 'Ubayd said that if it is read with *yā'*, it means: "Allah will erase…" Abū Ḥātim says that it means, "the giving will erase". Generally speaking, the view is that, if it is in the third person, it refers to the giving.

In the words "some of your bad actions" (*min sayyi'ātikum*) the "*min*" (some) is partitive. Aṭ-Ṭabarī reports that some have said that it is redundant, but Ibn 'Aṭiyya says that is a mistake on their part.

لَّيْسَ عَلَيْكَ هُدٰيهُمْ وَلَٰكِنَّ اللَّهَ يَهْدِي
مَن يَّشَآءُ وَمَا تُنفِقُواْ مِنْ خَيْرٍ فَلِأَنفُسِكُمْ
وَمَا تُنفِقُونَ إِلَّا ابْتِغَآءَ وَجْهِ اللَّهِ وَمَا تُنفِقُواْ
مِنْ خَيْرٍ يُوَفَّ إِلَيْكُمْ وَأَنتُمْ لَا تُظْلَمُونَ ﴿٢٧٢﴾

272 ***You are not responsible for their guidance,***
but Allah guides whoever He wills.
Whatever good you give away
is to your own benefit,
when you give desiring only the Face of Allah.
Whatever good you give away
will be repaid to you in full.
You will not be wronged.

You are not responsible for their guidance but Allah guides whoever He wills.

These words are connected to the mention of *ṣadaqa*. It is as if Allah were making it clear that it is permitted to give *ṣadaqa* to the idolaters. There is a *mursal ḥadīth* related by Sa'īd ibn Jubayr where the Prophet, may Allah bless him and grant him peace, said that the reason for the revelation of this *āyat* was that the Muslims used to give *ṣadaqa* to the poor among the People of Book. When there were a lot of poor Muslims, the Messenger of Allah said, "Only give *sadaqa* to the people of your own *dīn*." Then this *āyat* was revealed to make it clear that it is permitted to give *ṣadaqa* to those who are not part of the *dīn* of Islam. An-Naqqāsh mentioned that the Prophet was given *zakāt* and a Jew came and said, "Give to me." The Prophet said, "There is no share in the *zakāt* of the Muslims for you." The Jew went away and this *āyat* was revealed. The Messenger of Allah called for him and gave some to him. Then that was abrogated by the *āyat* of *zakāt*.

Ibn 'Abbās said, "Some of the Anṣār had relatives in the Jewish tribes of the Banū Qurayẓa and the Banū an-Naḍīr. They used to not give *ṣadaqa* to them, out of the desire that they would become Muslim if they were needy, and the *āyat* was revealed because of them."

One of the commentators related that Asmā' bint Abī Bakr wanted to give *ṣadaqa* to her grandfather, Abū Quhāfa, and then did not do so because he was an unbeliever, and the *āyat* was revealed about that. Aṭ-Ṭabarī related that the aim of the Prophet in not giving *ṣadaqa* was so that they would become Muslims and enter into the *dīn* and for that reason Allah said, *"You are not responsible for their guidance."* It is also said that this is not connected to the *āyat* before it, but is totally a new statement.

Our scholars say that the *ṣadaqa* which non-Muslims are permitted according to these traditions is voluntary *ṣadaqa*. As for *zakāt*, it is not permitted to give it to an unbeliever since the Prophet said, "I was commanded to take *ṣadaqa* (meaning here *zakāt*) from your rich and give it to your poor." Ibn al-Mundhir said, "The consensus among all the scholars I learned from is that a *dhimmī* is not given any of the *zakāt*." Then he mentioned a group who said something different to that. Al-Mahdawī said that this *āyat* is an allowance for the Muslims to give some of the *zakāt* to their relatives who are unbelievers. Ibn 'Aṭiyya said "This is rejected by consensus, and Allah knows best." Abū Ḥanīfa said that *zakāt al-fiṭr* can be given to them, but Ibn al-'Arabī says that this is baseless and weak. Our evidence is that *zakāt* on livestock and money is an obligatory purification and is not given to unbelievers. The Prophet said, "Spare them from having to beg on this day," meaning *'Īd al-Fiṭr.*

We reply that this is the case because the Muslims are busy with the *'īd* and the *'īd* prayer, while this is not the case with the idolaters. It is permitted to give it to non-Muslims if one holds the position that it is a *sunna* to do so. It is one of our positions, and it is also the position of Abū Ḥanīfa, as we mentioned. It is adopting the general meaning of the *āyat* about kindness, feeding people and general *ṣadaqa*. Ibn 'Aṭiyya said, "This ruling is conceivable for the Muslims when dealing with the *dhimmī*s and enslaved *ḥarbī*s."

In the Qur'ān we read: *"They give food, despite their love for it, to the poor and orphans and captives."* (76:8) A captive in the Abode of Islam can only be an idolater. The Almighty says: *"Allah does not forbid you from being good to those who have not fought you in the dīn or driven you from your homes, or from being just towards them."* (60:8). So the literal meaning of these *āyat*s allows *ṣadaqa* to be given to non-Muslims. The Prophet, however, excepted *zakāt* from that, saying, "Take *ṣadaqa* from their rich and give it to their poor," and scholars agree on that. So non-Muslims can be given voluntary *ṣadaqa* if they are needy, and Allah knows best.

Ibn al-'Arabī said, "There is no disagreement that *zakāt al-fiṭr* can be given to disobedient Muslims, unless they have abandoned the pillars of Islam: prayer and fasting. Then it may not be given to them until they repent. *Zakāt* is given to other disobedient Muslims because they are included under the general category of "Muslims".

but Allah guides whoever He wills.

This refutes the Qadariyya and groups of the Mu'tazilites as we have already explained (2:5).

Whatever good you give away is to your own benefit

The word "good" in this *āyat* refers to wealth because it is accompanied by the words "give away". The context indicates that it is wealth. In other contexts, the word "good" can have other meanings.

when you give desiring only the Face of Allah.

This indicates that the spending which is accepted is only that by which the Face of Allah is sought. It is also said that it is testimony by Allah for the Companions that they sought the Face of Allah when they spent. This is preference and praise of them.

لِلْفُقَرَآءِ ٱلَّذِينَ أُحْصِرُوا۟ فِى سَبِيلِ ٱللَّهِ لَا
يَسْتَطِيعُونَ ضَرْبًا فِى ٱلْأَرْضِ يَحْسَبُهُمُ ٱلْجَاهِلُ
أَغْنِيَآءَ مِنَ ٱلتَّعَفُّفِ تَعْرِفُهُم بِسِيمَٰهُمْ لَا
يَسْـَٔلُونَ ٱلنَّاسَ إِلْحَافًا ۗ وَمَا تُنفِقُوا۟ مِنْ
خَيْرٍ فَإِنَّ ٱللَّهَ بِهِۦ عَلِيمٌ ﴿٢٧٣﴾

273 ***It is for the poor***
who are held back in the Way of Allah,
unable to travel in the land.
The ignorant consider them rich
because of their reticence.
You will know them by their mark.
They do not ask from people insistently.
Whatever good you give away, Allah knows it.

It is for the poor

The words "for the poor" are connected to *"whatever good you give away"* in the previous *āyat*. It is said that it implies that spending or *ṣadaqa* is for the poor alone. As-Suddī, Mujāhid and others said that what is meant by poor in this instance are the poor Muhājirūn of Quraysh and others. Then the *āyat* is extended so that it is applied to all who are considered poor throughout time. The poor Muhājirūn are singled out because they were those who were poor at that time. They were the People of the Ṣuffa, who numbered about four hundred men. That was because the poor used to come to the Messenger of Allah, may Allah bless him and grant him peace. They had neither family nor property and so a verandah (*ṣuffa*) was built for them in the mosque of the Messenger of Allah, may Allah bless him and grant him peace, which is why they were called the People of the Ṣuffa.

Abū Dharr said, "I was one of the people of the Ṣuffa. In the evening, we presented ourselves at the door of the Messenger of Allah and he would order each of us to go with a man [as his guest for supper] until there remained ten or less of the people of the Ṣuffa and the Prophet would bring us his supper and we would eat with him. When we finished, the Messenger of Allah, may Allah bless him and grant him peace, said, 'Sleep in the mosque.'"

At-Tirmidhi transmitted that al-Barā' ibn 'Āzib quoted the *āyat "Do not have recourse to bad things when you give"* (2:267) and said, "It was revealed about us, the Anṣār. We owned some palm trees. A man would bring dates from his trees according to whether its fruits were a lot or a little. A man would bring a branch or two of dates and hang them in the mosque. The people of the Ṣuffa did not have any food, so when one of them was hungry, he would go to the bunch and hit it with his stick and some dates would fall and he would eat. People who did not truly desire to do good would bring branches of poor dates or broken ones and hang them in the mosque. Then Allah Almighty revealed, *'O you who believe, spend of the good things...'* (2:267). This means: 'If one of you had been given the like of what he gave, you would only take it with your eyes closed due to embarassment.' After that a man would only bring good things."

According to our scholars the people in the mosque were impoverished and ate from *ṣadaqa* due to their compelling need. When Allah gave victory to the Muslims, they were relieved from that and went out and then had property of their own.

who are held back in the Way of Allah, unable to travel in the land.

Allah then described the states of those poor Muhājirūn in a manner which obliges compassion for them. These words indicate the fact that they were restricted in their ability to move. Qatāda and Ibn Zayd said that this means they were kept from going about to earn a living due to fear of the enemy. This is why Allah says that they are unable to travel because every direction was full of unbelievers. This was at the beginning of Islam. So their excuse kept them from earning and *jihād*, and the unbelievers' dislike of them kept them from going out in trade and so they remained poor. It is also said that it means they held themselves back from *jihād*, but the first interpretation is more likely, and Allah knows best.

The ignorant consider them rich because of their reticence.

This means that they have withdrawn and do not ask, and rely on Allah so that someone who did not know would suppose them to be rich. This shows that the ascription of poverty can be applied to someone who has clothes of some value and that does not prevent *zakāt* being given to him. Allah commands that it be given to these people. They were among the Muhājirūn who fought with the Messenger of Allah, may Allah bless him and grant him peace, and were not ill or blind. "Reticence" (*ta'affuf*) in this context means to refrain from begging and put oneself above it.

You will know them by their mark.

This is evidence that the distinguishing marks of Islam have a legal bearing in respect of those on whom they appear so that if we find a corpse in the Abode of Islam who is wearing a Christian belt and is not circumcised, it is not buried in the graveyard of the Muslims. That takes precedence over the normal ruling that a dead person is deemed to belong to the *dīn* of the place where he is found according to most scholars. It also indicates the permissibility of giving *zakāt* to someone who has fine clothes and adornment. Scholars agree on that. Then they disagree about the amount he may take. Abū Ḥanīfa says that it is the same amount on which *zakāt* is obliged to be paid, ash-Shāfi'ī says that it is food for a year, and Mālik says it is forty dirhams.

Scholars disagree about what the *"sīmā"* (mark) referred to is. Mujāhid says that it is humility and humbleness. As-Suddī said that it is the sign of poverty and need which can be seen in their faces. Ibn Zayd said that it is their tattered clothes. Some people, including Makkī, said that it is the mark of prostration, and Ibn 'Aṭiyya says that this is better. That is because they were unoccupied and trusted in Allah and had no work except the prayer and so they had the mark of prostration on them.

This mark which is the mark of prostration was shared by all the Companions as Allah says at the end of *Sūrat al-Fatḥ, "Their mark is on their faces, the traces of prostration."* (48:29) So in this respect there can have been no difference between them and others. So the only thing that the "mark" can be is the effect of poverty and need, or an extra large mark of prostration. They were recognised by the sallowness of their faces from praying at night and fasting in the day, Allah knows best. As for humility, its place is the heart, and rich and poor share in it.

They do not ask from people insistently.

"*Ilḥāf*" (insistently) is derived from *liḥāf* (blanket). It is called that because it covers all manner of asking in the same way that a blanket covers everything; an insistent beggar is one who begs from everyone and pesters them with his asking. An-Nasā'ī and Muslim reported from Abū Hurayra that the Messenger of Allah, may Allah bless him and grant him peace, said, "The very poor man is not the one who is turned away by a date or two, or a bite or two; the very poor man is the one who does not ask. Recite if you like: *'They do not ask from people insistently.'*"

Scholars disagree about the meaning of this and take two positions. Some people, including aṭ-Ṭabarī and az-Zajjāj, say that the meaning is: "They do not beg at all." This would mean that they completely refrain from asking. This is the position of the majority of commentators, and refraining from asking is their firm quality. They do not ask people either insistently or not insistently. Other people say that what is meant is that they simply do not ask insistently which is what is first understood from the phrase. They ask, but not insistently.

In any case the *āyat* calls attention to the bad state of those who do ask people insistently. The Imāms related from Mu'āwiya ibn Abī Sufyān that the Messenger of Allah, may Allah bless him and grant him peace, said, "Do not be insistent in asking. By Allah, one of you may ask me for something and gets what he wants from me even though I dislike him doing it, and he is blessed in what I give him." In the *Muwaṭṭā'* we read that a man of the Banū Asad said, "My family and I dismounted to rest at Baqī' al-Gharfad. My family said to me, 'Go to the Messenger of Allah, may Allah bless him and grant him peace, and ask him for something to eat,' and they began to mention what they needed. I went to the Messenger of Allah, may Allah bless him and grant him peace, and found that a man was asking for something, and the Messenger of Allah, may Allah bless him and grant him peace, was saying, 'I do not have anything to give you.' The man turned away from him in anger, saying, 'By my life! You give to those you wish to give to!' The Messenger of Allah, may Allah bless him and grant him peace, remarked, 'He is angry with me because I do not have anything to give him. Whoever asks you for something while he has an *uqiyya* or its equivalent has asked insistently.'" The man continued, "I told myself that a camel we had was worth more than an *uqiyya*. (Mālik explained that an *uqiyya* was forty dirhams.) So I returned without having asked him for anything, and the Messenger of Allah, may Allah bless him and grant him peace, sent me barley and raisins later on. He gave us from his share until Allah, the Mighty, the Majestic, gave us relief."

This *ḥadīth* indicates that it is disliked for anyone who has an *uqiyya* of silver to beg. Anyone who begs when he has that amount of silver or what is equivalent to it is considered to be insistent. I do not know of anyone who possesses knowledge of the *dīn* who did not dislike someone begging when they have this amount of silver or its equivalent in gold according to the literal meaning of this *ḥadīth*. They are permitted to take what comes to them without asking, provided it is not *zakāt*. There is disagreement if it is *zakāt*.

Ibn 'Abdu'l-Barr said, "One of the best things related from the *fuqahā'* regarding begging and dislike of it, and the position of those who possess scrupulousness regarding it, is what al-Athram related from Aḥmad ibn Ḥanbal when he was asked when begging became lawful. He said, "When a person does not have enough for his lunch and supper. This is based on the *ḥadīth* of Sahl ibn al-Ḥanẓaliyya." Ibn Ḥanbal was then asked, "And if he is compelled to ask?" He replied, "It is permitted if he is in pressing need." He was asked, "And if he refrains?" He replied, "That is better for him." Then he added, "I do not think that anyone will die of hunger. Allah will bring him his provision." Then he mentioned the *ḥadīth* of Sa'īd al-Khudrī: "Whoever abstains, Allah will make him abstinent."

It is reported by Abū Dāwūd, an-Nasā'ī and others that a Persian asked the Messenger of Allah, may Allah bless him and grant him peace, "Should I beg, Messenger of Allah?" He said, "No, but if you must, then ask of the righteous." So he permitted asking the people of excellence and righteousness when that is necessary. Ibrāhīm ibn Adham said, "Asking for your needs from people is a veil between you and Allah Almighty. Place your need with the One who controls harm and benefit. Take refuge in Allah Almighty and Allah will spare you from others and you will live in happiness."

If something comes to someone without them asking for it, they should accept it and not reject it. It is provision which Allah has brought. Mālik reported from Zayd ibn Aslam from 'Aṭā' ibn

Yasār that the Messenger of Allah, may Allah bless him and grant him peace, sent a gift to 'Umar ibn al-Khaṭṭāb and 'Umar returned it. The Messenger of Allah, may Allah bless him and grant him peace, asked, "Why did you return it?" He replied, "Messenger of Allah, did you not tell us that it is better for us not to take anything from anyone?" The Messenger of Allah, may Allah bless him and grant him peace, said, "That is by asking. Provision which Allah gives you is not the same as asking." 'Umar ibn al-Khaṭṭāb said, "By the One in whose hand my self is, I will not ask anything from anyone, and anything that comes to me without my asking for it, I will accept." This is a definitive text.

Insistence in asking and being importunate in it when a person is wealthy is forbidden and not lawful. The Messenger of Allah, may Allah bless him and grant him peace, said, "Anyone who asks people for an increase over what he has, is asking for a hot ember. He can either seek to be independent or he is seeking increase."(Muslim, via Abū Hurayra) Ibn 'Umar reported that the Prophet, may Allah bless him and grant him peace, said, "One of you will continue to beg until he meets Allah without a single piece of flesh on his face." (Muslim)

If the asker is needy, there is no harm in him asking three times, informing people of his state and apologising. But it is best to leave it. If the one asked knows of his need and he is able to give him what he asks, he is obliged to give. If he does not know it, he gives to him out of fear that he is speaking truth.

Regarding someone who needs something to keep up appearances, such as having a good garment to wear on the *'Īd* and *Jumu'a*, Ibn al-'Arabī mentioned, "While I was in the mosque of the Khalif in Baghdād, I heard a man say, 'This is your brother who attends *Jumu'a* and he has no other garment with which to support the *sunna* of *Jumu'a*.' The following *Jumu'a* I saw him in another garment and was told, 'Abū'ṭ-Ṭāhir al-Burnusī gave it to him.'"

الَّذِينَ يُنفِقُونَ أَمْوَالَهُم بِاللَّيْلِ وَالنَّهَارِ سِرًّا
وَعَلَانِيَةً فَلَهُمْ أَجْرُهُمْ عِندَ رَبِّهِمْ وَلَا خَوْفٌ
عَلَيْهِمْ وَلَا هُمْ يَحْزَنُونَ ﴿٢٧٤﴾

274 ***Those who give away their wealth by night and day,***
secretly and openly,
will have their reward with their Lord.
They will feel no fear and will know no sorrow.

It is related from Ibn 'Abbās, Abū Dharr, Abu Umāma, Abū'd-Dardā', 'Abdullāh ibn Bishr al-Ghāfiqī and al-Awzā'ī that this *āyat* was revealed about the fodder of horses which are used for *jihād* in the Way of Allah. In the *Ṭabaqāt*, Ibn Sa'd mentioned that 'Arīb reported that the Messenger of Allah, may Allah bless him and grant him peace, was asked about *"Those who give away their wealth by night and day, secretly and openly, will have their reward with their Lord. They will feel no fear and will know no sorrow."* He said, "They are the owners of horses." By means of the same *isnād*, the Messenger of Allah, may Allah bless him and grant him peace, is reported as saying, "The one who gives to horses is like someone who stretches out his hand with *ṣadaqa* which is not immediately taken. Their urine and droppings will be like fragrant musk on the Day of Rising."

Ibn 'Abbās also reported that this *āyat* was revealed about 'Alī ibn Abī Ṭālib who had four dirhams and gave away one at night, one in the day and one secretly and one openly. Ibn Jurayj said that it was revealed about a man who did that but he did not name 'Alī or anyone else. Qatāda said that this *āyat* was revealed about those who spend without being either extravagant or tightfisted. "Their reward" is their repayment.

ٱلَّذِينَ يَأْكُلُونَ ٱلرِّبَوٰاْ لَا يَقُومُونَ إِلَّا كَمَا يَقُومُ
ٱلَّذِى يَتَخَبَّطُهُ ٱلشَّيْطَٰنُ مِنَ ٱلْمَسِّ ذَٰلِكَ بِأَنَّهُمْ
قَالُوٓاْ إِنَّمَا ٱلْبَيْعُ مِثْلُ ٱلرِّبَوٰاْ وَأَحَلَّ ٱللَّهُ ٱلْبَيْعَ
وَحَرَّمَ ٱلرِّبَوٰاْ فَمَن جَآءَهُۥ مَوْعِظَةٌ مِّن رَّبِّهِۦ فَٱنتَهَىٰ
فَلَهُۥ مَا سَلَفَ وَأَمْرُهُۥٓ إِلَى ٱللَّهِ وَمَنْ عَادَ فَأُوْلَٰٓئِكَ أَصْحَٰبُ
ٱلنَّارِ هُمْ فِيهَا خَٰلِدُونَ ٢٧٥ يَمْحَقُ ٱللَّهُ ٱلرِّبَوٰاْ وَيُرْبِى
ٱلصَّدَقَٰتِ وَٱللَّهُ لَا يُحِبُّ كُلَّ كَفَّارٍ أَثِيمٍ ٢٧٦ إِنَّ ٱلَّذِينَ
ءَامَنُواْ وَعَمِلُواْ ٱلصَّٰلِحَٰتِ وَأَقَامُواْ ٱلصَّلَوٰةَ وَءَاتَوُاْ ٱلزَّكَوٰةَ
لَهُمْ أَجْرُهُمْ عِندَ رَبِّهِمْ وَلَا خَوْفٌ عَلَيْهِمْ وَلَا هُمْ
يَحْزَنُونَ ٢٧٧ يَٰٓأَيُّهَا ٱلَّذِينَ ءَامَنُواْ ٱتَّقُواْ ٱللَّهَ وَذَرُواْ
مَا بَقِىَ مِنَ ٱلرِّبَوٰٓاْ إِن كُنتُم مُّؤْمِنِينَ ٢٧٨ فَإِن لَّمْ تَفْعَلُواْ
فَأْذَنُواْ بِحَرْبٍ مِّنَ ٱللَّهِ وَرَسُولِهِۦ وَإِن تُبْتُمْ فَلَكُمْ
رُءُوسُ أَمْوَٰلِكُمْ لَا تَظْلِمُونَ وَلَا تُظْلَمُونَ ٢٧٩

275 *Those who practise usury*
will not rise from the grave
except as someone driven mad by Shayṭān's touch.
That is because they say,
'Trade is the same as usury.'

But Allah has permitted trade
and He has forbidden usury.
Whoever is given a warning by his Lord
and then desists,
can keep what he received in the past
and his affair is Allah's concern.
But all who return to it
will be the Companions of the Fire,
remaining in it timelessly, for ever.
276 *Allah obliterates usury*
but makes ṣadaqa grow in value!
Allah does not love
any persistently ungrateful wrongdoer.
277 *Those who believe and do right actions*
and establish the prayer and pay zakāt,
will have their reward with their Lord.
They will feel no fear and will know no sorrow.
278 *You who believe! be fearful of Allah*
and forgo any remaining usury
if you are believers.
279 *If you do not, know that it means war from Allah*
and His Messenger.
But if you sincerely repent
you may have your capital,
without wronging and without being wronged.

These *āyat*s contain the ruling on usury and the permissibility of contracts in trade and a threat to those who consider usury lawful and persist in it. Many points emerge from them.

Those who practise usury

The word "practise" (lit. "eat") means here "take". Linguistically "*ribā*" (usury) means "increase" in general. Then the *Sharī'a* limited this general usage to certain specific practices. Sometimes the word is applied to unlawful earning, as when Allah Almighty says about the Jews, *"because of their practising usury when they were forbidden to do it."* (4:160) What is meant by usury here is not the kind which is unlawful for us. What is meant is unlawful property, as when Allah says, *"They are people who listen to lies and consume ill-gotten gains,"* (5:42) meaning unlawful wealth in the form of bribes and what they consider lawful of the property of the Gentiles when they say, *"We are under no obligation where the gentiles are concerned."* (3:75) So according to this, the prohibition against usury includes all unlawful wealth in whatever way it is earned.

The usury known in the *Sharī'a* takes two forms: the usury entailed by delay and the usury entailed by disparity in contracts and foodstuffs as will be explained. The Arabs had a practice whereby they would say to a debtor, "Will you settle now or pay more later?" The debtor could then increase the amount of money he owed, and the creditor would wait for it. This is all forbidden by the consensus of the Community. Most prohibited sales are forbidden because of the idea of increase either in money or in benefit to one of the parties incurred by delay and the like. Some forbidden sales do not have increase in them, like selling fruit before it is ripe or selling after the *adhān* has been called for *Jumu'a*, even if the one who does it is said metaphorically to practise usury.

The Imāms relate from Abū Sa'īd al-Khudrī that the Messenger of Allah, may Allah bless him and grant him peace, said. "Gold for gold, silver for silver, wheat for wheat, barley for barley, dates for dates and salt for salt, like for like, hand to hand. Anyone who increases or asks for increase practises usury. The taker and the giver are the same in respect of that." In the *ḥadīth* of 'Ubāda ibn aṣ-Ṣāmit we find, "When the categories are different, sell however you wish when it is hand to hand."

Abū Dāwūd related from 'Ubāda ibn aṣ-Ṣāmit that the Messenger of Allah, may Allah bless him and grant him peace, said, "Gold for gold, ore and coins, silver for silver, ore and coins, wheat for wheat, *mudd* for *mudd*, barley for barley, *mudd* for *mudd*, dates for dates, *mudd* for *mudd*, and salt for salt, *mudd* for *mudd*. Anyone who increases or asks for increase practises usury. There is no harm in selling gold for silver when the amount of silver is more, provided it is hand to hand, and no delay is permitted. There is no harm in selling wheat for barley when the amount of barley is more, provided it is hand to hand, and no delay is permitted."

Scholars agree that taking this position is following the *Sunna* and that is the position of the majority of the Muslim *fuqahā'* except in the case of wheat and barley. Mālik considers them one category and does not permit two of them for one. That is also the position of al-Layth, al-Awzā'ī, and a large number of the scholars of Madina and Syria. Mālik adds sult barley to them. Al-Layth considers them as one category and Ibn Wahb also holds that view.

The *Sunna* is confirmed and there is no position other than it. The Prophet, may Allah bless him and grant him peace, said, "When these categories are different, sell however you wish when it is hand to hand," and he said, "Wheat for wheat and barley for barley" which indicates that they are two different categories, just as wheat differs from dates and because their attributes differ and they have different names. One does not consider plants which the Sharī'a does not consider. They are different. This is the position of ash-Shāfi'ī, Abū Ḥanīfa, ath-Thawrī and the people who base their position on the *ḥadīth*.

Mu'āwiya ibn Abī Sufyān believed that the prohibition related from the Prophet was about minted dirhams and dinars, not gold and silver ore for coins nor about things made from gold and silver. It is said that this was his position until an incident occurred to him with 'Ubāda which is transmitted by Muslim and others:

> "We went on a sortie when Mu'āwiya was in command of the people and took a lot of booty. Part of our booty consisted of a silver vessel. Mu'āwiya ordered a man to sell it against the people's stipends. People argued about that. 'Ubāda ibn aṣ-Ṣāmit heard about it, went along and said, 'I heard the Messenger of Allah, may Allah bless him and grant him peace, forbid selling gold for gold, silver for silver, wheat for wheat, barley for barley, dates for dates, and salt for salt except like for like, item for item. Anyone who increases or asks for increase practises usury.' The people

> returned what they had been given. Mu'āwiya heard about that and stood up and said, 'What is the matter with men who relate *aḥādīth* from the Messenger of Allah, may Allah bless him and grant him peace, when we saw him and were his Companions and did not hear it from him!' 'Ubāda ibn aṣ-Ṣāmit stood up and repeated the story. He said, 'We will relate what we heard from the Messenger of Allah, may Allah bless him and grant him peace, even if Mu'āwiya dislikes it! – or 'in spite of him'. I do not care. I accompanied him in his army on a dark night.'"

Ibn 'Abdu'l-Barr said, "It is related that the story concerned Abū'd-Dardā' with Mu'āwiya. It is possible that that occurred to both of them together but the *ḥadīth* on the custom is recorded from 'Ubāda. It is what scholars rely on regarding the subject of usury. There is no disagreement that what Mu'āwiya did was not permitted and it is not denied that Abū'd-Dardā' and 'Ubāda knew something that was unknown to Mu'āwiya. They were respected men among the *fuqahā'* of the Companions and two of their great men. Certain things were unknown to Abū Bakr and 'Umar while they were known to lesser men and the same holds true for Mu'āwiya. It is also possible that his position was that of Ibn 'Abbās who was an ocean of knowledge, but did not see anything wrong in two dirhams for one until Abū Sa'īd dissuaded him from it. The incident of Mu'āwiya and 'Ubāda occurred while he was governor. Qabīṣa ibn Dhu'ayb said, ''Ubāda objected to something Mu'āwiya did and said, "I will not live in the same land as you!" and went back to Madina. 'Umar asked him, "What has brought you here?" and he told him. He said, "Go back to your place. May Allah make ugly a land which does not contain you and those like you." He wrote to Mu'āwiya, "You have no authority over him."'"

The Imāms related from 'Alī that the Messenger of Allah, may Allah bless him and grant him peace, said, "Dinar for dinar and dirham for dirham with no disparity between them. Anyone who needs silver, should buy it with gold. If he needs gold, he should buy it with silver, thus and thus." Scholars say that this indicates the genus of the coins. Silver is both white and black and gold is red and yellow. None of that can be exchanged except like for like, same for same, in every case. This is the position of the majority of the people of knowledge. The transmission from Mālik about minor coins of base metal (*filūs*) varies. He at times compared them to dirhams since they are used to pay for things, while at other times he forbade doing that since they are not currency in every land and vary from one land to another.

There is no consideration given to one view which is related from several Mālikīs. Some relate from Mālik that when a merchant is preparing to leave and requires minted dirhams or dinars, he can take his silver or gold bullion to the mint and tell the minter, "Take this silver or gold of mine and take out the fee for your work and give me minted dinars for my gold or minted dirhams for my silver because I am preparing to leave and I fear I will miss the people I am travelling with." That is permitted due to necessity, and it is something which some people have to do. Ibn al-'Arabī related it in what he took from Mālik about someone other than the merchant and said that Mālik lightened the usual ruling in that. The form of this transaction is that he sells his silver which weighs a hundred dirhams, adding five extra as the fee for minting the hundred. This is pure usury. A transaction which would be permissible would be if he told him, "Mint this for me," and then separately gives him the wage for it. When he mints it, he takes the whole amount from him and pays him the wage for doing it.

That which Mālik did first is what he did last. Mālik looked at property and imposed on it a judgement according to the specific situation. The rest of the *fuqahā'* reject it. Ibn al-'Arabī said, "Mālik's argument concerning it is clear." Abū 'Umar said, "This is the same usury which the Messenger of Allah, may Allah bless him and grant him peace, forbade when he said, 'Anyone who increases or asks for increase practises usury.'" Ibn Wahb denied that this was Mālik's position and denied it himself. Al-Abharī claimed that it was out of compassion in seeking trade and so that the market was not missed, and the judgement of usury is only applicable against someone who desires an increase and intends that. Al-Abharī forgets Mālik's basic principle of cutting off the means to wrong (*sadd adh-dharā'i'*), including his position about someone who sells a garment on credit which he has no intention of rebuying and then finds it being sold in the market: he is not permitted to buy it for less than the amount he sold it for, even if he did not intend or desire that originally. Such examples are numerous. If usury only existed in a transaction when someone actually intended it, it would only be made *ḥarām* for the *fuqahā'* [who would possess the necessary perspicacity to recognise it in the transaction]. 'Umar said, "No one should trade in our market except someone with *fiqh*. Otherwise usury will be practised." This is clear to anyone who is fair and inspired to right guidance.

Mālik went to great lengths to prevent forbidden increase, and so he considered something merely suspect to be the same as actual usury. He forbade exchanging a dinar and dirham for a dirham and dinar in order to block the means and to cut off suspicion, since they would not be exchanged except with some increase in mind. The reason for prohibiting that is the impossibility of making an equal distribution. It is exchanging gold and silver for gold, and it is evident that the intrinsic disparity in such an exchange is forbidden. Furthermore, he forbade exchanging a dinar of fine gold for a dinar of base gold as when a fine one would be worth two thousand base ones. This demonstrates the acuteness of his investigation into the matter and indicates that that transmission about paying extra for minting should be rejected and is not sound, and Allah knows best.

Al-Khaṭṭābī said, "Bullion is pieces of gold and silver before they are minted." *'Ayn* (specie) are minted dirhams and dinars. The Messenger of Allah, may Allah bless him and grant him peace, forbade selling a *mithqal* of gold coins for slightly over a *mithqal* of unminted gold bullion, and he forbade a disparity between minted silver and unminted silver. He said, "Bullion and coins have the same ruling."

Scholars agree that dates for dates can only be like for like. They disagree about selling one date for two dates and one grain of wheat for two. Ash-Shāfi'ī, Aḥmad, Isḥāq, and ath-Thawrī forbid it. That is analogous to the position of Mālik. It is sound because if there is usury in a lot of something, then a little of it is included in the ruling by analogy. Those who permit that argue that when only one or two dates are consumed, they have no price because they cannot be weighed or measured and therefore disparity is permitted.

Know that the issues concerning this subject are numerous and its secondary rulings widespread. A measure of that can be gained by looking at what each the scholars consider to be the legal reason (*'illa*) behind the prohibition of usury. Abū Ḥanīfa said that the reason is because it is a weighed or measured category. So in his view all that is subject to measurement or weight consists of one category. It is not permitted to sell some of it for the same category with disparity or with delay. So he forbids selling dirt for dirt with disparity because it can be measured, but permits one loaf of bread for two loaves because he does not think it falls under measurement which is its basis and so he removes it from a genus in which usury can exist.

Ash-Shāfi'ī says that the reason is that it is a category of food. This is his position in his new school. So he does not permit selling flour for bread or bread for bread with disparity or delay, whether the bread is leavened or unleavened. He thinks that it is not permitted to sell one egg for two, one pomegranate for two, or one melon for two melons, either hand to hand or with delay because all of those are consumable foods. In his old school, he said that the reason was that the prohibition was based on its being weighed or measured.

What the Mālikīs say about this matter varies. The best of what is said about it is that foodstuffs which can be stored form a general category, like wheat, barley, dates, and salt for which there is a text, as well as similar items like rice, millet, sorghum, sesame, and legumes like broad beans, lentils, cowpeas, and chickpeas. The same holds for conserved meats, milks, vinegars, oils and fruits like grapes, raisins, and olives. There is disagreement about figs. Honey and sugar are added to them. Usury can occur with all of those things with delay, but disparity is permitted in them by the words of the Prophet, may Allah bless him and grant him peace, "When these categories are different, sell however you wish when it is hand to hand." There is no usury in respect of fresh fruits which are perishable, like apples, melons, pomegranates, pears, cucumbers, aubergines and other vegetables. Mālik said, "It is not permitted to sell eggs for eggs with disparity because they can be stored." He permits like for like. Muḥammad ibn 'Abdullāh ibn 'Abdu'l-Ḥakam said, "It is permitted to sell one egg for two more because they are not stored." That is the position of al-Awzā'ī.

will not rise (from the grave) except as someone driven mad by Shayṭān's touch.

"Lā yaqūmūna" (they will not rise) here refers to rising from the grave according to Ibn 'Abbās, Mujāhid, Ibn Jubayr, Qatāda, ar-Rabī', aḍ-Ḍaḥḥāk, as-Suddī, and Ibn Zayd. One of them said, "Allah appoints a shayṭān to choke him." They all said, "He will be raised like a madman to punish him and make him hated by all the people in the Gathering." This agreed-upon interpretation is strengthened by the reading of Ibn Mas'ūd which is, "They will not rise on the Day of Rising except as someone rises…" Ibn 'Aṭiyya said, "The words of the *āyat* contain a simile for the state of someone who engages in trade in this world with avarice and greed, comparing him to a madman because greed and desire affect him to the extent that his limbs become disordered. This is like when you say, 'He's mad!' about someone walking quickly whose movements are addled, either by anxiety or something else."

Allah will make this disorder a sign of practising usury. That is because He enlarges the usury in their bellies and it makes them heavy, so when they rise from their graves they will stand and then fall over. It is said that they will be raised on the Day of Rising with their bellies inflated like pregnant women and whenever they stand, they will fall and people will walk over them. Some scholars say that that is the sign by which they will be known on the Day of Rising and then punishment comes after that. The image of "eating" is used here for the practice of usury because consumption is the greatest goal of a person in property, and it also indicates greed, which is the most severe form of avarice.

This *āyat* contains evidence against those who deny that epilepsy is from the jinn and claim that it is natural and that Shayṭān does not move inside a person nor touch him.

That is because they say, 'Trade is the same as usury.'

With all commentators this refers to the unbelievers and they are told to keep that which they received in the past. This is not what is said to a disobedient believer. He should cancel his sale and cancel what he did when he was ignorant of the prohibition. That is why the Prophet, may Allah bless him and grant him peace, said, "If anyone does an action which is not part of our business, it is rejected." The threat implicit in this *āyat* includes those who are disobedient.

They say that the increase at the end of the term is based on the price at the beginning of the contract. This is because of the way that the Arabs understood usury. Allah refuted them by saying, *"But Allah has permitted trade and He has forbidden usury."* It is clear that when the terms ends and he cannot pay it, he is given a deferral. This is what the Prophet cancelled when he stated on the Day of 'Arafa, "All usury is cancelled, and the first usury I cancel is our usury, that of 'Abbās ibn Abdu'l-Muṭṭalib. It is all cancelled." He began with his uncle. This is one of the customs which demonstrates justice in a ruler: to impose justice on himself and those close to him, and then on people in general.

But Allah has permitted trade and He has forbidden usury.

This is one of the generally applicable (*'āmm*) *āyat*s in the Qur'ān. The definite article before the word "trade" (*al-bay'*) is to indicate the genus, not to make it definite, since there is no prior mentioned trade to which it can refer. So trade is general, and then the usurious transactions we have mentioned and other things which are mentioned as being forbidden are specified. Such things include wine, carrion, the transaction known as *ḥabal al-ḥabala* and other things confirmed in the *Sunna* and by the consensus of the Community. This is the position of most of the *fuqahā'*. Some say that this *āyat* is included in the undefined (*mujmal*) parts of the Qur'an which, in turn, is further described by what is lawful and unlawful in sales, and so it is not possible to use it to make a sale lawful or unlawful unless that is accompanied by some clarification from the *Sunna* of the Prophet, may Allah bless him and grant him peace. It indicates the permissibility of sales in general, not particular transactions. This is the difference between *'āmm* and *mujmal*. The *'āmm* indicates the permissibility of sales in general when there is no evidence of a specific factor making them prohibited. The *mujmal* does not indicate the permissibility of the specific unless there is definite evidence of permissiblity. The first is sounder, and Allah knows best.

Linguistically "*bay'*" (trade) is a verbal noun of the verb "*bā'a*" (to sell), meaning to give goods and take something in return. It stipulates a seller, who is the owner or one who acts on his behalf, and a buyer, who is the one who pays the price, and the goods which are paid for. So the pillars of the sale are four: seller, buyer, price, and thing paid for. The sale involves a verbal offer and verbal acceptance, however it is expressed. The sale can also be made binding by a commonly understood allusion.

A usurious contract is void and is never permitted since the Imāms related from Abū Sa'īd al-Khudrī: "Bilāl brought some Barni dates and the Messenger of Allah, may Allah bless him and grant him peace, asked him, 'Where are these from?' Bilāl said, 'From dates which we consider low quality. I exchanged two *ṣā'*s of them for a *ṣā'* to feed the Prophet.' The Messenger of Allah said, 'Oh! usury itself! Do not do it, but if you want to buy dates, sell them in another sale and then buy them.'" In one variant, "This is usury. Return them. Then sell our dates and buy for us from the price." The words "return them" indicate that a usurious contract is void and not valid in any way. That is the position of the majority, except for Abū Ḥanīfa who said, "An usurious sale is permitted in as far as it is a sale, but forbidden since it entails usury. If the usury is removed, then the sale is permitted."

Any sale which is clearly *ḥarām* is null and void and so the buyer must return the goods themselves. If they have been lost while in his possession, he must return the price paid.

Whoever is given a warning by his Lord

Ja'far aṣ-Ṣādiq said, "Allah forbade usury so that people would lend to one another." Ibn Mas'ūd reported that the Prophet, may Allah bless him and grant him peace, said, "A loan is worth twice what *ṣadaqa* is worth." Some people said that Allah forbade it because it destroys wealth and thereby destroys people.

'Ā'isha recited this *āyat* when she was told about what Zayd ibn Arqam had done. Ad-Dāraquṭnī reported from al-'Āliyya bint Anfa': "Umm Muḥibba and I went to Makka and we visited 'A'isha, may Allah be pleased with her, and greeted her. She asked, 'Who are you?' We said, 'We are from the people of Kufa.' It was as if she turned away from us and Umm Muḥibba said to her, 'Umm al-Mu'minīn, I had a slavegirl and I sold her to Zayd ibn Arqam al-Anṣārī for eight hundred dirhams against his stipend. He wanted to sell her and then I bought her for six hundred dirhams cash.' She turned to us and said, 'Evil is what you sold and what you bought! Tell Zayd that he has nullified his *jihād* with the Messenger of Allah, may Allah bless him and grant him peace, unless he repents!' She asked her, 'What do you think of the transaction if I only take the capital from him?' She recited, *'Whoever is given a warning by his Lord and then desists, can keep what he received in the past.'*" Al-'Āliyya was the daughter of Abū Isḥāq al-Hamdānī al-Kūfī as-Sabī'ī.

Mālik relates this *ḥadīth* from Ibn Wahb regarding credit sales. If something leads to falling into the forbidden, then it is forbidden, even if it is outwardly a permissible sale. In this principle, Mālik differed from other *fuqahā'* who said, "Rulings are based on the outward, not an supposition." Our evidence is the position of "blocking the means" (*sadd adh-dharā'i'*). If the transaction is safe, we deduce its soundness, as already stated. This *ḥadīth* is a definitive text. What 'Ā'isha said for Zayd was only to deter him, since such things are not a matter of opinion. Nullification of actions can only be known by revelation.

We read in the *Ṣaḥīḥ* Muslim from an-Nu'mān ibn Bashīr that the Messenger of Allah, may Allah bless him and grant him peace, said, "The *ḥalāl* is clear and the *ḥarām* is clear. But between the two there are doubtful things about which most people have no knowledge. Whoever exercises caution with regard to what is doubtful, shows prudence in respect of his *dīn* and his honour. Whoever gets involved in the doubtful things is like a herdsman who grazes his animals near a private preserve (*ḥimā*). He is bound to enter it. Every king has a private preserve and the private preserve of Allah on His earth are the things that He has made forbidden."

The legal sense of this, in terms of evidence, is that he forbade doing doubtful things out of the fear of falling into the forbidden and it is that which constitutes the legal principle of "blocking the means" (*sadd adh-dharā'i'*). The Prophet, may Allah bless him and grant him peace, said, "One of the major wrong actions is for a man to abuse his parents." They said, "O Messenger of Allah, is it possible for a man to abuse his parents?" He replied, "He may curse another man's father who in turn curses his father, and curse his mother and he in turn curses his mother." So he made allusion to cursing parents in general like cursing one's own parents. The Prophet, however, did curse the Jews when they consumed the price for that which they were forbidden to eat.

In a letter, Abū Bakr, may Allah be pleased with him, said: "There is no joining separated animals nor separating joined animals out of fear of *zakāt*." Ibn 'Abbās forbade dirhams for dirhams when combining them would lead to an offence. Scholars agree that it is forbidden to combine a sale and a loan, that a little wine is *ḥarām*, even if it does not intoxicate, that being alone with an unrelated women is forbidden, even if a man is impotent, that it is forbidden to look at the face of a young woman, and several other things which are known to be definite. It is confirmed that the *Sharī'a* has forbidden them because they are the means to forbidden things. So it is more fitting that the potential causes of usury be defended against and its means blocked. If someone allows those means, he should allow digging wells and setting up ropes in situations where they might lead to the death of Muslim men and women. No one allows that.

There is also agreement that the *'īna* sale is forbidden, and Allah is the One who grants success. Abū 'Ubayd al-Harawī explained an *'īna* sale as being "a transaction in which someone sells goods to a man for a known price for a known term and then buys it back from him for less than the price for which he sold them." He said, "If he buys goods from someone else in the presence of the one who seeks the *'īna* for a known price and then takes possession of them and then sells them to the one who seeks the *'īna* for a higher price for a set term, and then the buyer buys them from the first seller for cash for a lower price, this is also *'īna,* but less disliked than the first, and some permit it." It is called *'īna* because of the presence of cash for the one with the *'īna*, *'ayn* meaning "ready money".

Abū Dāwūd reports that Ibn 'Umar said, "I heard the Messenger of Allah, may Allah bless him and grant him peace, say, 'When you sell by *'īna*, follow the tails of cattle, are content to be farmers and abandon *jihād*, then Allah will impose abasement on you which will not be removed from you until you return to your *dīn*." Abū 'Abdu'r-Raḥmān al-Khurāsānī says that the *isnād* of this *ḥadīth* contains someone who is not well known.

Our scholars say that if someone sells goods for a price on credit and then buys them for the same sort of payment for which he sold them, he must buy them for cash or with a term less than the term for which he sold to them or for a longer term for the same price, or greater or less. These are three possible situations. In the first and second, the transaction is permitted if the price paid is the same or greater, but it is not permitted if the price is less, according to 'Ā'isha's *ḥadīth.* As for the third case, which is to sell them for a longer term, if he buys the goods themselves or more, it is permitted to do so for the same price or less, but not for more. If he buys some of it, it is only permitted for the same price, not more or less.

He can keep what he received in the past

This refers to past usury with no consequence in this world or the Next. As-Suddī and others said that. This is the judgement of Allah for the unbelievers of Quraysh and Thaqīf and others who became Muslim who used to deal in usurious transactions.

and his affair is Allah's concern.

There are four interpretations of this. One is that the pronoun "his" refers to usury, meaning the business of usury is subject to Allah's command in making it unlawful or not. The second is that the pronoun refers to *"what was in the past"*, i.e. it is up to Allah to pardon that and remove its consequences. The third is that the pronoun refers to the one with the usury, meaning that his affair is up to Allah in making him firm in stopping or returning him to disobedience in usury. An-Naḥḥās preferred this position, saying that it is clear and good, i.e. his business is up to Allah in the future. If He wishes, He makes him firm in the prohibition, and if He wishes, he allows it. The fourth is that the pronoun refers to what is forbidden (i.e. "its" affair), but means to allow him to hope for the best.

But all who return to it

Meaning return to usury before they die. Sufyān said that. Another said, "Whoever returns and says that trade is like usury has disbelieved." Ibn 'Aṭiyya said, "We believe that the *āyat* is about the unbelievers, so being forever in the Fire is literal. In respect of the disobedient Muslim, it is metaphorical.

Allah obliterates usury

In this world: meaning that He removes blessing (*baraka*) from usury, even if it is a lot. Ibn Mas'ūd related that the Prophet, may Allah bless him and grant him peace, said, "Even if usury is a lot, its end is little." It is said that it means in the Next World. Regarding these words, Ibn 'Abbās said, "Neither *ṣadaqa, ḥajj, jihād* or gifts to relatives are accepted from a usurer." *Maḥaqa* (obliterating) has the meaning of "to decrease and vanish." The waning (*maḥāq*) of the moon is derived from the same root.

but makes ṣadaqa grow in value!

This means that He increases it in blessing in this world and makes its reward many times more in the Next World. In the *Ṣaḥīḥ* Muslim, "When someone gives *ṣadaqa*, Allah makes it grow, even if it is only a morsel of food, like one of you would raise his colt or foal until it comes on the Day of Rising the size of Uhud."

Allah does not love any persistently ungrateful wrongdoer.

The ungrateful person is also called a wrongdoer for emphasis.

Those who believe and do right actions and establish the prayer and pay zakāt, will have their reward with their Lord. They will feel no fear and will know no sorrow.

Here He singles out the prayer and *zakāt* although they are only a part of righteous deeds to honour them and point out their value since they are the best of actions: the prayer with respect to the body and the *zakāt* with respect to property.

You who believe! be fearful of Allah and forgo any remaining usury

Its outward meaning is that any uncollected usury is void, even if it was contracted before the revelation of the *āyat* of prohibition. It is said that this *āyat* was revealed because of Thaqīf. They made a treaty with the Prophet that they would claim the usury which people owed them while the usury they owed others would be cancelled. When the terms of their usury arrived, they went to Makka to settle them and the debts were against the Banū 'Abda and the Banū al-Mughīra. The Banū Mughīra said, "We will not give you anything. Usury has been abolished." They went to 'Attāb ibn Usayd and he wrote about it to the Messenger of Allah, may Allah bless him and grant him peace, and the *āyat* was revealed and the Messenger of Allah wrote it to 'Attāb, and Thaqīf learned it and refrained. This is the reason for the *āyat* as was reported by Ibn Isḥāq, Ibn Jurayj, as-Suddī and others. It means: place a screen between you and the punishment of Allah by abandoning any outstanding usury.

if you are believers.

This is a condition applying to Thaqīf because it was when they first became Muslim. We can suppose that, if the *āyat* is about those who affirm belief, it is a metaphorical condition. Muqātil ibn Sulaymān said that the word "if" here means "when". Ibn 'Aṭiyya said that this is not known linguistically.

If you do not, know that it means war from Allah and His Messenger.

This is a threat to anyone who does not abandon usury. War calls for killing. Ibn 'Abbās said that on the Day of Rising it will be said to the practiser of usury, "Take your weapons for war." Ibn 'Abbās also said, "If someone insists on usury and does not desist, it is a duty for the leader of the Muslims to ask him to repent. If he does not desist, he strikes off his head. Qatāda said, "Allah threatened the people of usury with killing and made them lawful for killing wherever they are found." It is said that the meaning is: "If you do not desist, you are at war with Allah and His Messenger," meaning their enemies. Ibn Khuwayzimandād said, "If the people of a land think usury to be lawful, they are apostates and the judgement regarding them is the same as that of the people of apostasy, and it is permitted for the ruler to fight them. Do you not see that Allah Almighty has announced that when He says, *'know that it means war from Allah and His Messenger'*?"

Ibn Bukayr narrated, "A man came to Mālik ibn Anas and said, 'Abū 'Abdullāh, I saw a drunkard, who was a chronic drinker, who was trying to catch the moon. I said, "My wife is divorced if there is anything worse than wine which enters a man's belly."' He said, 'Go away while I investigate your problem.' He came back to him the following day and he said the same thing. He came back the day after that and Mālik told him, 'Your wife is divorced. I have examined the Book of Allah and the *Sunna* of His Prophet and I did not see anything worse than usury because Allah has proclaimed war on account of it.'"

This *āyat* indicates that practising usury and making use of it is one of the major wrong actions. There is no disagreement about that as we will make clear. It is related that the Prophet, may Allah bless him and grant him peace, said, "A time will come upon people when there will not be anyone left who does not consume usury, and even one who does not consume it will be touched by its dust." Ad-Dāraquṭnī related that 'Abdullāh ibn al-Ḥanẓala reported that the Prophet, peace be upon him, said, "A dirham of usury is worse in the sight of Allah than thirty-six wrongful acts of fornication." It is related that he said, "Usury has ninety-nine gates, the least of which is like a man having sex with his mother."

Ibn Mas'ūd said, "Those who take usury, pay it, its witnesses and scribes if they know of it, are cursed on the tongue of Muḥammad, may Allah bless him and grant him peace." Al-Bukhārī related that Abū Juḥayfa said, "The Messenger of Allah forbade the price of blood, the price of dogs, and the earnings of prostitutes, and cursed those who consume usury and those who pay it, the tattooer and women who are tattooed." In the *Ṣaḥīḥ* Muslim, Abū Hurayra reported, "Avoid the seven deadly wrong actions." Usury was one of them. In Abū Dāwūd from Ibn Mas'ūd we find: "The Messenger of Allah cursed those who take usury, pay it, its scribes and its witnesses."

But if you sincerely repent, you may have your capital, without wronging and without being wronged.

Abu Dāwūd related that the father of Sulaymān ibn 'Amr said, "I heard the Messenger of Allah, may Allah bless him and grant him peace, say in the Farewell *Ḥajj*, "Every usury of the *Jāhiliyya* is cancelled. You have your capital, not wronging or being wronged." So when there is repentance, Allah returns to usurers their capital and tells them not to wrong others by taking usury *"and that they will not be wronged"* by their capital being retained so that they lose it. It is possible that *"not being wronged"* refers to procrastination because the procrastination of the wealthy is wrongdoing. The meaning is that it is settled straight away while the usury is removed. This is the *sunna* of righteousness, and is the closest thing to righteousness. Do you not see that when the Prophet indicated to Ka'b ibn Mālik to reduce the debt of Ibn Abī Ḥadrad by half, to which Ka'b agreed, the Messenger of Allah, peace be upon him, told the other, "Get up and pay it." Scholars agree that the command referred to settling the debt.

But if you sincerely repent you may have your capital,

This is to stress the invalidation of the usury which is still outstanding but permits receiving the capital in which there is no usury. Some scholars use this as evidence that anything that happens to the sale goods before they are received which would oblige the prohibition of the contract invalidates the contract, as when a Muslim buys game and then the buyer or seller assumes *iḥrām* before it is collected: the sale is forbidden because something has occurred which forbids the sale. Allah has invalidated what has not been collected because something has occurred which makes it forbidden before it has been collected. If it has already been collected before that happens, the sale is not affected. This is the school of Abū Ḥanīfa and the position of the Shāfi'īs. It is used as evidence that the destruction of the goods before they are collected and while they are still in the possession of the seller obliges that the contract be cancelled, although some early scholars disagree about this position according to Aḥmad ibn Ḥanbal.

This is in keeping with the position of those who say that the basic contract in which there is usury is permitted, but then it becomes invalidated by the ruling of Islam before it can be collected. As for those who forbid the usurious contract at its source, these words are not sound. That is because usury is forbidden in all religions, and what was done in the *Jāhiliyya* was the custom of the idolaters, and what they took of usury is like what they had by usurpation and looting, and so what they did is not considered.

According to this, it is not correct to call witnesses to any contract involving usury. The laws of the Prophets before us forbid usury, and this is well-known and mentioned in the Book of Allah as He relates about the Jews, *"because of their practising usury when they were forbidden to do it."* (4:161) Allah mentions in the story of Shu'ayb that his people rejected that and said, *"Do your prayers instruct you that we should abandon what our fathers worshipped or stop doing what we want to with our wealth?"* (11:87). So it is not valid to use testimony as evidence (i.e. for the validity of such contracts).

Some of the scrupulous who go to excess believe that when lawful property is mixed with the unlawful in such a way that it cannot really be separated, and then someone removes the unlawful amount mixed with it, what remains is not lawful or good because he might have removed the lawful and left the unlawful. Ibn al-'Arabī said, "This is excess in the *dīn*. In all that cannot be distinguished, what is desired in it is the value, not the thing itself. If it is destroyed, then its equivalent replaces it. Mixing is tantamount to destruction as the individual item cannot be distinguished." Allah knows best.

Our scholars say that the way to repent of unlawful property in one's possession if it is usury, is to return it to the person from whom it was taken and to seek him out if he is not present. If you despair of finding him, then you should give that amount away as *sadaqa*. If you took something through injustice, you should follow the same procedure in dealing with the one you wronged. If the matter is unclear to you, and you do not know how much is lawful and how much is unlawful, you should examine the amount and return an amount sufficient to preclude any doubt that any of the unlawful remains in your possession. You should return that to those you know that you wronged and from whom you took usury. If you despair of finding them, you must give *ṣadaqa* on their behalf. If your wrongs take up all you have and you know that you are obliged to pay what you can never do because it is so great, then your repentance is to give all of your possession either to the poor or for the best interests of the Muslims so that there only remains in your possession the minimum clothing necessary for the prayer and covering your private parts and food for the day.

In the eyes of most scholars there is a difference between this and someone who is bankrupt because the one who is bankrupt did not take people's property through transgression. They are the ones who go to him and so he is left with what will cover him in his normal dress. Abū 'Ubayd and others, however, think that the judgement is the same and a bankrupt is only left with what will be enough for the prayer and to cover his private parts.

This *āyat* is a threat from Allah about usury, and a similar threat about sharecropping (*mukhābara*)[1] is reported from the Prophet. In Abū Dāwūd, Jarir ibn 'Abdullāh is reported as saying, "Allah and His Messenger announce war against someone who does not abandon *mukhābara*." This is evidence for the prohibition of sharecropping, which is working land for a half, third or quarter of its produce. It is also called *muzāra'a*. All the Mālikīs, ash-Shāfi'ī, Abū Ḥanīfa and their followers and Dā'ud agree that it is not permitted to rent land for a third, a fourth, or part of its produce because that is unknown, although ash-Shāfi'ī and his people and Abū Ḥanīfa say that it is permitted to rent land for food when what it produces is known, as it is known that the Prophet, may Allah bless him and grant him peace, said, "As for something known and guaranteed, there is no harm in it." (Muslim) That is the position of Muḥammad ibn 'Abdu'l-Ḥakam, while Mālik and his adherents forbid it.

That is also based on what Muslim related, that Rāfi' ibn Khadīj said: "In the time of the Messenger of Allah, may Allah bless him and grant him peace, we used to let out the land for cultivation and we would rent it in return for a third, a fourth and for a specified amount of food. One day one of my uncles came to us and said, 'The Messenger of Allah, may Allah bless him and grant him peace, has forbidden us something which used to contain benefit for us, but obeying Allah and His Messenger is more beneficial for us. He forbade us to rent out the land for cultivation in return for a third, a fourth and a specified amount of food. He command-

1. Usually *mukhābara* is another name for the *musāqā*, a contract between the owner of a plantation of fruit trees and a worker who waters them in exchange for a share of the crop.

ed the owner of the land to cultivate it or give it for cultivation." He disliked renting it and the like of that.

It is agreed that it is not permitted to rent land in exchange for any type of food or drink because that would be tantamount to selling food for food on credit. Therefore they forbid renting land for any of what it produces even if that is not normally eaten or drunk, except in the case of wood, reeds and firewood, as they fall under the category of *muzābana* in their view. This is recorded from Mālik and his adherents. Ibn Saḥnūn mentioned from 'Abdu'r-Raḥmān al-Makhūmī al-Madanī that "There is no harm in renting land for food which is not produced from it." It is also related from al-Mughīra that it is not permitted, as the rest of the Mālikīs say.

وَإِن كَانَ ذُو عُسْرَةٍ فَنَظِرَةٌ إِلَىٰ مَيْسَرَةٍ وَأَن
تَصَدَّقُوا خَيْرٌ لَّكُمْ إِن كُنتُمْ تَعْلَمُونَ ﴿٢٨٠﴾

280 ***If someone is in difficult circumstances,***
there should be a deferral until things are easier.
But making a free gift of it would be better for you
if you only knew.

If someone is in difficult circumstances,

After Allah decreed that the usurers should receive their capital back from those to whom they lent it, He decrees that the one experiencing hardship should be granted a delay until a time when things are easier for him. The reason for the revelation of this *āyat* is that when Thaqīf asked for the property which was owed to them, the Banū'l-Mughīra complained of hardship and said, "We have nothing," and asked for a delay until the time when their fruits would be ready for harvesting.

It is affirmed that someone owed a debt can ask for it from the debtor and is permitted to take property without his consent. This indicates that when a debtor refuses to settle the debt when he is able to do so, he is a wrongdoer. Allah Almighty says, *"you may have your capital"* and so enabled people to seek their capital when it is not impossible for their debtor to pay it.

Al-Mahdawī and some scholars said, "This *āyat* abrogates what was done in the *Jāhiliyya* by way of selling people as slaves who were unable to pay their debts. Makkī related that the Prophet also instructed people to follow that practice at the beginning of Islam. Ibn 'Aṭiyya said, "If it is really confirmed that the Prophet did that, then it was abrogated." Aṭ-Ṭaḥāwī said, "A free man would be sold for a debt at the beginning of Islam if he did not have enough property to settle his debts until Allah abrogated that practice by His words: *"If someone is in difficult circumstances, there should be a deferral until things are easier."* Their evidence is a *ḥadīth* related by ad-Dāraquṭnī from the *ḥadīth* of Surrāq, "I owed a man some money – or a debt – and he took me to the Messenger of Allah, may Allah bless him and grant him peace, and I did not have any money and so he bought me from him – or I was bought for him." (al-Bazzār) Some say that it is not evidence.

there should be a deferral until things are easier.

These words are general to all people. Anyone who is in difficulty is given a deferral. This is the position of Abu Hūrayra, al-Ḥasan and most of the *fuqahā'*. An-Naḥḥās said, "The best of what is said on this *āyat* is the position of 'Aṭā', ad-Daḥḥāk and ar-Rabī'. They said that the deferral applies to everyone who is in difficulty both in respect of usury and in respect of all other debts. This combines all the positions because it can be an abrogation revealed about usury and then become another more general ruling. Ibn 'Abbās and Shurayḥ said that it is specific to usury and there is no deferral in other debts and dealings. The debtor must pay people what he owes or be imprisoned until he pays it. That is the position of Ibrāhīm [an-Nakhā'ī]. Their evidence is *"Allah commands you to return to their owners the things you hold on trust."* (4:58) Ibn 'Aṭiyya said, "This position applies when is there is no pressing poverty. If there is poverty, the judgement is that a deferral should be imposed."

If someone has a lot of debts and his creditors ask for their money, the judge can divest him of all his property and leave him with just his bare needs. Ibn Nāfi' related from Mālik that he is only left with what will conceal his private parts. The well-known position is that a debtor is left his normal clothing without excess and his cloak is not removed if he normally wears it, and the clothing of his wife is left. There is disagreement about selling his books if he is a scholar. He is not left a house or servant or Friday clothes unless they are inexpensive and in such a case, it is forbidden to imprison him. The basis for that is *"If someone is in difficult circumstances, there should be a deferral until things are easier."*

The Imāms related that Abū Sa'īd al-Khudrī said, "A man experienced loss in the time of the Messenger of Allah in respect of the produce which he sold and his debts mounted up. The Messenger of Allah, may Allah bless him and grant him peace, said, 'Give *ṣadaqa* to him.' The people gave him *ṣadaqa* but that did not amount to enough to settle his debt. So the Messenger of Allah told his creditors, 'Take what you find and you may only have that.'" In Abū Dāwūd we find: "The Messenger of Allah did not allow creditors more than the seizure of a debtor's property." This is a definitive text. The Messenger of Allah, may Allah bless him and grant him peace, did not order that the debtor be imprisoned or kept in confinement. According to Shurayḥ, the man concerned was Mu'ādh ibn Jabal. This differs from the position of Abū Ḥanīfa who said that he is kept in close confinement if there is a possibility that he might have money. He is not forced to work as we mentioned. Success is by Allah.

A bankrupt person is imprisoned according to Mālik, ash-Shāfi'ī, Abū Ḥanīfa and others until it becomes clear he has no property. Mālik says that he is not imprisoned if he has no property and it is clear that he does not have anything. He is not imprisoned if his difficulties are evident. If the property of a bankrupt man is collected and then destroyed before it reaches its owner and can be sold, the bankrupt man is liable and the debt remains. If the *qāḍī* sells the property and keeps the price and then the money is lost before the creditors get possession of it, they are responsible and the bankrupt man is free of further liability. Muḥammad ibn 'Abdu'l-Ḥakam says that the debtor is always liable until the money reaches the creditors.

"Difficulties" (*'usra*) refer to constricted circumstances due to lack of money. The name of the Army of Hardship is taken from it.

Nāfi' reads *"until things are easier"* as *maysura* while the others read it as *maysara*.

But making a free gift of it would be better for you if you only knew.

Here Allah recommends that *ṣadaqa* be given to a person faced with difficulties and makes that better than granting a deferral. As-Suddī, Ibn Zayd and aḍ-Ḍaḥḥāk said that. Aṭ-Ṭabarī and others said that the meaning of the *āyat* is, "That you make it a free gift to both rich and poor is better for you." The sound position is the first one. There is nothing about the rich in the *āyat*.

At-Taḥāwī mentioned that Burayda ibn al-Khaṣīb reported that the Messenger of Allah, may Allah bless him and grant him peace, said, "If someone grants time to a person in difficulties, he is considered to have given *ṣadaqa* on every day [of the deferral]." He said, "It is *ṣadaqa* for every day until the debt is due. When he defers it after it is due, he is considered to have given the same amount in *ṣadaqa* for every day." Muslim reported that Abū Mas'ūd narrated that the Messenger of Allah, may Allah bless him and grant him peace, said, "A man among those before you underwent the reckoning and no good at all was found for him except that, being a wealthy man, he used to do business with people and used to order his employees to make allowances for anyone in difficulties. So Allah, the Mighty and Exalted, said, 'We have more right to do that than you,' and he was pardoned."

It is related from Abu Qatāda that he looked for a debtor of his who concealed himself and found him. The man said, "I am in difficulties." "By Allah?" Abu Qatāda asked. "By Allah," he said. Abu Qatāda said, "I heard the Messenger of Allah, may Allah bless him and grant him peace, say, 'Whoever wants Allah to save him from the calamity of the Day of Rising should give more time to someone in financial difficulties or absolve him.'" In another *ḥadīth* we find: "If someone gives more time to someone in difficulties, Allah will shade him in His shade on the Day of Rising." There are many *aḥādīth* which encourage doing that. The *ḥadīth* reported by Abu Qatāda indicates that if the creditor know that the debtor is in difficulty, or even suspects it, it is forbidden for him to demand it from him, even if that has not been proven before a judge.

وَاتَّقُوا يَوْمًا تُرْجَعُونَ فِيهِ إِلَى اللَّهِ ثُمَّ تُوَفَّىٰ كُلُّ
نَفْسٍ مَّا كَسَبَتْ وَهُمْ لَا يُظْلَمُونَ ﴿٢٨١﴾

281 ***Be fearful of a Day***
when you will be returned to Allah.
Then every self will be paid in full
for what it earned.
They will not be wronged.

It is said that this *āyat* was revealed nine days before the death of the Prophet, may Allah bless him and grant him peace, and that nothing else was revealed after it. Ibn Jurayj said that. Ibn Jubayr and Muqātil said it was seven days before his death. Three days is also mentioned. It is related that it was three hours before his death, and the Prophet, may Allah bless him and grant him peace, ordered, "Put it between the *āyat*s of usury and the *āyat* of the debt." Makkī reported that the Prophet, may Allah bless him and grant him peace, said, "Jibrīl came to me and said put it at the beginning of *āyat* 280."

It is related from Ubayy ibn Ka'b, Ibn 'Abbās and Qatāda that the last *āyat* to be revealed was *"A Messenger has come to you from yourselves."* (9:128). The first position is more commonly reported, sounder and better known. It is related that Ibn 'Abbās said, "The last *āyat* to be revealed was *'Be fearful of a Day when you will be returned to Allah. Then every self will be paid in full for what it earned. They will not be wronged.'* Jibrīl told the Prophet, 'Muḥammad! Put it at the beginning of *āyat* 280 of *al-Baqara*.'" Abū Bakr al-Anbārī mentioned in *Kitāb ar-Radd* that the position of Ibn 'Umar was that this was the last *āyat* to be revealed and the Prophet, may Allah bless him and grant him peace, lived twenty-one days after it.

The *āyat* is a warning to all people and a command encouraging every human being. Ibn Jinnī said, "It was as if Allah showed kindness to the believers by directly addressing them when He mentions the return, since that is what awakens the hearts. Then He makes a grammatical change to the third person, which is also out of kindness tothem. The majority of scholars say that the day referred to is the Day of Rising and Reckoning, while some people say that it is the day a person dies. Ibn 'Aṭiyya said that the first is sounder because of the context. There is an implied elision: "you will be returned to the judgement and decision of Allah." "They" here means "all people". This *āyat* conveys to us that reward or punishment is connected to actions and so it refutes the Jabriyya, as we already mentioned.

يَٰٓأَيُّهَا ٱلَّذِينَ ءَامَنُوٓاْ إِذَا تَدَايَنتُم بِدَيۡنٍ إِلَىٰٓ أَجَلٖ
مُّسَمّٗى فَٱكۡتُبُوهُۚ وَلۡيَكۡتُب بَّيۡنَكُمۡ كَاتِبُۢ بِٱلۡعَدۡلِۚ وَلَا
يَأۡبَ كَاتِبٌ أَن يَكۡتُبَ كَمَا عَلَّمَهُ ٱللَّهُۚ فَلۡيَكۡتُبۡ وَلۡيُمۡلِلِ ٱلَّذِي
عَلَيۡهِ ٱلۡحَقُّ وَلۡيَتَّقِ ٱللَّهَ رَبَّهُۥ وَلَا يَبۡخَسۡ مِنۡهُ شَيۡـٔٗاۚ فَإِن
كَانَ ٱلَّذِي عَلَيۡهِ ٱلۡحَقُّ سَفِيهًا أَوۡ ضَعِيفًا أَوۡ لَا يَسۡتَطِيعُ
أَن يُمِلَّ هُوَ فَلۡيُمۡلِلۡ وَلِيُّهُۥ بِٱلۡعَدۡلِۚ وَٱسۡتَشۡهِدُواْ شَهِيدَيۡنِ
مِن رِّجَالِكُمۡۖ فَإِن لَّمۡ يَكُونَا رَجُلَيۡنِ فَرَجُلٞ وَٱمۡرَأَتَانِ مِمَّن تَرۡضَوۡنَ
مِنَ ٱلشُّهَدَآءِ أَن تَضِلَّ إِحۡدَىٰهُمَا فَتُذَكِّرَ إِحۡدَىٰهُمَا ٱلۡأُخۡرَىٰۚ

وَلَا يَأْبَ ٱلشُّهَدَآءُ إِذَا مَا دُعُوا۟ ۚ وَلَا تَسْـَٔمُوٓا۟ أَن تَكْتُبُوهُ
صَغِيرًا أَوْ كَبِيرًا إِلَىٰٓ أَجَلِهِۦ ۚ ذَٰلِكُمْ أَقْسَطُ عِندَ
ٱللَّهِ وَأَقْوَمُ لِلشَّهَٰدَةِ وَأَدْنَىٰٓ أَلَّا تَرْتَابُوٓا۟ ۖ إِلَّآ أَن تَكُونَ
تِجَٰرَةً حَاضِرَةً تُدِيرُونَهَا بَيْنَكُمْ فَلَيْسَ عَلَيْكُمْ جُنَاحٌ
أَلَّا تَكْتُبُوهَا ۗ وَأَشْهِدُوٓا۟ إِذَا تَبَايَعْتُمْ ۚ وَلَا يُضَآرَّ
كَاتِبٌ وَلَا شَهِيدٌ ۚ وَإِن تَفْعَلُوا۟ فَإِنَّهُۥ فُسُوقٌۢ بِكُمْ ۗ
وَٱتَّقُوا۟ ٱللَّهَ ۖ وَيُعَلِّمُكُمُ ٱللَّهُ ۗ وَٱللَّهُ بِكُلِّ شَىْءٍ عَلِيمٌ ٢٨٢

282 *You who believe! when you take on a debt*
for a specified period, write it down.
A writer should write it down between you justly.
No writer should refuse to write;
as Allah has taught him, so he should write.
The one incurring the debt should dictate
and should be fearful of Allah his Lord
and not reduce it in any way.
If the person incurring the debt is incompetent
or weak or unable to dictate,
then his guardian should dictate for him justly.
Two men among you should act as witnesses.
But if there are not two men,
then a man and two women
with whom you are satisfied as witnesses;
then if one of them is confused,
the other can remind her.
Witnesses should not refuse
when they are called upon.

Do not think it too trivial to write down,
whether small or large,
with the date that it falls due.
Doing that is more just in Allah's sight
and more helpful when bearing witness
and more likely to eliminate any doubt –
unless it is an immediate transaction hand to hand,
taken and given without delay.
There is nothing wrong in your not writing that down.
Call witnesses when you trade.
Neither writer nor witness
should be put under pressure.
If you do that, it is deviancy on your part.
Be fearful of Allah and Allah will give you knowledge.
Allah has knowledge of all things.

You who believe! when you take on a debt

Sa'īd ibn al-Musayyab said, "I heard that the closest *āyat* in time in relation to the *Āyat al-Kursī* was the *Āyat* of the Debt." Ibn 'Abbās said, "This *āyat* was revealed specifically about the *salam* sale," meaning the fact that the people of Madina used the *salam* sale was the reason for the revelation of the *āyat*. Our scholars define the *salam* sale as being a known sale on credit for goods which are present for a known term. It must be known and anything unknown must be avoided. For instance, in Madina at the time the Prophet came to them they used to give credit and make a loan on the basis of the expected fruits of the date-palms, and the Prophet forbade them to do that because of the uncertainty inherent in it, since the trees might not produce anything. *Salaf* and *salam* have the same meaning, however the term *salaf* can be used for a loan (*qarḍ*). But it is agreed that the *āyat* applies to all debts.

Ibn Khuwayzimandād said, "The *āyat* contains thirty rulings." Some of our scholars use it as evidence for the permission to put a term on loans according to what Mālik said, since there is no difference between a loan and any other contract which involves debts. The Shāfi'īs disagree with that and say that the *āyat* does not contain permission for delay on all debts. The command is for there to be witnesses if the debt has a set term.

The word "*dayn*" (debt) is the correct term for any transaction in which one person is owed cash and the other is granted a delay. The word *'ayn* refers to what is immediate and *dayn* refers to what is absent.

for a specified period

Ibn al-Mundhir said that this indicates that a *salam* sale without a known term is not permitted. The *Sunna* of the Messenger of Allah, may Allah bless him and grant him peace, indicates something similar to the Book of Allah. It is confirmed that when the Messenger of Allah came to Madina they used to give advances against fruit for two or three years ahead. The Messenger of Allah, may Allah bless him and grant him peace, said, "Whoever gives an advance on dates, should give an advance for a known measure and known weight for a known term." (Ibn 'Abbās in al-Bukhārī and Muslim)

Ibn 'Umar said, "The people of the *Jāhiliyya* used to sell meat to one another for the *ḥabal al-ḥabala* (the offspring of a pregnant camel). The Messenger of Allah, may Allah bless him and grant him peace, forbade them to do that. All scholars agree that the permitted *salam* is when a man gives an advance to his companion of known defined food with a known measure for a known term in known dinars or dirhams and the transaction is made before they leave the place." Our scholars say that the date set for when a *salam* becomes due can be the harvest, cutting of the fruit, or the festivals of Nayrūz or Mihrajān [New Year or the autumn equinox] since that is a particular time.

write it down.

"Write down the amount and the term." It is said that Allah commanded writing, but what is meant is writing and witnessing because writing without witnesses does not constitute proper evidence. It is said that He commanded us to write so that we will not forget. Abū Dāwūd reports in his *Sunan* that Ibn 'Abbās said that the Messenger of Allah, may Allah bless him and grant him peace, said about the words of Allah, *"when you take on a debt..."*, "The first disavowal of Ādam, peace be upon him, occurred in this manner. When Allah showed him his descendants, he saw a radiant man, shining with light, and asked, 'O Lord, who is this?' The answer was, 'This is your descendant, Dā'ūd.' He asked, 'O Lord, how long will he live?' 'Sixty years,' was the reply. He said, 'O lord, increase his life!' 'No,' He replied, 'unless you give him some of your life span.' He asked, 'What is my life span?' 'A thousand years,' He replied. He said, 'I have given him forty years.' So Allah wrote it for him and the angels testified to it. When the angels came to him as he was dying, he said, 'I still have forty years!' They said, 'You gave them to your descendant Dā'ūd.' 'I did not give anyone anything!' he said. So Allah produced the document and the angels testified to it."

Some people believe that writing accounts is obligatory for owners and obliged by this *āyat*, be it a sale or a loan, so that there will be no forgetfulness or disavowal. Aṭ-Ṭabarī prefers that. Ibn Jurayj said, "The one who borrows should write it down and the one who lends should act as witness." Ash-Sha'bī said, "They used to think that His words, *'If you leave things on trust with one another'* (2:283) were abrogated by the command to write. The like of this is related by Ibn Jurayj. Ibn Zayd also said that and he reported it from Abū Sa'īd al-Khudrī. Ar-Rabī' believed that this was obligatory by these words and then the ruling was lightened by His words, *"If you leave things on trust with one another."* Most say that the command to write is a recommendation to preserve property and remove uncertainty. If the debtor is trustworthy, writing the debt down does not harm him. If he is other than that, writing will put his debt in order and satisfy the need of the one with the right.

A writer should write it down between you justly.

'Aṭā' and others said that it is obligatory for a scribe to write, when he is the only available scribe. The word "justly" means "with trust and fairness". He should not write more or less than the amount. The words "between you" are used because both sides are involved and so that it is not suspected that the scribe has written the debt down incorrectly. He should not be moved by favouritism for either party. Mālik said that, based on this *āyat*, documents should only be written down by people who are known for being fair and trustworthy.

No writer should refuse to write.

The scribe is forbidden to refuse when called upon to fulfil his function.

The one incurring the debt should dictate

The one taking on the debt acknowledges his liability verbally so that it is known what he owes. The scribe must not reduce the amount owed and must have fear of Allah.

If the person incurring the debt is incompetent or weak

Some people say that this means young, but that is an error. An adult can also be an incompetent. The word "weak" here implies an adult without intelligence.

or unable to dictate,

Allah puts people who incur debts into four categories: an independent person who can dictate by himself and three others who do not dictate. They are always in existence. Their rights are also taken care of in matters other than business dealings, like inheritance when it is divided and other things. They are the incompetent, the weak and those unable to dictate. An incompetent (*safīh*) is someone with deficient sense regarding property and it is not proper for him to give or take for himself. He is like the *safīh* garment, which is one that is lightly woven. Someone with a vile tongue is called a fool (*safīh*) because foul language almost only occurs in ignorant people and people of defective intellect. Arabs sometimes use the word *safīh* for feebleness of the intellect and sometimes for weakness of the body.

Anas ibn Mālik reported that a man in the time of the Prophet, may Allah bless him and grant him peace, used to trade and he had some weakness in his intellect. His family went to the Prophet of Allah, may Allah bless him and grant him peace, and said, "Prophet of Allah, debar so-and-so. He trades and there is some weakness in his mind." So the Prophet, may Allah bless him and grant him peace, summoned him and forbade him to sell. He said, "Messenger of Allah, I cannot endure a time without trade." The Messenger of Allah said. "If you will not stop trading, then say, 'This for that, and no cheating.'" (at-Tirmidhī said it is *ṣaḥīḥ*.) The Messenger of Allah, may Allah bless him and grant him peace, also gave someone like this the option of three days on his contracts. Scholars disagree about someone who is deluded in sales due to lack of experience and lack of intelligence and whether he should be debarred based on this *āyat* and on the *ḥadīth*.

The "weak" are those who have some defect in their mind and so cannot dictate, either because of a stammer, muteness or ignorance of the language. Their guardian is their father or a trustee. Those who cannot dictate are children and their guardian is their trustee or father. If someone is ill, he has an agent. As for the dumb, they can be one of the weak or one who cannot dictate.

then his guardian should dictate for him justly.

Aṭ-Ṭabarī believed that the pronoun "him" refers to the "right," (meaning the guardian entitled to the right) and has an *isnād* to that effect from ar-Rabī' and Ibn 'Abbās. It is also said that it refers to the one who owes it, which is correct, and what is reported from Ibn 'Abbās is not sound. How could it be considered evidence if the one responsible for dictating the debt owed by an incompetent is the one owed the money! This is something which is not part of the *Sharī'a* unless the reason that the person is unable to dictate is that illness or great age make his words incomprehensible or he is mute. In such a case the one owed the debt can dictate while the one who is unable to do so listens and when it is finished, affirms it. But this is not what the *āyat* is about.

If it is confirmed that what is meant by the 'guardian' here is a *faqīh*, then the text indicates that the affirmation of the *faqīh* regarding the matter is accepted when he takes an oath.

The dealings of a debarred incompetent without the permission of his guardian are null and void by consensus and do not ever effect anything. There is disagreement about the dealings of an incompetent who is not debarred. That will be dealt with in *Sūrat an-Nisā'*.

Two men among you should act as witnesses.

They are called upon to act as witnesses. People disagree about whether this is obligatory or merely recommended. The sound position is that it is recommended. Allah regulates testimony by His wisdom in financial and physical matters and other *ḥudūd* and makes two witnesses necessary in each case except where fornication is concerned.

The word "men" (*rijāl*) does not apply to all men since unbelievers are excluded. The expression could include slaves but Mujāhid said that it means free men, which Qāḍī Abū Isḥāq prefers. Scholars disagree about the testimony of slaves. This also indicates that people who are blind can act as witnesses when they have definite knowledge about what they are testifying to, as is related from Ibn 'Abbās: "The Messenger of Allah, may Allah bless him and grant him peace, was asked about testimony and said, 'You can see this sun. So testify when you have the equivalent certainty about the matter or do not testify.'" This indicates that a witness should actually see what he testifies to, and that testimony on the basis of logical deduction, which might be wrong, is not permitted. For instance, a blind man is permitted to have intercourse with his wife when he recognises her voice because it is permitted to engage in intercourse on the basis of probability that it is lawful. If a woman is brought to him and he is told, "This is your wife," and he does not recognise her, he is permitted to have intercourse with her. He can accept a gift which comes to him by the statement of the messenger and he can testify to what he has been told.

The position of Mālik regarding the testimony of the blind on the basis of hearing the voice is that it is permitted in divorce and other things when he recognises the voice. Ibn al-Qāsim said, "I asked Mālik, 'A man hears his neighbour through a wall without seeing him and hears him divorce his wife. Can he testify to it if he recognises his voice?' Mālik answered, 'His testimony is allowed.' That position was also related from 'Alī ibn Abī Ṭālib, al-Qāsim ibn Muḥammad, Shurayḥ al-Kindī, ash-Sha'bī, 'Aṭā' ibn Abī Rabāḥ, Yaḥyā ibn Sa'īd, Rabī'a, Ibrāhīm an-Nakhā'ī, Mālik and al-Layth.

But if there are not two men, then a man and two women

This means that if the claimant does not bring two men, then a man and two women are sufficient. This is the position of the majority. Some say that the testimony of women is only permissible when there are no other men at all. Ibn 'Aṭiyya said that this is weak and not in accordance with the words of the *āyat*. The clear position is that of the majority, which simply permits one man and two women, even when there are other men available. According to the majority, this is particular to property and on condition that there is a man with them. It is for property rather than other matters because Allah gives many means for confirming property since there are many means of obtaining it and property is frequently subject to dispute. Sometimes confirmation is by writing, sometimes by witnessing, sometimes by pledges and sometimes by guarantee, and the testimony of women with men is part of that. Scholars permit the testimony of women alone regarding things which only they can know, as is also the case with the testimony of children, when it is necessary, about injuries. However scholars disagree about the testimony of children in such cases. Mālik allowed it as long as the children have not separated and do not disagree. 'Abdullāh ibn az-Zubayr gave judgement regarding injuries in such cases, and Mālik said, "It is the agreed practice here.' Ash-Shāfi'ī, Abū Ḥanīfa and the Ḥanafīs did not permit it because they are not "men".

Al-Mahdawī says that the testimony of women in cases involving *ḥudūd* is not permitted according to the position of most of the *fuqahā'* and most preclude it in marriage and divorce as well. That is the position of Mālik, ash-Shāfi'ī and others. They may testify about property but not about other things.

with whom you are satisfied as witnesses

This describes both the man and the two women. Ibn Bukayr and others said that this is addressed to judges. Ibn 'Aṭiyya said, "This is not an excellent interpretation. The *āyat* is addressed to all people, but someone confused by the context might think it referred to judges alone. This usage is frequent in the Book of Allah." These words indicate that there are witnesses who are not considered to be satisfactory. Those are people who are not considered to be of sufficient integrity. That is, of course, in addition to being Muslim. This is the position of the majority. Our scholars says that integrity entails uprightness in religious matters which includes avoiding major wrong actions and maintaining noble character and abandoning minor wrong actions and being clearly trustworthy. Abū Ḥanīfa says that outward affirmation of Islam is sufficient to qualify as a witness in matters involving property but not in cases involving the *ḥudūd*. This is false because property is one of people's rights, as Ibn al-'Arabī said. We say that integrity is a necessary requirement for testimony to marriage, which differs from Abū Ḥanīfa who says that a marriage may be contracted even if the witnesses are impious.

then if one of them is confused, the other can remind her.

Abū 'Ubayd says that the expression "is confused" (*ḍalla* lit. strays) here means "forgets". Straying from testimony happens by forgetting part of it and remembering another part so that a person is confused. That is not the case when someone forgets it all.

Witnesses should not refuse when they are called upon.

Al-Ḥasan says that this phrase deals with two issues. You should not refuse when you are asked to be a witness and you should not refuse to attest to the thing you are asked to bear witness to. Ibn 'Abbās said that. Qatāda, ar-Rabī' and Ibn 'Abbās said it means that people should not refuse to convey what they witnessed and confirm it in writing. Mujāhid said, "This means when you are called to perform the testimony and are in possession of the evidence." An-Naqqāsh reports that this is how the Prophet, may Allah bless him and grant him peace, explained the *āyat*. Mujāhid said, "When you are first called to testify, if you wish, then go, and if you do not wish, do not." Abū Miljaz, 'Aṭā', Ibrāhīm, Ibn Jubayr, as-Suddī, Ibn Zayd and as-Suddī all said that.

According to this, it is not obliged for witnesses to attend when summoned regarding two people who made a contract, but they must attend in the case of two people who contracted a debt if they were present at the transaction. When they were witnesses to the original contract and they are asked to affirm their testimony to the document, they should do so. This is the situation which is referred to in this *āyat*. What is involved is the confirmation of testimony already given. If the testimony is confirmed, then they are called upon to reconfirm it in the presence of the judge. So the being "called upon" refers to attending the court.

Ibn 'Aṭiyya said, "The *āyat*, as al-Ḥasan said, combines two recommended matters. The Muslims are encouraged to help their brothers. When there are many witnesses and there is confidence that the person will not be deprived of his right, then it is merely recommended for the one summoned, and he can fail to attend for any excuse whatsoever. If he fails to attend without any excuse, there is no wrong action or reward for him. If it is necessary and there is the slightest risk that the person will be deprived of his right, the recommendation is strengthened to the point that is close to an obligation. If a witness knows that someone will be completely deprived of his right by his failing to testify, then it is obligatory for him to testify, especially if he is summoned to do so.

This *āyat* provides evidence that it is permitted for a ruler to provide witnesses for people and to pay them from the treasury and for them to have no other work except attending to the preservation of people's rights. Otherwise those rights might be lost and rendered null and void. Then the meaning would imply: "witnesses should not refuse to testify when people demand what they are entitled to." Allah knows best. If it is said that this refers to testifying in exchange for a wage, we reply that it is simple testimony from people who have their needs fulfilled by the treasury. That is like paying judges and guardians and all the acts of public welfare which help the Muslims. This is part of it, and Allah knows best. The Almighty says, *"Those who collect it"* (9:60), giving a share of the *zakāt* to those who collect it.

This indicates that a witness is someone who comes before a judge. This is the basis of the *Sharī'a* and is acted on in every time and is understood by every nation.

Do not think it too trivial to write down, whether small or large, with the date that it falls due.

This is in order to avert the danger of tedium which may come about through the constant repetition of contracting debts as it is feared that people may become bored with writing them down. One of them may say, "This is so little that it does not need to be written down", so it is stressed for both small and large amounts.

Doing that is more just in Allah's sight

This means writing down both small and large transactions with witnesses. "*Aqwam*" (more just) here means "more correct and more likely to protect the rights of those concerned". It is also more likely to remove doubts and uncertainty.

and more helpful when bearing witness

This is evidence that if a witness sees the contractual document but does not remember giving the testimony, he should not confirm it since there is some doubt about it. He should only testify to what he is sure about and may say, for instance, "This is my handwriting, but I do not remember writing it." Ibn al-Mundhir said, "Most trustworthy scholars forbid a witness to testify to his writing when he does not remember giving the testimony." Mālik found evidence for the permissibility of doing that in Allah's words, *"We can do no more than to testify to what we know."* (12:81). Some scholars say that since Allah ascribed writing to justice, he can testify to his handwriting, even if he does not remember writing it.

unless it is an immediate transaction hand to hand,

This means that it takes place on the spot. That is because Allah knew that it would be difficult for them. That is in respect of small things. As-Suddī and aḍ-Ḍaḥḥāk said, "This is what is done hand to hand."

taken and given without delay.

The transaction is achieved by each party taking their goods or cash and separating. When it is a question of land or buildings or a lot of animals so that the conclusion of the contract is not subject to the two parties separating, then it is recommended that it be written down because a change in circumstances might occur in that instance. When the exchange is clearly made and they part, each with his goods, it is very unusual for there to be a dispute. The *Sharī'a* recommends this procedure as being in people's best interests in the case of credit sales whether the goods are absent or not, by means of writing, testimony and pledge. Ash-Shāfi'ī says: "There are three forms of sale: selling with a document and witnesses, selling with a pledge, and selling on trust." When Ibn 'Umar sold for cash, he called for witnesses and when he sold on credit, he wrote it down.

Call witnesses when you trade.

Aṭ-Ṭabarī says that this means that you should call witnesses to both small and large transactions. People disagree about whether that is obligatory or recommended. Abū Mūsā al-Ash'arī, Ibn 'Umar, aḍ-Ḍaḥḥāk, Sa'īd ibn al-Musayyab, Jābir ibn Zayd, Mujāhid, Dā'ūd ibn 'Alī and his son Abū Bakr say that it is obligatory. One of the strongest in respect of that position was 'Aṭā'. He said, "I call witnesses when I sell and buy for a dirham, or half a dirham, or a third or less. Allah says, *'Call witnesses when you trade.'"* Ibrāhīm said, "I call witnesses when I sell and buy, even for a bunch of onions. One of those who believed it to be obligatory and preferred that was aṭ-Ṭabarī. He said, "It is not lawful for a Muslim to buy and sell without calling witnesses. Otherwise he opposes the Book of Allah. If it is on credit, he must write it down and have witnesses if a scribe is at hand."

Ash-Sha'bī and al-Ḥasan believe that the *āyat* is just recommendation and guidance and not a definite injunction. That is reported to be the position of Mālik, ash-Shāfi'ī, and the People of Opinion. Ibn al-'Arabī claimed that this is the position of all and he said that it is sound. No one related that it is mandatory except aḍ-Ḍaḥḥāk. He said, "The Prophet, may Allah bless him and grant him peace, bought a slave and wrote: 'In the Name of Allah, the All-Merciful, Most Merciful. This is what Muḥammad, Messenger of Allah, has purchased from al-'Addā' ibn Khālid, a sale from one Muslim to another, with no hidden defect, no taint and no wickedness (*ghā'ila*) [i.e. in the slave sold.].'" He also bought without witnesses and left his armour in pawn to a Jew without witnesses being present. If having witnesses had been mandatory, it would have been obligatory when leaving a pledge out of fear of dispute.

We mentioned the view of it being obligatory from other than aḍ-Ḍaḥḥāk, namely the *ḥadīth* of al-'Addā' in ad-Dāraquṭnī and Abū Dāwūd. He became Muslim after the Conquest of Makka and Ḥunayn. Al-Mahdawī, an-Naḥḥās and Makkī report that some people say that *"Call witnesses when you trade"* was abrogated by *"If you leave things on trust with one another."* He reported from Abū Sa'īd al-Khudrī that the second *āyat* abrogated the one before it. An-Naḥḥās said that this is the position of al-Ḥasan, al-Ḥakam, and 'Abdu'r-Raḥmān ibn Zayd. Aṭ-Ṭabarī disagrees and says that the second *āyat* refers to someone who cannot find a scribe.

Neither writer nor witness should be put under pressure.

One meaning of this is that a scribe should not write anything other than what has been dictated to him nor should the witness add to his testimony nor decrease it. Al-Ḥasan, Qatāda, Ṭāwūs, Ibn Zayd and others said that. It is related from Ibn 'Abbās, Mujāhid and 'Aṭā' that the *āyat* means that the scribe should not be prevented from writing nor the witness from testifying.

Mujāhid, aḍ-Ḍaḥḥāk, Ṭāwūs, and as-Suddī said – and the same thing is also related from Ibn 'Abbās – that the *āyat* means that the witness should not be summoned to testify or the scribe to write when they are busy and they should not be made to come when they have an excuse nor should they be abused. They should not be told, "You have disobeyed Allah's command!" or similar things so as to put them under pressure. Allah forbade this because, if it was applied, it would distract them from their *dīn* and livelihood.

If you do that, it is deviancy on your part,

If you do put them under pressure it is disobedience to Allah, as Sufyān ath-Thawrī said. The scribe and witness disobey by adding or decreasing. That is a type of prevarication which harms property and people and invalidates their rights. Forcing the witness or scribe when they are busy is also disobedience and incorrect behaviour since it is disobeying Allah's command.

Be fearful of Allah and Allah will give you knowledge.

This is a promise from Allah that He will teach those who fear him, meaning that He will put a light in their hearts by which they will understand what comes to them. He may put discrimination in their hearts, so that they will be able to distinguish between truth and falsehood. Allah says, *"O you who believe, if you fear Allah, he will give you discrimination,"* (8:29) Allah knows best.

وَإِن كُنتُمْ عَلَىٰ سَفَرٍ وَلَمْ تَجِدُواْ كَاتِبًا فَرُهُنٌ مَّقْبُوضَةٌ
فَإِنْ أَمِنَ بَعْضُكُم بَعْضًا فَلْيُؤَدِّ الَّذِي اؤْتُمِنَ أَمَانَتَهُ وَلْيَتَّقِ
اللَّهَ رَبَّهُ وَلَا تَكْتُمُواْ الشَّهَادَةَ وَمَن يَكْتُمْهَا فَإِنَّهُ آثِمٌ
قَلْبُهُ وَاللَّهُ بِمَا تَعْمَلُونَ عَلِيمٌ ﴿٢٨٣﴾

283 *If you are on a journey and cannot find a writer,*
something can be left as a security.
If you leave things on trust with one another
the one who is trusted must deliver up his trust
and be fearful of Allah his Lord.
Do not conceal testimony.
If someone does conceal it, his heart commits a crime.
Allah knows what you do.

If you are on a journey and cannot find a writer,

After Allah has mentioned the recommendation to testify and write for the benefit of preserving property and the *dīn*, He follows that by mentioning the excuses which may prevent people from writing and enjoins them to leave a pledge in such cases. He clarifies what constitutes a valid excuse by mentioning a journey which is the usual reason, especially since there were a lot of expeditions at that time. But included in that are all valid excuses. There are often times when a person is resident and cannot make use of a scribe, as occurs when people are at work or during the night. Another instance is when there is fear for the loss of what the debtor owes and the lender seeks a pledge from him for that reason. The Prophet, may Allah bless him and grant him peace, left his armour in pledge with a Jew whom he asked for an advance of barley. He said, "Muḥammad wants to take away my property." The Prophet, may Allah bless him and grant him peace, said, "He lies. I am the one who is trustworthy on earth and trustworthy in heaven. If you trust me, I will pay. Take my armour to him." He died with his armour still in pledge.

Most scholars say that a pledge should be left when travelling going by the text of the Revelation. It is confirmed while a person is resident by the *sunna* of the Messenger. This is sound.

something can be left as a security.

The meaning of "leaving a security" is that an item be kept by the lender as a guarantee against what is owed so that the amount can be paid in full from selling the security or renting it out if the debt cannot be collected from the debtor. That is how scholars define it. The root of the verb (*rahana*) means "to remain or last". That which is *rāhin* continues and is fixed. Since the word means to be fixed and constant, the pledge is void according to the *fuqahā'* the moment it goes from the possession of the one who takes it to the one who pledged it. This is what we believe. If the pledge is taken from the possession of the one who accepted it and returned to the pledger by the choice of the one who has taken it on pledge, the pledge then becomes invalid. Abū Ḥanīfa says that, although he adds that if it is returned to his keeping, it is not invalid. Ash-Shāfi'ī also says that it is not invalidated.

If the pledge is verbal and not actually taken, no ruling applies since the *āyat* says "taken". Ash-Shāfi'ī says that Allah only gives a ruling to a pledge which is "taken". Without that, there is no ruling. This is very literal. The Mālikīs say that the pledge is binding by the contract and the pledger must hand over the pledge to the keeping of the person who takes it by the words of the Almighty, *"Fulfil your contract*s."(5:1). This is a contract. The Prophet, may Allah bless him and grant him peace, said, "The believers abide by their conditions," and this is a condition. We believe that taking possession of the pledge is a precondition for its being operative.

The word "taken" (*maqbūḍa*) implies that the person accepting the pledge or his agent must clearly take it. They disagree about a third party with integrity taking it and whether that effects it or not. Mālik and all his people and most other scholars say that the taking by a just person constitutes "taking", while Ibn Abī Laylā, Qatāda, al-Ḥakam, and 'Aṭā' said that it does not, and that it is only taken when it is actually in the possession of the person accepting the pledge. They see it as an act of worship. The position of the majority is sounder because, if a just person takes it, it is still taken. If the pledge is in the possession of a just person who took it and he loses it, the pledgee is not liable since there is nothing in his possession for which he is liable.

If you leave things on trust with one another the one who is trusted must deliver up his trust

This is an order from Allah to hand over what was left and not to procrastinate. The word for "*amāna*" (leave on trust) is a verbal noun meaning something for which one is responsible.

and be fearful of Allah his Lord.

He must not deprive anyone of what is rightfully theirs.

Do not conceal testimony.

This forbids a witness from causing harm by hiding the fact of his testimony. The prohibition is a threat. If there are several witnesses, it is a *farḍ kifāya* that they testify. When two have satisfied it, the obligation falls from the rest of them.

If someone does conceal it, his heart commits a crime.

The heart is mentioned since concealment is an action and the heart is that piece of flesh by whose soundness the entire body is sound, as the Prophet, may Allah bless him and grant him peace, said. This stresses the real nature of what occurs and it is part of eloquence and fine use of language. It is said that the crime of the heart is the reason for its transformation. When Allah transforms the heart, He makes the person a hypocrite and seals it. We seek refuge from Allah. This was already mentioned.

Know that Allah's commands concerning testimony and writing are in intended to rectify discord and to avoid disputes which might lead to conflict, thereby preventing Shayṭān from enticing people to deny others their rights and exceed what the *Sharī'a* has defined for them, or not to confine themselves to the amount they are owed. It is for this reason that the *Sharī'a* forbids unknown sales which would lead to disagreement and conflict and bring about mutual rancour and separation. One aspect of this is Allah's prohibition of gambling and games of chance and drinking wine. Allah says: *"Shayṭān wants to stir up enmity and hatred between you by means of wine and gambling,"* (5:91) Whoever is guided by Allah in respect of His commands and restraints, obtains the good of this world and the *dīn*. Allah Almighty says, *"But if they had done what they were urged to do, it would have been better for them."* (4:66)

Al-Bukhārī related from Abū Hurayra that the Prophet, may Allah bless him and grant him peace, said, "If someone takes something from another intending to repay it, Allah will repay it for him, and if someone takes it intending to destroy it, Allah will destroy him." An-Nasā'ī reported that Maymūna, the wife of the Prophet, used to have a lot of debts, and she was asked, "Umm al-Mu'minīn, do you incur debts when you have nothing with which to pay them?" She replied, "I heard the Messenger of Allah, may Allah bless him and grant him peace, say, 'If anyone takes on a debt intending to pay it, Allah will help him with it.'" Ath-Thawrī, aṭ-Ṭabarī and al-Ḥārith ibn Abī Usāma reported from 'Uqba ibn 'Āmir that the Messenger of Allah, may Allah bless him and grant him peace, said, "Do not frighten people when they are secure." They asked "Messenger of Allah, how can that happen?" "By debts," he replied. Al-Bukhārī reported from Anas that the Prophet said in a supplication, "O Allah, I seek refuge with You from worry, sorrow, incapacity, laziness, cowardice, miserliness, heavy debts and the oppression of men." Scholars say that heavy debts are those which the debtor can find no way to pay.

The Prophet, may Allah bless him and grant him peace, said, "A debt is the shame of the *dīn*." It is related that he said, "Debts are worry by night and abasement by day." Our scholars say that debts are shame and abasement because they preoccupy the heart and mind, and one is always concerned about paying them. There is abasement by the creditor when he meets him and he continues to endure the burden by the creditor's favour to him by delaying it to the end of its term. He may promise to pay and then put it off, or the creditor may abuse him because of it and he will lie, or he may give him an oath and then break it, and other such things. This is why the Prophet sought refuge from it. It was said to the Messenger of Allah, "How often you seek refuge from debts!" He said, "When a man is in debt, he will speak and lie and promise and break his promise." Furthermore, sometimes he may die without paying the debt and then be left in pledge for it, for the

Prophet, may Allah bless him and grant him peace, said, "The soul of the believer is pledged in the grave for his debts until they are paid." All of these things are shame in the *dīn* which removes its beauty and perfection. Allah knows best.

When Allah commands people to write down debts, to bear witness and to take pledges, that constitutes a clear text about preserving property and making it grow, refuting ignorant false Sufis and their riffraff who do not agree with that. They abandon all their wealth and do not leave enough for themselves and their families. Then, when they and their families are in need, they either turn to the generosity of brothers or friends, or take from the wealthy and unjust. This is blameworthy and forbidden. Abū'l-Faraj al-Jawzī said, "I do not wonder at those who practise asceticism when they are lacking in knowledge. I do wonder at how people who have knowledge and intellect encourage this and command it when it is contrary to the *Sharī'a* and logic." Al-Muḥāsibī talked a lot about this and Abū Ḥāmid al-Ghazālī praised it as well. I think al-Muḥāsibī has more of an excuse than Abū Ḥāmid because Abū Ḥāmid had more *fiqh*, although his entry into *taṣawwuf* obliged him to support what he had entered into.

Al-Muḥāsibī said, "I heard that when 'Abdu'r-Raḥmān ibn 'Awf died, some of the Companions of Messenger of Allah, may Allah bless him and grant him peace, said, 'We fear for 'Abdu'r-Raḥmān because of what he left.' Ka'b said, 'Glory be to Allah! What do you fear for 'Abdu'r-Raḥmān? He earned well, spent well and left well.' That reached Abū Dharr who went out angrily after Ka'b. He picked up the jawbone of a camel and then went after Ka'b. Ka'b was told, 'Abū Dharr is looking for you.' So he ran to 'Uthmān asking him for his help and telling him the story. Abū Dharr tracked down Ka'b until he came to 'Uthmān's house. When he entered, Ka'b got up and sat down behind 'Uthmān, fleeing from Abū Dharr. Abū Dharr said to him, 'Son of a Jewish woman, do you claim that there is no harm in what 'Abdu'r-Raḥmān left! The Messenger of Allah, may Allah bless him and grant him peace, went out one day and said, "The ones with the most will be the ones with the least on the Day of Rising except for those who say such-and-such.'"" Al-Muḥāsibī said, "In spite of his excellence, 'Abdu'r-Raḥmān will still be made to stand in the courtyard on the Day of Rising because of his lawful earnings which he used for the sake of abstinence and acts of charity, and so he will be prevented from hastening to the Garden with the poor and will have to crawl in behind them."

Al-Ghazālī mentioned this and strengthened it by the *ḥadīth* of Tha'laba. He was given money and then refused to pay *zakāt*. He said, "If anyone examines the states of the Prophets and *awliyā'* and their statements, he will not doubt that the absence of wealth is better than its existence, even if it is directed towards good ends since the least of the consequences of wealth is that attending to it distracts the *himma* (aspiration) from remembrance of Allah. So the *murīd* must leave his property so that he only has what he needs and not have a dirham to which his heart turns so that he is veiled from Allah."

Al-Jawzī said, "This is contrary to the *Sharī'a* and intelligence, and is poor understanding of what is desired in respect of property. Allah honoured and esteemed it and commanded it to be preserved since He made it the support of the human being and that which is the support of the noble human being is also noble. The Almighty says, *'Do not hand over to the simple-minded any property of theirs for which Allah has made you responsible.'* (4:5). He forbade property to be surrendered to someone without good sense and said, *'If you perceive that they have sound judgement hand over their property to them.'* (4:6) The Prophet, may Allah bless him and grant him peace, forbade squandering property and told Sa'd, 'It is better to leave rich heirs than to leave them poor, begging from other people,' and he said, 'Nothing helped me like the property of Abū Bakr.' He told 'Amr ibn al-'Āṣ, 'The best of property is the good property of a righteous man.' He prayed for Anas, 'O Allah, make his property and children plentiful and bless him in it.' Ka'b said, 'One thing I repent of is that I divested myself of my property as *ṣadaqa* for Allah and His Messenger.' He said, 'Keep part of your property for yourself. That will be better for you.'"

Al-Jawzī continued, "These *aḥādīth* are found in the sound collections and are contrary to what false Sufis believe about a lot of wealth being a veil and a punishment and that having it is contrary to reliance on Allah. It cannot be denied that its temptation is something to be feared, that a lot of people avoid it out of fear of that, that amassing it properly rarely occurs, that the safety of the heart from temptation by it is rare and that it is unusual for a heart to be busy with it while still remembering the Next World. This is why its temptation is feared. As for earning property, when someone confines himself to what will suffice him of what is lawful, that is necessary. As for someone who intends to amass it and have a lot of the lawful, one looks to his intention. If his intention is to boast, that is evil. If he intends a modest income for himself and his family, to save up for changes of fortune and bad times, and intends to expand things for his brothers, enrich the poor and do righteous actions, his intention will be rewarded, and his amassing it with this intention is better than many acts of obedience.

"The intention of many of the Companions was to amass sound wealth for good ends and so they encouraged it and asked for more. When the Prophet, may Allah bless him and grant him peace, gave az-Zubayr a land-grant, he summoned his horse and ran his horse until it stopped, and then threw his whip and he said, 'Give him up to where his whip lands.' Sa'id ibn 'Ubāda said in his supplication, 'O Allah, give me expansion.' The brothers of Yūsuf said, *'We can get an extra load.'* (12:65) Shu'ayb said to Mūsā, *'If you complete ten, then that is up to you.'* (28:27) When Ayyūb was healed and golden locusts began to fall on him, he began to collect them in his garment and collected a lot, he was asked, 'Are you not full?' He said, 'Lord, does a poor man have his fill of Your bounty?'

"This is something embedded in human nature. The words of al-Muḥāsibī are erroneous and indicate lack of knowledge. What he mentioned about Ka'b and Abū Dharr is impossible and forged by the ignorant. Its lack of soundness is concealed because of their attachment to the People [i.e. Sufis]. Its *isnād* is not firm. The truth of the matter is that Abū Dharr died in 25 AH and 'Abdu'r-

Raḥmān ibn 'Awf died in 32 AH so he lived seven years after Abū Dharr. The actual words of the account indicate that it is forged. How could the Companions say, 'We fear for 'Abdu'r-Raḥmān?' Is there not a consensus that it is permitted to amass lawful wealth, so what is the sense of fearing for someone because of something which is allowed? Would the *Sharī'a* permit something and then punish someone for it? This is poor understanding.

"How would Abū Dharr disapprove of 'Abdu'r-Raḥmān when 'Abdu'r-Raḥmān was far more excellent than him? Is its attribution to 'Abdu'r-Raḥmān alone evidence that he did not follow the path of the Companions? Ṭalḥa left three thousand measures and every measure weighed three hundredweight. Az-Zubayr left two hundred and fifty thousand. Ibn Mas'ūd left seventy thousand. Many of the Companions amassed wealth and left it and no one objected to that. As for the words, ''Abdu'r-Raḥmān will crawl on the Day of Rising,' this is proof that the transmitter does not know the *ḥadīth*. I seek refuge with Allah from 'Abdu'r-Raḥmān crawling on the Day of Rising! Do you think that one of the ten promised the Garden, one of the people present at the Battle of Badr and one of the people of the *Shūra* would have to crawl?

"The statement, 'It is better to abandon lawful wealth than to amass it' is not true. When the intention is sound, then amassing it is better without any disagreement among the scholars. Sa'īd ibn al-Musayyab said, 'There is no good in one who does not seek wealth with which to pay his debts and protect his reputation. If he dies, he leaves inheritance for those after him.' He himself left four hundred dinars. Sufyān left two hundred. He used to say. 'Wealth in this time is an armour.' The *Salaf* continued to praise wealth and collect it for recommended things and to help the poor."

Part of what indicates that preserving property and caring for it is correct is that one can fight for it and over it. The Prophet, may Allah bless him and grant him peace, said, "If someone is killed in defence of his property, he is a martyr." This will be mentioned further in *Sūrat al-Mā'ida,* Allah willing.

لِّلَّهِ مَا فِي ٱلسَّمَٰوَٰتِ وَمَا فِي ٱلْأَرْضِۗ وَإِن تُبْدُواْ مَا فِيٓ
أَنفُسِكُمْ أَوْ تُخْفُوهُ يُحَاسِبْكُم بِهِ ٱللَّهُۖ فَيَغْفِرُ
لِمَن يَشَآءُ وَيُعَذِّبُ مَن يَشَآءُۗ وَٱللَّهُ عَلَىٰ كُلِّ شَيْءٍ
قَدِيرٌ ٢٨٤

284 ***Everything in the heavens***
and everything in the earth belongs to Allah.
Whether you divulge what is in yourselves
or keep it hidden,
Allah will still call you to account for it.
He forgives whoever He wills
and He punishes whoever He wills.
Allah has power over all things.

Whether you divulge what is in yourselves or keep it hidden, Allah will still call you to account for it.

People disagree about this statement and there are several positions:

- One group say that it is abrogated. Ibn ʻAbbās, Ibn Masʻūd, ʻĀ'isha, Abū Hurayra, ash-Shaʻbī, ʻAṭā', Muḥammad ibn Sīrīn, Muḥammad ibn Kaʻb, Mūsā ibn ʻUbayda and a group of Companions and *Tābiʻūn* said that. This degree of responsibility remained until Allah revealed, *"Allah does not impose on any self any more than it can bear."* (2:286)

- Ibn ʻAbbās, ʻIkrima, ash-Shaʻbī and Mujāhid said that it is an *āyat* of judgement specifically about the testimony referred to earlier which it is forbidden to conceal and for which the person will be called to account.

- The *āyat* is about doubt and certainty which comes to the heart. Mujāhid said that.

• It is a general judgement and not abrogated. Allah will call His creatures to account for their actions and for things they did not do which were settled in themselves and which they concealed, desired and intended. He will forgive the believers and punish the people of disbelief and hypocrisy for that. Aṭ-Ṭabarī mentioned this position from some people including Ibn 'Abbās who said, "It was not abrogated. But when Allah gathers the creatures, He will say, 'I will tell you what you concealed in yourselves.' He will tell the believers and then forgive them. As for the people of doubt and uncertainty, He will tell them of the denial they concealed. That is what He means when He says, *'He forgives whoever He wills and He punishes whoever He wills.'* and the meaning of His words, *'He will take you to task for the intention your hearts have made'* (2:225) referring to doubt and hypocrisy."

Aḍ-Ḍaḥḥāk said, "On the Day of Rising Allah will tell the person what he was concealing so that he knows that he does not have to fear on account of it." In a report we read, "Allah Almighty will say on the Day of Rising 'This is the day on which secrets are revealed and consciences probed. My scribes only record your actions which appear on your limbs and tongues. I know what they do not know and know what they do not report or write down. I will inform you of that and reckon you for it and then I will forgive whoever I wish and punish whoever I wish.' So He will forgive the believers and punish the unbelievers."

This is the soundest position on the topic. It is indicated by the *ḥadīth* in which the Prophet, may Allah bless him and grant him peace, said, "Allah will pardon My Community for what their selves suggest to them when they do not articulate that nor act on it." We say that this refers to the judgements of this world, like divorce, emancipation and sales whose rulings are not binding as long as they are not spoken. That which is mentioned in the *āyat* is what is between the slave and Allah in the Next World.

- Al-Ḥasan said that the *āyat* is one whose judgement is not abrogated. Aṭ-Ṭabarī mentioned that other scholars said things similar to what has been quoted from Ibn 'Abbās, although they added that the punishment which is a repayment for what occurs in the selves and is accompanied by thought occurs through the misfortunes of this world, its pains and all the things which are disliked in it. Ibn 'Aṭā' said, "This [that it is not abrogated] is correct. Allah's words: *'Whether you divulge what is in yourselves or keep it hidden...'* refer to things which are within your capacity and ability accompanied by conviction and thought, since the words of the *āyat* include thoughts which worried the Companions and the Prophet, may Allah bless him and grant him peace, and so Allah explained to them what He meant by another *āyat* and stipulated that the judgement is that a person is only obliged to do what he is capable of doing. It is not possible to repel thoughts. They predominate and they are not part of what people are held accountable for. This explanation gave them relief and removed their anxiety."

The rest of the *āyat* is one of judgement and is not abrogated. One thing which refutes the claim of abrogation is that the *āyat* is a report, not an order or instruction, and abrogation does not occur in respect of reports. If someone believes that there is abrogation, it can only be in the judgement which was connected to the Companions when they were alarmed by the *āyat*. That was that the Prophet, may Allah bless him and grant him peace, said, "Say, 'We hear and obey.'" That conveys the command to be firm in this and cling to Allah and see the kindness of Allah in His forgiveness. If this is the case, the ruling can be abrogated. The best position is to take the *āyat* as being general and not specific, which is the position of Ibn 'Abbās. It is also said that it was revealed about those who took unbelievers as friends rather than the believers.

He forgives whoever He wills and He punishes whoever He wills.

Ibn Kathīr, Nāfi‘, Abu ‘Amr, Ḥamza and al-Kisā’ī recited this in the apocopate form, *yaghfir – yu‘adhdhib,* while Ibn ‘Āmir and ‘Āṣim read it *yaghfiru – yu‘adhdhibu.*

ءَامَنَ ٱلرَّسُولُ بِمَآ أُنزِلَ إِلَيْهِ مِن رَّبِّهِۦ وَٱلْمُؤْمِنُونَ كُلٌّ
ءَامَنَ بِٱللَّهِ وَمَلَٰٓئِكَتِهِۦ وَكُتُبِهِۦ وَرُسُلِهِۦ لَا نُفَرِّقُ بَيْنَ أَحَدٍ
مِّن رُّسُلِهِۦ وَقَالُوا۟ سَمِعْنَا وَأَطَعْنَا غُفْرَانَكَ رَبَّنَا وَإِلَيْكَ
ٱلْمَصِيرُ ﴿٢٨٥﴾ لَا يُكَلِّفُ ٱللَّهُ نَفْسًا إِلَّا وُسْعَهَا لَهَا مَا
كَسَبَتْ وَعَلَيْهَا مَا ٱكْتَسَبَتْ رَبَّنَا لَا تُؤَاخِذْنَآ
إِن نَّسِينَآ أَوْ أَخْطَأْنَا رَبَّنَا وَلَا تَحْمِلْ عَلَيْنَآ إِصْرًا
كَمَا حَمَلْتَهُۥ عَلَى ٱلَّذِينَ مِن قَبْلِنَا رَبَّنَا وَلَا تُحَمِّلْنَا مَا لَا
طَاقَةَ لَنَا بِهِۦ وَٱعْفُ عَنَّا وَٱغْفِرْ لَنَا وَٱرْحَمْنَآ أَنتَ
مَوْلَىٰنَا فَٱنصُرْنَا عَلَى ٱلْقَوْمِ ٱلْكَٰفِرِينَ ﴿٢٨٦﴾

285 ***The Messenger believes in what has been***
sent down to him from his Lord,
and so do the believers.
Each one believes in Allah and His angels
and His Books and His Messengers.
We do not differentiate
between any of His Messengers.
They say, ‘We hear and we obey.
Forgive us, our Lord!
You are our journey’s end.’
286 ***Allah does not impose on any self***
any more than it can bear.

For it is what it has earned;
against it, what it has merited.
Our Lord, do not take us to task
if we forget or make a mistake!
Our Lord, do not place on us a load
like the one You placed on those before us!
Our Lord, do not place on us a load
we have not the strength to bear!
And pardon us;
and forgive us;
and have mercy on us.
You are our Master ,
so help us against the people of the unbelievers.

The Messenger believes in what has been sent down to him from his Lord.

It is related from al-Ḥasan, Mujāhid and aḍ-Ḍaḥḥāk that this *āyat* is about the Night Journey (*al-Mi'rāj*). The same *tafsīr* is transmitted from Ibn 'Abbās. Some of them say that the entire Qur'ān was brought down by Jibrīl to Muḥammad, may Allah bless him and grant him peace, except for this *āyat*. One of them said, "It is what he heard during the *Mi'rāj*." Others say that it was not about the *Mi'rāj* because the Night Journey occurred in Makka while this entire *sūra* is Madinan.

As for those who say that this *āyat* is about the Night Journey, they say, "When the Prophet, may Allah bless him and grant him peace, ascended and reached a high place in the heavens, Jibrīl accompanied him until he reached the Lote Tree of the Furthest Limit. Then Jibrīl said to him, 'I cannot go beyond this place. No one except you has been commanded to go beyond it. So the Prophet went beyond the Lote Tree until he reached what Allah wished. Jibrīl indicated that the Prophet should greet his Lord and so he said, 'Greetings are for Allah and prayers and good words.'[1] Allah said, 'Peace be upon you, O Prophet and the mercy of Allah and His blessings.' The Prophet desired that his Community

1. This is the *taḥīyāt* used in the *tashahhud* in the prayer.

should have a share of the greeting and so he said, 'Peace be upon us and on the righteous slaves of Allah.' Jibrīl and all the people of the heavens said, 'I bear witness that there is no god except Allah alone without partner and I bear witness that Muḥammad is His slave and Messenger,' and then Allah Almighty said, *'The Messenger believes...'* meaning that he is thankful and that the Messenger affirms *'what has been sent down to him from his Lord.'"* The Prophet wanted his Community to share in the honour and said, *'So do the believers. Each one believes in Allah and His angels and His Books and His Messengers. We do not differentiate between any of His Messengers.'*

In defining the extent of Allah's help, the Prophet, may Allah bless him and grant him peace, reported, "I was helped by terror going before me for the distance of a month." It is said that when those going on a military expedition leave their houses with a sincere intention and beat the drums, terror and awe falls into the hearts of the unbelievers the distance of a month away, whether they know that they have set out or not." When the Prophet returned from his Night Journey, Allah revealed these *āyat*s so that he could inform his Community of that.

There is another aspect to the interpretation of this *āyat*. Az-Zajjāj said, "In this *sūra*, after Allah has mentioned the obligation of the prayer and *zakāt* and clarified the principles of *ḥajj,* the ruling of menstruation, divorce, *īlā'*, the stories of the Prophets and clarified the ruling on usury, He mentions His own worth since He said, *'Everything in the heavens and everything in the earth belongs to Allah.'* Then He mentions that all this is affirmed by the Prophet and the believers.

It is said that the reason for its revelation was the *āyat* before it. When the former *āyat* was revealed to the Prophet, it was hard on the Companions of the Messenger of Allah, so they went to the Messenger of Allah and then knelt and said, "Messenger of Allah, we have been given as obligations actions we can do: prayer, fasting, *jihād* and *ṣadaqa*. But, in this *āyat*, Allah has revealed something it is impossible for us to do." The Messenger of Allah said, "Do you mean to say what the people of the two Books before you said: 'We hear and we disobey'? Say: 'We hear and we obey. Forgive us, our Lord! You are our journey's end.'" When the people recited it, their tongues were humbled and then Allah revealed this *āyat*. When they said that, Allah abrogated the *āyat* and revealed, *"Allah does not impose on any self ...."*

Allah confirmed them when they said "We hear and obey". He praised them in this *āyat* and removed from them the hardship they experienced about thoughts which occur to them. This favour is the fruit of obedience and devotion to Allah. What happened to the tribe of Israel was the opposite of that. They were censured and made to endure the hardships of abasement, wretchedness and exile since they said, "We hear and we disobey." Such is the result of disobedience and recalcitrance towards Allah. We seek refuge with Allah from His vengeance by His grace and generosity!

The Prophet, may Allah bless him and grant him peace, was told, "The house of Thābit ibn Qays is adorned with lamps every night." He replied, "Perhaps he is reciting *Sūrat al-Baqara*." Thābit was told about this and said, "I recited *'The Messenger believes...'* from *Sūrat al-Baqara*. It was revealed when the Companions of the Prophet were experiencing hardship because Allah threatened to call them to account for what their selves concealed. They complained about that to the Prophet, may Allah bless him and grant him peace, and he said, 'Perhaps you say, "We hear and we disobey" as the tribe of Israel said?' They said, 'We hear and we obey!' and so Allah revealed this *āyat* to him."

This *āyat* shows that the believers are not like the Jews and Christians who believe in some of the revelation and reject some of it.

They say, 'We hear and we obey.'

This suggests some elision such as "We hear as those who accept hear." It is said that "hear" means "accept" as in the prayer when it is said, "Allah hears whoever praises Him," and so there is no elision. This entails praise of the speaker. Obedience is acceptance of the command.

Forgive us, our Lord!

The word "*ghufrān*" (forgive) is a verbal noun and the object of it is implied, so what is literally "Your forgiveness" means "grant us Your forgiveness," as az-Zajjaj said. Others say that it means, "We ask (or I ask) for Your forgiveness."

You are our journey's end.'

This is an affirmation of the Resurrection and the fact that we will stand before Allah. It is related that when this *āyat* was revealed, Jibrīl told the Prophet, may Allah bless him and grant him peace, "Allah has allowed praise of you and your Community. Ask and you will be given," and the following *āyat* was what he asked.

Allah does not impose on any self any more than it can bear.

Imposition implies a command to do something which is difficult. The word "*wus'*" (bear) denotes capacity and effort. This is a definite report and it is a declaration from Allah that, from the moment of the revelation of the *āyat,* He has not imposed on His slaves any kind of worship demanded of the hearts or the limbs which is not within the capacity of the one on whom it is imposed. Through this *āyat*, anxiety was removed from the Muslims in the matter regarding their thoughts.

People disagree about whether it is permissible that a ruling in worldly matters be imposed on someone when that is not within his capacity. They do, however, agree that there is no imposition in the *dīn* which is beyond a person's capacity. This *āyat* informs us that such an imposition does not occur in the *Sharī'a*. Abū'l-Ḥasan al-Ash'arī and a group of *mutakallimūn* say that it is logically permissible that someone be charged with doing something he is not capable of doing, and that does not detract at all from the tenets of belief (*'aqīda*) in the *Sharī'a*. That sort of command can be meant to be a punishment for the person on whom it is imposed, as when someone who made images is ordered to create a barley-seed on the Day of Judgement. Those who say that it is permitted disagree about whether it occurred in respect of the Message of Muḥammad, may Allah bless him and grant him peace, or not.

One group say that such an imposition occurred in the case of Abū Lahab,[1] because he was obliged to believe in all of the *Sharī'a* and yet part of the revelation was that he would never believe because his judgement was that his hands would be ruined and he would burn in the Fire. It was announced that he would not believe and so he was charged with believing something which he could not believe. Another group says that such an imposition does not occur at all and report that there is a consensus on that. They say, *"He will burn in a Flaming Fire"* (111:3) means "He will be brought to it." Ibn 'Aṭiyya related that.

The word *"yukallifu"* (impose) is a transitive verb with two objects one of which is elided so that "worship" or "something" is implied. By His kindness and blessing to us, even though He imposed on us what is hard and difficult, like odds of one against ten and *hijra*, which entails leaving one's homeland and separation from family, homeland and traditions, Allah did not impose on us burdensome hardships or painful matters, such as those He imposed on those before us which involved killing themselves and cutting out the patch soiled by urine on clothes and skins. Rather He made things easy for us and reduced the burden and the chains which He had placed on those before us. To Allah belongs praise, grace, favour and blessing.

For it is what it has earned; against it, what it has merited.

The words refer to good actions and bad actions, according to as-Suddī. The majority of scholars do not disagree with that. Ibn 'Aṭiyya said that. It is like His words, *"No bearer of a burden can bear the burden of another,"* (6:164) and *"What each self earns is for itself alone."* (6:164) Thoughts and their like are not part of what the human being earns. The expression for good actions is in the words *"for it"* since a person rejoices in earning them and adds them to his property. Bad actions are *"against it"* since they are

1. Abū Lahab ("Father of Flame"), the nickname of one of the uncles of the Prophet who was an obdurate enemy of Islam. He is mentioned in Sūra 111.

weights and burdens and hard to bear, as one says, "I have property," and "There is a debt against me." The root *kasaba,* which has the basic meaning of acquisition, is repeated and the meaning differs according to the form the word takes [*kasabat* = earned, *iktasabat* = merited]. Ibn 'Aṭiyya says, "It is clear to me regarding this that good actions are part of what is acquired without being a burden since their acquirer is following the path of Allah's command and His *Sharī'a*. Evil deeds are acquired since their acquirer burdens himself through them by rending the veil which Allah has forbidden.

This *āyat* indicates that it is valid to call people's actions "acquisitions". People do not create them. Aṭ-Ṭabarī said that the *āyat* is evidence that someone who kills someone else by crushing, choking or drowning is personally responsible in respect of retaliation or blood money as opposed to someone whose blood money is the responsibility of the clan (*'āqila*).

Our Lord, do not take us to task if we forget or make a mistake!

This *āyat* means: "Pardon our wrong actions if we forget and make a mistake or simply forget or simply make a mistake," as the Prophet, may Allah bless him and grant him peace, said, "Error and forgetfulness have been removed from my Community and from what they are forced to do," i.e. its being a wrong action in those cases. There is no disagreement that the wrong action is cancelled out. There is disagreement about the judgements connected to that action. Does that cancellation of the action mean that the action has no legal consequences or does it still entail all its legal consequences? There is disagreement about that, and the sound position is that it varies according to the circumstances. It is agreed that some consequences are not cancelled, like penalties, blood money and obligatory prayers, and others are agreed to be cancelled, like retaliation and speaking words which can be construed as disbelief. There is disagreement about a third category, like eating out of forgetfulness in Ramaḍān or breaking an oath out of forgetfulness.

Our Lord, do not place on us a load like the one You placed on those before us!

Mālik and ar-Rabī' say that the word "*iṣr*" (load) denotes a difficult onerous thing. Sa'īd ibn Jubayr said that it is severe commands and what was hard for the tribe of Israel regarding urine and the like. Aḍ-Ḍaḥḥāk said "They endured hard things." This is similar to what the others said. 'Aṭā' said that it refers to being turned into pigs and monkeys. Ibn Zayd also said that. He also said that it means wrong actions for which there is no repentance or expiation. The word linguistically means "charge or undertaking", as when Allah says, *"Do you agree and undertake my charge (iṣrī) on that condition?"* (3:81) Another form of the word means constriction, wrong action and burdensomeness. The word *iṣār* denotes a short rope which is used to bind loads and the like. The verb means "to confine." A place of confinement is called a *ma'ṣir*.

Ibn Khuwayzimandād said, "It is possible to infer from the literal meaning of this *āyat* that this refers to the burden which opponents claim that every act of worship entails. That resembles the words of Allah: *"He has not placed any constraint on you in the dīn,"* (22:78) and the words of the Prophet, may Allah bless him and grant him peace: "The *dīn* is ease, so make things easy. Do not make things difficult."

O Allah, be hard on those who are hard on the Community of Muhammad, may Allah bless him and grant him peace!

Glossary

adab: correct behaviour, inward and outward.

adhān: the call to prayer

aḥādīth: plural of *ḥadīth.*

amīr: the one who commands, the source of authority in a situation; a military commander.

Amīr al-Mu'minīn: "the Commander of the Believers," the khalif.

'āmm: generally applicable, in reference to a Qur'ānic ruling.

'Amwas Plague: a major plague in Syria in 18/639 which killed many of the Companions.

Anṣār: the "Helpers", the people of Madina who welcomed and aided the Prophet.

'āqila: the paternal kinsmen of an offender who are liable for the payment of blood money.

'Aṣr: the mid-afternoon prayer.

'Arafa: a plain 15 miles to the east of Makka. One of the essential rites of the *ḥajj is* to stand on 'Arafa on the 9th of Dhū'l-Ḥijja.

'Āshūrā': the 10th day of Muḥarram, the first month of the Muslim lunar calendar. It is considered a highly desirable day to fast.

athar: (plural *āthār*) lit. impact, trace, vestige; synonym of *khabar*, but usually reserved for deeds and precedents of the Companions.

awliyā': the plural of *walī.*

āyat: a verse of the Qur'ān

Ayyūb: the Prophet Job.

Badr: a place near the coast, about 95 miles to the south of Madina where, in 2 AH in the first battle fought by the newly established Muslim community, the 313 outnumbered Muslims led by the Messenger of Allah overwhelmingly defeated 1000 Makkan idolaters.

Banū: lit. sons, meaning a tribe or clan.

basmala: the expression "In the name of Allah, the All-Merciful, the All-Compassionate".

Bilqīs: the Queen of Saba' or Sheba.

Dajjāl: the false Messiah whose appearance marks the imminent end of the world. The root in Arabic means "to deceive, cheat, take in".

Dā'ūd: the Prophet David.

deen: see *dīn.*

dhikr: lit. remembrance, mention. Commonly used, it means invocation of Allah by repetition of His names or particular formulae.

dhimma: obligation or contract, in particular a treaty of protection for non-Muslims living in Muslim territory.

dhimmī: a non-Muslim living under the protection of Muslim rule.

Dhū'l-Ḥijja: the twelfth month of the Muslim calendar, the month of the hajj.

Dhū'l-Qarnayn: "the two-horned", a name given to a great ruler in the past who ruled the world, and was a true believer. It is often thought to refer to Alexander the Great.

dīn: the life-transaction, lit. the debt between two parties, in this usage between the Creator and created.

Fajr: the dawn prayer.

farḍ: obligatory, an obligatory act of worship or practice of the *dīn* as defined by the Sharī'a.

farḍ kifāya: a collective obligation, something which is obligatory for the community as a whole and is satisfied if one adult performs it.

faqīh: pl. *fuqahā'*, a man learned in knowledge of *fiqh* who by virtue of his knowledge can give a legal judgement.

Fātiḥa: "the Opener," the first *sūra* of the Qur'ān.

fatwā: an authoritative statement on a point of law.

fidya: a ransom, compensation paid for rites or acts of worship missed or wrongly performed because of ignorance or ill health.

fiqh: the science of the application of the Sharī'a. A practitioner or expert in *fiqh* is called a faqīh.

fitna: civil strife, sedition, schism, trial, temptation.

fuqahā': plural of *faqīh.*

gharīb: a *ḥadīth* which has a single reporter at some stage of the *isnād.*

ghusl: major ablution of the whole body with water required to regain purity after menstruation, lochia and sexual intercourse.

ḥabal al-ḥabala: a forbidden business transaction in which a man buys the unborn offspring of a female animal.

ḥadd: Allah's boundary limits for the lawful and unlawful. The *ḥadd* punishments are specific fixed penalties laid down by Allah for specified crimes.

ḥadīth: reported speech of the Prophet.

ḥadīth qudsī: those words of Allah on the tongue of His Prophet which are not part of the Revelation of the Qur'ān.

ḥāfiẓ: pl. *ḥuffāẓ*, someone who has memorised the Qur'ān.

ḥajj: the annual pilgrimage to Makka which is one of the five pillars of Islam.

ḥalāl: lawful in the Sharī'a.

hamza: the character in Arabic which designates a glottal stop.

ḥarbī: a belligerent.

ḥarām: unlawful in the Sharī'a.

Ḥaram: Sacred Precinct, a protected area in which certain behaviour is forbidden and other behaviour necessary. The area around the Ka'ba in Makka is a Ḥaram, and the area around the Prophet's Mosque in Madina is a Ḥaram. They are referred to together as al-Ḥaramayn, 'the two Ḥarams'.

al-Ḥarra: a stony tract of black volcanic rock east of Madina where a terrible battle took place in 63 AH (26 August 683) between the forces of Yazīd I and 'Abdullāh ibn az-Zubayr which ended in Madina being sacked and plundered.

Hārūn: the Prophet Aaron, the brother of Mūsā.

Hārūt and Mārūt: the two angels mentioned in the Qur'ān (2:102) in Babel from whom people learned magic. Some commentators state that they are two kings rather than two angels (*malik* rather than *malak*).

ḥasan: good, excellent, often used to describe a *ḥadīth* which is reliable, but which is not as well authenticated as one which is *ṣaḥīḥ*.

Ḥashwiyya: a sect who took the verses of the Qur'an literally and hence became anthropormorphists. They also espoused other innovations.

Ḥawwā': Eve, the first woman.

ḥijāb: a partition which separates two things; a curtain; in modern times used to describe a form of women's dress.

Ḥijāz: the region along the western seaboard of Arabia in which Makka, Madina, Jidda and Ṭā'if are situated.

Hijra: emigration in the way of Allah. Islamic dating begins with the *Hijra* of the Prophet Muhammad from Makka to Madina in 622 AD.

ḥizb: pl. *aḥzāb,* a sixtieth part of the Qur'ān.

Ḥudaybiyya: a well-known place ten miles from Makka on the way to Jidda where the Homage of ar-Riḍwān took place.

ḥudūd: plural of *ḥadd.*

ḥuffāẓ: plural of *ḥāfiẓ.*

Ḥulūlī: someone who espouses incarnation.

Ḥunayn: a valley between Makka and Ṭā'if where the battle took place between the Prophet and Quraysh pagans in 8/630.

'ibāda: act of worship.

Iblīs: the personal name of the Devil. He is also called Shayṭān or the "enemy of Allah".

Ibrāhīm: the Prophet Abraham.

'Īd: a festival, either the festival at the end of Ramaḍān or at the time of the *Ḥajj.*

'idda: a period after divorce or the death of her husband for which a woman must wait before re-marrying.

idghām: In Qur'ān recitation, to assimilate one letter into another. Thus *an-ya'bud* becomes *ay-ya'bud*, *qad tabayyan* becomes *qat-tabayyan*, etc.

Idrīs: a Prophet, possibly Enoch.

ifrād: a form of *ḥajj* in which the *ḥajj* is performed before *'umra.*

iḥrām: the conditions of clothing and behaviour adopted by someone on *ḥajj* or *'umra.*

ijtihād: to exercise personal judgement in legal matters.

īlā': a vow by a husband to abstain from sexual relations with his wife. If four months pass, it is considered a divorce.

Ilyās: also Ilyāsīn, the Prophet Elijah or Elias.

imām: Muslim religious or political leader; leader of Muslim congregational worship.

īmān: belief, faith.

'īna: a transaction in which the price in paid in advance, based on the description of the goods purchased.

iqāma: the call which announces that the obligatory prayer is about to begin.

i'rāb: grammatical inflection; the rules for the vowel endings.

'Īsā: the Prophet Jesus.

'Ishā': the obligatory evening prayer.

Isḥāq: the Prophet Isaac.

ishārāt: allusions, hints, indications of meanings too fine to be expressed directly.

ishbā': lengthening a vowel.

Ismā'īl: the Prophet Ishmael.

isnād: a *ḥadīth*'s chain of transmission from individual to individual.

istiḥāḍa: bleeding from the womb of a woman outside her ordinary periods.

i'tikāf: seclusion, while fasting, in a mosque, particularly in the last ten days of Ramadān.

iẓhār: clear articulation of the letter without nasalisation. This occurs when *nūn* or *tanwīn* is followed by one of six guttural letters (*hamza*, *hā'*, *'ayn*, *ḥā'*, *ghayn* and *khā'*).

Jabriyya: pre-determinism, the name given to those who, in opposition to the Qadarīya, deny the freedom of the will, and on this point make no distinction between man and inanimate nature, inasmuch as his actions are subordinate to the compulsion (*jabr*) of God. Thus everything has been pre-determined and man has no responsibility whatsoever for his actions.

Jahannam: Hell.

Jāhiliyya: the Time of Ignorance before the coming of Islam.

Jamra: lit. a small walled place, but in this usage a stone-built pillar. There are three *jamra*s at Mina. One of the rites of *ḥajj* is to stone them.

janāba: major ritual impurity requiring a ghusl: intercourse, sexual discharge, menstruation, childbirth.

jihād: struggle, particularly fighting in the way of Allah to establish Islam.

jinn: inhabitants of the heavens and the earth made of smokeless fire who are usually invisible.

jizya: a protection tax payable by non-Muslims living under Muslim rule as a tribute to the Muslim ruler.

Jumu'a: the day of gathering, Friday, and particularly the *Jumu'a* prayer which is performed instead of *Ẓuhr* by those who attend it.

juz': pl. *ajzā'*, a thirtieth part of the Qur'ān.

Ka'ba: the cube-shaped building at the centre of the Ḥaram in Makka, originally built by the Prophet Ibrāhīm. Also known as the House of Allah.

kaffāra: atonement, prescribed way of making amends for wrong actions, especially missed obligatory actions.

kāfir: (pl. *kāfirūn* or *kuffār)*: an unbeliever, a person who rejects Allah and His Messenger. The opposite is believer or *mu'min.*

kalām: 'theology' and dogmatics. *Kalām* starts with the revealed tradition and employs rationalistic methods in order to understand it and resolve contradictions.

kasra: the Arabic vowel i.

Kawthar: "Abundance", a river in the Garden.

Khalīl: "Friend", a title of the Prophet Ibrāhīm.

Khārijites: the earliest sect, who separated themselves from the body of the Muslims and declared war on all those who disagreed with them, stating that a wrong action turns a Muslim into an unbeliever.

al-Khiḍr: or al-Khāḍir, "the green one," whose journey with Mūsā is mentioned in the Qur'ān 18:65. He may or may not be a Prophet, and often appears to people.

khimār: a veil or yashmaq which covers the head and lower part of the face but leaves the eyes exposed.

Khorasan: Persian province southeast of the Caspian Sea; a centre of many dissident movements in early Islamic history.

khul': a form of divorce initiated by the wife from her husband by giving him a certain compensation, or by returning back the bride price (*mahr*) which he gave her.

khums: the fifth taken from the booty which is given to the ruler for distribution.

khuṭba: a speech, and in particular a standing speech given by the imām before the *Jumu'a* prayer and after the two *'Īd* prayers.

kitābī: Someone who is one of the People of the Book, i.e. a Jew or Christian.

kufr: disbelief, to cover up the truth, to reject Allah and refuse to believe that Muḥammad is His Messenger.

kunya: a respectful but intimate way of addressing people as "the father of so-and-so" or "the mother of so-and-so."

Lūṭ: the Prophet Lot.

madda: prolongation. There are three letters which are subject to prolongation in recitation of the Qur'ān: *alif*, *wāw* and *yā'*.

Maghrib: the sunset prayer; the western part of Muslim lands. Today it means Morocco.

al-Mahdī: "the Divinely Guided", the descendant of the Prophet who will return at the end of time to establish justice.

maḥram: a male relative with whom marriage is forbidden.

Maqām of Ibrāhīm: the place of the stone on which the Prophet Ibrāhīm stood while he and Ismā'īl were building the Ka'ba, which marks the place of the two *rak'āt* prayer following *ṭawāf* of the Ka'ba.

marfū': 'elevated', a narration from the Prophet mentioned by a Companion, e.g. "The Messenger of Allah said..."

Maryam: Mary, the mother of 'Īsā.

Masjid al-Ḥaram: the great mosque in Makka.

Mathānī: lit. "the often recited", said to be the first long *sūra*s, or the *Fātiḥa* and also various other things.

Mawqif: lit. a standing or stopping place. There are two places where pilgrims must stop on the *ḥajj*: 'Arafa and Muzdalifa.

Mina: a valley five miles on the road to 'Arafa where the three *jamra*s stand. It is part of the *ḥajj* to spend four or possibly three nights there over the course of the *ḥajj*.

mithqāl (plural *mathāqīl*): "miskal", the weight of one dinar, the equivalent of 72 grains of barley (equals 4.4 grams).

Mīzāb ar-Raḥma: "the Spout of Mercy," the rainspout at the top of the Ka'ba on its northeast side.

mu'adhdhin: someone who calls the *adhān* or call to prayer.

muḍāraba: *commenda*, co-partnership, *qirāḍ*.

mudabbar: a slave who has been given a *tadbīr*, a contract that he be freed after his master's death.

Muḍar: the ancestor of the Arabs.

mudd: a measure of volume, approximately a double-handed scoop.

Mufaṣṣal: the *sūras* of the Qur'ān starting from *Sūrat al-Hujurāt* (49) or *Sūrat Qāf* (50) to the end of the Qur'ān.

muftī: someone qualified to give a legal opinion or *fatwā*.

Muhājirūn: Companions of the Messenger of Allah who accepted Islam in Makka and made *hijra* to Madina.

muḥkam: perspicuous, a word or text conveying a firm and unequivocal meaning.

muḥrim: a person in *iḥrām.*

mujtahid: a scholar who is qualified to carry out *ijtihād.*

mujmal: ambivalent, requires details and explanation, ambiguous, referring to a category of unclear words.

munkar: "denounced", a narration reported by a weak reporter which goes against another authentic *ḥadīth.*

mukhābara: see *muzāra'a*

munqaṭi': a *ḥadīth* whose *isnād* has a link which is omitted.

muqallid: a person who practises *taqlīd*, not performing *ijtihād* himself but instead following the legal opinion already arrived at by a *mujtahid.*

murīd: disciple. He is the one who is stripped of his will (*irāda*) and hands himself over to his shaykh, his guide.

Murji'ites: the opponents of the Khārijites. The held that it is faith and not actions which are important. There is also a political position which suspends judgement on a person guilty of major sins.

mursal: a *ḥadīth* where a man in the generation after the Companions quotes directly from the Prophet without mentioning the Companion from whom he got it.

Mūsā: the Prophet Moses.

musnad: a collection of *āḥādīth* arranged according to the first authority in its *isnād*; also a *ḥadīth* which can be traced back through an unbroken *isnād* to the Prophet.

mutakallimūn: those who study the science of *kalām*, the science of investigating theological doctrine.

mutashābih: intricate, unintelligible, referring to a word or text whose meaning is not totally clear.

mutawātir: a *ḥadīth* which is reported by a large number of reporters at all stages of the *isnād.*

Mu'tazilite: someone who adheres to the school of the Mu'tazila which is rationalist in its approach to existence. Originally they held that anyone who commits a sin is neither a believer nor an unbeliever. They also held the Qur'ān to be created.

muzābana: a forbidden sale in which something whose number, weight, or measure is known is sold for something whose number, weight or measure is not known.

muzāra'a: farming partnership, in which someone allows his land to be cultivated in exchange for a portion of the produce.

Muzdalifa: a place between 'Arafa and Mina where the pilgrims returning from 'Arafa spend a night in the open between the ninth and tenth day of Dhū'l-Ḥijja after performing *Maghrib* and *'Ishā'* there.

nāfila: (plural *nawāfil*): supererogatory act of worship.

naskh: abrogation.

naṣṣ: unequivocal, clear injunction or prohibition; an explicit textual meaning.

Nūḥ: the Prophet Noah.

People of the Book: principally the Jews and Christians whose religions are based on the Divine Books revealed to Mūsā and 'Īsā; a term also used to refer to any other group who claim to be following a Book revealed prior to the Qur'ān.

People of the Cave: *Aṣḥāb al-Kahf,* the Seven Sleepers, the seven believers who slept for 309 years (in a cave near Ephesus) and who attained high status because of their emigrating to another place in order not to lose their faith when disbelievers invaded their land. Mentioned in *Sūrat* 18:9-27 of the Qur'ān.

People of Opinion (*ra'y*): a term used to describe those who use personal opinion to deduce judgement. It was a term used particularly to describe the early Ḥanafīs.

Qadariyya: sect who said that people have power (*qadar*) over their actions and hence free will.

qāḍī: a judge, qualified to judge all matters in accordance with the Shari'a and to dispense and enforce legal punishments.

Qādisīya: a decisive four day battle fought against the Persians in Iraq in 15/636.

qinṭār (plural *qanāṭīr)*: "kantar", a relatively large weight-measure for food-grains.

qasāma: an oath taken by fifty members of a tribe or locality to refute or establish accusations of complicity in unclear cases of homicide.

qibla: the direction faced in the prayer which is towards the Ka'ba in Makka.

qirāḍ: wealth put by an investor in the trust of an agent for use for commercial purposes, the agent receiving no wage, but taking a designated share of the profits after the capital has been paid.

qirā'a (plural *qirā'āt*): the method of recitation, punctuation and vocalisation of the Qur'ān. There are seven main readings: Abū 'Amr ibn al-'Alā', Ḥamza, 'Āsim, Ibn 'Āmir, Ibn Kathīr, Nāfi' and al-Kisā'ī. The two most used today are the qirā'a of 'Asim in the *riwaya* of Ḥafs (d. 190/805) and that of Nāfi' in the *riwāya* of Warsh (d. 197/812).

qirān: performing *ḥajj* and *'umra* simultaneously.

Qubā': a village on the outskirts of Madina (originally about 5 km/3 miles outside the city) where the first mosque in Islam was built, also known as the Masjid at-Taqwā (Mosque of Fear of God).

Quraysh: one of the great tribes of Arabia. The Prophet Muḥammad belonged to this tribe, which had great powers spiritually and financially both before and after Islam came. Someone from this tribe is called a Qurayshī.

Rāfiḍites: the *Rawāfiḍ,* a group of the Shī'a known for rejecting Abū Bakr and 'Umar as well as 'Uthmān. It is a nickname, meaning "deserters".

Rajab: the seventh month of the Muslim calendar.

Rajī': an incident which took place in 4/625, when, at the request of a tribe, some Muslims were sent to instruct them in Islam, but they betrayed them to their enemies.

rak'at: a unit of the prayer consisting of a series of standings, bowing, prostrations and sittings.

Ramaḍān: the month of fasting, the ninth month in the Muslim lunar calendar.

ra'y: opinion, personal discretion. (see also *People of Opinion.*)

ribā: usury.

Ridda: the defection of various Arab tribes after the death of the Prophet, may Allah bless him and grant him peace, which brought about the Ridda War.

rūḥ: (plural *arwāḥ*) the soul, vital spirit.

rukū': the bowing position in the prayer.

ṣā': a measure of volume equal to four *mudds.*

Sabians: a group of believers. It is not entirely clear who they were. Possibly they were Gnostics or Mandaeans.

ṣadāq: dower given by a husband to his wife on marriage.

ṣadaqa: charitable giving in the Cause of Allah.

sadd adh-dharā'i': the blocking of a means which might lead to undesired consequences.

ṣaḥīḥ: healthy and sound with no defects, used to describe an authentic *ḥadīth*.

Ṣaḥīḥ: "the Sound", the title of the *ḥadīth* collections of al-Bukhārī and Muslim.

saḥūr: pre-dawn meal before a day of fasting.

Salaf: the early generations of the Muslims.

salaf: loan, advance payment.

salām: the expression, *"as-salāmu 'alaykum,"* or "Peace be upon you," used as a greeting and to end the prayer.

salam: a sale in which the price is paid at once for goods to be delivered later; ownership in the goods passes at the time the contract is made.

sa'y: the main rite of *'umra* and part of *ḥajj*. It is going between the hills of Ṣafā and Marwa seven times.

Sha'bān: the eighth month in the Muslim calendar

shahāda: bearing witness, particularly bearing witness that there is no god but Allah and that Muhammad is the Messenger of Allah. It is one of the pillars of Islam. It is also used to describe legal testimony in a court of law.

Sharī'a: The legal modality of a people based on the revelation of their Prophet. The final *Sharī'a* is that of Islam.

Shawwāl: the tenth month of the Muslim calendar.

Shayṭān: devil, particularly Iblīs, one of the jinn.

shirk: the unforgiveable wrong action of worshipping something or someone other than Allah or associating something or someone as a partner with Him.

Shu'ayb: the Prophet Jethro.

shūrā: consultation, especially used for the council of six Companions who met after the death of 'Umar to choose the next khalif.

ṣiddīq: a man of truth, the *ṣiddīq* is the one who believes in Allah and His Messenger by the statement of the one who reports it, not from any proof except the light of belief which he experiences in his heart and which prevents him from hesitating and prevents any doubt entering him about the word of the Messenger who reported.

Ṣirāṭ: the narrow bridge which spans the Fire and must be crossed to enter the Garden. It is described as sharper than a sword and thinner than a hair. It will have hooks over it to catch people as they cross it.

siwāk: a small stick, usually from the arak tree, whose tip is softened and used for cleaning the teeth.

Ṣubḥ: dawn prayer

Ṣuffa: a verandah attached to the Prophet's Mosque where the poor Muslims used to sleep.

Sulaymān: the Prophet Solomon.

sunan: plural of *sunna.*

Sunna: the customary practice of a person or group of people. It has come to refer almost exclusively to the practice of the Messenger of Allah.

sūra: a chapter of the Qur'ān.

Ṭā'if: a walled town south of Makka known for its fertility. It was the home of the tribe of Thaqīf.

Tābi'ūn: the second generation of the early Muslims who did not meet the Prophet Muhammad, may Allah bless him and grant him peace, but learned the *dīn* of Islam from his Companions.

tadbīr: a contract given by a master to a slave whereby the slave will be freed after the master dies.

tafsīr: commentary or explanation of the meanings of the Qur'ān.

tafwīḍ: delegation of authority, proxy.

takbīr: saying "*Allāhu Akbar*," "Allah is greater".

takbīr al-iḥrām: the *takbīr* which begins the prayer.

talbīya: saying "*Labbayk*" ("At Your service") during the *ḥajj.*

tamattu': a form of *ḥajj* in which *'umra* is done first, and then the *ḥajji* comes out of *iḥrām* before going back into *iḥrām* for the *ḥajj* itself.

taqwā: awe or fear of Allah, which inspires a person to be on guard against wrong action and eager for actions which please Him.

taqlīd: imitation; following the opinion of a *mujtahid* without considering the evidence.

tarjī': making the voice quaver.

tartīl: slow recitation of the Qur'ān.

Tarwiya: 'drawing water', on the 8th of Dhu'l-Hijja, the day before 'Arafa when the pilgrims gather water in preparation for the days of the *Ḥajj* which lie ahead.

tashahhud: lit. to pronounce the *shahāda*. In the context of the prayer, it is a formula which includes the *shahāda* and is recited in the final sitting position of each two *rak'at* cycle.

tashrīq: "drying meat in the sun", the days of the 10th, 11th, 12th and 13th of Dhū'l-Ḥijja when the pilgrims sacrifice their animals and stone the *jamra*s at Mina.

ṭawāf: circumambulation of the Ka'ba, done in sets of seven circuits.

tawḥīd: the doctrine of Divine Unity.

tayammum: purification for the prayer with clean dust, earth, or stone, when water for *ghusl* or *wuḍū'* is unavailable or would be detrimental to health.

Tha'alibiyya: a Khārijite sect.

Thamūd: a people to whom the Prophet Ṣāliḥ was sent, possibly a group of Nabateans. Madā'in Ṣāliḥ is located at al-Ḥijr in Najd about 180 miles north of Madina. The inscriptions on the tombs there date from 3 BC to 79 CE which are probably after the culture which once flourished there was destroyed.

Thaqīf: a tribe based in the town of Ṭā'if, a branch of the tribe of Hawāzin.

Uḥud: a mountain just outside of Madina where five years after the Hijra, the Muslims lost a battle against the Makkan idolaters. Many great Companions, and in particular Ḥamza, the uncle of the Prophet, were killed in this battle.

Umm al-Mu'minīn: lit. "Mother of the Believers", an honorary title given to the wives of the Prophet.

Umma: the body of Muslims as one distinct Community.

'umra: the lesser pilgrimage to the Ka'ba in Makka performed at any time of the year.

uṣūl: plural of *aṣl*, the basic principles of any source, used in *fiqh*.

'Uzayr: Ezra.

wājib: a necessary part of the Sharī'a but not obligatory, although it is sometimes used as a synonym for *farḍ*.

walī: (plural *awliyā'*) someone who is a "friend" of Allah, thus possessing the quality of *wilāya*. Also a relative who acts as a guardian.

wasq: a measure of volume equal to sixty *ṣā'*s.

wuḍū': ritual washing to be pure for the prayer.

Yaḥyā: the Prophet John the Baptist, the son of Zakariyyā.

Yamāma, Battle of: also known as the Battle of 'Aqrabā, the major battle of the Ridda War in which the Muslims defeated the forces of the false Prophet Musaylima in 12/633.

Ya'qūb: the Prophet Jacob, also called Isrā'īl.

Yathrib: the ancient name for Madina.

Yūnus: the Prophet Jonah.

Yūsuf: the Prophet Joseph.

Zabāniya: "the violent thrusters", the angels who thrust people into Hellfire, who are nineteen in number.

Zabūr: the Psalms of Dā'ūd.

Zakariyyā: the Prophet Zacharia, the father of Yaḥyā, John the Baptist, and guardian of Maryam.

zakāt: a wealth tax, one of the five pillars of Islam.

zakāt al-fiṭr: a small obligatory head-tax imposed on every Muslim who has the means for himself and his dependants. It is paid at the end of Ramaḍān.

Zamzam: the well in the Ḥaram of Makka.

zandaqa: heresy. This is an Arabicised Persian word. The term had been used for heterodox groups, especially Manichaeans, in pre-Islamic Persia, and hence it was originally applied to Magians.

az-Zaqqūm: a tree with bitter fruit which grows at the bottom of the Fire. Its fruit resembles the heads of devils.

zindīq: a term used to describe a heretic whose teaching is a danger to the community or state.

zuhd: making do with little of this world and leaving what you do not need.

Ẓuhr: the midday prayer.

Index